The Disability Studies Reader

The fifth edition of *The Disability Studies Reader* addresses the post-identity theoretical landscape by emphasizing questions of interdependency and independence, the human–animal relationship, and issues around the construction or materiality of gender, the body, and sexuality. Selections explore the underlying biases of medical and scientific experiments and explode the binary of the sound and the diseased mind. The collection addresses physical disabilities, but as always investigates issues around pain, mental disability, and invisible disabilities as well. Featuring a new generation of scholars who are dealing with the most current issues, the fifth edition continues the *Reader*'s tradition of remaining timely, urgent, and critical.

Lennard J. Davis is Distinguished Professor of Liberal Arts and Sciences at the University of Illinois at Chicago in the Departments of Disability and Human Development, English, and Medical Education. He is the author of, among other works, *Enforcing Normalcy: Disability, Deafness, and the Body*; *Bending Over Backwards: Disability, Dismodernism, and Other Difficult Positions*; *My Sense of Silence: Memoirs of a Childhood with Deafness*; *Obsession: A History*, for which he received a Guggenheim Fellowship, and *The End of Normal: Identity in a Biocultural Era*.

The fifth edition of Lennard Davis' *The Disability Studies Reader* adds a range of new essays on topics from disability and work to disability and sexual abuse. It remains the gold standard to teach your introductory course on disability studies or as the perfect supplement to a medical humanities course to provide materials on disability and culture

Sander L. Gilman, Distinguished Professor of the Liberal Arts and Sciences;
Professor of Psychiatry, Emory University, USA

What is disability? What is disability studies? The first edition of *The Disability Studies Reader* played a foundational role in leading beginning students and advanced scholars to these questions. The newest edition of this canonical anthology, the best one yet, offers an ideal selection of texts through which to explore how both the field and the concept of disability itself are being reconsidered, resisted, extended and reclaimed.

Susan Schweik, Professor of English, University of California, Berkeley, USA

Disability experiences are diverse, nuanced and deeply political. As scholars, advocates and policy-makers, we need to think more and better — and this volume is the best place to start.

Tom Shakespeare, Professor of Disability Research, University of East Anglia, UK

The Disability Studies Reader remains the indispensable volume for all scholars and students working in the interdisciplinary field of disability studies. The new edition continues a solid tradition of providing readers with foundational essays in the field, even as it opens out onto the most exciting new work centering disability and social justice, insisting on the centrality of race to a critical disability studies, or locating disability in a global context.

Robert McRuer, Professor of English, George Washington University, USA;
author of Crip Theory: Cultural Signs of Queerness and Disability

The Disability Studies Reader provides critical information for scholars of the field. The thoughtful essays in this text explore the ways in which disability intersects with law, technology, medicine, education, and the world of media. Lennard Davis guides readers through our disability history with fascinating insights and surprising information. This is an excellent book through which to understand disability in today's increasingly interdependent world.

Haben Girma, Global Accessibility Leader

The Disability Studies Reader

Fifth Edition

Lennard J. Davis

Routledge
Taylor & Francis Group

NEW YORK AND LONDON

Fifth edition published 2017
by Routledge
711 Third Avenue, New York, NY 10017

and Routledge
2 Park Square, Milton Park, Abingdon, Oxon, OX14 4RN

Routledge is an imprint of the Taylor & Francis Group, an informa business

© 2017 Taylor & Francis

First edition published by Routledge 1997
Fourth edition published by Routledge 2013

Library of Congress Cataloging in Publication Data
Names: Davis, Lennard J., 1949- editor.
Title: The disability studies reader / [edited by] Lennard J. Davis.
Description: Fifth edition. | New York, NY: Routledge, 2016. | Includes
bibliographical references and index.
Identifiers: LCCN 2016013306 | ISBN 9781138930230 (pbk.) |
ISBN 9781315680668 (e-book)
Subjects: LCSH: People with disabilities. | Sociology of disability. |
Disability studies.
Classification: LCC HV1568 .D5696 2016 | DDC 362.4–dc23
LC record available at https://lccn.loc.gov/2016013306

ISBN: 978-1-138-93022-3 (hbk)
ISBN: 978-1-138-93023-0 (pbk)
ISBN: 978-1-315-68066-8 (ebk)

Typeset in Utopia
by Sunrise Setting Ltd, Brixham, UK

Printed and bound in the United States of America by Sheridan

CONTENTS

As many as 40 percent of current Americans can trace their ancestry to Ellis Island, a place that Jay Dolmage asks us to consider as a "rhetorical space." Dolmage argues that the policies and practices at Ellis Island created new and influential ways of seeing the body and categorizing deviations.

PART II: THE POLITICS OF DISABILITY

PART III: STIGMA AND ILLNESS

This essay argues that postmodernism has failed to deconstruct the schizophrenic, keeping a monolithic view based on some canonical writings rather than seeing the schizophrenic as part of a new emerging group that is active, multivocal, and seeking to fight for its rights.

PART V: IDENTITIES AND INTERSECTIONALITIES

PREFACE TO THE FIFTH EDITION

This fifth edition of the *Disability Studies Reader* appears in the wake of the 25th anniversary of the Americans with Disabilities Act. This benchmark gives us a way of remembering that before 1990 people with disabilities and Deaf people in the United States (and most of the world) had limited rights and did not enjoy the protections afforded to people of color and women by the 1964 Civil Rights Act and other legislation. Just a quarter of a century ago people with disabilities were second-class citizens. So many people know the story of Martin Luther King, Rosa Parks, Malcolm X, and others, but so few people know the stories of the leaders of the disability rights movement and the accomplishments of the activists, politicians, and others who helped move forward civil rights for people with disabilities. There is a task ahead of disability studies: while much has been accomplished in the past 25 years, so much more remains.

The rise of disabilities studies in the humanities and social sciences in the United States and the United Kingdom really began around the same time as the 1990 Act, reminding us that political rights and academic discourses are intricately linked.

Areas covered by this *Reader* and not so easy to legislate are the social, cultural, and political manifestations around disability and Deafness. In these less directly tangible but equally important arenas, attitudes and habits directly affect the daily lives of people with disabilities. The struggle for equality still remains in areas like the arts, for example, where films and television rarely include the true stories of Deaf and disabled people. When disabled people exist in the media their stories are written and acted by people without disabilities. You can't legislate routine everyday interactions. Disabled people, as a matter of course, encounter bias in the encounters of everyday life—sexuality and dating, education, and employment where micro-aggressions and discriminations fleetingly appear in a glance, a phrase, or much worse. Only education, familiarity, and allied activity will reshape the way people think and feel about the different body and mind. Disability Studies, as a discourse, therefore has an important role to play. The more the disability experience is analyzed, understood, parsed, explored, witnessed, testified to and put into writing, the quicker we will all come to see disability and Deafness as on a par with and intersected by other identities.

In each of the previous four editions I began the preface by taking the pulse of the field of disability studies at the current moment. In the first edition I lamented the lack of traction disability studies was having in getting attention. In the second I saw disability studies on the rise. In the third edition I wrote, "disability studies is definitely part of the academic world and civil society." In the fourth edition I said that disability is not only accepted but also has become very much a critical term in discussions of being, posthumanism, political theory, transgender theory, philosophy, and the like. Indeed as we begin to think through the complexities of being and post-identity, disability has become an almost necessary aspect of understanding the human–animal relationship, questions of interdependency and independence as well as issues around the construction or materiality of gender, the body, and sexuality. The turn to the neurological and affect theory has made us think through the underlying biases of medical and scientific experiments and focus more on continua and less on abstract and discrete categories. So in the world of neurodiversity, we are asked to think not of the sound mind and the diseased mind but of the range of possibilities and variations in the construction of human brains and neural networks.

Because of the frequency with which Routledge has indicated its willingness to have new editions of this text, I have been able to replace some excellent essays in good conscience, feeling that those authors removed may well reappear in future issues, while also having the excitement of including many new and younger scholars who are dealing with the most current issues. The *Disability Studies Reader* has this advantage over many other Readers in that it is able to stay up to date and relevant with new editions appearing on a regular basis.

Indeed, in this edition we reprise two essays that had been previously removed. One is really back by popular demand and relevance—the late Chris Bell's essay (Chapter 28) critiquing the whiteness of disability studies. While there are many more people of color writing about disability now, the field still remains more monolithic than one would like. Many readers wanted to see the Bell essay back, and so it is now. With the rise of Black Lives Matter and the renewed awareness of racism it brings, Bell's essay serves as a reminder of work to be done. A reprise of Erving Goffman's seminal work on stigma (Chapter 9) also reminds us of where disability studies covertly hid before it came out clearly.

As always, I have had a tough time selecting which works will remain and which will be newly included. With the aid of Routledge's very helpful marketing department, I have been able to see which essays are being used in courses and which are not. My decisions are not made completely on a utilitarian basis, but at least the marketing information provides a bit of perspective on these factors. I am ever mindful of providing a balance between essays of foundational and historic interest in disability studies and newer ones that provide continuing conversation with current and past moments. I also want to thank the many people who responded to my call on various Internet lists for suggestions of topics and particular essays to showcase. These responses really do make a difference and help me with my difficult task.

I would particularly like to offer kudos to Steve Rutter, my longtime editor at Routledge who recognized the importance of disability studies and encouraged me to come on board and edit this Reader. With his retirement to rural Maine, he is very ably followed by my current editor Samantha Barbaro and her assistants Athena Bryan, Margaret Moore, and Drew Acuff. Alexander Luft, my research assistant, was extremely adept in providing organization and support. As always, my own departments at the University of Illinois at Chicago were very helpful, as were my colleagues in Disability Studies and English.

One of the challenges in publishing books on disability is to ensure that the works are accessible to a wide variety of readers. The fourth edition was the first one that had an e-book version. The fifth edition will aim to do more than that. Following the guidelines generated by a group of disability scholars and approved by several disability organizations, it will make available versions for screenreaders that meet the standards necessary for the widest distribution. Those guidelines can be found at http://disstudies.org/Publishing%20Accessible%20Books

A word on the cover. It is very difficult to find adequate photographs about disability. The mainstream media like to proliferate upbeat pictures of supercrips—mostly attractive, buff athletes using wheelchairs or prostheses. I've chosen not to use such pictures as I feel they further a kind of disability inspiration porn. I tried to go in the direction of ASL but seemingly all ASL photos use the sign for "I love you" or spelling out "LOVE" which is relatively easy to read. Not everything about being Deaf is part of this "feel-good" signage, so I've opted not to use those. The wheelchair of course is the ubiquitous symbol of disability, despite the fact that a very small percentage of people with disabilities use wheelchairs. So I've eschewed that symbol. What's left? That is when the seagull appeared. At first I thought the cover was too whimsical, but a number of people said they liked it. So the bird settled onto the cover. What I do like about it is that it opens conversations. Is the bird one-legged or simply does it have its leg pulled up and tucked under its feathers? Why does either theory matter? Do we see the bird differently when we consider it impaired versus if we keep the "normal" status of the bird? The animal–human connection comes into play. Does its environment disable an animal or is it simply impaired? Social model or medical model? I expect classes on disability could discuss the seagull for quite a while.

I would finally like to thank the actual people who both taught the *Disability Studies Reader* and provided feedback for us. They are: Jami Anderson, Kathleen Brian, Jeffrey Brune, Megan Conway, Kerry Dobransky, Julie Passanante Elman, Karla Erickson, Jonathan Hsy, David Kociemba, David Mitchell, Joseph Murray, Lawrence Nelson, Margaret Price, Benjamin Reiss, Lou Thompson, Karyn Valerius, and Diane Wiener.

CHAPTER 1

Introduction: Disability, Normality, and Power

Lennard J. Davis

SUMMARY

In this introduction to the *Disability Studies Reader*, Lennard J. Davis tells us that "we live in a world of norms" that influences every part of contemporary life. Understanding how and why we think of something as normal is an important part of understanding the disabled body. Davis tells us that the "problem" of disability does not lie with the person with disabilities but rather in the way that normalcy is constructed.

Davis makes the point that despite appearing to be universal, norms haven't always existed. The concept of a norm is constructed, historically speaking, as a reaction to the concept of the ideal human body, and it "implies that the majority of the population must or should be somehow part of the norm." Instead of accepting that all bodies are not ideal, the power of the norm makes it so that people are described as deviant if their bodies don't match the norm.

By deviating from the norm, people become defined and identified by these irrepressible physical qualities. Davis shows how eugenics and statistics developed in tandem to criminalize and dehumanize people with these qualities while the idea of progressive human perfectibility created a dominant idea of what the body should be. Believing that norms were scientifically true led to the idea that those norms were desirable, and this association permeated everything from political ideology to psychoanalytic practice and literature. This is a legacy that people with disabilities are still having trouble living down. Davis introduces the critical approach to this Reader by pointing out that a disabilities-studies consciousness can open new possibilities for the way we read novels, analyze cultural forces, and think about the history of normality.

We live in a world of norms. Each of us endeavors to be normal or else deliberately tries to avoid that state. We consider what the average person does, thinks, earns, or consumes. We rank our intelligence, our cholesterol level, our weight, height, sex drive, bodily dimensions along some conceptual line from subnormal to above-average. We consume a minimum daily balance of vitamins and nutrients based on what an average human should consume. Our children are ranked in school and tested to determine where they fit into a normal curve of learning, of intelligence. Doctors measure and weigh them to see if they are above or below average on the height and weight curves. There is probably no area of contemporary life in which some idea of a norm, mean, or average has not been calculated.

To understand the disabled body, one must return to the concept of the norm, the normal body. So much of writing about disability has focused on the disabled person as the object of study, just as the study of race has focused on the person of color. But as with recent scholarship on race, which has turned its attention to whiteness and intersectionality, I would like to focus not so much on the construction of disability as on the construction of normalcy. I do this because the "problem" is not the person with disabilities; the problem is the way that normalcy is constructed to create the "problem" of the disabled person.

A common assumption would be that some concept of the norm must have always existed. After all, people seem to have an inherent desire to compare themselves to others. But the idea of a norm is less a condition of human nature than it is a feature of a certain kind of society. Recent work on the ancient Greeks, on preindustrial Europe, and on tribal peoples, for example, shows that disability was once regarded very differently from the way it is now. As we will see, the social process of disabling arrived with industrialization and with the set of practices and discourses that are linked to late eighteenth- and nineteenth-century notions of nationality, race, gender, criminality, sexual orientation, and so on.

I begin with the rather remarkable fact that the constellation of words describing this concept "normal," "normalcy," "normality," "norm," "average," "abnormal"—all entered the European languages rather late in human history. The word "normal" as "constituting, conforming to, not deviating or different from, the common type or standard, regular, usual" only enters the English language around 1840. (Previously, the word had meant "perpendicular"; the carpenter's square, called a "norm," provided the root meaning.) Likewise, the word "norm," in the modern sense, has only been in use since around 1855, and "normality" and "normalcy" appeared in 1849 and 1857, respectively. If the lexicographical information is relevant, it is possible to date the coming into consciousness in English of an idea of "the norm" over the period 1840–1860.

If we rethink our assumptions about the universality of the concept of the norm, what we might arrive at is the concept that preceded it: that of the "ideal," a word we find dating from the seventeenth century. Without making too simplistic a division in the history, one can nevertheless try to imagine a world in which the concept of normality does not exist. Rather, what we have is the ideal body, as exemplified in the tradition of nude Venuses, for example. This idea presents a mytho-poetic body that is linked to that of the gods (in traditions in which the god's body is visualized). This divine body, then, this ideal body, is not attainable by a human. The notion of an ideal implies that, in this case, the human body as visualized in art or imagination must be composed from the ideal parts of living models. These models individually can never embody the ideal since an ideal, by definition, can never be found in this world. Pliny tells us that the Greek artist Zeuxis tried to paint Aphrodite, the goddess of love, by using as his models all the beautiful women of Crotona in order to select in each her ideal feature or body part and combine these into the ideal figure of the goddess. One young woman provides a face and another her breasts. The central point here is that in a culture with an ideal form of the body, all members of the population are below the ideal. No one young lady of Crotona can be the ideal. By definition, one can never have an ideal body. And there is no social pressure, we would imagine, that populations have bodies that conform to the ideal.

If the concept of the norm or average enters European culture, or at least the European languages, only in the nineteenth century, one has to ask what is the cause of this conceptualization? One of the logical places to turn in trying to understand concepts like "norm" and "average" is that branch of knowledge known as statistics. It was the French statistician Adolphe Quetelet (1796–1847) who contributed the most to a generalized notion of the normal as an imperative. He noticed that the "law of error," used by astronomers to locate a star by plotting all the sightings and then averaging the errors, could be equally applied to the distribution of human features such as height and weight. He then took a further step of formulating the concept of "l'homme moyen" or the average man. Quetelet maintained that this abstract human was the average of all human attributes in a given country. Quetelet's average man was a combination of *l'homme moyen physique* and *l'homme moyen morale*, both a physically average and a morally average construct.

With such thinking, the average then becomes paradoxically a kind of ideal, a position devoutly to be wished. As Quetelet wrote, "an individual who epitomized in himself, at a given time, all the qualities of the average man, would represent at once all the greatness, beauty and goodness of that being" (cited in Porter 1986, 102). Furthermore, one must observe that Quetelet meant this hegemony of the middle to apply not only to moral qualities but to the body as well. He wrote: "deviations more or less great from the mean have constituted [for artists] ugliness in body as well as vice in morals and a state of sickness with regard to the constitution" (ibid., 103). Here Zeuxis's notion of physical beauty as an exceptional ideal becomes transformed into beauty as the average.

Quetelet foresaw a kind of utopia of the norm associated with progress, just as Marx foresaw a utopia of the norm in so far as wealth and production is concerned. Marx actually cites Quetelet's notion of the average man in a discussion of the labor theory of value.

The concept of a norm, unlike that of an ideal, implies that the majority of the population must or should somehow be part of the norm. The norm pins down that majority of the population that falls under the arch of the standard bell-shaped curve. This curve, the graph of an exponential function, that was known variously as the astronomer's "error law," the "normal distribution," the "Gaussian density function," or simply "the bell curve," became in its own way a symbol of the tyranny of the norm. Any bell curve will always have at its extremities those characteristics that deviate from the norm. So, with the concept of the norm comes the concept of deviations or extremes. When we think of bodies, in a society where the concept of the norm is operative, then people with disabilities will be thought of as deviants. This, as we have seen, is in contrast to societies with the concept of an ideal, in which all people have a non-ideal status.[1]

In England, there was a burst of interest in statistics during the 1830s. A statistical office was set up at the Board of Trade in 1832, and the General Register Office was created in 1837 to collect vital statistics. The use of statistics began an important movement, and there is a telling connection for the purposes of this essay between the founders of statistics and their larger intentions. The rather amazing fact is that almost all the early statisticians had one thing in common: they were eugenicists. The same is true of key figures in the eugenics movement: Sir Francis Galton, Karl Pearson, and R. A. Fisher.[2] While this coincidence seems almost too striking to be true, we must remember that there is a real connection between figuring the statistical measure of humans and then hoping to improve humans so that deviations from the norm diminish. Statistics is bound up with eugenics because the central insight of statistics is the idea that a population can be normed. An important consequence of the idea of the norm is that it divides the total population into standard and nonstandard subpopulations. The next step in conceiving of the population as norm and non-norm is for the state to attempt to norm the nonstandard—the aim of eugenics. Of course such an activity is profoundly paradoxical since the inviolable rule of statistics is that all phenomena will always conform to a bell curve. So norming the non-normal is an activity as problematic as untying the Gordian knot.

MacKenzie asserts that it is not so much that Galton's statistics made possible eugenics but rather that "the needs of eugenics in large part determined the content of Galton's statistical theory" (1981, 52). In any case, a symbiotic relationship exists between statistical science and eugenic concerns. Both bring into society the concept of a norm, particularly a normal body, and thus in effect create the concept of the disabled body.

It is also worth noting the interesting triangulation of eugenicist interests. On the one hand Sir Francis Galton was cousin to Charles Darwin, whose notion of the evolutionary advantage of the fittest lays the foundation for eugenics and also for the idea of a perfectible body undergoing progressive improvement. As one scholar has put it, "Eugenics was in reality applied biology based on the central biological theory of the day, namely the Darwinian theory of evolution" (Farrall 1985, 55). Darwin's ideas serve to place disabled people along the wayside as evolutionary defectives to be surpassed by natural selection. So, eugenics became obsessed with the elimination of "defectives," a category which included the "feebleminded," the deaf, the blind, the physically defective, and so on.

In a related discourse, Galton created the modern system of fingerprinting for personal identification. Galton's interest came out of a desire to show that certain physical traits could be inherited. As he wrote:

> one of the inducements to making these inquiries into personal identification has been to discover independent features suitable for hereditary investigation. ...it is not improbable, and worth taking pains to inquire whether each person may not carry visibly about his body undeniable evidence of his parentage and near kinships.
>
> (cited in MacKenzie 1981, 65)

Fingerprinting was seen as a physical mark of parentage, a kind of serial number written on the body. But further, one can say that the notion of fingerprinting pushes forward the idea that the human body is standardized and contains a serial number, as it were, embedded in its corporeality. Thus the body has an identity that coincides with its essence and cannot be altered by moral, artistic, or human will. This indelibility of corporeal identity only furthers the mark placed on the body by other physical qualities—intelligence, height, reaction time. By this logic, the person enters into an identical relationship with the body, the body forms the identity, and the identity is unchangeable and indelible as one's place on the normal curve. For our purposes, then, this fingerprinting of the body means that the marks of physical difference become synonymous with the identity of the person.

Finally, Galton can be linked to that other major figure connected with the discourse of disability in the nineteenth century—Alexander Graham Bell. In 1883, the same year that Galton coined the term "eugenics," Bell delivered his eugenicist speech *Memoir upon the Formation of a Deaf Variety of the Human Race*, warning of the "tendency among deaf-mutes to select deaf-mutes as their partners in marriage" (1969, 19) with the dire consequence that a race of deaf people might be created. This echoing of

Dr. Frankenstein's fear that his monster might mate and produce a race of monsters emphasizes the terror with which the "normal" beholds the differently abled.[3] Noting how the various interests come together in Galton, we can see evolution, fingerprinting, and the attempt to control the reproductive rights of the deaf as all pointing to a conception of the body as perfectible but only when subject to the necessary control of the eugenicists. The identity of people becomes defined by irrepressible identificatory physical qualities that can be measured. Deviance from the norm can be identified and indeed criminalized, particularly in the sense that fingerprints came to be associated with identifying deviants who wished to hide their identities.

Galton made significant changes in statistical theory that created the concept of the norm. He took what had been called "error theory," a technique by which astronomers attempted to show that one could locate a star by taking into account the variety of sightings. The sightings, all of which could not be correct, if plotted would fall into a bell curve, with most sightings falling into the center, that is to say, the correct location of the star. The errors would fall to the sides of the bell curve. Galton's contribution to statistics was to change the name of the curve from "the law of frequency of error" or "error curve," the term used by Quetelet, to the "normal distribution" curve.

The significance of these changes relates directly to Galton's eugenicist interests. In an "error curve" the extremes of the curve are the most mistaken in accuracy. But if one is looking at human traits, then the extremes, particularly what Galton saw as positive extremes—tallness, high intelligence, ambitiousness, strength, fertility—would have to be seen as errors. Rather than "errors" Galton wanted to think of the extremes as distributions of a trait. As MacKenzie notes:

> Thus there was a gradual transition from use of the term "probable error" to the term "standard deviation" (which is free of the implication that a deviation is in any sense an error), and from the term "law of error" to the term "normal distribution."
>
> (1981, 59)

But even without the idea of error, Galton still faced the problem that in a normal distribution curve that graphed height, for example, both tallness and shortness would be seen as extremes in a continuum where average stature would be the norm. The problem for Galton was that, given his desire to perfect the human race, or at least its British segment, tallness was preferable to shortness. How could both extremes be considered equally deviant from the norm? So Galton substituted the idea of ranking for the concept of averaging. That is, he changed the way one might look at the curve from one that used the mean to one that used the median—a significant change in thinking eugenically.

If a trait, say intelligence, is considered by its average, then the majority of people would determine what intelligence should be—and intelligence would be defined by the mediocre middle. Galton, wanting to avoid the middling of desired traits, would prefer to think of intelligence in ranked order. Although high intelligence in a normal distribution would simply be an extreme, under a ranked system it would become the highest ranked trait. Galton divided his curve into quartiles, so that he was able to emphasize ranked orders of intelligence; that someone was in the first quartile in intelligence (low intelligence) or the fourth quartile (high intelligence). Galton's work led directly to current "intelligence quotient" (IQ) and scholastic achievement tests. In fact, Galton revised Gauss's bell curve to show the superiority of the desired trait (for example, high intelligence). He created what he called an "ogive," which is arranged in quartiles with an ascending curve that features the desired trait as "higher" than the undesirable deviation. As Stigler notes:

> If a hundred individuals' talents were ordered, each could be assigned the numerical value corresponding to its percentile in the curve of "deviations from an average": the middlemost (or median) talent had value 0 (representing mediocrity), an individual at the upper quartile was assigned the value 1 (representing one probable error above mediocrity), and so on.
>
> (1986, 271)

What these revisions by Galton signify is an attempt to redefine the concept of the "ideal" in relation to the general population. First, the application of the idea of a norm to the human body creates the idea of deviance or a "deviant" body. Second, the idea of a norm pushes the normal variation of the body through a stricter template guiding the way the body "should" be. Third, the revision of the "normal curve of distribution" into quartiles, ranked in order, and so on, creates a new kind of "ideal." This statistical ideal is unlike the classical notion of the ideal, which contains no imperative that everyone should strive to be perfect. The new ideal of ranked order is powered by the imperative of the norm, and then is supplemented by the notion of progress, human perfectibility, and the elimination of deviance, to create a dominating, hegemonic vision of what the human body should be.

While we tend to associate eugenics with a Nazi-like racial supremacy, it is important to realize that eugenics was not the trade of a fringe group of right-wing, fascist maniacs. Rather, it became the common belief and practice of many, if not most, European and American citizens. When Marx used Quetelet's idea of the average in his formulation of average wage and abstract labor, socialists as well as others embraced eugenic claims, seeing in the perfectibility of the human body a utopian hope for social and economic improvement. Once people allowed that there were norms and ranks in human physiology, then the idea that we might want to, for example, increase the intelligence of humans, or decrease birth defects, did not seem so farfetched. These ideas were widely influential and the influence of eugenicist ideas persisted well into the twentieth century, so that someone like Emma Goldman could write that unless birth control was encouraged, the state would "legally encourage the increase of paupers, syphilitics, epileptics, dipsomaniacs, cripples, criminals, and degenerates" (Kevles 1985, 90).

One problem for people with disabilities was that eugenicists tended to group together all allegedly "undesirable" traits. So, for example, criminals, the poor, and people with disabilities might be mentioned in the same breath. Take Karl Pearson, a leading figure in the eugenics movement, who defined the "unfit" as follows: "the habitual criminal, the professional tramp, the tuberculous, the insane, the mentally defective, the alcoholic, the diseased from birth or from excess" (cited in Kevles 1985, 33). In 1911, Pearson headed the Department of Applied Statistics, which included Galton and the Biometric Laboratories at University College in London. This department gathered eugenic information on the inheritance of physical and mental traits including "scientific, commercial, and legal ability, but also hermaphroditism, hemophilia, cleft palate, harelip, tuberculosis, diabetes, deaf-mutism, polydactyly (more than five fingers) or brachydactyly (stub fingers), insanity, and mental deficiency" (ibid., 38–39). Here again one sees a strange selection of disabilities merged with other types of human variations. All of these deviations from the norm were regarded in the long run as contributing to the disease of the nation. As one official in the Eugenics Record Office asserted: "the only way to keep a nation strong mentally and physically is to see that each new generation is derived chiefly from the fitter members of the generation before" (ibid., 39–40).

The emphasis on nation and national fitness obviously plays into the metaphor of the body. If individual citizens are not fit, if they do not fit into the nation, then the national body will not be fit. Of course, such arguments are based on a false idea of the body politic—by that notion a hunchbacked citizenry would make a hunchbacked nation. Nevertheless, the eugenic "logic" that individual variations would accumulate into a composite national identity was a powerful one. This belief combined with an industrial mentality that saw workers as interchangeable and therefore sought to create a universal worker whose physical characteristics would be uniform, as would the result of their labors—a uniform product.

One of the central foci of eugenics was what was broadly called "feeblemindedness."[4] This term included low intelligence, mental illness, and even "pauperism," since low income was equated with "relative inefficiency" (ibid., 46).[5] Likewise, certain ethnic groups were associated with feeblemindedness and pauperism. Charles Davenport, an American eugenicist, thought that the influx of European immigrants would make the American population "darker in pigmentation, smaller in stature ... more given to crimes of larceny, assault, murder, rape, and sex-immorality" (cited in ibid., 48). In his research, Davenport scrutinized the records of "prisons, hospitals, almshouses, and institutions for the mentally deficient, the deaf, the blind, and the insane" (ibid., 55).

The association between what we would now call disability and criminal activity, mental incompetence, sexual license, and so on established a legacy that people with disabilities are still having trouble living down. This equation was so strong that an American journalist writing in the early twentieth century could celebrate "the inspiring, the wonderful, message of the new heredity" as opposed to the sorrow of bearing children who were "diseased or crippled or depraved" (ibid., 67). The conflation of disability with depravity expressed itself in the formulation "defective class." As the president of the University of Wisconsin declared after World War One, "we know enough about eugenics so that if the knowledge were applied, the defective classes would disappear within a generation" (ibid., 68). And it must be reiterated that the eugenics movement was not stocked with eccentrics. Averell Harriman's sister Mary Harriman, as well as John D. Rockefeller, funded Davenport. Prime Ministers A. J. Balfour, Neville Chamberlain, and Winston Churchill, along with President Theodore Roosevelt, H. G. Wells, and John Maynard Keynes, among many others, were members of eugenicist organizations. Francis Galton was knighted in 1909 for his work, and in 1910 he received the Copley Medal, the Royal Society's highest honor. A Galton Society met regularly in the American Museum of Natural History in New York City. In 1911 the Oxford University Union moved approval of the main principles behind eugenics by a vote of almost two to one. In Kansas, the 1920 state fair held a contest for "fitter families" based on their eugenic family histories; a brochure for the contest noted about the awards, "this trophy and medal are worth more than livestock sweepstakes. ... For health is wealth and a sound mind in a sound body is the most priceless of human possessions" (ibid., 62). County fairs like these also administered intelligence tests, medical exams, and screened for venereal disease.

In England, bills were introduced in Parliament to control mentally disabled people, and in 1933 the prestigious scientific magazine *Nature* approved the Nazis' proposal of a bill for "the avoidance of inherited diseases in posterity" by sterilizing the disabled. The magazine editorial said "the Bill, as it reads, will command the appreciative attention of all who are interested in the controlled and deliberate improvement of human stock." The list of disabilities for which sterilization would be appropriate were "congenital feeblemindedness, manic depressive insanity, schizophrenia, hereditary epilepsy, hereditary St Vitus's dance, hereditary blindness and deafness, hereditary bodily malformation and habitual alcoholism" (cited in MacKenzie 1981, 44). We have largely forgotten that what Hitler did in developing a hideous policy of eugenics was just to implement the theories of the British and American eugenicists. Hitler's statement in *Mein Kampf* that "the struggle for the daily livelihood [between species] leaves behind, in the ruck, everything that is weak or diseased or wavering" (cited in Blacker 1952, 143) is not qualitatively different from any of the many similar statements we have seen before. And even the conclusions Hitler draws are not very different from those of the likes of Galton, Bell, and others.

> In this matter, the State must assert itself as the trustee of a millennial future. ... In order to fulfill this duty in a practical manner, the State will have to avail itself of modern medical discoveries. It must proclaim as unfit for procreation all those who are afflicted with some visible hereditary disease or are the carriers of it; and practical measures must be adopted to have such people rendered sterile.
>
> (cited in Blacker 1952, 144)

One might want to add here a set of speculations about Sigmund Freud. His work was made especially possible by the idea of the normal. In fact, it is hard to imagine the existence of psychoanalysis without the concept of normalcy. Indeed, one of the core principles behind psychoanalysis was "if the *vita sexualis* is normal, there can be no neurosis" (Freud 1977, 386). Psychoanalysis through talk therapy bring patients back to their normal selves. Although I cannot go into a close analysis of Freud's work here, it is instructive to think of the ways in which Freud is producing a eugenics of the mind—creating the concepts of normal sexuality, normal function, and then contrasting them with the perverse, abnormal, pathological, and even criminal.

The first depiction in literature of an attempt to norm an individual member of the population occurred in the 1850s during the development of the idea of the normal body. In Flaubert's *Madame Bovary*, Charles Bovary performs a trendy operation that would correct the clubfoot of Hippolyte, the stable boy of the local inn. This corrective operation is seen as "new" and related to "progress" (Flaubert 1965, 125). Hippolyte is assailed with reasons why he should alter his foot. He is told, it "must considerably interfere with the proper performance of your work" (ibid., 126). And in addition to redefining him in terms of his ability to carry out work, Homais adds: "Think what would have happened if you had been called into the army, and had to fight under our national banner!" (ibid., 126). So national interests and again productivity are emphasized. But Hippolyte has been doing fine in his job as stable boy; his disability has not interfered with his performance in the community under traditional standards. In fact, Hippolyte seems to use his club foot to his advantage, as the narrator notes:

> But on the equine foot, wide indeed as a horse's hoof, with is horny skin, and large toes ... the cripple ran about like a deer from morn till night. He was constantly to be seen on the Square,

jumping round the carts, thrusting his limping foot forwards. He seemed even stronger on that leg than the other. By dint of hard service it had acquired, as it were, moral qualities of patience and energy; and when he was given some heavy work to do, he would support himself on it in preference to the sound one.

(ibid., 126)

Hippolyte's disability is in fact an ability, one which he relies on, and from which he gets extra horsepower, as it were. But although Hippolyte is more than capable, the operation must be performed to bring him back to the human and away from the equine, which the first syllable of his name suggests. To have a disability is to be an animal, to be part of the Other. Davis

A newspaper article appears after the operation's apparent initial success, praising the spirit of progress. The article envisages Hippolyte's welcome back into the human community adding: "Hasn't the time come to cry out that the blind shall see, the deaf hear, the lame walk?" (ibid., 128) The imperative is clear: science will eradicate disability. However, by a touch of Flaubertian irony, Hippolyte's leg becomes gangrenous and has to be amputated. The older doctor lectures Charles about his attempt to norm this individual.

This is what you get from listening to the fads from Paris! ... We are practitioners; we cure people, and we wouldn't dream of operating on someone who is in perfect health. Straighten club feet! As if one could straighten club feet indeed! It is as if one wished to make a hunchback straight!

(ibid., 131)

While Flaubert's work illustrates some of the points I have been making, it is important that we do no simply think of the novel as merely an example of how an historical development lodges within a particular text. Rather, I think there is a larger claim to be made about novels and norms.

While Flaubert may parody current ideas about normalcy in medicine, there is another sense in which the novel as a form promotes and symbolically produces normative structures. Indeed, the whole focus of *Madame Bovary* is on Emma's abnormality and Flaubert's abhorrence of normal life. If we accept that novels are a social practice that arose as part of the project of middle-class hegemony,[6] then we can see that the plot and character development of novels tend to pull toward the normative. For example, most characters in nineteenth-century novels are somewhat ordinary people who are put in abnormal circumstances, as opposed to the heroic characters who represent the ideal in earlier forms such as the epic.

If disability appears in a novel, it is rarely centrally represented. It is unusual for a main character to be a person with disabilities, although minor characters, like Tiny Tim, can be deformed in ways that arouse pity. In the case of Esther Summerson, of Dickens' *Bleak House*, who is scarred by smallpox, her scars are made virtually to disappear through the agency of love. Dinah Craik's *Olive* is one of the few nineteenth-century novels in which the main character has a disability (a slight spinal deformity), but even with her the emphasis on the deformity diminishes over the course of the novel so by the end it is no longer an issue. On the other hand, as sufficient research has shown, more often than not villains tend to be physically abnormal: scarred, deformed, or mutilated.[7]

I am not saying simply that novels embody the prejudices of society toward people with disabilities. That is clearly a truism. Rather, I am asserting that the very structures on which the novel rests tend to be normative, ideologically emphasizing the universal quality of the central character whose normativity encourages us to identify with him or her.[8] Furthermore, the novel's goal is to reproduce, on some level, the semiologically normative signs surrounding the reader, that paradoxically help the reader to read those signs in the world as well as the text. This normativity in narrative will by definition create the abnormal, the Other, the disabled, the native, the colonized subject, and so on.

Even on the level of plot, one can see the implication of eugenic notions of normativity. The parentage of characters in novels plays a crucial role. Rather than being self-creating beings, characters in novels have deep biological debts to their forebears, even if the characters are orphans—or perhaps especially if they are orphans. The great Heliodoric plots of romance, in which lower-class characters are found actually to be noble, take a new turn in the novel. While nobility may be less important, characters nevertheless inherit bourgeois respectability, moral rectitude, and eventually money and position through their genetic connection. In the novelistic world of nature versus nurture, nature almost always wins out. Thus Oliver Twist will naturally bear the banner of bourgeois morality and linguistic normativity, even though he grows up in the workhouse. Oliver will always be normal, even in abnormal circumstances.[9]

A further development in the novel can be seen in Zola's works. Before Zola, for example in the work of Balzac, the author attempted to show how the inherently good character of a protagonist was affected by the material world. Thus we read of the journey of the soul, of everyman or everywoman, through a trying and corrupting world. But Zola's theory of the novel depends on the idea of inherited traits and biological determinism. As Zola wrote in *The Experimental Novel*:

> Determinism dominates everything. It is scientific investigation, it is experimental reasoning, which combats one by one the hypotheses of the idealists, and which replaces purely imaginary novels by novels of observation and experimentation.
>
> (1964, 18)

In this view, the author is a kind of scientist watching how humans, with their naturally inherited dispositions, interact with each other. As Zola wrote, his intention in the Rougon–Macquart series was to show how heredity would influence a family "making superhuman efforts but always failing because of its own nature and the influences upon it" (Zola 1993, viii). This series would be a study of the "singular effect of heredity" (ibid.). "These young girls so pure, these young men so loyal, represented to us in certain novels, do not belong to the earth. ... We tell everything, we do not make a choice, neither do we idealize" (ibid., 127).

My point is that a disabilities-studies consciousness can alter the way we see not just novels that have main characters who are disabled but any novel. In thinking through the issue of disability, I have come to see that almost any literary work will have some reference to the abnormal, to disability, and so on. I would explain this phenomenon as a result of the hegemony of normalcy. This normalcy must constantly be enforced in public venues (like the novel), must always be creating and bolstering its image by processing, comparing, constructing, deconstructing images of normalcy and the abnormal. In fact, once one begins to notice, there really is a rare novel that does not have some characters with disabilities—characters who are lame, tubercular, dying of AIDS, chronically ill, depressed, mentally ill, and so on.

Let me take the example of some novels by Joseph Conrad. I pick Conrad not because he is especially representative, but just because I happen to be teaching a course on Conrad. Although he is not remembered in any sense as a writer on disability, Conrad is a good test case, as it turns out, because he wrote during a period when eugenics had permeated British society and when Freud had begun to write about normal and abnormal psychology. Conrad, too, was somewhat influenced by Zola, particularly in *The Secret Agent*.

The first thing I noticed about Conrad's work is that metaphors of disability abound. Each book has numerous instances of phrases like the following selections from *Lord Jim*:

a dance of lame, blind, mute thoughts—a whirl of awful cripples.

(Conrad 1986, 114)

[he] comported himself in that clatter as though he had been stone-deaf.

(ibid., 183)

there was nothing of the cripple about him.

(ibid., 234)

Her broken figure hovered in crippled little jumps . . .

(ibid., 263)

he was made blind and deaf and without pity . . .

(ibid., 300)

a blind belief in the righteousness of his will against all mankind . . .

(ibid., 317)

They were erring men whom suffering had made blind to right and wrong.

(ibid., 333)

you dismal cripples, you . . .

(ibid., 340)

unmoved like a deaf man . . .

(ibid., 319)

These references are almost like tics, appearing at regular intervals. They tend to focus on deafness, blindness, dumbness, and lameness, and they tend to use these metaphors to represent limitations on normal morals, ethics, and of course language. While it is entirely possible to maintain that these figures of speech are hardly more than mere linguistic convention, I would argue that the very regularity of these occurrences speaks to a reflexive patrolling function in which the author continuously checks and notes.

The use of phrenology, too, is linked to the patrolling of normalcy, through the construction of character. So, in *Heart of Darkness*, for example, when Marlow is about to leave for Africa a doctor measures the dimensions of his skull to enable him to discern if any quantitative changes subsequently occur as a result of the colonial encounter. So many of the characters in novels are formed from the ableist cultural repertoire of normalized head, face, and body features that characteristically signify personal qualities. Thus in *The Secret Agent*, the corpulent, lazy body of Verloc indicates his moral sleaziness, and Stevie's large ears and head shape are explicitly seen by Ossipon as characteristic of degeneracy and criminality as described in the theories of the nineteenth-century eugenic phrenologist Cesare Lombroso.

In a Zolaesque moment of insight, Ossipon sees Stevie's degeneracy as linked to his sister Winnie:

> he gazed scientifically at that woman, the sister of a degenerate, a degenerate herself—of a murdering type. He gazed at her and invoked Lombroso. . . . He gazed scientifically. He gazed at her cheeks, at her nose, at her eyes, at her ears . . . Bad! . . . Fatal!
>
> (Conrad 1968, 269)

This eugenic gaze that scrutinizes Winnie and Stevie is really only a recapitulation of the novelistic gaze that sees meaning in normative and non-normative features. In fact, every member of the Verloc family has something "wrong" with them, including Winnie's mother who has trouble walking on her edematous legs. The moral turpitude and physical grimness of London is embodied in Verloc's inner circle. Michaelis, too, is obese and "wheezed as if deadened and oppressed by the layer of fat on his chest" (ibid., 73). Karl Yundt is toothless, gouty, and walks with a cane. Ossipon is racially abnormal having "crinkly yellow hair . . . a flattened nose and prominent mouth cast in the rough mould of the Negro type . . . [and] almond-shaped eyes [that] leered languidly over high cheek-bones" (ibid., 75)—all features indicating African and Asian qualities, particularly the cunning, opiated glance. The latter links up the eugenic with the racialized and nationalized matrix of identity.

I am not claiming that this reading of Conrad is brilliant or definitive. But I do want to show that even in texts that do not appear to be about disability, the issue of normalcy is fully deployed. One can find in almost any novel, I would argue, a kind of surveying of the terrain of the body, an attention to difference—physical, mental, and national. This activity of consolidating the hegemony of normalcy is one that needs more attention, in addition to the kinds of work that have been done in locating the thematics of disability in literature.

What I have tried to show here is that the very term that permeates our contemporary life—the normal—is a configuration that arises in a particular historical moment. It is part of a notion of progress, of industrialization, and of ideological consolidation of the power of the bourgeoisie. The implications of the hegemony of normalcy are profound and extend into the very heart of cultural production. The novel form, that proliferator of ideology, is intricately connected with concepts of the norm. From the typicality of the central character, to the normalizing devices of plot to bring deviant characters back into the norms of society, to the normalizing coda of endings, the nineteenth- and twentieth-century novel promulgates and disburses notions of normalcy and by extension makes of physical differences ideological differences. Characters with disabilities are always marked with ideological meaning, as are moments of disease or accident that transform such characters. One of the tasks for a developing consciousness of disability issues is the attempt, then, to reverse the hegemony of the normal and to institute alternative ways of thinking about the abnormal.

Many of the essays in this collection do just that. As disability studies progresses along with postmodernism and posthumanism, we are seeing that normality continues to hold sway insofar as the body, the medical, and the push to diagnose disabilities are concerned. But the writers in this reader are not simply trying to include disability under the rubric of normal but to question the idea of normality, and to expand the definition of disability into such concepts as neurodiversity, debility and capacity, chronic illness, invisible conditions, and the like. In other words while consolidating the idea of disability, these critics are at the same time disarticulating the elements of disability to ponder how part and whole fit together. It's less a question of segregating the normal from the abnormal, the old eugenic game, as it is to describe, detail, theorize, and occupy the category of disability. Along these lines, intersectionality—the subject position of holding multiple identities—makes complex the general rubric of disability itself. If anything, this collection of essays serves to render complex the simple fact of impairment while rendering simple the ideological screen of normality.

NOTES

1. One wants to make sure that Aristotle's idea of the mean is not confused with the norm. The Aristotelian mean is a kind of fictional construct. Aristotle advocates that in choosing between personal traits, one should tend to choose between the extremes. He does not however think of the population as falling generally into that mean. The mean, for Aristotle, is more of a heuristic device to assist in moral and ethical choices. In the sense of being a middle term or a middle way, it carries more of a spatial sense than does the term "average" or "norm."
2. This rather remarkable confluence between eugenics and statistics has been pointed out by Donald A. MacKenzie, but I do not believe his observations have had the impact they should.
3. See my *Enforcing Normalcy* Chapter 6 for more on the novel *Frankenstein* and its relation to notions of disability.
4. Many twentieth-century prejudices against the learning disabled come from this period. The founder of the intelligence test still in use, Alfred Binet, was a Galton acolyte. The American psychologist Henry H. Goddard used Binet's tests in America and turned the numbers into categories—"idiots" being those whose mental age was 1 or 2, "imbeciles" ranged in mental age from 3 to 7. Goddard invented the term "moron" (which he took from the Greek for "dull" or "stupid") for those between 8 and 12. Pejorative terms like "moron" or "retarded" have by now found their way into common usage (Kevles 1985, 78). And even the term "mongoloid idiot" to describe a person with Down's syndrome was used as recently as 1970s not as a pejorative term but in medical texts as a diagnosis. [See Michael Bérubé's fascinating article "Life As We Know It" for more on this phenomenon of labelling.]
5. If this argument sounds strangely familiar, it is being repeated and promulgated in the neo-conservative book *The Bell Curve* which claims that poverty and intelligence are linked through inherited characteristics.
6. This assumption is based on my previous works—*Factual Fictions: Origins of the English Novel* and *Resisting Novels: Ideology and Fiction*—as well as the cumulative body of writing about the relationship between capitalism, material life, culture, and fiction. The work of Raymond Williams, Terry Eagleton, Nancy Armstrong, Mary Poovey, John Bender, Michael McKeon, and others points in similar directions.
7. The issue of people with disabilities in literature is a well-documented one and is one I want generally to avoid in this work. Excellent books abound on the subject, including Alan Gartner and Tom Joe, eds., *Images of the Disabled, Disabling Images* (New York: Praeger, 1987) and the work of Deborah Kent including "In Search of a Heroine: Images of Women with Disabilities in Fiction and Drama" in Michelle Fine and Adrienne Asch, eds. *Women with Disabilities: Essays in Psychology, Culture, and Politics* (Philadelphia: Temple University Press, 1988).
8. And if the main character has a major disability, then we are encouraged to identify with that character's ability to overcome their disability.
9. The genealogical family line is both hereditary and financial in the bourgeois novel. The role of the family is defined by Jürgen Habermas thus: "as a genealogical link it [the family] guaranteed a continuity of personnel

that consisted materially in the accumulation of capital and was anchored in the absence of legal restrictions concerning the inheritance of property" (47). The fact that the biological connectedness and the financial connectedness are conflated in the novel only furthers the point that normality is an enforced condition that upholds the totality of the bourgeois system.

WORKS CITED

Bell, Alexander Graham. 1969. *Memoir upon the Formation of a Deaf Variety of the Human Race*. Washington, DC: Alexander Graham Bell Association for the Deaf.

Blacker, C. P. 1952. *Eugenics: Galton and After*. Cambridge, MA: Harvard University Press.

Conrad, Joseph. 1986. *Lord Jim*. London: Penguin.

——. 1990 [1968]. *The Secret Agent*. London: Penguin.

Davis, Lennard J. 1995. *Enforcing Normalcy*. New York: Verso Books.

Farrall, Lyndsay Andrew. 1985. *The Origin and Growth of the English Eugenics Movement 1865–1925*. New York: Garland.

Flaubert, Gustave. 1965. *Madam Bovary*. Trans. Paul de Man. New York: Norton.

Freud, Sigmund. 1977. *Introductory Lectures on Psychoanalysis*. Trans. James Strachey. New York: Norton.

Habermas, Jürgen. 1989. *The Structural Transformation of the Public Sphere: An Inquiry into a Category of Bourgeois Society*. Trans. Thomas Burger. Cambridge, MA: MIT Press.

Kevles, Daniel J. 1985. *In the Name of Eugenics: Genetics and the Uses of Human* Heredity. New York: Alfred A. Knopf.

MacKenzie, Donald. A. 1981. *Statistics in Britain, 1865–1930*. Edinburgh: Edinburgh University Press.

Marx, Karl. 1970. *Capital*. Vol. 1. Trans. Samuel Moore and Edward Aveling. New York: International Publishers.

Porter, Theodore M. 1986. *The Rise of Statistical Thinking 1820–1900*. Princeton, NJ: Princeton University Press.

Stigler, Stephen M. 1986. *The History of Statistics: The Measurement of Uncertainty before 1900*. Cambridge, MA: Harvard University Press.

Zola, Emile. 1964. *The Experimental Novel and Other Essays*. Trans. Belle M. Sherman. New York: Haskel House.

——. 1993. *The Masterpiece*. Trans. Thomas Walton. London: Oxford University Press.

PART I

*H*istorical Perspectives

CHAPTER 2

Disability and the Justification of Inequality in American History

Douglas C. Baynton

SUMMARY

Baynton argues that disability has been one of the most prevalent justifications for inequality in American history, and yet it has been rarely studied by historians. This essay focuses on three groups—women, African Americans, and immigrants—whose inequitable treatment has been justified when the concept of disability has been applied to them. Oppressed groups were routinely charged with myriad physical or intellectual flaws that both explained and justified their inferior social status. Even as the oppressed groups fought against inequality, they most often did so by insisting that they were not disabled rather than arguing that disability did not justify inequality.

As the concept of normality became intertwined with social progress in the mid-1800s, nonwhite races were routinely understood as both disabled and lagging behind in human evolution. For example, pro-slavery advocates argued that African Americans lacked the intelligence to participate in society and were more prone to disease, physical impairments, and immoral behavior. This line of thinking served as a justification for slavery as a way to protect the slaves themselves.

Similarly, opponents of women's suffrage argued that women were frail, irrational, and excessively emotional. Thus women could be accused of being incapable of using the vote correctly and were imagined to be in danger of exhausting themselves if exposed to political participation. Baynton argues that even though historians acknowledge disability as a way of limiting women's rights, they tend to focus on gender inequality rather than the ways disability is used to structure social hierarchies.

Baynton provides an overview of such a structure in the history of American immigration policy, which not only explicitly barred disabled people but also established quotas for particular ethnic groups by insisting they were unable to function as laborers or citizens. But when immigrants or any other group attain equality by arguing they are not disabled, Baynton says, this strategy "tacitly accepts the idea that disability is a legitimate reason for inequality." Rather than continuing to operate on this assumption that disability implies the power to discredit a group, historians can now bring disability to the center of their historical inquiries.

Since the social and political revolutions of the eighteenth century, the trend in western political thought has been to refuse to take for granted inequalities between persons or groups. Differential and unequal treatment has continued, of course, but it has been considered incumbent on modern societies to produce a rational explanation for such treatment. In recent decades, historians and other scholars in the humanities have studied intensely and often challenged the ostensibly rational explanations for inequalities based on identity—in particular, gender, race, and ethnicity.

Disability, however, one of the most prevalent justifications for inequality, has rarely been the subject of historical inquiry.

Disability has functioned historically to justify inequality for disabled people themselves, but it has also done so for women and minority groups. That is, not only has it been considered justifiable to treat disabled people unequally, but the *concept* of disability has been used to justify discrimination against other groups by attributing disability to them. Disability was a significant factor in the three great citizenship debates of the nineteenth and early twentieth centuries: women's suffrage, African American freedom and civil rights, and the restriction of immigration. When categories of citizenship were questioned, challenged, and disrupted, disability was called on to clarify and define who deserved, and who was deservedly excluded from, citizenship. Opponents of political and social equality for women cited their supposed physical, intellectual, and psychological flaws, deficits, and deviations from the male norm. These flaws—irrationality, excessive emotionality, physical weakness—are in essence mental, emotional, and physical disabilities, although they are rarely discussed or examined as such. Arguments for racial inequality and immigration restrictions invoked supposed tendencies to feeblemindedness, mental illness, deafness, blindness, and other disabilities in particular races and ethnic groups. Furthermore, disability figured prominently not just in arguments *for* the inequality of women and minorities but also in arguments *against* those inequalities. Such arguments took the form of vigorous denials that the groups in question actually had these disabilities; they were not disabled, the argument went, and therefore were not proper subjects for discrimination. Rarely have oppressed groups denied that disability is an adequate justification for social and political inequality. Thus, while disabled people can be considered one of the minority groups historically assigned inferior status and subjected to discrimination, disability has functioned for all such groups as a sign of and justification for inferiority.

It is this use of disability as a marker of hierarchical relations that historians of disability must demonstrate in order to bring disability into the mainstream of historical study. Over a decade ago, Joan Scott made a similar argument about the difficulty of persuading historians to take gender seriously. Scott noted that despite a substantial number of works on women's history, the topic remained marginal in the discipline as a whole. A typical response to women's history was "Women had a history separate from men's, therefore let feminists do women's history, which need not concern us," or "My understanding of the French Revolution is not changed by knowing that women participated in it." Scott argued that research on the role of women in history was necessary but not sufficient to change the paradigms of the profession. To change the way in which most historians went about their work, feminists had to demonstrate not just that women participated in the making of history but that gender is "a constitutive element of social relationships" and "a primary way of signifying relationships of power."[1]

To demonstrate the ubiquity of gender in social thought, Scott focused on political history, a field in which historians were especially apt to argue that gender was unimportant, and where most historians today would imagine disability to be equally so. She chose as an example Edmund Burke's attack on the French Revolution, noting that it was "built around a contrast between ugly, murderous *sans-culottes* hags ('the furies of hell, in the abused shape of the vilest of women') and the soft femininity of

Marie-Antoinette." The contrast Scott highlights calls on not only gender but also notions of beauty, disfigurement, and misshapen bodies that would be amenable to an analysis informed by disability. Even more striking, however, is that in addition to the rhetoric of gender, Burke's argument rested just as fundamentally on a rhetorical contrast between the natural constitution of the body politic and the *monstrous* deformity that the revolution had brought forth. Burke repeatedly referred to "public measures...deformed into monsters," "monstrous democratic assemblies," "this monster of a constitution," "unnatural and monstrous activity," and the like (as well as evoking "blind prejudice," actions taken "blindly," "blind followers," and "blind obedience" and alluding to the madness, imbecility, and idiocy of the revolutionary leaders). This rhetoric of monstrosity was by no means peculiar to the conservative cause. Tom Paine, in his response to Burke, also found the monster metaphor an apt and useful one but turned it around: "Exterminate the monster aristocracy," he wrote.[2]

The metaphor of the natural versus the monstrous was a fundamental way of constructing social reality in Burke's time. By the late nineteenth and early twentieth centuries, however, the concept of the natural was to a great extent displaced or subsumed by the concept of normality.[3] Since then, normality has been deployed in all aspects of modern life as a means of measuring, categorizing, and managing populations (and resisting such management). Normality is a complex concept, with an etiology that includes the rise of the social sciences, the science of statistics, and industrialization with its need for interchangeable parts and interchangeable workers. It has been used in a remarkable range of contexts and with a bewildering variety of connotations. The natural and the normal both are ways of establishing the universal, unquestionable good and right. Both are also ways of establishing social hierarchies that justify the denial of legitimacy and certain rights to individuals or groups. Both are constituted in large part by being set in opposition to culturally variable notions of disability—just as the natural was meaningful in relation to the monstrous and the deformed, so are the cultural meanings of the normal produced in tandem with disability.[4]

The concept of normality in its modern sense arose in the mid-nineteenth century in the context of a pervasive belief in progress. It became a culturally powerful idea with the advent of evolutionary theory. The ideal of the natural had been a static concept for what was seen as an essentially unchanging world, dominant at a time when "the book of nature" was represented as the guidebook of God. The natural was good and right because it conformed to the intent or design of Nature or the Creator of nature. Normality, in contrast, was an empirical and dynamic concept for a changing and progressing world, the premise of which was that one could discern in human behavior the direction of human evolution and progress and use that as a guide. The ascendance of normality signaled a shift in the locus of faith from a God-centered to a human-centered world, from a culture that looked within to a core and backward to lost Edenic origins toward one that looked outward to behavior and forward to a perfected future.

Just as the counterpart to the natural was the monstrous, so the opposite of the normal person was the defective. Although normality ostensibly denoted the average, the usual, and the ordinary, in actual usage it functioned as an ideal and excluded only those defined as *below* average. "Is the child normal?" was never a question that expressed fear about whether a child had *above*-average intelligence, motor skills, or beauty. Abnormal signified the *sub*normal.[5] In the context of a pervasive belief that the tendency of the human race was to improve itself constantly, that barring something out of the ordinary humanity moved ever upward away from its animal origins and toward greater perfection, normality was implicitly defined as that which advanced progress (or at least did not impede it). Abnormality, conversely, was that which pulled humanity back toward its past, toward its animal origins.

As an evolutionary concept, normality was intimately connected to the western notion of progress. By the mid-nineteenth century, nonwhite races were routinely connected to people with disabilities, both of whom were depicted as evolutionary laggards or throwbacks. As a consequence, the concept of disability, intertwined with the concept of race, was also caught up in ideas of evolutionary progress. Physical or mental abnormalities were commonly depicted as instances of atavism, reversions to earlier stages of evolutionary development. Down's syndrome, for example, was called Mongolism by the doctor who first identified it in 1866 because he believed the syndrome to be the result of a biological reversion by Caucasians to the Mongol racial type. Teachers of the deaf at the end of the century spoke of making deaf children more like "normal" people and less like savages by forbidding them the use of sign language, and they opposed deaf marriages with a rhetoric of evolutionary progress and decline. Recent work on late nineteenth-century freak shows has highlighted how disability and race intersected with an ideology of evolutionary hierarchy. James W. Trent argued in a recent article that at the 1904 World's Fair, displays of "defectives" alongside displays of "primitives" signaled similar and interconnected classification schemes for both defective individuals and defective races. Both were placed in hierarchies constructed on the basis of whether they were seen as "improvable" or not—capable of being educated, cured, or civilized. Whether it was individual atavism or a group's lack of evolutionary development, the common element in all was the presence or attribution of disability.[6]

Disability arguments were prominent in justifications of slavery in the early to mid-nineteenth century and of other forms of unequal relations between white and black Americans after slavery's demise. The most common disability argument for slavery was simply that African Americans lacked sufficient intelligence to participate or compete on an equal basis in society with white Americans. This alleged deficit was sometimes attributed to physical causes, as when an article on the "diseases and physical peculiarities of the negro race" in the *New Orleans Medical and Surgical Journal* helpfully explained, "It is this defective hematosis, or atmospherization of the blood, conjoined with a deficiency of cerebral matter in the cranium, and an excess of nervous matter distributed to the organs of sensation and assimilation, that is the true cause of that debasement of mind, which has rendered the people of Africa unable to take care of themselves." Diseases of blacks were commonly attributed to "inferior organisms and constitutional weaknesses," which were claimed to be among "the most pronounced race characteristics of the American negro." While the supposedly higher intelligence of "mulattos" compared to "pure" blacks was offered as evidence for the superiority of whites, those who argued against "miscegenation" claimed to the contrary that the products of "race-mixing" were themselves less intelligent and less healthy than members of either race in "pure" form.[7] A medical doctor, John Van Evrie of New York, avowed that the "disease and disorganiz-ation" in the "abnormal," "blotched, deformed" offspring of this "monstrous" act "could no more exist beyond a given period than any other physical degener-ation, no more than tumors, cancers, or other abnormal growths or physical dis-ease can become permanent." Some claimed greater "corporeal vigor" for "mixed offspring" but a deterioration in "moral and intellectual endowments," while still others saw greater intelligence but "frailty," "less stamina," and "inherent physical weakness."[8]

A second line of disability argument was that African Americans, because of their inherent physical and mental weaknesses, were prone to become disabled under conditions of freedom and equality. A New York medical journal reported that deafness was three times more common and blind-ness twice as common among free blacks in the North compared to slaves in the South. John C. Calhoun, senator from South Carolina and one of the most influential spokesmen for the slave states, thought it a powerful argument in defense of slavery that the "number of deaf and dumb, blind, idiots, and insane, of the negroes in the States that have changed the ancient relation between the races" was seven times higher than in the slave states.[9]

While much has been written about the justification of slavery by religious leaders in the South, more needs to be said about similar justifications by medical doctors. Dr. Samuel Cartwright, in 1851, for example, described two types of mental illness to which African Americans were especially subject. The first, Drapetoma-nia, a condition that caused slaves to run away—"as much a disease of the mind as any other species of mental alienation"—was common among slaves whose masters had "made themselves too familiar with them, treating them as equals." The need to submit to a master was built into the very bodies of African Americans, in whom "we see *'genu flexit'* written in the physical structure of his knees, being more flexed or bent, than any other kind of man." The second mental disease peculiar to African Americans, Dysaesthesia Aechiopis—a unique ailment differing "from every other species of mental disease, as it is accompanied with physical signs or lesions of the body"—resulted in a desire to avoid work and generally to cause mischief. It was commonly known to overseers as "rascal-ity." Its cause, similar to that of Drapetoma-nia, was a lack of firm governance, and it was therefore far more common among free blacks than among slaves—indeed, nearly universal among them—although it was a "common occurrence on badly-governed plantations" as well.[10]

Dr. Van Evrie also contributed to this line of thought when he wrote in the 1860s that education of African Americans came "at the expense of the body, shortening the existence" and resulted in bodies "dwarfed or destroyed" by the unnatural exertion. "An 'educated negro,' like a 'free negro,' is a social monstrosity, even more unnatural and repulsive than the latter." He argued further that, since they belonged to a race inferior by nature, *all* blacks were necess-arily inferior to (nearly) *all* whites. It occasionally happened that a particular white person might not be superior to all black people because of a condition that "deforms or blights individuals; they may be idiotic, insane, or otherwise incapable." But these unnatural exceptions to the rule were "the result of human vices, crimes, or ignorance, immediate or remote." Only disability might lower a white person in the scale of life to the level of a being of a marked race.[11]

By the turn of the century, medical doctors were still arguing that African Americans were disabled by freedom and therefore in need of greater oversight. J. F. Miller, writing in the *North Carolina Medical*

Journal, thought it important to inquire whether "the effect of freedom upon the mental and physical health of the negroes of the South" had been "damaging or otherwise." His conclusion was that there were "more congenital defects" and a dramatic increase in mental illness and tuberculosis, which supposedly had been rare among enslaved African Americans. Freedom, for which the African American's weak mind and constitution were ill suited, had brought to the former slave "a beautiful harvest of mental and physical degeneration and he is now becoming a martyr to an heredity thus established."[12]

While these arguments were often contradictory, incoherent, or simply ludicrous, disability was central to all of them. If freedom for African Americans was undesirable and slavery good, then it was sufficient to note that free blacks were more likely than slaves to be disabled. The decisive argument for miscegenation being morally wrong or socially injurious was that it produced disability. The contention had to be countered, and no argument on other grounds could trump it. Samuel Forry, for example, writing in the *New York Journal of Medicine* in 1844, noted that the supposedly higher rates of insanity among free blacks compared to slaves had been "seized upon by journals devoted to the peculiar institutions of the Southern States, as a powerful argument." Forry retorted, first, that the census did not allow a reliable comparison of deafness, blindness, idiocy, and insanity in free and enslaved blacks and, second, that even were it the case that free blacks in the North suffered more disability than slaves, slavery and freedom might not be the determinants. Instead, perhaps "the whole constitution of the black is adapted to a tropical region," and their mental and physical health was therefore bound to suffer in the northern climate.[13] The argument that a people might be enslaved to protect them from disability he left unchallenged.

Race and disability intersected in the concept of the normal, as both prescription and description. American blacks, for example, were said to flourish in their "normal condition" of slavery, while the "'free' or abnormal negro" inevitably fell into illness, disability, and eventually extinction. The hierarchy of races was itself depicted as a continuum of normality. Just as medical textbook illustrations compared the normal body with the abnormal, so social science textbooks illustrated the normal race and the abnormal ones. Arnold Guyot, in his 1873 textbook *Physical Geography*, under the heading "The White Race the Normal, or Typical, Race," compared the beauty, regularity of features, and "harmony in all the proportions of the figure" of the white race with those who have "gradually deviated" from the normal ideal. Similarly, Dr. John C. Nott, writing in the *American Journal of Medical Sciences* in 1843, invited the reader to "look first upon the Caucasian female with her rose and lily skin, silky hair. Venus form, and well-chiseled features—and then upon the African wench with her black and odorous skin, woolly head and animal features—and compare their intellectual and moral qualities, and their whole anatomical structure." He added for good measure that the American Indian "has many peculiarities which are just as striking." In nineteenth-century freak shows, where disability and race intersected to illustrate familiar narratives of evolutionary progress, disabled adults were displayed as less-evolved creatures from far-off jungles. P. T. Barnum promoted his American Museum exhibit "What Is It?" as the "missing link" between human and animal, a "man-monkey." At least two different men played the role: a white actor with unusually short legs of uneven length and a mentally retarded black man with microcephaly who later became known by the stage name Zip. The presence of disability in both cases, in addition to race in one of them, was in effect the costume that signified the role of "subhuman."[14]

It is not new to point out that images of American blacks have commonly shown them with exaggerated lips, amusingly long or bowed legs, grotesquely big feet, bad posture, missing teeth, crossed or bulging eyes, and otherwise deformed bodies. At least since 1792, when Benjamin Rush explained that the skin color of Africans was due to their suffering from congenital leprosy, black skin itself has been treated as anomalous, a defect and a disfigurement, something akin to an all-body birthmark and often a sign of sin or degeneracy. Advertisements for soap in the nineteenth century often played on this idea of dark skin as defect with, for example, a pink-cheeked child asking an African American child, "Why doesn't your mamma wash you with Fairy Soap?"[15] Another advertisement told a tale of children who were bathed daily, "Because their mother did believe/That white they could be made/So on them with a scrubbing brush/Unmerciful she laid." The mother's efforts were fruitless until she found the right brand of soap: "Sweet and clean her sons became/it's true, as I'm a workman/And both are now completely white, Washed by this soap of Kirkman."[16] Dreydoppel Soap told a similar story of an African American boy ("A mite of queer humanity/As dark as a cloudy night") who scrubbed himself with acids, fasted, took sulfur baths, and "sampled all the medicine that ever was made or brewed" in the attempt to cure his unfortunate skin color. "He built an air-tight sweat box with the/Hope that he would bleach/The sweat poured down in rivers/but the Black stuck like a leech." That is, until he discovered Dreydoppel soap: "One trial was all he needed/Realized was his fondest hope/His face was white as white could be/There's nothing like Dreydoppel Soap."[17]

Daryl Michael Scott has described how both conservatives and liberals have long used an extensive repertory of "damage imagery" to describe African Americans. Conservatives "operated primarily from within a biological framework and argued for the innate inferiority of people of African descent" in order to justify social and political exclusion. Liberals maintained that social conditions were responsible for black inferiority and used damage imagery to argue for inclusion and rehabilitation; but regardless of their intentions, Scott argues, liberal damage imagery "reinforced the belief system that made whites feel superior in the first place." Both the "contempt and pity" of conservatives and liberals—a phrase that equally well describes historically prevalent attitudes toward disabled people—framed Americans of African descent as defective. Scott cites the example of Charles S. Johnson, chair of the social science department and later president of Fisk University, who told students in a 1928 speech that "the sociologists classify Negroes with cripples, persons with recognized physical handicaps." Like Johnson, Scott is critical of the fact that "African Americans were often lumped with the 'defective,' 'delinquent,' and dependent classes." This is obviously a bad place to be "lumped." Scott does not ask, however, why that might be the case.[18] The attribution of disease or disability to racial minorities has a long history. Yet, while many have pointed out the injustice and perniciousness of attributing these qualities to a racial or ethnic group, little has been written about why these attributions are such powerful weapons for inequality, why they were so furiously denied and condemned by their targets, and what this tells us about our attitudes toward disability.

During the long-running debate over women's suffrage in the nineteenth and early twentieth centuries, one of the rhetorical tactics of suffrage opponents was to point to the physical, intellectual, and psychological flaws of women, their frailty, irrationality, and emotional excesses. By the late nineteenth century, those claims were sometimes expressed in terms of evolutionary progress; like racial and ethnic minorities, women were said to be less evolved than white men, their disabilities a result of lesser evolutionary development. Cynthia Eagle Russett has noted that "women and savages, together with idiots, criminals, and pathological monstrosities [those with congenital disabilities] were a constant source of anxiety to male intellectuals in the late nineteenth century."[19] What all shared was an evolutionary inferiority, the result of arrested development or atavism.

Paralleling the arguments made in defense of slavery, two types of disability argument were used in opposition to women's suffrage: that women had disabilities that made them incapable of using the franchise responsibly, and that because of their frailty women would become disabled if exposed to the rigors of political participation. The American antisuffragist Grace Goodwin, for example, pointed to the "great temperamental disabilities" with which women had to contend: "woman lacks endurance in things mental. ... She lacks nervous stability. The suffragists who dismay England are nerve-sick women." The second line of argument, which was not incompatible with the first and often accompanied it, went beyond the claim that women's flaws made them incapable of exercising equal political and social rights with men to warn that if women were given those rights, disability would surely follow. This argument is most closely identified with Edward Clarke, author of *Sex in Education; or, A Fair Chance for Girls.* Clarke's argument chiefly concerned education for women, though it was often applied to suffrage as well. Clarke maintained that overuse of the brain among

young women was in large part responsible for the "numberless pale, weak, neuralgic, dyspeptic, hysterical, menorraghic, dysmenorrhoeic girls and women" of America. The result of excessive education in this country was "bloodless female faces, that suggest consumption, scrofula, anemia, and neuralgia." An appropriate education designed for their frail constitutions would ensure "a future secure from neuralgia, uterine disease, hysteria, and other derangements of the nervous system."[20]

Similarly, Dr. William Warren Potter, addressing the Medical Society of New York in 1891, suggested that many a mother was made invalid by inappropriate education: "her reproductive organs are dwarfed, deformed, weakened, and diseased, by artificial causes imposed upon her during their development."[21] Dr. A. Lapthorn Smith asserted in *Popular Science Monthly* that educated women were increasingly "sick and suffering before marriage and are physically disabled from performing physiological functions in a normal manner." Antisuffragists likewise warned that female participation in politics invariably led to "nervous prostration" and "hysteria," while Dr. Almroth E. Wright noted the "fact that there is mixed up with the woman's movement much mental disorder." A prominent late nineteenth-century neurophysiologist, Charles L. Dana, estimated that enfranchising women would result in a 25 percent increase in insanity among them and "throw into the electorate a mass of voters of delicate nervous stability ... which might do injury to itself without promoting the community's good." The answer for Clarke, Potter, and others of like mind was special education suited to women's special needs. As with disabled people today, women's social position was treated as a medical problem that necessitated separate and special care. Those who wrote with acknowledged authority on the "woman question" were doctors. As Clarke wrote, the answer to the "problem of woman's sphere...must be obtained from physiology, not from ethics or metaphysics."[22]

While historians have not overlooked the use of disability to deny women's rights, they have given their attention entirely to gender inequality and not at all to the construction and maintenance of cultural hierarchies based on disability. Lois Magner has described how women were said to bear the "onerous functions of the female," which incapacitated them for "active life" and produced a "mental disability that rendered women unfit" for political engagement. Nancy Woloch has noted that a "major antisuffragist point was that women were physically, mentally, and emotionally incapable of duties associated with the vote. Lacking rationality and sound judgment, they suffered from 'logical infirmity of mind.'...Unable to withstand the pressure of political life, they would be prone to paroxysms of hysteria." Aileen Kraditor, in her intellectual history of the women's suffrage movement, wrote that antisuffragists "described woman's physical constitution as too delicate to withstand the turbulence of political life. Her alleged weakness, nervousness, and proneness to fainting would certainly be out of place in polling booths and party conventions." On the one hand, this was of course an unfounded stereotype deserving of ridicule, as Kraditor's ironic tone suggests. On the other hand, just as it was left unchallenged at the time, historians today leave unchallenged the notion that weakness, nervousness, or proneness to fainting might legitimately disqualify one for suffrage.[23]

Disability figured not just in arguments *for* the inequality of women and minorities but also in arguments *against those* inequalities. Suffragists rarely challenged the notion that disability justified political inequality and instead disputed the claim that women suffered from these disabilities. Their arguments took three forms: one, women were not disabled and therefore deserved the vote; two, women were being erroneously and slanderously classed with disabled people, with those who were legitimately denied suffrage; and three, women were not naturally or inherently disabled but were *made* disabled by inequality—suffrage would ameliorate or cure these disabilities.

References to the intelligence and abilities of women, countering the imputations of female inferiority, pervaded suffrage rhetoric. Although more common later in the century, this form of argument was already in evidence in 1848 at the Seneca Falls Woman's Rights Convention. Delegates resolved that "the equality of human rights results necessarily from the fact of the identity of the race in capabilities and responsibilities," and further, that "being invested by the Creator with the same capabilities...it is demonstrably the right and duty of woman" to participate in public political life. Rebecca M. Sandford avowed, "Our intellect is as capable as man's to assume, and at once to hold, these rights...for if we did not believe it, we would not contend for them." Frederick Douglass proclaimed that "the true basis of rights was the capacity of individuals."[24] The converse of their premise that equality in capacity justified political equality, was a warrant too basic to be considered explicitly: differences in capacity, if present, would be justification for political inequality.

A second powerful and recurrent rhetorical device for suffragists was to charge that women were wrongly categorized with those legitimately excluded from political life. A popular theme in both British and American suffrage posters was to depict a thoughtful-looking woman, perhaps wearing the gown of a college graduate, surrounded by slope-browed, wild-eyed, or "degenerate" men identified implicitly or explicitly as "idiots" and "lunatics." The caption might read, "Women and her Political Peers," or, "It's time I got out of this place. Where shall I find the key?" Echoing this theme, suffrage supporter George William Curtis rhetorically asked a New York constitutional convention in 1867 why women should be classed with "idiots, lunatics, persons under guardianship and felons," and at the national Woman Suffrage Convention in 1869, Elizabeth Cady Stanton protested that women were "thrust outside the pale of political consideration with minors, paupers, lunatics, traitors, [and] idiots."[25]

These challenges directly confronted the euphemisms used by the antisuffragists, whose attributions of mental and psychological inferiority to women were couched in less direct language. Antisuffragists were wont to counter that it was "a noble sort of disfranchisement" that women enjoyed, "something wholly different from the disfranchisement of the pauper, the criminal, the insane. . . . These are set aside as persons not human; women are absolved as constituting a higher class. There is a very real distinction between being placed among the beasts, and being placed among the 'ministering angels.'"[26] The suffragist answer to these sentimental claims made clear that the antisuffrage argument was rooted in the attribution of disability.

Suffragists did on occasion take issue with the argument that rights rested on capacity. Lucretia Mott, speaking at Seneca Falls, conceded that "woman's intellect may be feeble, because she had been so long crushed; but is that any reason why she should be deprived of her equal rights? Does one man have fewer rights than another because his intellect is inferior? If not, why should woman?" But she immediately undercut the point by avowing, "Let woman arise and demand her rights, and in a few years we shall see a different mental development." Charlotte Perkins Gilman

was the most prominent of those who argued that women's capacities had been stunted over time by restricted activity, which had come to represent a genetic inheritance that could be undone only by access to an unfettered social and political life. Matilda Gage similarly suggested that "obedience to outside authority to which woman has everywhere been trained, has not only dwarfed her capacity, but made her a retarding force in civilization."[27] These arguments were an implicit acknowledgment that capacity was indeed relevant to the question of rights. They are also examples of the third variant on the suffrage disability argument, that women were disabled by exclusion from political equality. This argument answered the antisuffrage accusation that women were inherently and unchangeably disabled with the claim that, given equal rights, they would attain equality in capacity. Like the antisuffrage position, it was a powerful argument precisely because of the cultural power of disability to discredit.

Ethnicity also has been defined by disability. One of the fundamental imperatives in the initial formation of American immigration policy at the end of the nineteenth century was the exclusion of disabled people. Beyond the targeting of disabled people, the concept of disability was instrumental in crafting the image of the undesirable immigrant. The first major federal immigration law, the Act of 1882, prohibited entry to any "lunatic, idiot, or any person unable to take care of himself or herself without becoming a public charge." Those placed in the categories "lunatic" and "idiot" were automatically excluded. The "public charge" provision was intended to encompass people with disabilities more generally and was left to the examining officer's discretion. The criteria for excluding disabled people were steadily tightened as the eugenics movement and popular fears about the decline of the national stock gathered strength. The Act of 1891 replaced the phrase *"unable* to take care of himself or herself without becoming a public charge," with *"likely* to become a public charge." The 1907 law then denied entry to anyone judged "mentally or physically defective, such mental or physical defect being of a nature which *may affect* the ability of such alien to earn a living." These changes considerably lowered the threshold for exclusion and expanded the latitude of immigration officials to deny entry.[28]

The category of persons *automatically* excluded was also steadily expanded. In 1903, people with epilepsy were added and, in addition to those judged insane, "persons who have been insane within five years previous [or] who have had two or more attacks of insanity at any time previously." This was reduced to one "attack" in the 1917 law; the classification of "constitutional psychopathic inferiority" was also added, which inspection regulations described as including "various unstable individuals on the border line between sanity and insanity...and persons with abnormal sex instincts."[29] This was the regulation under which, until recently, gays and lesbians were excluded. One of the significant factors in lifting this ban, along with other forms of discrimination against gays and lesbians, was the decision by the American Psychiatric Association in 1973 to remove homosexuality from its list of mental illnesses. That is, once gays and lesbians were declared not to be disabled, discrimination became less justifiable.

Legislation in 1907 added "imbeciles" and "feeble-minded persons" to the list, in addition to "idiots," and regulations for inspectors directed them to exclude persons with "any mental abnormality whatever...which justifies the statement that the alien is mentally defective." These changes encompassed a much larger number of people and again granted officials considerably more discretion to judge the

fitness of immigrants for American life. Fiorello H. LaGuardia, who worked his way through law school as an interpreter at Ellis Island, later wrote that "over fifty percent of the deportations for alleged mental disease were unjustified," based as they often were on "ignorance on the part of the immigrants or the doctors and the inability of the doctors to understand the particular immigrant's norm, or standard."[30]

The detection of physical disabilities was a major aspect of the immigration inspector's work. The Regulations for the medical inspection of immigrants in 1917 included a long list of diseases and disabilities that could be cause for exclusion, among them arthritis, asthma, bunions, deafness, deformities, flat feet, heart disease, hernia, hysteria, poor eyesight, poor physical development, spinal curvature, vascular disease of the heart, and varicose veins. A visiting physician in 1893, when admission standards were still relatively liberal, described the initial inspection: "If a man has a hand done up, or any physical injury in any way ..., or if a person has but one leg or one arm, or one eye, or there is any physical or mental defect, if the person seems unsteady and in any way physically incapacitated to earn his livelihood, he is passed to one side to be examined later."[31] An immigration official later recalled a young Italian couple who would have been deported (the man had a "game leg" that required use of a crutch) had not a wealthy philanthropist visiting Ellis Island taken an interest in the couple and intervened, guaranteeing that they would not become a public charge.[32]

In short, the exclusion of disabled people was central to the laws and the work of the immigration service. As the Commissioner General of Immigration reported in 1907, "The exclusion from this country of the morally, mentally, and physically deficient is the principal object to be accomplished by the immigration laws." Once the laws and procedures limiting the entry of disabled people were firmly established and functioning well, attention turned to limiting the entry of undesirable ethnic groups. Discussion on this topic often began by pointing to the general public agreement that the laws excluding disabled people had been a positive, if insufficient, step. In 1896, for example, Francis Walker noted in the *Atlantic Monthly* that the necessity of "straining out" immigrants who were "deaf, dumb, blind, idiotic, insane, pauper, or criminal" was "now conceded by men of all shades of opinion"; indeed there was a widespread "resentment at the attempt of such persons to impose themselves upon us." As one restrictionist wrote, the need to exclude the disabled was "self evident."[33]

For the more controversial business of defining and excluding undesirable ethnic groups, however, restrictionists found the *concept* of disability to be a powerful tool. That is, while people with disabilities constituted a distinct category of persons unwelcome in the United States, the charge that certain ethnic groups were mentally and physically deficient was instrumental in arguing for *their* exclusion. The belief that discriminating on the basis of disability was justifiable in turn helped justify the creation of immigration quotas based on ethnic origin. The 1924 Immigration Act instituted a national quota system that severely limited the numbers of immigrants from southern and eastern Europe but, long before that, disabilities stood in for nationality. Superintendents of institutions, philanthropists, immigration reformers, and politicians had been warning for decades before 1924 that immigrants were disproportionately prone to be mentally defective—up to half the immigrants from southern and eastern Europe were feebleminded, according to expert opinion.[34] Rhetoric about "the slow-witted Slav," the "neurotic condition of our Jewish immigrants," and, in general, the "degenerate and psychopathic types, which are so conspicuous and numerous among the immigrants," was pervasive in the debate over restriction.[35] The laws forbidding entry to the feebleminded were motivated in part by the desire to limit immigration from inferior nations, and conversely, it was assumed that the 1924 act would reduce the number of feebleminded immigrants. The issues of ethnicity and disability were so intertwined in the immigration debate as to be inseparable.

Arguments for immigration restriction often emphasized the inferior appearance of immigrants, and here also ethnicity and disability overlapped and intertwined. Disability scholars have emphasized the uncertain and shifting line between an impairment of appearance and one of function. Martin Pernick, for example, has described the importance of aesthetics in eugenics literature—how fitness was equated with beauty and disability with ugliness. Lennard Davis has maintained that disability presents itself "through two main modalities—function and appearance." Restrictionists often emphasized the impaired appearance of immigrants. An Ellis Island inspector claimed that "no one can stand at Ellis Island and see the physical and mental wrecks who are stopped there...without becoming a firm believer in restriction."[36] A proponent of restriction avowed, "To the practised eye, the physiognomy of certain groups unmistakably proclaims inferiority of type." When he observed immigrants, he saw that "in every face there was something wrong. ...There were so many sugar-loaf heads, moon-faces, slit mouths, lantern-jaws, and goose-bill noses that one might imagine a malicious jinn had amused himself by casting human beings in a set of skew-molds discarded by the Creator." Most new immigrants were physically inadequate in some way: "South Europeans run to low stature. A gang of Italian navvies filing along the street present, by their dwarfishness, a curious contrast to other people. The Portuguese, the Greeks, and the Syrians are, from our point of view, undersized. The Hebrew immigrants are very poor in physique ... the polar opposite of our pioneer breed."[37]

The initial screening of immigrants was mostly a matter of detecting visible abnormality. Inspectors, who prided themselves on their ability to make a "snapshot diagnosis," had only a few seconds to detect the signs of disability or disease as immigrants streamed past them in single file. Inspection regulations specified that "each individual should be seen first at rest and then in motion," in order to detect "irregularities in movement" and "abnormalities of any description." If possible, inspectors watched immigrants as they carried their luggage upstairs to see if "the exertion would reveal deformities and defective posture."[38] As one inspector wrote, "It is no more difficult to detect poorly built, defective or broken down human beings than to recognize a cheap or defective automobile. ... The wise man who really wants to find out all he can about an automobile or an immigrant, will want to see both in action, performing as well as at rest."[39]

For most immigrants, a normal appearance meant a quick, uneventful passage through the immigration station. An abnormal appearance, however, meant a chalked letter on the back: "L for lameness, K for hernia, G for goiter, X for mental illness," and so on.[40] Once chalked, a closer inspection was required. The inspection then would be general, not confined to the abnormality that set them apart, which meant that visibly disabled people—as well as those whose ethnic appearance was abnormal to the inspectors—were more likely to be set apart for close examination and therefore were also more likely to have other problems discovered and to be excluded.

Aesthetic and eugenic considerations were at least as important as concerns about the functional limitations of disabled immigrants. For example, on June 30, 1922, Israel Raskin was refused entry to the United States as "physically defective and likely to become a public charge." The diagnosis on the medical certificate was "lack of sexual development which may affect his ability to earn a living." The United States Surgeon General explained that the diagnosis warranted exclusion because "these persons present bad economic risks ... due to the fact that their abnormality soon becomes known to their associates who make them the butt of coarse jokes to their own despair, and to the impairment of the work in hand." Since this was "recognized pretty generally among employers, it is difficult for these unfortunates to get or retain jobs, their facial and bodily appearance, at least in adult life, furnishing a patent advertisement of their condition."[41]

Medical exclusions on the basis of "poor physique" and "lack of physical development" began to appear around the turn of the century. The immigration service defined it as covering individuals "who have frail frame, flat chest, and are generally deficient in muscular development," or those who are "undersized—markedly of short stature—dwarf"[42] In part, this diagnosis represented a judgment of employability, and in part it was a eugenic judgment. Both concerns were expressed in a letter from the Bureau of Immigration, which explained that "a certificate of this nature implies that the alien concerned is afflicted with a body but illy adapted ... to the work necessary to earn his bread." The diagnosis further indicated that the immigrant was "undersized, poorly developed [and] physically degenerate, and as such, not only unlikely to become a desirable citizen, but also very likely to transmit his undesirable qualities to his offspring, should he unfortunately for the country in which he is domiciled, have any."[43]

As one medical officer explained it, the "immigrant of poor physique is not able to perform rough labor, and *even if he were able*, employers of labor would not hire him."[44] The belief that an immigrant with a disability was unfit to work was justification for exclusion; but the belief that an immigrant was *likely to encounter discrimination* because of a disability was equally justification for exclusion. The disability that justified exclusion in these cases was largely or entirely a matter of an abnormal appearance that might invite employment discrimination.

The laws excluding disabled immigrants could be used by inspectors to target particular ethnic groups. The Hebrew Sheltering and Immigrant Aid Society in New York expressed concern in 1909 that the "lack of physical development" diagnosis was "constantly increasing" and being applied to Jewish immigrants disproportionately. An investigation by the Jewish Immigrants' Information Bureau in 1910 discovered that an inspector in Galveston was using the diagnosis to discriminate against Jewish immigrants. Nationality and disability might be implicitly linked in anti-immigration rhetoric, as when William Green, president of the American Federation of Labor, argued that quotas were "necessary to the preservation of our national characteristics and to our physical and our mental health."[45] They also were explicitly connected, as when a New York Supreme Court justice worried that the new immigrants were "adding to that appalling number of our inhabitants who handicap us by reason of their mental and physical disabilities."[46]

Historians have scrutinized the attribution of mental and physical inferiority based on race and ethnicity, but only to condemn the slander. With their attention confined to ethnic stereotypes, they have largely ignored what the attribution of disability might also tell us about attitudes toward disabled people. Racial and ethnic prejudice is exposed while prejudice against people with disabilities is passed over as insignificant and understandable. As a prominent advocate of restriction wrote in 1930, "The necessity of the exclusion of the crippled, the blind, those who are likely to become public charges, and, of course, those with a criminal record is self evidenc."[47] The necessity has been treated as self-evident by historians as well, so much so that even the possibility of discrimination against people with disabilities in immigration law has gone unrecognized. In historical accounts, disability is present but rendered invisible or insignificant. While it is certain that immigration restriction tests in good part on a fear of "strangers in the land," in John Higham's phrase, American immigration restriction at the turn of the century was also clearly fueled by a fear of *defectives* in the land.

Still today, women and other groups who face discrimination on the basis of identity respond angrily to accusations that they might be characterized by physical, mental, or emotional disabilities. Rather than challenging the basic assumptions behind the hierarchy, they instead work to remove themselves from the negatively marked categories—that is, to disassociate themselves from those people who "really are" disabled—knowing that such categorization invites discrimination. For example, a recent proposal in Louisiana to permit pregnant women to use parking spaces reserved for people with mobility impairments was opposed by women's organizations. A lobbyist for the Women's Health Foundation said, "We've spent a long time trying to dispel the myth that pregnancy is a disability, for obvious reasons of discrimination." She added, "I have no problem with it being a courtesy, but not when a legislative mandate provides for pregnancy in the same way as for disabled persons."[48] To be associated with disabled people or with the accommodations accorded disabled people is stigmatizing.

Even disabled people have used this strategy to try to deflect discrimination. Rosemarie Garland-Thomson notes that "disabled people also often avoid and stereotype one another in attempting to normalize their own social identities." Deaf people throughout the twentieth century have rejected the label of disability, knowing its dangers; and the tendency of those with less-stigmatized disabilities to distance themselves from those with more highly stigmatized disabilities is a common phenomenon. In 1918, the associate director of what was known as the "Cleveland Cripple Survey" reported that some of those surveyed "were amazed that they should be considered cripples, even though they were without an arm or leg, or perhaps seriously crippled as a result of infantile paralysis. They had never considered themselves handicapped in any way."[49]

This common strategy for attaining equal rights, which seeks to distance one's own group from imputations of disability and therefore tacitly accepts the idea that disability is a legitimate reason for inequality, is perhaps one of the factors responsible for making discrimination against people with disabilities so persistent and the struggle for disability rights so difficult. As Harlan Hahn has noted, "Unlike other disadvantaged groups, citizens with disabilities have not yet fully succeeded in refuting the presumption that their subordinate status can be ascribed to an innate biological inferiority."[50] If Hahn is perhaps too optimistic about the extent to which women and minority groups have managed to do away with such presumptions, nevertheless it is true that such views are no longer an accepted part of public discourse. Yet the same views regarding disability are still espoused widely and openly.

Disability is everywhere in history, once you begin looking for it, but conspicuously absent in the histories we write. When historians do take note of disability, they usually treat it merely as personal tragedy or an insult to be deplored and a label to be denied, rather than as a cultural construct to be questioned and explored. Those of us who specialize in the history of disability, like the early historians of other minority groups, have concentrated on writing histories of disabled people and the institutions and laws associated with disability. This is necessary and exciting work. It is through this work that we are building the case that disability is culturally constructed rather than natural and timeless—that disabled people have a history, and a history worth studying. Disability, however, more than an identity, is a fundamental element in cultural signification and indispensable for *any* historian seeking to make sense of the past. It may well be that all social hierarchies have drawn on culturally constructed and socially sanctioned notions of disability. If this is so, then there is much work to do. It is time to bring disability from the margins to the center of historical inquiry.

NOTES

1. Joan Scott, "Gender: A Useful Category of Historical Analysis," *American Historical Review* 91 (December 1986): 1053–75.

2. Edmund Burke, *Reflections on the Revolution in France* ("Books-on-Line" Internet edition—gopher://gopher.vt.edu.10010/02/55/l): for rhetoric of monstrosity, see 13–14, 63, 118–19, 261, 355, 384, 396, 412; for blindness, see 70, 89, 171, 308, 378; for imbecility and madness, see 165, 173, 217, 346, 394, 419, 444, 448. Tom Paine, *The Rights of Man* ("Books-on-Line" Internet edition), 86; see also 12, 15.

3. Ian Hacking, *The Taming of Chance* (Cambridge: Cambridge University Press, 1990), 160–66. See also Georges Canguilhem, *The Normal and the Pathological* (New York: Zone Books, 1989); Douglas C. Baynton, *Forbidden Signs: American Culture and the Campaign against Sign Language* (Chicago: University of Chicago Press, 1996), chaps. 5–6.

4. Francois Ewald, "Norms Discipline, and the Law," *Representations* 30 (Spring 1990): 146, 149–50, 154; Lennard Davis, *Enforcing Normalcy: Disability, Deafness, and the Body* (London: Verso, 1995); Baynton, *Forbidden Signs*, chaps. 5 and 6.

5. Late nineteenth-century educators began using "normal child" as the counterpart to "deaf child" instead of the "hearing" and "deaf" of previous generations. "Normal" appears to refer to an average, since the "average" person is hearing. Since it does not exclude those with superior hearing, however, it does not denote the average but those *above* a certain standard.

6. Daniel J. Kevles, *In the Name of Eugenics: Genetics and the Uses of Human Heredity* (Berkeley: University of California Press, 1985), 160; Baynton, *Forbidden Signs*, chap. 2; James W. Cook, Jr., "Of Men, Missing Links, and Nondescripts: The Strange Career of P. T. Barnum's 'What Is It?' Exhibition," in Rosemarie Garland-Thomson, ed., *Freakery: Cultural Spectacles of the Extraordinary Body* (New York: New York University Press, 1996); James W. Trent, Jr., "Defectives at the World's Fair: Constructing Disability in 1904," *Remedial and Special Education* 19 (July/August 1998): 201–11.

7. Samuel A. Cartwright, "Report on the Diseases and Physical Peculiarities of the Negro Race," *New Orleans Medical and Surgical Journal* 7 (May 1851): 693; George M. Fredrickson, *The Black Image in the White Mind* (New York: Harper and Row, 1971), 250–51; J. C. Nott, "The Mulatto a Hybrid," *American Journal of Medical Sciences* (July 1843), quoted in Samuel Forry, "Vital Statistics Furnished by the Sixth Census of the United States," *New York Journal of Medicine and the Collateral Sciences* 1 (September 1843): 151–53.

8. John H. Van Evrie, *White Supremacy and Negro Subordination, or Negroes a Subordinate Race* (New York: Van Evrie, Horton, & Co., 1868), 153–55; Forry, "Vital Statistics," 159; Paul B. Barringer, *The American Negro: His Past and Future* (Raleigh, NC: Edwards & Broughton, 1900), 10.

9. Cited in Forry, "Vital Statistics," 162–63. John C. Calhoun, "Mr. Calhoun to Mr. Pakenham," in Richard K. Cralle, ed., *The Works of John C. Calhoun* (New York: D. Appleton, 1888), 5: 337.

10. Cartwright, "Report," 707–10. See also Thomas S. Szasz, "The Sane Slave: A Historical Note on the Use of Medical Diagnosis as Justificatory Rhetoric," *American Journal of Psychotherapy* 25 (1971): 228–39.

11. Van Evrie, *White Supremacy*, 121, 181, 221. Van Evrie notes in his preface that the book was completed "about the time of Mr. Lincoln's election" and was therefore originally an argument in favor of the continuation of slavery but presently constituted an argument for its restoration.

12. J. F. Miller, "The Effects of Emancipation upon the Mental and Physical Health of the Negro of the South," *North Carolina Medical Journal* 38 (November 20, 1896): 285–94.

13. Samuel Forry, "On the Relative Proportion of Centenarians, of Deaf and Dumb, of Blind, and of Insane in the Races of European and African Origin," *New York Journal of Medicine and the Collateral Sciences* 2 (May 1844): 313.

14. Van Evrie, *White Supremacy* 199, chap. 15 *passim*; Arnold Guyot, *Physical Geography* (1873; reprint, New York: American Book Co., 1885), 114–18; Nott, "Mulatto a Hybrid," quoted in Forry, "Vital Statistics," 163–64; Cook, "Of Men, Missing Links, and Nondescripts," 139–57; Robert Bogdan, *Freak Show: Presenting Human Oddities for Amusement and Profit* (Chicago: University of Chicago Press, 1988), 134–42.

15. Winthrop D. Jordan. *White over Black: American Attitudes toward the Negro, 1550–1812* (Chapel Hill: University of North Carolina Press, 1968), 518–25; Rush explained not only African skin this way but the nose, lips, and hair as well. Smithsonian Institution Archives, Collection 60—Warshaw Collection, "Soap," Box 4 Folder: Fairbanks; dated 1893 or 1898 (illegible).

16. Smithsonian Institution Archives, Collection 60—Warshaw Collection, "Afro-Americana," Box 4, Folder 7, n.d.

17. Smithsonian Institution Archives, Collection 60—Warshaw Collection, "AfroAmericana," Box 4, Folder 4, n.d., ca. 1893.

18. Daryl Michael Scott, *Contempt and Pity: Social Policy and the Image of the Damaged Black Soul, 1880–1996* (Chapel Hill: University of North Carolina Press, 1997) xi–xvii; 12, 208 n. 52.

19. Cynthia Eagle Russett, *Sexual Science: The Victorian Construction of Womanhood* (Cambridge, MA: Harvard University Press, 1989), 63. See also Lois N. Magner, "Darwinism and the Woman Question: The Evolving Views of Charlotte Perkins Gilman," in Joanne Karpinski, *Critical Essays on Charlotte Perkins Gilman* (New York: G. K. Hall, 1992), 119–20.

20. Grace Duffield Goodwin, *Anti-Suffrage: Ten Good Reasons* (New York: Duffield and Co., 1913), 91–92

(in Smithsonian Institution Archives, Collection 60—Warshaw Collection, "Women," Box 3). Edward Clarke, *Sex in Education; or, A Fair Chance for Girls* (1873; reprint, New York: Arno Press, 1972), 18, 22, 62.

21. William Warren Potter, "How Should Girls Be Educated? A Public Health Problem for Mothers, Educators, and Physicians," *Transactions of the Medical Society of the State of New York* (1891): 48, quoted in Martha H. Verbrugge, *Able Bodied Womanhood: Personal Health and Social Change in Nineteenth-Century Boston* (Oxford: Oxford University Press, 1988), 121.

22. A. Lapthorn Smith, "Higher Education of Women and Race Suicide," *Popular Science Monthly* (March 1905), reprinted in Louise Michele Newman, ed., *Men's Ideas/Women's Realities: Popular Science, 1870–1915* (New York: Pergamon Press, 1985), 149; Almroth E. Wright quoted in Mara Mayor, "Fears and Fantasies of the Anti-Suffragists," *Connecticut Review 7* (April 1974): 67; Charles L. Dana quoted in Jane Jerome Camhi, *Women against Women: American Anti-Suffragism, 1880–1920* (New York: Carlson Publishing, 1994), 18; Clarke, *Sex in Education,* 12.

23. Magner, "Darwinism," 119–20; Nancy Woloch, *Women and the American Experience, Vol. 1: To 1920* (New York: McGraw-Hill, 1994), 339: Aileen S. Kraditor, *The Ideas of the Woman Suffrage Movement* (New York: W. W. Norton, 1981), 20. See also Anne Digby, "Woman's Biological Straitjacket," in Susan Mendas and Jane Randall, eds., *Sexuality and Subordination: Interdisciplinary Studies of Gender in the Nineteenth Century* (New York: Routledge, 1989), 192–220.

24. *Woman's Rights Conventions: Seneca Falls and Rochester, 1848* (New York: Arno Press, 1969), 4–6; originally published as *Proceedings of the Woman's Rights Convention, Held at Seneca Falls and Rochester, N.Y., July and August, 1848* (New York: Robert J. Johnston, 1870), 4–6.

25. Lisa Tickner, *The Spectacle of Women: Imagery of the Suffrage Campaign, 1907–14* (Chicago: University of Chicago Press, 1988), illustration IV; Alice Sheppard, *Cartooning for Suffrage* (Albuquerque: University of New Mexico Press, 1994), 30; Elizabeth Cady Stanton, Susan B. Anthony, and Matilda Joslyn Gage, eds., *History of Woman Suffrage* (1881; reprint, New York: Arno Press, 1969), 2: 288, quoted in Yvonne Pitts, "'Under This Disability of Nature': Women and Constructions of Disability in the National Suffrage Debates, 1870–1920" (paper presented to the Berkshire Conference on the History of Women, June 1999); Elizabeth Cady Stanton, "Address to the National Woman Suffrage Convention, Washington, D.C., January 19, 1869," in Mari Jo Buhle and Paul Buhle, eds., *The Concise History of Woman Suffrage* (Urbana: University of Illinois Press, 1978), 256.

26. O. B. Frothingham, "The Real Case of the 'Remonstrants' against Woman Suffrage," *The Arena* 2 (July 1890): 177.

27. *Woman's Rights Conventions,* 11; on Charlotte Perkins Gilman, see Kraditor, *Ideas of the Woman Suffrage Movement,* 97–101; "Preceding Causes, written by Matilda Joslyn Gage, in 1881," in Buhle and Buhle, eds., *Concise History,* 53.

28. *United States Statutes at Large* (Washington, D.C.: Government Printing Office, 1883), 22:214. *United States Statutes at Large* (Washington, D.C.: Government Printing Office, 1891), 26:1084; *United States Statutes at Large* (Washington, DC: Government Printing Office, 1907), 34:899. Emphases added.

29. *United States Statutes at Large* (Washington, D.C.: Government Printing Office, 1903), 32:1213; United States Public Health Service, *Regulations Governing the Medical Inspection of Aliens* (Washington, D.C.: Government Printing Office, 1917), 28–29.

30. *Statutes* (1907), 34:899; United States Public Health Service, *Regulations,* 30–31, Fiorello H. LaGuardia, *The Making of an Insurgent: An Autobiography, 1882–1919* (1948; reprint, New York: Capricorn, 1961), 65.

31. United States Public Health Service, *Regulations,* 16–19; U. O. B. Wingate, "Quarenteen Immigration at the Port of New York," *Milwaukee Medical Journal* 1 (1893): 181, quoted in Elizabeth Yew, "Medical Inspection of Immigrants at Ellis Island, 1891–1924," *Bulletin of the New York Academy of Medicine* 56 (June 1980): 494.

32. Philip Cowen, *Memories of an American Jew* (1932; reprint, New York: Arno Press, 1975) 148–49.

33. U.S. Bureau of Immigration, *Annual Report of the Commissioner of Immigration* (Washington, D.C.: Government Printing Office, 1907), 62; Francis A. Walker, "Restriction of Immigration," *Atlantic Monthly* 77 (June 1896): 822; Ellsworth Eliot, Jr., M. D., "Immigration," in Madison Grant and Charles Steward Davison, eds., *The Alien in Our Midst, or Selling our Birthright for a Mess of Industrial Pottage* (New York: Galton Publishing, 1930), 101.

34. See James W. Trent, Jr., *Inventing the Feeble Mind: A History of Mental Retardation in the United States* (Berkeley: University of California Press, 1994), 166–69.

35. Thomas Wray Grayson, "The Effect of the Modern Immigrant on Our Industrial Centers," in *Medical Problems of Immigration* (Easton, PA: American Academy of Medicine, 1913), 103, 107–9.

36. Martin Pernick, *The Black Stork: Eugenics and the Death of "Defective" Babies in American Medicine and Motion Pictures since 1915* (Oxford: Oxford University Press, 1996), 60–71; Davis, *Enforcing Normalcy*, 11–12. See also Harlan Hahn, "Antidiscrimination Laws and Social Research on Disability: The Minority Group Perspective," *Behavioral Sciences and the Law* 14 (1996): 54; Alfred C. Reed, "Going through Ellis Island," *Popular Science Monthly* 82 (January 1913): 8–9.

37. Edward Alsworth Ross, *The Old World and the New: The Significance of Past and Present Immigration to the American People* (New York: Century, 1914), 285–90.

38. Elizabeth Yew, "Medical Inspection of Immigrants at Ellis Island, 1891–1924," *Bulletin of the New York Academy of Medicine* 56 (June 1980): 497–98; United States Public Health Service, *Regulations*, 16–19; Alan M. Kraut, *Silent Travelers: Germs, Genes, and the "Immigrant Menace"* (New York: Basic Books, 1994), 54–57.

39. Victor Safford, *Immigration Problems: Personal Experiences of an Official* (New York: Dodd, Mead, 1925), 244–46.

40. Kraut, *Silent Travelers*, 55.

41. Letter from W. W. Husband, Commissioner General, Bureau of Immigration, to H. S. Cumming, Surgeon General, United States Public Health Service, September 27, 1922; and reply from Cumming to Husband, September 29, 1922; National Archives, RG 90, Entry 10, File 219.

42. Letter from George Stoner, Chief Medical Officer, Public Health and Marine Hospital Service, to Surgeon General of the Public Health and Marine Hospital, November 29, 1912, National Archives, RG 90, Entry 10, File 219.

43. Letter from F. P. Sargent, Commissioner-General of the Bureau of Immigration, to the Commissioner of Immigration on Ellis Island, April 17, 1905, National Archives, RG90, E10, File 219.

44. Allan McLaughlin, "The Problem of Immigration," *Popular Science Monthly* 66 (April 1905): 532 (emphasis added).

45. Letter from Leon Sanders, President of the Hebrew Sheltering and Immigrant Aid Society, to Surgeon General of the Public Health and Marine Hospital, November 14, 1909, National Archives, RG 90, Entry 10, File 219. Kraut, *Silent Travelers*, 65. William Green, "Immigration Should Be Regulated," in Grant and Davison, *Alien in Our Midst*, 2.

46. Norman S. Dike, "Aliens and Crime," in Grant and Davison, *Alien in Our Midst*, 81.

47. Ellsworth Eliot, Jr., M.D., "Immigration," in Grant and Davison, *Alien in Our Midst*, 101.

48. Heather Salerno, "Mother's Little Dividend: Parking," *Washington Post* (September 16, 1997): Al.

49. Rosemarie Garland-Thomson, *Extraordinary Bodies: Figuring Physical Disability in American Culture and Literature* (New York: Columbia University Press, 1997), 15. Amy Hamburger, "The Cripple and His Place in the Community," *Annals of the American Academy of Political and Social Science* 77 (1918): 39.

50. Harlan Hahn, "Antidiscrimination Laws and Social Research on Disability: The Minority Group Perspective," *Behavioral Sciences and the Law* 14 (1996): 43.

CHAPTER 3

"Heaven's Special Child": The Making of Poster Children

Paul K. Longmore

SUMMARY

Paul Longmore opens his discussion about disabled poster children by suggesting that modern charity telethons operate on the same ideological grounds perpetuated by Tiny Tim from Charles Dickens's *A Christmas Carol*. Telethon hosts encouraged the public to care for the "most weak" out of moral responsibility.

Longmore points to a long history of children receiving greater charitable support than adults because they were imagined as more innocent. Thus charities deployed the image of the helpless child for a number of causes. For example, the Warm Springs Foundation grounded its fundraising campaign for polio with a poster featuring a disabled child, and other similar campaigns stressed the visibility of children's disabilities as a strategy for inspiring public support.

The children used in such campaigns were chosen for marketing reasons and were supposed "to appear helpless" without seeming "too disabled." On the other hand, marketing executives rarely focused on disabled adults that they might have seen as customers, employees, or colleagues. The use of poster children reinforced the medical model of disability that encouraged the public to think of disability as a "weakness" to be addressed through medical means and to think of disabled people as objects of beneficence.

Tiny Tim was a little "crippled" boy whose sweetness and courage and pathetic plight melted the heart of miserly Ebenezer Scrooge. Scrooge's charity toward Tim secured his own redemption. Dickens's *A Christmas Carol* was a Yuletide staple. Between 1901 and 2009, the entertainment industry produced 56 live-action and 15 animated movie and television versions. Many were available on video and were rerun on television each December.[1] Book retailers sold illustrated volumes as a holiday gift.[2] And each December it seemed that every theater in the U.S. staged the story as a play.[3] Americans saw a lot of Tim.

But Tiny Tim was more than a character in Dickens's tale. He was a ubiquitous cultural figure. The annual return of *A Christmas Carol* did not exhaust his appearances or significance. He arrived not just seasonally but almost year-round. Or rather, not Tim himself, but the Tiny Tim image was made into a constant and powerful cultural symbol, especially on telethons. Its main purveyors were the disability charities. Within both the charity tradition and the operation of the medical model, that personal helped to shape the identities of millions of people with disabilities. Disability rights advocates challenged the ideology behind that imposed identity.

Telethons in effect reenacted a version of *A Christmas Carol.* The hosts and audiences were huge Cratchit clans, with disabled children—and adults—playing Tiny Tim. Jerry Lewis on the MDA pageant, Dennis James in the UCP spectacle, Pat Boone on the Easter Seals rite, and the other hosts, male and female, conflated the roles of the Christmas Ghosts and Bob and Mrs. Cratchit. They were moral preceptors to potential donors, instructing them in their duty to look after Tiny Tim's siblings. At the same time, the hosts and the givers were the Cratchits gathered around the sweet pathetic children. Viewers at risk of becoming Scrooges peered through their TV screens and learned that they could join the family by opening their hearts to the afflicted Tims. By looking after the "most weak," they could buy a place at the telethon hearth.

Telethon Tiny Tims were not just *Jerry's* kids. They belonged to anyone who phoned in a pledge to any of the telethons. Some Easter Seals posters declared "He's yours too." Easter Seals local hosts touted "Adopt-a-Child." As with charities for Third World children, sponsors supported a particular youngster, who would write them a personal thank-you.[4] On some Easter Seals telecasts, Pat Boone spoke for those children in song:

> I am your child.
> Wherever you go,
> You take me too.
> Whatever I'll know,
> I'll learn from you.
> Whatever I do,
> You'll teach me to do.
> I am your child ...
> You are my hope.
> You are my chance.
> And I am your child.[5]

"Believe me," declared UCP's Dennis James, "we're all taking care of heaven's special child."[6]

Through much of Western history, disabled and sick children were central to the practice of charity. In early modern Britain, children's hospitals drew more support than those treating adults with venereal disease. Though the latter were desperately needed, philanthropists feared they would be seen as supporting vice and debauchery. Beneficence to children instead associated them with innocent suffering. In any era, donation typically went to institutions that promised the greatest public approbation. That was one reason children were always popular as objects of charity. Older people were much less likely to receive such relief and remained desperately in need until establishment of state pensions in the twentieth century.[7]

The eighteenth-century English artist William Hogarth may have pioneered images of children as a charity fundraising tool. A governor of London's first foundling hospital, established in 1737, he designed both "a distinctive uniform" for the infant inmates and "an affecting coat-of-arms" for the institution. The latter displayed "a new-born child flanked by the figures of Nature and Britannia, with the plaintive motto 'Help!'" He and other artists exhibited their paintings at the hospital, inviting wealthy patrons to buy them. This advanced Hogarth's aim to make British art competitive with Continental art in the British marketplace. It also anticipated twentieth-century fundraising that linked charity with commerce and patriotism.[8]

In 1930s America, the National Society for Crippled Children and Adults and the polio crusade invented child-based methods that became standard in disability-related soliciting. As the Society (founded in 1919) launched its 1934 drive, finance chair Paul King asked *Cleveland Plain Dealer* cartoonist J. H. Donahey to design a stamp supporters could purchase for a penny and place on envelopes and letters. That first Easter

Seal pictured a boy wearing leg braces and leaning on crutches, his head bent sadly. Behind him was a white cross and—reminiscent of Hogarth's coat-of-arms—the words "Help Crippled Children." The design expressed clients' alleged plea "simply for the right to live a normal life." The huge public response eventually prompted the organization to rename itself the National Easter Seal Society. In 1952, it made the lily part of its logo. The flower explicitly represented spring, while implicitly referring to the season's religious holiday and the charity's "quasi-religious tenor." The Society also held annual contests in each state to select children as the public faces of its affiliates' fundraising.[9]

Meanwhile, the polio campaign crafted its own child-centered strategy. As early as 1932, the Warm Springs Foundation enlisted illustrator Howard Chandler Christy—famous for his World War I Uncle Sam "I–Want–You" recruiting poster—to design a poster featuring a disabled child. He also drew program covers for the President's Birthday Balls. Unlike later images, these drawings did not make the children's disabilities visible.[10] But as time went on, the drive began to stress those physical differences. In 1934, exhorting his audience to support the Birthday Balls, nicknamed "Paralysis Dances," syndicated columnist and radio personality Walter Winchell invoked the image of a paralyzed child. "If you buy a ticket to dance," he said, "then some little child who can't even walk may be able to dance some day." Polio publicists blazoned the slogan "Dance so that a child may walk." They filled the nation's newspapers with studies in physical contrast, photos of nondisabled adult dancers alongside pictures of children *crippled* by polio.[11]

In 1937, strategists at the new National Foundation for Infantile Paralysis "shifted the main appeal" from paying tribute to FDR as a victor over polio to "unashamed exploitation of the pathetic appeals of crippled children." NFIP's March of Dimes hammered at the radical difference between *crippled* children and *normal* kids. Its first drive in 1938 featured nondisabled children wearing buttons that proclaimed, "I'm glad I'm well."[12] In 1946, it begat its first poster child.[13] And its ominous film "The Crippler" blended sentimentality and pity with terror, fear, and hope. "A figure leaning on a crutch—sinister in its invisibility—stalks the land like death itself . . . 'And I'm *especially* fond of children,' the voice-over intones with fiendish glee."[14]

The strategies contrived in the 1930s persisted over the next seven decades. Disability charities drew on the cult of sentimentalism's traditional tropes as they focused public attention on the icon of the innocent helpless child.[15] The agencies also used adults to illustrate their services, but the grown-ups got nowhere near the publicity beamed at the kids. Poster children were, by design, the most visible symbols of fundraising. At the back of their stages, the UCP, MDA, and Easter Seals telethons displayed photos of children. Easter Seals' 1994 opening scrolled images from past programs; nine out of ten showed children. Later, there was a montage of 48 years of poster children but no retrospective of adult representatives. Besides "national" children, Easter Seals and MDA exhibited state and local poster kids. UCP had only local poster children, but its national telecasts were filled with images of youngsters.[16] Even the Arthritis Telethon used children to elicit alms. Of the 37 million Americans with connective-tissue diseases, 200,000 were kids or teens with juvenile rheumatoid arthritis. Still, the telethon showcased a disproportionate number of children.[17]

At a 1986 workshop on the how-to's of telethon success, Easter Seals officials told local chapter executives: "Children raise more money than adults." Youngsters were effective fundraising tools, they explained, because the public sympathized with images of "the most weak." They also reported that girls pulled in larger amounts than boys.[18] Of the 48 national poster children chosen between 1947 and 1994, two out of three were girls. For MDA, the gender pattern seemed the reverse, with boys—in particular, boys with Duchenne Muscular Dystrophy—attracting more money.

Easter Seals' strategists also said that White kids drew more donations than children of color, though more nonwhite children would appear by the later decades of the twentieth century. The ethnic ratios on all telethons reflected that strategic judgment, even though disability prevalence rates were higher in minority communities.[19] Among those 48 Easter Seals poster children, just one—a girl—was African-American, while another girl was born in India. The selections reflected historic patterns of discrimination in health care. During the 1930s and 1940s, African-American community leaders criticized the Warm Springs Foundation and the National Foundation for Infantile Paralysis for neglecting black polio patients and then treating them in segregated facilities. Following World War II, in response to the civil rights movement and Cold War race politics, the NFIP slowly began to fund integrated training programs and medical rehabilitation facilities. Concurrently, beginning in 1947 a few African-American children were selected as poster children for local, regional, and national campaigns.[20] Beginning in the 1990s, perhaps because of the growth of the middle class in minority communities as well as the impact of civil rights movements, more disabled people of color, adults as well as children, were featured on telethons. For example,

those African-American and Indian girls were Easter Seals National Child Representatives in the early 1990s, and in 1996 and 1997 MDA chose a Latino lad and an African-American youngster as National Ambassadors.[21]

Given poster children's important function, their selection became an art. Fashions changed in the charity business, noted the *Los Angeles Times* in 1986, but choosing child spokespersons remained highly competitive. It had "earmarks of a beauty pageant: stage mothers trying to boost their youngsters to fame and fortune, children trying too hard to impress, and local Easter Seals officials going to great lengths to promote their nominees." One chapter "arranged for [national communications director Sandi Gordon] Perkins to be flown in on a sponsor's corporate airplane, gave her a party featuring California wine—and followed up with an angry letter when the chapter's candidate was not selected." Local leaders promoted their favorites as embodying sentimental stereotypes. Of one finalist, a functionary wrote: "His clear, sweet, high-pitched voice . . . together with his angelic face, breaks hearts." Another declared that a girl had "a special magnetism that will draw you near and steal your heart."[22]

Each charity chose youngsters who embodied its particular message. MDA and Arthritis kids were heart-tuggingly dependent; Easter Seals and UCP children were plucky overcomers. But all poster children had this much in common: picked for "practical marketing reasons," they must be congenial and presentable. They must be attractive, telegenic. "The national child doesn't have to be gorgeous," said Easter Seals' Perkins, "as long as they look OK." Poster kids must not look too different. According to the MDA telethon's producer, Jerry Lewis "prefer[red] his poster child to be ambulatory.

He says he doesn't want to bend over a wheelchair to raise a buck." But in fact, Lewis was often shown bending over his "kids" seated on wheelchairs. It was a tricky balance: they had to appear helpless but they mustn't be too disabled.[23]

These considerations were crucial because poster children did far more than appear on the telethons. The charities displayed Tiny Tim's siblings year-round. A blizzard of poster-kid pictures blanketed the nation. Their images looked out from drugstore and supermarket displays tied to Easter Seals and MDA promotions. Their photos were fixed on MDA and UCP "banks" beside restaurant and grocery-store cash registers. Newspapers and magazines featured stories about them. They went to charity fund raisers: "bowl-a-thons," golf tournaments, and dinners honoring local business leaders. They posed with sports heroes and Hollywood celebrities. Over the song "You've Got to Have Friends," the Easter Seals Telethon screened a photo montage of national poster children with movie and TV stars.[24]

Poster kids were "seen and listened to by millions of Americans," noted the *L.A. Times.* Just halfway through his "reign" the 1986 National Easter Seals Child had flown tens of thousands of miles, every-*where* from Washington, DC, to Las Vegas to Puerto Rico. He had addressed conventions of every*one* from realtors to truck drivers. And his image had appeared "on every*thing* from Easter Seals' seals to Crayola crayons posters to Safeway delivery trucks." His image had been reproduced "roughly 70 million times." And he still had six months to go as a poster child.[25]

Especially important, these dependent children were introduced to the executives whose corporations were the charities' most prominent supporters. A review of hundreds of hours of telethons found a few segments featuring executives visiting therapy centers that served adults and just one that showed them meeting an adult with a disability in a business setting. Telethons did not present executives or their employees encountering disabled adults in situations that portrayed them as colleagues or even *potential* co-workers. But they met lots of children.

Poster children also had their pictures taken with elected officials—state governors and legislators, members of Congress, even the President of the United States.[26] From Harry S. Truman to William Jefferson Clinton, presidents annually met the national poster children of the several disability charities. A photo of MDA's 1993 national child with Clinton ran in 3,900 newspapers.[27] In 1995, First Lady Hillary Rodham Clinton appeared on the UCP Telethon with a 4-year-old girl, a UCP client, to urge viewers to support that charity. In 1992, Easter Seals aired a medley of photos of its national children meeting every president from George H. W. Bush all the way back to Truman while viewers heard the song "Stand By Me."[28]

"The poster child is our major ambassador to the public," explained a March of Dimes spokeswoman.[29] That icon influenced business executives' attitudes about the millions of adults they might have seen as customers, employees, or colleagues, instead of recipients of their charity. It instructed lawmakers as they formulated policies that affected disabled citizens. It defined who Americans with disabilities really were and what they really needed. Reinforcing the medical model, charity images portrayed them as dependent objects of beneficence whose most important needs were medical. In late twentieth-century America, the Tiny Tim persona was central to framing the cultural, social, and political meaning of disability. The charities depicted the representative disabled person as a vulnerable child, one of "the most weak."

NOTES

1. The names of many of the actors who played Scrooge are included with each entry. Live-action motion pictures and television programs: *A Christmas Carol* (1901), *A Christmas Carol* (Essanay, 1908); *A Christmas Carol* (Edison, 1910), Mark McDermott; *A Christmas Carol*, (1912); *A Christmas Carol* (dir. Leedham Bantock, Zenith Film Company, 1913), Seymour Hicks; *A Christmas Carol* (dir. Harold M. Shaw, Fenning London Film Company, 1914), Charles Rock; *The Right to Be Happy* aka *A Christmas Carol* (dir. Rupert Julian, Universal, 1916); *Scrooge* (dir. George Wynn, 1922), H. V. Esmond; *Tense Moments with Great Authors: "#7 Scrooge"* (dir. H. B. Parkinson, W. Courtney Rowden, 1922), H. V. Esmond; *Scrooge* (dir. Edwin Greenwood, 1923), Russell Thorndike; *Scrooge* (dir. Hugh Croise, 1928), Bransby Williams; *Scrooge* (dir. Henry Edwards, Julius Hagen-Twickenham, 1935), Seymour Hicks; *A Christmas Carol* (dir. Edwin L. Marin, MGM, 1938), Reginald Owen; *A Christmas Carol* (dir. George Lowther, 1943), William Podmore, this version was 60 minutes and, at the time, was the longest U.S. TV program yet broadcast; *A Christmas Carol* (dir. James Caddigan, 1947), John Carradine; *The Philco Television Playhouse: "A Christmas Carol"* (dir. Fred Coe, 1948), Dennis King; *The Christmas Carol* (dir. Arthur Pierson, 1949), was a U.S. TV film narrated by Vincent Price with Taylor Holmes as Scrooge; *A Christmas Carol* (British TV, 1950), Bransby Williams; *Fireside Theatre: "A Christmas Carol"* (dir. Gordon Duff, 1951), Ralph Richardson; *Scrooge*, aka *A Christmas Carol* (dir. Brian Desmond Hurst, Showcorporation/George Minter/Renown, 1951), Alistair Sim; *Kraft Television Theatre: "A Christmas Carol"* (1952), Malcolm Keen; *Shower of Stars: "A Christmas Carol"* (dir. Ralph Levy, 1954), Fredric March; *The Alcoa Hour: "The Stingiest Man in Town"* (dir. Daniel Petrie, 1955), Basil Rathbone; *Story of the Christmas Carol* (dir. David Barnheizer, 1955), Norman Gottschalk; *General Electric Theater: "The Trail to Christmas"* (dir. James Stewart, 1957), a cowboy tells a boy the Dickens tale with John McIntire as Scrooge; *Tales from Dickens: A Dickens Christmas: "A Christmas Carol"* (dir. Neil McGuire, 1958), TV series hosted by Fredric March with Basil Rathbone as Scrooge; *Mr. Scrooge* (dir. Bob Jarvis, 1964), Cyril Ritchard; *Carry on Christmas* (dir. Ronnie Baxter, 1969), comedy with Sid James; *Scrooge* (dir. Ronald Neame, Cinema Center, 1970), musical version with Albert Finney; *A Christmas Carol* (dir. Richard Williams, 1971), British TV movie with Alistair Sim; *A Christmas Carol* (dir. Moira Armstrong, BBC, 1976), Michael Hordern; *Scrooge* (dir. John Blanchard, Canadian TV movie, 1978); *An American Christmas Carol* (Scherick-Chase-Slan/Scrooge Productions/Smith-Hemion, 1979), Henry Winkler as a New England "Scrooge" during the Great Depression, who is redeemed by helping the family of a boy (Chris Crabb) who needs rehabilitation from polio; *A Christmas Carol at Ford's Theatre* (1979); *Skinflint: A Country Christmas Carol* (1979), a country music version with Hoyt Axton as Cyrus Flint; *A Christmas Carol* (dir. Laird Williamson, 1981), William Paterson, a U.S. TV movie; *The Guthrie Theatre Presents a Christmas Carol* (The Entertainment Channel, 1982), film of stage production, narrated by John Gielgud; *The Gospel According to Scrooge* (dir. Mark S. Vegh, 1983); *A Christmas Carol* (dir. Clive Donner, CBS, 1984), George C. Scott; *A Christmas Carol* (1994), U.S. ballet; *Ebbie* (dir. George Kazcender, Victor Television Productions/Maverick Crescent Entertainment Limited, 1994), Susan Lucci as a hard-driving department store owner Elizabeth "Ebbie" Scrooge, whose widowed assistant Roberta Cratchit has a son named Timmy who needs medical treatment; Ebbie decides to provide adequate health insurance for all her employees; *John Grin's Christmas* (1986), features an African-American Scrooge, Robert Guillaume, and no Tiny Tim, but does feature a generous and insightful blind woman; *Scrooged* (dir. Richard Donner, 1988), Bill Murray as a heartless executive producing a telecast of *A Christmas Carol* with Buddy Hackett as Scrooge; *Bah! Humbug!: The Story of Charles Dickens' "A Christmas Carol"* (dir. Derek Bailey, PBS, 1994), a reading by actors James Earl Jones and Martin Sheen; *Ebenezer* (dir. Ken Jubenvill, 1997), a Wild West version with Jack Palance as a ruthless cattle baron; *Ms Scrooge* (Wilshire Court/Power Pictures, 1997), Cicely Tyson as Ebenita Scrooge who, like "Ebbie," decides to pay for medical treatment for Tim (who this time has a slow-growing congenital tumor in his leg) and health insurance for her employees; *A Christmas Carol* (dir. David Hugh Jones, Flying Freehold, 1999), Patrick Stewart; *A Christmas Carol* (dir. Catherine Morshead, 2000), British TV movie, Ross Kemp as Eddie Scrooge; *A Diva's Christmas Carol* (dir. Richard Shankman, 2000), a TV movie made for VH1 with Vanessa L. Williams as pop singing star Ebony Scrooge; *Scrooge and Marley* (dir. Fred Holmes, 2001), an evangelical Christian version with Dean Jones; *A Carol Christmas* (dir. Matthew Imas, Hallmark, 2003), Tori Spelling as Carol Cartman, a selfish TV talk show host; *A Christmas Carol: The Musical* (dir. Arthur Alan Seidelman, 2004), Kelsey Grammer; *A Carol of*

Christmas (dir. Roland Black, 2005); *Chasing Christmas* (dir. Ron Oliver, 2005), a time-traveling version with Tom Arnold as a Scrooge-like single dad; *The Carol Project* (dir. Tim Folkmann, 2006), musical; *The Nutcracker: A Christmas Story* (2007), a ballet combining the E.T.A. Hoffman story with the Dickens tale. Animated productions: *Mister Magoo's Christmas Carol* (dir. Abe Levitow, UPA, 1962); *Bah, Humduck! A Looney Tunes Christmas* (dir. Charles Visser, Warner, 2006), Daffy Duck; *A Christmas Carol* (dir. Zoran Janjic, Australia, Air Programs International, 1969), screened on U.S. TV 1970; *The Stingiest Man in Town* (dirs. Jules Bass, Arthur Rankin Jr., Rankin-Bass, 1978), Walter Matthau as the voice of Scrooge and Robert Morse as the voice of Young Scrooge; *A Christmas Carol* (Australia, 1982); *A Christmas Carol* (Burbank Productions, 1982), narrated by Michael Redgrave; *Mickey's Christmas Carol* (dir. Burny Mattinson, Disney, 1983), Alan Young as the voice of Scrooge McDuck; *The Muppet Christmas Carol* (dir. Brian Henson, 1992), Michael Caine as the voice of Scrooge; *A Christmas Carol* (dirs. Toshiyuki Hiruma, Takashi Masunaga, Jetlag, 1994); *A Flintstones Christmas Carol* (dir. Joanna Romersa, 1994); *A Christmas Carol* (dir. Stan Phillips, DIC Entertainment, 1997), narrated by Tim Curry; *Christmas Carol: The Movie* (dir. Jimmy T. Murakami, 2001), Simon Callow as the voice of Scrooge; *A Sesame Street Christmas Carol* (dirs. Ken Diego, Victor DiNapoli, Emily Squires, Jon Stone, 2006); *Barbie in A Christmas Carol* (Australia, 2008); *A Christmas Carol* (dir. Robert Zemeckis, Disney, 2009), Jim Carrey as the voice of Scrooge. Internet Movie Database, www.imdb.com (accessed 20–22 November 2009); Martin F. Norden, *The Cinema of Isolation, A History of Physical Disability in the Movies* (New Brunswick, NJ: Rutgers University Press, 1994), 33; Patricia King Harrison and Alan Gevinson, ed., *American Film Institute Catalog 1931–1940* (Berkeley: University of California Press, 1993), 347.

2. In June 1999, *Books in Print* listed 66 different editions of the story, including adaptations based on Dickens's basic plot.

3. In the late 1930s, the WPA Federal Theater Project in Los Angeles and other places made a theatrical version part of every Christmas Season program. William F. McDonald, *Federal Relief Administration and the Arts* (Columbus: Ohio State University Press, 1969), 554. That customary programming continued decades later. A sampling of the myriad stage productions from 1998 alone included not only major theaters such as Radio City Music Hall in New York City, the San Diego Repertory Theater, and the Geary Theater in San Francisco, but also the Totempole Playhouse in Chambersberg,

Pennsylvania; the Bardavon Opera House in Poughkeepsie, New York; Triangle Church in Chapel Hill, North Carolina; Hale Center Theater in Orem, Utah; the Hippodrome State Theater in Gainesville, Florida; the Alley Theater in Houston; and *Scrooge: The Ballet!* at the Hawaii Theater Center in Honolulu. In 1999, comedian and composer Steve Allen was reportedly writing songs for a stage musical adaptation. Reed Johnson, "Steve Allen Writes Songs for 'Christmas Carol' Musical," *San Francisco Chronicle*, 24 November 1999. In 2007, playwright Christopher Durang satirized the Dickens's tale. Robert Hurwitt, "'Christmas Carol' Meets 'Wonderful Life' in 'Wild Binge,'" *San Francisco Chronicle*, 4 December 2007, www.sfgate.com (accessed 4 December 2007).

4. "Adopt-a-Child" donors received a statuette of a disabled child leaning on crutches behind a small dog. Easter Seals Telethon, 1990.

5. Ibid.

6. UCP Telethon, 1993.

7. William B. Cohen, "Epilogue: The European Comparison," in *Charity, Philanthropy, and Civility in American History*, ed., Lawrence J. Friedman and Mark D. McGarvie (New York: Cambridge University Press, 2003), 393.

8. Linda Colley, *Britons: Forging the Nation 1707–1837* (New Haven, CT: Yale University Press, 1992), 59. The London Foundling Hospital cared for children with many kinds of disabilities, medically and vocationally rehabilitating some and providing lifelong maintenance for others. Alysa Levene, *Childcare-Health and Mortality at the London Foundling Hospital 1741–1800: "Left to the Mercy of the World"* (Manchester: Manchester University Press, 2007), 165–8.

9. The organization officially adopted the name National Easter Seal Society in 1979. Charles A. Riley, II, *Disability and the Media: Prescriptions for Change* (Lebanon, NH: University Press of New England, 2005), 110–11; Easter Seals Telethon, 1991; James E. Williams, Jr., "Easter Seals Transforms the Telethon," *Fund Raising Management* 26, no. 7 (September 1995): 28–32; Charlotte Snow, "Rehab Rival: Easter Seals is a Healthcare Force to be Reckoned With," *Modern Healthcare* 27, no. 17 (28 April 1997), 18–19, www.lexisnexis.com (accessed 1 June 2007).

10. Scott M. Cutlip, *The Unseen Power: Public Relations. A History* (Hillsdale, NJ: Lawrence Erlbaum, 1994), 558–60, 561; Riley, *Disability and the Media*, 111–12. Christy's illustrations for the 1936, 1937, and 1938 Birthday Balls program covers are reproduced online at www.disabilitymuseum.org (accessed 7 July 2007).

11. Scott M. Cutlip, *Fund Raising in the United States, Its Role in America's Philanthropy* (New Brunswick, NJ: Rutgers University Press, 1965), 361, 365–71.

12. Ibid., 376, 383–7, quotes from 384 and 387; Richard Carter, *The Gentle Legions* (Garden City, NY: Doubleday, 1961), 112; David L. Sills, *The Volunteers: Means and Ends in a National Organization* (1957; repr., New York: Arno Press, 1980), 126–7, 169–70.

13. David Zinman, "Many Former Poster Kids Lead Normal Lives Today," *Los Angeles Times*, 16 December 1984; David M. Oshinsky, *Polio: An American Story* (New York: Oxford University Press, 2005), 83.

14. Tony Gould, *A Summer Plague: Polio and Its Survivors* (New Haven, CT: Yale University Press, 1995), xi; Oshinsky, *Polio: An American Story*, 68, 81–3. In 1974, MDA presented a video monologue entitled "I Hate People, Especially Children," in which an actor personified muscular dystrophy and, like "The Crippler," "ominously hovers over the figure of a healthy child." The vignette was written by Budd Schulberg and directed by Jerry Lewis. Lawrence Joseph Londino, "A Descriptive Analysis of 'The Jerry Lewis Labor Day Telethon for Muscular Dystrophy,'" (PhD diss.: University of Michigan, 1975), 127–8.

15. See Chapters 7–8. Cutlip, *Fund Raising in the United States*, 51; Riley, *Disability and the Media*, 111–12; Zinman, "Many Former Poster Kids Lead Normal Lives Today"; Ellen L. Barton, "Textual Practices of Erasure: Representations of Disability and the Founding of the United Way," in *Embodied Rhetorics: Disability in Language and Culture*, ed. James C. Wilson and Cynthia Lewiecki-Wilson (Carbondale: Southern Illinois University Press, 2001), 178–9, 184, 187, 193.

16. See for instance Shawn Hubler, "After Initial Anguish, Family of Cerebral Palsy Poster Child is Picture of Happiness," *Los Angeles Times*, 21 January 1990, South Bay edition.

17. The 1988 Arthritis Telethon paraded photos of kids with arthritis while a singer urged: "Share your love with all the children of the world." See also Herbert J. Vida, "Dana Point Boy Works Hard as Arthritis Foundation Poster Child," *Los Angeles Times*, 8 June 1986, Orange County edition, www.proquest.com (accessed 7 July 2007).

18. *Disability Rag* 7, no. 2 (March/April 1986): 22; Dennis Hall and Susan G. Hall, *American Icons: An Encyclopedia of the People, Places, and Things That Have Shaped Our Culture*, vol. 1 (Westport, CT: Greenwood Publishing, 2006), 574.

19. For a summary of disability prevalence rates in the 1990s U.S. population among African-Americans, Asian-Americans/Pacific Islanders, Hispanic Americans, and Native Americans as compared to European Americans see Rhoda Olkin, *What Psychotherapists Should Know about Disability* (New York: Guilford Press, 1999), 19–20.

20. Naomi Rogers, "Race and the Politics of Polio: Warm Springs, Tuskegee, and the March of Dimes," *American Journal of Public Health* 97, no. 5 (May 2007), 784–95; Oshinsky, *Polio: An American Story*, 65–7.

21. MDA Telethon, 1996; "Benjamin Gives Hope to Others—Again," *Parade* (31 August 1997). In 1986, the MDA poster child for the District of Columbia was an African-American lad. Anne Simpson, "People: MDA Poster Child," *Washington Post*, 8 May 1986. Service organizations in the black community supplied volunteers for the disability charities that may have, over the years, won them greater attention from those agencies. "First Year of Service Noted by AKA Chapter," *Los Angeles Sentinel*, 23 August 1979. The Chicago UCPA's 1991 poster child was a 10-year-old Latino boy. "Mutual Admiration," *Chicago Sun-Times*, 8 January 1991.

22. Scott Kraft, "Poster Child Quest: Cute Isn't Enough," *Los Angeles Times*, 7 April 1986. See also Laura Kavesh, "It Takes a Tough Kid to Be a Poster Child," *Chicago Tribune*, 29 March 1985, c edition. On the March of Dimes selecting poster children for both medical and cosmetic reasons see Zinman, "Many Former Poster Kids Lead Normal Lives Today."

23. Kraft, "Poster Child Quest"; David Zinman, "Critics Say Drives Foster Stereotyping of Disabled," *Los Angeles Times*, 16 December 1984; Kavesh, "It Takes a Tough Kid to Be a Poster Child"; Fred Rothenberg, "Waking up Telethon's Wee Hours," *Toronto Globe and Mail*, 3 September 1982, early edition. In a TV commercial publicizing "Aisles of Smiles," he appeared with his "friend," that year's national poster child. The boy sat on a wheelchair, not a power chair he could have operated on his own, but a manual chair pushed by his paternal benefactor Lewis. The spot created an image of helplessness and dependency. Likewise, the 1993 MDA extravaganza opened with a musical number and then showed Lewis approaching and then bending to embrace the national poster child who was sitting on a wheelchair.

24. Easter Seals Telethon, 1993; Kavesh, "It Takes a Tough Kid to Be a Poster Child."

25. Kraft, "Poster Child Quest," emphasis added. See also Kavesh, "It Takes a Tough Kid to Be a Poster Child."

26. Kavesh, "It Takes a Tough Kid to Be a Poster Child."

27. Reported on MDA Telethon, 1993.

28. Easter Seals Telethon, 1991 and 1992.

29. Zinman, "Many Former Poster Kids Lead Normal Lives Today."

CHAPTER 4

Disabled Upon Arrival: The Rhetorical Construction of Disability and Race at Ellis Island

Jay Dolmage

SUMMARY

As many as 40 percent of current Americans can trace their ancestry to Ellis Island, a place that Jay Dolmage asks us to consider as a "rhetorical space." Dolmage argues that the policies and practices at Ellis Island created new and influential ways of seeing the body and categorizing deviations. The labels of disability and race then applied to immigrant bodies still permeate contemporary culture. In this chapter, Dolmage argues that Ellis Island served as a testing ground for American eugenics and the imbrication of race, sex, and disability.

Immigrants were routinely subjected to cursory medical inspections or a "six-second physical" designed to quickly label some as "likely to become a public charge." Having a "poor physique" meant that they would be unproductive citizens. Undesirable bodies were shaded with attributions of disability; and disabled bodies were "raced" as nonwhite, or as disqualified white. Race and disability rhetorically reinforced one another to differentiate and create a hierarchy of bodies under the gaze of immigration officials. As a focal point for Americans intent on controlling immigration and the country's genetic makeup, Ellis Island manufactured a new rhetoric around visible differentiations of race and visibility.

From these visible differences, officials developed conclusions about interior inferiorities—whether they be moral, biological, or mental—that led to the rhetoric of feeblemindedness. Whether intentional or not, Ellis Island promoted the reading of bodies to determine all kinds of social fitness. Terms like "moron" that originated on the island permeated national discourse, allowing the nation to eventually dispatch with Ellis Island inspectors and enlist us all in enforcing exclusions. Ellis Island is remembered in triumphant narratives about becoming American, but the legacy of the island also includes countless mechanisms for oppressing Americans marked by race and disability.

I'm going to ask you to come with me on a short trip. We'll travel to New York City, approaching from the west, over the southern tip of Manhattan and out across New York Bay to Ellis Island, the way-station for millions of new Americans at the turn of the twentieth century. During our visit to Ellis Island for this essay, I will examine what the Ellis Island experience entailed, paying attention specifically to the ways that Ellis Island policed and limited immigration in the early twentieth century, leading up to the highly restrictive immigration laws of the 1920s. This tour will concentrate on the ways that Ellis Island rhetorically constructed disability, and contingently race. Today, you can go on a tour of the grounds, and you can learn about the success stories of plucky migrants, on the cusp of freedom and opportunity. You can buy a mug and a

T-shirt. But, in the past, if you were traveling to Ellis Island from the other direction, your experience of the island might have been quite different. It is estimated that 40 percent of the current American population can trace their ancestry through Ellis Island.[1] More than 22 million people entered the country through this immigration station. In the years of peak immigration, from the late 1800s until the clampdown on immigration in the 1920s, you might have arrived as one of thousands of steerage passengers on an ocean liner from Europe. Were you of eastern European, southern European, African, or Jewish heritage, you would have been subject to a restrictive squeeze not unlike the cramping you felt in your boat's close quarters as you came across the Atlantic.[2] As you were processed through Ellis Island, you became part of an indelible marking, your body was interrogated, written across, and read into.

RHETORICAL SPACES

In this essay I will examine Ellis Island from a rhetorical perspective—rhetoric defined here as a framework for exploring "the relationship of discourse and power, a rhetoric . . . being a set of rules that privilege particular power relations" (Berlin, 12). I define rhetoric as the function and circulation of power in language, and I will use this definition to guide my inquiry here. Further, I will look at Ellis Island as what Roxanne Mountford calls a "rhetorical space." Mountford urges us to consider "the effect of physical spaces on communicative event[s]"; the ways that "rhetorical spaces carry the residue of history upon them, but also, perhaps, something else: a physical representation of relationships and ideas" (42). She argues that space "carries with it the sediment of cultural tradition, of the social imaginary" (63). Richard Marback elaborates, claiming that a given space can be seen as a "nexus of cultural, historical,

and material conditions" of oppression, and can become a "physical representation of . . . injustice" (8). Thus, in revisiting Ellis Island, rhetorical analysis will allow me to pay attention not just to how power structures and travels through proliferating discourses of ability, ethnicity, racialization, and citizenship, but also how this charging and circulation imbricates, and is proscribed by, the space of Ellis Island.

Richard Marback has written that any island is a "special rhetorical space" (1). Ato Quayson, in his study of Robben Island in South Africa, also argues that, in looking at this island as a space for the detention of society's unwanted, we should "take both the totality of its history and the rhetoricity of its space seriously as points for productive cross-fertilization" (175). Robben Island housed a hospital for leprosy, a hospital for the chronically sick, a lunatic asylum, and became a sequestered colony. I will show that Ellis Island, like Robben, was a space where, in Quayson's words, "stipulations of undesirability placed in close and volatile proximity ideas of illness, deformity, insanity, and criminality, sometimes interweaving the various terms and leaving none of them stable." The legacy of both of these islands echoes today as "denominations of bodily difference . . . have been [repeatedly] incorporated into racial and other hierarchies" (176). Foucault has suggested that our epoch's primary spatial concern has been "knowing what relations of propinquity, what type of storage, circulation, marking and classification of human elements should be adopted." This has led us to create what he calls "*heterotopias of deviation:* those in which individuals whose behavior is deviant in relation to the required mean or norm are placed" (1986, 25, italics added). These spaces are "capable of juxtaposing in a single real space several spaces, several sites that are in themselves incompatible" (ibid.). Unlike the postmodern notion of the heterotopia as an ideal in which "nothing is left out of the grand mix," a heterotopia of deviation divides and isolates difference, suggesting that this situation (of purifying by extraction) is ideal for the "normals" in mainstream society, yet also creating a dystopian space for the minoritized (Siebers, 32; see also Vattimo; Hetherington). Ellis Island was just such a space.

Interestingly, the word *heterotopia* was first used (and is still used) in a biological and pathological sense to refer to abnormal anatomy—a displacement, a missing or extra element, a tumor that appears out of place, an alien growth (see *OED*; Hetherington, 42). The social processing that Ellis Island engendered was all about identifying and sometimes manufacturing abnormal bodies: these elements are out of place; these bodies are disordered. Ellis Island created a physical space in which abnormality could be arrested or deposited. But it also created powerful social practices of stigmatization. A heterotopia of deviation was placed at the edge of North America, and alienation was placed upon racial groups and individuals. At Ellis Island, the categories of defect and disability that adhere today were strongly grounded if not created, as was the diagnostic gaze that allowed for the nebulous application of the stigma of disability as we know it today.[3] The space of Ellis Island circumscribed certain patterns of movement and practices of visualizing the body. The product was, often, the spectacle of Otherness. And all who passed through Ellis Island also became subject to—and then possessor and executor of—a certain gaze and a certain bodily attitude. Ellis Island functioned as a heterotopic space. And not simply so—always in a tangle of definitions and as a repository of bad science and overlapping oppressions.

I will examine Ellis Island in the early twentieth century as a "special rhetorical space," a heterotopia for the invention of new categories of deviation. And I will suggest that Ellis Island floats into every aspect of contemporary American society. As Robert Chang has argued, "The border is not just a peripheral phenomenon. . . . To be an immigrant is to be marked [always] by the border." Further, "it is through its flexible operation that the border helps to construct and contain the nation and the national community" (27). Ellis Island has been rhetorically used, internalized, incorporated, embodied.

RHETORICAL BODIES

Ellis Island was designed to process the immigrant body—through an industrialized choreography, through a regime of vision, and through layers of anti-immigration discourse. Ellis Island became the key laboratory and operating theater for American eugenics, the scientific racism that can be seen to define a unique era of Western history, the effects of which can still be felt today. I will argue that Ellis Island, as a rhetorical space, can be seen as a nexus—and a special point of origin—for eugenics and the rhetorical construction of disability and race in the early twentieth century. Importantly, constructions of class, sex, and sexuality were also always part of this racializing and normalizing process.[4] Race and disability are always imbricated with gender, sex, sexuality, and class. And, as Eithne Luibheid suggests, "Immigration scholarship virtually ignores the connections among heteronormativity, sexuality, and immigration" (2004, 227). It is not my intention to further this occlusion here. Indeed, the categories of "defect" used to sort bodies at Ellis Island always also referenced gender, sex, and sexuality norms, and were also always classed. But because these intersections and transsections deserve dedicated and extensive analysis, I may elide explicit discussion of the vectors of gender, sex, sexuality, and class in this essay, but not in the larger project of which this is one part. This essay lays out the foundation upon which further analysis of these constructions can develop footings.

As I begin, I will provide a legend for the key concepts of this exploration—beginning with a definition of eugenics. Charles Davenport, perhaps the eugenics movement's greatest proponent, defined the movement as "the science of the improvement of the human race by better breeding" (1911, 1). Disability Studies scholars David Mitchell and Sharon Snyder define eugenics as "the hegemonic formation of exclusionary practices based on scientific formulas of deviancy" (73). And Nancy Ordover notes that in the early twentieth century "eugenics gave racism and nationalism substance by bringing to bear the rationalizing technologies of the day" (6). Looking at Ellis Island, then, allows me to recognize the development and use of these rationalizing technologies in a specific rhetorical space, as well as the discursive currents that surrounded and buttressed the island; the flow of relationships and ideas, the sediments of cultural tradition, and the social imaginary swirling around Ellis Island between 1890 and 1925. Ellis Island was a genetic experiment. This genetic experiment has, in many ways, created the frame for how we now see both race and disability.

Building on my definitions of rhetoric and rhetorical space, the idea of the "rhetorical construction" of disability develops out of the social and the postmodern models of disability, both put forward in the field of disability studies—I'll define these ideas next. The social model of disability posits that disability is purely social, an oppression stacked upon people *on top of* their impairments, which are real. The view is that, as Michael Oliver writes, "Disablement is nothing to do with the body, impairment is nothing less than a description of the body" (34). Adrienne Asch qualifies that, "saying that disability is socially constructed does not imply that the characteristics are not real or do not have describable effects on physiological or cognitive functions that persist in many environments" (18). Bodies and spaces are undeniably material, yet they are also undeniably rhetorical. The point is to draw attention to the fictive and oppressive cultural meanings of disability, without diminishing the lived experience of disability. Yet so-called postmodern disability studies contradicts this social model by suggesting that the strict separation of impairment and disability is a chimera (see Tremain). Judith Butler's definition of a "partial" social construction of the body, from her introduction to *Bodies That Matter,* nicely distills this idea: "To claim that discourse is formative is not to claim that it originates, causes, or exhaustively composes that which it concedes; rather, it is to claim that there is no reference to a pure body which is not at the same time a further formation of that body" (5). Following this, I suggest that we can see the "formation" of disability as being both material and rhetorical—characterized in vital ways by my definition of rhetoric as the "circulation and function of power in language." To see bodies as rhetorically constructed rather than socially constructed is to focus more closely on the power dynamics of the process of construction itself, rather than on its products, however transient. In the history and the geography that I chart, we will see how rhetorically invested the creation of disability has been—shaped by material spaces and corporeal experiences, and also by languages and grammars. This move to see disability rhetorically justifies a focus on the architectures and discourses surrounding bodies. A rhetorical perspective suggests that these spaces and discourses must be seen as formed by bodies and as, in part, *forming* bodies. I refer to rhetoric here and throughout the essay in a capacious sense—not as the duplicitous or obscurant art that we often see rhetoric as, but as the investigation of how meaning is made and negotiated, focusing not on reified products and transcendent truths, but on the power dynamics involved in the effort to make meaning. This rhetorical perspective disallows the canonization of any one definition of disability, yet allows me to challenge the accrued negative meanings as well as the social structures that have circumscribed the experience of disability. Finally, this rhetorical method asks each of us to examine critically the spaces and discourses that shape *any* body.

As I hope to show, this rhetorical perspective then also interacts with a critical perspective on race—allowing me to examine the ways that race is (at least partially) constructed through spaces and discourses. To say that race and disability are rhetorically constructed, importantly, is not to deny either concept materially or ontologically—but rather to bring into focus their shifting cultural meanings. Further, in aligning race and disability in this analysis, I am seeking to understand their rhetorical connections, not to conflate or compare, and never to deny the particularity and complexity of either race or disability. Yet these constructions of race and disability overlap, I will show, throughout the history of American eugenics. Their entwined narrative is best examined, I will also show, through the structures, practices, bodies, and discourses that make Ellis Island such a compelling rhetorical space.

SPECTACLES OF DIFFERENCE: THE INSPECTION PROCESS

Cursory medical inspections most strongly characterized the experience of Ellis Island for the arriving alien. In the years of peak immigration, as immigrants landed at Ellis Island they were almost immediately paraded up a set of steep stairs, some immigrants still carrying all of their possessions in their arms, afraid to leave them unattended in the baggage room. Here the inspection began. Immigration agents positioned themselves so that they could view individual bodies from several angles, and so that they could pick out deficient bodies as they labored up the stairs and into the registry room. As Victor Safford, a medical doctor and officer at Ellis Island in this peak period, wrote in his memoir, "A man's posture, a movement of his head or the appearance of his ears . . . may disclose more than could be detected by puttering around a man's chest with a stethoscope for a week, [thus] an attempt was made to utilize this general scheme" at Ellis Island (247). The "scheme" allowed for views of each immigrant "systematically both in rest and in motion at a distance of about twenty or twenty-five feet"; carrying his or her bags, hopefully, because "carrying baggage makes lameness from any cause more noticeable"; and creating a situation wherein each immigrant "while under inspection [would] make two right hand turns" to help "to bring out imperfections in muscular coordination" (Safford, 247–49). Officers would also stamp cards, and then hand the cards to immigrants. Because the immigrant was curious about what the stamp said, this was an opportunity for further inspection: "The way he held [the card] showed if his vision was defective" (Safford, 247–49).

The inspection process, facilitated by the space of the Ellis Island immigration station, looked like the choreographic and architectural brainchild of Jeremy Bentham and Henry Ford—a panopticon and an assembly line.[5] Indeed, Safford used the automobile metaphor at great length in describing Ellis Island inspections, and justifying the use and the efficacy of the glancing appraisal employed by inspectors to recognize defective bodies, what Emmanuelle Birn calls "snapshot diagnosis" (281). Safford wrote that "it is no more difficult a task to detect poorly built or broken down human beings than to recognize a cheap or defective automobile" (244). This metaphor both equates the functioning of the body to that of the machine, as it argues for the efficiency of the assembly line: "One can see on glancing at an automobile at rest that the paint is damaged or a headlight broken . . . [likewise] defects, derangements, and symptoms of disease which would not be disclosed by a so-called 'careful physical examination' are often easily recognizable watching a person twenty-five feet away" and in action (Safford, 245). Thus only cursory physical examinations—known as the six-second physical—were imposed upon newly-arriving immigrants, and the agents were trained to notice, immediately, inferior stock. These practices effectively "turned entry into the U.S. into a passage partially defined by a medical vocabulary and pathology of health" (Markel and Minna-Stern, 1315).[6] This medical lexicon was repeatedly imprinted upon the immigrant, and this printing was done hastily, efficiently, mechanically.

In the beginning at Ellis Island, pre-1900, there were few categories of physical (and perceived mental) defect that would warrant marking aliens out for further inspection and possible rejection. The first capacious terminology was the category of "LPC" or "likely to become a public charge," introduced in 1891. Inspectors could use their judgment to determine whether an immigrant looked like he or she could work for a living. William Williams, the Ellis Island commissioner at the time, wrote in his annual report that he hoped that this category would allow inspectors to weed out the "worst" immigrants (n.p). Yet by 1904, the commissioner was suggesting that the LPC terminology be expanded, as it was difficult to prove that someone would become a public charge, particularly once individual cases made it to boards of inquiry on the island, and family members, church representatives, or others were willing to vouch for immigrants. This shows that perhaps the calculus of exclusion was never purely economic, as the LPC label might suggest—there needed to be other ways to exclude the genetically "threatening." And in this period, we begin to see the ways that eugenic ideas of bodily "fitness" begin to structure the rhetoric of Ellis administrators. In 1904, Commissioner Williams called for the use of categories for exclusion such as "poor physique" or "low vitality," with one's appearance itself warranting rejection, without having to be mediated through an overt economic consideration. A body with a "poor physique" was defined as "ill proportioned, with defective circulatory system and poorly developed relaxed muscular system and flabby muscles . . . frail . . . a slender build, whose physical proportions with respect to chest and weight fall below the minimum requirements of the naval service, who are deficient in muscular development" ("Definitions of Various Terms"). In 1905, F. P. Sargent, commissioner general of the Bureau of Immigration, notified inspection officers and boards of special inquiry that

"poor physique" means afflicted with a body but illy adapted not only to the work necessary to earn his bread, but is also poorly able to withstand the onslaught of disease . . . undersized, poorly developed . . . physically degenerate, and as such not likely to become a desirable citizen, but also very likely to transmit his undesirable qualities to his offspring. . . . Of all causes for rejection, outside of dangerous, loathsome, or contagious diseases, or for mental disease, that of "poor physique" should receive the most weight, for, in admitting such aliens, not only do we increase the number of public charges by their inability to gain their bread . . . but we admit likewise progenitors to this country whose offspring will reproduce, often in an exaggerated degree, the physical degeneracy of their parents.

(n.p.)

This type of starkly eugenic language came to characterize much of Ellis Island policy. And, clearly, very little about these definitions could be reliably sensed, visually. Yet this was no impediment to their implementation.

The classification of "poor physique" would expand when, in 1907, the category of "feebleminded" was also officially adopted. Howard Markel and Alexandra Minna-Stern show that "poor physique" became a "favorite wastebasket" label of nativist groups, and was highly diagnosed during inspections in the 1910s (1319). They also reveal "the fluid nature of exclusionary labels themselves. If one label failed to work in rejecting the most objectionable, a new one was soon created, whether of contagion, mental disorder, chronic disability, or physique" (1327). The category of the "feebleminded" soon became the new wastebasket. As David Mitchell and Sharon Snyder show, "'feeblemindedness' became the primary category that allowed eugenics to consolidate a host of defective types under a shared heading" (79). Importantly, as Anna Stubblefield has shown, "White elites deployed the concept of feeblemindedness to link the different versions of white impurity" (163). As well, the insinuation of *mental* disability was conflated with a semiotics of exterior markers. In the heterotopia of deviation created at Ellis Island, undesirable bodies were shaded with attributions of disability; and disabled bodies were "raced" as nonwhite, or as disqualified whites.

Further aiding in the flexible application of stigma, as Safford's description suggests, these cursory inspections were largely a matter of intuition, a kind of magical medical view—in his words, "From long experience physicians sometimes acquire[d] a most remarkable intuitive power" (245). As Samuel Grubbs wrote, recalling his work as an officer, "I wanted to acquire this magical intuition but found there were few

rules. Even the keenist [*sic*] of these medical detectives did not know just why they suspected at a glance a handicap which later might require a week to prove" (quoted in Fairchild, 91). Regardless of the provenance of the process, suspect bodies were identified and sorted out from the stream of immigrants; these individuals were marked with chalk codes, letters written on the lapels of their jackets, inscrutable to those immigrants who had been inscribed.[7] Thelma Matje, an immigrant who arrived in August 1912, wrote of her experience that, "on disembarking upon our arrival at Ellis Island we were herded through the portals of this haven for the lost and destitute souls and tagged with more labels on our clothing than a pedigreed dog" (n.p.).

The marked were removed for further mental and physical examination. I won't look in great detail at the further testing and examination that took place beyond the initial inspection here. Instead, I'll suggest that, though line officers could not deport immigrants, their inspections and markings had an indelible rhetorical effect. This effect reached three distinct audiences:

1. Those immigrants who were not marked, and yet learned something about the danger of difference, gained a self-consciousness of their own possible defects, and were empowered and encouraged to diagnose others.
2. Those who were marked and were thus in danger of rejection.
3. The medical doctors themselves, who would later inspect the immigrants in greater detail.[8]

As Safford writes, the cursory inspection processes may actually have had greater power than the detailed inspections that followed upon detainment. For instance, he suggests that "if after taking into an examination room a person regarding whom suspicion has been aroused" due to the snapshot diagnosis "appears normal," then "the medical officer knows the passenger should not be released without looking further" (248). Without alleging that defect was manufactured by this process, clearly Safford and other officers strongly believed in the power of the medical glance. And the power of the glance was transferred to every immigrant who passed through this space.

Ellis Island, then, can be seen as a rhetorical space in which Foucault's history of "punishment" reaches a sort of climax. Ellis Island both provided a classical "spectacle"—the body publicly inscribed— and it inculcated new forms of self- and other-surveillance (see *Discipline and Punish*, 32–69).[9] The alien body could be publicly stigmatized and displayed, or removed to the back rooms at Ellis Island for further medical inspection, or passed along, yet always formatively imbued with the spirit of the investigation and the power of the gaze. Each of these acts carried significant rhetorical power, structuring the "heterotopia of deviation." Foucault wrote that the classical use of the spectacle to discipline and punish was "a manifestation of the strongest power over the body" of the condemned, whose punishment "made the crime explode into its truth." Yet he suggests that through modernity, "the ideal point of penalty would [evolve to become] an indefinite discipline: an interrogation without end, an investigation that would be extended without limit to a meticulous and ever more analytical observation" (1979, 227). While Ellis Island centered many spectacles, it also diffused innumerable investigations and unlimited surveillance into the nation.[10]

As Terry and Urla write, "The scopic regimes associated with looking for semantic markings of deviance position the expert simultaneously as objective scientist, informed interpreter, and voyeur" (11).[11] This might describe the role of the Ellis Island line inspector. When other immigrants also became privy to this gaze, they were granted the same diagnostic power, and this access to Other bodies, combined with access to these mechanisms of Othering, was a formative American experience. Through this processing and marking, and through the possibility of detainment, Ellis Island made a spectacle of inspection and exclusion, made the focus on defect *the* initiation rite for hopeful immigrants.[12] When H. G. Wells visited Ellis Island in 1906, he commented on the "wholesale and multitudinous quality of that place and its work" (43). He left with an overwhelming impression that Ellis Island was a "dirty spectacle of hopeless failure" (44). His impressions summarize the ways that Ellis Island manufactured and focused an exclusionary gaze. And his feelings perhaps understate the general impression of the immigrant, as Wells was just a visitor, and a welcome visitor at that.[13] Of course, the dominant cultural memory of Ellis Island celebrates the process as a rite of passage, arrival as celebratory. I am arguing against this whitewashed narrative in this essay, even as I would acknowledge that hope and triumph also always circulated in this space—as did subversion. For all of the interpellative power of this gaze, one would expect that there was also resistance to its power.

DISABILITY AND "NEW" RACISM

Throughout history, as Aristide Zolberg shows, American immigration policy has always had a double logic: "boldly inclusive" *and* "brutally exclusive" (2006a, 432). He argues that the United States has never been laissez-faire about immigration (2). That is, immigration has always been a matter of keen public and political concern— as the public has shaped immigration, so has it shaped the public. Yet, starting in the late 1800s, the stakes were raised. Immigration debates became a rhetorical arena through which one of the most powerful and dangerous ideas of our civilization took form: eugenics. The Immigration Restriction League (IRL) began in 1894, and was to have a remarkable influence on the political, intellectual, and business leadership of the country, and on the U.S. public. The immigrant was reframed as a menace, as a possible strain on resources, and as an undesirable undercurrent in the national gene pool. Eugenics, the "science" of positively advocating for particular forms of human regeneration, coupled with the negative restriction of the propagation of certain classes and ethnicities, beginning at the turn of the twentieth century, was the modus operandi of North American national health and immigration policy. Eugenics was "anointed guardian of national health and character," as Nancy Ordover has shown, "constructing immigrants as both contaminated and contaminators" (xiv). IRL cofounder Prescott F. Hall, in his article "Immigration Restriction and World Eugenics," wrote at the time that "immigration restriction is a species of segregation on a large scale, by which inferior stocks can be prevented from both diluting and supplanting good stocks. ... The superior races, more self-limiting than the others, with the benefits of more space and nourishment will tend to still higher levels" (126). Robert De Courcey Ward, another cofounder (with Hall) of the IRL, wrote at the time of the ways that America would map out its eugenic future: "A policy of national eugenics, for the United States as for every other nation, means the prevention of the breeding of the unfit native. For us it means, in addition, the prevention of the immigration of the unfit alien" (1912, 38). Ellis Island was a key reference point for this new mapping of America.

The rhetoric employed by the IRL and other proponents of eugenics held that certain races and ethnicities were characterized by embodied deviance. Such uses of disability as a mode of derogation grafted onto Other bodies might be seen as one of the primary corporeal grammars available to us. Douglas Baynton has shown that "the *concept* of disability has been used to justify discrimination against other groups by attributing disability to them" (33).[14] The disabled body becomes a loose, flexible, and magnetic symbol easily layered over insinuations of deficiency of all colors, shapes, and locations. In this negative sense, disability functions rhetorically. Eugenic rhetoric, seeking to identify inferior genes, necessarily constructed deviant phenotypes, creating investigatory techniques, a visual shorthand for identifying and marking out undesirable elements. At Ellis Island, through the inspection process, a medical and a penological gaze were incorporated, in the service of both identifying some bodies for detention and rejection, and in the process, through a logic of negation, constructing the U.S. citizen. As Matthew Frye-Jacobson shows, for anyone who arrived at Ellis Island before 1924, "Race was the prevailing idiom for discussing citizenship and the relative merits of a given people" (9). Within this racial idiom, disability was the accent applied to differentiate and hierarchize. Race and disability rhetorically reinforced each other and worked together to stigmatize. Markel and Minna Stern summarize this propensity: "In an era in which differences of skin color and physical characteristics were becoming increasingly medicalized, it is not surprising that exclusionary labels of disease and disability became an essential aspect" of immigration restriction (1328). Frye-Jacobson adds that the categories of the physically and mentally defective were created and used in service of racism, as a means of darkening a group of ethnic others with the stigma of disability. Frye-Jacobson writes that the "scientific probabilities for such conditions [of mental and physical defect] were themselves determined by a calculus of race" (69). The use of disability as a darkening mark applied to the singular body of an arriving immigrant later allowed for the accent of disability to be applied to entire (designated) racial groups. The probability of exclusion was determined by an exponential interaction of race and disability. As Anna Stubblefield has shown, "[disability and] ability [were] constructed as the touchstone in a way that linked race to class and gender and created the tangled mess that we are still untangling today" (179).

Racialized immigration restriction officially began with the Page Law of 1875 and the Chinese Exclusion Act of 1882, through which the nation effectively halted Chinese immigration. From this point on, restriction tightened as quickly as the immigration machine itself expanded. Roger Daniels argues that, although Chinese exclusion is often seen as a small matter, affecting only Chinese Americans, it is "now apparent that [this exclusion] became the pivot upon which all American immigration policy turned, the hinge upon which the 'golden door' of immigration began its swing towards a nearly closed position" (Daniels and Graham, 8). This exclusion also characterizes the enduring fusion of racism and attributions of disability. The February 28, 1877, "Report of the Joint Special Committee to Investigate Chinese Immigration" to the U.S. Congress found that "there is not sufficient brain capacity in the Chinese to furnish motive power for self-government. ... Upon the point of morals, there is no Aryan or European who is not far superior" (159). This synthesis of race classification and attributions of inferiority would set a powerful precedent for future prejudice, prejudice that would become medicalized, industrialized, and bureaucratized through Ellis Island.[15] Between 1891 and 1906, the immigration bureaucracy in the United States grew by 4200 percent (Daniels and Graham, 15).[16] This explosion would be matched by an

unprecedented "production of racial knowledge" (Ngai, 7). As this knowledge grew, its flaws would also multiply, as racial knowledge tangled with emerging eugenic ideas about bodily fitness, confusion between race, ethnicity, and nationality, and the bad science that Ellis Island allowed.

A major aspect of this proliferation of flawed racial knowledge was the Dillingham Immigration Commission's "Dictionary of Races or Peoples." The atmosphere of eugenic panic in the United States in this period led to the creation of this special commission, made up of eugenics proponents such as Henry Cabot Lodge, to investigate immigration. The commission presented this famous (and huge) document as part of an even larger report to Congress in 1911. The goal of the "Dictionary" was to classify races, and it did so according to physical and linguistic difference from the Caucasian norm. The "Dictionary" presented as part of the 1911 Dillingham Report relied on "ethnical factors" and "racial classification" to identify immigrant groups, signaling a shift from the old system of classification based on country of birth or nativity. The commission focused on color (white, black, yellow, red, and brown); on head measurements; and on not just language but also perceptions of literacy. This "Dictionary" both borrowed from and slightly evolved from the key preceding ethnological text, William Z. Ripley's 1899 *The Races of Europe*, which divided Europe into Alpines, Nordics, and Mediterraneans, basing these divisions on physiognomy, somatotype, and skin color, as well as social and cultural distinctions, and rooting all divergence in heredity. The key innovation of the "Dictionary" was its subcategorization: moving beyond the five primary colors of ethnology to create hierarchies within ethnic groups.

The "Dictionary" was built out of an informal "list of races or peoples" that Ellis Island officials had been keeping for years, and using to compile a crude count of immigrants for statistical purposes (Weil, 370). But the "Dictionary" signals a shift in that it makes a concerted effort to create divisions that might be useful beyond counting and broadly classifying newcomers—the text repeatedly strives for further divisions and discriminations. For instance, under the entry for "Negro, Negroid, African, Black, Ethiopian or Austafrican," the "Dictionary" begins by describing "that grand division of mankind distinguished by its black color" (100). The document's authors concede that "in a simple classification for immigration purposes it is preferable to include all of the above under the term 'Negroes.' They are alike in inhabiting hot countries and in belonging to the lowest division of mankind from an evolutionary standpoint" (ibid.). Yet the "Dictionary" offers ever more qualified and subtle categorizations when considering the "bewildering confusion in terms used to indicate the different mixture of white and dark races" (101). As a huge group of Others, "Negroes" seemingly required minimal taxonomy. Yet when the challenge was to differentiate within many shades of black and white, the project of generating "racial knowledge" gained momentum—at stake was exposure to the "lowest division of mankind," from a eugenic perspective. As Thomas Guglielmo, David Theo Goldberg, Anna Stubblefield, Matthew Frye-Jacobson, Jennifer Guglielmo, and others have shown, this "new" racial "knowledge" manufactured shades of nonwhiteness, using darkness to symbolize genetic inferiority and using the implication of genetic inferiority to rescind whiteness. A result was that "black color" and "dark races" came to be loaded rhetorical terms and tools, facilitated in their usage by eugenic constructions of disability.

As Patrick Weil has argued, the "Dictionary" was used primarily "for the purpose of demonstrating the inferior capacity of certain races and peoples, primarily from Eastern and Southern Europe" and Africa. Notably, the influence of the document "on the future course of immigration policy was enormous" (373). Just as the bureaucracy of immigration was multiplying, so too were the powers given to immigration officials to differentiate between individuals. There were now many more ways to be racially abnormal.

Roger Daniels shows that the Dillingham Report "popularized, if it did not invent, the category of 'old' and 'new' immigrants" with new immigrants being "both different from and inferior to" old (pre-1880) immigrants (1997, 62). And Foucault suggested that the proliferation of categorization that the "Dictionary" engendered also typifies a "new racism": "a racism against the abnormal, against individuals who, as carriers of stigmata, or any defect whatsoever" allows them to be detected and seen as a danger. This, in his words, "is an internal racism that permits the screening of every individual within a given society" (1999, 317). This "new" racism always interacts with the "old" racism of identifying differences *between* larger ethnic groups. As Martin Pernick points out, there are historical bases for this shift—movements more gradual and diffuse than Foucault suggests, yet still recognizable. Pernick writes that early twentieth-century eugenic rhetoric helped to convert ethnicity into race—linking race to the idea of "heredity as immutable" (56). For instance, people of the Jewish religion from varying backgrounds and geographies became Jews; then they also became, as Ellis Island doctor J. G. Wilson wrote in 1908, "a highly inbred and psychopathically inclined race," whose defects are "almost entirely due to heredity" (493). Jewish ethnicity may have been characterized by the religious and cultural habits that made a "people" unique. The Jewish "race" would be classified by genetic characteristics that mark a group as defective. Race became a *"project* in which human bodies and social structures [were] represented and organized" (Chang, 29). This was both a project (noun) in that it was the result of concerted and organized rhetorical action on the part of groups like the IRL, and it was a *projection* of the nation's fear of difference onto the bodies of immigrants.[17] Robert Chang suggests that immigrants *became racialized* as they entered Ellis Island. Chang calls this new racism "nativistic racism" because racism and nativism became "mutually constitutive" (30).[18] Ellis Island was a key part of this process, conveniently extracting (or manufacturing) from the stream of newcomers a range of dark, disabled, sexually ambiguous others who, when marked out, allowed a white, Western European, heteronormative, normal, able (and wholly fictional) American body to rise out of the negative space. The "new racism" at Ellis Island gave this process prominent grammars of race and ethnicity, with the accent of defect and disability. Foucault argued that these two types of racism—old and new—were most fully "grafted" by Nazism. Yet Ellis Island was perhaps the place where these forces were *first* successfully grafted and used. Of course, immigrants carried race and racisms across the Atlantic with them, and disability was not created immediately or solely upon their arrival; but the Ellis Island rhetorical space was constitutive of both race and disability in important (though never monolithic) ways.

As Foucault has noted, medicine constructs bodies by "limiting and filtering" what we see through classification systems, and then transcribing difference into language (1973, 135). This might proceed according to what Foucault called "the nomination of the visible," wherein the definition and coherence of difference is located in the skin and skull (132). Recall the inspection process itself. But also recall that the language used to attribute defectiveness

to Chinese immigrants referred to brain capacity, based on skull measurements.[19] The situated practices of Ellis Island were enabled by texts like the "Dictionary," just as the situated practices of Ellis Island provided the pseudoscientific basis for such texts to be created—rhetorical discourse and rhetorical space were mutually constitutive. Ellis Island manufactured both newly nominal and newly visible difference. The island, as a "heterotopia of deviation" and as a "special rhetorical space," processed the aforementioned "new racism." In this new cartography, Ellis Island functioned to filter and remap the bodies of immigrants.[20] To figure out who was American, one had to scientifically create, locate, mark, and showcase the expulsion of he and she who were not.[21] Thus Ellis Island, as a rhetorical space, was a conduit or centrifuge through which race and defect could be redefined. Ellis Island offered a page—not a blank page, but an available surface—upon which racial Others could be newly mapped, always located offshore from an American ideal.[22]

Kevin Hetherington writes of heterotopias that "they exist only in relation" (43). A heterotopia is established based upon its opposition to other sites, not based on an Otherness derived solely from itself. Ellis Island perfectly exemplifies this relation—its rhetorical purpose was always to establish the normalcy of the American mainland, the white mainstream. Looked at in and of itself, Ellis was just an island. But viewed from a foothold in North America—then, and now—it is something much different, something capable of setting terms through which difference is established and mandated.

THE TERMS OF RHETORICAL DISABILITY

When, in 1907, the term "feebleminded" was adopted as a class for exclusion at Ellis

Island, eugenicists and immigration restrictionists found a broad brush for the application of derogation and the attribution of deviance. Feeblemindedness was classified as "an awkward mentality which is beyond much hope of improvement. ...Appearance, stigmata, and physical signs may confirm such diagnosis" (Knox 1914, 80). This term had been used in America since the 1850s, when state asylums emerged. Anyone deemed unproductive or otherwise "backward" could be excluded from society and housed in these asylums or "idiot schools" (Kline, 15). Then, as at Ellis Island, the term "feebleminded" was useful for its flexibility. The term took on greater meaning in the early twentieth century, when it was charged with eugenic rhetoric. Undesirable people were now not just to be kept out of sight—they needed to be kept out of the genetic pool as well. "Feeblemindedness" was often interpreted as a purely statistical—and use fully tautological—category. The *Eugenical News,* in 1916, stated that the lowest 3 percent of the community at large "determined by definitely standardized mental tests, are to be called feeble-minded" (39). The authors admitted that "objections may be urged against such a standard based on the "community at large," which would differ from area to area and time to time. But "incidentally, the new method solves the problem of estimating the proportion of feeble-minded in the population. It is three per cent by definition" (ibid.). Of course, this is perhaps the strongest evidence of the bad science of eugenics, as it is also clear evidence of the subjective nature of this eugenic project: the goal was not to diagnose clearly and scientifically or to understand feeblemindedness, it was to exclude a certain quotient of the population.[23]

Howard Knox, arguably the most powerful man at Ellis Island and the number-one surgeon at Ellis Island from 1912 to 1916, in the textbook he created for his officers on the mental testing of aliens, wrote that "fortunately the term 'feeble-mindedness' is regarded by most alienists as a sort of waste basket for many forms and degrees of weak-mindedness, and since it is incorporated in the law as a mandatorily [*sic*] excludable defect, it is especially suited to the needs of the examiners who for the sake of conservatism and certain fairness include many imbeciles under the term" (1914, 125). Knox's motivations of course were always eugenic: "Fortunately," he wrote, "the laws are such that feebleminded aliens may be certified and deported before they have had an opportunity to contaminate the blood of the nation or to commit any crime" (122).

Ellis Island, and eugenics writ large, projected suggestions of interior (mental, moral, biological) inferiority onto the surface of the body and into gesture and bearing.[24] Officers (and then every immigrant) became well versed in this symbology—this rhetoric. Howard Knox wrote that "in the higher and more refined grades of deficiency, the most important element in the diagnosis is the 'human test' or the ability of one human being to take the mental measurement of another by conversing and associating with him. This intuitive ability can be very highly developed in persons of a strong and pleasing personality and good physique" (1914, 127).[25] The better looking you are, the better you will be able to pick out inferiors. The conflation of perceived mental or physical disability with differences of ethnicity, class, gender, and sexuality gels in the development of each of these snapshot glances, and also frames how we look at ourselves and one another. Whether or not this outcome was desired, Ellis Island helped to strengthen or validate this propensity for body-reading in everyone.[26] This "human test" became a form of interpellation at Ellis Island—the idea that one can size up a "defective" is one of the most pervasive social attitudes about disability.

Knox even developed a visual manual for Ellis Island inspectors, showing the supposed facial characteristics of different forms of feeblemindedness.

When Ellis Island surgeon E. H. Mullan later wrote about the mental inspection process for *Public Health Reports,* he emphasized the ways that the mental and the physical overlapped, and the ways that "feeble-mindedness" might be a way to enforce racial typing and exclusion as well.[27] Mullan wrote that "the physical details in the medical inspection of immigrants have been dwelt on at some length, and necessarily so, because a sizing up of the mentality is not complete without considering them. Speech, pupil symptoms, goiters, palsies, atrophies, scars, skin lesions, gaits, and other physical signs, all have their meaning in mental medicine. . . . Knowledge of racial characteristics in physique, costume and behavior are important in this primary sifting process" (733). Mullan went on to echo Knox, and reinforce the idea that any good American should be able to co-identify racial, mental, and physical deficiency, suggesting that "experience enables the inspecting officer to tell at a glance the race of an alien. . . . Those who have inspected immigrants know that almost every race has its own type of reaction during the line inspection. On the line if an Englishman reacts to questions in the manner of an Irishman, his lack of mental balance would be suspected. The converse is also true. If the Italian responded to questions as the Russian Finn responds, the former would in all probability be suffering with a depressive psychosis" (ibid.). Clearly, those who trespassed racial categories and stereotypes could be quickly and easily disciplined. The ability to view racial trespass as deficiency was meant to be made innate within the American citizen. This mandate interacted with a very active rhetorical push to identify and stigmatize racial trespass within the country, closely policing the color line through antimiscegenation laws, for instance, and attributing a perceived wayward genetic stream within the country to mixed blood.

The invention of the term "moron" then became another important move for immigration restriction. This term was invented by Henry Goddard in 1910, and the classification was key to research he performed on immigrants at Ellis Island beginning in 1913—the term should be seen as, in part, a product of this rhetorical space.[28] As Anna Stubblefield has argued, Goddard's invention of this term as a "signifier of tainted whiteness" was the "most important contribution to the concept of feeble-mindedness as a signifier of a racial taint," through the diagnosis of the menace of alien races, but also as a way to divide out the impure elements of the white race (173, 162). The moron was seen as, in the words of Goddard's contemporary, Margaret Sanger, "the mental defective who is glib and plausible, bright looking and attractive." This person "may not merely lower the whole level of intelligence in a school or in a society, but may . . . increase and multiply until he dominates and gives the prevailing 'color'—culturally speaking—to an entire community" (210). The "moron," designated as a high-functioning feebleminded individual, yet capable of "passing" as normal, being attractive to normals, highly sexualized and thus an even greater menace to the gene pool, was a threat that created the need for greater diligence and surveillance, and inspection and worry, in the whole population and on the borders. This desire to detect, detain, and deport the confusing border creatures, and thus somehow protect the supposedly clear delineation of an untainted norm, was achieved through linguistic and symbolic finesse. "Feeblemindedness" became a useful categorical wastebasket. The "moron" upped the stakes.

Feeblemindedness and the classification "moron," as wastebasket terms, incorporated many biases into bodily signs. As June Dwyer has written of immigration law in this period, despite the specificity of the catalogue of restrictions that each new law introduced, "generalizing phrases" such as feeblemindedness, "moral turpitude," and "psychopathic inferiority" "were easily read as catch-all terms and invited blanket condemnation." "It was quite easy, for those who were so inclined, to elide . . . specific restrictions into manifestations of a root condition: the mental and physical inferiority of the immigrant body" (3). That is, the flexibility of terms allowed *any* noticeably foreign body to be made inferior.

Importantly, while the location of defect in the face of the immigrant was still the dominant visual trope of immigration restriction, the moron needed to be less detectable to be more menacing. As Goddard wrote, what "we are struggling very hard to overcome in the popular mind . . . is the idea that these defective children ['morons'] show their defect in their faces. The real fact . . . is that the most dangerous children in a community are those that look entirely normal" (2). By creating a category of "defective" that eludes visual investigation, the inspection process could reach further into the bodies of immigrants, and the sweep of exclusion could be even further extended. This move also allowed for a further *combination* of the disciplining power of the spectacle, and the disciplining power of diffuse surveillance. The invention of the "moron," while originating in the special rhetorical space of Ellis Island, had the power to float into the consciousness of the nation. In this way, this microhistory shows clearly how the disciplinary shift from spectacle to surveillance also results in a proliferation of discourses, architectures, and choreographies, the tangle of which is best investigated rhetorically. As I will show in the following, final section, the discourses of power and surveillance engendered by the invention of terms like "moron" allowed the nation eventually to dispatch with Ellis Island inspectors altogether, and enlist us all in enforcing exclusions.

THE REGIME OF "NORMALCY"

As Francis Galton wrote in his 1909 *Essays in Eugenics,* "The first and main point is to secure the general intellectual acceptance of Eugenics as a hopeful and most important study. Then let its principles work into the heart of the nation, who will gradually give practical effect to them in ways that we may not wholly foresee" (43). The spectacle of the denial or detainment of aliens at Ellis Island, and the inculcated, incorporated practices of Other-assessment, of marking the alien as defective and the assumedly defective as alien, allowed eugenics to march from Ellis Island into the heart of the nation, and indeed to lead to unprecedented practical applications. Interestingly, as eugenic sentiment flowered, as the national immigration bureaucracy grew by 4200 percent, as the classifications within and between races multiplied, Ellis Island itself was also growing physically. Originally it had an area of 3.3 acres. In 1892, it was expanded to 11.07 acres; in 1896, 14.2; in 1898, 15.52; in 1906, 20.27; in 1924, 24.37; it now has an area of 27.5 acres (Moreno, 127). Ellis Island expanded geographically as it expanded ideologically and, conversely, constricted access to the American frontier just a few miles away. Garbage and landfill from New York was added to the island to increase its size, as was soil from the construction of the new New York subway system. The garbage metaphor seems almost too apt: not just because many saw immigrants as the waste of other countries, but because the rhetorical growth of pseudosciences and racisms were matched by a physical growth that was equally odorous.[29]

Another irony: this island, the end of the line for the immigrant, a cul-de-sac for many, was also built out of the dirt that was cleared away to make mass subway transit possible in New York City.

In 1921, President Warren G. Harding passed the first immigration quota law, the Johnson-Reed Act, intended to be temporary. This law limited immigration numerically by nation. When such quotas were first proposed in 1919, census data for 1910 were used to set thresholds—immigration was then capped at 3 percent of the total of any nation's residents in the United States, according to this census. In effect, the immigration service was able to turn back the clock, to arrest the growth of the country and to call time-out, hearkening back to the years before the waves of southern and eastern Europeans and Jews began to arrive in large numbers. The quota law adopted in 1921 went back even further, using the 1890 census numbers (with the cap again at 3 percent), essentially rewinding 30 years of American immigration, in an attempt to reverse the melting of certain races into the American pot.[30] The 1921 quota law was so restrictive that Italians reached their monthly quota the second day after it passed, and thousands more Italians were stranded at Ellis Island or in ships in New York harbor waiting for the next month's allotment.[31] The final quota law, the National Origins Act, was passed in 1924. The "per centum" number was lowered to 2 percent, and again based on the 1890 census. As eugenics proponent Charles Davenport stated in a lecture on American Immigration Policy, the 1924 act "now added the eugenic principle in selection and new legislation was enacted which was directed toward retaining in our population a prevalence of that high quality which it had from the beginning" (2). Essentially, any group tainted by the possibility of genetic inferiority was to be excluded.[32]

With President Harding's passage of this National Origins Act in 1924, the door essentially shut. As Roger Daniels wrote, with this act, Congress "wrote the assumptions of the Immigration Restriction League and other nativist [and eugenicist] groups into the statute book of the United States" (2004, 55). The eugenic message was clear. Prescott Hall, writing on behalf of the IRL in 1920, simply stated that America must "exclude the black, the brown, and the yellow altogether. As to the white, favor the immigration of Nordic and nordicized stock." "We need to become and to remain a strong, self-reliant, united country, with the only unity that counts, viz, that of race" (1920–21, 6). And this is essentially what the Johnson-Reed Act of 1921 and the National Origins Act of 1924 did. These developments were celebrated by eugenicists on both sides of the ocean—from Henry Laughlin to Adolf Hitler.

President Harding's own rise to power was fueled by the immigration restriction rooted at Ellis Island, and he relied on some of the same rhetorical tools that restrictionists had made useful. In his famous 1920 speech on "Readjustment," Harding used (or perhaps even invented) the term "normalcy" to describe an idealized state, attainable once America was again at peace and had closed its doors to foreigners (see Murray). While many believed this was a lexical mistake, the word perhaps nicely summed up a new system of making-normal. Of particular note is Harding's strong push for "not submergence in internationality but sustainment [sic] in triumphant nationality" (n.p.). He was referring here both to the end of war overseas and the end of the stream of immigration. He promised to close the gates, and he did just that. As Roger Daniels points out, his speech "served as a stimulus for congressional action on immigration restriction" (Daniels and Graham, 18).[33] The rhetoric of an idealized American "normalcy" is what allowed Harding and others to paint the international world as irrational, crooked, impaired, while the new America would be straight and sure on its feet. The traditional concept of the norm, defined by Canguilhem as "a polemical concept which negatively qualifies" also applies to Harding's "normalcy"—he does not have to say what America will be, only to qualify what it will not be. In such cases, "the abnormal, while logically second, is existentially first" (243).[34] The Jew, the Asian with "insufficient brain capacity," the black, the brown and the yellow, the "tainted" white, and all other conveniently unfit or enfeebled aliens, are the ground against which some fiction of the "normal" American comes into relief.

What is remarkable about the "normalcy" that Ellis Island spawned in the United States was not that racist and eugenic sentiments and policies were new, but that now the mechanisms for marking out difference, and thus fortifying the "normal" position only ever in contrast, were multiplied. While the National Origins Act was blunt and finite, the bodily attitudes interpellated at Ellis Island were nuanced and profligate. Post-1924, eugenics became a widespread projection of Ellis Island across the entire country. The rhetoric surrounding the Ellis Island process and spectacle helped to inculcate "normalcy" into the American everyday, to bury systems of downward comparison and stigmatization into the citizen's psyche. When Harding used the term "normalcy" in his presidential campaign of 1920, he solidified an ongoing rhetorical reality: America had defined and would continue to define itself most successfully by what it rejected, not by what it was.

Within a year of the 1924 act, the Commissioner of Immigration at Ellis Island, Henry Curran, reported proudly, though ridiculously, that "all immigrants now look exactly like Americans" (n.p.). The dangerous hope and the seeming lack of logic in a statement such as this nicely sums up the frantic play for "normalcy" and the tragic comedy of this drama.[35] To say that "all immigrants now look like Americans" simply reveals that, all along, the idea of American-ness had been an opportunistic projection. Restrictionists shifted more emphasis to the deportation of new Americans within the country, communists, and other threats, and the eugenic focus shifted to the lower classes within America, maintaining racial and ethnic prejudice that had been defined and applied at Ellis Island.[36]

One specific relocation for Ellis Island as a rhetorical space has been the U.S.–Mexico border. The U.S.–Mexico border patrol was founded on May 28, 1924—three days after the passage of the National Origins Act. As Kyle Lytle Hernandez has shown, the patrol, to this day, allows for "perseverance of racially differentiated systems of coercive force . . . racial profiling [by the border patrol is] a wormhole of racial domination; a practice in which past articulations of white supremacy live in the present" (13). In this way, Ellis Island lives on in current American anti-immigration rhetoric.

Further, as Gary Gerstle has shown, it was no coincidence that "the kind of eugenics-inflected revulsion against 'mongrelization' that informed Congressional immigration debates" leading up to the 1921 and 1924 crackdowns "also triggered an expansion of and hardening of state anti-miscegenation laws," including the 1924 Virginia law, which "powerfully strengthened the nation's substantial body of racially and eugenically-based marriage laws" (114). On March 20, 1924, the Virginia legislature passed two closely related eugenics laws: SB 219, entitled "The Racial Integrity Act [1]" and SB 281, "An act to provide for the sexual sterilization of inmates of State institutions in certain cases," referred to as "The Sterilization Act." The alien "feebleminded" became larger targets within the country as eugenic sterilization became widespread.

By 1932, 30 states had sterilization statutes on the books, thanks in large part to the rhetoric of immigration restriction. In the United States, there were 70,000 total known sterilizations between 1907 and end of World War II.[37] Eugenic anti-immigrant rhetoric reached into the bodies of those racialized others made alien within the country. The "integrity" of racial groups could be qualified and policed in multiple, overlapping ways. For instance, sterilization was always explicitly linked to class, and black Americans were specifically targeted for sterilization when they could also be labeled as mentally defective, because they were then seen as more likely to be sexually promiscuous and to thus breed interracially (Holloway, 56).[38] Ellis Island's rhetorical "success" allowed Americans to pick up the border, so to speak, and lay it down across the bodies of thousands of Others within the country.[39]

Perhaps most notably, U.S. immigration restriction efforts shifted from "filtering" arriving bodies to detecting and deporting within the country. The raids on Mexican workers in the Southwest in the 1950s (and that continue today) are one notable example of this new emphasis. But these raids were preceded (and in some ways, anticipated and allowed) by the "Palmer Raids" between 1918 and 1921, exemplified by the "Red Raids" of 1920, during which 3000 suspected communists were detained and deported, many of these bodies held at Ellis Island (see "500 Reds").[40] During the "Tong Wars" of the later 1920s, many more Chinese immigrants were removed from New York to Ellis Island for eventual deportation (see "More Tong Wars"). Ellis Island became a space, like Guantánamo Bay Prison today, where suspect bodies could be held indefinitely, all rights and protections countermanded in this "special rhetorical space." The aggressiveness of current ICE (Immigration and Customs Enforcement) efforts clearly relies on similar suspensions of legal protections and rights, and no longer relies on the fixity of the physical border to apply these powers. In fact, ICE detention centers can be seen as contemporary Ellis Islands, towed onto the mainland.

Daniel J. Tichenor has argued that, following the 1924 clampdown, immigration restriction also gained more "remote control" (117).[41] This was allowed not just because American restrictionists began to have more control over the ways immigration was restricted in other countries, before an immigrant even made it to Ellis Island, but also because of the rhetorical power of the "new racial and ethnic map" drawn at Ellis Island (Ngai, 3).[42] As Mae Ngai has argued, post-1924, there was a new "global racial and national hierarchy," as this new map articulated an unprecedented "production of racial knowledge" and a "new sense of territoriality, which was marked by unprecedented awareness and state surveillance" of borders (7, 3). Snyder and Mitchell reveal the ways that the eugenics movement created new connections across the Atlantic. In the evolving relationship between the United States and Europe, commonality across the Atlantic "was marked not in the likeness of their valued citizens, but rather in the existence of a common social disease with the biologically stigmatized. ... Racialized and disabled others were catapulted to the status of transatlantic pariahs" (129). Clearly, we can see similar influences in current transnational "exports" of American norms, and in the ways that race and ability continue to strongly inflect immigration control internationally. Further, a clear line can be drawn from Ellis Island and the rhetoric of immigration restrictionists and American eugenicists in this period, across the Atlantic, to Germany and the Nazi T4 program.[43] Nazi doctors named American eugenicists as their ideological mentors at Nuremberg. The chalk marks at Ellis Island might be seen as a precursor to the armbands and the tattooing of the Nazi regime.[44] In 1936, Nazis gave a medal to Harry Laughlin, IRL founder. He was recognized by Hitler for his "model eugenic law" (Carlson, 12). Hitler also praised the eugenic provenance of the 1924 American Immigration Restriction Act in *Mein Kampf.*

The attitudes incubated or accelerated at Ellis Island led to the eugenic "racial knowledge" that can be seen clearly in a text such as the "Dictionary of Races or Peoples." There was a new catalogue of races, ordered by deviancy.[45] The use of terms such as "moron" and "feebleminded," applied nimbly for eugenic purposes, created the rhetorical potential for opportunistic disablement and incorporated a look and a lexicon of eugenics into the American psyche. As mentioned, the island was gradually expanded with landfill, subterranean mazes connecting every building. Ellis Island was also constantly regenerating and redoubling its rhetorical powers, connecting forms of discrimination and derogation. Its ideological spread was vast.[46]

As a "heterotopia of deviation" and a "special rhetorical space," Ellis Island helped to invent—and rhetorically construct—disability as we know it today. This construction continues to inflect our understandings of race, "normalcy," and difference, continues to electrify and transport our borders, continues to exist as a bodily attitude, continues to shade and shadow how we look at others and ourselves. The stories of Ellis Island write and map for us much broader narratives and cultural geographies. We see not just the ways that spaces and discourses work together to impose social order, creating spaces in which deviation is sequestered; we also see how spaces and discourses in part *create* deviation and difference. Recall the original use of the word heterotopia to refer to abnormal anatomy—a displacement, a missing or extra element, a tumor that appears out of place, an alien growth. Ellis Island was both a eugenically "hopeful" experiment wherein threats to American purity could be isolated and arrested, and it inculcated an act of diagnosis, the discursive and rhetorical and spatial terms through which any "abnormal" anatomy might be marked. Recall also that the heterotopia only ever exists "in relation." Hopefully, retelling these stories and remapping this space also demands that we develop a new relation to the history of Ellis Island and to immigration that reevaluates the rhetorical uses of difference. I suggested, at the beginning of this essay, that we all take a trip to Ellis Island. But Ellis Island visits us, too. We might recognize the ways that the chalk marks can be read on all of our bodies, the ways that Ellis Island travels with each of us wherever we go. As we recognize the ghosts and ruins of this space elsewhere, as we view its regeneration and persistence, we can make an effort to challenge its spectacles and interpellations, and to imagine the resistance and subversion it might have engendered and might still. Finally, in viewing this island as a rhetorically constructed space in which the key grammars were derogation and exclusion, we might also recognize the possible power of any rhetorical or cartographic construction for reimagining the individual, social, and political body more carefully and critically.

NOTES

I would like to thank the archivists at Ellis Island, particularly Jeffrey Dosik, George Tselos, and Doug Tarr, for invaluable research assistance. I would also like to thank West Virginia University for a Senate Summer Research Grant to support this project in 2007. Finally, I would like to thank the wonderful Faculty Research Group of the WVU Department of English: Jonathan Burton, Ryan Claycomb, Pat Conner, John Ernest, Lara Farina, Marilyn Francus, Michael Germana, Donald Hall, Tim Sweet, Lisa Weihman, and Scott Wible.

1. Of course, another way to state this statistic is to say that 60 percent of Americans cannot and do

not trace ancestry through the Island—which calls into question the myth of Ellis Island's seminal status. Yet in this essay I hope to suggest that the island had a powerful rhetorical effect even on those who never stepped there, even as there have always been many other spaces and stories and histories of origin, arrival, or lineage that have also exerted rhetorical influence over the formation of the American body.

2. You wouldn't have been arriving from China, after the Chinese Exclusion Act of 1882, the legislative move that became a precedent for much of this "squeeze," and for later legislation that would close U.S. doors to immigrants.

3. David Mitchell and Sharon Snyder, whose work is heavily indebted to Foucault, also put forward the idea of "cultural locations of disability"—locations "in which disabled people find themselves deposited, often against their will" (3). These locations are revealed to be "sites of violence, restriction, confinement, and absence of liberty" (x). As you will see, Ellis Island became a place in which disability, and people who were seen as disabled, could be detained or deposited. Importantly, you will see the ways that "formulas of abnormality develop and serve to discount entire populations as biologically inferior" rooted to specific sites of enforcement like Ellis Island, capable of great rhetorical influence (3). But understanding disability as not fixed, but rather as culturally located, we can also see that the formulas can be rhetorically challenged and the spaces can be renovated and reimagined.

4. For instance, questions about sexual preferences and histories were part of almost every medical inspection at Ellis Island. The 1917 Immigration Act listed "abnormal sex instincts" as a "constitutional psychopathic inferiority" (29). As Jennifer Terry has written, "Eugenic doctrine of the first half of the twentieth century placed both racial and sexual purity at the top of its agenda. . . . White phobia about miscegenation and racial passing paralleled a growing sex panic that inverts and perverts were everywhere, but difficult to detect visually hence, an apparatus for identifying and isolating them could be justified as a matter of social hygiene" (138). Ellis Island offered just such an apparatus.

5. Henry Ford's Model T assembly lines began to produce cars in 1914. The appeal of mechanized industry was huge in this period, and the idea of mechanization had import even outside the automobile plant—it became a cultural logic. Christina Cogdell, in an interesting book on the confluence between eugenics and American modern architecture and design, goes a step further, drawing attention to "the interconnectedness of streamline design with eugenic ideology," in particular through the analogy of digestion (ix). Ellis Island works as an excellent application of this metaphorical alliance: eugenicists wanted the nation, and thus its immigration, to "run like an unobstructed colon" (Cogdell, 132). Ellis Island could not be constipated, as "constipation was seen as stunting national evolutionary advancement" (133). Thus the spectacle of expulsion and a steady diet of restriction at the island could be seen as healthy.

6. As Ellis Island expanded, it grew in the direction of this lexicon of pathology, and expanded the island's use as a massive "laboratory and operating theater." The huge Contagious Disease Hospital built on the island centered around "an autopsy amphitheater that enabled visiting physicians and medical students to study the pathology of exotic diseases" (Conway, 9). Immigrants who had died on the trip overseas or while at Ellis Island could be exhibited, their "exotic" bodies used to develop new medical knowledge. This amphitheater is itself an analogue to the architecture of the entire island—a means of dispassionately focusing on bodies in order to alienate, Other, and exoticize difference. The hospital functioned not just as a place to heal and inoculate but also as a space for framing defect.

7. As Mullan describes in his mental inspection guide, "Should the immigrant appear stupid and inattentive to such an extent that mental defect is suspected, an X is made on his coat at the anterior aspect of his right shoulder. Should definite signs of mental disease be observed, a circle would be used. In like manner, a chalk mark is placed . . . in all cases where physical deformity or disease is suspected" (740). Some of the other code letters were "L" for lameness, "Pg" for pregnancy, and "H" for heart.

8. In an article in *Pearson's Magazine* in 1910, Mary Grace Quackenbos also suggested that the steamship lines were involved in this mechanical process of alienation. She writes that the majority of undesirable immigrants were transported to the United States via the "superior power of a vast and intricate 'machine.' In its main outlines this 'machine' may be likened to an enormous dredging apparatus stretching forth gigantic cranes to every port of Europe, catching up and heaving back loads of emigrants collected from every corner of the Eastern Hemisphere by the tireless efforts of no less than fifty steamship agents and their canvassers. The fuel which energizes this colossal structure is an equally colossal greed for yearly dividends, and the combined

intellects controlling [these companies] ... may be said to represent the engineer. The pivot upon which the entire mechanism turns is fraud and evasion of the U.S. Immigration Law." She concludes that, finally, all immigrants are "tarnished by the corroding influence of the 'machine'" and suggests that this influence will always affect their ability to become good citizens (737).

9. Mae Ngai also suggests that the alien has always been a "kind of specter" (7). I find the metaphorical interaction between the spectacle and the specter interesting here—the spectacle being the hypervisible text, the specter being the ghostly presence. Through the spectacles of Ellis Island, it seems that specters of racialized and disabled otherness were given rhetorical power. In this way, Ellis Island continues to ghost our understandings of citizenship, the body, race, normalcy, and so on.

10. As Eithne Luibhéid asserts, the examination process at Ellis Island "individuated" each person examined and "tied [her or him] in to [a] wider network of surveillance," placing "immigrants within lifelong networks of surveillance and disciplinary relations" (2002, xii; xvii).

11. Often the Public Health Service stationed its newest doctors to work as inspectors at Ellis Island as an extension of their training, thus initiating these doctors through the Ellis Island diagnostic process. Many inspectors were also former immigrants themselves, who had come through Ellis Island and then returned to work there. Thus while the inspection process may have inculcated an ableist and "racist" scopic regime, many inspectors may also have seen Ellis Island more positively, as a gateway to opportunities they hoped to share with other immigrants.

12. Alexandra Minna Stern has shown that such techniques were expanded for use at the border of Texas and Mexico in the first decade of the century (at El Paso, Naco, Nogales, Douglas, Tucson, Laredo, Eagle Pass, Rio Grande, Brownsville, and Hidalgo). At stations on this border, every immigrant was stripped, their clothing "chemically scoured," their hair clipped and burned, they were showered with kerosene and water, and then subjected to a medical exam and psychological profile (Minna Stern, 63). Ostensibly this process was used because of the threat of typhus. But these processing stations, called "sanitation plants," were later "enlarged and further equipped ... despite the disappearance of any typhus threat" (65). This spectacular rendering allowed for the "pathologization of Mexicans" and the "association of immigrants with disease" to expand "into new racial and metaphorical terrain"

(67). The embodied rhetorical effects of these plants and their processing then "contributed to the culture of segregation, suspicion, and violence that took shape in the Southwest and California in the first half of the twentieth century" (70). There is some evidence that similar showers were used on ships traveling to Ellis Island. Emmie Kremer, an immigrant reflecting on his Ellis Island experience in 1986, wrote that "third class passengers had to go through a disinfecting shower" on a boat coming from Germany in 1926. "I believe about two years later or so, they did away with that process," he wrote (Kremer, n.p.). In the space of Ellis Island, the space of the ship, and the space of the U.S.–Mexico border, initiation through inspection and inoculation served key rhetorical purposes.

13. Amy Fairchild argues that examination of arriving immigrants on the inspection line and in more intensive exams following detention was "chiefly a spectacle" (99). Her work shows just how powerful the Ellis Island process was, rhetorically, specifically in influencing the first group I identified in my previous list: "Those immigrants who were not marked and yet learned something about the danger of difference gained a self-consciousness of their own possible defects, and were empowered and encouraged to diagnose others."

14. It is worthwhile to quote Baynton at greater length here to clarify this point. He suggests that "disability has functioned historically to justify inequality for disabled people themselves, but it has also done so for women and minority groups." For instance, "opponents of political and social equality for women cited their supposed physical, intellectual, and psychological flaws, deficits, and deviations from the male norm" (Baynton, 33). In similar ways, "disability was a significant factor in the three great citizenship debates of the nineteenth and early twentieth centuries: women's suffrage, African American freedom and civil rights, and the restriction of immigration. When categories of citizenship were questioned, challenged, and disrupted, disability was called on to clarify and define who deserved, and who was deservedly excluded from, citizenship" (ibid.).

15. Of course the American Naturalization Act of 1870 was a precedent for, yet also consonant and contemporaneous with, the sentiment of this document—limiting American citizenship to "white persons and persons of African descent" and thus excluding the Chinese specifically, even as it extended citizenship rights to African Americans, overwriting the 1790 act, which limited citizenship to "any alien, being a free white person."

16. Unlike any other federal bureaucracy before it, these officials were tasked not to serve as advocates or service-providers, but to *protect* America *from* certain constituents (Daniels and Graham, 15).

17. As Catherine Kudlick has written, every Ellis Island rejection "reinforced the ideal of a healthy nation" (61). This reinforcement of course was repeatedly unsuccessful, as any desire for normalcy goes unrequited. As David Gerber adds, "When we see normality asserted in regards to the body and the mind, we are usually seeing anxious and aggressive projections of boundary-drawing that are meaningful in understanding a society's felt need and points of stress" (50).

18. Chang's definition of "nativistic racism" emerges from the work of Étienne Balibar and of Omi and Winant, the latter developing the idea of "racial formation," the former the concept of this new "differentialist racism" (quoted in Chang, 30). Lisa Lowe also cites Omi and Winant in her book *Immigrant Acts,* and she similarly suggests that racialization happens "along the legal access of definitions of citizenship" (11).

19. Martha Gardner also suggests that the "Dictionary" "argued for a link between sexual deviance and visible racial-ethnic otherness" (66). Through this "Dictionary," "immigration officials...defined moral deviance as a *visible procedure long* before federal courts would confirm the visual common sense of racialized and sexualized identities" (51, italics added).

20. James Tyner argues that "the idea that bodies belong to specific places is a peculiar construct of...the last few decades of the nineteenth century" (23). This was "a period of knowledge production that centered on embodied spaces" and "the disciplining of bodies through space" (24). Indeed, the connection of a given body with a "naturalized" ethnicized space was a relatively new concept. This was one of the main functions of the "Dictionary," linking bodies to geographical regions—spaces were given bodies, but bodies were given spaces, too.

21. Mitchell and Snyder suggest that the "commonality" of the majority "was marked not in the likeness of their valued citizens, but rather in the existence of a common social disease with the biologically stigmatized. In this way racialized and disabled others were catapulted to the status of transatlantic pariahs" (Mitchell and Snyder, 129). To be American was to be *not* the racialized, disabled alien. As Étienne Balibar writes, "The racial-cultural identity of 'true nationals' remains invisible, but it can be inferred (and is ensured) a contrario by the alleged, quasi-hallucinatory visibility of the 'false nationals.' ... In other words, it remains constantly in doubt and in danger; the fact that the 'false' is too visible will never guarantee that the 'true' is visible enough" (1991, 60). We might also look at Žižek's Lacanian reading of the ethnic Other: "In the perceived deficiency of the Other, each perceives—without knowing it—the falsity of his/her own subject position. The deficiency of the Other is just an objectification of the distortion of our own point of view" (196). In these ways, the American subject requires a deviant Other, and creates him or her from the rhetorical material of his or her own panic about normalcy and belonging.

22. The heterotopia of deviation and the special rhetorical space come together at Ellis Island as what Gareth Hoskins calls a "racialized landscape," "where racial categories frame a discourse of national identity" and where race was a "geographical project," "a social category constructed to consolidate claims to space by alienating others from it" (96, 109, paraphrasing Mitchell, 230).

23. As I will explore further, this quotient approach to exclusion would soon carry over to the enterprise of immigration legislation—when the doors to Ellis Island closed in 1921, the "quota" for immigration by nation would also be capped at 3 percent. This would later be lowered to 2 percent in 1924.

24. This became what Mitchell and Snyder call a "corporeal regime," in which "the body must be made to bear witness to an otherwise internal deviance" (141). Such a regime is, in their words, "essentially a discursive order grafted onto the body to visually articulate morals and laws," calling for an "over-reliance on readings of the symbology of the body" (142).

25. Knox continues, further explaining the construction of the norm only ever in reference to "positive cases": "It must be based on the experience of having seen and examined many positive and also normal cases and the examiner must be a broad-minded, big-souled man keenly alive to the frailties and shortcomings of the human race in general, including himself" (1914, 127).

26. The inculcation of an investigatory gaze worked its way across the Atlantic as well: by 1907, "about ten times as many people were refused transportation for medical reasons as were barred upon arrival at U.S. ports" ("Annual Report of the Commissioner General," 62, 83).

27. The faces in Knox's "Manual" are seemingly all "white." The vision that this text trained for would allow these "feebleminded" faces and bodies to be effectively "colored" as exceptions to the genetic superiority of Western European "white" stock.

28. Steven Gelb argues that it is important also to recognize the discourses that preceded Goddard's invention of this term. As Gelb writes:

Henry H. Goddard first coined the term moron and applied it to mature persons who scored between eight and twelve years of mental age on the 1908 Binet-Simon test. His contemporaries argued that Goddard had actually discovered a milder type of deficiency than had been identified before, and this claim is still widely accepted. However, that belief is erroneous because it ignores the development of ideas about mild states of mental deficiency in the late eighteenth and nineteenth centuries which defined and shaped Goddard's work in 1910. This mythology sanitizes the modern construct by distancing it from earlier, scientifically discredited paradigms—including faculty and religious psychologies, phrenology, degeneracy theory, and criminal anthropology—in which its roots are planted.

(360)

Gelb's argument is that many have seen Goddard's coining of the term "moron" as the beginning of a modern and more valid paradigm of mental testing and classification, and he suggests we recognize the full pseudoscientific history as a way to challenge the validity of all later testing and classification.

29. Vice President Calvin Coolidge wrote in 1921 that America had become a "dumping ground," explaining his eugenic view that "the Nordics propagate themselves successfully. With other races, the outcome shows deterioration on both sides" (14). Coolidge wrote this in an article entitled "Whose Country Is This?" for *Good Housekeeping* magazine in 1921.

30. The final quota law of 1924 also took the added step of barring all Japanese immigrants, even though the quota would have limited their immigration to just 200 persons a year. This move was intended as a slap in the face and was rightly interpreted as an insult by the Japanese government (see Daniels 2002).

31. The Johnson amendment eventually let them in— basically allowing entry for those who were on the seas when the law passed. Still, ships would wait in the harbor and race to Ellis Island at midnight of each new month. See "Six Big Liners in Thrilling Race to Land Aliens," *New York Evening World*, September 1, 1921.

32. Restrictionist Robert De Courcey Ward, writing in *Scientific Monthly,* celebrated the idea that although this act "contains no specific provisions looking towards a more rigid exclusion of eugenically undesirable aliens, it will accomplish a better selection than has hitherto been possible" through the "distinct improvement in the mental and physical conditions of our immigrants" (538). Eugenic principles had been largely camouflaged. The quota law also acted against the socially constructed category of "new immigrants," genetically distinct from "old immigrants" pre-1880 (see Daniels 1997, 61).

33. It helped that the House was "dominated by radical anti-immigration forces" (*Debating,* 18). For instance, Albert Johnson, chair of the House Committee on Immigration in 1924, made specific reference to the danger of incoming "abnormally twisted" and "unassimilable" Jews: "filthy, un-American and often dangerous in their habits" (quoted in Daniels and Graham, 20).

34. For more from the field of Disability Studies on the concept of normalcy, see Lennard J. Davis, "Constructing Normalcy."

35. This reference to "normalcy" pertains to a subject position around which this rhetoric of difference swivels. Disability Studies scholars use the term "normate" to designate the unexamined and privileged subject position of the supposedly (or temporarily) able-bodied individual and the ways in which our culture valorizes that position. As with the concepts of whiteness or of heteronormativity, the normate occupies a supposedly preordained, unproblematic, and unexamined central position. In Disability Studies, this concept has come to symbolize how norms are used to control bodies—normalcy, as a social construct, *acts* upon people with disabilities. Rosemarie Garland-Thomson defines the normate as "the constructed identity of those who, by way of the bodily configurations and cultural capital they assume, can step into a position of authority and wield the power it grants them" (8). A normate culture, then, continuously reinscribes the centrality, naturality, neutrality, and unquestionability of this normate position. Such cultures demand normalcy and enforce norms, marking out and marginalizing those bodies and minds that do not conform. Norms circulate, have cultural ubiquity, and ensure their own systemic enforcement.

36. The rhetoric of "normalcy" and the impetus for immigration restriction also gained important momentum from the Red Scare between 1917 and 1920.

37. At this time, Margaret Sanger wrote that "every feeble-minded girl or woman of the hereditary type, especially of the moron class, should be segregated during the reproductive period. ... Moreover, when we realize that each feebleminded person is a potential source of an endless progeny of defect,

we prefer the policy of immediate sterilization, of making sure that parenthood is absolutely prohibited to the feeble-minded" (n.p.).

38. As Holloway writes, the "class bias in sterilization" was always "openly articulated" (55). She also explains that many whites believed that "mentally unfit African Americans were especially likely to be sexually promiscuous and engage in interracial sex . . . [thus] this population was more likely to pollute the white races and should be sterilized" (56).

39. Étienne Balibar has written about the ways that physical borders have become "inner borders." That is, to establish "national normality," the mode of discrimination between the national and the alien "is *internalized* by individuals" (2002, 78). These inner borders allow for "some borders [to be] no longer situated at the borders at all" and reside instead "wherever selective controls are to be found" (89).

40. Ellis Island continued to be the space that many East Coast political dissidents (such as C. L. R. James) were "removed to" before deportation, from the 1920s through the 1960s. It is also interesting to note that the overwhelming emphasis of much anticommunist rhetoric was put upon the foreign-ness of possible dissidents, seen as what Woodrow Wilson called "hyphenated Americans."

41. Aristide Zolberg suggests that "remote control amounted to a projection of the country of destination's borders into the world at large" (2006b, 224). Matthew Coleman has written about this phenomenon more abstractly, by suggesting that there has been a historical shift from the "geopolitics of containment," characterized by hard borders, to a "geopolitics of engagement," which "reaches inward to 'local' spaces and at once outward to 'regional' spaces beyond the state" (610).

42. One example of this "remote control" was that American restrictionists began to experiment with the use of field workers at American consuls overseas. These workers examined would-be immigrants in their own countries. As Henry Laughlin wrote, in a personal letter in 1923, "We have demonstrated that in friendly countries the American Consul can, without giving international offence, make first-hand studies in the field, of the would-be immigrants. The minute of any objection to the field-studies appears, the Consul and his workers simply withdraw to the American consulate, and announce that if the would-be immigrant desires to have his passport vised [*sic*], he must provide the information concerning his own 'case history' and 'family pedigree.' Because of the immigrants' desire to come to the United States, they smooth the way for perfecting these field studies, and give their consent to medical examinations. In the future, doubtless the cost of these examinations would be placed upon the immigrant, so that ready and prompt co-operation means less expense than hesitancy or non-cooperation" (1923, 3). He continues: "I do not expect the field studies to be as perfect as they could be made if the Law were established, [but the Consul can get information] which under no circumstances could be secured at Ellis Island" (4). Laughlin's trip abroad had been made possible by an honorary appointment by the secretary of labor, designating Laughlin as "United States Immigration Agent to Europe."

43. "Aktion T4" was a Nazi eugenic program that systematically killed between 200,000 to 250,000 people with intellectual or physical disabilities between 1939 and 1941 in Germany.

44. In 1927, Charles Davenport of the American Eugenics Society was in contact with Professor Eugen Fischer of the newly formed Kaiser Wilhelm Institute in Berlin. He made a note to send to Fischer "all publications of the Eugenics Record Office so far as they are available. The Institut was opened two weeks ago and is almost without a library. We want to work in close cooperation with them" (Davenport 1927, n.p.). The Kaiser Wilhelm Institute, it has now been recognized, was the key location for German eugenic science and racial hygiene—undertaking mass sterilizations and performing experiments on skulls and body parts received from Auschwitz in order to "establish" the genetic inferiority of those killed.

45. This racial knowledge was highly flawed of course, and in this way it was *defective knowledge*—yet it is defective also because the terms by which each race was differentiated from Caucasian or white normalcy was always through perceived defect. Only through defect did difference come into view. The alien, always somewhat spectral, always convenient for the projection of the nation's own insecurities, was also useful for his or her key role in the spectacle of inspection and exclusion—warning every citizen that they too were being watched, that their humanity might also be qualified.

46. The American Eugenics Society, for instance, began to reach out to American intellectuals to insinuate eugenic rhetoric into American higher education. Henry Laughlin, reporting on the activities of the society in 1922, wrote that university "teachers of biology, sociology and psychology are finding it profitable to include in their practical laboratory work, provisions for building up, by the research method, authentic family histories with special reference to the descent and

recombination of natural physical and mental qualities. ... The average University student is able to compile a valuable biological record of the family within a few months." This record "centers about the student himself, and, thus, when analyzed, throws light upon the origin of his natural capacities and limitations, and upon his potentiality as a parent in passing on particular traits" (1922, 3).

WORKS CITED

"500 Reds at Ellis Island: Prisoners Taken in Raids Hurried to This Port for Deportation." 1920. *New York Times*, January 4, p. 1.

Asch, Adrienne. 2004. "Critical Race Theory, Feminism, and Disability." In *Gendering Disability*. Ed. Bonnie G. Smith and Beth Huchinson, 9–44. New Brunswick, NJ: Rutgers University Press.

Balibar, Étienne. 1991. *Race, Nation, Class: Ambiguous Identities*. With Immanuel Wallerstein. Trans. Chris Turner. New York: Verso.

——. 2002. *Politics and the Other Scene*. New York: Verso.

Baynton, Douglas. 2001. "Disability and the Justification of Inequality in American History." In *The New Disability History: American Perspectives*. Ed. Paul K. Longmore and Lauri Umansky, 33–57. New York: New York University Press.

Berlin, James, Susan Jarratt, Sharon Crowley, and Victor J. Vitanza *et al.* 1988. "Octlog: The Politics of Historiography." *Rhetoric Review* 7:5–49.

Birn, Anne-Emanuelle. 1997. "Six Seconds Per Eyelid: The Medical Inspection of Immigrants at Ellis Island, 1892–1914." *Dynamis* 17:281–316.

Butler, Judith. 1993. *Bodies That Matter: On the Discursive Limits of "Sex."* London: Routledge.

Canguilhem, George. 1989. *The Normal and the Pathological*. New York: Zone Books.

Carlson, Elof Axel. 2001. *The Unfit: A History of a Bad Idea*. Cold Spring Harbor, N.Y.: Cold Spring Harbor Laboratory Press.

Chang, Robert. 1999. *Disoriented: Asian-Americans, Law, and the Nation-State*. New York: New York University Press.

Cogdell, Christina. 2004. *Eugenic Design: Streamlining America in the 1930s*. Philadelphia: University of Pennsylvania Press.

Coleman, Matthew. 2007. "A Geopolitics of Engagement: Neoliberalism, the War on Terrorism, and the Reconfiguration of US Immigration Enforcement." *Geopolitics* 12:607–34.

Conway, Lorie. 2007. *Forgotten Ellis Island*. New York: HarperCollins.

Coolidge, Calvin. 1921. "Whose Country Is This?" *Good Housekeeping*, February, pp. 13–14.

Curran, Henry H. 1925. "The New Immigrant." *Saturday Evening Post*, August 15.

Daniels, Roger. 1997. *Not Like Us: Immigrants and Minorities in America, 1890–1924*. Chicago: Ivan R. Dee.

——. 2002. *Coming to America: A History of Immigration and Ethnicity in American Life*. New York: Harper Perennial.

——. 2004. *Guarding the Golden Door: American Immigration Policy and Immigrants Since 1882*. New York: Hill and Wang.

Daniels, Roger, and Otis Graham. 2001. *Debating American Immigration, 1882–Present*. Lanham, MD: Rowman and Littlefield.

Davenport, Charles B. 1911. *Heredity in Relation to Eugenics*. New York: Henry Holt.

——. "Lecture: Immigration Policy of the U.S." Charles B. Davenport Papers, American Philosophical Society.

——. 1927. "Memorandum for Dr. Laughlin, October 6, 1927." Charles B. Davenport Papers, American Philosophical Society.

Davis, Lennard J. 1995. *Enforcing Normalcy: Disability, Deafness, and the Body*. New York: Verso.

——. 2006. "Constructing Normalcy: The Bell Curve, the Novel, and the Invention of the Disabled Body in the Nineteenth Century." In *The Disability Studies Reader*, 2nd ed. Ed. Lennard J. Davis, 3–16. New York: Routledge.

"Definition of Feeble-Minded." 1916. *Eugenical News*, vol. 1: n.p.

"Definitions of Various Terms Used in Medical Certificates." BMS Am 2245 (1059) Compositions, 1906. Houghton Library, Harvard College Library, Harvard University.

Dillingham Commission. "Dictionary of Races or Peoples" [Serial set no. 5867, Senate document 662, session 61-3, session date: 1910, 1911]. *Reports of the Immigration Commission*. Washington, D.C.: Government Printing Office, 1911.

Dwyer, June. 2003. "Disease, Deformity, and Defiance: Writing the Language of Immigration Law and the Eugenics Movement on the Immigrant Body." *MELUS* 28, no. 1 (Spring): 105–21.

Fairchild, Amy. 2004. *Science at the Borders: Immigrant Medical Inspection and the Shaping of the Modern Industrial Labor Force*. Baltimore: Johns Hopkins University Press.

Foucault, Michel. 1973. *The Order of Things: An Archeology of the Human Sciences*. New York: Vintage.

——. 1979. *Discipline and Punish: The Birth of the Prison*. New York: Vintage.

——. 1986. "Of Other Spaces." *Diacritics* 16 (Spring): 22–7.

———. 1999. *Abnormal: Lectures at the Collège de France, 1974–1975*. New York: Picador.

Frye-Jacobson, Matthew. 1999. *Whiteness of a Different Color*. Cambridge, MA: Harvard University Press.

Galton, Francis. 1909. *Essays in Eugenics*. London: Macmillan.

Gardner, Martha. 2005. *The Qualities of a Citizen: Women, Immigration, and Citizenship, 1870–1965*. Princeton, NJ: Princeton University Press.

Garland-Thomson, Rosemarie. 1997. *Extraordinary Bodies*. New York: Columbia University Press.

Gelb, Steven A. 1989. "'Not Simply Bad and Incorrigible': Science, Morality, and Intellectual Deficiency." *History of Education Quarterly* 29, no. 3:359–79.

Gerber, David. 2009. "Comment: Immigration History and Disability History." *Journal of American Ethnic History* 28, no. 3 (Spring): 49–53.

Gerstle, Gary. 2001. *American Crucible: Race and Nation in the Twentieth Century*. Princeton, NJ: Princeton University Press.

Goddard, Henry H. 1917. "Mental Tests and the Immigrant." *Journal of Delinquency* 2:243–77.

Goldberg, David Theo. 2001. *The Racial State*. Oxford: Basil Blackwell.

Guglielmo, Jennifer, and eds. 2003. *Are Italians White? How Race Is Made in America*. London: Routledge.

Guglielmo, Thomas A. 2003. *White on Arrival: Italians, Race, Color, and Power in Chicago, 1890–1945*. New York: Oxford University Press.

Hall, Prescott F. 1919. "Immigration Restriction and World Eugenics." *Journal of Heredity* 10, no. 3 (March): 125–27.

———. "Immigration and the World War." Immigration Restriction League Records. BMS Am 2245 (1070) Compositions, 1920–21. Houghton Library, Harvard College Library, Harvard University.

Hernandez, Kelly Lytle. 2002. "Distant Origins: The Mexican Roots of Border Patrol Practice and American Racism, 1924–1954." UCLA Second Annual Interdisciplinary Conference on Race, Ethnicity, and Immigration. May 18. Ellis Island Manuscript Collection IM-158.

Hetherington, Kevin. K. 1997. *The Badlands of Modernity: Heterotopia and Social Ordering*. London: Routledge.

Holloway, Pippa. 2006. *Sexuality, Politics, and Social Control in Virginia, 1920–1945*. Chapel Hill: University of North Carolina Press.

Hoskins, Gareth. 2006. "Poetic Landscapes of Exclusion: Chinese Immigration at Angel Island, San Francisco." In *Landscape and Race in the United States*. Ed. Richard H. Schein, 95–112. New York: Routledge.

Kline, Wendy. 2001. *Building a Better Race*. Berkeley and Los Angeles: University of California Press.

Knox, Howard A. 1913. "A Diagnostic Study of the Face." *New York Medical Journal* (June 14): 1227–28.

———. 1914. "Tests for Mental Defects: How the Public Health Service Prevents Contamination of Our Racial Stock by Turning Back Feeble-Minded Immigrants—General Characteristics Noted and Progressive Series of Tests Applied to Determine Exact Mentality." *Journal of Heredity* 5, no. 3:122–30.

———. 1918. *Manual of the Mental Examination of Aliens*. Treasury Department of the United States Public Health Service, Miscellaneous Publication no. 18.

Kotker, Norman, Shirley C. Burden, Charles Hagen, Robert Twombly, Susan Jonas, Klaus Schnitzer, and Brian Feeney. 1991. *Ellis Island: Echoes of a Nation's Past*. New York: Aperture.

Kremer, Emmie. "Personal Correspondence with AARP." Ellis Island Archive Metaform Collection, Box 39, no. 1 (New Box 99), "General Research Files: AARP Letters."

Kudlick, Catherine. 2005. "Comment: Comparative Observations on Disability in History." *Journal of American Ethnic History* 29, no. 3 (Spring): 59–63.

Kraut, Alan. 1994. *Silent Travelers: Germs, Genes, and the "Immigrant Menace."* New York: Basic Books.

La Guardia, Fiorello H. 1948. *The Making of an Insurgent: An Autobiography, 1882–1919*. Westport, CT: Greenwood Press.

Laughlin, Henry H. 1922. "Report of H.H. Laughlin for the Year Ending August 31, 1922." Charles B. Davenport Papers, American Philosophical Society.

———. 1923. "Correspondence with Charles B. Davenport, Eugenics Record Office, November 22, 1923." Charles B. Davenport Papers, American Philosophical Society.

Lowe, Lisa. 1996. *Immigrant Acts*. Durham, NC: Duke University Press.

Luibheid, Eithne. 2002. *Entry Denied: Controlling Sexuality at the Border*. Minneapolis: University of Minnesota Press.

———. 2004. "Heteronormativity and Immigration Scholarship: A Call for Change." *GLQ: A Journal of Lesbian and Gay Studies* 10, no. 2:227–35.

Marback, Richard. 2004. "The Rhetorical Space of Robben Island." *Rhetoric Society Quarterly* 24, no. 2 (Spring): 7–28.

Markel, Howard, and Alexandra Minna Stern. 1999. "Which Face? Whose Nation?" *American Behavioral Scientist* 42, no. 9:1314–31.

Matje, Thelma I. "A Pursuit of Happiness Through Ellis Island." Ellis Island Archive Metaform Collection,

Box 39, no. 1 (New Box 99). "General Research Files," "Immigration Experiences: First-Person Accounts."

Minna Stern, Alexandra. 2005. *Eugenic Nation: Faults and Frontiers of Better Breeding in Modern America.* Berkeley and Los Angeles: University of California Press.

Mitchell, David, and Sharon Snyder. 2006. *Cultural Locations of Disability.* Chicago: University of Chicago Press.

Mitchell, Don. 2000. *Cultural Geography: An Introduction.* Oxford: Blackwell.

"More Tong Wars." 1925. *Time Magazine,* October 5.

Moreno, Barry. 2004. *The Encyclopedia of Ellis Island.* Westport, CT: Greenwood Press.

Mountford, Roxanne. 2001. "On Gender and Rhetorical Space." *Rhetoric Society Quarterly* 31, no. 1 (Winter): 41–71.

Mullan, E. H. 1917. "Mental Examination of Immigrants: Administration and Line Inspection at Ellis Island." *Public Health Reports* 33, no. 20 (May 18): 733–46.

Murray, Robert K. 1917. *The Politics of Normalcy.* New York: W. W. Norton.

Ngai, Mae M. 2004. *Impossible Subjects: Illegal Aliens and the Making of Modern America.* Princeton, NJ: Princeton University Press.

New York Evening World. 1921. "Six Big Liners in Thrilling Race to Land Aliens." September 1.

Oliver, Michael. 1990. *The Politics of Disablement: A Sociological Approach.* London: St. Martin's Press.

Ordover, Nancy. 2003. *American Eugenics: Race, Queer Anatomy, and the Science of Nationalism.* Minneapolis: University of Minnesota Press.

Oxford English Dictionary Online, 2nd ed. 1989. "Heterotopy." http://www.oed.com

Pernick, Martin. 1996. *The Black Stork: Eugenics and the Death of "Defective" Babies in American Medicine and Motion Pictures Since 1915.* New York: Oxford University Press.

Quackenbos, Mary Grace. 1910. "Why They Come." *Pearson's Magazine* (December): 737–47.

Quayson, Ato. 2007. *Aesthetic Nervousness: Disability and the Crisis of Representation.* New York: Columbia University Press.

Rand, Erica. 2005. *The Ellis Island Snow Globe.* Durham, NC: Duke University Press.

"Report of the Joint Special Committee to Investigate Chinese Immigration, 1877." Senate Reprint no. 689, 44th Cong., 2nd sess. at p. 1172 (1877).

Ripley, William Z. 1899. *The Races of Europe: A Sociological Study.* New York: D. Appleton.

Safford, Victor. 1925. *Immigration Problems: Personal Experiences of an Official.* New York: Dodd, Mead.

Sanger, Margaret. 1922. *The Pivot of Civilization.* New York: Brentano's Press.

Sargent, Frank P. 1905. "Dept. of Commerce and Labor, Bureau of Immigration Correspondence with Immigration Restriction League," April 17. BMS Am 2245 (916) U.S. Immigration and Naturalization Service. Correspondence with IRL, 1896–1920. Houghton Library, Harvard College Library, Harvard University.

Siebers, Tobin, ed. 1994. *Heterotopia: Postmodern Utopia and the Body Politic.* Ann Arbor: University of Michigan Press.

Stubblefield, Anna. 2007. "Beyond the Pale: Tainted Whiteness, Cognitive Disability, and Eugenic Sterilization." *Hypatia* 22, no. 2:162–81.

Terry, Jennifer, and Jacqueline Urla. 1995. "Introduction." In *Deviant Bodies: Critical Perspectives on Difference in Science and Culture.* Ed. Jennifer Terry and Jacqueline Urla. Bloomington: Indiana University Press.

Tichenor, Daniel J. 2002. *Dividing Lines: The Politics of Immigration Control in America.* Princeton, NJ: Princeton University Press.

Tifft, Wilton S. 1990. *Ellis Island.* Chicago: Contemporary Books.

Tremain, Shelley. 2002. "On the Subject of Impairment." In *Disability/Postmodernity: Embodying Political Theory.* Ed. Mairian Corker and Tom Shakespeare, 32–47. London: Continuum Press.

Tyner, James. 2006. *Oriental Bodies: Discourse and Discipline in U.S. Immigration Policy, 1875–1943.* Lexington: University of Kentucky Press.

Vattimo, Gianni. 1992. "From Utopia to Heterotopia." In *The Transparent Society.* Trans. David Webb, 62–75. Cambridge: Polity Press.

Ward Robert De Courcey. 1912. "Our Immigration Law from the Viewpoint of National Eugenics." *National Geographic* (January): 38–41.

——. 1922. "Some Thoughts on Immigration Restriction." *Scientific Monthly* (October).

Weil, Patrick. 2003. "Races at the Gate: Racial Distinctions in Immigration Policy: A Comparison Between France and the United States." In *From Europe to North America, Migration Control in the Nineteenth Century: The Evolution of State Practices in Europe and the United States from the French Revolution to the Inter-War Period.* Ed. Andreas Fahrmeir, Olivier Faron, and Patrick Weil, 368–402. New York: Berghahn Books.

Wells, H. G. 1987. *The Future in America: A Search After Realities.* Boston: St. Martin's Press.

Williams, William. "Annual Reports of the Commissioner of Ellis Island, 1902–09, 1909–13," William

Williams Papers, box 5, Rare Book and Manuscript Collections, New York Public Library, New York.

——. 1907. "Annual Report of the Commissioner General of Immigration 1907," 62–83. Washington, D.C.: Government Printing Office.

Wilson, J. G. 1911. "The Crossing of the Races." *Popular Science Monthly* 79 (November): 493–95.

Žižek, Slavoj. 2006. *The Universal Exception.* New York: Continuum.

Zolberg. Aristide R. 2006a. *A Nation by Design: Immigration Policy in the Fashioning of America.* New York: Russell Sage Foundation with Harvard University Press.

——. 2006b. "Managing a World on the Move." *Population and Development Review* 32: 222–53.

PART II

The Politics of Disability

CHAPTER 5

Disability Rights and Selective Abortion

Marsha Saxton

SUMMARY

Marsha Saxton writes that it's "ironic that just when disabled citizens have achieved so much, the new reproductive and genetic technologies are promising to eliminate births of disabled children." Many disabled people who would have been the target of prenatal screening and abortion find themselves in the position to nonetheless defend abortion rights and activism. In this essay, Saxton writes that while the abortion rights movement is about the right to have an abortion, the disability rights movement can instead emphasize the right not to have an abortion.

Although some Americans would consider it a "commonsense" measure to terminate the pregnancy of a disabled child, the growing interest in prenatal screening and abortion follows from a history of eugenics. Saxton calls for a clarification between the control of so-called "defective fetuses" and the control of women's bodies. When fetal anomalies are used as justification for abortion, it reinforces the idea that disabled children oppress mothers. To blame a woman's oppression on characteristics of the fetus, Saxon argues, obscures the core of the "choice" touted by reproductive rights in the first place—the choice should include the option of giving birth to a disabled child.

Saxton ends this essay with a list of proposals for the reproductive rights movement, which she says should recognize disability as a feminist issue. In addition to including disabled people in reproductive rights organizations, the movement should call for an end to "wrongful birth" suits and overcome discomfort when applying feminist ideals to the discussions of the fetus. These measures may one day help combat selective abortion's central message that some people are too flawed to even exist.

Disability rights activists are now articulating a critical view of the widespread practice of prenatal diagnosis with the intent to abort if the pregnancy might result in a child with a disability. Underlying this critique are historical factors behind a growing activism in the United States, Germany, Great Britain, and many other countries, an activism that confronts the social stigmatization of people with disabilities.

For disabled persons, women's consciousness-raising groups in the 1960s and 1970s offered a model for connecting with others in an "invisible" oppressed social group and confirming the experience of pervasive social oppression. ("That happened to you, too?") Participants in such groups began to challenge a basic tenet of disability oppression: that disability *causes* the low socioeconomic status of disabled persons.

Collective consciousness-raising has made it clear that stigma is the cause.

Effective medical and rehabilitation resources since the 1950s have also contributed to activism. Antibiotics and improved surgical techniques have helped to alleviate previously fatal conditions. Consequently, disabled people are living longer and healthier lives, and the population of people with severely disabling conditions has increased. Motorized wheelchairs, lift-equipped wheelchair vans, mobile respirators, and computer and communication technologies have increased the mobility and access to education and employment for people previously ostracized because of their disabilities.

Effective community organizing by blind, deaf, and mobility-impaired citizen groups and disabled student groups flourished in the late 1960s and resulted in new legislation. In 1973 the Rehabilitation Act Amendments (Section 504) prohibited discrimination in federally funded programs. The Americans with Disabilities Act of 1990 (ADA) provides substantial civil rights protection and has helped bring about a profound change in the collective self-image of an estimated 45 million Americans. Today, many disabled people view themselves as part of a distinct minority and reject the pervasive stereotypes of disabled people as defective, burdensome, and unattractive.

It is ironic that just when disabled citizens have achieved so much, the new reproductive and genetic technologies are promising to eliminate births of disabled children—children with Down's syndrome, spina bifida, muscular dystrophy, sickle cell anemia, and hundreds of other conditions. The American public has apparently accepted these screening technologies based on the "commonsense" assumptions that prenatal screening and selective abortion can potentially reduce the incidence of disease and disability and

thus improve the quality of life. A deeper look into the medical system's views of disability and the broader social factors contributing to disability discrimination challenges these assumptions.

REPRODUCTIVE RIGHTS IN A DISABILITY CONTEXT

There is a key difference between the goals of the reproductive rights movement and the disability rights movement regarding reproductive freedom: the reproductive rights movement emphasizes the right to have an abortion; the disability rights movement, the right *not to have to have* an abortion. Disability rights advocates believe that disabled women have the right to bear children and be mothers, and that all women have the right to resist pressure to abort when the fetus is identified as potentially having a disability.

Women with disabilities raised these issues at a conference on new reproductive technologies (NRTs) in Vancouver in 1994.[1] For many of the conference participants, we were an unsettling group: women in wheelchairs; blind women with guide dogs; deaf women who required a sign-language interpreter; women with scarring from burns or facial anomalies; women with missing limbs, crutches, or canes. I noticed there what we often experience from people who first encounter us: averted eyes or stolen glances, pinched smiles, awkward or overeager helpfulness—in other words, discomfort accompanied by the struggle to pretend there was none.

It was clear to me that this situation was constraining communication, and I decided to do something about it. I approached several of the nondisabled women, asking them how they felt about meeting such a diverse group of disabled women. Many of the women were honest when invited to be: "I'm nervous. Am I going to say something offensive?" "I feel pretty awkward. Some of these women's bodies are so different!" One woman, herself disabled, said that she'd had a nightmare image of a disabled woman's very different body. One woman confessed: "I feel terrible for some of these unfortunate disabled women, but I know I'm not supposed to feel pity. That's awful of me, right?"

This awkwardness reveals how isolated the broader society and even progressive feminists are from people with disabilities. The dangerous void of information about disability is the *context* in which the public's attitudes about prenatal diagnosis and selective abortion are formed. In the United States this information void has yielded a number of unexamined assumptions, including the belief that the quality and enjoyment of life for disabled people is necessarily inferior, that raising a child with a disability is a wholly undesirable experience, that selective abortion will save mothers from the burdens of raising disabled children, and that ultimately we as a society have the means and the right to decide who is better off not being born.

What the women with disabilities were trying to do at the Vancouver conference, and what I wish to do in this essay, is explain how selective abortion or *eugenic abortion,* as some disability activists have called it, not only oppresses people with disabilities but also hurts all women.

EUGENICS AND THE BIRTH CONTROL MOVEMENT

The eugenic interest that stimulates reliance on prenatal screening and selective abortion today has had a central place in reproductive politics for more than half a century. In the nineteenth century, eugenicists believed that most traits, including such human "failings" as pauperism, alcoholism, and thievery, as well as such desired traits as intelligence, musical

ability, and "good character," were hereditary. They sought to perfect the human race through controlled procreation, encouraging those from "healthy stock" to mate and discouraging reproduction of those eugenicists defined as socially "unfit," that is, with undesirable traits. Through a series of laws and court decisions American eugenicists mandated a program of social engineering. The most famous of these was the 1927 U.S. Supreme Court ruling in *Buck v. Bell.*[2]

Leaders in the early birth control movement in the United States, including Margaret Sanger, generally embraced a eugenic view, encouraging white Anglo-Saxon women to reproduce while discouraging reproduction among nonwhite, immigrant, and disabled people. Proponents of eugenics portrayed disabled women in particular as unfit for procreation and as incompetent mothers. In the 1920s Margaret Sanger's group, the American Birth Control League, allied itself with the director of the American Eugenics Society, Guy Irving Burch. The resulting coalition supported the forced sterilization of people with epilepsy, as well as those diagnosed as mentally retarded and mentally ill. By 1937, in the midst of the Great Depression, 28 states had adopted eugenics sterilization laws aimed primarily at women for whom "procreation was deemed inadvisable." These laws sanctioned the sterilizations of over 200,000 women between the 1930s and the 1970s.[3]

While today's feminists are not responsible for the eugenic biases of their foremothers, some of these prejudices have persisted or gone unchallenged in the reproductive rights movement today.[4] Consequently, many women with disabilities feel alienated from this movement. On the other hand, some pro-choice feminists have felt so deeply alienated from the disability community that they have been willing to claim, "The right wing wants to force us to have defective babies."[5] Clearly, there is work to be done.

DISABILITY-POSITIVE IDENTITY VERSUS SELECTIVE ABORTION

It is clear that some medical professionals and public health officials are promoting prenatal diagnosis and abortion with the intention of eliminating categories of disabled people, people with Down's syndrome and my own disability, spina bifida, for example. For this reason and others, many disability activists and feminists regard selective abortion as "the new eugenics." These people resist the use of prenatal diagnosis and selective abortion.

The resistance to selective abortion in the disability activist community is ultimately related to how we define ourselves. As feminists have transformed women's sense of self, the disability community has reframed the experience of having a disability. In part, through developing a sense of community, we've come to realize that the stereotyped notions of the "tragedy" and "suffering" of "the disabled" result from the *isolation* of disabled people in society. Disabled people with no connections to others with disabilities in their communities are, indeed, afflicted with the social role assignment of a tragic, burdensome existence. It is true, most disabled people I know have told me with certainty, that the disability, the pain, the need for compensatory devices and assistance can produce considerable inconvenience. But the inconvenience becomes minimal once the disabled person makes the transition to a typical everyday life. It is discriminatory attitudes and thoughtless behaviors, and the ensuing ostracism and lack of accommodation, that make life difficult. That oppression is what's most disabling about disability.

Many disabled people have a growing but still precarious sense of pride in an identity as "people with disabilities." With decades of hard work, disability activists have fought institutionalization and challenged discrimination in employment, education, transportation, and housing. We have fought for rehabilitation and Independent Living programs, and we have proved that disabled people can participate in and contribute to society.

As a political movement, the disability rights community has conducted protests and effective civil disobedience to publicize our demand for full citizenship. Many of our tactics were inspired by the women's movement and the black civil rights movement in the 1960s. In the United States we fought for and won one of the most far-reaching pieces of civil rights legislation ever, the Americans with Disabilities Act. This piece of legislation is the envy of the international community of disability activists, most of whom live in countries where disabled people are viewed with pity and charity, and accorded low social and legal status. Disability activists have fought for mentor programs led by adults with disabilities. We see disabled children as "the youth" of the movement, the ones who offer hope that life will continue to improve for people with disabilities for generations to come.

In part because of our hopes for disabled children, the "Baby Doe" cases of the 1980s caught the attention of the growing disability rights movement. These cases revealed that "selective nontreatment" of disabled infants (leaving disabled infants to starve because the parents or doctors choose not to intervene with even routine treatments such as antibiotics) was not a thing of the past. In this same period, we also took note of the growing number of "wrongful birth" suits—medical malpractice suits brought against physicians, purportedly on behalf of disabled children, by parents who feel that the child's condition should have been identified prenatally.[6] These lawsuits claim that disabled babies, once born, are too great a burden, and that the doctors who failed to eliminate the "damaged" fetuses should be financially punished.

But many parents of disabled children have spoken up to validate the joys and satisfactions of raising a disabled child. The many books and articles by these parents confirm the view that discriminatory attitudes make raising a disabled child much more difficult than the actual logistics of care.[7] Having developed a disability-centered perspective on these cases, disabled adults have joined with many parents of disabled children in challenging the notion that raising a child with a disability is necessarily undesirable.

The attitudes that disabled people are frightening or inhuman result from lack of meaningful interaction with disabled people. Segregation in this case, as in all cases, allows stereotypes to abound. But beyond advocating contact with disabled people, disability rights proponents claim that it is crucial to challenge limiting definitions of "acceptably human." Many parents of children with Down's syndrome say that their children bring them joy. But among people with little exposure to disabled people, it is common to think that this is a romanticization or rationalization of someone stuck with the burden of a damaged child.

Many who resist selective abortion insist that there is something deeply valuable and profoundly human (though difficult to articulate in the sound bites of contemporary thought) in meeting and loving a child or adult with a severe disability. Thus, contributions of human beings cannot be judged by how we fit into the mold of normalcy, productivity, or cost-benefit. People who are different from us (whether in color, ability, age, or ethnic origin) have much to share about what it means to be human. We must not deny ourselves the opportunity for connection to basic humanness by dismissing the existence of people labeled "severely disabled."

MIXED FEELINGS: DISABLED PEOPLE RESPOND TO SELECTIVE ABORTION

The disability *activist* community has begun to challenge selective abortion. But among disabled people as a whole, there is no agreement about these issues. After all, the "disability community" is as diverse as any other broad constituency, like "the working class" or "women." Aspects of this issue can be perplexing to people with disabilities because of the nature of the prejudice we experience. For example, the culture typically invalidates our bodies, denying our sexuality and our potential as parents. These cultural impulses are complexly intertwined with the issue of prenatal testing. Since the early 1990s, disability rights activists have been exploring and debating our views on selective abortion in the disability community's literature.[8] In addition, just like the general population's attitudes about *abortion*, views held by people with disabilities about *selective abortion* relate to personal experience (in this case, personal history with disability) and to class, ethnic, and religious backgrounds.

People with different kinds of disabilities may have complex feelings about prenatal screening tests. While some disabled people regard the tests as a kind of genocide, others choose to use screening tests during their own pregnancies to avoid the birth of a disabled child. But disabled people may also use the tests differently from women who share the larger culture's anti-disability bias.

Many people with dwarfism, for example, are incensed by the idea that a woman or couple would choose to abort simply because the fetus would become a dwarf.

When someone who carries the dwarfism trait mates with another with the same trait, there is a likelihood of each partner contributing one dominant dwarfism gene to the fetus. This results in a condition called "double dominance" for the offspring, which, in this "extra dose of the gene" form, is invariably accompanied by severe medical complications and early death. So prospective parents who are carriers of the dwarfism gene, or are themselves dwarfs, who would readily welcome a dwarf child, might still elect to use the screening test to avoid the birth of a fetus identified with "double dominance."

Deafness provides an entirely different example. There is as yet no prenatal test for deafness, but if, goes the ethical conundrum, a hearing couple could eliminate the fetus that would become a deaf child, why shouldn't deaf people, proud of their own distinct sign-language culture, elect for a deaf child and abort a fetus (that would become a hearing person) on a similar basis?

Those who challenge selective or eugenic abortion claim that people with disabilities are the ones who have the information about what having a disability is like. The medical system, unable to cure or fix us, exaggerates the suffering and burden of disability. The media, especially the movies, distort our lives by using disability as a metaphor for evil, impotence, eternal dependence, or tragedy—or conversely as a metaphor for courage, inspiration, or sainthood. Disabled people alone can speak to the women facing these tests. Only we can speak about our real lives, our ordinary lives, and the lives of disabled children.

"DID YOU GET YOUR AMNIO YET?": THE PRESSURE TO TEST AND ABORT

How do women decide about tests, and how do attitudes about disability affect women's choices? The reproductive technology market has, since the mid-1970s, gradually changed the experience of pregnancy. Some prenatal care facilities now present patients with their ultrasound photo in a pink or blue frame. Women are increasingly pressured to use prenatal testing under a cultural imperative claiming that this is the "responsible thing to do." Strangers in the supermarket, even characters in TV sit-coms, readily ask a woman with a pregnant belly, "Did you get your amnio yet?" While the ostensible justification is "reassurance that the baby is fine," the underlying communication is clear: screening out disabled fetuses is the right thing, "the healthy thing," to do. As feminist biologist Ruth Hubbard put it, "Women are expected to implement the society's eugenic prejudices by 'choosing' to have the appropriate tests and 'electing' not to initiate or to terminate pregnancies if it looks as though the outcome will offend."[9]

Often prospective parents have never considered the issue of disability until it is raised in relation to prenatal testing. What comes to the minds of parents at the mention of the term *birth defects*? Usually prospective parents summon up the most stereotyped visions of disabled people derived from telethons and checkout-counter charity displays. This is not to say that all women who elect selective abortion do so based on simple, mindless stereotypes. I have met women who have aborted on the basis of test results. Their stories and their difficult decisions were very moving. They made the decisions they felt were the only ones possible for them, given information they had been provided by doctors, counselors, and society.

Indeed, some doctors and counselors do make a good-faith effort to explore with prospective parents the point at which selective abortion may seem clearly "justifiable," with respect to the severity of the condition or the emotional or financial costs involved. These efforts are fraught with enormous social and ethical difficulty. Often, however, unacknowledged stereotypes prevail, as does a commitment to a libertarian view ("Let people do whatever they want!"). Together, these strains frequently push prospective parents to succumb to the medical control of birth, while passively colluding with pervasive disability discrimination.

Among the most common justifications of selective abortion is that it "ends suffering." Women as cultural nurturers and medical providers as official guardians of well-being are both vulnerable to this message. Health care providers are trying, despite the profit-based health care system, to improve life for people they serve. But the medical system takes a very narrow view of disease and "the alleviation of suffering." What is too often missed in medical training and treatment are the *social factors* that contribute to suffering. Physicians, by the very nature of their work, often have a distorted picture of the lives of disabled people. They encounter disabled persons having health problems, complicated by the stresses of a marginalized life, perhaps exacerbated by poverty and race or gender discrimination, but because of their training, the doctors tend to project the individual's overall struggle onto the disability as the "cause" of distress. Most doctors have few opportunities to see ordinary disabled individuals living in their communities among friends and family.

Conditions receiving priority attention for prenatal screening include Down's syndrome, spina bifida, cystic fibrosis, and fragile X, all of which are associated with mildly to moderately disabling clinical outcomes. Individuals with these conditions can live good lives. There are severe cases, but the medical system tends to underestimate the functional abilities and overestimate the "burden" and suffering of people with these conditions. Moreover, among the priority conditions for prenatal screening are diseases that occur very infrequently. Tay–Sachs disease, for example, a debilitating, fatal disease that affects primarily Jews of eastern European descent, is often cited as a condition that justifies prenatal screening. But as a rare disease, it's a poor basis for a treatment mandate.

Those who advocate selective abortion to alleviate the suffering of children may often raise that cornerstone of contemporary political rhetoric, *cost–benefit*. Of course, cost–benefit analysis is not woman-centered, yet women can be directly pressured or subtly intimidated by both arguments. It may be difficult for some to resist the argument that it is their duty to "save scarce health care dollars," by eliminating the expense of disabled children. But those who resist these arguments believe the value of a child's life cannot be measured in dollars. It is notable that families with disabled children who are familiar with the actual impact of the disabilities tend not to seek the tests for subsequent children.[10] The bottom line is that the cost–benefit argument disintegrates when the outlay of funds required to provide services for disabled persons is measured against the enormous resources expended to test for a few rare genetic disorders. In addition, it is important to recognize that promotion and funding of prenatal tests distract attention and resources from addressing possible environmental causes of disability and disease.

DISABLED PEOPLE AND THE FETUS

I mentioned to a friend, an experienced disability activist, that I planned to call a conference for disabled people and genetics professionals to discuss these controversial issues. She said, "I think the conference is important, but I have to tell you, I have trouble being in the same room with professionals who are trying to eliminate my people." I was struck by her identification with fetuses as "our people."

Are those in the disability rights movement who question or resist selective abortion trying to save the "endangered species" of disabled fetuses? When this metaphor first surfaced, I was shocked to think of disabled people as the target of intentional elimination, shocked to realize that I identified with the fetus as one of my "species" that I must try to protect.

When we refer to the fetus as a *disabled* (rather than defective) fetus, we *personify* the fetus via a term of pride in the disability community. The fetus is named as a member of our community. The connection disabled people feel with the "disabled fetus" may seem to be in conflict with the pro-choice stance that the fetus is only a part of the woman's body, with no independent human status.[11]

Many of us with disabilities might have been prenatally screened and aborted if tests had been available to our mothers. I've actually heard people say, "Too bad that baby with [x disease] didn't 'get caught' in prenatal screening." (This is the sentiment of "wrongful birth" suits.) It is important to make the distinction between a pregnant woman who chooses to terminate the pregnancy because she *doesn't want to be pregnant* as opposed to a pregnant woman who *wanted to be pregnant* but rejects a particular fetus, a particular potential child. Fetuses that are wanted are called "babies." Prenatal screening results can turn a "wanted baby" into an "unwanted fetus."

It is difficult to contemplate one's own hypothetical nonexistence. But I know several disabled teenagers, born in an era when they could have been "screened out," for whom this is not at all an abstraction.

In biology class their teachers, believing themselves to be liberal, raised abortion issues. These teachers, however, were less than sensitive to the disabled students when they talked about "eliminating the burden of the disabled" through technological innovation.

In the context of screening tests, those of us with screenable conditions represent living adult fetuses that didn't get aborted. We are the constituency of the potentially aborted. Our resistance to the systematic abortion of "our young" is a challenge to the "nonhumanness," the nonstatus of the fetus. This issue of the humanness of the fetus is a tricky one for those of us who identify both as pro-choice feminists and as disability rights activists. Our dual perspective offers important insights for those who are debating the ethics of the new reproductive technologies.

DISENTANGLING PATRIARCHAL CONTROL AND EUGENICS FROM REPRODUCTIVE FREEDOM

The issue of selective abortion is not just about the rights or considerations of disabled people. Women's rights and the rights of all human beings are implicated here.

When disability rights activists challenge the practice of selective abortion, as we did in Vancouver, many feminists react with alarm. They feel "uncomfortable" with language that accords human status to the fetus. One woman said: "You can't talk about the fetus as an entity being supported by advocates. It's too 'right to life.'" Disabled women activists do not want to be associated with the violent anti-choice movement. In the disability community we make a clear distinction between our views and those of anti-abortion groups. There may have been efforts to court disabled people to support anti-abortion ideology, but anti-abortion groups have never taken up the issues of expanding resources for disabled people or parents of disabled children, never lobbied for disability legislation. They have shown no interest in disabled people after they are born.[12]

But a crucial issue compels some of us to risk making people uncomfortable by discussing the fetus: we must clarify the connection between control of "defective fetuses" and the control of women as vessels or producers of quality-controllable products. This continuum between control of women's bodies and control of the *products of women's bodies* must be examined and discussed if we are going to make headway in challenging the ways that new reproductive technologies can increasingly take control of reproduction away from women and place it within the commercial medical system.

A consideration of selective abortion as a control mechanism must include a view of the procedure as a wedge into the "quality control" of all humans. If a condition (like Down's syndrome) is unacceptable, how long will it be before experts use selective abortion to manipulate—eliminate or enhance—other (presumed genetic) socially charged characteristics: sexual orientation, race, attractiveness, height, intelligence? Preimplantation diagnosis, now used with in vitro fertilization, offers the prospect of "admission standards" for all fetuses.

Some of the pro-screening arguments masquerade today as "feminist" when they are not. Selective abortion is promoted in many doctors' offices as a "reproductive option" and "personal choice." But as anthropologist Rayna Rapp notes, "Private choices always have public consequences."[13] When a woman's individual decision is the result of social pressure, it can have repercussions for all others in the society.

How is it possible to defend selective abortion on the basis of "a woman's right to choose" when this "choice" is so constrained by oppressive values and attitudes? Consider the use of selective abortion for sex selection. The feminist community generally regards the abortion of fetuses on the basis of gender—widely practiced in some countries to eliminate female fetuses—as furthering the devaluation of women. Yet women have been pressed to "choose" to perpetuate their own devaluation.[14] For those with "disability-positive" attitudes, the analogy with sex selection is obvious. Oppressive assumptions, not inherent characteristics, have devalued who this fetus will grow into.

Fetal anomaly has sometimes been used as a *justification* for legal abortion. This justification reinforces the idea that women are horribly oppressed by disabled children. When disability is sanctioned as a justification for legal abortion, then abortion for sex selection may be more easily sanctioned as well. If "choice" is made to mean choosing the "perfect child," or the child of the "right gender," then pregnancy is turned into a process and children are turned into products that are perfectible through technology. Those of us who believe that pregnancy and children must not be commodified believe that real "choice" must include the birth of a child with a disability.

To blame a woman's oppression on the characteristics of the fetus is to obscure and distract us from the core of the "choice" position: women's control over our own bodies and reproductive capacities. It also obscures the different access to "choice" of different groups of women. At conferences I've been asked, "Would I want to force a poor black woman to bear a disabled child?" That question reinforces what feminists of color have been saying, that the framework of "choice" trivializes the issues for non-privileged women. It reveals distortions in the public's perception of users of prenatal screening; in fact, it is the middle and upper class who most often can purchase these "reproductive choices." It's not poor women, or families with problematic genetic traits, who are creating the market for tests. Women with aspirations for the "perfect baby" are establishing new "standards of care." Responding to the lure of consumerism, they are helping create a lucrative market that exploits the culture's fear of disability and makes huge profits for the biotech industry.

Some proponents argue that prenatal tests are feminist tools because they save women from the excessive burdens associated with raising disabled children.[15] This is like calling the washer-dryer a feminist tool; technological innovation may "save time," even allow women to work outside the home, but it has not changed who does the housework. Women still do the vast majority of child care, and child care is not valued as real work. Rather, raising children is regarded as women's "duty" and is not valued as "worth" paying mothers for (or worth paying teachers or day-care workers well). Selective abortion will not challenge the sexism of the family structure in which women provide most of the care for children, for elderly parents, and for those disabled in accidents or from nongenetic diseases. We are being sold an illusion that the "burden" and problems of motherhood are being alleviated by medical science. But using selective abortion to eliminate the "burden" of disabled children is like taking aspirin for an ulcer. It provides temporary relief that both masks and exacerbates the underlying problems.

The job of helping disabled people must not be confused with the traditional devaluing of women in the caregiver role. Indeed, women can be overwhelmed and oppressed by their work of caring for disabled family members. But this is *not caused by the disabilities per se*. It is caused by lack of community services and inaccessibility, and greatly exacerbated by the sexism that isolates and overworks women caregivers. Almost any kind of work with people, if sufficiently shared and validated, can be meaningful, important, joyful, and productive.

I believe that at this point in history the decision to abort a fetus with a disability even because it "just seems too difficult" must be respected. A woman who makes this decision is best suited to assess her own resources. But it is important for her to realize this "choice" is actually made under duress. Our society profoundly limits the "choice" to love and care for a baby with a disability. This failure of society should not be projected onto the disabled fetus or child. No child is "defective." A child's disability doesn't ruin a woman's dream of motherhood. Our society's inability to appreciate and support people is what threatens our dreams.

In our struggle to lead our individual lives, we all fall short of adhering to our own highest values. We forget to recycle. We ride in cars that pollute the planet. We buy sneakers from "developing countries" that exploit workers and perpetuate the distortions in world economic power. Every day we have to make judgment calls as we assess our ability to live well and right, and it is always difficult, especially in relation to raising our own children—perhaps in this era more so than ever—to include a vision of social change in our personal decisions.

Women sometimes conclude, "I'm not saintly or brave enough to raise a disabled child." This objectifies and distorts the experience of mothers of disabled children. They're not saints; they're ordinary women, as are the women who care for spouses or their own parents who become disabled. It doesn't take a "special woman" to mother a disabled child. It takes a caring parent to raise any child.

If her child became disabled, any mother would do the best job she could caring for that child. It is everyday life that trains people to do the right thing, sometimes to be leaders.

DISABLED WOMEN HAVE A LEGITIMATE VOICE IN THE ABORTION DEBATE!

Unfortunately, I've heard some ethicists and pro-choice advocates say that disabled people should not be allowed a voice in the selective abortion debate because "they make women feel guilty." The problem with this perspective is evident when one considers that there is no meaningful distinction between "disabled people" and "women." Fifty percent of adults with disabilities are women, and up to 20 percent of the female population have disabilities. The many prospective mothers who have disabilities or who are carriers of genetic traits for disabling conditions may have particular interests either in challenging or in utilizing reproductive technologies, *and* these women have key perspectives to contribute.

Why should hearing the perspectives of disabled people "make women feel guilty"? The unhappy truth is that so many decisions that women make about procreation are fraught with guilt and anxiety because sexism makes women feel guilty about their decisions. One might ask whether white people feel guilty when people of color challenge them about racism. And if so, doesn't that ultimately benefit everyone?

Do I think a woman who has utilized selective abortion intended to oppress *me* or wishes I were not born? Of course not. No more than any woman who has had an abortion means to eliminate the human race. Surely one must never condemn a woman for making the best choice she can with the information and resources available to her in the crisis of decision. In resisting prenatal testing, we do not aim to blame any individual woman or compromise her individual control over her own life or body. We *do* mean to offer information to empower her and to raise her awareness of the stakes involved for her as a woman and member of the community of all women.

A PROPOSAL FOR THE REPRODUCTIVE RIGHTS MOVEMENT

The feminist community is making some headway in demanding that women's perspectives be included in formulating policies and practices for new reproductive technologies, but the disability-centered aspects of prenatal diagnosis remain marginalized. Because the technologies have emerged in a society with entrenched attitudes about disability and illness, the tests have become embedded in medical "standards of care." They have also become an integral part of the biotech industry, a new "bright hope" of capitalist health care and the national economy. The challenge is great, the odds discouraging.

Our tasks are to gain clarity about prenatal diagnosis, challenge eugenic uses of reproductive technologies, and support the rights of all women to maintain control over reproduction. Here are some suggestions for action:

- We must actively pursue close connections between reproductive rights groups and disabled women's groups with the long-range goal of uniting our communities, as we intend to do with all other marginalized groups.
- We must make the issue of selective abortion a high priority in our movements' agendas, pushing women's groups and disability and parent groups

to take a stand in the debate on selective abortion, instead of evading the issue.

- We must recognize disability as a feminist issue. All females (including teenagers and girls) will benefit from information and discussion about disability *before* they consider pregnancy, so they can avoid poorly informed decisions.

- Inclusion of people with disabilities must be part of the planning and outreach of reproductive rights organizations. Inclusion involves not only use of appropriate language and terminology for disability issues but also *involvement of disabled people* as resources. Women's organizations must learn about and comply with the Americans with Disabilities Act (or related laws in other countries). If we are going to promote far-reaching radical feminist programs for justice and equality, we must surely comply with minimal standards set by the U.S. Congress.

- We must support family initiatives—such as parental leave for mothers and fathers, flex- and part-time work, child care resources, programs for low-income families, and comprehensive health care programs—that help *all* parents and thus make parenting children with disabilities more feasible.

- We must convince legislatures, the courts, and our communities that fetal anomaly must never be used again as a justification or a defense for safe and legal abortion. This is a disservice to the disability community and an insupportable argument for abortion rights.

- We must make the case that "wrongful life" suits should be eliminated. "Wrongful birth" suits (that seek damages for the cost of caring for a disabled child) should be carefully controlled only to protect against medical malpractice, not to punish medical practitioners for not complying with eugenic policy.

- We must break the *taboo* in the feminist movement against discussing the fetus.

Getting "uncomfortable" will move us toward clarity, deepening the discussion about women's control of our bodies and reproduction.

- In response to the imperative from medical providers to utilize reproductive technologies, we can create programs to train "NRT peer counselors" to help women to learn more about new reproductive technologies, become truly informed consumers, and avoid being pressured to undergo unwanted tests. *People with disabilities must be included as NRT peer counselors.*

- We can help ourselves and each other gain clarity regarding the decision to abort a fetus with a disability. To begin with, we can encourage women to examine their motivations for having children, ideally before becoming pregnant. We can ask ourselves and each other: What needs are we trying to satisfy in becoming a mother? How will the characteristics of the potential child figure into these motivations? What opportunities might there be for welcoming a child who does not meet our ideals of motherhood? What are the benefits of taking on the expectations and prejudices of family and friends? Have we met and interacted meaningfully with children and adults with disabilities? Do we have sufficient knowledge about disability, and sufficient awareness of our own feelings about disabled people, for our choices to be based on real information, not stereotypes?

Taking these steps and responding to these questions will be a start toward increasing our clarity about selective abortion.

CARING ABOUT OURSELVES AND EACH OTHER

Here are some things I have learned while working to educate others on this issue. I try to be patient with potential allies, to take time to explain my feelings. I try to take nothing for granted, try not to get defensive when people show their confusion or disagreement. I must remember that these issues are hard to understand; they run contrary to common and pervasive assumptions about people and life. I have to remember that it took me a long time to begin to understand disability stereotyping myself. At the same time, I have very high expectations for people. I believe it is possible to be pushy but patient and loving at the same time.

To feminist organizations attempting to include disabled women in discussions of abortion and other feminist issues: forgive us for our occasional impatience. To disabled people: forgive potential allies for their ignorance and awkwardness. At meetings we disabled people hope to be heard, but we also perceive the "discomfort" that nondisabled people reveal, based on lack of real information about who we are. *There is no way around this awkward phase.* Better to reveal ignorance than to pretend and thereby preclude getting to know each other as people. Ask questions; make mistakes!

I sometimes remember that not only have I taken on this cutting-edge work for future generations, but I'm doing this *for myself now.* The message at the heart of widespread selective abortion on the basis of prenatal diagnosis is the greatest insult: some of us are "too flawed" in our very DNA to exist; we are unworthy of being born. This message is painful to confront. It seems tempting to take on easier battles, or even just to give in. But fighting for this issue, our right and worthiness to be born, is the fundamental challenge to disability oppression; it underpins our most basic claim to justice and equality—we are indeed worthy of being born, worth the help and expense, and we know it! The great opportunity with this issue is to think and act and take leadership in the place

where feminism, disability rights, and human liberation meet.

NOTES

1. *New reproductive technologies* is the term often used to describe procreative medical technologies, including such prenatal diagnostic tests as ultrasound, alpha fetal protein (AFP) blood screening, amniocentesis, chorionic villi screening (CVS, a sampling of a segment of the amniotic sac), and the whole host of other screening tests for fetal anomalies. NRTs also include in vitro fertilization and related fertility-enhancing technologies. The conference, "New Reproductive Technologies: The Contradictions of Choice; the Common Ground between Disability Rights and Feminist Analysis," held in Vancouver, November 1994, was sponsored by the DisAbled Women's Network (DAWN), and the National Action Council on the Status of Women (NAC).

2. David J. Kevles, *In the Name of Eugenics* (New York: Knopf, 1985).

3. Not long after eugenics became a respectable science in the United States, Nazi leaders modeled state policies on their brutal reading of U.S. laws and practices. After their rise to power in 1933 the Nazis began their "therapeutic elimination" of people with mental disabilities, and they killed 120,000 people with disabilities during the Holocaust. See Robert J. Lifton, *The Nazi Doctors: Medical Killing and the Psychology of Genocide* (New York: Basic Books, 1986).

4. Marlene Fried, ed., *From Abortion to Reproductive Freedom: Transforming a Movement* (Boston: South End Press, 1990), 159.

5. Michelle Fine and Adrienne Asch, "The Question of Disability: No Easy Answers for the Women's Movement," *Reproductive Rights Newsletter* 4, no. 3 (Fall 1982). See also Rita Arditti, Renate Duelli Klein, and Shelley Minden, *Test-Tube Women: What Future for Motherhood?* (London: Routledge and Kegan Paul, 1984); Adrienne Asch, "The Human Genome and Disability Rights," *Disability Rag and Resource,* February 1994, 12–13; Adrienne Asch and Michelle Fine, "Shared Dreams: A Left Perspective on Disability Rights and Reproductive Rights," in *From Abortion to Reproductive Freedom,* ed. Fried; Lisa Blumberg, "The Politics of Prenatal Testing and Selective Abortion," in *Women with Disabilities: Reproduction and Motherhood,* special issue of *Sexuality and Disability Journal* 12, no. 2 (Summer 1994); Michelle Fine and Adrienne Asch, *Women with Disabilities: Essays in Psychology, Culture, and Politics* (Philadelphia: Temple

University Press, 1988); Laura Hershey, "Choosing Disability," *Ms.*, July/August 1994; Ruth Hubbard and Elijah Wald, *Exploding the Gene Myth: How Genetic Information Is Produced and Manipulated by Scientists, Physicians, Employers, Insurance Companies, Educators and Law Enforcers* (Boston: Beacon Press, 1993); Marsha Saxton, "The Politics of Genetics," *Women's Review of Books* 9, no. 10–11 (July 1994); Marsha Saxton, "Prenatal Screening and Discriminatory Attitudes about Disability," in *Embryos, Ethics and Women's Rights: Exploring the New Reproductive Technologies*, ed. Elaine Hoffman Baruch, Amadeo F. D'Adamo, and Joni Seager (New York: Haworth Press, 1988); Marsha Saxton and Florence Howe, eds., *With Wings: An Anthology by and about Women with Disabilities* (New York: Feminist Press, 1987).

6. Adrienne Asch, "Reproductive Technology and Disability," in *Reproductive Laws for the 1990s: A Briefing Handbook*, ed. Nadine Taub and Sherrill Cohen (New Brunswick, NJ: Rutgers University Press, 1989).

7. Helen Featherstone, *A Difference in the Family: Life with a Disabled Child* (New York: Basic Books, 1980).

8. To my knowledge, Anne Finger was the first disability activist to raise this issue in the U.S. women's literature. In her book *Past Due: Disability, Pregnancy, and Birth* (Seattle, WA: Seal Press, 1990), which includes references to her earlier writings. Finger describes a small conference where feminists and disability activists discussed this topic. German and British disability activists and feminists pioneered this issue.

9. Ruth Hubbard, *The Politics of Women's Biology* (New Brunswick, NJ: Rutgers University Press, 1990), 197.

10. Dorothy Wertz, "Attitudes toward Abortion among Parents of Children with Cystic Fibrosis," *American Journal of Public Health* 81, no. 8 (1991).

11. This view must be reevaluated in the era of in vitro fertilization (IVF), where the embryo or a genetically prescreened embryo (following "pre-implantation diagnosis") can be fertilized outside the woman's body and frozen or can be implanted in another woman. Such a fetus has come to have legal status apart from the mother's body: for example, in divorce cases where the fate of these fetuses is decided by the courts.

12. Many "pro-life" groups support abortion for "defective fetuses." Most state laws, even conservative ones, allow later-stage abortions when the fetus is "defective."

13. Rayna Rapp, "Accounting for Amniocentesis," in *Knowledge, Power, and Practice: The Anthropology of Medicine in Everyday Life*, ed. Shirley Lindenbaum and Margaret Lock (Berkeley: University of California Press, 1993).

14. Suneri Thobani, "From Reproduction to Mal[e] Production: Women and Sex Selection Technology," in *Misconceptions: The Social Construction of Choice and the New Reproductive Technologies*, vol. I, ed. Gwynne Basen, Margaret Eichler, and Abby Lippman (Quebec: Voyager Publishing, 1994).

15. Dorothy C. Wertz and John C. Fletcher, "A Critique of Some Feminist Challenges to Prenatal Diagnosis," *Journal of Women's Health* 2 (1993).

CHAPTER 6

Disability, Democracy, and the New Genetics

Michael Bérubé

SUMMARY

Does it serve a democracy to prohibit or permit parents to engage in genetic selection? In this essay, Michael Bérubé investigates the possibilities of not-too-distant technologies to select against genetic features and how our laws should restrict or allow certain reproductive practices.

Bérubé provides a reading of the science-fiction film *Gattaca* in which he points out that the movie's futuristic setting takes for granted that society would endorse genetic screening. In the film, detecting a genetic anomaly is self-evident justification for terminating an embryo. Bérubé argues against this assumption, but only as far as childbirth isn't considered mandatory for such embryos either. Rather, he insists that it is more consistent with democratic principles to allow prospective parents to choose for themselves. Citing the work of Ruth Hubbard, this essay explains the difficulties in maintaining an individual's abortion rights while also fighting a social stigma against disabled people that shapes prenatal choices. Bérubé envisions a world in which rigorous debate focuses on screening certain conditions while also refusing to equate disability with disease or consider disabilities solely in the terms of cure or elimination. Democracy, he tells us, does not have to honor all personal preferences in order to honor individual autonomy in decision-making.

Although eugenicists have historically focused on larger populations, modern genetic screening can be understood as a "private" or individual version of the same principles. But taking a libertarian stance by making genetics a private choice doesn't adequately account for any kind of social good. For disabled people, Bérubé claims, there is no realm of the wholly private because living with disability is always a matter for public policy. Disabled people must play a part in the democratic deliberation that shapes these policies.

In this essay I will try to suggest ways of thinking about biotechnology, bioethics, and disability that are compatible with democratic values. I will start with the uncontroversial proposition that we have entered an era in which our capacity for manipulating genetic material will determine what it means to be human—and in which our deliberations about what it means to be human will guide our capacity for manipulating genetic material. In saying this, I am presuming not only that political deliberations can determine the scope and direction of scientific research— that much seems obvious—but also that democratic values should prevail with regard both to the procedures and the substance of such deliberations. Affirming at the outset one's commitment to deliberative democracy in such matters does not foreordain their outcome: it remains to be determined, for instance, whether it is consonant with democracy to prohibit or permit prospective parents to engage in genetic selection for Huntington's disease or for myopia, or to prohibit or permit potential genetic therapies for Alzheimer's or multiple sclerosis. Deliberative democrats can plausibly come to different conclusions on these questions, based on opposing yet reasonable assessments of how to understand and adjudicate competing claims with regard to individual liberties (positive and negative), ideas of distributive justice, legitimate scientific objectives, moral injunctions to prevent suffering, and beliefs about human dignity and nascent human life. However, deliberative democrats must nevertheless agree to insist at the outset that democracy is the primary value to be upheld in the deliberations—that although participants in the debate may rely on and express strongly held religious beliefs, religious beliefs in and of themselves cannot and must not determine the course or the scope of the debate.

This might sound uncontroversial, but in practice and in theory, it has important consequences that many of my fellow citizens (and many of my fellow humans) will not be willing to accept. In the course of this essay, for example, I will rehearse my position on prenatal screening for fetuses with disabilities, a position I set forth in chapter 2 of *Life As We Know It*, and I want to acknowledge immediately that there are many people of sound mind and good will who disagree with that position. Some of them, as I have learned over the past few years, dispute not only my calculations of the relative social goods and harms of prenatal testing, but also, and more stringently, my primary assumption that public access to and public uses of prenatal testing should be thought of in terms consonant with democratic values. As one of my interlocutors once put it, in the course of a discussion

at Syracuse University's Center for Human Policy, it may be that democracy is not the highest value in such affairs. To people who start from the premise that there are divine laws the meanings of which are not subject to human deliberation, and which therefore must be imposed on humanity by the representatives of the deity, nothing I say in this essay will have sufficient persuasive force. And this is but one example of a pervasive philosophical problem that some have called, for better or worse, "postmodern": when the claims of two systems of belief—democracy and theocracy, perhaps—are opposed, there may not be any way to reconcile them under the heading of a third, more universal term. We may instead be faced with a fundamental incommensurability between discourses of justification, such that we may not even have the language in which to agree to disagree. Understanding this problem, then, and admitting that I will have no common ground with some participants in debates over genomics even as I appeal to the practice of deliberative democracy, I will begin my discussion of biotechnology and disability by talking about a Hollywood movie. But not just any Hollywood movie: the film in question, *Gattaca*, might well be the new *locus classicus* for discussions of genetic screening and enhancement, and one of its plots offers a vivid illustration of what Michael Sandel would argue some years later in *The Case Against Perfection*: namely, that a designer baby might spend its life laboring under the burdens imposed by his or her design, and that our sense of human freedom (for such children, and for their designing parents) would thereby be paradoxically diminished rather than enhanced by our increasing mastery over the genome.

Gattaca depicts a dystopian world, set in the "not-too-distant future," of widespread *in vitro* fertilization and pre-implantation screening, in which school placements, job interviews, and indeed life prospects consist of blood tests and urine samples. Children conceived the "old-fashioned" way—for example, by means of sex in the back seat of a car, as is the case for our protagonist and narrator, Vincent Freeman—are called "in-valids," "de-generates," "faith births," or "God children"; they are increasingly rare, and they make up the lower echelons of society, assigned to various forms of menial labor. Vincent, played by Ethan Hawke, is excluded from school as a child because the school cannot afford the insurance costs he entails, and consigned to a life of janitorial work even though he dreams of space flight, hoping against hope to work someday at the giant aerospace corporation, Gattaca. Throughout his childhood, he had been fascinated with space and space travel; we see him, as a scrawny, bespectacled teen, reading a book titled *Careers in Space*—and we witness his father, venting his frustration and anger by telling his son, "For God's sake, Vincent, don't you understand. The only way you'll see the inside of a space ship is if you're cleaning it." The moment Vincent is born, his initial genetic analysis, drawn from a blood sample and read instantaneously by an attending nurse, reveals the following: he will have a 60 percent probability of a neurological condition, a 42 percent probability of manic depression, an 89 percent probability of attention deficit disorder, a 99 percent probability of heart disease, and a life expectancy of 30.2 years. No, this is not a plausible representation of what genes can tell us. But my argument does not depend on this scene; what matters for my purposes is that Vincent's devastated parents, Marie and Antonio, decide to have a second child *in vitro*; "like most other parents of their day, they were determined that their next child would be brought into the world in what has become the natural way." The genetic technician/counselor informs Marie and Antonio that four eggs have

been fertilized—two boys, two girls—and that they have been fully screened for "critical predispositions to any of the major inheritable diseases." Marie and Antonio indicate that they would like to have another boy, a brother for Vincent to play with. The geneticist nods. "You have specified," he goes on:

> hazel eyes, dark hair, fair skin. I've taken the liberty of eradicating any potentially prejudicial conditions—premature baldness, myopia, alcoholism and addictive susceptibility, propensity for violence and obesity—
>
> MARIE: We didn't want—I mean, diseases, yes, but—
>
> ANTONIO: Right, we were just wondering if it's good to leave just a few things to chance.
>
> GENETICIST: You want to give your child the best possible start. Believe me, we have enough imperfection built in already. Your child doesn't need any additional burdens. And keep in mind, this child is still you— simply the best of you. You could conceive naturally a thousand times and never get such a result.

The geneticist smiles indulgently when he refers to the parents' preference for "fair skin," because, as it happens, he himself is black (he is played by Blair Underwood). By this we are led to understand that in *this* brave new world, genetic discrimination is common but racial discrimination is a thing of the past. The point is reinforced a few minutes later, when Vincent recounts his experience as a young man seeking employment: "Of course," he tells us, "it's illegal to discriminate— genoism, it's called—but no one takes the law seriously. If you refuse to disclose, they can always take a sample from a door handle, or a handshake, even the saliva on your application form. If in doubt, a legal drug test can just as easily become an illegal peek at your future in the company." And we see a human-resources manager wordlessly challenging Vincent to provide a urine sample. The manager, like the genetic counselor, is black.

I find this aspect of the movie's premise fascinating for two reasons—not only because the film so clearly (if counterintuitively and counterfactually) disarticulates racism from genoism, but also because it establishes *Gattaca* as a film about civil rights and employment discrimination. Disability in science fiction is not often discussed in such mundane terms, but perhaps it should be. Readers of Philip K. Dick will remember that one of the things that got lost in translation between the 1969 novel *Do Androids Dream of Electric Sheep?* and the 1982 film *Blade Runner* is the category of human "specials," people neurologically damaged by the nuclear fallout of World War Terminus and derisively referred to as "chickenheads" or, in severe cases, "antheads."[1] The Voight–Kampff empathy test, central to both the novel and the film, is a device bounty hunters ("blade runners") employ to distinguish humans from androids trying to pass as human; it was originally devised, as Dick's novel explains, to identify "specials" so that they could be sterilized and consigned to the lower echelons of society. *Blade Runner* drops Dick's treatment of the relation between disability and employment by taking the novel's despised and lonely "chickenhead," J. R. Isidore, a driver for an artificial animal repair shop, and rewriting him as J. F. Sebastian, a lonely high-ranking engineer for the Tyrell Corporation (though the film does give Sebastian another disability, "Methusaleh syndrome," a premature-aging disorder that effectively links him to the Nexus-6 androids who have lifespans of only four years). *Gattaca*, by contrast, builds its plot around the relation between employment and disability; its central drama focuses entirely on whether Vincent will be discovered and thrown out of work and into jail. That drama of detection and evasion, in turn, transforms the relation between race and disability into one of mutual implication: once it become inescapably clear that he will be unable to pursue a career in space exploration because of his genetic makeup, Vincent decides to become a "borrowed ladder," using the bodily fluids and effluvia of Jerome Morrow in order to obtain the clearance necessary for employment at Gattaca. Jerome (played by Jude Law) is a former world-class athlete who was struck by a car (we learn later that he tried to kill himself after failing to win an Olympic gold medal); paraplegic and visually marked by the most common sign for physical disability, his wheelchair, he literally sells his genetic identity to Vincent as he descends into bitterness and alcoholism, finally committing suicide in the film's final sequence. In other words, *Gattaca* is not only a science-fictional exploration of employment discrimination; it is also a member of one of the oldest genres in African American fiction, the passing narrative.

Scholars in disability studies have tended to see Jerome's character as a regrettable and gratuitous reinforcement of stereotypes of disability. Anne Finger's 1998 review has largely set the terms of the debate: arguing that the film is ultimately "scared of the radicalness of its critique," Finger suggests that Jerome's suicide is meant to reassure the contemporary able-bodied audience who largely identify with Vincent and hope that they, too, would have the determination to fight genetic determinism and succeed. "In its futuristic world," Finger notes:

> virtually everyone watching the film would be classified as a 'de-generate,' an 'invalid.' Rather than leave the audience members in the uncomfortable position of thinking of themselves as disabled, the film had to create a 'really disabled' person,

someone who fits our social stereotype of what a crip is. In the end, despite its possibilities, *Gattaca* doesn't really challenge the terms of the debate. It tells us that with hard work and 'spirit' we can overcome, but it still leaves intact a division between 'us' and 'them,' those whose bodies succeed and those whose bodies fail.
(Finger)

Likewise, Kathleen Ellis argues that "movies such as *Gattaca* contribute to the discrimination" against people with disabilities insofar as Jerome is presented as a weak, contemptible character, wallowing in vodka and self-pity (Ellis). What these critiques overlook, however, is that Jerome is not bitter and suicidal because he is disabled; he tried to commit suicide before he was disabled, solely because he had to settle for a silver medal, and he is bitter because his attempt failed: "Jerome Morrow," he tells Vincent, "was never meant to be one step down on the podium." Jerome's story is not that of *Million Dollar Baby*, in which an athlete decides that a physically disabled life is not worth living; it is an illustration of Sandel's argument against genetic enhancement—or, as Vincent's voiceover puts it, a warning about "the burden of perfection."

That said, it is notable that there are no accommodations for Jerome in this society: it is otherwise impressively high-tech, featuring 12-fingered pianists and space travel to the moons of Saturn, but it does not appear to have a single elevator, ramp, or kneeling bus. Perhaps Jerome has reason to be bitter. He does not own a power chair (apparently such things no longer exist), and his apartment has no elevator—just a spiral staircase, an echo of the double helix, by which Jerome has to drag himself upstairs at a critical moment in the narrative. Notably, there are no wheelchair users at Gattaca Corporation, even though physical disability is clearly no impediment to becoming

a first-rate computer programmer or aeronautical engineer. One is left to infer that disability discrimination in this society is severe indeed, though the film leaves this point implicit, just as it does not call attention to its representation of race. Of course, it's possible to say that the film is simply bizarrely optimistic that a society so obsessed with genetics will be a society without racism; it certainly appears to be a society composed entirely of able-bodied heterosexuals, so it is not clear why one form of pervasive bigotry has been overcome while other forms seem to rule the world. But let me turn from the implicit aspects of the film to the film's explicit presentation of what counts as uncontroversial genetic screening in this society: the elimination of all major inheritable diseases, as well as "potentially prejudicial conditions" such as premature baldness, myopia, alcoholism and addictive susceptibility, propensity for violence, and obesity. When Victor's mother demurs, saying "we didn't want—I mean, diseases, yes," surely the phrase she's thinking of and not uttering is something like "a designer baby." Which is, of course, precisely what she gets—still you, just the best of you. And the reason she goes along with it is that her child doesn't need any additional burdens—especially barriers to meaningful education and employment.

The *Gattaca* scenario presents a challenge especially to liberals who (like me) have thus far combined political support for reproductive rights, a defense of technologies of prenatal screening, a critique of cost-benefit analyses of human worth, a stringent skepticism about the workings of the United States' deeply inegalitarian insurance and health care system, and, last but not least, a defense of an aggressive social welfare state that provides need-based benefits to children and adults with disabilities. Granted, abortion is not an issue in *Gattaca*, precisely because IVF and genetic screening seem to have taken it off the table (though one does not know if there are abortion providers who cater to prospective parents who conceive accidentally in the back seats of cars). But the film does raise the question of what happens to the embryos Marie and Antonio do not select, and more importantly, it raises the question of what conditions we should screen for, and what we should do if and when we detect them. The larger question at stake, of course, is the question of who should inhabit the world, and on what terms. My own position on what is now called the ethics of "selective abortion" with regard to fetuses with disabilities is substantially identical to that of the 1999 Hastings Center Report on the Disability Rights Critique of Prenatal Genetic Testing (Parens and Asch 2000), which defended reproductive rights and prospective parents' access to prenatal screening while critiquing the idea that the detection of genetic anomaly is a self-evident justification for terminating a pregnancy.[2] Though I do not consider disability sufficient grounds for abortion, I believe that the fetus does not have a moral status equivalent to that of a child unless and until it is viable outside the womb, and I support the right of prospective parents to terminate pregnancies even for reasons that I would regard as trivial or wrongheaded.

Rayna Rapp's *Testing Women, Testing the Fetus* is replete with accounts of such parents, including the one who told Rapp that "having a 'tard, that's a bummer for life" (91) or the one who insisted that if the baby "can't grow up to have a shot at becoming the president, we don't want him" (92)—in regard to a fetus with Klinefelter's syndrome, on the basis of whose diagnosis the parents terminated the pregnancy. I remain unpersuaded that there are transcendent moral virtues to be advanced by compelling such parents to bear children with disabilities, even though the disabilities in question are relatively benign; indeed, I shudder to think how

such parents will treat their disabled children if they are compelled to bear them against their will. Nor do I see why it is virtuous to compel parents to bear children with far more severe conditions that involve profound physical and emotional suffering for all concerned, such as Lesch–Nyhan syndrome or Tay–Sachs disease; I submit that in a democratic society it is better to allow prospective parents to make such decisions for themselves. For that reason I have insisted (and continue to insist) that it is more consistent with the principles of democracy for people like me to *persuade* prospective parents and genetics counselors not to think of amniocentesis as part of a search-and-destroy mission, and to persuade them that many people with disabilities, even those disabilities detectable *in utero* (like Down syndrome), are capable of living lives that not only bring joy and wonder to those around them but are fulfilling and fascinating to the people living them as well. But I will not argue that some forms of childbirth should be made mandatory, nor will I demand that prospective parents be barred from obtaining genetic information about the fetus if they so desire such information.

As Rapp writes, "at the intersection of the disability rights movement and the feminist movement for reproductive rights lies a thorny problem: How is it possible to contest the eugenic and stigmatizing definition of disabilities which seems to underlie prenatal diagnosis, while still upholding the rights of individual women to determine what kind of medical care, and what sorts of pregnancy decisions, are in their own best interests?" (51) Rapp eventually crafts two moral imperatives— as well as the meta-imperative to see these two as complementary rather than contradictory: "The first is the need to champion the reproductive rights of women to carry or refuse to carry to term a pregnancy that would result in a baby with a serious disability. The second is the need to support adequate, nonstigmatizing, integrative services for all the children, including disabled children, that women bear" (7–8). The difficulty of balancing these needs is exemplified by the excruciating tensions in Ruth Hubbard's essay, "Abortion and Disability: Who Should and Should Not Inhabit the World?", which insists—four times, for good measure (three times emphatically in the course of its seven final paragraphs)—that "a woman must have the right to abort a fetus, whatever her reasons" while arguing that some of those reasons are (a) continuous with the logic of Nazi eugenics and (b) influenced by forces that appear to undermine Hubbard's faith that a woman's reasons can be her own. "Women are expected to implement the society's eugenic prejudices by 'choosing' to have the appropriate tests and 'electing' not to initiate or to terminate pregnancies if it looks as though the outcome will offend," Hubbard writes, pointedly questioning the choices she does not endorse by employing scare quotes to suggest that they are not "choices" at all. "And to a considerable extent not initiating or terminating these pregnancies may indeed be what women want to do. But one reason we want to is that society promises much grief to parents of children it deems unfit to inhabit the world" (118). What's striking about Hubbard's argument is not only that it discounts the decisions of prospective parents whose justifications for abortion she (and I) might find trivial or wrongheaded, suggesting that such decisions are imposed by "society" and on a continuum with Nazism, but also, and more remarkably, that it manages to criticize women *who choose not to become pregnant in the first place*—who do not "initiate" pregnancies—in an essay ostensibly devoted (as its title indicates) to abortion and disability. But surely a democratic society can find some way of honoring and respecting the decisions of women who do not want to

pass a genetic disability on to their children. And one does not (by which, of course, I mean I do not) want to see disability rights advocates elide the difference between abortion and contraception, so that they wind up taking the position Hubbard suggests here—that the decision not to initiate a pregnancy, for reasons related to disability, is as censurable as the decision to terminate one.

For the moment, our society seems to have achieved a shaky but substantial consensus that it is morally acceptable to screen fetuses for profoundly debilitating conditions such as Tay–Sachs disease, which involves severe and ceaseless suffering over a nasty, brutish, and short life span, but morally unacceptable to terminate a pregnancy solely with regard to gender.[3] Everything else—Down syndrome, Huntington's disease, multiple sclerosis, leukemia—falls at various points in the capacious area between, and thus far the people of the United States have apparently decided to leave decisions concerning such conditions up to the people who will be most affected by them. But the *Gattaca* scenario compels us to ask which "potentially prejudicial conditions" we would allow prospective parents to eliminate if the technology were available. That is to say, even in the not-too-distant-future, we might feel a profound moral repugnance at the idea of terminating a pregnancy simply on the basis of the finding that the fetus has a genetic propensity for obesity, myopia, or premature baldness. But if we could select against these features at fertilization, would we do so, and what moral grounds would we offer for refusing to do so and preventing others, by law, from doing so?

In recent years I have taught *Gattaca* alongside Sandel's *The Case Against Perfection* and Jonathan Glover's *Choosing Children: Genes, Disability, and Design*, noting that Glover, in the course of an argument for genetic enhancement in "a regulated market, on a European model," where "which choices, if any, should be excluded would be part of democratic debate" (77), sees no problem with eliminating many "potentially prejudicial conditions": "Elim inating a genetic disposition to shyness or laziness might help someone flourish, as might making them more cheerful or boosting their ability to sing or to learn languages" (75–76). In Glover's ideal regulated-market democracy, apparently, a social consensus has been achieved that it is acceptable to tinker with character traits like shyness or cheerfulness, just as it goes without saying in the world of *Gattaca* that we should screen for premature baldness— despite the fact that the genetic counselor himself is bald (and, in my humble opinion, rather attractively so). My students have overwhelmingly found Glover's position repugnant, arguing that such traits as laziness and shyness do not rise to the level of diseases one would want to delete from the random reconfigurations of our genetic possibilities. (Some argue, however, along Sandel's lines, that it is acceptable to intervene pharmaceutically to bring someone to a baseline of health, as when one is prescribed medication for severe and debilitating shyness, anxiety, or depression.) Interestingly, however, many of my students report that they would welcome a genetic test that would screen for "propensity to violence," considering this a trait well worth deleting whenever possible. Upon noting that in class after class, my female students were nearly unanimous on this point, I began to reflect on the question of gendered violence (which, I realized, had been implicit in the discussions all along), and to suggest to students that this is one of the questions posed to us by Margaret Atwood's *Oryx and Crake*: though Crake's attempt to redesign the human species from scratch is monstrous—he is, after all, Victor Frankenstein as sophisticated genetic engineer—there is surely something to be

said for a world in which there is "no more prostitution, no sexual abuse of children, no haggling over the price, no pimps, no sex slaves. No more rape" (165).

My own answer to the question of how we might determine how and why to screen for genetic traits, tentative though it be, runs as follows. In a world that possesses the kind of genetic knowledge we envision in *Gattaca*, bioethicists, philosophers, Presidential commissions, and humanists like me would have made the argument that while it is acceptable to screen for major inheritable diseases, screening out the "potentially prejudicial conditions" enumerated above—even the propensity for violence—would be highly controversial and far from routine. Our society would have had, and would still be engaged in, a wide-ranging debate about what kinds of disabilities do involve profound suffering or significantly diminished life chances for those who have them, and (by contrast) what varieties of human embodiment may be undesirable or inconvenient but, on the whole, do not constitute conditions so prejudicial as to jeopardize significantly the life chances of those who have them. Such a debate would acknowledge, moreover, that many disabilities are not detectable genetically, and that no amount and no degree of prenatal screening or *in vitro* engineering will produce a world free of people with cerebral palsy, autism, or pneumonia, not to mention people who are hit by cars.[4] Some of the debate's participants would have learned not to think of disability as synonymous with disease, and would continually try to persuade other participants that not all disabilities have disease etiologies and not all disabilities need to be considered in terms of cure or elimination (though in many cases, amelioration might be perfectly acceptable).[5] And finally, such a debate would focus not only on potentially prejudicial conditions but on actually existing prejudices, extending the protection of the social welfare state to stigmatized populations while working also to de-stigmatize previously stigmatized identities (as had been done, evidently, with regard to people of African descent in the world of *Gattaca*). The debate would produce a boundary of the unacceptable, just as we now have agreement on the desirability of forbidding human cloning to produce children and a looser agreement on the permissibility but undesirability of selective abortion for gender. And in democratic fashion, the debate would seek to honor liberal freedoms and ideas of individual autonomy in decision-making while insisting nonetheless, as both Mill and Rawls would tell us, that democracy does not have to honor all the preferences and desires of every person participant therein.

It pains me deeply to admit it, but in such a society, the vast majority of people with Down syndrome would be those among the "faith births," those conceived without the benefits of IVF and genetic screening. There would still be a good number Deaf people in this society, despite screening and despite the widespread availability of cochlear implants, partly because our social debate would have concluded that Deafness is far less damaging to one's life prospects and one's ability to participate fully in the social and political life of the polity than is Down syndrome and partly because some of our fellow humans (Deaf and hearing) would have determined that Deaf culture is valuable, distinctive, and worth preserving in its own right, and that it has no linguistic or cultural counterpart among people with Down syndrome. I say this not because I desire to see a world absent of people with Down syndrome; I cannot even imagine what it would be like to desire such a thing. But I can imagine that if we had the power to screen for major disabilities, inheritable diseases, and potentially prejudicial conditions, many (but by no means all) of

my fellow humans would see the elimination of Down syndrome as a social good; fewer would see the eradication of Deafness as a good; and fewer still would see the eradication of myopia or baldness in those terms. Such would be, on my best guess, the results of a democratic deliberation about disability and genomics.[6]

Yet one of the factors that makes this discussion so difficult is the fact that, as I mentioned at the beginning of this essay, some of us do not agree that societies should decide such matters by democratic deliberation. The debate over genetic screening, in other words, necessarily includes the voices of those who do not believe that it should be taking place, or who believe that it should take place but that it should not be morally binding or dispositive when it comes into conflict with moral absolutes. Those moral absolutes concern the destruction of "nascent human life," whether by means of abortion, by means of the discarding of embryos not selected for implantation (three out of four of Marie and Antonio's options), or by means of the use of embryos for stem-cell research. For example, in a discussion of *Life As We Know It* for the Christian book review *Books and Culture*, Jean Bethke Elshtain responded to my defense of abortion rights and prenatal testing by accusing me of "subtly but inexorably blowing out the moral lights among us, as Lincoln said of Douglas's defense of popular sovereignty in the matter of slavery" (18). I find this remark at once exceptionally offensive and insufficiently morally serious, partly because it rests on Elshtain's remarkably unelaborated claim that "the fetus, of course, is human all along—what else can it be?" For Elshtain, apparently, there can be no debate about the morality of prenatal screening and selective abortion, because there can be no debate about the moral status of the fetus: there is one correct position, that the fetus is fully human (even as a zygote and embryo, for that is what "all along" must mean) and deserves all the protections associated with ideas of inviolable human dignity, and those who disagree are simply blowing out the moral lights among us.[7]

When that hard-line position on nascent human life becomes part of a broader democratic deliberation, it produces distinctive distortions that can skew debate decisively. Take for instance the deliberation conducted by President George W. Bush's Council on Bioethics, published under the title *Human Cloning and Human Dignity: An Ethical Inquiry*. That Council unanimously endorsed a ban on "reproductive cloning," which the Council called "cloning-to-produce-children," and, by a complicated ten-to-seven margin, a four-year moratorium on "therapeutic cloning," which the Council called "cloning-for-biomedical-research." As Council chairman Leon Kass argued in *The Public Interest*, the Council construed the debate over cloning-for-biomedical-research as a clash between competing moral imperatives:

> On the one hand, we acknowledge that the research offers the prospect, though speculative at the moment, of gaining valuable knowledge and treatments for many diseases. On the other hand, this practice would require the exploitation and destruction of nascent human life created solely for the purpose of research.
>
> (40)

This seems to me a reasonable statement of the conflict, even though the second sentence is almost a word-for-word repetition of Charles Krauthammer's partisan account of the debate in his personal statement in the report's Appendix. Yet within only a few sentences, Kass reframes it in a way that can only be called tendentious:

> Each side recognized that we must face up to the moral burden of either approving or disapproving this research, namely, on the one hand, that some who might be healed more rapidly might not be; and on the other hand, that we will become a society that creates and uses some human lives in the service of others
>
> (40)

Note what has happened between these two passages: both hands have changed substantially. On the one hand, at first we had speculative research that offers the prospect of treating many diseases; but now, blocking that research means only that "some who might be healed more rapidly might not be," and not that "some who might be healed *will never be*." On the other hand, at first we were faced with the admittedly dicey prospect of "the exploitation and destruction of *nascent* human life"; but now if we permit cloning-for-biomedical-research "we will become a society that creates and uses some human lives in the service of others," and there is no longer anything "nascent" about the embryo.

The reason the President's Council did not advocate an outright ban on cloning-for-biomedical-research is that it could not get a majority of its members, even among those who oppose abortion as a matter of principle, to agree that such cloning constituted an exploitation and destruction of human life in the sense that five-day-old embryos bear the same moral weight as do five-month-old fetuses or 5-year-old children or 55-year-old adults. Social conservative James Q. Wilson, for instance, held to a position that would permit "biomedical research on cloned embryos provided the blastocyst is no more than fourteen days old and would not allow implantation in a uterus, human or animal" (297). The Council settled therefore for a moratorium that, as the report's executive summary puts it,

> provides time for further democratic deliberation about cloning-for-biomedical research,

a subject about which the nation is divided and where there remains great uncertainty. A national discourse on this subject has not yet taken place in full, and a moratorium, by making it impossible for either side to cling to the status-quo, would force both to make their full case before the public. By banning all cloning for a time, it allows us to seek moral consensus on whether or not we should cross a major moral boundary (creating nascent cloned human life solely for research) and prevents our crossing it without deliberate decision. It would afford time for scientific evidence, now sorely lacking, to be gathered—from animal models and other avenues of human research— that might give us a better sense of whether cloning-for-biomedical-research would work as promised, and whether other morally nonproblematic approaches might be available.

(xxxvi)

In one respect the statement is question-begging, insofar as it presumes the very point that needs to be argued—namely, that cloning for biomedical research involves crossing a major moral boundary. This claim is precisely what many proponents of stem-cell research wish to contest. But the ancillary claim that biomedical research itself might benefit from this moratorium is simply disingenuous, as Council member Elizabeth Blackburn pointed out in her personal statement in the Appendix to the report: "It may sound tempting," Blackburn wrote, "to impose a moratorium to get more information, since, despite very promising results, it is true, at this early stage of the research, that we still know only a little. But that information can *only* be gained by performing he same research that the moratorium proposes to halt" (246). Nor is it clear—and this is the distorting effect I mentioned above—that the appeal to "further democratic deliberation" is not a stalling tactic: since the nation remains divided between people who believe that stem-cell research is legitimate and people who

believe it is immoral, there is no "moral consensus" to be had, and therefore no need for a waiting period during which such a consensus can be allowed to form.

Perhaps, then, the Council's appeal to democratic deliberation might be understood cynically as a temporizing move that will allow pro-life proponents to marshal their arguments and their social forces. Should that happen, and should we find ourselves living in a society whose democratic deliberations wind up by banning stem-cell research, then we will have become a society in which the value placed on the moral status of the human embryo trumps all other considerations, including the moral injunction to alleviate plausibly remediable suffering. It is altogether possible to achieve such a society by democratic means, and I want to argue strenuously against it, for it would install essentially theocratic views about human life at the center of moral debate.

Having made clear my antipathy to theocratic conceptions of human life, I should immediately make it clear that I am by no means sanguine or unworried about the life prospects for people with disabilities in a society in which it is widely assumed that identifiable disabilities should either be cured or prevented. For the *Gattaca* scenario is just another vision of the world of eugenics, and the world of eugenics is already too much with us. On this count, contemporary professions of good faith among geneticists are no guarantee that they've learned the lessons of history. As Dorothy Roberts argues in *Killing the Black Body*, the discourse of eugenics is not really "history" at all, and certainly not ancient history. And yet the new eugenics is not precisely the same as the old. Our era differs from the era of the Kansas State Fair in critically important ways: one might call these "public" and "private" eugenics, or one might call them macro and micro eugenics, as

Barbara Katz Rothman has done in *Genetic Maps and Human Imaginations*, or one might say (as I will proceed to) that the old eugenics saw the human population as an aggregate of various ethnic and racial traits some of which were not beneficial to the enlightened propagation of the species, whereas the new eugenics sees individuals as aggregates of biochemical traits some of which are not beneficial to the families or populations in which they occur. I believe that this molecular view of the human is inadequate and incomplete, partly because genetics is an inexact science, a science of probabilities in which we cannot be sure how a biochemical predisposition may express itself, and partly because we have limited but conscious, self-reflexive control over how we express some of the traits with which we are born. (This too is one of the lessons of *Gattaca*, unfortunately summed up by the movie's tag line, "there is no gene for the human spirit": much depends on what one does with the genetic hand one is dealt.) It is one thing, in other words, to promote genetic research on the grounds that it will eradicate Tay–Sachs or Huntington's or Alzheimer's; I would regard each of these as a universal, species-wide good comparable to the universal species-wide good of eradicating smallpox or tuberculosis or HIV. But it would be foolish and destructive, I think, to think of individuals as agglomerations of traits like "propensity to become impatient," "sense of how to arrange a room" or "ability to memorize geographical maps"—or shyness, or laziness, or plumb-cussedness—and to try to order an individual's genetic makeup accordingly.[8]

And yet this is what the libertarian position on genetic engineering would invite us to do. For bioethicists such as Julian Savulescu and Nicholas Agar, the *Gattaca* scenario represents not a dystopia but a utopia, in which prospective parents have the opportunity and the obligation to avail themselves of the technology that will allow them to design the "best" possible child—still you, just the best of you. For advocates of what Sandel calls forms of "liberal eugenics," the evil of eugenics as practiced in the first decades of the twentieth century was not that it was eugenics, but that the policies of involuntary sterilization and institutionalization represented forms of coercion visited on individuals by the state. "Private" eugenics, from this standpoint, is not an evil at all; it consists simply of individuals, in various familial arrangements, making rational decisions about what is best for them and their children. In democratic deliberation over genetics and disability, therefore, I will want to argue against both the theocratic and the libertarian positions, the former because I believe it has an inadequate account of the social basis of moral debate and the latter because I believe it has an inadequate account of the social good. Additionally (and, I think, tellingly), in some circumstances the libertarian position can rely on beliefs about eugenics that are not merely untroubled by history but also hostile to disability. It is as if individual choices about genetic enhancement are just fine, but decisions to screen *for* disability, rather than against, require state regulation. Or, perhaps, it is as if some libertarians tend to imagine that everyone who is allowed to design a child will share a moral consensus that disability is to be avoided or eliminated—that it is, as Jonathan Glover writes, to be "contrasted with human flourishing" (88), if not indeed inimical to human flourishing.

I draw from these debates two political paradoxes. The first is this: many of the people who supported the passage of the Americans with Disabilities Act of 1990 were, like White House counsel C. Boyden Gray, diehard antistatist conservatives, deeply opposed to gender-equity initiatives and race-based affirmative action and civil rights laws generally. The reason that the ADA enjoyed such bipartisan support, however, was that its conservative and libertarian advocates championed it as a law that would free people with disabilities from dependence on the state. For them, the purpose of this public law was to return individuals with disabilities to the realm of the private. The second paradox is this: for people involved with disability, even for those of us who support reproductive rights, there is no realm of the private. Disability is always and everywhere a public issue, a matter for public policy, even or especially for political thinkers who otherwise have no conception of the public good. I want to suggest, then, that one way to think about disability, democracy, and genetics is to imagine that the public is not public enough and the private is not private enough. Those of us who support reproductive rights *and* a woman's right to pre-natal testing *and* stem-cell research *and* the egalitarian provisions of the welfare state need to make the argument that intimate decisions about childbearing and care for people with disabilities should be protected from state coercion yet supported by the state's apparatus of social welfare; at the same time we need to make the argument that the state's apparatus of social welfare should seek to enhance the independence of people with disabilities from the state, but in order to do so must recognize the very real dependencies associated with some disabilities, and must expand and enhance the roles of state-funded dependency workers. These are matters to be determined by democratic deliberation, a deliberation that must include the voices of people with disabilities, their advocates, their family members, surrogates, and guardians. On one side of this deliberation, people like me will engage with moral absolutists for whom one value, one religious interpretation of human life, will always supersede all others; on the other side, we will engage with moral absolutists for whom one value, the value of individual freedom from state regulation, will supersede all others—except when some individual decisions about disability impose social costs on other individuals. This dual engagement, I submit, is central to the challenge of thinking democratically about disability in the age of genomics.

NOTES

1. Critics seem not to have noticed that disability is pervasive in the work of Philip K. Dick. *Martian Time-Slip* features a largely nonverbal character with autism (understood in 1964, both by Dick and the DSM-III, as a form of "childhood schizophrenia") who subtly controls the plot and warps the narrative; he, like many of Dick's "precogs," can see the future only because they are anomalies akin to mutants. And in *Total Recall*, the film version of "We Can Remember It for You Wholesale," the mutants on Mars are the result of genetic anomalies induced by exposure to radiation; they are the turbinium miners who were not given adequate protection from cosmic rays by their employers. If *Gattaca* is a film about disability-related discrimination, *Total Recall* is a film about employment-related disability. The "mutants" may have exotically anomalous bodies and minds (and at least one of them possesses psychic powers), but they are basically Martian versions of coal miners with black lung disease.

2. Apparently the feeling is mutual, insofar as the Hastings Center report cites *Life As We Know It* approvingly at crucial moments in its argument.

3. This is not to say that a child with Tay–Sachs falls under the infamous Nazi category of "life unworthy of life." I do not believe that any human being has the capacity or the right to so designate another human being. (For a compelling account of what it is like to care for a young child with Tay–Sachs, see Emily Rapp, "Notes From a Dragon Mom.") It is simply to acknowledge that the Chevra Dor Yesurim Program ("Organization for the Generations") was, as Rapp notes, "originally developed by an Orthodox rabbi living in Brooklyn who had lost three children to Tay-Sachs disease" (157). Rapp writes, "modern biomedical genetic technology here undergirds and enhances a traditional patriarchal practice" (157)—namely, arranged marriage. Insofar as no

American conservative (or liberal) spokesperson has denounced any Orthodox Jewish organization for screening for Tay–Sachs, I submit that we have achieved some consensus on the acceptability of doing so.

4. This was my argument in "We Still Don't Know What 'Normal' Really Is," and here I fondly hope that the argument has won broad popular agreement—not an unreasonable hope, I submit, insofar as the proposition that many disabilities are undetectable has the virtue of being true.

5. For two regrettable examples of how disability is elided with and collapsed into disease, see Glover's analogy between disability and cancer (35) and Dan Hurley's repeated references to Down syndrome as a "disease" in his *New York Times Magazine* essay, "A Drug for Down Syndrome." My critique of Glover on this count can be found in "Humans, Disabilities, and the Humanities?"

6. At present, as Amy Julia Becker points out, "only 2 percent of all women seek a definitive diagnosis of Down syndrome or other chromosomal abnormalities through amniocentesis or chorionic villa sampling during pregnancy. But of the women who receive that definitive diagnosis, the vast majority (90 percent) choose to terminate their pregnancies." The fear, which I believe to be well founded (and which I share), is that more prospective parents will screen for Down syndrome if they can do so in the first trimester of pregnancy and without the risk of miscarriage associated with amniocentesis. See, e.g., Pollack (both essays).

7. I call Elshtain's remark "offensive" not simply because I disagree with it, but because I believe it falls short of the standard of intellectual honesty one should expect in serious debate. First, Elshtain ignores passages in which I explicitly say things like "a fetal diagnosis of Down syndrome should not be understood, either by medical personnel or by parents, as a finding to which abortion is the most logical response" (79). Second, Elshtain argues that I caricature the pro-life position:

> Bèrubè's [*sic*] cardboard cutout pro-life politician denies rights to living persons. One wonders who does this. Who are these people? He calls the implications of holding that humans have a right to life "only until they're born" staggering, and this would be true if anybody held to that view. But I can't think of a single pro-lifer who does, certainly not to judge from the literature I received from a number of pro-life groups.
>
> (18)

I submit that Elshtain is too intelligent to intend this as a serious argument. Surely she is aware of pro-life

politicians who support the death penalty. Take the example of the Texas pro-life politician who not only executed dozens of living persons in his home state but publicly mocked one such person's pleas for clemency. Is he the only pro-life politician who believes that the state can take the life of a person? And whatever became of him, anyway?

Last, and far more seriously, Elshtain illegitimately interpolates her own words into a passage she cites, severely misconstruing the passage in the process:

> If you had told me in August 1991—or, for that matter, after an amniocentesis in April 1991—that I'd have to feed my infant by dipping a small plastic tube in K-Y jelly and slipping it into his nose and down his pharynx into his teeny tummy, I'd have told you that I wasn't capable of caring for such a child. [In other words, had they had amniocentesis, they would likely have opted for abortion.] But by mid-October, I felt as if I had grown new limbs and new areas of the brain to direct them.
>
> (89; Elshtain's addition in brackets.)

There are three things wrong with this interpolation. First, most children with Down syndrome do not require such care as this; therefore, amniocentesis would not have "told" us that we would need to feed Jamie with a gavage tube. Second, the bracketed sentence allows Elshtain to ignore my discussion of prenatal-care counseling and the provision of prospective parents with information about disabilities on pages 67–88 of my book. The reason *that's* important, in turn, is that my discussion of prenatal testing is targeted in part at genetics counselors, whom I am trying to persuade not to think of the detection of trisomy-21 as a search-and-destroy operation. Third, I am also trying here to persuade prospective parents not to decide in advance that they cannot care for a child with disabilities. Before Jamie was born, I did not know how to feed an infant with a gavage tube, and I would have been terrified at the thought; after he was born, I learned how to do it, just as I learned to care for my first child without knowing how beforehand. Elshtain's "in other words" gets this important point exactly wrong.

8. I choose the traits "propensity to become impatient," "sense of how to arrange a room," and "ability to memorize geographical maps" because these traits happen to describe my own family. The first pertains to me, the second to my partner Janet, and the third to both our children—the one with Down syndrome and the one without.

WORKS CITED

Atwood, Margaret. *Oryx and Crake*. New York: Anchor, 2003.

Becker, Amy Julia. "Has Down Syndrome Hurt Us?" *New York Times* blog, "Motherlode: Adventures in Parenting." Published under the byline of Lisa Belkin. 3 Oct. 2011. http://parenting.blogs.nytimes.com/2011/10/03/has-down-syndrome-hurt-us/.

Bérubé, Michael. *Life As We Know It: A Father, a Family, and an Exceptional Child*. New York: Pantheon, 1996.

——. "We Still Don't Know What 'Normal' Is." *The Globe and Mail* 3 March 2007: F8.

——. "Humans, Disabilities, and the Humanities." *On the Human: A Project of the National Humanities Center*. 17 January 2011. http://onthehuman.org/2011/01/humans-disabilities-humanities/

Ellis, Kathleen. "Reinforcing the Stigma: The Representation of Disability in Gattaca." *Australian Screen Education* 32 (2003): 111–14.

Elshtain, Jean Bethke. "Idiots, Imbeciles, Cretins." *Books and Culture: A Christian Review* 4.1 (January/February 1998): 18.

Finger, Anne. "Invalids, De-generates, High-Tech Zombies and Old-Fashioned Hollywood Cripples." *Electric Edge: Web Edition of The Ragged Edge*, January/February 1998. www.ragged-edge-mag.com/jan98/movie01.htm

Gattaca. Dir. Andrew Niccol. Perf. Ethan Hawke, Uma Thurman, Jude Law. Columbia/Tristar, 1997.

Glover, Jonathan. *Choosing Children: Genes, Disability, and Design*. Oxford: Oxford University Press, 2006.

Hubbard, Ruth. "Abortion and Disability: Who Should and Should Not Inhabit the World?" *Disability Studies Reader*. 4th ed. Routledge, 2013.

Hurley, Dan. "A Father's Search for a Drug for Down Syndrome." *New York Times Magazine* 31 July 2011. www.nytimes.com/2011/07/31/magazine/a-fathers-search-for-a-drug-for-down-syndrome.html?_r=1

Kass, Leon. "The Public's Stake." Introduction to "Biotechnology: A House Divided." Symposium with Diana Schaub, Charles Murray, William A. Galston, and J. Bottum. *The Public Interest* 150 (Winter 2003): 38–62.

Parens, Erik, and Adrienne Asch, eds. *Prenatal Testing and Disability Rights*. Hastings Center Studies in Ethics. Washington, DC: Georgetown University Press, 2000.

Pollack, Andrew. "A Less Risky Down Syndrome Test is Developed." *New York Times* 17 October 2011. www.nytimes.com/2011/10/18/business/sequenom-test-for-down-syndrome-raises-hopes-and-questions.html?pagewanted=all

——. "The Quandary Posed by a New Down Syndrome Test." New York Times *blog*, "Prescriptions: The Business of Health Care." 18 October 2011. http://prescriptions.blogs.nytimes.com/2011/10/18/the-quandary-posed-by-a-new-down-syndrome-test/

President's Council on Bioethics. *Human Cloning and Human Dignity: An Ethical Inquiry*. Washington, DC: The White House, 2002. http://bioethics.georgetown.edu/pcbe/reports/cloningreport/pcbe_cloning_report.pdf

Rapp, Emily. "Notes from a Dragon Mom." *New York Times* 16 October 2011: SR12. www.nytimes.com/2011/10/16/opinion/sunday/notes-from-a-dragon-mom.html

Rapp, Rayna. *Testing Women, Testing the Fetus: The Social Impact of Amniocentesis in America*. New York: Routledge, 1999.

Roberts, Dorothy. *Killing the Black Body: Race, Reproduction, and the Meaning of Liberty*. New York: Pantheon, 1997.

Rothman, Barbara Katz. *Genetic Maps and Human Imaginations: The Limits of Science in Understanding Who We Are*. New York: W. W. Norton, 1998.

Sandel, Michael. *The Case Against Perfection: Ethics in the Age of Genetic Engineering*. Cambridge: Harvard University Press, 2007.

CHAPTER 7

A Mad Fight: Psychiatry and Disability Activism

Bradley Lewis

SUMMARY

The Mad Pride movement is made up of activists resisting and critiquing physician-centered psychiatric systems, finding alternative approaches to mental health and helping people choose minimal involvement with psychiatric institutions. They believe mainstream psychiatry over exaggerates pathology and forces conformity though diagnosis and treatment. In this chapter, Bradley Lewis highlights the political and epistemological similarities between the Mad Pride movement and other areas of disability studies. For instance, the social categories of normal and abnormal legitimize the medicalization of different bodies and minds and exert pressure on institutions to stay on the side of normality, or in this case, sanity.

Lewis briefly traces the historical roots of Mad Pride to show how diagnoses of insanity were often political abuses aimed at normalizing differing opinions and experiences. The movement entered into the debate to fight involuntary hospitalization and recast mental illness as a myth rather than an objective reality. Today's Mad Pride often works within mental health services systems by bringing together "consumers" (rather than "survivors" or "ex-patients") who contribute real input for psychiatric policy.

Nevertheless, Mad Pride still wages an epistemological and political struggle with psychiatry, which has undergone a "scientific revolution" that values "objective" data and undervalues humanistic inquiries. For example, biopsychiatric methods led to Prozac-type drugs being prescribed to 67.5 million Americans between 1987 and 2002. Mad Pride staged a hunger strike to protest the reduction of mental illness to a brain disease, arguing this model couldn't be proved by evidence and limited consumers' options for treatments like therapy or peer-support. By opposing mental illness screening and other policies that advance pharmaceutical interests, Mad Pride continues to work to open peer-run mental health services and reduce the coercive connections between psychiatry and state power.

In the late summer of 2003, six people gathered at a small building in Pasadena, California, and starved themselves for 22 days. The small group of hunger strikers were later joined by over a dozen "solidarity strikers" around the world. Their strike was about "human rights in mental health" and, in particular, it sought to protest the "international domination" of biological approaches to psychiatry and the ever-increasing and widespread use of prescription drugs to treat "mental and emotional crises" (MindFreedom, July 28, 2003).

The hunger strike caught the attention of the *LA Times*, *The Washington Post* and, most important for those involved, the attention of the American Psychiatric Association (APA). One of the central aims of the strike was to challenge the main institutions in psychiatry—namely the American Psychiatric Association, the National Alliance of the Mentally Ill (NAMI) and U.S Surgeon General—and to rouse them into providing "evidence that clearly establishes the validity of 'schizophrenia,' 'depression' or other 'major mental illnesses' as biologically-based brain diseases" (MindFreedom, July 28, 2003). The fasters demanded evidence that mental and emotional distress results from "chemical imbalances" in the brain; a view that underpins the biopsychiatric medical model and which currently dominates mental health treatment in the West.

In demanding this evidence, the strikers were taking a risk. Using a hunger strike to challenge psychiatry and its scientific findings (which are now almost ubiquitously accepted throughout the medical world and wider culture), the protestors faced the possibility of being labeled "mad." After all, isn't psychiatry a science? Shouldn't scientific questions be decided in laboratories and in peer-reviewed articles filled with graphs and statistical analysis? What sense does it make to hold a hunger strike to challenge contemporary scientific beliefs?

The hunger strikers took the risk because, indeed, they are mad. They are all members of a psychiatry disability activist group known among their friends and allies as "Mad Pride." This activist group is an international coalition devoted to resisting and critiquing clinician-centered psychiatric systems, finding alternative and peer-run approaches to mental health recovery, and helping those who wish to do so minimize their involvement with current psychiatric institutions. They affectionately call themselves "Mad Pride" because they believe mainstream psychiatry over exaggerates psychic pathology and over

enforces psychic conformity in the guise of diagnostic labeling and treatment—which all too often comes in the form of forced or manipulated hospitalizations, restraints, seclusions, and medications. Like the celebratory and reappropriative uses of the terms "Crip," "Queer," and "Black Pride," the term "Mad Pride" overturns traditional distinctions and hierarchies. It signifies a reversal of standard pathological connotations of "madness." Rather than pathologizing mental difference, Mad Pride signifies a stance of respect, appreciation, and affirmation.

In this essay, I discuss the relation of Mad Pride to disability studies, review the history of the movement, and work through its contemporary struggles with psychiatry. Throughout the discussion, I highlight the importance of Mad Pride's efforts to go beyond "politics-as-usual." Mad Pride, like other forms of "biocultural" activisms (such as Women's Health Movement and AIDS Coalition to Unleash Power), is located at the interface of bioscience and politics. As such, Mad Pride continuously struggles with epistemological issues along with more typical political issues. In short, the people in Mad Pride struggle over *both* truth and values.

This commingling of politics, power, and truth is familiar ground for disability studies. Similar to Mad Pride, disability studies unpacks and undermines stereotyped representations of disability in science and popular culture to understand and intervene in how "representation attaches meanings to bodies" (Garland-Thomson, 1997, 5). Michael Oliver gives a good sense of these stereotyped disability representations by dividing them into key themes of "individualism," "medicalization," and "normality" (Oliver, 1990, 56, 58). *Individualism* refers to the perspective that disability is a "personal tragedy." This frame undergirds a "hegemony of disability" which views disability as "pathological and problem-oriented" (1996, 129). It leads to a ubiquitous *medicalization* that legitimizes the medical infrastructure for acquiring knowledge about the disabled individual. The logic of this medical infrastructure rests on notions of *normality* and the dichotomy between normal and pathological. The able-bodied and the disabled, the valued and the devalued, become co-constituted cultural divisions which structure medical and cultural preoccupations (Davis, 1995). One side of the binary defines the other and both operate together as "opposing twin figures that legitimate a system of social, economic, and political empowerment justified by physiological differences" (Garland-Thomson, 1997, 8).

Together, these stereotyped disability representations direct the health care industry toward a near exclusive focus on individual biomedical cures. Rather than adjust social environments to meet differing bodily needs, medical interventions seek to cure the individual "abnormal" body. Disability activists resist these individualizing and medicalizing approaches by reframing disability as a social restriction and oppression rather than simply a medical problem. Emphasizing a social model rather than a medical model they call attention to the fact that much of the suffering of different bodies comes from social exclusion, isolation, and lack of opportunity, along with the often pernicious side effects of a medical industry bent on aggressive intervention to achieve "normal" bodies.[1]

The task of undermining stereotyped representations of individualism, medicalization, and normality are also central to the Mad Pride movement. Individualistic approaches to mental difference and distress blame and punish the victim for structural problems that are often better understood as located in families, communities, and society. Medicalization, or psychiatrization, legitimizes the medical community's expert authority over the domain of mental difference. And the binary between normal and abnormal shores up this psychiatrization by providing tremendous social and psychological pressure to stay on the side of normality, or sanity. Disability studies scholars refer to social stigma and oppression against the physically different as "ableism"; those in Mad Pride refer to social stigma and oppression against mental difference as "mentalism" or "sanism" (Chamberlin, 1977, 219; Perlin, 2000, 21).

Despite these similarities, disability activists and Mad Pride members have had difficulty forming a sustained coalition. Part of this difficulty involves the simple fact that two groups are composed of different subcultures—with different histories, different cultural artifacts, and different networks of association. But, beyond this, there are other, deeper reasons. Some disability advocates continue to harbor sanist style associations toward mental difference and do not wish to be associated or "tarnished" by Mad Pride. Likewise, many in Mad Pride (like many in the Deaf community) express discomfort with the "disability" label. They do not see their mental difference as a disability, but rather as a valued capacity. In addition, many in Mad Pride feel that disability struggles are separate from their concerns because physical disability does not involve the same level of state coercion. People with physical differences are often inappropriately confined (through limited choices and multiple manipulations), but Mad Pride activists must deal with an additional layer of state-sponsored coercion in the forms of involuntary commitment and forced medication laws.[2]

Like many in both movements, however, I believe it is wise to foreground the similarities between disability activism and Mad Pride. Clearly, all of the new social movements, in one way or another, have to struggle with both truth and values—largely because biomedical science has been used to justify such a broad range of subordination practices. But, more than most, Mad Pride and disability activism face a combined political and epistemological struggle. The very heart of these activisms begins with expressly biomedical assignments of impairment. This comes not in the form of a general pronouncement of inferiority, but in a direct and specific diagnosis and treatment process. Because of this, Mad Pride and disability activist efforts to reduce individualization, medicalization, and ableism require a dual struggle that goes beyond politics-as-usual. The challenge of this dual epistemological and political struggle requires all the allies you can get. When disability activist and Mad Pride work together, they can form a formidable coalition.

THE BIRTH OF MAD PRIDE MOVEMENT

Mad Pride activists have had extensive experience going beyond politics-as-usual. Their lesson of dual engagement goes back to the nineteenth century efforts of Mrs. Elizabeth Ware Packard, an early precursor to today's Mad Pride movement. In 1886, Packard, a former mental hospital patient and founder of the Anti-Insane Asylum Society, began publishing a series of books and pamphlets critical of psychiatry. Packard's writings challenged the subordination of women to their husbands and the remarkable complicity of the political and psychiatric establishment to this subordination (Packard 1868, 1874). As Gerald Grob explains, "When Packard refused to play the role of obedient [minister's] wife and expressed religious ideas bordering on mysticism, her husband had her committed in 1860 to the Illinois State Hospital for the Insane" (Grob, 1994, 84). Packard remained incarcerated for three years and only won her

freedom by going to court to challenge her confinement. The trial received national publicity and eventually led to Packard being declared sane by the court and released from the asylum. She spent the next 20 years campaigning for personal liberty laws that would protect individuals from wrongful commitment and retention in the asylums.

Even in this early precursor to today's movement, the issues of epistemological struggle and political struggle are inseparably intertwined. Packard challenged pathologizing diagnostic practices that would treat people as insane "simply for the expression of opinions, no matter how absurd these opinions may appear for others" (quoted in Geller and Harris, 1994, 66). And she challenged the political abuses that occurred once the insanity diagnosis had been made. Lunatic asylums, she argued, too often left people at the complete mercy of hospital despotism where they were treated worse than convicts or criminals. Packard's dual stress on both the "facts" of insanity and the inhumane treatment of those considered to be insane reverberate into today's resistance to psychiatry.

The more proximate antecedents to today's Mad Pride movement began in the 1970s. Mad Pride activists, during these years, gained momentum from the black civil rights movement, the women's movement, and from the early stages of lesbian and gay movement and the disability movement. Like Elizabeth Packard almost a century before, the key experience that motivated Mad Pride activists was their negative treatment within the psychiatric system. Early founders of the movement shared common experiences of being treated with disrespect, disregard, and discrimination at the hands of psychiatry. Many also suffered from unjustified confinement, verbal and physical abuse, and exclusion from treatment planning.

The testimony of Leonard Roy Frank, co-founder of the Network Against Psychiatric Assault (1972), provides a helpful glimpse into the experiences of many. After graduating from Wharton, Frank moved to San Francisco to sell commercial real estate. He was in his own words "an extraordinarily conventional person" (Farber, 1993, 191). Gradually, during his late twenties, he started discovering a new world within himself and began going through an "obvious clash between . . . my emerging self and that of my old self" (191). He later thought of this as a "spiritual transformation." But, at the time, he responded by doing serious reading and reflection on his emerging insights. He ended up rethinking everything in his life: "what was happening to me was that I was busy being born" (191).

A key text for Frank during his transformation was Mohandas Gandhi's autobiography. Frank took seriously Gandhi's message that one's inner life and outer life should interact and complement each other. Reading Gandhi opened his eyes to the violence of political injustice and to the power of non-violent resistance. It also raised his awareness that animals had feelings and could suffer. The more Frank thought about Gandhi's writings on meat-eating, the more he concluded it was inescapably cruel to both animals and to humans: "We can't avoid harming ourselves when we harm other beings, whether human or animal. Meat-eating was an excellent example of how this principle played out in real life. . . . Because it was inherently cruel to animals and morally wrong, it affected the wrong doers by causing them to become sick and cutting short their lives" (206). This combination of insights made it difficult for Frank to continue his previous lifestyle and his work selling commercial real estate; he soon lost his job, grew a beard, became vegetarian, and devoted himself to full time spiritual exploration.

Frank was exhilarated by the process, but his parents were deeply concerned. Seeing Frank's transition through the stereotyped frames of individualization, psychiatrization, and sanism, they thought he was having a "breakdown." They tried to persuade him to see a psychiatrist, but Frank resisted. They responded by arranging an involuntary commitment. The hospital records show that Frank's psychiatrists document symptoms of "not working, withdrawal, growing a beard, becoming a vegetarian, bizarre behavior, negativism, strong beliefs, piercing eyes, and religious preoccupations" (193). The psychiatrists diagnosed him as "paranoid schizophrenia," and they started a sustained course of court authorized insulin-electroshock treatments that lasted nine months and included 50 insulin comas and 35 electroshocks.

When the psychiatrists were not giving him shock treatments, their "therapeutic" interactions with Frank revolved around his behavior, particularly his refusal to shave or eat meat. There was never any discussion of his emerging beliefs or his spirituality. Instead, Frank's psychiatrists focused on changing overt signs of "abnormality." They even went so far as to shave his beard while he was unconscious from an insulin treatment. Frank eventually came to realize that his hospital resistance was futile, and, with the ever-increasing numbers of shock treatments, he also came to fear he was in a "life or death" situation: "These so-called [shock] treatments literally wiped out all my memory for the [previous] two-year period. . . . I realized that my high-school and college were all but gone; educationally, I was at about the eighth-grade level" (196).

Rather than risk more "treatments," Frank surrendered. He played the psychiatrists' game and did what they wanted: "I shaved voluntarily, ate some non vegetarian foods like clam chowder and eggs, was somewhat sociable, and smiled 'appropriately' at my jailers" (196). After his release, it took six years to recover from his treatment. But, throughout it all, he never gave up on his beliefs, and he never saw another psychiatrist for treatment. He went on to become a major figure in early Mad Pride activism.

During the early 1970s, people like Frank began to recognize they were not alone and started organizing local consciousness-raising groups. U.S. examples include the Insane Liberation Front in Portland Oregon (1970), the Mental Patient's Liberation Project in New York City (1971), and the Mental Patients' Liberation Front in Boston (1971). These groups built support programs, advocated for hospitalized patients, lobbied for changes in the laws, and educated the public through guest lectures and newsletters. In addition, they began the process of developing alternative, creative, and artistic ways of dealing with emotional suffering and psychological difference outside the medical models of psychiatry. The publication of Mad Pride activist Judi Chamberlin's book *On Our Own* (1977) in the mainstream press was a milestone in the development of peer-run alternatives (Van Tosh and del Vecchio, 2000, 9). Chamberlin used the book to expose her own abuse at the hands of psychiatry and to give a detailed account of burgeoning consumer-run alternatives. The eloquence, optimism, and timing of the book was a critical catalyst for many in the movement. As ex-patient Mary O'Hagan puts it: "When my mood swings died away I was angry and amazed at how the mental health system could be so ineffective. There had to be a better way. I searched the library not quite knowing what I was looking for. And there it was, a book called *On Our Own* by Judi Chamberlin. It was all about ex-patients who set up their own alternatives to the mental health system and it set me on my journey in to the psychiatric survivor movement" (quoted in Chamberlin, 1977, back cover).

The newly formed local Mad Pride groups also organized an annual Conference on Human Rights and Psychiatric Oppression to help connect local members with the wider movement. At these meetings, activists from across the country gathered to socialize, strategize, and share experiences. They gained solidarity and increasing momentum from the experience of being with like-minded activists. Between meetings local groups communicated through a newspaper forum. The San Francisco local newsletter, *Madness Network News,* evolved into a newspaper format which covered ex-patient activities across North America and around the world. This publication became the major voice of the movement, with each issue containing a rich selection of personal memoirs, creative writing, cartoons, humor, art, political commentary, and factual reporting—all from the ex-patient point of view (Hirsch, 1974; Chamberlin, 1990, 327).

This early period of the Mad Pride movement was also the most radical in its epistemological critique. Early leaders of the movement drew philosophical support from high-profile critical writers that, as a group, came to be known as "anti-psychiatry." Writers such as Erving Goffman (1961), R. D. Laing (1967), Thomas Scheff (1966), and Thomas Szasz (1961) may have differed widely in their philosophies, but collectively their main tenets were clear. Mental illness is not an objective medical reality but rather either a negative label or a strategy for coping in a mad world. As Laing put it, "the apparent irrationality of the single 'psychotic' individual" may often be understood "within the context of the family." And, in turn, the irrationality of the family can be understood if it is placed "within the context of yet larger organizations and institutions" (Laing, 1968, 15). Put in context in this way, madness has a legitimacy of its own which is erased by medical-model approaches that can only pathologize it. For many anti-psychiatry writers, mental suffering can be the beginning of a healing process and should not be suppressed through aggressive behavioral or biological interventions.

The most epistemologically radical of the anti-psychiatry writers, Thomas Szasz, had the most influence on U.S. activists. Szasz, a dissident psychiatrist, was shunned within his own field, but his prolific writings (over 25 books) and forceful prose gave him tremendous influence outside psychiatry (Leifer, 1997). Throughout his work, Szasz's argument was always two-fold: (1) mental illness is a myth and (2) there should be complete separation between psychiatry and the state. As Szasz put it in a summary statement, "Involuntary mental hospitalization is imprisonment under the guise of treatment; it is a covert form of social control that subverts the rule of law. No one ought to be deprived of liberty except for a criminal offense, after a trial by jury guided by legal rules of evidence. No one ought to be detained against their will in a building called 'hospital,' or any other medical institution, on the basis of expert opinion" (Szasz, 1998).

Consistent with others in the Mad Pride movement, Szasz combined his epistemology and his politics. Szasz's insistence on the autonomy of mental health clients rested directly on his epistemology, which he based on a strong positivist philosophy of science that emphasized a sharp demarcation between observation and conjecture. For Szasz, *physical illness* was real because it was based on actual observation, but *mental illness* was at best a metaphor. A broken leg is real because you can see the X-ray, but a "broken brain" is a myth because there is no X-ray that will show it. For Szasz, to see mental illness as "real" rather than as a metaphor was to make a serious category

mistake. "Mental illness" is not objectively observable; it is a myth.

MAD PRIDE TODAY

During the last 30 years of their struggle, Mad Pride has increasingly infiltrated the mental health system rather than simply criticizing it from outside. Despite the fact that institutional psychiatry continues to ignore and denigrate their efforts, important government agencies involved in mental health policy have begun to pay attention. Mad Pride activists have been particularly successful in increasing consumer participation in treatment planning and facility governance. In addition, they have gained increasing respect for the work developing peer-run treatment alternatives.

The most important agency to pay attention to Mad Pride perspectives has been the national Center for Mental Health Services (CMHS). This little known public agency is "charged with leading the national system that delivers mental health services" (Center for Mental Health Services, 2002). Following on the success of Chamberlin's *On Our Own*, the agency worked with a local California peer group to publish *Reaching Across: Mental Health Clients Helping Each Other*, a "how to" manual for peer-run services (Zinnman, Harp, and Budd, 1987). For too long, CMHS explains, "decisions about mental health policies and services were made without any input from people who have mental illnesses or their families. As a result, some policies and programs failed to meet the needs of the people they were intended to serve" (Center for Mental Health Services, 2004). CMHS worked to change this by sponsoring peer-run research, training, and technical assistance centers, and producing federally mandated documents encouraging states to include consumer-operated alternatives to traditional treatment programs. Since 1985, CMHS has also sponsored an annual, national level,

Alternatives Conference that brings together consumers and ex-patients to network and to share the results of their scholarship and program development.

These political successes have gradually necessitated a change in Mad Pride's epistemological critique. Szasz's strong epistemological critique of psychiatry was useful in the early days of the movement, but it became less so as Mad Pride shifted into its more contemporary formations. The early anti-psychiatry literature set up an either/or relation between consumers and providers. People had to either be with psychiatry or against it. Szasz's rigid positivist epistemology left little room for contradiction and coalition politics. As sociologist and Mad Pride activist Linda Morrison points out, with increasing infiltration of the mental health system, many members no longer took a hard-line approach to psychiatry. These members identified themselves more as "consumers" than "survivors" or "ex-patients." Consumers, by definition, were critical of aspects of psychiatry but were willing to legitimize and participate in other aspects (Morrison, 2005). Mad Pride needed to embrace these contradictions and adopt coalition politics to avoid losing these members.

Contemporary Mad Pride members have made just this kind of epistemological shift. Though activists still reference Szasz favorably, they now draw more on his political values (of autonomy and separation of psychiatry and state) than on his epistemology. Mad Pride members mark this shifting epistemology by referring to themselves as "consumer/survivor/ex-patient" groups. This hyphenated designation, usually shortened to "c/s/x" or "consumer/ survivors," highlights that today's Mad Pride is a coalition of critical activists—some of whom have a more radical epistemological critique than others (Morrison, 2005).

This shift has set the stage for additional coalitional possibilities between Mad Pride and critical psychiatrists. Increasingly, critical psychiatrists are moving beyond the narrow approaches of their training and drawing from interdisciplinary theory in science studies, disability studies, and the humanities. Like Mad Pride, they are developing alternative perspectives on psychiatry that emphasizes the importance of social models and of democratic research and treatment. In Britain, an influential Critical Psychiatry Network (www.critpsynet.freeuk.com/ critpsynet.htm) has recently formed, bringing together a coalition of critical providers and consumer/survivors (Double, 2004).[3]

Contemporary Mad Pride's political success at getting a seat at the table of mental health policy has also necessitated a change in the more radical infrastructure of the movement. The Conference on Human Rights and Psychiatric Oppression no longer meets and has now been replaced by the Alternatives Conference sponsored by CMHS. The different name of the conference is consistent with a shift in emphasis from psychiatric oppression to peer-run support and service involvement. The change is subtle as both oppression and support remain paramount for Mad Pride, but the change does mark a shift of the emphasis within the movement.

In addition, the newspaper *Madness Network News* is no longer being published. Today's Mad Pride connects its members largely through the activities of the Support Coalitions International (SCI) which brings together 100 international local groups. Under the leadership of David Oaks, SCI has become "the epicenter of the Mad Movement" ("Windows into madness," 2002). It runs a website (www. mindfreedom.com), an email list, a magazine (*MindFreedom Journal*), and an online "Mad Market" (where interested parties can find "a little library of dangerous books"). Much of the success of the center comes from Oaks' capacity to build a coalition of consumers, survivors, and ex-patients. Like Packard, Frank, and Chamberlin before him, Oaks' motivation for mental health activism comes from his experiences of psychiatric abuse: including forced hospitalization and forced treatment. Like so many others, he has taken those experiences and turned them into political action.

RECENT STRUGGLES WITH PSYCHIATRY

Despite the successes Mad Pride has had within the mental health system, their epistemological and political struggle with psychiatry continues. These struggles are often complicated, and they require impressive political savvy. In this section, I work through some examples of these struggles to give a sense of the political terrain and the critical importance of today's consumer/survivor activism. The 2003 hunger strike is a good example of Mad Pride's contemporary epistemological battles. To understand the context of the strike, it is important to note that during the same time Mad Pride has complicated its epistemology, psychiatry has gone in the exact opposite direction. The last 30 years have seen a "scientific revolution" in psychiatry that primarily values quantitative, positivistic protocols for research (Lewis, 2006). The emphasis on "objective" data has created a preference for neuroscience and genetics at the expense of an array of cultural and humanistic styles of inquiry. This new scientific psychiatry, working in tandem with pharmaceutical funding, has gone on to create today's dominant clinical model of psychiatry, "biopsychiatry"— whose emphasis is almost exclusively biomedical style diagnoses and pharmacological treatments.

The blockbuster medication, Prozac, gives a window into biopsychiatry's dominance.

Between 1987 and 2002 (the year Prozac came off patent), new prescriptions for the drug reached over 27 million. Combined with the multiple "me too" drugs it inspired—the class of antidepressants known as "selective serotonin inhibitors" (SSRI)—that total reached 67.5 million in the U.S. alone (Alliance for Human Research Protection, 2004). That means almost one in four people in the U.S. were started on a Prozac-type drug between 1987 and 2002. These same one in four people were dealing with sufficient emotional issues that someone thought they needed help.

For some of these people, the SSRIs may have been the best choice. But was it the best choice for 67.5 million people? Psychiatry's professional literature, its patient hand-outs, and the popular press all tell us "yes." They tout "scientific progress in the treatment of depression" as the main reason for the SSRIs extensive use (Gardner, 2003; Metzl, 2003; Lewis, 2006). But, if we scratch the surface, we find that the SSRIs are highly controversial, and researchers have not been able to agree on even simple questions like: Do the drugs work? or, Are they safe? The *Handbook of Psychiatric Drug Therapy*, typical of most clinical reviews, claims with great authority that the SSRIs are highly effective and that they have a mild side effect profile (Arana and Rosenbaum, 2000, 57, 76). But critical analysts conclude just the opposite: that the SSRIs are not much better than sugar pills and that they have major side effects—including sexual dysfunction, suicidality, and even violence (Breggin, 1994, 65; Fisher and Fisher, 1996; Kirsch and Sapirstein, 1998; Glenmullen, 2000; Healy, 2004). Going further, scientific opinion is also at odds regarding the question of explanation. Some argue that the SSRIs have effects because they treat biological disease. But others argue these drugs are simply stimulants like cocaine and amphetamines.

These researchers conclude that SSRIs are mood brighteners and psychic energizers because they work on the same neurotransmitters as other stimulants (Breggin 1994; Glenmullen, 2000).

When we take these controversies surrounding the Prozac-type drugs into account, it seems highly questionable that the SSRIs were the best choice for 67.5 million people. For most of these people, alternatives like psychotherapy, peer-support, and personal and political activism would have likely been better options than taking drugs that are expensive, are possibly no better than placebo, have multiple side effects, and may be little more than a dressed-up version of speed. But, because of the hype of biopsychiatry, these controversies are not well known and alternatives are not given a chance. The SSRIs are seen as quick and easy solutions backed by advances in psychiatric science and individual medical recommendations. For most people thrown in that situation, they are seen as the only viable option.

Mad Pride's hunger strike was directed squarely at this so-called "biological revolution" in psychiatry. The fasters, organized by David Oaks and Support Coalition International, demanded evidence that emotional and mental distress can be deemed "biologically-based" brain diseases, and also evidence that psychopharmaceutical treatments can correct those "chemical imbalances" attributed to a psychiatric diagnoses (MindFreedom, July 28, 2003).

The strikers were not trying to show that the biopsychiatric model of mental illness is myth, and they were not touting another model of mental distress as better or more accurate. The protestors stated from the outset that they were aware that psychopharmaceuticals work for some people, and that they were not judging individuals who choose to employ biopsychiatric approaches in an effort to seek relief. For Oaks and his fellow protestors, there are

> many ways to help people experiencing severe mental and emotional crises. ... We respect the right of people to choose the option of prescribed psychiatric drugs. Many of us have made this personal choice. ... However, choice in the mental health field is severely limited. One approach dominates, and that is a belief in chemical imbalances, genetic determinism and psychiatric drugs as the treatment of choice. Far too often this limited choice has been exceedingly harmful to both the body and the spirit.
>
> (MindFreedom, July 28, 2003)

In demanding evidence, the strikers hoped to show that the "chemical imbalance" theory of mental distress is not watertight, and to therefore challenge the overinvestment in this "biopsychiatric approach" by the mental health institutions.

In the early days of the strike, the APA brushed off the strikers' demands for evidence and told them to consult introductory textbooks on psychiatry. The strikers responded by persisting in their demands and by sending a letter to the APA written by a panel of 14 critical scholars. The letter showed that within the very textbooks that the APA had recommended there were numerous statements that invalidated the notion that mental illnesses have specific biological bases (MindFreedom, August 22, 2003). Using psychiatry's own knowledge against itself, the hunger strikers prompted the APA to respond more fully, and a follow-up communiqué from APA finally conceded that "brain science has not advanced to the point where scientists or clinicians can point to readily discernible pathological lesions or genetic abnormalities that in and of themselves serve as a reliable or predictive biomarkers of a given mental disorder" (American Psychiatric Association, 2003). This reluctant admission from the APA marked an important epistemological victory for Mad Pride. In an interview, Oaks said: "They acknowledged that they didn't have the biological evidence [of mental illness], so that's on the record" (Davis, 2003). The hunger strike vividly demonstrated how problematic it is to accept without question the "truths" of biopsychiatry.[4]

Despite this small success, Mad Pride's epistemological struggle continues to be a tough one. They are battling against a veritable superpower whose main ally is the hugely profitable and very influential pharmaceutical industry. As David Davis reports in his *LA Times* article on the hunger strike, Mad Pride is up against both an American Psychiatric Association, whose conventions bustle with "brightly colored" booths of the drug companies, and a booming pharmaceutical industry whose "sales of psychotherapeutics reached $21 billion in 2002, almost double the $11 billion in sales in 1998" (Davis, 2003).[5]

Because of the influence and clout of biopsychiatry, Mad Pride knows all too well that skirmishes over epistemology are only part of the struggle. While it is vital to strike at the heart of mainstream psychiatry's "knowledge" and "truths," it is just as vital to realize that the epistemology game is hard to win. Science studies scholar Bruno Latour explains that dissenters of science can only go so far by using scientific literature against itself. For alternative perspectives to successfully join in the process of science (and truth) in the making, they must build their own "counter-laboratories," which of course requires tremendous resources (Latour, 1987, 79). Mad Pride clearly does not have the resources to compete laboratory for laboratory with the institutions of psychiatry and their pharmaceutical supporters. Thus, while Mad Pride continues to play the game of epistemology, and continues to have some successes destabilizing psychiatry's biomedical model, it also

struggles with psychiatry on the more typically political and economic terrain.

This was particularly evident in 2002 when President George W. Bush's administration initiated what David Oaks dubbed "the Bush triple play," which prompted Mad Pride to mobilize swiftly and energetically to fight on the political front (Oaks, 2002–2003). The triple play included (1) the planned appointment of a controversial conservative psychiatrist, Dr. Sally Satel, to the important National Advisory Council for Mental Health, (2) the announcement of budget cuts to key government-sponsored consumer/survivor technical support centers, and (3) the creation of a New Freedom Commission to study U.S. mental health services. All aspects of this triple play posed direct threats to Mad Pride and the consumer/survivor movement, and they threatened the freedoms and rights of those suffering mental and emotional crises.

The first part of the triple play began with a White House leak, with word coming out that Dr. Sally Satel was being selected by the Bush administration for a position on the advisory council for the CMHS (the very organization which has been most receptive to consumer/survivor initiatives). Dr. Satel—a fellow at the American Enterprise Institute (a conservative political think tank)—is the author of the controversial book *P.C., M.D.: How Political Correctness is Corrupting Medicine* (2000). She is not only a vociferous advocate of the biopsychiatric model of mental illness; she is also an outspoken critic of the consumer survivor movement, and an insistent lobbyist for involuntary commitment and treatment laws. In *P.C., M.D.*, under a chapter titled "Inmates Take Over the Asylum," Satel names the leaders of the Mad Pride movement and attacks their hard fought efforts to increase peer-run services and reduce involuntary treatments. She denigrates mental health administrators who have taken Mad Pride seriously: "Tragically, they [mental health administrators] seem to be willing to sacrifice the needs of those with the most severe illnesses to political correctness and to the expediency of placating the vocal and annoying consumer/survivor lobby" (76). And she even goes so far as to describe the Alternatives Conference as the "guinea pig rebellion" (50).

For Mad Pride, Satel's appointment and her public vilification of consumer-run organizations signaled an overall Bush administration strategy to aggressively push a controversial biopsychiatry paradigm, to abandon consumer-run self-help and peer-support programs, and to increase forced psychiatric medication.

These concerns were reinforced by the second part of the Bush triple play. Soon after the leak about Dr. Satel, the Bush administration announced budget cuts to CMHS-sponsored consumer/survivor technical assistance centers. Although the cuts totaled only $2 million out of the total CMHS budget, they were targeted directly at consumer/survivors. Three out of five of these centers were consumer run, which represented a clear about face for CMHS. Joseph Rogers, director of one of the programs to be cut, the National Mental Health Consumer Self-Help Clearinghouse, commented that "We had no warning. The cuts just came out of the blue, and we've had no explanation since that makes any sense" (Mulligan, 2002).

The third part of the Bush triple play was the creation of a New Freedom Commission on mental health. Bush hailed the Commission as a major step toward improving mental health services, and he charged it with the ambitious goals of reviewing the quality of mental health services, identifying innovative programs, and formulating federal, state, and local level policy options. The administration stipulated that the Commission be composed of 15 members and that these members be selected from a range of stakeholder groups, including providers, payers, administrators, consumers, and family members (Bush, 2002). Although all of this sounded laudable enough, but true to Mad Pride concerns, when the New Freedom Commission's 15 members were made public, only one person self-identified as having personally experienced the mental health system or as involved in the consumer/survivor movement. The New Freedom Commission's choice of members appeared not to be about true stakeholder inclusion, but only a crude form of tokenism.

For many consumer/survivors, the Bush triple play was not only an outrage, it was a serious danger. These three deft moves threatened to undo all the gains consumer/survivors had made over the past 30 years. Oaks put it this way: "Mental health consumers and psychiatric survivors have experienced fierce repression. But to have a well-funded think tank unite with a Presidential administration to openly attack our movement in such a way is unprecedented. As the enormity of the attacks set in, several activists said they were numb with disbelief" (Oaks, 2002–2003).

Mad Pride activists could have reasonably given up at this juncture. Instead, they held a strategy meeting with colleagues from the international movement, and they decided to directly oppose each part of the Bush triple play. Opposition to Dr. Satel's appointment and the cuts to CHMS programs took the form of a blitz of emails to consumer/survivor list-servs, active lobbying of mental health administrators, and a barrage of critical faxes to Secretary Tommy Thompson of the US Department of Health and Human Services. And, rather than being dismayed by the non-democratic message of the New Freedom Commission's selection process, consumer/survivors took full advantage of the Commission's plan to hold public hearings on psychiatric services. Four days before the first scheduled hearing, consumer/survivors gathered for an emergency meeting with a network of physical disability activists. Judi Chamberlin, who has been a longtime advocate of disability and Mad Pride coalitions, explained the rationale for involving the larger disability movement, "When a wolf wants to target a whole flock, it looks for the most vulnerable lamb. The Bush administration is targeting psychiatric survivors today, but the whole disability movement is the target tomorrow" (Oaks, 2002–2003).

The meeting turned out to be a major inspiration for consumer/survivors. The first speaker that night was Justin Dart, who many call the "Martin Luther King" of the disability movement. Dart, struggling with the last stages of terminal illness (he died just eight days later), gave a rousing speech which set the tone for the meeting. Dart proposed that:

> we in the disability communities must unite with all who love justice to lead a revolution of empowerment. A revolution, to create a culture that will empower every single individual including all people with psychiatric disabilities, to live his or her God given potential for self determination, productivity and quality of life.
>
> Empowerment means choices—individual choices about where we live, how we live, where we work, choices about health care. We have a right to complete quality health care of our own choosing.
> NO FORCED TREATMENT EVER.
> We choose our own doctors and medication. We choose the places of care. No denial of treatment ever.
> NO FORCED TREATMENT EVER.
>
> (Oaks, 2002)

The combined presence of Dart and several other disability representatives created the strategic capacity to get the word out and rally support and resistance far beyond the usual consumer/survivor community. It also further advanced a cross-disability activist connection between the disability movement and consumer/survivors.

On the day of the New Freedom Commission's first public meeting, consumer/survivor activists and their disability activist comrades made their presence known. Not only did they hand out their own press release and talk individually to members of the Bush Commission, they also made public announcements. Judi Chamberlin's testimony was typical. Announcing that she was a "psychiatric survivor" and "an advocate" on consumer/survivor issues for more than 30 years," she pointed out:

> A basic premise of the disability rights movement is simply this: Nothing About Us Without Us. The makeup of the Commission violates this basic principle. Just as women would not accept the legitimacy of a commission of "expert" men to define women's needs, or ethnic and racial minorities would not accept a panel of "expert" white people to define their needs, we similarly see the Commission as basically irrelevant to our struggle to define our own needs.
>
> (Chamberlin, 2002)

Chamberlin argued that the Commission lacked the "expertise on the consumer/survivor experience" and also the "expertise of disability rights activists, those knowledgeable about the legal and civil rights of people diagnosed with mental illness, and experts in community integration." And she went on to detail how the Commission should get the extra expertise it needed.

Unlike the results of the hunger strike, however, the results of Mad Pride's efforts to resist the Bush triple play can only be described as mixed. With regard to part one of the triple play, Mad Pride was unable to stop Sally Satel's appointment to the advisory board. Once on the board, she predictably advocated for more forced treatment and for discontinuation of consumer-run programs. But part two of the triple play, the planned budget cuts to peer-support programs never materialized. The three technical centers sponsored by CMHS continued to be funded.

The New Freedom Commission results were also contradictory. On the one hand, the Commission ended up quite friendly to Mad Pride concerns. It agreed with Mad Pride that the mental health system is fundamentally broken, that it needs extensive overhaul (not just piecemeal reform), that mental health services must be consumer and family centered, that modern psychiatry overemphasizes reductionist biomedical approaches, and that consumers must be protected from unjust incarceration and the use of seclusion and restraints. Together these recommendations signified an impressive success for Mad Pride's and their disability allies' efforts to reach the Commission and have their voices included in their report.

But, on the other hand, all was not rosy with the Commission's report. In addition to the above recommendations, the New Freedom Commission also recommended nationwide mental health screenings in schools, primary care offices, prisons, and the welfare system. The ominous dimension of this plan was pointed out in the *British Medical Journal* (BMJ) in an exposé titled "Bush plans to screen whole US population for mental illness." The BMJ explained that the New Freedom Commission recommendation for nationwide screening was linked to their recommendation for "evidence-based" treatment protocols. In psychiatry, these protocols are code words for the Texas Medication Algorithm Project (TMAP). TMAP was started in 1995 as an alliance between the pharmaceutical industry, the University of Texas, and the mental health system to set up expert guidelines for psychiatric practices. But a whistle

blower at TMAP, Allen Jones, revealed that key officials received money and perks from the drug companies to unnecessarily promote expensive on-patent drugs. As Jones explained "the same political/pharmaceutical alliance" behind TMAP is also behind the New Freedom Commission. This alliance is "poised to consolidate the TMAP effort into a comprehensive national policy" of over-treating mental illness with expensive medications (Lenzer, 2004). When you add to this state of affairs the recent National Institute of Health conclusion that half of all Americans will meet the criteria for a *DSM-IV* disorder some time in their life, the profiteering possibilities of the New Freedom Commission's political/pharmaceutical alliance is easy to imagine (Kessler, 2005).

Of course, none of this screening will go forward without resistance. In quick response to the BMJ exposé, MindFreedom sent out a news release "What You Gonna Do When They Screen For You" and set up a section of its website titled "President Bush and the Shrinking of the USA" (see www. mindfreedom.org/mindfreedom/bush_p-sychiatry.shtml). This news board gives access to breaking stories and commentary, plus it provides answers to frequently asked questions concerning the controversy. In addition, the Mad Pride advocacy group Alliance for Human Research Protection (AHRP) has begun to monitor closely the outcomes of the New Freedom Commission (see www.ahrp.org/about/about.php). At the time of this writing, AHRP reports that lawsuits are already being filed in Indiana to resist the effects of "TeenScreen Depression"—a program funded partly with new federal grants initiated by the New Freedom Commission.[6]

CONCLUSION

These recent conflicts with psychiatry provide an important window into Mad Pride's ongoing epistemological and political struggles. Against tremendous odds, the movement has worked impressively to expose psychiatry as a limited field of inquiry, to open up its clinical services to more peer-run alternatives, and to reduce coercive connections between psychiatry and the state. Their fight to reduce individualization, psychiatrization, and sanist approaches to psychic life is arduous, and at times a little "mad." But the stakes are high and the struggle must continue. With the increasing coalition with the broader disability movement and the emergence of a critical psychiatry network, the fight is becoming more and more mainstream. Soon the battle will be one about which we all know and in which we can all participate. Active biocultural citizenship regarding mental difference and distress requires nothing less.

As the editors of *Adbusters* sum up in their issue on Mad Pride, in a culture of hardening isolation, status, materialism, and environmental degradation,

> Mad Pride can be a broad embrace. It is a signal that we will allow ourselves our deep sorrow, our manic hope, or fierce anxiety, our imperfect rage. These will be our feedback into the system. We reserve the right to seek relief from both our most troubling symptoms and from society's most punitive norms. The sickness runs deep; without madness, there is no hope of cure.
>
> ("Deep sadness, manic hope," 2002)

NOTES

1. Public health scholar Barbara Starfield estimates that the combined effect of medical adverse effects in the United States are as follows:

   - 12,000 deaths/year from unnecessary surgery
   - 7000 deaths/year from medication errors in hospitals
   - 20,000 deaths/year from other errors in hospitals
   - 80,000 deaths/year from nosocomial infections in hospitals
   - 106,000 deaths/year from nonerror, adverse effects of medications.

   That comes to a total to 225,000 deaths per year from iatrogenic causes—which constitutes the third leading cause of death in the United States. Just after heart disease and cancer (Starfield 2000, 484).

2. For an extended discussion of confinement and disability see the "Confinement" entry in the *Encyclopedia of Disability* (Lewis, 2005).

3. The Critical Psychiatry Network organizes its members less under the banner of "anti-psychiatry" and more under the banner of "post-psychiatry" (Thomas and Bracken, 2004). The epistemological underpinning of post-psychiatry avoids the either/or problems of anti-psychiatry. Relying on the philosophy of Michel Foucault, a post-psychiatric perspective blurs the binary between truth and myth as all forms of human knowledge making are understood to be both material and semantic (Foucault, 1965 and 2003; Bracken and Thomas 2001; Lewis, 2006). This shift moves the legitimacy question of psychiatric knowledge from "truth" to "consequences." The issue is not whether psychiatric knowledge magically mirrors the world, but who is allowed to participate in making the knowledge? What kinds of consequences (and for who) will follow from the knowledge?

4. For an extended analysis of the exchange between Mad Pride and the APA see critical psychiatrists Duncan Double's review: "Biomedical Bias of the American Psychiatric Association" (Double, 2004).

5. See former editor-in-chief of the *New England Journal of Medicine* Marcia Angell's book, *The Truth about Drug Companies: How They Deceive Us and What to Do About It* (2004), for an extended discussion of the influence of the pharmaceuticals on medical research and practice. Also see Pulitzer Prize finalist Robert Whitaker's book, *Mad in America: Bad Science, Bad Medicine, and the Enduring Mistreatment of the Mentally Ill* (2002) for an historical perspective specific to psychiatry.

6. Theresa and Michael Rhoades, who filed the first suit, claim that TeenScreen sent their daughter home from school telling her she had been diagnosed with obsessive compulsive disorder and social anxiety disorder. The Rhoades "claim that the survey was erroneous, improper, and done with reckless disregard for their daughter's welfare and that they did not give the school permission to give the test" (Pringle, 2005). High-profile attorney John Whitehead calls the situation an "Orwellian Nightmare" and has agreed to take on the Rhoades case. However, "because of the financial backing of pharmaceutical companies and the Bush

administration's support through the New Freedom Commission," even Whitehead is concerned and considers his opposition to be formidable foes (Alliance for Human Research Protection, 2005).

REFERENCES

Alliance for Human Research Protection (2005). "The Rutherford Institute takes on TeenScreen case in Indiana." Retrieved on July 25 from www.ahrp.org/infomail/05/06/13.php.

American Psychiatric Association (2003) *Statement on Diagnosis and Treatment of Mental Disorders.* Release no. 03-39, September 25, 2003. Retrieved on July 15, 2005 from www.psych.org/news_room/press_releases/mentaldisorders0339.pdf.

Angell, M. (2004). *The truth about drug companies: How they deceive us and what to do about it.* New York: Random House.

Arana, G. and Rosenbaum, J. (2000). *Handbook of psychiatric drug therapy.* 4th ed. Philadelphia: Lippincott Williams and Wilkins.

Bracken, P. and Thomas, P. (2001). "Postpsychiatry: A new direction for mental health." *British Medical Journal* 322: 724–727.

Breggin, P. (1994). *Talking back to Prozac: What doctors aren't telling you about today's most controversial drugs.* New York: St. Martin's Press.

Bush, G. W. (2002). "President's New Freedom Commission on Mental Health: Executive Order." The White House President George W. Bush On line. Released on April 29, 2002. Retrieved on June 17, 2005 from www.whitehouse.gov/news/releases/2002/04/20020429-2.html.

Center for Mental Health Services (2002). "About CMHS." Retrieved on July 20, 2005 from www.mentalhealth.samhsa.gov/cmhs/about.asp.

Center for Mental Health Services (2004). "Consumer affairs program." Retrieved on July 20, 2005 from www.mentalhealth.samhsa.gov/consumersurvivor/about.asp.

Chamberlin, J. (1977). *On our own: Patient-controlled alternatives to the mental health system.* Lawrence, MA: National Empowerment Center.

Chamberlin, J. (1990). "The ex-patients' movement: Where we've been and where we are going." *Journal of Mind and Behavior* 11 (3 & 4): 323–336.

Chamberlin, J. (2002). "Testimony of Judi Chamberlin." American Association of People with Disabilities On line. Retrieved on June 17, 2005 from www.aapd-dc.org/News/disability/testjudichamberlin.html.

Davis, D. (2003). "David Oaks and others in the "Mad Pride" movement believe drugs are being overused in treating mental illness, and they want the abuse stopped." *L.A. Times Magazine*, Sunday,

October 23, 2003. Retrieved on July 20, 2005 from www.latimes.com.

Davis, L. (1995). *Enforcing normalcy: Disability, deafness, and the body.* London: Verso.

"Deep sadness, manic hope: A movement for liberty, and the pursuit of madness." (2002). *Adbusters* (10) 3.

Double, D. (2004). "Biomedical bias of the American Psychiatric Association." Critical Psychiatry Website. Retrieved on June 22, 2005 from www.critpsynet.freeuk.com/biomedicalbias.htm.

Farber, S. (1993). "From victim to revolutionary: An interview with Lennard Frank." In *Madness, heresy, and the rumor of angels: The revolt against the mental health system.* Chicago: Open Court.

Fisher, R. and Fisher, S. (1996). Antidepressants for children: Is scientific support necessary? *Journal of Nervous and Mental Disease* 184: 99–102.

Foucault, M. (1965). *Madness and civilization: A history of insanity in the age of reason.* New York: Vintage Books.

Foucault, M. (2003) *Abnormal: Lectures at the College of France 1974–1975.* New York: Picador.

Gardner, P. (2003). "Distorted packaging: Marketing depression as illness, drugs as cures." *Journal of Medical Humanities* 24 (1/2): 105–130.

Garland-Thomson, R. (1997). *Extraordinary bodies: Figuring physical disability in American culture and literature.* New York: Columbia University Press.

Geller, J. and Harris, M. (1994). *Women of asylum: Voices from behind the walls 1840–1945.* New York: Doubleday.

Glenmullen, J. (2000). *Prozac backlash: Overcoming the dangers of Prozac, Zoloft, Paxil, and other antidepressants with safe, effective alternatives.* New York: Touchstone.

Goffman, E. (1961). *Asylums: Essays on the social situation of mental patients and other inmates.* New York: Doubleday.

Grob, G. (1994). *The mad among us: A history of the care of America's mentally ill.* Cambridge, MA: Harvard University Press.

Healy, D. (2004). *Let them eat Prozac: The unhealthy relationship between the pharmaceutical industry and depression.* New York: New York University Press.

Hirsch, S. (Ed.) (1974). *Madness Network News Reader.* San Francisco: Glide Publications.

Hogan, M. (2003) "Cover letter: President's New Freedom Commission on Mental Health." Retrieved on June 17, 2005 from www.mentalhealthcommission.gov/reports/FinalReport/CoverLetter.htm.

Kessler, R. *et al.* (2005). "Lifetime prevalence and age-of-onset distributions of *DSM-IV* disorders in the national comorbidity survey replication."

Archives of General Psychiatry 62. Retrieved on July 25, 2005 from www.archgenpsychiatry.com.

Kirsch, I. and Sapirstein, G. (1998). "Listening to Prozac but hearing placebo: A meta-analysis of antidepressant medications." *Prevention and Treatment* 1 art. 2a. http://journals.apa.org/prevention/volume1.

Laing, R. (1967). *The politics of experience*. New York: Ballantine.

Laing, R. D. (1968) "The obvious." In D. Cooper (Ed.). *The dialectics of liberation*. Harmondsworth: Penguin.

Latour, B. (1987). *Science in action*. Cambridge, MA: Harvard University Press.

Leifer, R. (1997). The psychiatric repression of Dr. Thomas Szasz: Its social and political significance. *Review of Existential Psychology and Psychiatry* 23 (1, 2 & 3): 85–107.

Lenzer, J. (2004) "Bush plans to screen whole US population for mental illness." *British Medical Journal* 328. June 19. Retrieved on August 10, 2004 from www.bmj.com.

Lewis, B. (2005). "Confinement." In G. Albrecht (Ed.). *The encyclopedia of disability*. Thousand Oaks, CA: Sage Publications.

Lewis, B. (2006). *Moving beyond Prozac, DSM, and the new psychiatry: The birth of postpsychiatry*. Ann Arbor: University of Michigan Press.

Metzl, J. (2003). "Selling sanity through gender: The psychodynamics of psychotropic advertising." *Journal of Medical Humanities* 24 (1/2): 79–105.

MindFreedom (July 28, 2003). "Original statement by the Fast for Freedom in Mental Health to the American Psychiatric Association, National Alliance for the Mentally Ill, and the US Office of the Surgeon General." Retrieved on July 10, 2005 from www.mindfreedom.org/mindfreedom/hungerstrike1.shtml#original.

Morrison, L. (2005). *Talking back to psychiatry: The consumer/survivor/ex-patient movement*. New York: Routledge.

Mulligan, K. (2002). "CMHS budget cuts harm consumer involvement." *Psychiatric News* 37(6): 17.

Oaks, D. (2002). "From patients to passion: A call for nonviolent revolution in the mental health system." Plenary Address Alternatives 2002 Convention. Retrieved on March 3, 2003 from www.mindfreedom.org/mindfreedom/conference.shtml.

Oaks, D. (2002–2003). "President Bush's position on people with psychiatric labels." *MindFreedom Journal* (Winter): 4–6.

Oliver, M. (1990). *The Politics of disablement: A sociological approach*. New York: St. Martin's Press.

Oliver, M. (1996). *Understanding disability: From theory to practice*. London: Macmillan.

Packard, E. (1868). *The prisoner's hidden life, or insane asylums unveiled: As demonstrated by the report of the Investigating Committee of the Legislature of Illinois*. Chicago: Published by the Author, A. D. Case.

Packard, E. (1874). *Modern persecutions, or married woman's liabilities*. Hartford, CT: Case, Lockwood and Brainard.

Perlin, M. (2000). *The hidden prejudice: Mental disability on trial*. Washington, DC: American Psychological Association.

President's New Freedom Commission (2003) "Executive Summary." Retrieved on June 17, 2005 from www.mentalhealthcommission.gov/reports/FinalReport/FullReport.htm.

Pringle, E. (2005). TeenScreen: The lawsuits begin. *CounterPunch* June 13, 2005. Retrieved July 25, 2005 from www.counterpunch.org/pringle06132005.html.

Richman, S. (2004). "Bush's brave new world." *The Washington Times*. October 17, 2004. Retrieved on July 25, 2005 from www.washingtontimes.com/commentary/20041016-115126-9840r.htm.

Satel, S. (2000). *P.C., M.D.: How political correctness is corrupting medicine*. New York: Basic Books.

Scheff, T. (1966). *Being mentally ill*. Chicago: Aldine.

Starfield, B. (2000). "Is US health really the best in the world?" *Journal of the American Medical Association* 284 (4): 483–485.

Support Coalition News (May 15, 2002). "Stop the appointment of extremist psychiatrist Sally Satel!" Retrieved on June 15, 2005 from www.mindfreedom.org/mindfreedom/satel_f.shtml.

Szasz, T. (1961). *The myth of mental illness: Foundations of a theory of personal conduct*. New York: Hoeber-Harper.

Szasz, T. (1998). "Thomas Szasz's summary statement and manifesto." Retrieved on July 20, 2005 from www.szasz.com/manifesto.html.

Thomas, P. and Bracken, P. (2004). "Critical psychiatry in practice." *Advances in Psychiatric Treatment* 10: 361–370.

Van Tosh, L. and del Vecchio, P. (2000). *Consumer-operated and self-help programs: A technical report*. Rockville, MD: U.S. Center for Mental Health Services.

Whitaker, R. (2002). *Mad in America: Bad science, bad medicine, and the enduring mistreatment of the mentally ill*. Cambridge, MA: Perseus Publishing.

"Windows into madness" (2002). *Adbusters* (10) 3.

Zinnman, S., Howie the Harp, and Budd, S. (Eds.) (1987). *Reaching across: Mental health clients helping each other*. Sacramento, CA: California Network of Mental Health Clients.

CHAPTER 8

"The Institution Yet to Come": Analyzing Incarceration Through a Disability Lens

Liat Ben-Moshe

SUMMARY

Disabled people have historically inhabited institutions ranging from group homes to prisons, and in this essay Liat Ben-Moshe calls for critical attention for those who are incarcerated in these facilities. Whether disabled people occupy a jail or a mental institution, they become subject to dehumanization and denial of rights. Ben-Moshe points out that race, gender, and disability play significant roles in shaping the population of institutions. Analyzing incarceration through a disability studies lens needs to account for social and economic conditions of disablement while also scrutinizing how the environment of incarceration is disabling.

The connection between incarceration and notions of "abnormality" has a long history in the wake of modernity. The power of normality can be cloaked by medical definitions of illness (mental illness or "feeblemindedness") or legal definitions of recidivism (criminality), both of which make it seem "normal" for certain people to be incarcerated. Even arguments that would remove "mentally ill" people from prisons and (re)hospitalize them reinforce a logic that it is appropriate to place disabled people into some kind of institution.

The problems of incarceration and institutionalization have spurred two competing forms of activism: institutional reform and abolition. Just as prison reformers might focus on reforms of today's conditions as part of a chain leading to eventual abolition, disability activists can improve institutions even while aiming to eliminate them someday. Focusing on abolition is a way to envision a more just society that doesn't use prisons and hospitals as a catch-all for "problematic populations." This means that deinstitutionalization isn't only about helping prisoners or disabled people; abolishing these institutions will improve the lives of all people inside and outside their walls.

Grandmother lost her mother in the early 1900's to what was considered progressive policy. To protect society from the insane, feebleminded and physically defective, states invested enormous public capital in institutions, often scattered in remote areas. Into this state-created disability gulag people disappeared, one by one. Today, more than 1.7 million mothers and fathers, daughters and sons, are lost in America's disability gulag. Today's gulag characterizes isolation and control as care and protection, and the disappearances are often called voluntary placements. However, you don't vanish because that's what you want or need. You vanish because that's what the state offers. You make your choice from an array of one.

(McBryde Johnson 2003)

"THE INSTITUTION YET TO COME"

Institutional life, whether in a prison, hospital, mental institution, nursing home, group home, or segregated "school," has been the reality, not the exception, for disabled people throughout North American history (and globally). In this paper I suggest analyzing the reality of incarceration through the prism of disability, by showcasing the connections between institutions and prisons and the populations that inhabit them, including disabled prisoners and those institutionalized. I will also highlight those who resist incarceration by calling for the abolition of repressive institutions such as prisons and institutions for those with labels of psychiatric and intellectual disabilities.

Harriet McBryde Johnson (2003) describes in the opening paragraph her experiences and fear of the "disability gulag," the warehouse for disabled people that is often called "the institution." As she describes in her narrative, many people with significant disabilities fear that one day they will be sent there and lose their independence, if they are not living there already. In *Crip Theory: Cultural Signs of Queerness and Disability*, Robert McRuer (2006) discusses what he calls "the disability yet to come," describing both the fear that non-disabled people have of becoming disabled and the notion that if anyone lives long enough, they will eventually become disabled in some way. Intersecting Johnson with McRuer, we can conceptualize "the institution yet to come" as a looming presence in the lives of all people with disabilities, even those who don't reside in them (for the time being). The ghost of forced confinement haunts us all, but does so much more materially and immediately for marginalized populations, especially poor people, people of color, disabled people and any amalgamation of these groups (Chapman, Ben-Moshe, and Carey 2014).

This call for connecting analysis of incarceration with disability, is also a call to pay attention to the lives of mostly poor people of color who are incarcerated

worldwide in nursing homes, institutions for those with labels of mental illness and/or intellectual/developmental disabilities and prisons, and bring their perspective to bear on what Chris Bell (2006) characterized as "white Disability Studies." I want to add that the field of Disability Studies had historically not only privileged the experiences of white bodies, but in fact focused on bodies in general, at times to its detriment. Feminist and critical analysis of disability brought to the forefront a new conceptualization of disability, not just as a socially excluded category, but as an embodied identity (Garland-Thomson 1997; Wendell 1996). This focus on embodiment challenges the medical model of disability which conceives of disability as a lack and deficiency inherent in non normative bodies. It also challenges the social model of disability which encourages us to focus solely on processes of disablement as a critical framework that will end the oppression of people with disabilities (Morris 2001; Tremain 2002).

Not discounting such achievements, the (often unintended) consequence of such an enterprise is the concern of overrepresentation of the body and visible disabilities in the field of Disability Studies. Such focus obscures the myriad disabilities and impairments that could and should be analyzed under the purview of Disability Studies. I am not trying to suggest that the experiences and analysis of various impairments and forms of oppression should be conflated into one meta-field, called Disability Studies or anything else. I am also not suggesting that being psychiatrized, or being labeled intellectually disabled, or having a physical or sensory disability are all the same. What I am trying to push for is the understanding that the logic of compulsory ablebodiedness (McRuer 2002), handicapism (Bogdan and Biklen 1977), ableism, normalcy (Davis 1995), and disablement (Oliver 1990) are not just similar but related to forces of sanism or mentalism (Chamberlin 1977; Perlin 2000). I thus argue that Disability Studies could benefit immensely by actively taking up the theorizations and lived experiences in the field of Developmental Disability and Mad Studies. What such expansive formulations achieve is an understanding of incarceration in its broadest way in relation to hospitalization, institutionalization, and imprisonment and a fuller understanding of the forces that construct medicalization and criminalization. This analysis is especially pressing because of the immense growth of the prison machine in the US.

SOME BACKGROUND ON IMPRISONMENT AND (DE)INSTITUTIONALIZATION

For the first time in US history, in 2008, more than one in 100 American adults is behind bars. In 2009 the adult incarcerated population in prisons and jails in the US had reached 2,284,900 (BJS 2010). Another whopping 5,018,900 people are under "community corrections" which include parole and probation (BJS 2010). Race, gender, and disability play a significant role in incarceration rates. By 2006, one in fifteen black men over the age of 18 and one in nine black men age 20–34 were incarcerated. The overall incarceration rate for women increased 832 percent from 1997 to 2007 (Human Rights Index 2009/10). The imprisonment rate for African-American women was almost double that of Hispanic women and three times the rate of white women. If these seem like mere numbers consider the reality that today more African-Americans find themselves in penal institutions than in institutions of higher learning (Thompson 2010).

Although several attempts have been made to estimate the number of prisoners who have psychiatric diagnosis, it is impossible to quantify their number with any degree of precision, even if taking the label of "mental illness" as a viable construct. The American Psychiatric Association reports in 2000 that up to 5% of prisoners are actively psychotic and that as many as one in five prisoners were "seriously mentally ill" (APA 2000). Other attempts to estimate the prevalence appear to have used a substantially more expansive definition of mental illness. Bureau of Justice Statistics reports that in 2005 more than half of all prison and jail inmates were reported as having a mental health problem. They also report that women inmates had higher rates of "mental health problems" than men (Human Rights Watch 2006). Researchers also found that the prevalence of "mental health problems" varied by racial or ethnic group. White inmates appear to have higher rates of reported "mental health problems" than African-Americans or Hispanics (Erickson and Erickson 2008). Yet African-Americans, and especially African-American men, seem to be labeled "seriously mentally ill" more often than their white counterparts.[1]

Analyzing imprisonment from a disability studies lens also necessitates a closer look at the social and economic conditions of disablement and incarceration rather than looking at disability as a cause for criminal acts. Prisoners are not randomly selected and do not represent all statuses of society. The majority of prisoners are poor, and are people of color. Poverty is known to cause a variety of impairments and disabling conditions. In addition, the prison environment itself is disabling— from hard labor in toxic conditions and materials; to closed wards with poor air quality; circulation of drugs and unsanitary needles; and lack of medical equipment and medication (Russell and Stewart 2001). It is also crucial to take an expansive view of what constitutes as "disability" in such environments. For instance, the high prevalence of HIV/AIDS amongst prisoners and the various impairments that come with aging in a disabling environment such as a prison, as a result of prolonged sentencing policies, should be of concern to Disability Studies scholars and those studying the effects of incarceration. Disability in this framework is not a natural biological entity, but related to economic and social conditions which lead to an increased chance of both disablement and imprisonment.

Similarly, conditions of confinement may cause further mental deterioration in prisoners entering the system with diagnoses of "mental retardation" or intellectual disabilities. Most court cases show that the right to (re)habilitation is often not fulfilled in jails, prisons, and institutions, and that this further distresses those incarcerated and worsens their mental and physical health overall. Those incarcerated (in institutions or prisons) with labels of intellectual and developmental disabilities may in fact lose crucial life skills that they had before they were imprisoned such as "loss of the ability to communicate, perform daily self-care, remain physically safe, and to maintain even rudimentary emotional stability" (American Association of Mental Retardation et al. amicus brief in *Goodman v. Georgia 2005*). Prisoners who are identified as mentally ill or exhibit "disruptive behaviors" are often sanctioned to "administrative segregation" in separate units, which are often isolation units. These segregated forms of incarceration, such as supermax or SHU (security housing units), are likely to cause or exacerbate mental and physical ill-health of those incarcerated.

In contrast to the constant expansion of prisons, deinstitutionalization and closure of large state institutions for people with labels of mental health and "mental retardation" have been a major policy trend in most US states in the past few decades. Deinstitutionalization of people who were labeled as mentally ill begun in the 1950s onwards. The deinstitutionalization of people labeled as intellectually and developmentally disabled gained prominence in the 1970s, although this of course varied by state. The population of people with intellectual disabilities living in large public institutions (serving over 16 people) peaked at 194,650 in 1967. In 2009, the number had declined to 33,732 (Braddock et al. 2011). The shift from large facility-centered to community residential services can be viewed from the fact that in 1977, an estimated 83.7% of the people with developmental disability labels who were receiving residential services lived in residences of 16 or more people. By 2009, an estimated 86.4% lived in community settings of 15 or fewer people, and 73.1% lived in residential settings with 6 or fewer people (Lakin et al. 2010). The trend in deinstitutionalization of people with intellectual disabilities resulted in closures of large state institutions across most of the US. By 2010, 11 states had closed all of their state-operated institutions for people with intellectual/developmental disabilities (Braddock et al. 2011). In contrast, seven states had not closed any public institutions (Lakin et al. 2010).

An accompanying shift occurred in the field of mental health with the establishment of community mental health centers in the 1960s and the closure of large state mental hospitals in most major cities. In 1955, the state mental health population was 559,000, nearly as large on a per capita basis as the prison population today. By 2000, it had fallen to below 100,000 (Gottschalk 2010; Harcourt 2011). In the public's eye, the first half of the twentieth century is conceived as an era of relative stability in terms of incarceration, with a later explosion in the form of the growth of prisons and jails, a phenomenon which is referred to as "mass incarceration" (Gottschalk 2010) or "hyper Incarceration" (Wacquant 2010). However, as Harcourt (2006) suggests, if mental hospitalization and institutionalization were also covered in such analyses, the "rise in incarceration" would have reached its peak in 1955, when mental hospitals reached their highest capacity. Put differently, the incarceration rates in prisons and jails barely scrape the levels of incarceration during the early part of the twentieth century (controlling for population growth).

What needs to be empirically assessed, then, is not "the rise in incarceration" but the systemic and lingering effects of the continuity of confinement in modern times. What such arguments highlight is the need to reconceptualize institutionalization and imprisonment as not merely analogues but as in fact interconnected, in their logic, historical enactment, and social effects. The theoretical and policy implications of such interconnectedness will also necessitate bringing in disability (psychiatric, developmental, physical, etc.) as a focus in studies on incarceration, as well as working out questions of criminality and danger in studies of institutionalization and disablement.

CONNECTIONS BETWEEN PRISON AND INSTITUTIONS

First, we need to examine some of the ways in which prisons and institutions for those with intellectual and psychiatric disabilities are connected and interrelated. As Goffman described in *Asylums* (1961), the incarcerated populations in institutions and prisons are subjected to stripping of their identities and to processes of dehumanization. Also, especially for people with intellectual and psychiatric disabilities, their citizenship and personhood is questioned. This can be done in the form of taking away or denying voting rights or

performing medical experimentation and, for women, denying reproductive rights, including forced sterilization (Waldman and Levi 2011).

On a theoretical level, the imperative to understand incarceration through both the prism of the prison but also that of the institution, as this paper suggests, is crucial to unveiling the underlying relations that legitimate confinement in a variety of settings. Such analysis also underscores the relation between penal and medical notions of danger, as they relate to both criminalization and medicalization. Historically, the connection between imprisonment and definitions of "abnormality" seems to have arisen out of the modernity project, as a result of a new configuration of notions of danger. From the nineteenth century the webs of the medical and the judicial start to intertwine with the rise of a hybrid discourse, according to Foucault (2003). Its hybridity lies not just in the sense of amalgamation of several discourses (legal, medical) but also in the creation of a new power/knowledge structure in which "doctors laying claim to judicial power and judges laying claim to medical power" (2003: 39) lay down an intertwined system of surveillance, which includes psychiatric progress reports of the incarcerated, examination in court of the accused, and surveillance of "at risk" groups. According to Foucault (2003), this medico-judicial discourse does not originate from medicine or law or in between, but from another external discourse—that of abnormality. The power of normalization is cloaked by medical notions of illness and legal notions of recidivism. The history of treatment and categorization of those labeled as feebleminded, and later "mentally retarded," is also paved on cobblestones of notions of social danger, as prominent eugenicists tried to "scientifically" establish that those whom they characterized as feebleminded had a tendency to commit violent crimes. In the late nineteenth century, as the eugenics movement gained momentum, it was declared that all feebleminded people were potential criminals (Rafter 2004; Trent 1995).

Another pervasive connection between institutionalization and imprisonment, both historically and at present, is offered through the framework of political economy. Many (including scholars and policy makers) believe that disabled people are a strain on the economy, especially under neoliberal ideology. But political economists of disability argue that disability supports a whole industry of professionals that keeps the economy afloat, such as service providers, case managers, medical professionals, health care specialists, etc. (Charlton 1998; Oliver 1990). Elsewhere (Ben-Moshe 2012) I suggest that the forces of incarceration of disabled people should be understood under the growth of both the prison industry and the institution–industrial complex, in the form of a growing private industry of nursing homes, boarding homes, for-profit psychiatric hospitals, and group homes. As an example, figures show that there is no correlation between the increase of the non-governmental institutional–industrial complex and percentage of those "needing" these services. Between 1977 and 2009, the total number of residential settings in which people with developmental disability labels received residential services grew from 11,008 to an estimated 173,042 (1,500%), while total service recipients increased from about 247,780 to an estimated 439,515 individuals (an increase of 77.4%) (Lakin et. al. 2010).

In a similar vein, for those drawing on the conceptualization of the prison–industrial complex, the increase in the number of prisons and cells is not seen as related to similar increases in crime, but as driven by capitalist and racist impetuses (Christie 2000; Goldberg and Evans 1997; Gilmore 2006). According to Parenti (1999), the criminal (in)justice system generally and the privatization of prisons specifically exist to "manage and contain the new surplus populations created by neo-liberal economic policies," and the global flow of capital. Under this new configuration, men of color in particular have turned into commodities in high demand for the growing prison industry. The prison comprises a solution to one of the deepest inherent contradictions of capitalism itself: how to maintain a proletariat class (in this case mostly poor people of color), while controlling them from rising up against their conditions of being. The prison solves this dilemma almost seamlessly. Some perceive the carceral system as a failing system, in that it actually creates criminality rather than reduces it. The prison thus becomes a hub and training school for criminal behavior (Morris 1995). Foucault (1995) aids us in the realization that the prison has not failed, but indeed, has succeeded. Its success lies in the making of docile bodies and an underclass to imprison. This political economic analysis of imprisonment and institutionalization should therefore be of great interest to critical scholars and activists who are interested in understanding the phenomenon of "mass incarceration" from an intersectional lens.

FROM ANALOGIES TO INTERSECTIONS

While such comparisons help crystallize the coalition building potential between those placed in institutions and in prisons, they also obscure the important ways in which one identity or form of oppression is used to discredit the other. In an essay in *Justice Matters*, Bird (2006) posits the important connections she finds between the two populations but cautions: "In 1995

I began sharing my story publicly of how being paralyzed in a drunk driving crash has changed my life. I'll never forget the first time that someone said to me 'but you got a life sentence sitting in that wheelchair and all he got was a year in a restitution center!?'" (Bird 2006). Such comparisons seem to create an equation of disability with punishment, which is not a new phenomenon. One of the earliest sources of stigmatization of disability can be found in religious or magical thinking that assumed that disability is a result of punishment from the gods or a result of witchcraft.

In addition, if one listens to the narratives of disabled people who were segregated in institutions, another obvious connection emerges in which many describe their time there as a form of incarceration. Self advocates (activists with intellectual disability labels) compare institutions to living in prisons, and characterize their existence there as incarceration or being jailed while committing no apparent crime (Hayden, Lakin and Taylor 1995/6; Hayden 1997). Such statements, combined with McBride Johnson's epigraph and Bird's narrative above, help crystallize the vital connections between prisoners and people with disabilities, but may also pit one group against the other and ignore both the differences and intersections between the two populations.

I argue that today one cannot analyze the forces of incarceration without having a disability lens. For instance, a disproportionate number of persons incarcerated in US prisons and jails are disabled. As suggested above, prisoners with disabilities are a population that is hard to count (and account for) but is definitely at the intersection of the disability and imprisonment juggernaut. There is much at stake in counting the percentage of disabled prisoners. In terms of policy and legislation, if one can prove sufficiently that there is a large percentage of prisoners

with a specific disability, then it would require a specific solution such as requesting more hospital units to be built in specific prisons or prescribing more medications on a particular unit. For activists, using statistics that demonstrate the high prevalence of disabled prisoners could go in several directions. If one is an activist in NAMI (National Alliance of Mental Illness), for instance, then these statistics are used to show that deinstitutionalization failed and that prisons and jails had become a dumping ground for those labeled as mentally ill with the lack of other alternatives. Such campaigns, which have been ongoing since the early 1990s, call in essence for the (re)hospitalization of those with psychiatric diagnosis (see Torrey 1996 for example). However, such critiques from activists and scholars about inappropriately placing disabled people in nursing homes or prisons reproduce the sentiment that there are those who are somehow *appropriately* placed in nursing homes and prisons. In other words, it reinscribes the notion that there are those who really need to be segregated in carceral edifices, while those who are young and disabled do not.

However, others might use these statistics to showcase the cruelty of the criminal "justice" system and call for the just treatment of all prisoners (such as abolishing the use of isolation units as a whole). The downturn of such arguments, much like those in the calls to abolish the death penalty for those who are labeled as intellectually disabled, is that they can turn into arguments which reproduce ableist rhetoric and may seem to call for the release of some prisoners (i.e., those most disabled) but not others. A similar tactic is used by those who find conditions of disabled prisoners and those institutionalized so deplorable that they call for the creation of more hospital beds in prisons, reform and overhaul of psychiatric hospitals and institutions for those labeled as intellectually disabled and the creation of more accessible prisons. Others call not for reforming these edifices, but for abolishing them altogether.

ABOLITION AS A FORM OF RESISTANCE TO INCARCERATION

In addition to the connections between the forces of incarceration and decarceration in prisons and institutions, I would like to end with an analysis of the connections between the movements that resist these forces. Instead of incarcerating people and segregating them, movements such as factions in anti-psychiatry, deinstitutionalization, and prison abolition propose radical new ways of treatment, care, and governance that do not require the segregation of people from their peers.

Deinstitutionalization could be characterized not only as a process or an exodus of oppressed people outside the walls of institutions. In the eyes of those who pushed for institutional closure and community living, deinstitutionalization is perceived as a philosophy (Ben-Moshe 2011). The resistance to institutionalization and psychiatric hospitals arose from a broader social critique of medicalization and medical authority (Conrad and Schneider 1992; Zola 1991) and a new understanding of human value, especially in regards to people with disabilities, as seen in the principles of normalization (Wolfensberger 1972), the anti-psychiatry and ex-patients movement (Chamberlin 1977; Szasz 1961), and the People First movement (Williams and Shoultz 1982). Although these ideological shifts did not solely bring about deinstitutionalization nationwide, I believe that any significant decrease in institutionalized populations would have been impossible without them. Furthermore, deinstitutionalization is not just something that happened, but something for which

many were relentlessly advocating. As such, deinstitutionalization can be construed as an active form of activism and as a social movement.

There are many ways in which one can fight for social justice or social change. In the struggle to eliminate institutional settings for those labeled as developmentally or psychiatrically disabled, and replacing them with community living and community-based services, there were myriad possibilities through which the struggle could have taken place. But what is illuminating in these cases is that some took the view that the *only* route for successful social change was to abolish these institutions and close them down, while others advocated for improving or reforming them. This tension between reform and abolition is a key characteristic of the prison abolitionist stance in particular, and there is no agreement as to how to resolve it, as the movement is diverse and ranges from calls for focusing on the present circumstances of prisoners and advocating for gradual changes, to those who contend that any type of reform would lead to the growth of the prison–industrial-complex and should be avoided by activists. Some (such as Knopp et al. 1976) suggest conceptualizing the long term goal of prison abolition as a chain for shorter campaigns around specific issues—like jail diversion, restitution programs, or the move of those released to community placements. Such strategic use of abolition and reform can also be applied to the context of abolishing psychiatric confinement and forced medical treatments, as suggested by anti-psychiatry activist Bonnie Burstow. In her keynote speech in the 2009 PsychOut conference, Burstow suggests that the short term goals of anti-psychiatry activists, such as reform efforts, should be kept as such, as concrete and direct partial abolitions (or reforms) on the road to long term change of abolishing psychiatry.

This contention between abolition and reform is not only a scholarly debate but one with pragmatic implications. For instance, Angela Y. Davis (2003), as a practicing abolitionist, suggests to question what kinds of reforms are sought and whether they will strengthen the system in the long run. For instance, fighting for health care for prisoners is something activists should support, as integral to abolitionist and decarcerating strategies. However, some health care initiatives are opposed by abolitionists, such as attempts to open prison hospitals or separate clinical wards, as these would only expand the scope of incarceration in the long haul. Many prison abolition and anti-psychiatry activists are insistent that the trend to develop mental health services within the prison only serves to criminalize (mostly women) with psychiatric and cognitive disabilities further, as quality health services of this nature are sparse outside the walls of the prison, while funds go to operate them within an already oppressive system.

Abolition can become a useful strategy for resistance to all forms of incarceration, as it does not acknowledge the structure as it is but envisions and creates a new worldview in which oppressive structures do not exist. It thus goes beyond protesting the current circumstances, to creating new conditions of possibility by collectively contesting the status quo. Norwegian sociologist Thomas Mathiesen conceptualizes abolition as an alternative in the making: "The alternative lies in the 'unfinished', in the sketch, in what is not yet fully existing" (Mathiesen 1974: 1). According to Mathiesen, abolition takes place when one breaks with the established order and simultaneously breaks new ground. Abolition is triggered by making people aware of the necessary dilemma they are faced with—continuing with the existing order with some changes (i.e. reform) or transitioning to something unknown.

The question becomes not "what is the best alternative?" in its final formulation, but how this new order shall begin from the old.

The most powerful relevance of the prison abolitionist and anti-institutional stance is to analyze imprisonment and institutional segregation as a core structure that shapes social relations in society, not just for those affected directly but for everyone. It is not merely about closure of prisons or institutions, but it is a revolutionary framework, which transforms the way we analyze and understand forces that shape our histories and everyday lives: notions like "crime" or "innocence" (what gets to be defined as crime, and who gets to be defined as criminal); "disability" (as an identity not just a medical diagnosis) and rehabilitation (a benign process or a force of assimilation and normalization); ideas of punishment (justice vs. revenge or retribution); notions of community (as in "living in the community" or "community re-entry"); or "institution" (who defines what gets to be called an institution); notions of freedom and equality (can we feel free and safe without locking others away?) and on the other hand concepts of danger and protection (who do we protect by segregating people behind bars in psychiatric hospitals and prisons? Is it for "their own good?").

As Angela Y. Davis (2003) suggests, there is no one single alternative to imprisonment, but a vision of a more just society—revamping of the education system, comprehensive health care for all, demilitarization, and a justice system based on reparation and reconciliation. One of the main problems with prisons and institutions is that they become a catch-all for "problematic populations" that are deemed socially undesirable or dangerous. The alternative to incarceration therefore cannot be a catch-all solution, but an individual one, in relation to the harm done and the community in which one is involved. Prison abolition and deinstitutionalization, therefore, is not about helping prisoners or people with disabilities, but is about societal change that will improve the lives of all, inside and outside prisons and institutions.

According to liberal discourses that call for social change, change entails incorporating excluded groups into current structures—such as education systems, the government, corporations, and politics. But these frameworks only change the hierarchy of the structures in which marginalized populations are placed, and not the structures themselves. Under a more abolitionary mindset it is clear that forms of oppression are not always characterized by exclusion, but by pervasive inclusion that sometimes does more damage. The goal of a non-carceral society is not to replace one form of control, such as a hospital, institution, and prison, with another, such as psychopharmaceuticals, nursing homes, and group homes in the community. The aspiration is to fundamentally change the way we react to each other, the way we respond to difference or harm, the way normalcy is defined, and the ways resources are distributed and accessed. It is no wonder then that the abolitionary approach to institutionalization and imprisonment, as an epistemic change that breaks down the segregationist model altogether, did not occur overall. Or at least not yet …

CONCLUSION

This article suggests the pressing need to expand notions of what comes to be classified as "incarceration," as including institutionalization in a wide variety of enclosed settings, including prisons, jails, detention centers, institutions for the intellectually disabled, treatment centers, and psychiatric hospitals. Such formulations conceptualize incarceration as a continuum and a multifaceted phenomenon, not one that occurs in one locale or in one historical period, in contrast to current interpretations of "the rise in incarceration" or the success (or failure) of deinstitutionalization. Closure of large institutions has not led to freedom for disabled people, nor has it resulted in the radical acceptance of the fact of difference amongst us. My main argument here is that the (his)story of disability is the (his)story of incarceration and there is a need to connect them in terms of their history, as medico-judicial hybrids; their present, in the disproportionate number of disabled prisoners and those still institutionalized; and the future, in terms of movements that seek to abolish the segregationist model that underpins systems of incarceration. It is only through such coalitions that we can truly analyze, and perhaps circumvent, "the institution yet to come."

ACKNOWLEDGMENTS

Parts of this chapter appeared in *Critical Sociology* 37 (7) (2012) as "Disabling Incarceration: Connecting Disability to Divergent Confinements in the USA." I want to thank Dr. Michael Rembis for providing me with some of the data on disabled prisoners. I want to also acknowledge NIDRR Advanced Training in Translational and Transformational Research to Improve Outcomes for People with Disabilities, Grant No. H133P110004 and University Center for Excellence in Developmental Disabilities, Grant No. 90-DD-0655/01 for funding my postdoctoral position at the University of Illinois-Chicago that enabled me to write this chapter.

NOTE

1. Jonathan Metzl's *The protest psychosis: How schizophrenia became a black disease* (Beacon Press, 2010) can provide a possible explanation of this phenomenon.

BIBLIOGRAPHY

American Psychiatric Association (APA) (2000) *Psychiatric services in jails and prisons* (2d edition). Washington, DC: American Psychiatric Association: xix.

Bell, C. (2006) Introducing White Disability Studies: A Modest Proposal. In Davis, L. J. (ed.) *The disability studies reader* (2nd ed.). New York: Routledge.

Ben-Moshe, L. (2011) *Genealogies of resistance to incarceration: Abolition politics in anti-prison and deinstitutionalization activism in the U.S.* Unpublished dissertation. Syracuse, NY: Syracuse University.

Ben-Moshe, L. (2012) Disabling Incarceration: Connecting Disability to Divergent Confinements in the USA. *Critical Sociology* 37 (7).

Bird, A. (2006) *Disability and the dehumanization of prisoners*. Retrieved August 2006 from www.safetyandjustice.org/story/842

Bogdan, R. and Biklen, D. (1977) Handicapism. *Social Policy* 7 (5) March/April: 14–19.

Braddock, D., Hemp, R., Rizzolo, M. C., Haffer, L., Tanis, E. S., and Wu, J. (2011) *The state of the states in developmental disabilities 2011*. Boulder: University of Colorado, Department of Psychiatry and Coleman Institute for Cognitive Disabilities.

Brief of the American Association on Mental Retardation et al. in Support of Petitioners, *Goodman v. Georgia*, No. 02-10168, 11th Circuit (July 29, 2005).

Bureau of Justice Statistics (BJS) (2010) *Correctional populations in the United States 2009*. Washington, DC: U.S. Department of Justice.

Chamberlin, J. (1977) *On our own: Patient-controlled alternatives to the mental health system*. Lawrence, MA: National Empowerment Center.

Chapman, C., Ben-Moshe, L., and Carey, A. C. (2014) Reconsidering confinement: Interlocking locations and logics of confinement. In Ben-Moshe, L., Carey, A., and Chapman, C. (eds.) *Disability incarcerated: Imprisonment and dis/ability in North America*. New York: Palgrave Macmillan.

Charlton, J. I. (1998) *Nothing about us without us: Disability oppression and empowerment*. Berkeley: University of California Press.

Christie, N. (2000) *Crime control as industry: Towards gulags, Western style* (3rd ed.). New York: Routledge.

Conrad, P. and Schneider, J. W. (1992) *Deviance and medicalization: From badness to sickness; with a new afterword by the authors* (Expanded ed.). Philadelphia: Temple University Press.

Davis, A. Y. (2003) *Are prisons obsolete?* New York: Seven Stories Press.

Davis, L. J. (1995) *Enforcing normalcy: Disability, deafness, and the body*. New York: Verso.

Erickson, P. E. and Erickson, S. K. (2008) *Crime, punishment, and mental illness: Law and the behavioral sciences in conflict*. New Brunswick, NJ: Rutgers University Press.

Foucault, M. (1995) *Discipline and punish: The birth of the prison* (2nd Vintage Books ed.). New York: Vintage Books.

Foucault, M. (2003) *Abnormal: Lectures at the Collège de France, 1974–1975*. New York: Picador.

Garland-Thomson, R. (1997) *Extraordinary bodies: Figuring physical disability in American culture and literature*. New York: Columbia University Press.

Gilmore, R. W. (2006) *Golden gulag: Prisons, surplus, crisis, and opposition in globalizing California*. Berkeley: University of California Press.

Goffman, E. (1961) *Asylums: Essays on the social situation of mental patients and other inmates* (1st ed.). Garden City, NY: Anchor Books.

Goldberg, E. and Evans, L. (1997) *The prison industrial complex and the global economy*. Pamphlet. Published by Prison Activist Resource Center.

Gottschalk, M. (2010) Cell Blocks and Red Ink: Mass Incarceration, the Great Recession and Penal Reform. *Daedalus* 139 (3): 62–73.

Harcourt, B. (2006) From the Asylum to the Prison: Rethinking the Incarceration Revolution. *Texas Law Review* 84: 1751–1786.

Harcourt, B. (2011) Reducing Mass Incarceration: Lessons from the Deinstitutionalization of Mental Hospitals in the 1960s. University of Chicago Law and Economics, Olin Working Paper No. 542; University of Chicago, Public Law Working Paper No. 335. Available at SSRN: http://ssrn.com/abstract=1748796

Hayden, M. F. (1997) *Living in the Freedom World*. Minneapolis: University of Minnesota, Research and Training Center on Community Living, Institute on Community Integration.

Hayden, M. F., Lakin, K. C., and Taylor, S. J. (Eds.) (1995/6) *IMPACT: Feature Issue on Institution Closures*, 9 (1): 8–9. Publication of the Institute on Community Integration, University of Minnesota.

Human Rights Index: US Prisons (2009–2010) *International Accents* 26 (Winter). University of Iowa Center for Human Rights. Retrieved February 12, 2012 from http://accents.international.uiowa.edu/worldviews/human-rights-index-us-prisons-winter-2009-2010-26/

Human Rights Watch, U.S. (September 5, 2006) Number of Mentally Ill in Prisons Quadrupled: Prisons Ill Equipped to Cope. Retrieved February 12, 2012 from www.hrw.org/print/news/2006/09/05/us-number-mentally-ill-prisons-quadrupled

Knopp, F. H. and Prison Research Education Action Project (1976) *Instead of prisons: A handbook for abolitionists.* Syracuse, NY: Prison Research Education Action Project.

Lakin, K. C., Larson, S. A., Salmi, P., and A. Webster (2010) *Residential services for persons with developmental disabilities: Statues and trends through 2009.* Minneapolis: University of Minnesota, Research and Training Center on Community Living, Institute on Community Integration.

McBryde Johnson, H. (2003) The Disability Gulag. *New York Times*, November 23.

McRuer, R. (2002) Compulsory able-bodiedness and queer/disabled existence. In Snyder, S. Brueggemann, B., and Garland-Thomson, R. (Eds.). *Disability studies: Enabling the humanities.* New York: MLA Press.

McRuer, R. (2006) *Crip theory: Cultural signs of queerness and disability.* New York: New York University Press.

Mathiesen, T. (1974) *The politics of abolition.* New York: Halsted Press.

Morris, J. (2001) Impairment and Disability: Constructing an Ethics of Care that Promotes Human Rights. *Hypatia* 16 (4): 1–16.

Morris, R. (1995) *Penal abolition, the practical choice: A practical manual on penal abolition.* Toronto: Canadian Scholars' Press.

Oliver, M. (1990) *The politics of disablement: A sociological approach.* New York: St. Martin's Press.

Parenti, C. (1999) *Lockdown America: Police and prisons in the age of crisis.* New York: Verso.

Perlin, M. (2000) *The hidden prejudice: Mental disability on trial.* Washington, DC: American Psychological Association.

Rafter, N. (2004) The Criminalization of Mental Retardation. In Noll, S. and Trent, J. (eds.) *Mental retardation in America: A historical reader.* New York: New York University Press.

Russell, M. and Stewart, J. (2001) Disability, Prison and Historical Segregation. *Monthly Review*, July–August issue.

Szasz, T. S. (1961) *The myth of mental illness. Foundations of a theory of personal conduct.* New York: Hoeber-Harper.

Thompson, H. A. (2010) Why Mass Incarceration Matters: Rethinking Crisis, Decline, and Transformation in Postwar American History. *Journal of American History* 97: 3.

Torrey, E. F. (1996) *Out of the shadows: Confronting America's mental illness crisis.* Hoboken, NJ: John Wiley.

Tremain, S. (2002) On the subject of impairment. In Corker, M. and Shakespeare, T. (Eds.). *Disability/postmodernity: Embodying disability theory.* London: Continuum.

Trent, J. W. (1995) *Inventing the feeble mind: A history of mental retardation in the United States.* Berkeley: University of California Press.

Wacquant, L. (2010) Class, Race and Hyperincarceration in Revanchist America. *Daedalus* 139 (3): 74–90.

Waldman, A. and Levi, R. (2011) *Inside this place, not of it: Narratives from women's prisons.* San Francisco: McSweeney Press.

Wendell, S. (1996) *The rejected body: Feminist philosophical reflections on disability.* New York: Routledge.

Williams, P. and Shoultz, B. (1982) *We can speak for ourselves.* London: Souvenir Press.

Wolfensberger, W. (1972) *The principle of normalization in human services.* Toronto: National Institute on Mental Retardation.

Zola, I. K. (1991) The Medicalization of Aging and Disability. *Advances in Medical Sociology* 2: 299–315.

PART III

Stigma and Illness

CHAPTER 9

Selections from *Stigma*

Erving Goffman

SUMMARY

A stigma is an attribute that makes a person different from others in a social category, and it reduces the person to a tainted or discounted status. A stigma is sometimes called a handicap, and it is made up of a discrepancy between the virtual (or perceived) identity and the actual identity of the stigma's bearer. In these passages from *Stigma*, Erving Goffman suggests that a stigma is really a special kind of relation between an attribute and the stereotype that causes a person to be "discredited" by others. For Goffman, stigma can be understood in three grossly different types: physical differences, perceived character deficiencies, and "tribal" stigma of race, nation, or religion. In all these various instances, an individual who might have been received easily in ordinary social intercourse possesses a trait that demands the attention of others and turns them away.

Drawing on the testimony of stigmatized individuals, Goffman focuses on the moments of interaction between the stigmatized and "normals." These can be anxious social interactions in which the presence of the stigma is a source of discomfort for both parties. For example, a visible disability might draw stares from other people; the stigmatized person dreads the stares while the "normal" must choose between looking or intentionally ignoring the stigma. This uneasiness often leads to the stigmatized individual being treated (or trying to act) as if he or she were a "non-person" and not present at all.

Goffman suggests that a person with a stigma is, by social definition, not quite human. On this assumption, people exercise varieties of discrimination that limit the life chances of the stigmatized person. This stigma-theory is an ideology meant to explain a person's inferiority, account for a person's danger, or rationalize an animosity based on other grounds.

STIGMA AND SOCIAL IDENTITY

The Greeks, who were apparently strong on visual aids, originated the term *stigma* to refer to bodily signs designed to expose something unusual and bad about the moral status of the signifier. The signs were cut or burnt into the body and advertised that the bearer was a slave, a criminal, or a traitor—a blemished person, ritually polluted, to be avoided, especially in public places. Later, in Christian times, two layers of metaphor were added to the term: the first referred to bodily signs of holy grace that took the form of eruptive blossoms on the skin; the second, a medical allusion to this religious allusion, referred to bodily signs of physical disorder. Today the term is widely used in something like the original literal sense, but is applied more to the disgrace itself than to the bodily evidence of it. Furthermore, shifts have occurred in the kinds of disgrace that arouse concern. Students, however, have made little effort to describe the structural preconditions of stigma, or even to provide a definition of the concept itself. It seems necessary, therefore, to try at the beginning to sketch in some very general assumptions and definitions.

PRELIMINARY CONCEPTIONS

Society establishes the means of categorizing persons and the complement of attributes felt to be ordinary and natural for members of each of these categories. Social settings establish the categories of persons likely to be encountered there. The routines of social intercourse in established settings allow us to deal with anticipated others without special attention or thought. When a stranger comes into our presence, then, first appearances are likely to enable us to anticipate his category and attributes, his "social identity"—to use a term that is better than "social status" because personal attributes such as "honesty" are involved, as well as structural ones, like "occupation." We lean on these anticipations that we have, transforming them into normative expectations, into righteously presented demands. Typically, we do not become aware that we have made these demands or aware of what they are until an active question arises as to whether or not they will be fulfilled. It is then that we are likely to realize that all along we had been making certain assumptions as to what the individual before us ought to be. Thus, the demands we make might better be called demands made "in effect" and the character we impute to the individual might better be seen as an imputation made in potential retrospect— a characterization "in effect," a *virtual*

social identity. The category and attributes he could in fact be proved to possess will be called his *actual social identity*.

While the stranger is present before us, evidence can arise of his possessing an attribute that makes him different from others in the category of persons available for him to be, and of a less desirable kind— in the extreme, a person who is quite thoroughly bad, or dangerous, or weak. He is thus reduced in our minds from a whole and usual person to a tainted, discounted one. Such an attribute is a stigma, especially when its discrediting effect is very extensive; sometimes it is also called a failing, a shortcoming, a handicap. It constitutes a special discrepancy between virtual and actual social identity. Note that there are other types of discrepancy between virtual and actual social identity, for example the kind that causes us to reclassify an individual from one socially anticipated category to a different but equally well-anticipated one, and the kind that causes us to alter our estimation of the individual upward. Note, too, that not all undesirable attributes are at issue, but only those which are incongruous with our stereotype of what a given type of individual should be.

The term stigma, then, will be used to refer to an attribute that is deeply discrediting, but it should be seen that a language of relationships, not attributes, is really needed. An attribute that stigmatizes one type of possessor can confirm the usualness of another, and therefore is neither creditable nor discreditable as a thing in itself. For example, some jobs in America cause holders without the expected college education to conceal this fact; other jobs, however, can lead the few of their holders who have a higher education to keep this a secret, lest they be marked as failures and outsiders. Similarly, a middle class boy may feel no compunction in being seen going to the library; a professional criminal, however, writes:

I can remember before now on more than one occasion, for instance, going into a public library near where I was living, and looking over my shoulder a couple of times before I actually went in just to make sure no one who knew me was standing about and seeing me do it.[1]

So, too, an individual who desires to fight for his country may conceal a physical defect, lest his claimed physical status be discredited; later, the same individual, embittered and trying to get out of the army, may succeed in gaining admission to the army hospital, where he would be discredited if discovered in not really having an acute sickness.[2] A stigma, then, is really a special kind of relationship between attribute and stereotype, although I don't propose to continue to say so, in part because there are important attributes that almost everywhere in our society are discrediting.

The term stigma and its synonyms conceal a double perspective: does the stigmatized individual assume his differentness is known about already or is evident on the spot, or does he assume it is neither known about by those present nor immediately perceivable by them? In the first case one deals with the plight of the *discredited*, in the second with that of the *discreditable*. This is an important difference, even though a particular stigmatized individual is likely to have experience with both situations. I will begin with the situation of the discredited and move on to the discreditable but not always separate the two.

Three grossly different types of stigma may be mentioned. First there are abominations of the body—the various physical deformities. Next there are blemishes of individual character perceived as weak will,

domineering or unnatural passions, treacherous and rigid beliefs, and dishonesty, these being inferred from a known record of, for example, mental disorder, imprisonment, addiction, alcoholism, homosexuality, unemployment, suicidal attempts, and radical political behavior. Finally there are the tribal stigma of race, nation, and religion, these being stigma that can be transmitted through lineages and equally contaminate all members of a family.[3] In all of these various instances of stigma, however, including those the Greeks had in mind, the same sociological features are found: an individual who might have been received easily in ordinary social intercourse possesses a trait that can obtrude itself upon attention and turn those of us whom he meets away from him, breaking the claim that his other attributes have on us. He possesses a stigma, an undesired differentness from what we had anticipated. We and those who do not depart negatively from the particular expectations at issue I shall call the *normals*.

The attitudes we normals have toward a person with a stigma and the actions we take in regard to him, are well known, since these responses are what benevolent social action is designed to soften and ameliorate. By definition, of course, we believe the person with a stigma is not quite human. On this assumption we exercise varieties of discrimination, through which we effectively, if often unthinkingly, reduce his life chances. We construct a stigma-theory, an ideology to explain his inferiority and account for the danger he represents, sometimes rationalizing an animosity based on other differences, such as those of social class.[4] We use specific stigma terms such as cripple, bastard, moron in our daily discourse as a source of metaphor and imagery, typically without giving thought to the original meaning.[5] We tend to impute a wide range of imperfections on the basis of the original one,[6] and at the same time to impute some desirable but undesired attributes, often of a supernatural cast, such as "sixth sense," or "understanding":[7]

> For some, there may be a hesitancy about touching or steering the blind, while for others, the perceived failure to see may be generalized into a gestalt of disability, so that the individual shouts at the blind as if they were deaf or attempts to lift them as if they were crippled. Those confronting the blind may have a whole range of belief that is anchored in the stereotype. For instance, they think they are subject to unique judgment, assuming the blinded individual draws on special channels of information unavailable to others.[8]

Further, we may perceive his defensive response to his situation as a direct expression of his defect, and then see both defect and response as just retribution for something he or his parents or his tribe did, and hence a justification of the way we treat him.[9]

Now turn from the normal to the person he is normal against. It seems generally true that members of a social category may strongly support a standard of judgment that they and others agree does not directly apply to them. Thus it is that a businessman may demand womanly behavior from females or ascetic behavior from monks, and not construe himself as someone who ought to realize either of these styles of conduct. The distinction is between realizing a norm and merely supporting it. The issue of stigma does not arise here, but only where there is some expectation on all sides that those in a given category should not only support a particular norm but also realize it.

Also, it seems possible for an individual to fail to live up to what we effectively demand of him, and yet be relatively untouched by this failure; insulated by his alienation, protected by identity beliefs of his own, he feels that he is a full-fledged normal human being, and that we are the ones who are not quite human. He hears a stigma but does not seem to be impressed or repentant about doing so. This possibility is celebrated in exemplary tales about Mennonites, Gypsies, shameless scoundrels, and very orthodox Jews.

In America at present, however, separate systems of honor seem to be on the decline. The stigmatized individual tends to hold the same beliefs about identity that we do; this is a pivotal fact. His deepest feelings about what he is may be his sense of being a "normal person," a human being like anyone else, a person, therefore, who deserves a fair chance and a fair break.[10] (Actually, however phrased, he bases his claims not on what he thinks is due *everyone*, but only everyone of a selected social category into which he unquestionably fits, for example, anyone of his age, sex, profession, and so forth.) Yet he may perceive, usually quite correctly, that whatever others profess, they do not really "accept" him and are not ready to make contact with him on "equal grounds."[11] Further, the standards he has incorporated from the wider society equip him to be intimately alive to what others see as his failing, inevitably causing him, if only for moments, to agree that he does indeed fall short of what he really ought to be. Shame becomes a central possibility, arising from the individual's perception of one of his own attributes as being a defiling thing to possess, and one he can readily see himself as not possessing.

The immediate presence of normals is likely to reinforce this split between self-demands and self, but in fact self-hate and self-derogation can also occur when only he and a mirror are about:

> When I got up at last... and had learned to walk again, one day I took a hand glass and went to a long mirror to look at myself, and I went alone. I didn't want anyone... to know how I felt when I saw myself for the first time.

But here was no noise, no outcry; I didn't scream with rage when I saw myself. I just felt numb. That person in the mirror *couldn't* be me. I felt inside like a healthy, ordinary, lucky person—oh, not like the one in the mirror! Yet when I turned my face to the mirror there were my own eyes looking back, hot with shame . . . when I did not cry or make any sound, it became impossible that I should speak of it to anyone, and the confusion and the panic of my discovery were locked inside me then and there, to be faced alone, for a very long time to come.[12]

Over and over I forgot what I had seen in the mirror. It could not penetrate into the interior of my mind and become an integral part of me. I felt as if it had nothing to do with me; it was only a disguise. But it was not the kind of disguise which is put on voluntarily by the person who wears it, and which is intended to confuse other people as to one's identity. My disguise had been put on me without my consent or knowledge like the ones in fairy tales, and it was I myself who was confused by it, as to my own identity. I looked in the mirror, and was horror-struck because I did not recognize myself. In the place where I was standing, with that persistent romantic elation in me, as if I were a favored fortunate person to whom everything was possible, I saw a stranger, a little, pitiable, hideous figure, and a face that became, as I stared at it, painful and blushing with shame. It was only a disguise, but it was on me, for life. It was there, it was there, it was real. Everyone of those encounters was like a blow on the head. They left me dazed and dumb and senseless every time, until slowly and stubbornly my robust persistent illusion of well-being and of personal beauty spread all through me again, and I forgot the irrelevant reality and was all unprepared and vulnerable again.[13]

The central feature of the stigmatized individual's situation in life can now be stated. It is a question of what is often, if vaguely, called "acceptance." Those who have dealings with him fail to accord him the respect and regard which the uncontaminated aspects of his social identity have led them to anticipate extending, and have led him to anticipate receiving; he echoes this denial by finding that some of his own attributes warrant it.

How does the stigmatized person respond to his situation? In some cases it will be possible for him to make a direct attempt to correct what he sees as the objective basis of his failing, as when a physically deformed person undergoes plastic surgery, a blind person eye treatment, an illiterate remedial education, a homosexual psychotherapy. (Where such repair is possible, what often results is not the acquisition of fully normal status, but a transformation of self from someone with a particular blemish into someone with a record of having corrected a particular blemish.) Here proneness to "victimization" is to be cited, a result of the stigmatized person's exposure to fraudulent servers selling speech correction, skin lighteners, body stretchers, youth restorers (as in rejuvenation through fertilized egg yolk treatment), cures through faith, and poise in conversation. Whether a practical technique or fraud is involved, the quest, often secret, that results provides a special indication of the extremes to which the stigmatized can be willing to go, and hence the painfulness of the situation that leads them to these extremes. One illustration may be cited:

Miss Peck [a pioneer New York social worker for the hard of hearing] said that in the early days the quacks and get-rich-quick medicine men who abounded saw the League [for the hard of hearing] as their happy hunting ground, ideal for the promotion of magnetic head caps, miraculous vibrating machines, artificial eardrums, blowers, inhalers, massagers, magic oils, balsams, and other guaranteed, sure-fire, positive, and permanent cure-alls for incurable deafness. Advertisements for such hokum (until the 1920s when the American Medical Association moved in with an investigation campaign) beset the hard of hearing in the pages of the daily press, even in reputable magazines.[14]

The stigmatized individual can also attempt to correct his condition indirectly by devoting much private effort to the mastery of areas of activity ordinarily felt to be closed on incidental and physical grounds to one with his shortcoming. This is illustrated by the lame person who learns or re-learns to swim, ride, play tennis, or fly an airplane, or the blind person who becomes expert at skiing and mountain climbing.[15] Tortured learning may be associated, of course, with the tortured performance of what is learned, as when an individual, confined to a wheelchair, manages to take to the dance floor with a girl in some kind of mimicry of dancing.[16] Finally, the person with a shameful differentness can break with what is called reality, and obstinately attempt to employ an unconventional interpretation of the character of his social identity.

The stigmatized individual is likely to use his stigma for "secondary gains," as an excuse for ill success that has come his way for other reasons:

> For years the scar, harelip or misshapen nose has been looked on as a handicap, and its importance in the social and emotional adjustment is unconsciously all embracing. It is the "hook" on which the patient has hung all inadequacies, all dissatisfactions, all procrastinations and all unpleasant duties of social life, and he has come to depend on it not only as a reasonable escape from competition but as a protection from social responsibility.

When one removes this factor by surgical repair, the patient is cast adrift from the more or less acceptable emotional protection it has offered and soon he finds, to his surprise and discomfort, that life is not all smooth sailing even for those with unblemished, "ordinary" faces. He is unprepared to cope with this situation without the support of a "handicap," and he may turn to the less simple, but similar, protection of the behavior patterns of neurasthenia, hysterical conversion, hypochondriasis or the acute anxiety states.[17]

He may also see the trials he has suffered as a blessing in disguise, especially because of what it is felt that suffering can teach one about life and people:

> But now, far away from the hospital experience, I can evaluate what I have learned. [A mother permanently disabled by polio writes.] For it wasn't only suffering: it was also learning through suffering. I know my awareness of people has deepened and increased, that those who are close to me can count on me to turn all my mind and heart and attention to their problems. I could not have learned *that* dashing all over a tennis court.[18]

Correspondingly, he can come to reassess the limitations of normals, as a multiple sclerotic suggests:

> Both healthy minds and healthy bodies may be crippled. The fact that "normal" people can get around, can see, can hear, doesn't mean that they are seeing or hearing. They can be very blind to the things that spoil their happiness, very deaf to the pleas of others for kindness; when I think of them I do not feel any more crippled or disabled than they. Perhaps in some way I can be the means of opening their eyes to the beauties around us: things like a warm handclasp, a voice that is anxious to cheer, a spring breeze, music to listen to, a friendly nod. These are important to me, and I like to feel that I can help them.[19]

And a blind writer.

> That would lead immediately to the thought that there are many occurrences which can diminish satisfaction in living far more effectively than blindness, and that lead

would be an entirely healthy one to take. In this light, we can perceive, for instance, that some inadequacy like the inability to accept human love, which can effectively diminish satisfaction of living almost to the vanishing point, is far more a tragedy than blindness. But it is unusual for the man who suffers from such a malady even to know he has it and self pity is, therefore, impossible for him.[20]

And a cripple:

> As life went on, I learned of many, many different kinds of handicap, not only the physical ones, and I began to realize that the words of the crippled girl in the extract above [words of bitterness] could just as well have been spoken by young women who had never needed crutches, women who felt inferior and different because of ugliness, or inability to bear children, or helplessness in contacting people, or many other reasons.[21]

The responses of the normal and of the stigmatized that have been considered so far are ones which can occur over protracted periods of time and in isolation from current contacts between normals and stigmatized.[22] This book, however, is specifically concerned with the issue of "mixed contacts"—the moments when stigmatized and normal are in the same "social situation," that is, in one another's immediate physical presence, whether in a conversation-like encounter or in the mere co-presence of an unfocused gathering.

The very anticipation of such contacts can of course lead normals and the stigmatized to arrange life so as to avoid them. Presumably this will have larger consequences for the stigmatized, since more arranging will usually be necessary on their part:

> Before her disfigurement [amputation of the distal half of her nose] Mrs. Dover, who lived with one of her two married daughters, had been an independent, warm and friendly woman who enjoyed traveling, shopping, and visiting her many relatives. The disfigurement of her face, however, resulted in a definite alteration in her way of living. The first two or three years she seldom left her daughter's home, preferring to remain in her room or to sit in the backyard. "I was heartsick," she said; "the door had been shut on my life."[23]

Lacking the salutary feed-back of daily social intercourse with others, the self-isolate can become suspicious, depressed, hostile, anxious, and bewildered. Sullivan's version may be cited:

> The awareness of inferiority means that one is unable to keep out of consciousness the formulation of some chronic feeling of the worst sort of insecurity, and this means that one suffers anxiety and perhaps even something worse, if jealousy is really worse than anxiety. The fear that others can disrespect a person because of something he shows means that he is always insecure in his contact with other people; and this insecurity arises, not from mysterious and somewhat disguised, sources, as a great deal of our anxiety does, but from something which he knows he cannot fix. Now that represents an almost fatal deficiency of the self-system, since the self is unable to disguise or exclude a definite formulation that reads, "I am inferior. Therefore people will dislike me and I cannot be secure with them."[24]

When normals and stigmatized do in fact enter one another's immediate presence, especially when they there attempt to sustain a joint conversational encounter, there occurs one of the primal scenes of sociology; for, in many cases, these moments will be the ones when the causes and effects of stigma must be directly confronted on both sides.

These stigmatized individual may find that he feels unsure of how we normals will identify him and receive him.[25] An illustration may be cited from a student of physical disability:

> Uncertainty of status for the disabled person obtains over a wide range of social interactions in addition to that of employment. The blind, the ill, the deaf, the crippled can never be sure what the attitude of a new acquaintance will be, whether it will be rejective or accepting, until the contact has been made. This is exactly the position of the adolescent, the light-skinned Negro, the second generation immigrant, the socially mobile person and the woman who has entered a predominantly masculine occupation.[26]

This uncertainty arises not merely from the stigmatized individual's not knowing which of several categories he will be placed in, but also, where the placement is favorable, from his knowing that in their hearts the others may be defining him in terms of his stigma:

> And I always feel this with straight people— that whenever they're being nice to me, pleasant to me, all the time really, under- neath they're only assessing me as a crim- inal and nothing else. It's too late for me to be any different now to what I am, but I still feel this keenly, that that's their only approach, and they're quite incapable of accepting me as anything else.[27]

Thus in the stigmatized arises the sense of not knowing what the others present are "really" thinking about him.

Further, during mixed contacts, the stigmatized individual is likely to feel that he is "on,"[28] having to be self-conscious and calculating about the impression he is making, to a degree and in areas of con- duct which he assumes others are not.

Also, he is likely to feel that the usual scheme of interpretation for everyday events has been undermined. His minor accomplishments, he feels, may be assessed as signs of remarkable and noteworthy capacities in the circumstances. A pro- fessional criminal provides an illustration:

> "You know, it's really amazing you should read books like this, I'm staggered I am. I should've thought you'd read paper-backed thrillers, things with lurid covers, books like that. And here you are with Claud Cockburn, Hugh Klare, Simone de Beauvoir, and Law- rence Durrell!"
>
> You know, he didn't see this as an insulting remark at all: in fact, I think he thought he was being honest in telling me how mistaken he was. And that's exactly the sort of patronizing you get from straight people if you're a criminal. "Fancy that!" they say. "In some ways you're just like a human being!" I'm not kidding, it makes me want to choke the bleeding life out of them.[29]

A blind person provides another illustration:

> His once most ordinary deeds—walking nonchalantly up the street, locating the peas on his plate, lighting a cigarette—are no longer ordinary. He becomes an unusual person. If he performs them with finesse and assurance they excite the same kind of wonderment inspired by a magician who pulls rabbits out of hats.[30]

At the same time, minor failings or incid- ental impropriety may, he feels, be inter- preted as a direct expression of his stigmatized differentness. Ex-mental patients, for example, are sometimes afraid to engage in sharp interchanges with spouse or employer because of what a show of emotion might be taken as a sign of. Mental defectives face a similar contingency:

> It also happens that if a person of low intel- lectual ability gets into some sort of trouble the difficulty is more or less automatically attrib- uted to "mental defect" whereas if a person of "normal intelligence" gets into a similar dif- ficulty, it is not regarded as symptomatic of anything in particular.[31]

A one-legged girl, recalling her experience with sports, provides other illustrations:

> Whenever I fell, out swarmed the women in droves, clucking and fretting like a bunch of bereft mother hens. It was kind of them, and in retrospect I appreciate their solicitude, but at the time I resented and was greatly embarrassed by their interference. For they assumed that no routine hazard to skating—no stick or stone—upset my flying wheels. It was a foregone conclusion that *I* fell because I was a poor, helpless cripple.[32]
>
> Not one of them shouted with outrage, "That dangerous wild bronco threw her!"—which, God forgive, he did technically. It was like a horrible ghostly visitation of my old roller-skating days. All the good people lamented in chorus, "That poor, poor girl fell off!"[33]

When the stigmatized person's failing can be perceived by our merely directing attention (typically, visual) to him—when, in short, he is a discredited, not discreditable, person—he is likely to feel that to be present among normals nakedly exposes him to invasions of privacy,[34] experienced most pointedly perhaps when children simply stare at him.[35] This displeasure in being exposed can be increased by the conversations strangers may feel free to strike up with him, conversations in which they express what he takes to be morbid curiosity about his condition, or in which they proffer help that he does not need or want.[36] One might add that there are certain classic formulae for these kinds of conversations: "My dear girl, how did you get your quiggle"; "My great uncle had a quiggle, so I feel I know all about your problem"; "You know I've always said that Quiggles are good family men and look after their own poor"; "Tell me, how do you manage to bathe with a quiggle?" The implication of these overtures is that the stigmatized individual is a person who can be approached by strangers at will, providing only that they are sympathetic to the plight of persons of his kind.

Given what the stigmatized individual may well face upon entering a mixed social situation, he may anticipatorily respond by defensive cowering. This may be illustrated from an early study of some German unemployed during the Depression, the words being those of a 43-year-old mason:

> How hard and humiliating it is to bear the name of an unemployed man. When I go out, I cast down my eyes because I feel myself wholly inferior. When I go along the street, it seems to me that I can't be compared with an average citizen, that everybody is pointing at me with his finger. I instinctively avoid meeting anyone. Former acquaintances and friends of better times are no longer so cordial. They greet me indifferently when we meet. They no longer offer me a cigarette and their eyes seem to say, "You are not worth it, you don't work."[37]

A crippled girl provides an illustrative analysis:

> When . . . I began to walk out alone in the streets of our town . . . I found then that wherever I had to pass three or four children together on the sidewalk, if I happened to be alone, they would shout at me, . . . Sometimes they even ran after me, shouting and jeering. This was something I didn't know how to face, and it seemed as if I couldn't bear it . . . .
>
> For awhile those encounters in the street filled me with a cold dread of all unknown children . . .
>
> One day I suddenly realized that I had become so self-conscious and afraid of all strange children that, like animals, they knew I was afraid, so that even the mildest and most amiable of them were automatically prompted to derision by my own shrinking and dread.[38]

Instead of cowering, the stigmatized individual may attempt to approach mixed contacts with hostile bravado, but this can induce from others its own set of troublesome reciprocation. It may be added that the stigmatized person sometimes vacillates between cowering and bravado, racing from one to the other, thus demonstrating one central way in which ordinary face-to-face interaction can run wild.

I am suggesting, then, that the stigmatized individual—at least "visibly" stigmatized one—will have special reasons for feeling that mixed social situations make for anxious unanchored interaction. But if this is so, then it is to be suspected that we normals will find these situations shaky too. We will feel that the stigmatized individual is either too aggressive or too shamefaced, and in either case too ready to read unintended meanings into our actions. We ourselves may feel that if we show direct sympathetic concern for his condition, we may be overstepping ourselves; and yet if we actually forget that he has a failing we are likely to make impossible demands of him or unthinkingly slight his fellow-sufferers. Each potential source of discomfort for him when we are with him can become something we sense he is aware of, aware that we are aware of, and even aware of our state of awareness about his awareness; the stage is then set for the infinite regress of mutual consideration that Meadian social psychology tells us how to begin but not how to terminate.

Given what both the stigmatized and we normals introduce into mixed social situations, it is understandable that all will not go smoothly. We are likely to attempt to carry on as though in fact he wholly fitted one of the types of person naturally available to us in the situation, whether this means treating him as someone better than we feel he might be or someone worse than we feel he probably is. If neither of these tacks is possible, then we may try to act as if he were a "non-person," and not present at all as someone of whom ritual notice is to be taken. He, in turn, is likely to go along with these strategies, at least initially.

In consequence, attention is furtively withdrawn from its obligatory targets, and self-consciousness and "other-consciousness" occurs, expressed in the pathology of interaction—uneasiness.[39] As described in the case of the physically handicapped:

> Whether the handicap is overtly and tactlessly responded to as such or, as is more commonly the case, no explicit reference is made to it, the underlying condition of heightened, narrowed, awareness causes the interaction to be articulated too exclusively in terms of it. This, as my informants described it, is usually accompanied by one or more of the familiar signs of discomfort and stickiness: the guarded references, the common everyday words suddenly made taboo, the fixed stare elsewhere, the artificial levity, the compulsive loquaciousness, the awkward solemnity.[40]

In social situations with an individual known or perceived to have a stigma, we are likely, then, to employ categorizations that do not fit, and we and he are likely to experience uneasiness. Of course, there is often significant movement from this starting point. And since the stigmatized person is likely to be more often faced with these situations than are we, he is likely to become the more adept at managing them.

NOTES

1. T. Parker and R. Allerton, *The Courage of His Convictions* (London: Hutchinson & Co., 1962), p. 109.
2. In this connection see the review by M. Meltzer, "Countermanipulation through Malingering," in A. Biderman and H. Zimmer, eds., *The Manipulation of Human Behavior* (New York: John Wiley & Sons, 1961), pp. 277–304.

3. In recent history, especially in Britain, low class status functioned as an important tribal stigma, the sins of the parents, or at least their milieu, being visited on the child, should the child rise improperly far above his initial station. The management of class stigma is of course a central theme in the English novel.

4. D. Riesman, "Some Observations Concerning Marginality," *Phylon,* Second Quarter, 1951, 122.

5. The case regarding mental patients is represented by T. J. Scheff in a forthcoming paper.

6. In regard to the blind, see E. Henrich and L. Kriegel, eds., *Experiments in Survival* (New York: Association for the Aid of Crippled Children, 1961), pp. 152 and 186; and H. Chevigny, *My Eyes Have a Cold Nose* (New Haven, CT: Yale University Press, paperbound, 1962), p. 201.

7. In the words of one blind woman, "I was asked to endorse a perfume, presumably because being sightless my sense of smell was super-discriminating." See T. Keitlen (with N. Lobsenz), *Farewell to Fear* (New York: Avon, 1962), p. 10.

8. A. G. Gowman, *The War Blind in American Social Structure* (New York: American Foundation for the Blind, 1957), p. 198.

9. For examples, see F. Macgregor et al., *Facial Deformities and Plastic Surgery* (Springfield, IL: Charles C. Thomas, 1953), throughout.

10. The notion of "normal human being" may have its source in the medical approach to humanity or in the tendency of large-scale bureaucratic organizations, such as the nation state, to treat all members in some respects as equal. Whatever its origins, it seems to provide the basic imagery through which laymen currently conceive of themselves. Interestingly, a convention seems to have emerged in popular life-story writing where a questionable person proves his claim to normalcy by citing his acquisition of a spouse and children, and, oddly, by attesting to his spending Christmas and Thanksgiving with them.

11. A criminal's view of this nonacceptance is presented in Parker and Allerton, *op. cit.,* pp. 110–111.

12. K. B. Hathaway, *The Little Locksmith* (New York: Coward-McCann, 1943), p. 41, in B. Wright, *Physical Disability—A Psychological Approach* (New York: Harper & Row, 1960), p. 157.

13. *Ibid.,* pp. 46–47. For general treatments of the self-disliking sentiments, see K. Lewin, *Resolving Social Conflicts,* Part III (New York: Harper & Row, 1948); A. Kardiner and L. Ovesey, *The Mark of Oppression: A Psychological Study of the American Negro* (New York: W. W. Norton & Company, 1951); and E. H. Erikson, *Childhood and Society* (New York: W. W. Norton & Company, 1950).

14. F. Warfield, *Keep Listening* (New York: The Viking Press, 1957), p. 76. See also H. von Hentig, *The Criminal and His Victim* (New Haven, CT: Yale University Press, 1948), p. 101.

15. Keitlen, *op. cit.,* Chap. 12, pp. 117–129 and Chap. 14, pp. 137–149. See also Chevigny, *op. cit.,* pp. 85–86.

16. Henrich and Kriegel, *op. cit.,* p. 49.

17. W. Y. Baker and L. H. Smith, "Facial Disfigurement and Personality," *Journal of the American Medical Association,* CXII (1939), 303. Macgregor et al., *op. cit.,* p. 57ff., provide an illustration of a man who used his big red nose for a crutch.

18. Henrich and Kriegel, *op. cit.,* p. 19.

19. *Ibid.,* p. 35.

20. Chevigny, *op. cit.,* p. 154.

21. F. Carlin, *And Yet We Are Human* (London: Chatto & Windus, 1962), pp. 23–24.

22. For one review, see G. W. Allport, *The Nature of Prejudice* (New York: Anchor Books, 1958).

23. Macgregor et al., *op. cit.,* pp. 91–92.

24. From *Clinical Studies in Psychiatry,* H. S. Perry, M. L. Gawel, and M. Gibbon, eds. (New York: W. W. Norton & Company, 1956), p. 145.

25. R. Barker, "The Social Psychology of Physical Disability," *Journal of Social Issues,* IV (1948), 34, suggests that stigmatized persons "live on a social–psychological frontier," constantly facing new situations. See also Macgregor et al., *op. cit.,* p. 87, where the suggestion is made that the grossly deformed need suffer less doubt about their reception in interaction than the less visibly deformed.

26. Barker, *op. cit.,* p. 33.

27. Parker and Allerton, *op. cit.,* p. III.

28. This special kind of self-consciousness is analyzed in S. Messinger, *et al.,* "Life as Theater: Some Notes on the Dramaturgic Approach to Social Reality," *Sociometry,* XXV (1962), 98–110.

29. Parker and Allerton, *op. cit.,* p. III.

30. Chevigny, *op. cit.,* p. 140.

31. L. A. Dexter, "A Social Theory of Mental Deficiency," *American Journal of Mental Deficiency,* LXII (1958), 923. For another study of the mental defective as a stigmatized person, see S. E. Perry, "Some Theoretical Problems of Mental Deficiency and Their Action Implications," *Psychiatry,* XVII (1954), 45–73.

32. Baker, *Out on a Limb* (New York: McGraw-Hill Book Company, n.d.), p. 22.

33. *Ibid.,* p. 73.

34. This theme is well treated in R. K. White, B. A. Wright, and T. Dembo, "Studies in Adjustment to Visible Injuries: Evaluation of Curiosity by the Injured," *Journal of Abnormal and Social Psychology,* XLIII (1948), 13–28.

35. For example, Henrich and Kriegel, *op. cit.*, p. 184.

36. See Wright, *op. cit.*, "The Problem of Sympathy," pp. 233–237.

37. S. Zawadski and P. Lazarsfeld, "The Psychological Consequences of Unemployment," *Journal of Social Psychology*, VI (1935), 239.

38. Hathaway, *op. cit.*, pp. 155–157, in S. Richardson, "The Social Psychological Consequences of Handicapping," unpublished paper presented at the 1962 American Sociological Association Convention, Washington, D.C., 7–8.

39. For a general treatment, see E. Goffman, "Alienation from Interaction," *Human Relations*, X (1957), 47–60.

40. F. Davis, "Deviance Disavowal: The Management of Strained Interaction by the Visibly Handicapped," *Social Problems*, IX (1961), 123. See also White, Wright, and Dembo, *op. cit.*, pp. 26–27.

CHAPTER 10

Stigma: An Enigma Demystified

Lerita M. Coleman-Brown

SUMMARY

Why are some human differences valued and desired while others are devalued, feared or stigmatized? No two human beings are exactly alike, and any difference between human beings has the potential of being stigmatized. In this essay, Lerita Coleman-Brown builds on Erving Goffman's theory of stigma to argue for a view of stigma that would reveal it as a response to the dilemma of difference. Assuming that flawless people don't exist and that some traits are quantifiable (age, for example), relative comparisons can give rise to feelings of superiority, at least in context. In some instances, it might be considered desirable to be older; in others, younger. Thus the sense of being stigmatized is inextricably tied to social context. Moving from one context to another can change both the definition and consequences of a stigma.

The origin of a stigma lies with the perpetual processing of human differences; stigmatizing is a natural response to difference for humans who want to believe in an ordered world. Maintaining the status quo of the social order, then, is often a matter of "marking" individuals with a stigma that stereotypes and exploits them.

Coleman-Brown theorizes that the relation between stigmatized and nonstigmatized people is always an inferior/superior one, and yet she also asks whether stigma would persist if stigmatized people did not feel inferior. The most pernicious consequence of bearing a stigma is that stigmatized people might develop the same concept of false superiority that a stigmatizer must maintain. Thus, stigmatized people might view normality with exaggerated importance, choosing to deny a stigma rather than to identify with it.

At some level, the fear and concern over stigma is a fear of the unpredictability of nature. Stigma represents the uncontrollability of human difference. Coleman-Brown suggests that stigma persists because these fears help to maintain existing social hierarchy, and responsibility for change lies with both the stigmatized and the nonstigmatized alike.

Nature caused us all to be born equal; if fate is pleased to disturb this plan of the general law, it is our responsibility to correct its caprice, and to repair by our attention the usurpations of the stronger.

(Maurice Blanchot)

What is stigma and why does stigma remain? Because stigmas mirror culture and society, they are in constant flux, and therefore the answers to these two questions continue to elude social scientists. Viewing stigma from multiple perspectives exposes its intricate nature and helps us to disentangle its web of complexities and paradoxes. Stigma represents a view of life; a set of personal and social constructs; a set of social relations and social relationships; a form of social reality. Stigma has been a difficult concept to conceptualize because it reflects a property, a process, a form of social categorization, and an affective state.

Two primary questions, then, that we as social scientists have addressed are how and why during certain historical periods, in specific cultures or within particular social groups, some human differences are valued and desired, and other human differences are devalued, feared, or stigmatized. In attempting to answer these questions, I propose another view of stigma, one that takes into account its behavioral, cognitive, and affective components and reveals that stigma is a response to the dilemma of difference.

THE DILEMMA

No two human beings are exactly alike: there are countless ways to differ. Shape, size, skin color, gender, age, cultural background, personality, and years of formal education are just a few of the infinite number of ways in which people can vary. Perceptually, and in actuality, there is greater variation on some of these dimensions than on others. Age and gender, for example, are dimensions with limited and quantifiable ranges; yet they interact exponentially with other physical or social characteristics that have larger continua (e.g., body shape, income, cultural background) to create a vast number of human differences. Goffman states, though, that "stigma is equivalent to an undesired differentness" (see Stafford & Scott, 1986). The infinite variety of human attributes suggests that what is undesired or stigmatized is heavily dependent on the social context and to some extent arbitrarily defined. The large number of stigmatizable attributes and several taxonomies of stigmas in the literature offer further evidence of how arbitrary the selection of

undesired differences may be (see Ainlay & Crosby, 1986; Becker & Arnold, 1986; Solomon, 1900, Stafford & Scott, 1986).

What is most poignant about Goffman's description of stigma is that it suggests that all human differences are potentially stigmatizable. As we move out of one social context where a difference is desired into another context where the difference is undesired, we begin to feel the effects of stigma. This conceptualization of stigma also indicates that those possessing power, the dominant group, can determine which human differences are desired and undesired. In part, stigmas reflect the value judgments of a dominant group.

Many people, however, especially those who have some role in determining the desired and undesired differences of the zeitgeist, often think of stigma only as a property of individuals. They operate under the illusion that stigma exists only for certain segments of the population. But the truth is that any "nonstigmatized" person can easily become "stigmatized." "Nearly everyone at some point in life will experience stigma either temporarily or permanently. ... Why do we persist in this denial?" (Zola, 1979, p. 454). Given that human differences serve as the basis for stigmas, being or feeling stigmatized is virtually an inescapable fate. Because stigmas differ depending upon the culture and the historical period, it becomes evident that it is mere chance whether a person is born into a nonstigmatized or severely stigmatized group.

Because stigmatization often occurs within the confines of a psychologically constructed or actual social relationship, the experience itself reflects relative comparisons, the contrasting of desired and undesired differences. Assuming that flawless people do not exist, relative comparisons give rise to a feeling of superiority in some contexts (where one possesses a desired trait that another person is lacking) but perhaps a feeling of inferiority in other contexts (where one lacks a desired trait that another person possesses). It is also important to note that it is only when we make comparisons that we can feel different. Stigmatization or feeling stigmatized is a consequence of social comparison. For this reason, stigma represents a continuum of undesired differences that depend upon many factors (e.g., geographical location, culture, life cycle stage) (see Becker & Arnold, 1986).

Although some stigmatized conditions appear escapable or may be temporary, some undesired traits have graver social consequences than others. Being a medical resident, being a new professor, being 7 feet tall, having cancer, being black, or being physically disfigured or mentally retarded can all lead to feelings of stigmatization (feeling discredited or devalued in a particular role), but obviously these are not equally stigmatizing conditions. The degree of stigmatization might depend on how undesired the difference is in a particular social group.

Physical abnormalities, for example, may be the most severely stigmatized differences because they are physically salient, represent some deficiency or distortion in the bodily form, and in most cases are unalterable. Other physically salient differences, such as skin color or nationality, are considered very stigmatizing because they also are permanent conditions and cannot be changed. Yet the stigmatization that one feels as a result of being black or Jewish or Japanese depends on the social context, specifically social contexts in which one's skin color or nationality is not a desired one. A white American could feel temporarily stigmatized when visiting Japan due to a difference in height. A black student could feel stigmatized in a predominantly white university because the majority of the students are white and white skin is a desired trait. But a black student in a predominantly black university is not likely to feel the effects of stigma. Thus, the sense of being stigmatized or having a stigma is inextricably tied to social context. Of equal importance are the norms in that context that determine which are desirable and undesirable attributes. Moving from one social or cultural context to another can change both the definitions and the consequences of stigma.

Stigma often results in a special kind of downward mobility. Part of the power of stigmatization lies in the realization that people who are stigmatized or acquire a stigma lose their place in the social hierarchy. Consequently, most people want to ensure that they are counted in the nonstigmatized "majority." This, of course, leads to more stigmatization.

Stigma, then, is also a term that connotes a relationship. It seems that this relationship is vital to understanding the stigmatizing process. Stigma allows some individuals to feel superior to others. Superiority and inferiority, however, are two sides of the same coin. In order for one person to feel superior, there must be another person who is perceived to be or who actually feels inferior. Stigmatized people are needed in order for the many nonstigmatized people to feel good about themselves.

On the other hand, there are many stigmatized people who feel inferior and concede that other persons are superior because they possess certain attributes. In order for the process to occur (for one person to stigmatize another and have the stigmatized person feel the effects of stigma), there must be some agreement that the differentness is inherently undesirable. Moreover, even among stigmatized people, relative comparisons are made, and people are reassured by the fact that there is someone else who is worse off. The dilemma of difference, therefore, affects both stigmatized and nonstigmatized people.

Some might contend that this is the very old scapegoat argument, and there is some truth to that contention. But the issues here are more finely intertwined. If stigma is a social construct, constructed by cultures, by social groups, and by individuals to designate some human differences as discrediting, then the stigmatization process is indeed a powerful and pernicious social tool. The inferiority/superiority issue is a most interesting way of understanding how and why people continue to stigmatize.

Some stigmas are more physically salient than others, and some people are more capable of concealing their stigmas or escaping from the negative social consequences of being stigmatized. The ideal prototype (e.g., young, white, tall, married, male, with a recent record in sports) that Stafford cites may actually possess traits that would be the source of much scorn and derision in another social context. Yet, by insulating himself in his own community, a man like the one described in the example can ensure that his "differentness" will receive approbation rather than rejection, and he will not be subject to constant and severe stigmatization. This is a common response to stigma among people with some social influence (e.g., artists, academics, millionaires). Often, attributes or behaviors that might otherwise be considered "abnormal" or stigmatized are labeled as "eccentric" among persons of power or influence. The fact that what is perceived as the "ideal" person varies from one social context to another, however, is tied to Martin's notion that people learn ways to stigmatize in each new situation.

In contrast, some categories of stigmatized people (e.g., the physically disabled, members of ethnic groups, poor people) cannot alter their stigmas nor easily disguise them. People, then, feel permanently stigmatized in contexts where their differentness is undesired and in social environments that they cannot easily escape. Hence, power,

social influence, and social control play a major role in the stigmatization process.

In summary, stigma stems from differences. By focusing on differences we actively create stigmas because any attribute or difference is potentially stigmatizable. Often we attend to a single different attribute rather than to the large number of similar attributes that any two individuals share. Why people focus on differences and denigrate people on the basis of them is important to understanding how some stigmas originate and persist. By reexamining the historical origins of stigma and the way children develop the propensity to stigmatize, we can see how some differences evolve into stigmas and how the process is linked to the behavioral (social control), affective (fear, dislike), and cognitive (perception of differences, social categorization) components of stigma.

THE ORIGINS OF STIGMA

The phrase *to stigmatize* originally referred to the branding or marking of certain people (e.g., criminals, prostitutes) in order to make them appear different and separate from others (Goffman, 1963). The act of marking people in this way resulted in exile or avoidance. In most cultures, physical marking or branding has declined, but a more cognitive manifestation of stigmatization—social marking—has increased and has become the basis for most stigmas (Jones *et al.*, 1984). Goffman points out, though, that stigma has retained much of its original connotation. People use differences to exile or avoid others. In addition, what is most intriguing about the ontogenesis of the stigma concept is the broadening of its predominant affective responses such as dislike and disgust to include the emotional reaction of fear. Presently, *fear* may be instrumental in the perpetuation of stigma and in maintaining its original social functions. Yet as the developmental literature reveals, fear is not a natural but an acquired response to differences of stigmas.

Sigelman and Singleton (1986) offer a number of insightful observations about how children learn to stigmatize. Children develop a natural wariness of strangers as their ability to differentiate familiar from novel objects increases (Sroufe, 1977). Developmental psychologists note that stranger anxiety is a universal phenomenon in infants and appears around the age of seven months. This reaction to differences (e.g., women versus men, children versus adults, blacks versus whites) is an interesting one and, as Sigelman and Singleton point out, may serve as a prototype for stigmatizing. Many children respond in a positive (friendly) or negative (fearful, apprehensive) manner to strangers. Strangers often arouse the interest (Brooks & Lewis, 1976) of children but elicit negative reactions if they intrude on their personal space (Sroufe, 1977). Stranger anxiety tends to fade with age, but when coupled with self-referencing it may create the conditions for a child to learn how to respond to human differences or how to stigmatize.

Self-referencing, or the use of another's interpretation of a situation to form one's own understanding of it, commonly occurs in young children. Infants often look toward caregivers when encountering something different, such as a novel object, person, or event (Feinman, 1982). The response to novel stimuli in an ambiguous situation may depend on the emotional displays of the caregiver; young children have been known to respond positively to situations if their mothers respond reassuringly (Feinman, 1982). Self-referencing is instrumental to understanding the development of stigmatization because it may be through this process that caregivers shape young children's responses to people, especially those who possess physically salient differences (Klinnert, Campos, Sorce, Emde, & Svejda, 1983). We may continue to learn

about how to stigmatize from other important figures (e.g., mentors, role models) as we progress through the life cycle. Powerful authority figures may serve as the source of self-referencing behavior in new social contexts (Martin, 1986).

Sigelman and Singleton (1986) also point out that preschoolers notice differences and tend to establish preferences but do not necessarily stigmatize. Even on meeting other children with physical disabilities, children do not automatically eschew them but may respond to actual physical and behavioral similarities and differences. There is evidence, moreover, indicating that young children are curious about human differences and often stare at novel stimuli (Brooks & Lewis, 1976). Children frequently inquire of their parents or of stigmatized persons about their distinctive physical attributes. In many cases, the affective response of young children is interest rather than fear.

Barbarin (1986) offers a poignant example of the difference between interest and fear in his vignette about Myra, a child with cancer. She talks about young children who are honest and direct about her illness, an attitude that does not cause her consternation. What does disturb her, though, are parents who will not permit her to baby-sit with their children for *fear* that she might give them cancer. Thus, interest and curiosity about stigma or human differences may be natural for children, but they must *learn* fear and avoidance as well as which categories or attributes to dislike, *fear*, or stigmatize. Children may learn to stigmatize without ever grasping "why" they do so (Martin, 1986), just as adults have beliefs about members of stigmatized groups without ever having met any individuals from the group (Crocker & Lutsky, 1986). The predisposition to stigmatize is passed from one generation to the next through social learning (Martin, 1986) or socialization (Crocker & Lutsky, 1986; Stafford & Scott, 1986).

Sigelman and Singleton agree with Martin that social norms subtly impinge upon the information-processing capacities of young children so that negative responses to stigma later become automatic. At some point, the development of social cognition must intersect with the affective responses that parents or adults display toward stigmatized people. Certain negative emotions become attached to social categories (e.g., *all* ex-mental patients are dangerous, *all* blacks are angry or harmful). Although the attitudes (cognitions) about stigma assessed in paper-and-pencil tasks may change in the direction of what is socially acceptable, the affect and behavior of elementary- and secondary-school children as well as adults reflect the early negative affective associations with stigma. The norms about stigma, though, are ambiguous and confusing. They teach young children to avoid or dislike stigmatized people, even though similar behavior in adults is considered socially unacceptable.

STIGMA AS A FORM OF COGNITIVE PROCESSING

The perceptual processing of human differences appears to be universal. Ainlay and Crosby (1986) suggest that differences arouse us; they can please or distress us. From a phenomenological perspective, we carry around "recipes" and "typifications" as structures for categorizing and ordering stimuli. Similarly, social psychologists speak of our need to categorize social stimuli in such terms as *schemas* and *stereotypes* (Crocker & Lutsky, 1986). These approaches to the perception of human differences indirectly posit that stigmatizing is a natural response, a way to maintain order in a potentially chaotic world of social stimuli. People want to believe that the world is ordered.

Although various approaches to social categorization may explain how people stereotype on the basis of a specific attribute (e.g., skin color, religious beliefs, deafness), they do not explain the next step—the negative imputations. Traditional approaches to sociocognitive processing also do not offer ideas about how people can perceptually move beyond the stereotype, the typification, or stigma to perceive an individual. Studies of stereotyping and stigma regularly reveal that beliefs about the inferiority of a person predominate in the thoughts of the perceiver (Crocker & Lutsky, 1986).

Stigma appears to be a special and insidious kind of social categorization or, as Martin explains, a process of generalizing from a single experience. People are treated categorically rather than individually, and in the process are devalued (Ainlay & Crosby, 1986; Barbarin, 1986; Crocker & Lutsky, 1986; Stafford & Scott, 1986). In addition, as Crocker and Lutsky point out, coding people in terms of categories (e.g., "X is a redhead") instead of specific attributes ("X has red hair") allows people to feel that stigmatized persons are fundamentally different and establishes greater psychological and social distance.

A discussion of the perceptual basis of stigma inevitably leads back to the notion of master status (Goffman, 1963). Perceptually, stigma becomes the master status, the attribute that colors the perception of the entire person. All other aspects of the person are ignored except those that fit the stereotype associated with the stigma (Kanter, 1979). Stigma as a form of negative stereotyping has a way of neutralizing positive qualities and undermining the identity of stigmatized individuals (Barbarin, 1986). This kind of social categorization has also been described by one sociologist as a "discordance with personal attributes" (Davis, 1964). Thus, many stigmatized people are not expected to be intelligent, attractive, or upper class.

Another important issue in the perception of human differences or social cognition is the relative comparisons that are made between and within stigmatized and nonstigmatized groups. Several authors discuss the need for people to accentuate between-group differences and minimize within-group differences as a requisite for group identity (Ainlay & Crosby, 1986; Crocker & Lutsky, 1986; Sigelman & Singleton, 1986). Yet these authors do not explore in depth the reasons for denigrating the attributes of the out-group members and elevating the attributes of one's own group, unless there is some feeling that the out-group could threaten the balance of power. Crocker and Lutsky note, however, that stereotyping is frequently tied to the need for self-enhancement. People with low self-esteem are more likely to identify and maintain negative stereotypes about members of stigmatized groups; such people are more negative in general. This line of reasoning takes us back to viewing stigma as a means of maintaining the status quo through social control. Could it be that stigma as a perceptual tool helps to reinforce the differentiation of the population that in earlier times was deliberately designated by marking? One explanation offered by many theorists is that stereotypes about stigmatized groups help to maintain the exploitation of such groups and preserve the existing societal structure.

Are there special arrangements or special circumstance, Ainlay and Crosby ask, that allow people to notice differences but not denigrate those who have them? On occasion, nonstigmatized people are able to "break through" and to see a stigmatized person as a real, whole person with a variety of attributes, some similar traits and some different from their own (Davis, 1964). Just how frequently and in what ways does this happen?

Ainlay and Crosby suggest that we begin to note differences within a type when we *need* to do so. The example they give about telephones is a good one. We learn differences among types of telephones, appliances, schools, or even groups of people when we need to. Hence stereotyping or stigmatizing is not necessarily automatic; when we want to perceive differences we perceive them, just as we perceive similarities when we *want* to. In some historical instances, society appears to have recognized full human potential when it was required, while ignoring certain devalued traits. When women were needed to occupy traditionally male occupations in the United States during World War II, gender differences were ignored as they have been ignored in other societies when women were needed for combat. Similarly, the U.S. armed forces became racially integrated when there was a need for more soldiers to fight in World War II (Terry, 1984).

Thus, schemas or stereotypes about stigmatized individuals can be modified but only under specific conditions. When stigmatized people have essential information or possess needed expertise, we discover that some of their attributes are not so different, or that they are more similar to us than different. "Cooperative interdependence" stemming from shared goals may change the nature of perceptions and the nature of relationships (Crocker & Lutsky, 1986). Future research on stigma and on social perception might continue to investigate the conditions under which people are less likely to stereotype and more likely to respond to individuals rather than categories (cf., Locksley, Borgida, Brekke, & Hepburn, 1980; Locksley, Hepburn & Ortiz, 1982).

THE MEANING OF STIGMA FOR SOCIAL RELATIONS

I have intimated that "stigmatized" and "nonstigmatized" people are tied together in a perpetual inferior/superior relationship. This relationship is key to understanding the meaning of stigma. To conceptualize stigma as a social relationship raises some vital questions about stigma. These questions include (a) when and under what conditions does an attribute become a stigmatized one? (b) can a person experience stigmatization without knowing that a trait is devalued in a specific social context? (c) does a person feel stigmatized even though in a particular social context the attribute is not stigmatized or the stigma is not physically or behaviorally apparent? (d) can a person refuse to be stigmatized or destigmatize an attribute by ignoring the prevailing norms that define it as a stigma?

These questions lead to another one: Would stigma persist if stigmatized people did not feel stigmatized or inferior? Certainly, a national pride did not lessen the persecution of the Jews, nor does it provide freedom for blacks in South Africa. These two examples illustrate how pervasive and powerful the social control aspects of stigma are, empowering the stigmatizer and stripping the stigmatized of power. Yet a personal awakening, a discovery that the responsibility for being stigmatized does not lie with oneself, is important. Understanding that the rationale for discrimination and segregation based on stigma lies in the mind of the stigmatizer has led people like Mahatma Gandhi and civil rights activist Rosa Parks to rise above the feeling of stigmatization, to ignore the norms, and to disobey the existing laws based on stigma. There have been women, elderly adults, gays, disabled people, and many others who at some point realized that their fundamental similarities outweighed and outnumbered their differences. It becomes clear that in most oppressive situations the primary problem lies with the stigmatizer and not with the stigmatized (Sartre, 1948; Schur, 1980, 1983). Many stigmatized people also begin to understand that the stigmatizer, having established a position of false superiority and consequently the need

to maintain it, is enslaved to the concept that stigmatized people are fundamentally inferior. In fact, some stigmatized individuals question the norms about stigma and attempt to change the social environments for their peers.

In contrast, there are some stigmatized persons who accept their devalued status as legitimate. Attempting to "pass" and derogating others like themselves are two ways in which stigmatized people effectively accept the society's negative perceptions of their stigma (Goffman, cited in Gibbons, 1986). It is clear, especially from accounts of those who move from a nonstigmatized to a stigmatized role, that stigmatization is difficult to resist if everyone begins to reinforce the inferior status with their behavior. Two of the most common ways in which nonstigmatized people convey a sense of fundamental inferiority to stigmatized people are social rejection or social isolation and lowered expectations.

There are many ways in which people communicate social rejection such as speech, eye contact, and interpersonal distance. The stigmatized role, as conceptualized by the symbolic interactionism approach, is similar to any other role (e.g., professor, doctor) in which we behave according to the role expectations of others and change our identity to be congruent with them. Thus, in the case of stigma, role expectations are often the same as the stereotypes. Some stigmatized people become dependent, passive, helpless, and childlike because that is what is expected of them.

Social rejection or avoidance affects not only the stigmatized individual but everyone who is socially involved, such as family, friends, and relatives (Barbarin, 1986). This permanent form of social quarantine forces people to limit their relationships to other stigmatized people and to those for whom the social bond outweighs the stigma, such as family members. In this way, avoidance or social rejection also acts as a form of social control or containment (Edgerton, 1967; Goffman, 1963; Schur, 1983; Scott, 1969). Social rejection is perhaps most difficult for younger children who are banned from most social activities of their peers.

Social exile conveys another message about expectations. Many stigmatized people are not encouraged to develop or grow, to have aspirations or to be successful. Barbarin reports that children with cancer lose friendships and receive special, lenient treatment from teachers. They are not expected to achieve in the same manner as other children. Parents, too, sometimes allow stigmatized children to behave in ways that "normal" children in the same family are not permitted to do. Social exclusion as well as overprotection can lead to decreased performance. Lowered expectations also lead to decreased self-esteem.

The negative identity that ensues becomes a pervasive personality trait and inhibits the stigmatized person from developing other parts of the self. Another detrimental aspect of stigmatization is the practice of treating people, such as the ex-con and ex-mental patient who are attempting to reintegrate themselves into society, as if they still had the stigma. Even the terms we use to describe such persons suggest that role expectations remain the same despite the stigmatized person's efforts to relinquish them. It seems that the paradoxical societal norms that establish a subordinate and dependent position for stigmatized people while ostracizing them for it may stem from the need of nonstigmatized people to maintain a sense of superiority. Their position is supported and reinforced by their perceptions that stigmatized people are fundamentally inferior, passive, helpless, and childlike.

The most pernicious consequence of bearing a stigma is that stigmatized people may develop the same perceptual problems that nonstigmatized people have. They begin to see themselves and their lives through the stigma, or as Sartre (1948) writes about the Jews, they "allow themselves to be poisoned by the stereotype and live in fear that they will correspond to it" (p. 95). As Gibbons observes, stigmatized individuals sometimes blame their difficulties on the stigmatized trait, rather than confronting the root of their personal difficulties. Thus, normal issues that one encounters in life often act as a barrier to growth for stigmatized people because of the attributional process involved.

The need to maintain one's identity manifests itself in a number of ways, such as the mischievous behavior of the adolescent boy with cancer cited in Barbarin's chapter. "Attaining normalcy within the limits of stigma" (Tracy & Gussow, 1978) seems to be another way of describing the need to establish or recapture one's identity (Weiner, 1975).

Stigma uniquely alters perceptions in other ways, especially with respect to the notion of "normality," and raises other questions about the dilemma of difference. Most people do not want to be perceived as different or "abnormal." Becker and Arnold and Gibbons discuss normalization as attempts to be "not different" and to appear "normal." Such strategies include "passing" or disguising the stigma and acting "normal" by "covering up"—keeping up with the pace of nonstigmatized individuals (Davis, 1964; Gibbons, 1986; Goffman, 1963; Weiner, 1975). For stigmatized people, the idea of normality takes on an exaggerated importance. Normality becomes the supreme goal for many stigmatized individuals until they realize that there is no precise definition of normality except what they would be without their stigma. Given the dilemma of difference that stigma reflects, it is not clear whether anyone can ever feel "normal."

Out of this state of social isolation and lowered expectations, though, can arise some positive consequences. Although the process can be fraught with pain and difficulty, stigmatized people who manage to reject the perceptions of themselves as inferior often come away with greater inner strength (Jones *et al.*, 1984). They learn to depend on their own resources and, like the earlier examples of Mahatma Gandhi and Rosa Parks, they begin to question the bases for defining normality. Many stigmatized people regain their identity through redefining normality and realizing that it is acceptable to be who they are (Ablon, 1981; Barbarin, 1986; Becker, 1980; Becker & Arnold, 1986).

FEAR AND STIGMA

Fear is important to a discussion of how and why stigma persists. In many cultures that do not use the term *stigma*, there is some emotional reaction beyond interest or curiosity to differences such as children who are born with birthmarks, epilepsy, or a caul. Certain physical characteristics or illnesses elicit fear because the etiology of the attribute or disease is unknown, unpredictable, and unexpected (Sontag, 1979). People even have fears about the sexuality of certain stigmatized groups such as persons who are mentally retarded, feeling that if they are allowed to reproduce they will have retarded offspring (Gibbons, 1986). It seems that what gives stigma its intensity and reality is fear.

The nature of the fear appears to vary with the type of stigma. For most stigmas stemming from physical or mental problems, including cancer, people experience fear of contagion even though they know that the stigma cannot be developed through contact (see Barbarin, 1986). This fear usually stems from not knowing about the etiology of a condition, its predictability, and its course.

The stigmatization of certain racial, ethnic, and gender categories may also be based on fear. This fear, though, cannot stem from contagion because attributes (of skin color, ethnic background, and gender) cannot possibly be transmitted to non-stigmatized people. One explanation for the fear is that people want to avoid "courtesy stigmas" or stigmatization by association (Goffman, 1963). Another explanation underlying this type of fear may be the notion of scarce resources. This is the perception that if certain groups of people are allowed to have a share in all resources, there will not be enough: not enough jobs, not enough land, not enough water, or not enough food. Similar explanations from the deviance literature suggest that people who stigmatize feel threatened and collectively feel that their position of social, economic, and political dominance will be dismantled by members of stigmatized groups (Schur, 1980, 1983). A related explanation is provided by Hughes, who states, "that it may be that those whose positions are insecure and whose hopes for the higher goals are already fading express more violent hostility to new people" (1945, p. 356 [in Hughes & Coser, 1994, p. 155]). This attitude may account for the increased aggression toward members of stigmatized groups during dire economic periods.

Fear affects not only nonstigmatized but stigmatized individuals as well. Many stigmatized people (e.g., ex-cons, mentally retarded adults) who are attempting to "pass" live in fear that their stigmatized attribute will be discovered (Gibbons, 1986). These fears are grounded in a realistic assessment of the negative social consequences of stigmatization and reflect the long-term social and psychological damage to individuals resulting from stigma.

At some level, therefore, most people are concerned with stigma because they are fearful of its unpredictable and uncontrollable nature. Stigmatization appears uncontrollable because human differences serve as the basis for stigmas. Therefore, *any* attribute can become a stigma. No one really ever knows when or if he or she will acquire a stigma or when societal norms might change to stigmatize a trait he or she already possesses. To deny this truth by attempting to isolate stigmatized people or escape from stigma is a manifestation of the underlying fear.

The unpredictability of stigma is similar to the unpredictability of death. Both Gibbons and Barbarin note that the development of a stigmatized condition in a loved one or in oneself represents a major breach of trust—a destruction of the belief that life is predictable. In a sense, stigma represents a kind of death—a social death. Nonstigmatized people, through avoidance and social rejection, often treat stigmatized people as if they were invisible, nonexistent, or dead. Many stigmas, in particular childhood cancer, remove the usual disguises of mortality. Such stigmas can act as a symbolic reminder of everyone's inevitable death (see Barbarin's discussion of Ernest Becker's, *The Denial of Death*). These same fears can be applied to the acquisition of other stigmas (e.g., mental illness, physical disabilities) and help to intensify and perpetuate the negative responses to most stigmatized categories. Thus, irrational fears may help stigmatization to be self-perpetuating with little encouragement needed in the form of forced segregation from the political and social structure.

The ultimate answers about why stigma persists may lie in an examination of why people fear differences, fear the future, fear the unknown, and therefore stigmatize that which is different and unknown. An equally important issue to investigate is how stigmatization may be linked to the fear of being different.

CONCLUSION

Stigma is clearly a very complex multidisciplinary issue, with each additional perspective containing another piece of this enigma. A multidisciplinary approach allowed us as social scientists to perceive stigma as a whole; to see from within it rather than to look down upon it. Our joint perspectives have also demonstrated that there are many shared ideas across disciplines, and in many cases only the terminology is different.

Three important aspects of stigma emerge from this multidisciplinary examination and may forecast its future. They are fear, stigma's primary affective component; stereotyping, its primary cognitive component; and social control, its primary behavioral component. The study of the relationship of stigma to fear, stereotyping, and social control may elucidate our understanding of the paradoxes that a multidisciplinary perspective reveals. It may also bring us closer to understanding what stigma really is—not primarily a property of individuals as many have conceptualized it to be but a humanly constructed perception, constantly in flux and legitimizing our negative responses to human differences (Ainlay & Crosby, 1986). To further clarify the definition of stigma, one must differentiate between an "undesired differentness" that is likely to lead to feelings of stigmatization and actual forms of stigmatization. *It appears that stigmatization occurs only when the social control component is imposed, or when the undesired differentness leads to some restriction in physical and social mobility and access to opportunities that allow an individual to develop his or her potential. This definition combines the original meaning of stigma with more contemporary connotations and uses.*

In another vein, stigma is a statement about personal and social responsibility. People irrationally feel that, by separating themselves from stigmatized individuals, they may reduce their own risk of acquiring the stigma (Barbarin, 1986). By isolating individuals, people feel they can also isolate the problem. If stigma is ignored, the responsibility for its existence and perpetuation can be shifted elsewhere. Making stigmatized people feel responsible for their own stigma allows nonstigmatized people to relinquish the onus for creating or perpetuating the conditions that surround it.

Changing political and economic climates are also important to the stigmatization and destigmatization process. What is economically feasible or politically enhancing for a group in power will partially determine what attributes are stigmatized, or at least how they are stigmatized. As many sociologists have suggested, some people are stigmatized for violating norms, whereas others are stigmatized for being of little economic or political value (Birenbaum & Sagarin, 1976, cited in Stafford & Scott, 1986). We should admit that stigma persists as a social problem because it continues to have some of its original social utility as a means of controlling certain segments of the population and ensuring that power is not easily exchanged. Stigma helps to maintain the existing social hierarchy.

One might then ask if there will ever be societies or historical periods without stigma. Some authors hold a positive vision of the future. Gibbons, for example, suggests that as traditionally stigmatized groups become more integrated into the general population, stigmatizing attributes will lose some of their onus. But historical analysis would suggest that new stigmas will replace old ones. Educational programs are probably of only limited help, as learning to stigmatize is a part of early social learning experiences (Martin, 1986; Sigelman & Singleton, 1986). The social learning of stigma is indeed very different from learning about the concept abstractly in a classroom. School experiences sometimes merely reinforce what children learn about stigmatization from parents and significant others.

From a sociological perspective, the economic, psychological, and social benefits of stigma sustain it. Stigmas will disappear when we no longer need to legitimize social exclusion and segregation (Zola, 1979). From the perspective of cognitive psychology, when people find it necessary or beneficial to perceive the fundamental similarities they share with stigmatized people rather than the differences, we will see the beginnings of a real elimination of stigma. This process may have already occurred during some particular historical period or within particular societies. It is certainly an important area for historians, anthropologists, and psychologists to explore.

Although it would seem that the core of the problem lies with the nonstigmatized individuals, stigmatized people also play an important role in the destigmatization process. Stigma contests, or the struggles to determine which attributes are devalued and to what extent they are devalued, involve stigmatized and nonstigmatized individuals alike (Schur, 1980). Stigmatized people, too, have choices as to whether to accept their stigmatized condition and the negative social consequences or continue to fight for more integration into nonstigmatized communities. Their cognitive and affective attitudes toward themselves as individuals and as a group are no small element in shaping societal responses to them. As long as they continue to focus on the negative, affective components of stigma, such as low self-esteem, it is not likely that their devalued status will change. Self-help groups may play an important role in countering this tendency.

There is volition or personal choice. Each stigmatized or nonstigmatized individual can choose to feel superior or inferior, and each individual can make choices about social control and about fear. Sartre (1948) views this as the choice between authenticity or authentic freedom, and inauthenticity or fear of being oneself. Each individual can choose to ignore social norms regarding stigma. Personal beliefs about a situation or circumstance often differ from norms, but people usually follow the social norms anyway, fearing to step beyond conformity to exercise their own personal beliefs about stigma (see Ainlay & Crosby, 1986; and Stafford & Scott, 1986, discussions of personal versus socially shared forms of stigma). Changing human behavior is not as simple as encouraging people to exercise their personal beliefs. As social scientists, we know a number of issues may be involved in the way personal volition interacts with social norms and personal values.

The multidisciplinary approach could be used in a variety of creative ways to study stigma and other social problems. Different models of how stigma has evolved and is perpetuated could be subject to test by a number of social scientists. They could combine their efforts to examine whether stigma evolves in a similar manner in different cultures, or among children of different cultural and social backgrounds, or during different historical periods. The study of stigma encompasses as many factors and dimensions as are represented in a multidisciplinary approach. All of the elements are interactive and in constant flux. The effective, cognitive, and behavioral dimensions are subject to the current cultural, historical, political, and economic climates, which are in turn linked to the norms and laws. We know that the responses of stigmatized and nonstigmatized individuals may at times appear to be separate, we know that they are also interconnected and may produce other responses when considered together. This portrayal of the issues vital to the study of stigma is neither exhaustive nor definitive. It does suggest, however, that a multidimensional model of stigma is needed to understand how these factors, dimensions, and responses co-vary.

We need more cross-disciplinary research from researchers who do not commonly study stigma. For example, a joint project among historians, psychologists, economists, and political scientists might examine the relationship between economic climate, perceptions of scarcity, and stigmatization. Other joint ventures by anthropologists and economists could design research on how much income is lost over a lifetime by members of a stigmatized category (e.g., blind, deaf, overweight), and how this loss adversely affects the gross national product (GNP) and the overall economy. Another example would be work by political scientists and historians or anthropologists to understand the links between the stigmatization of specific attributes and the maintenance of social control and power by certain political groups. Psychologists might team up with novelists or anthropologists to use case studies to understand individual differences or to examine how some stigmatized persons overcome their discredited status. Other studies of the positive consequences of stigma might include a joint investigation by anthropologists and psychologists of cultures that successfully integrate stigmatized individuals into nonstigmatized communities and utilize whatever resources or talents a stigmatized person has to offer (as the shaman is used in many societies) (Halifax, 1979, 1982).

The study of stigma by developmental and social psychologists, sociologists, anthropologists, economists, and historians may also offer new insights into the evolution of sex roles and sex role identity across the life cycle and during changing economic climates. Indeed, linguists, psychologists, and sociologists may be able to chronicle the changes in identity and self-concept of stigmatized and nonstigmatized alike, by studying the way people describe themselves and the language they use in their interactions with stigmatized and nonstigmatized others (Coleman, 1985; Edelsky & Rosengrant, 1981).

The real challenge for social scientists will be to better understand the need to stigmatize; the need for people to reject rather than accept others; the need for people to denigrate rather than uplift others. We need to know more about the relationship between stigma and perceived threat, and how stigma may represent "the kinds of deviance that it seeks out" (Schur, 1980, p. 22). Finally, social scientists need to concentrate on designing an optimal system in which every member of society is permitted to develop one's talents and experience one's full potential regardless of any particular attribute. If such a society were to come about, then perhaps some positive consequences would arise from the dilemma of difference.

REFERENCES

Ablon, J. 1981. "Stigmatized health conditions." *Social Science and Medicine* 15: 5–9.

Ainlay, S. and F. Crosby. 1986. "Stigma, Justice and the Dilemma of Difference." In S. Ainlay, G. Becker, and L. M. Coleman, *The Dilemma of Difference: A Multicultural View of Stigma*. New York: Plenum, 17–38.

Barbarin, O. 1986. "Family Experience of Stigma in Childhood Cancer." In S. Ainlay, G. Becker, and L. M. Coleman, *The Dilemma of Difference: A Multicultural View of Stigma*. New York: Plenum, 163–184.

Becker, G. 1980. *Growing Old in Silence*. Berkeley: University of California Press.

Becker, G. and R. Arnold. 1986. "Stigma as Social and Cultural Construct." In S. Ainlay, G. Becker, and L. M. Coleman, *The Dilemma of Difference: A Multicultural View of Stigma*. New York. Plenum, 39–58.

Brooks, J. and Lewis, M. 1976. "Infants' responses to strangers: Midget, adult, and child." *Child Development* 47: 323–332.

Coleman, L. 1985. "Language and the Evolution of Identity and Self-concept." In F. Kessel, ed., *The Development of Language And Language Researchers: Essays in Honor of Roger Brown*. Hillsdale, NJ: Erlbaum.

Crocker, J. and N. Lutsky. 1986. "Stigma and the Dynamics of Social Cognition." In S. Ainlay, G. Becker, and L. M. Coleman, *The Dilemma of Difference: A Multicultural View of Stigma*. New York. Plenum, 95–122.

Davis, F. 1964. "Deviance Disavowal: The Management of Strained Interaction by the Visibly Handicapped." In H. Becker, ed., *The Other Side*. New York: Free Press, 119–138.

Edelsky, C. and T. Rosengrant. 1981. "Interactions with handicapped children: Who's handicapped?" *Sociolinguistic Working Paper* 92. Austin, TX: Southwest Educational Development Laboratory.

Edgerton, R. G. 1967. *The Cloak of Competence: Stigma in the Lives of the Mentally Retarded*. Berkeley: University of California Press.

Feinman, S. 1982. "Social referencing in infancy." *Merrill-Palmer Quarterly* 28: 445–70.

Gibbons, F. X. 1986. "Stigma and Interpersonal Relations." In S. Ainlay, G. Becker, and L. M. Coleman, *The Dilemma of Difference: A Multicultural View of Stigma*. New York. Plenum, 123–144.

Goffman. E. 1963. *Stigma: Notes on the Management of Spoiled Identity*. Englewood Cliffs, NJ: Prentice Hall.

Halifax, J. 1979. *Shamanic Voices: A Survey of Visionary Narratives*. New York: Dutton.

———. 1982. *Shaman: The Wounded Healer*. London: Thames and Hudson.

Hughes, E. C. and L. A. Coser. 1994. *On Work, Race, and the Sociological Imagination*. Chicago: University of Chicago Press.

Jones. E. E., A. Farina, A. H. Hastof, H. Markus, D. T. Miller, and R. A. Scott. 1984. *Social Stigma: The Psychology of Marked Relationships*. New York: Freeman.

Kanter, R. M. 1979. *Men and Women of the Corporation*. New York: Basic Books.

Klinnert, M. D., J. J. Campos, J. F. Sorce, R. Emde, and M. Svejda. 1983. "Emotions as Behavior Regulators: Social Referencing in Infancy." In R. Plutchik and H. Kellerman, eds. *Emotion Theory, Research, and Experience. Vol. II. Emotions in Early Development*. New York: Academic Press, 57–88.

Locksley, A., E. Borgida, N. Brekke, and C. Hepburn. 1980. "Sexual stereotypes and social judgment." *Journal of Personality and Social Psychology* 39: 821–31.

Locksley, A., C. Hepburn, and V. Ortiz. 1982. "Social stereotypes and judgments of individuals: An instance of the base-rate fallacy." *Journal of Experimental Social Psychology* 18: 23–42.

Martin, L. G. 1986. "Stigma: A Social Learning Perspective." In S. Ainlay, G. Becker, and L. M. Coleman, *The Dilemma of Difference: A Multicultural View of Stigma*. New York. Plenum, 1–16.

Sartre, J. 1948. *Anti-Semite and Jew*. New York: Schocken Books.

Schur, E. 1980. *The Politics of Deviance: A Sociological Introduction*. Englewood Cliffs, NJ: Prentice Hall.

———. 1983. *Labeling Women Deviant: Gender, Stigma, and Social Control*. Philadelphia: Temple University Press.

Scott, R., 1969. *The Making of Blind Men.* New York: Russel Sage Foundation.

Sigelman, C. and L. C. Singleton. 1986. "Stigmatization in Childhood: A Survey of Developmental Trends and Issues." In S. Ainlay, G. Becker, and L. M. Coleman, *The Dilemma of Difference: A Multicultural View of Stigma.* New York. Plenum, 185–210.

Solomon, Howard M. 1986. "Stigma and Western Culture: A Historical Approach." In S. Ainlay, G. Becker, and L. M. Coleman, *The Dilemma of Difference: A Multicultural View of Stigma.* New York: Plenum, 59–76.

Sontag, S. 1979. *Illness as Metaphor.* New York: Random House.

Sroufe, L. A. 1977. "Wariness of strangers and the study of infant development." *Child Development* 48: 731–46.

Stafford, M. and R. Scott. 1986. "Stigma, Deviance and Social Control: Some Conceptual Issues." In S. Ainlay, G. Becker, and L. M. Coleman, *The Dilemma of Difference: A Multicultural View of Stigma.* New York. Plenum, 77–94.

Terry, W. 1984. *Bloods: An Oral History of the Vietnam War by Black Veterans.* New York: Random House.

Tracy, G. S. and Z. Gussow. 1978. "Self-help health groups: A grass-roots response to a need for services." *Journal of Applied Behavioral Science:* 81–396.

Weiner, C. L., 1975. "The burden of rheumatoid arthritis: Tolerating the uncertainty." *Social Science and Medicine* 99: 97–104.

Zola, I. Z. 1979. "Helping one another: A speculative history of the self-help movement." *Archive of Physical Medicine and Rehabilitation* 60: 452.

CHAPTER 11

Unhealthy Disabled: Treating Chronic Illnesses as Disabilities

Susan Wendell

SUMMARY

Identifying disability with illness can foster the myth that disabled people are always incapacitated, and this often motivates disabled activists to distinguish themselves from people who are ill. But by refusing to represent the disabled body as a body in need of a cure, disability scholars can overlook disabled people who are sick or diseased. In this essay, Susan Wendell clarifies the differences between healthy disabled and unhealthy disabled to find a better understanding of the problematic relationship between illness and disability.

For Wendell, a person who is healthy disabled has physical conditions or limitations that are relatively stable and predictable. An unhealthy disabled person, on the other hand, is motivated to seek medical treatment for the onset of conditions. These categories remain in flux, as a person may be stable at one point and in need of treatment at another. Chronic illnesses, which do not go away on their own and cannot be reliably cured, highlight the ways in which a person may not be obviously disabled but nevertheless experience similar conditions and limitations as a healthy disabled person. For example, people with chronic illness commonly experience fatigue that is more debilitating than that experienced by healthy people. Though this is similar to the impairment associated with disability, this condition of chronic illness might not be accommodated or treated as disability in social or political contexts.

Writing from her own experiences, Wendell suggests that in activist movements, dedication can be equated with expending energy. People with chronic illnesses might not have the energy considered appropriate for activism in either feminist or disability communities, and accommodating (or even just claiming) chronic illness can draw suspicion in these communities and others. Similarly, people who express gratitude for good health make it difficult for people with chronic illnesses to find pride in being ill. Wendell urges us to understand illness as a way of being human even while contemplating ways to prevent and relieve suffering.

The relationship between disability and illness is a problematic one. Many people are disabled by chronic and/or life-threatening illnesses, and many people with disabilities not caused by illness have chronic health problems as consequences of their disabilities; but modern movements for the rights of people with disabilities have fought the identification of disability with illness, and for good reasons. This identification contributes to the medicalization of disability, in which disability is regarded as an individual misfortune, and people with disabilities are assumed to suffer primarily from physical and/or mental abnormalities that medicine can and should treat, cure, or at least prevent (Oliver 1990; Morris 1991). Moreover, Ron Amundson argues that, since illness is perceived as "globally incapacitating," identifying disability with illness fosters the myth that people with disabilities are globally incapacitated, which in turn contributes to the social devaluation of disabled people (Amundson 1992, 113–14). Perhaps most importantly, in the recent past, many healthy people with disabilities were forced to live in long-term care institutions under medical supervision simply because they needed services to perform tasks of daily living. In those institutions, medical personnel controlled every aspect of their lives, and little or no provision was made for them to work, to receive education, or to participate in life outside the institutions. At least in Canada, not everyone who could live outside an institution has achieved that goal, and institutionalization (especially when support networks break down) remains a threat to some people with disabilities who have achieved independent living (for example, see Snow 1992). All these reasons motivate disabled activists and other people with disabilities to distinguish themselves from those who are ill.

For example, in her recent book *Exile and Pride: Disability, Queerness and Liberation* (1999), Eli Clare describes her resistance to the medical model of disability in terms that emphasize her distance from sick people:

> To frame disability in terms of a cure is to accept the medical model of disability, to think of disabled people as sick, diseased, ill people. . . . My CP simply is not a *medical* condition. I need no specific medical care, medication, or treatment for my CP; the adaptive equipment I use can be found in a computer catalog, not a hospital. Of course, disability comes in many varieties. Some disabled people, depending on their disabilities, may indeed have pressing medical needs for a specific period of time or on an ongoing basis. But having particular medical needs differs from labeling a person with multiple sclerosis

as sick, or thinking of quadriplegia as a disease. The disability rights movement, like other social change movements, names systems of oppression as the problem, not individual bodies. In short it is ableism that needs the cure, not our bodies.

> (Clare 1999, 105–6)

Although she acknowledges that some people with disabilities have medical needs, including someone with multiple sclerosis (MS, which qualifies as a chronic illness), Clare criticizes the medical model for thinking of disabled people as "sick, diseased, ill people" and says that their bodies do not need cure. Yet some people with disabilities *are* sick, diseased, and ill. Social constructionist analyses of disability, in which oppressive institutions and policies, prejudiced attitudes, discrimination, cultural misrepresentation, and other social injustices are seen as the primary causes of disability, can reduce attention to those disabled people whose bodies are highly medicalized because of their suffering, their deteriorating health, or the threat of death. Moreover, some unhealthy disabled people, as well as some healthy people with disabilities, experience physical or psychological burdens that no amount of social justice can eliminate. Therefore, some very much want to have their bodies cured, not as a substitute for curing ableism, but in addition to it. There is a danger that acknowledging these facts might provide support for those who prefer the individualized, medicalized picture of disability. Thus, in promoting the liberatory vision of social constructionism, it is safer and more comfortable for disability activism to focus on people who are healthy disabled.

Despite the problematic relationship between disability and illness, many people who are disabled by chronic illnesses are involved in disability politics and contribute to social constructionist analyses, and disability groups have increasingly welcomed into their activities people with HIV/AIDS, fibromyalgia, myalgic encephalomyelitis/chronic fatigue immune dysfunction syndrome (ME/CFIDS), and other chronic illnesses. However, there are important differences between healthy disabled and unhealthy disabled people that are likely to affect such issues as treatment of impairment in disability politics and feminism, accommodation of disability in activism and employment, identification of persons as disabled, disability pride, and prevention and so-called "cure" of disabilities. Here I hope to introduce and perhaps clarify some of those differences, and to open a conversation about the relationships between illness and disability and between unhealthy and healthy people with disabilities.

The issues I will be raising are particularly important to women because women are more likely than men to be disabled by chronic illnesses (Morris 1994; Trypuc 1994), and women (including women with other disabilities) suffer more ill health than men (Carroll and Niven 1993). Women live longer than men, but much of that extra living is done with a disabling chronic illness (Carroll and Niven 1993; *Report on the Health of Canadians* 1996). Accommodating chronic illnesses in disability politics and feminism is essential to many disabled women's participation in them. Thus, as we shall see, it is women with disabilities who have been most outspoken about some of these issues.

WHO IS WHO?

When I speak of people who are "healthy disabled," I mean people whose physical conditions and functional limitations are relatively stable and predictable for the foreseeable future. They may be people who were born with disabilities or people who were disabled by accidents or illnesses later in life, but they regard themselves as healthy, not sick, they do not expect to die

any sooner than any other healthy person their age, and they do not need or seek much more medical attention than other healthy people (I will not try to give a definition of health, which is too big a topic to discuss here, but I am assuming that healthy people's functional limitations and bodily suffering are fairly stable and do not motivate them to seek medical treatment or cures).

Notice that "healthy disabled" is a category with fluctuating and sometimes uncertain membership. Many people who seem to have stable disabilities now will encounter illness and changing disability later in life (for example, post-polio syndrome has destabilized the health and abilities of some people who had recovered from polio, with residual disability, decades ago), and some people who seem to have stable disabilities also have chronic or recurrent health problems, either as consequences of their disabilities or independently of them. Thus, many of the problems I describe here as problems of unhealthy disabled people have been or will be problems of people who are now healthy disabled.

Defining what I mean by chronic illness would help to clarify the distinction between healthy and unhealthy people with disabilities, but it is not easy to pin down chronic illnesses with a definition.[1] Usually, they are understood to be illnesses that do not go away by themselves within six months, that cannot reliably be cured, and that will not kill the patient any time soon. I think that any practical concept of chronic illness has to be patient-centered or illness-centered, rather than based on diagnosis or disease classification, because many diseases cannot reliably be categorized into chronic and non-chronic. Nevertheless, a brief discussion of the variety of ways that diseases can cause chronic illness may be helpful.

Some diseases, such as lupus or diabetes, are known to be *typically* chronic. Physicians do not expect to cure them, and, once diagnosed, patients more or less expect to have to live with them (depending on how informed they are and how inclined they are to believe in miraculous cures or rapid progress in scientific medicine). A few patients with these diseases do recover their health instead of remaining chronically ill, but most do not. On the other hand, patients do not expect to die soon from these diseases. Nevertheless, many of the recognized chronic diseases, such as lupus, sometimes occur in acute forms that kill the patient quickly, and many of them, such as diabetes, are expected to kill the patient eventually, either by wearing down the patient's health or by creating severe, life-threatening episodes of illness.

Other diseases, such as infectious mononucleosis or Lyme disease, are usually acute but can last for years in some patients, making them chronically ill by any patient-centered definition. People who are chronically ill with these diseases are likely to have trouble getting recognition of their illnesses—if not by the medical profession, then by friends, relatives, acquaintances, employers, insurers, and others who believe that they should have recovered from their diseases long ago. Still other diseases are acute or chronic, depending on the treatment available to patients. HIV infection most often becomes the acute and deadly disease AIDS in poor countries, but in wealthy countries, where expensive treatment can slow its progress, it can frequently be a chronic disease.

Some diseases, such as MS and rheumatoid arthritis, can behave like recurring acute illnesses, with periods of extreme debility and periods of normal (or nearly normal) health, or they can have virtually constant symptoms (such as fatigue or pain) and/or be characterized by recurring acute episodes that leave behind permanent losses of function (such as paralysis caused by MS). Mental illnesses are sometimes acute, sometime recurring, and sometimes chronically debilitating. For example, schizophrenia and depression go in and out of remission for many people. Whether the mental illnesses are diseases is still controversial (see Agich 1997, 229–37), but clearly any adequate concept of illness includes them because of the involuntary suffering and loss of function they cause. I consider illnesses that go into remission chronic when they require prolonged medical treatment or surveillance, or when patients must fear recurrences because there is no reasonable expectation of cure.

The questions "Is my illness temporary?" and "How long will it last?" are often unanswered or answered uncertainly by medicine. This creates difficulties of identity both for the person who is ill (am I disabled or just sick for a while?) and for other people. Christine Overall describes an experience of being ill for more than a year with a painful, debilitating condition initially diagnosed as rheumatoid arthritis and then re-diagnosed as viral arthritis. She says that during the time she was ill, she identified with people with disabilities, was constructed as a person with disabilities, and inhabited the world of people with disabilities. However, she also experienced a strong pressure to "*pass* for normal" (Overall 1998, 155). People minimized her illness, ignored it, denied it, and urged her to get over it. Overall attributes some of this reaction to ageism, speculating that disability is "easier to recognize and tolerate ... in older people than in younger ones" (1998, 162).

My own analysis is that young and middle-aged people with chronic illnesses inhabit a category not easily understood or accepted. We are considered too young to be ill for the rest of our lives, yet we are not expecting cure or recovery.[2] We cannot be granted the time-out that is normally granted to the acutely ill (or we were given it at first and have now used it up, overused it), yet we seem to refuse to return to pre-illness life. We are not old enough to have finished making our contributions of productivity and/or caregiving; old people with chronic illnesses may be seen to be entitled to rest until they die. And we are not expected to die any time soon, so we are going to hang around being sick for a long while. Cheri Register calls us "the interminably ill" (Register 1987, ix).

Moreover, those of us with chronic illnesses do not fit most people's picture of disability. The paradigmatic person with a disability is healthy disabled and permanently and predictably impaired. Both attitudes toward people with disabilities and programs designed to remove obstacles to their full participation are based on that paradigm. Many of us with chronic illnesses are not obviously disabled; to be recognized as disabled, we have to remind people frequently of our needs and limitations. That in itself can be a source of alienation from other people with disabilities, because it requires repeatedly calling attention to our impairments.

IMPAIRMENT

Many of the issues I raise in this article would be classified as issues of *impairment* in the literature of disability activism and disability studies. Disability activists and scholars usually distinguish impairment from disability, treating impairment as the medically defined condition of a person's body/mind, and disability as the socially constructed disadvantage based upon impairment. This distinction follows the United Nations' definition of impairment as "any loss or abnormality of psychological, physiological, or anatomical structure or function" (U.N. 1983, I.c., 6–7). The U.N.'s attempt to give an objective, universal definition of impairment, which I have criticized elsewhere (Wendell 1996), connects impairment to the medical institutions that measure structure and function and set the standards of "normality." I believe this connection has contributed to neglect of the realities of impairment in disability activism and disability studies, because it makes attention to impairment seem irrelevant to or in conflict with the social constructionist analyses of disability they employ.

Illness is equated with impairment, even by disability activists and scholars, in ways that disability is not; hence there is anxiety to assure nondisabled people that disability is not illness. Another consequence is the pressure to be (or to pass as) healthy disabled both within disability activism and outside it. Because disability activists have worked hard to resist medicalization and promote the social model of disability, activists sometimes feel pressured to downplay the realities of fluctuating impairment or ill health. Cheryl Marie Wade (1994, 35) has criticized the new image of "the able-disabled" and the reluctance among disability activists to admit to weakness and vulnerability. She found that her identity as an activist made it difficult to acknowledge her physical limitations until her body broke down, endangering both her health and her self-esteem. Outside disability activism, there is pressure to conform to an inspiring version of the paradigm of disability. Those people with disabilities who can best approximate the activities and appearance of nondisabled people (that is, those who can make others forget they are disabled) will be allowed to participate most fully in the activities of their society.

British feminist disability activist Liz Crow has written a powerful critique of "our silence about impairment" within disability movements. She says:

> Our insistence that disadvantage and exclusion are the result of discrimination and prejudice, and our criticisms of the medical model of disability, have made us wary of acknowledging our experiences of impairment. Impairment is safer not mentioned at all.
>
> This silence prevents us from dealing effectively with the difficult aspects of impairment. Many of us remain frustrated and

disheartened by pain, fatigue, depression and chronic illness, including the way they prevent us from realizing our potential or railing fully against disability (our experience of exclusion and discrimination); many of us fear for our futures with progressive or additional impairments; we mourn past activities that are no longer possible for us; we are afraid we may die early or that suicide may seem our only option; we desperately seek some effective medical intervention; we feel ambivalent about the possibilities of our children having impairments; and we are motivated to work for the prevention of impairments. Yet our silence about impairment has made many of these things taboo and created a whole new series of constraints on our self-expression.

(Crow 1996, 209–10)

Crow emphasizes the need to focus on both disability *and* impairment, and she acknowledges that "impairment *in itself* can be a negative, painful experience" (Crow 1996, 219). She urges people with disabilities to adopt a new approach to impairment that includes not only the medically based descriptions of our bodies/minds but also our experiences of our bodies/ minds over time and in variable circumstances, the effects they have on our activities, the feelings they produce, and any concerns about them that impaired individuals might have.

It seems possible to pay more attention to impairment while supporting a social constructionist analysis of disability, especially if we focus our attention on the phenomenology of impairment, rather than accepting a medical approach to it. Knowing more about how people experience, live with, and think about their own impairments could contribute to an appreciation of disability as a valuable difference from the medical norms of body and mind. Moreover, recognition of impairment is crucial to the inclusion of people with chronic illnesses in disability politics. Chronic illness

frequently involves pain, fatigue, dizziness, nausea, weakness, depression, and/or other impairments that are hard to ignore. Everything one does, including politics, must be done within the limitations they present. The need to accommodate them is just as great, if more problematic (see below), as the need to accommodate blindness or hemiplegia, but they cannot be accommodated if they are not acknowledged and discussed openly.

Liz Crow points out that ignoring impairment can reduce the relevance of the social model of disability to certain groups, such as women, among whom (in England) arthritis is the most common cause of impairment, manifested in pain (1996, 221). I would add that pain and/or fatigue are major sources of impairment in many chronic illnesses that are more common in women than in men, including rheumatoid arthritis, fibromyalgia, lupus, ME/CFIDS, migraine headache, MS, and depression. This is not to say that men do not suffer from impairments of chronic illness, but that attempting to ignore impairment in disability politics may alienate or marginalize more women than men. Jenny Morris reports that restoring the experience of impairment to disability politics was regarded as a women's issue in the series of meetings of disabled women that led to the book, *Encounters with Strangers: Feminism and Disability*, in which Crow's critique of the social model was published (Morris 1996, 13).

When feminist politics ignores their experience of impairment, there are different but equally disturbing sources of disabled women's alienation from feminism or their marginalization within it. Feminist organizations have become more aware of the need to make their activities accessible to women who use wheelchairs, women who need written material in alternative formats, and women who need Sign Language translation, but much feminist practice still assumes a consistently energetic, high-functioning body and mind, and certainly not a body and mind that are impaired by illness. (I will discuss accommodating chronic illnesses in political practice in the next section.) More over, in their writing and organizing, most feminists still assume that feminists are giving, and not receiving, care, and that all significant contributions to feminist movements happen in meetings, at public events, and in demonstrations on the streets. The accepted image of a good feminist still includes handling paid work and family responsibilities and having plenty of energy left over for political activity in the evenings or on weekends. In these circumstances, women with chronic illnesses are likely to find it difficult to participate in feminist movements or to identify themselves as feminists.

Not only unhealthy people with disabilities but many healthy disabled people would benefit from more recognition of impairment in both disability and feminist politics. Some disabilities that are not illnesses and do not cause illnesses do involve impairments similar to those caused by chronic illnesses. It has been difficult, for example, for people with some brain injuries to have their impairments understood and accommodated, because they are more like impairments of chronic illnesses— transitory and unpredictable—than those of paradigmatic, stable disabilities. They may include both fatigue and intermittent cognitive impairments that are exacerbated by fatigue, such as difficulty concentrating and recalling words.

Fatigue is one of the most common and misunderstood impairments of chronic illness. The fatigue of illness is different in three critical respects from the ordinary fatigue experienced by healthy people: it is more debilitating, it lasts longer, and it is less predictable. Every activity, including thinking, watching, listening, speaking, and eating, requires energy. It is possible to be too fatigued to do any of these. Anyone who has had severe influenza may recall being too fatigued to have a conversation, to follow a simple story, or to make a decision. That experience of fatigue is closer to the fatigue of MS, rheumatoid arthritis, fibromyalgia, depression, or ME/CFIDS than the fatigue of a healthy person at the end of a hard day. A good night's sleep rarely cures the profound fatigue of illness; it may last for days or weeks with no apparent improvement, or it may fluctuate, allowing some activity punctuated by periods of total exhaustion. And unlike the fatigue of influenza, which will gradually improve as one's body recovers from infection, the fatigue of chronic illness is unpredictable. It may appear first thing in the morning on the tenth day of a restful vacation or in the middle of an energetic day's work. Reasonable precautions may help to prevent it, but it resists control.

Fatigue may be a primary symptom of a chronic illness, or it may be caused by other symptoms, such as pain, anorexia, or depressed mood. Thus, fluctuating and severely limited energy is a common impairment of people with chronic illnesses. Of course, not everyone with a chronic illness experiences this impairment, but it is an important example, not only because many of us have impaired energy, but because it is one of the most challenging impairments to accommodate.

ACCOMMODATING CHRONIC ILLNESSES

Fluctuating abilities and limitations can make people with chronic illnesses seem like unreliable activists, given the ways that political activity in both disability and feminist movements are structured. On a bad day of physical or mental illness, we may be unable to attend a meeting or workshop, to write a letter, to answer the phone, or to respond to e-mail. We may need notice in advance of work to be done, in order to work only on good days or more slowly on days when we are very ill. We may need to work in teams, so that someone else can take over when we cannot work at all. We may need to send a written speech to a meeting to be read by someone else because we are too sick to attend and read it in person. We need others to understand that our not showing up does not mean that we are not committed to the group, event, or cause.

Commitment to a cause is usually equated to energy expended, even to pushing one's body and mind excessively, if not cruelly. But pushing our bodies and minds excessively means something different to people with chronic illnesses: it means danger, risk of relapse, hospitalization, long-lasting or permanent damage to our capacities to function (as for some people with MS). And sometimes it is simply impossible; people get too tired to sit up, to think, to speak, to listen, and there are no reserves of energy to call upon. Yet in political activity, all-day meetings and evening events after a full day's work are assumed to be appropriate. Stamina is required for commitment to a cause.

I feel uneasy describing these conflicts between the demands of activism and the realities of chronic illness, because I do not want to supply good reasons for regarding those of us who are perpetually ill as social burdens rather than social contributors. This is probably the same uneasiness that healthy disabled people feel about focusing attention on their impairments. I can only hope, as Liz Crow does (Crow 1996, 222–25), that probing these threatening topics will lead eventually to facing and solving some problems. If there is to be more than token participation by unhealthy disabled people over the long term, there will have to be changes in the structure, culture, and traditions of political activism. People will have to think differently about energy and commitment, pace and cooperation.

Implementing the accommodations of pace and scheduling needed by people with chronic illnesses may inconvenience a lot of other people in a group (although, given the general silence about limitations of energy, perhaps many more people will be relieved). Moreover, everyone knows that the people who commit the most time and energy to a group will usually acquire the most power to influence the group's activities. In order for people with impaired energy to participate as equals, the relationships between time, energy, and power will have to be discussed openly and negotiated.

None of this will be easy. Conflicts and suspicions are inevitable. Management of energy is an issue, and at times a challenge, for every adult, whether nondisabled, healthy disabled, or unhealthy disabled. And it is sometimes hard to tell the difference between someone's mismanaging her/his own energy and other people's failure to accommodate her/his impaired energy. Even those of us who have lived a long time with chronic fatigue cannot always tell whether we are not trying hard enough or experiencing a physical/mental limitation, whether we need inspiration, self-discipline, or a nap. In political activism, where external pressures such as publication deadlines or responding to governmental announcements can virtually dictate the pace of the group, someone's claim to need rest may seem like shirking responsibility, especially to people who resent contributing more time or energy than others. Thus, pace and flexibility about time are bound to be controversial in any group that tries to negotiate them. Yet the only alternative is to take them for granted and make it difficult or impossible for people with impaired energy to participate.

Pace and flexibility about time are also issues of employment access for people with chronic illnesses, and here too conflict may arise—in this case, between the goals of healthy disabled people and the needs of unhealthy disabled people. We have learned that, even with strong legislation such as the Americans with Disabilities Act, it is hard to achieve accommodation of permanent, predictable disabilities in workplaces. Many employers (and nondisabled workers) resist the most straightforward requirements of wheelchair accessibility or Deaf translation. Understandably, disability activists want to stress the message "Remove the barriers that have been erected arbitrarily against our participation, and we will perform as well as anyone else." Insisting on accommodations of pace and time threaten this message, because working according to the employer's schedule and at the pace he/she requires are usually considered to be aspects of job performance, even in jobs where they are not critical to the adequate completion of tasks.

Iris Marion Young has pointed out that, from the perspective of most employers, "the norm of the 'hale and hearty' worker" makes a necessary contribution to workplace discipline. "The 'normal' worker is supposed to be energetic, have high concentration abilities, be alert to adapt to changing conditions, and be able to withstand physical, mental or interactive stress in good humor. Workers who fail to measure up to one or more of these standards are 'normally' considered lazy, slackers, uncooperative or otherwise inadequate. All workers must worry about *failing* in the eyes of their employers ..." (Young 2000, 172). Because many workers fail, either temporarily or permanently, to live up to this "norm," requiring accommodation of a wide range of disabilities would call the "norm" into question and challenge employers' power to set the standards of workplace performance. Employers would prefer to define disability narrowly and regard the vast majority of workers who do not meet their standards as unsuitable for their jobs.

Moreover, if people with chronic illnesses demand accommodations of pace and time,

they may encounter resistance from other workers because of the "politics of resentment," described here by Young:

> Most workers feel put-upon and frustrated by their working conditions and the demands of their employers on their time and energy. They have to stand up all day, or have few bathroom breaks, or work overtime or at night, and their employer refuses to accommodate to their aching backs, their family pressures, their sleeplessness or difficulty in concentrating. Many workers, that is, find the demands placed on them next to overwhelming at times, and they feel barely able to cope. Rarely do they get a sympathetic ear to voice their frustrations, however, and the only agents they are allowed to blame for their difficulties are themselves. It is little wonder that they may resent people that the law requires employers to accommodate in order to enable them better to fit the work situation.
>
> ... Disability is a matter of degree, and it is arbitrary where the line is drawn between not disabled enough to warrant accommodation, and disabled enough. A politics of resentment motivates some people to draw that line as far down the extreme end of the continuum as possible so that almost everyone will be legally expected to conform to the *normal* workplace demands.
>
> (Young 2000, 171)

On the basis of Young's analysis, I think we should expect strong resistance from both employers and workers to accommodating chronic illnesses in the workplace. This resistance may strain the resources and the solidarity of disability rights movements. Yet access to work for unhealthy disabled people will require taking what Young calls "the next step toward equal opportunity for people with disabilities," that is, challenging the prerogative of employers to define the content, qualifications, and performance criteria of work (Young 2000, 173). There are some reasons for optimism: we have a lot of potential allies to whom pace and flexibility about time make the difference between working and not working, including many nondisabled women caring for children and disabled older family members; and, as Young points out, there are many other workers, who do not identify themselves as disabled, who would benefit from "more humane and individualized workplace accommodation" (2000, 173).

WHO BELONGS?

Controversy about the appropriateness of accommodations of pace and time often leads to doubts about the legitimacy of the disability for which accommodation is requested. Suspicion surrounds people with chronic illnesses—suspicion about how ill/disabled we really are, how or why we became ill, whether we are doing everything possible to get well, and how mismanaging our lives, minds, or souls may be contributing to our continuing illness (Wendell 1996). Suspicion comes from medical professionals, friends, relatives, coworkers, and, understandably, from other people with disabilities.

In her study of a group of people with disabilities in Britain, Jill C. Humphrey found that there was a conspicuous silence about impairment and an associated suspicion as to whether some people belonged in the group—in other words, whether they were really disabled. In her interviews with them, group members raised this suspicion about people whose impairments were not readily apparent. Humphrey comments: "the propensity to treat only tangible impairments as evidence of a *bona fide* disability identity clearly marginalizes those with non-apparent impairments ... whilst the reluctance or refusal to differentiate between impairments by identifying them bolsters up the claim by people with apparent impairments that they represent all disabled people" (Humphrey 2000, 67). Of course, suspicions about whether people

with non-apparent impairments are really disabled are common, being the flip side of the ability to pass as nondisabled.

The ability to pass is a frequent, though not a universal, difference between unhealthy and healthy people with disabilities. Its advantages include avoiding the prejudices and daily acts of discrimination and patronizing behavior that people with obvious disabilities are subjected to at school, at work, and in other public places. Passing is sometimes voluntary, but it can also be involuntary, in that some of us will be perceived as nondisabled unless we draw attention to our disability, and sometimes even after we draw attention to it. The ability to pass makes a person *not* the paradigmatic person with a disability. Whether it makes her/him more or less acceptable to nondisabled people is unclear; someone who can pass but chooses not to may be seen as soliciting sympathy and special treatment. In either case, our ability to pass means that having our disabilities recognized as genuine is a major issue for many unhealthy disabled people. So much depends on that recognition—accommodation of our impairments, inclusion in disability politics, and, of course, our moral reputations. Because of what Young calls "the politics of resentment" (Young 2000, 171), people wonder whether someone whose disability is not obvious is faking or exaggerating it; the trustworthiness of people who claim to be disabled but do not look disabled is always in question.

Even when our disabilities are considered genuine, there is often suspicion about our role in causing them. Blame and responsibility for our disabilities are more persistent issues for unhealthy than for healthy people with disabilities. Although people disabled by accidents that they themselves caused (for example, by driving drunk) or risked unreasonably (by not wearing a helmet on a motorcycle, for example) may be blamed at first for their disabilities, that blame does not usually follow them for long, perhaps because their disabilities are relatively stable, and thus holding them responsible seems more and more pointless as time goes on. In contrast, people with chronic illnesses are likely to be blamed or held responsible not only during the process of seeking a diagnosis, but also during every relapse or deterioration of their condition, which they are expected (by doctors, loved ones, employers, and the general public) to control (Register 1987; Charmaz 1991). Fluctuations in our illnesses and abilities—which *can* be affected by our emotions, changes in our lives, and stress, but which may occur independently of them—contribute to the perception that we are responsible for our disabilities. In addition, an abundance of popular theories claim or imply that anyone can control her/his health with the right diet, exercise, attitudes, relationships, or religious beliefs; it follows from most of them that those who are unhealthy are doing something wrong, and that, if they have been told how to take better care of themselves, they are acting irresponsibly (see Wendell 1999).

PRIDE, PREVENTION, AND "CURE"

Health is regarded as a virtue or a blessing, depending on how well a person or group of people understands that it cannot be controlled, but it is almost always regarded as a good. Among people who have the political savvy not to give thanks publicly for being nondisabled, giving thanks for being healthy is acceptable, even commendable. Healthy people with disabilities express gratitude for being healthy, people with progressive chronic illnesses express gratitude for not having gotten sicker than they have, and people with recurring or fluctuating chronic illnesses express gratitude for coming out of a relapse (as I know I do).

Of course, many people, especially non-disabled people who have little knowledge of the lives of people with disabilities, fear other kinds of disability as much as, or more than, illness, and regard physical and mental "normality" as blessings, if not virtues. Because fear of disability contributes to the social stigma of being disabled, it is one of the goals of disability politics to replace fear with the understanding that disability can be a valuable difference and that people with disabilities can be proud of their differences from nondisabled people. The question is, does this goal make sense in relation to disabling chronic illnesses? At first glance, it seems to, because chronic illness is a kind of disability, but compare "Thank God I'm not disabled" with "Thank God I'm healthy," and you see the difficulty of applying disability pride to a chronic illness.

Is illness *by definition* an evil, or have we made less progress in recognizing chronic illnesses as potentially valuable differences than we have in relation to other disabilities? (There is a third possibility: perhaps acute illness is by definition an evil, chronic illness is not, and people confuse them. Yet if that were the case, the news that you are not going to recover from an illness and will have to live with it would be good news; but, unless you were expecting death, it is not good news. Illness, chronic or acute, is widely regarded as an evil.) Certainly it is difficult to say that one is glad to have been ill and be believed, despite the fact that many people who are or have been ill testify that it has changed them for the better. Of everything I said in my book about disability, *The Rejected Body* (1996), readers have most often questioned or been shocked by my statements that, although I would joyfully accept a cure if it were offered me, I do not need a cure and I do not regret having become ill (Wendell 1996, 83–84, 175). I suppose many people suspect I am making the best of a miserable fate, but then they probably think something very similar about other expressions of disability pride.

I do not think that those of us who appreciate having become ill are making a mistake or deceiving ourselves. Illness is not by definition an evil, but people fear and try to avoid illness because of the suffering it causes. Some of that suffering is social and could be eliminated by social justice for people with disabilities, but some of it is not. Solidarity between people with chronic illnesses and people with other disabilities depends on acknowledging the existence of the suffering that justice cannot eliminate (and therefore on our willingness to talk about impairment). It also depends on acknowledging that illness is not *only* suffering. Like living with cerebral palsy or blindness, living with pain, fatigue, nausea, unpredictable abilities, and/or the imminent threat of death creates different *ways of being* that give valuable perspectives on life and the world. Thus, although most of us want to avoid suffering if possible, suffering is part of some valuable ways of being. If we could live the ways of being without the suffering, some of us would choose to live them. Some of us would choose to live them even if they were inseparable from the suffering. And some of us are glad to have been forced to live them, would choose to be rid of the suffering even if it meant losing the ways of being, but would hope to hold on to what we have learned from them. There are, I think, many versions of disability pride.

Disability pride has come into conflict with medical efforts to prevent disability, especially by selective abortion of potentially disabled fetuses, and with medical efforts to "cure" certain disabilities, especially deafness in children. Moreover, disability movements have criticized spending enormous amounts of public and donated money searching for "cures" while neglecting to provide the most basic services and opportunities that would improve the lives of people with disabilities. Prevention and cure both focus public attention on the medical model, which can lead us to ignore the social conditions that are causing or increasing disability among people who have impairments. Moreover, given the history of eugenics, there is reason to be skeptical about whether prevention and cure are intended primarily to prevent suffering or to eliminate "abnormalities" and "abnormal" people.

However, it is striking that everyone, including disability scholars and activists, tends to assume that prevention is desirable when the cause of disability is war, famine, poor medical care, accident, or illness, and that cure is desirable when the cause is illness. Perhaps, in these instances, it seems heartless to insist on preserving difference instead of preventing or ending suffering. Whatever our reasons, we sometimes insist on people's rights to have impairments and sometimes assume that they would not want them, depending on the causes and circumstances of disability. I think that when we explore these different responses further, we will discover different beliefs about how much suffering is an acceptable price to pay for a difference we value, and even different beliefs about the value of suffering itself. The perspectives of people with chronic illnesses will be essential to such an exploration, because it may be as difficult for healthy disabled people to see the value of illness as for nondisabled people to see the value of disability. Only some people know what is at stake when we contemplate preventing and curing illnesses: not only the relief of suffering, but also, as with other disabilities, ways of being human.

NOTES

Many thanks to Anita Silvers and three anonymous referees for their helpful comments on an earlier version of this paper.

1. In this article, I am using "sickness" and "illness" synonymously to mean suffering, limitation, and/or

loss of function experienced by a person and attributed by her/him (or others) to a loss of health and not to a physical or mental condition present from birth or acquired by an injury to a specific part of the body. I am using "disease" to refer to some medically recognized diagnostic categories of physical or mental "abnormality." Not all sicknesses and illnesses are diseases recognized by medicine, and not all medically recognized diseases cause a person to feel sick or ill. My definitions are based on ordinary use of the words; unfortunately, ordinary use does not make precise distinctions, so there are afflictions that do not fit the definitions neatly (such as chronic inflammation of an injured limb). There is a considerable philosophical literature debating the definitions of "disease," "sickness," "illness," and related concepts. For a recent overview and samples of those debates, see Humber and Almeder (1997).

2. I have lived with ME/CFIDS since 1985. During the first two years of illness, I was severely impaired by fatigue, muscle pain, muscle weakness, dizziness, nausea, headaches, depression, and problems with short-term memory (especially verbal recall). All these impairments are still with me, but now they are intermittent and less severe than they were. I am able to work three-quarter-time as a professor by living a quiet, careful life. An account of my personal experience of being disabled by chronic illness can be found in *The Rejected Body: Feminist Philosophical Reflections on Disability* (1996).

REFERENCES

Agich, George J. 1997. Toward a pragmatic theory of disease. In *What is disease?* ed. James M. Humber and Robert F. Almeder. Totowa, NJ: Humana Press.

Amundson, Ron. 1992. Disability, handicap, and the environment. *Journal of Social Philosophy* 23 (1): 105–18.

Carroll, Douglas, and Catherine A. Niven. 1993. Gender, health and stress. In *The health psychology of women*, ed. Catherine A. Niven and Douglas Carroll. Chur, Switzerland: Harwood Academic Publishers.

Charmaz, Kathy. 1991. *Good days, bad days: The self in chronic illness*. New Brunswick, NJ: Rutgers University Press.

Clare, Eli. 1999. *Exile and pride: Disability, queerness and liberation*. Cambridge, MA: South End Press.

Crow, Liz. 1996. Including all of our lives: Renewing the social model of disability. In *Encounters with strangers: Feminism and disability*, ed. Jenny Morris. London: Women's Press.

Humber, James M., and Robert F. Almeder, eds. 1997. *What is disease?* Totowa, NJ: Humana Press.

Humphrey, Jill C. 2000. Researching disability politics, or, some problems with the social model in practice. *Disability and Society* 15 (1): 63–85.

Morris, Jenny. 1991. *Pride against prejudice: Transforming attitudes to disability*. Philadelphia: New Society Publishers.

——. 1994. Gender and disability. In *On equal terms: Working with disabled people*, ed. Sally French. Oxford: Butterworth-Heinemann.

——. ed. 1996. *Encounters with strangers: Feminism and disability*. London: Women's Press.

Oliver, Michael. 1990. *The politics of disablement*. London: Macmillan.

Overall, Christine. 1998. *A feminist I: Reflections from academia*. Peterborough, Ont.: Broadview Press.

Register, Cheri. 1987. *Living with chronic illness: Days of patience and passion*. New York: Bantam.

Report on the health of Canadians. 1996. Ottawa: Minister of Supply and Services Canada.

Snow, Judith A. 1992. Living at home. In *Imprinting our image: An international anthology by women with disabilities*, ed. Diane Driedger and Susan Gray. Charlottetown, P.E.I.: Gynergy Books.

Trypuc, Joann M. 1994. Gender based mortality and morbidity patterns and health risks. In *Women, medicine and health*, ed. B. Singh Bolaria and Rosemary Bolaria. Halifax, N.S.: Fernwood.

U.N. Decade of Disabled Persons 1983–1992. 1983. *World programme of action concerning disabled persons*. New York: United Nations.

Wade, Cheryl Marie. 1994. Identity. *The Disability Rag and ReSource* (September/October): 32–36.

Wendell, Susan. 1996. *The rejected body: Feminist philosophical reflections on disability*. New York: Routledge.

——. 1999. Old women out of control: Some thoughts on aging, ethics and psychosomatic medicine. In *Mother time: Women, aging and ethics*, ed. Margaret Walker. Lanham, MD: Rowman and Littlefield.

Young, Iris Marion. 2000. Disability and the definition of work. In *Americans with disabilities: Exploring implications of the law for individuals and institutions*, ed. Leslie Francis and Anita Silvers. New York: Routledge.

PART IV

*T*heorizing Disability

CHAPTER 12

What's So "Critical" about Critical Disability Studies?

Helen Meekosha and Russell Shuttleworth

SUMMARY

Critical Disability Studies, or CDS, is increasingly becoming the preferred name for the work of disability scholars. In this chapter, Helen Meekosha and Russell Shuttleworth investigate whether this renaming is the signal of a paradigm shift or simply the maturation of the discipline.

Disability studies emerged as a growing area of academic research and professional education across much of the Western world in the 1970s. It has continued to expand with the growing presence of disabled people in society and increasing influence on other fields of inquiry. CDS has emerged in the last decade as a way to reevaluate the critical underpinnings of past work in disability studies, most notably its focus on the social model of disability. CDS calls instead upon critical social theory, which challenges the very way that the status quo is construed and maintains a space for critical reason to achieve a more participatory and egalitarian society.

In CDS the question has become how to conceptualize diversity among disabled people to restructure cultural meanings, social processes, and politics. Rather than emphasizing the materialism of older disability discourses, CDS draws on the idea of biopower to analyze how practices attempt to manage bodily differences and variations from a norm. Similarly, the self-reflexivity of feminist scholarship has helped CDS to reconsider the importance of disability identity, especially as informed by the concept of intersectionality. Gender, disability, race and class, among others, are available for critique through CDS.

CDS intends to build an alternative body of work that will necessarily be subversive. As Meekosha and Shuttleworth argue, the disability movement's struggle was about more than ramps; now CDS can help to highlight how societies exclude "abnormal" bodies and reformulate who is eligible for participation in civic life. Investigating difficult problems that disability studies tended to shy away from will now contribute to an expanded understanding of disabled people's place in the world.

This article self-reflexively turns the focus on disability studies to consider why critical disability studies (CDS) is emerging as the preferred nomenclature and whether this constitutes a radical paradigm shift, or simply signifies a maturing of the discipline. We first trace the emergence of disability studies as part of the disability rights movement, which harbored a primarily materialist critique against the normative status quo. The diversification of critical social theory that has occurred in recent years has opened up new modes of critical enquiry. Yet there are nevertheless several principles that we feel it is important to maintain and we briefly outline these: (1) the irreducibility of social life to objective facts; (2) the requirement of linking theory with praxis in the struggle for an autonomous and participatory society; (3) the necessity that a discipline or field of study be aware of its own historicity and critically reflect on its conceptual framework; and (4) the need to engage in a dialogue with other cultures on the issues and concepts of current significance. We subsequently trace some of the areas where critical theory has been employed in the study of disability. Critical social thought, grounded in the principles we discuss and developing innovative lines of enquiry, has the potential to render a wide range of issues and discourses heretofore obscured visible in the study of disability.

INTRODUCTION

> As with any new discourse, disability studies must claim space in a contested area, trace its continuities and discontinuities, argue for its existence, and justify its assertions
>
> (Lennard Davis 1997, xv)

The politics of knowledge creation is a critical dimension in the success of any social movement. The creation of knowledge and meaning is also implicated in maintaining structures of control and exclusion. In tracing the emergence of disability studies as part of the disability rights movement, this article will be mindful of these sometimes paradoxical dimensions in the politics of knowledge creation. In any academic offshoot of a social movement, the terms of engagement and debate must adapt to newly perceived articulations of oppressive structures, even if some of those structures are discerned within the movement itself.

This article self-reflexively turns the focus on disability studies to consider the question of why critical disability studies (CDS) is emerging as the preferred nomenclature by many scholars, and whether this constitutes a radical paradigm shift or simply signifies a maturing of the discipline. While the influence of critical theory in disability studies has often been assumed because of its critique of the status quo in

the study of disability, the influence of critical theorists is not always acknowledged. We seek to unpack this complexity in the formulation of CDS.

The diversification of critical social theory that has occurred in recent years has opened up new modes of critical enquiry. Yet there are nevertheless several principles that we feel it is important to maintain and we briefly examine these. We then review where critical theory has been used in disability research. CDS is still in its infancy, so a review of the literature, as such, is not appropriate, but we intend to draw out instances of scholarly work that we consider reflect some of the major developments in critical theory. Emancipation is a cornerstone of critical theory, so it is inevitable that CDS also encapsulates questions of human rights such as those identified in the recent UN Convention on the Rights of Persons with Disabilities that came into force in 2008. This article is selective and is intended to stimulate debate on the meanings and interpretations of CDS, not to provide definitive answers.

EVOLUTION OF CRITICAL DISABILITY STUDIES

Disability studies emerged as a growing area of academic research and professional education across much of the Western world in the 1970s and has continued to expand into the twenty-first century. The International Year of Disabled People in 1981 raised disability as a human rights issues in the global public discourse. The rise of the contemporary disability movement in the latter decades of the twentieth century, and the vocal demand for relevant curricula by disabled people and their allies, lent weight to the legitimacy of the new discipline.

The growing presence of disabled people in society, in particular their presence in the community following centuries of institutionalization, has further contributed to an awareness of the responsibilities of educational institutions to disabled citizens. At the same time, the limitations of medical and individual pathology models of disability, in both explaining the situation of disabled people and enabling their full citizenship, have resulted in the flowering of new explanatory paradigms—particularly in the humanities and social sciences. While the dominant discourse is still framed within the concerns of the global north, writers from the global south and the majority world are adding their voices to the expanding discipline (Ariotti 1999; Ghai 2002; Soldatic and Biyanwila 2006; Watermeyer et al. 2006; Ingstad and Reynolds Whyte 2007; Meekosha 2008).

Disability studies has made an impact on the research agendas of many other disciplines. Starting with the social sciences and the humanities, disability studies has also been increasingly taken on board by the applied sciences such as architecture, design, engineering and, more recently, medicine and pure science. The Society for Disability Studies (SDS), in its working guidelines, argues that disability studies is interdisciplinary and multidisciplinary and that programs in disability studies should engage with various disciplinary perspectives (SDS 2009). Thus, disability studies can be thought of as a critique of specific approaches to disability; a project to evolve an interdisciplinary frame that can be incorporated into multiple disciplines; and a new sphere of scholarly work that has a similar legitimacy to women's studies, black studies and queer studies (Linton 1998; Meekosha 2004). Disability studies, as a discipline in its own right (Lorenzo, Mzolisika, and Priestley 2006, 179), boasts a discrete body of knowledge and research and specialist journals devoted to the subject, such as *Disability Studies Quarterly* and *Disability and Society*. Yet a troubling trend concerns the cooption of some of the

language of disability studies that is also taking place. More traditional rehabilitation and special education departments are re-badging themselves as disability studies, but without going far enough in rewriting the script. This is evidenced by courses within universities whose primary allegiance is to medical models, while only weakly acknowledging the sociopolitical analysis of disability (Longmore 2003; Meekosha and Green 2004).

The term "critical disability studies" has been increasingly employed in scholarly work over the last decade (Tremain 2005; Erevelles 2005; Meekosha 2006; Pothier and Devlin 2006; Shildrick 2007a; Gustafson 2007; Roets and Goodley 2008; Hosking 2008; Campbell 2008), and York University in Canada now offers a postgraduate research program in CDS. CDS has accompanied a social, political, and intellectual re-evaluation of explanatory paradigms used to understand the lived experience of disabled people and potential ways forward for social, political, and economic change. Shildrick (2007a, 233) notes that CDS: "is broadly aligned with a postconventional theoretical approach. It seeks to extend and productively critique the achievements of working through more modernist paradigms of disability, such as the social constructionist model."

There are a number of factors influencing this re-evaluation that has led to the development of CDS. First, the social model of disability argued for a conceptual distinction between "impairment" as a functional limitation and "disability" as a socially generated system of discrimination. This binary way of thinking about disability has undergone a number of critiques from feminists, cultural studies scholars, and postmodernists, which has led to tensions and splits within the disability studies community, particularly in Britain (for example, Hughes and Paterson 1997; Corker 1999; Shakespeare and Watson 2001;

Shakespeare 2006). Using the term "CDS" is a move away from the preoccupation with binary understandings—social vs medical model, British vs American disability studies, disability vs impairment.

While critical legal studies emerged in opposition to North American liberalism and individualism (Pothier and Devlin 2006), CDS partly emerged as an outcome of the tensions that surfaced as a reaction to the more authoritarian Marxism and economic determinism associated with the social model. Paradoxically, the social model drew directly from critical theory, examining as it did the interrelations between the capitalist system of production, class, and disability, as well as arguing for an emancipatory perspective within disability studies. Hosking (2008), in his formulation of critical disability theory, argues that it includes the social model of disability. We believe that it is not a question of including the social model as one of a number of separate tools in our analysis, but rather of incorporating a more complex conceptual understanding of disability oppression in our work that nevertheless still employs key ideas about disability that saw the light of day with the ascendance of the social model.

Second, the influx of humanities and cultural studies scholars with their postmodern leanings and decentering of subjectivity during the 1990s, especially in the US, enabled a more self-conscious focus on critical theorizing to take hold in disability studies. Use of CDS signifies an implicit understanding that the terms of engagement in disability studies have changed; that the struggle for social justice and diversity continues but on another plane of development—one that is not simply social, economic, and political, but also psychological, cultural, discursive, and carnal. Evidence for these new terms of engagement can be seen in the recent openness to perspectives, such as psychological and psychoanalytic, that would have been stigmatized in the past as reinforcing an individual model of disability (for example, Goodley and Lawthom 2005; Shildrick 2007b).

A third factor for the divergence of CDS from disability studies concerns the cooption of the language of disability studies by the institutions of government, along with the professional areas of rehabilitation and special education taught within higher educational institutions (Meekosha and Dowse 2007). These traditional human service professions, for the most part, "conceive, discuss and treat disability within a diagnostic perspective that emphasises individual deficiency" (Meekosha and Dowse 2007, 172). The normalization and quality of life paradigms, even if subsumed under the rubric of disability studies, still carry regulatory and controlling undertones. We would call these applied disciplines to task to more fully integrate a critique of disabling structures into their approaches.[1] Thus, CDS represents a distancing from those who have coopted disability studies for simply normalizing ends.

Identification with critical race theory, critical legal theory, and the newly emerging critical criminology and critical queer studies sets up the fourth factor. Critical legal theory, which separated politics and law as separate discourses, drew on the Frankfurt School and post-structuralism in its critique of the dominant ideologies in legal studies. Critical race theory followed critical legal theory with an emphasis on examining racism, discrimination, and race as a socially constructed concept. Critical race theory recognizes the historical context, is interdisciplinary, and works towards eliminating oppression (Dixson and Rousseau 2006, 4). Thus, both critical legal theory and critical race theory have set theoretical, conceptual and methodological examples for CDS to follow.

WHAT IS CRITICAL SOCIAL THEORY?

Critical social theory, as a group of approaches to the study of society, has its origins in the critical theory of the Frankfurt School in the 1930s. The Frankfurt theorists perceived the historical convergence of capitalism, bureaucracy, and science as progressively restricting the development of critical consciousness and an autonomous society. They moved well beyond the typical Marxian model of social analysis to take up issues such as the ascendance of instrumental reason, the rise of authoritarianism, and the emergence of the culture industry. These cultural trends were viewed as evidence of a crisis for critical reason (Horkheimer and Adorno 1972; Horkheimer 1974, 1986; Held 1980).

The current purview of critical social theory appears much wider than that envisioned by the first-generation Frankfurt theorists, who were constrained by the pressing issues of their day. The current sociopolitical climate demands that attention be paid to other crucial issues as well— that is, the crisis of representation, the rise of new social movements and identity politics, globalization, and the fragmentation and compartmentalization of everyday life. Additionally, new conceptualizations of what it means to render a critique have further opened up the critical vista. Post-Marxists, post-structuralists, postmodernists, post-positive and critical realists problematize these issues, among others, and apply diverse methods of critique. While some retain a faith in the emancipatory project and the struggle for autonomy, others are more skeptical of this project's possibility of success (Torney and Townshend 2006).

A healthy skepticism, of course, has its place in critical thinking, but must nevertheless maintain its applicability to emancipatory political practice. In our view, it is important to incorporate the following four principles in the current conceptualization of CDS.

Critical Social Theory Is Irreducible to Facts

Critical social theory rejects a vision of the social sciences modeled on the natural sciences. While critical social theory is not averse to strategically employing quantitative approaches, it views the working of society and culture as much more dynamic than what can be captured quantitatively. Undergoing continual historical and sociocultural transformation, society cannot be described adequately without reference to changing social relations and cultural meanings.

A challenge to the very way the status quo is construed permeated the Frankfurt theorists' writings from the beginning. Their early criticism of appearances—that is, the raw facts of a case and exaltation of the underlying social relations obscured by a focus on their facticity—while conceptually connected to Marx's analysis of ideology and the economic infrastructure (Marcuse 1965), more importantly opens out to a wholesale condemnation of scientistic practice—that is, belief in an atheoretical, context-free science. Indeed, the Frankfurt theorists, and especially Horkheimer (1974, 1986) in his sustained critique of empiricism and positivism as naively viewing as "real" that which is constituted by a narrowly construed reason, bequeathed to critical theorists one of their major principles. Their critique is aimed squarely at maintaining a space for the application of critical reason in the struggle for autonomy and a more participatory and egalitarian society.

Critical Social Theory Links Theory with Praxis in the Struggle for an Autonomous and Participatory Society

While the cultural specificity of notions such as civil rights and equality cannot be denied, it is our belief that they have their roots in a more general understanding of human protest of suffering, and human need for both autonomy and social participation. Analysis of the social processes and cultural meanings that impinge on social actors and restrict their ability to reflexively choose a more participatory society has been a primary focus of critical social theory. Moreover, autonomy, as conceived by critical theorists, has always been a more complex notion than the idea of independent living which dominated much of the discourse on disability during the 1970s through to the 1990s in the US. Critical theorists themselves continue to argue about what precisely constitutes autonomy and its relation to social participation (Kalyvas 2001). The defining feature of autonomy that interweaves throughout critical theory's history is its meaning as emancipation from hegemonic and hierarchical ideologies that structure personal consciousness, representations, social relations and practices in everyday life. Critical social thought is aimed squarely at revealing the power relational dynamics within societies as manifested and reinforced via these seemingly innocuous means, at both the individual and the societal levels. Furthermore, this critical analysis of appearances is specifically meant to provide insight for the goal of social change towards a society in which individuals can discuss and debate the future of their institutions without the constraints imposed by power-relational mystifications. Indeed, critical social theories, whether more traditional or postmodern, posit certain hierarchies and structures, processes or discourses as constraining people's conceptions and experience (such as false consciousness, reification, hegemony, metaphysics of presence, governmentality) (Agger 1998). Current schools of critical social theory differ in their approaches to critique and by the ways in which they elucidate the restrictions on autonomy.[2]

Critical Social Theory Is Self-aware of its Historicity

Since critical social theory recognizes the inherent historicity of society—that it is susceptible to change—the concepts critical social theory employs are always an investment in bringing about social change. However, critical theory also recognizes its own situatedness within a particular historical moment. Thus, it is obliged to maintain a critical self-reflexivity toward its own theories and praxis. It is not as if an unmasking of the oppressive dynamics within a particular society or concerning a particular social group can be theorized and acted upon definitively. The ever-changing social relations, cultural meanings, and thus self-understandings necessitate a hypervigilance towards the possibility of changed terms of engagement. In hindsight, theories that were once thought to adequately elucidate inequalities and oppressive circumstances and practices are often flawed in some way. This is exemplified early on in the history of the Frankfurt School as it broke from a traditional Marxist materialism, viewing it as deterministic and inadequate to comprehend the full extent of modern structures of hierarchy and domination. It is this commitment to critical self-reflexivity that has sustained critical social theory throughout the waxing and waning of many other theoretical perspectives (such as functionalism, structuralism, and existentialism) and that can be considered the hallmark of a mature field of study committed to social transformation.

Thus, the upswell of critique within disability studies during the past decade of its "big idea," the socially constructed exclusions inherent in materialist and political structures, may signify the maturation of disability enquiry.

Critical Social Theory Engages in Dialogue among Cultures

Calhoun states that critical theory is "a theory that is self-conscious about its historicity, its place in dialogue among cultures, its irreducibility to facts, and its engagement in the practical world" (1995, 11). While we would agree with him on three of these counts, we beg to differ regarding critical theory's engagement in dialogue among cultures. Calhoun is likely projecting an international ideal here. Critical theory, it can be argued, conceived in Western Europe and North America, has traditionally not taken on board the perspectives of non-Western cultures. As Held argues, "the importance of non-European societies in world politics . . . [is not] adequately recognized by the critical theorists" (1980, 400). More recent social theorists, such as Foucault, also focus on a critical analysis of the emergence of Western institutions and their discourses (for example, Foucault 1978; Burchell, Gordon, and Miller 1991)—or, as in the case of Castoriadis (1997), explicitly locate the origins of critical self-reflection of our instituted traditions, the politics of autonomy, and the impetus for social change in that fulcrum of Western society, ancient Greece. However, the relevance to non-Western societies of this history and concepts derived from the study of Western societies is an issue that demands more attention than it has received.[3] While critical theory that elides engaging with non-Western scholarship is not without its significance, we would call for an explicit dialogue with human rights and emancipatory thinking from the diversity of cultures.

This is crucial for CDS when the global majority of disabled people are excluded from the dominant disability discourse.

These then are what we consider key principles to incorporate in the application of critical social theory to the struggle for emancipation of marginalized groups, including disabled people. What follows is a discussion of some topical areas in CDS in which critical social thought has been and is being brought to bear.

CRITICAL SOCIAL THEORY AND DISABILITY STUDIES

The Trials and Tribulations of Emancipatory Research

A critical, emancipatory orientation lies at the core of disability studies' raison d'être (Mercer 2004). A social transformative perspective underlies the search for knowledge in this field of study. As Pfeiffer (2003, 104) notes, an implication of "the disability studies paradigm" is progressive social change. However, the influence of critical theory, especially in the UK, was early on narrowly construed within certain Marxist parameters. The Frankfurt School's broader vision for critical theory was largely ignored in favor of a heavily materialist-oriented understanding of disabled people's social situation in modern society. Indeed, in the 1980s and early 1990s, even though disability studies was not primarily about class struggle, blame for disabled people's oppression was laid clearly at the feet of economic relations in capitalistic society, with allusions to an agrarian past in which disabled people were, if not idyllically, at least pragmatically integrated into the family system (Finkelstein 1980; Oliver 1990).

The 1980s and 1990s saw the ascendance of participatory research approaches, which were influenced by Habermas's (1973) differentiation of knowledge constitutive interests—positivistic, interpretive, and emancipatory. In the UK, disability studies developed a radicalized interpretation of participatory research, a so-called emancipatory approach (Oliver 1992; Stone and Priestley 1996), which while democratizing the research process diminished the conceptual contribution of the researcher. The researcher's methodological and theoretical expertise were considered technical skills in the rearrangement of commonsense precepts, not critical-interpretive skills, in the analysis of interaction and meaning and in the unmasking of ideologies and hierarchies. Further, a naive opposing of emancipatory research to positivistic and interpretive research downplayed the significance of the latter kinds of approaches in a broader understanding of autonomy (the importance of disability statistics and politically informed interpretations of disabled people's embodied lived experience). One assumption in this emancipatory discourse was that disabled people could reach a consensus on what constituted emancipation (Davis 2000). The result was over a decade of dogmatic policing of disciplinary, researcher, theoretical, and practice boundaries. Those who argued for a widening of the disability studies agenda, both empirically and theoretically, were perceived as heretical to the materialist truths that constituted disabled people's social situation (for example, Morris 1991; Shakespeare 1994; Corker 1998, 1999; Meekosha 1998).

In hindsight, this view of emancipation appears simplistic. In fact, the sheer diversity of disabled people—that is, the variety and degrees of their impairments and their intersection with other relevant social categories of experience—demands a much broader and contextual interrogation of their restrictions. To that effect, CDS draws from a much more eclectic mix of critical theories than earlier work in disability studies.

Dichotomizing Disability

In CDS the question has become how to conceptualize a diversity within a radical agenda to restructure cultural meanings, social processes, and a carnally relevant politics. Mairian Corker, a British sociolinguist, feminist, deaf disability studies scholar, was at the forefront of the turn from a strictly narrowly conceived materialist approach to this broader conception of disability studies—one that included interrogation of discourses and cultural meanings and theorization of diversity. During the late 1990s, she began employing a post-structural critique to challenge dichotomous and binary modes of thinking and models of disability (see, for example, Corker 1998, 1999). Using the post-structural notions of Jacques Derrida, among other postmodern theorists, she deconstructs the dichotomous, modernist assumptions underlying the social model of disability—that is, individual/society, impairment/disability—and notes their hierarchical ordering and instability. Recognizing that "the social model of disability" has been hugely pragmatic for disabled people within certain political parameters, Corker contended that it nevertheless could not easily articulate an understanding of the complexity of postmodern culture with its social flux, the contextual fluidity of identity formations and transformations, and changing micro-macro social relations and cultural meanings. Corker argued for a dialogic relation between impairment and disability, not an analytical privileging of one over the other, in a broader approach that adds to the preoccupation with structure a discursive theory of communication.

One of Corker's aims was to open up the productive space between modernist dichotomies of individual–society and impairment–disability for exploration, in order to reveal the issues and agency of disabled people who were overlooked by modernist sociopolitical models of disability (Shuttleworth 2006). Corker's thinking demonstrates a disciplinary self-reflexivity that is a hallmark of critical social theory and her incisive critique of the "social model" was ahead of its time (see, for example, Corker 1998, 1999). While according the social model its historical and pragmatic due, she argued for a critical re-evaluation of the very model that had garnered personal and political power for disabled people. Of course, there were others in the late 1990s who were also arguing for a reassessment of disability binaries, including Meekosha (1998) and Hughes and Paterson (1997; Paterson and Hughes 1999), and this stance is almost de rigueur in CDS today.

Power and the Politics of Resistance

Foucault's innovative understanding of power/knowledge continues to grow exponentially in influence across the humanities and social sciences. It is also becoming an important critical perspective, as disability studies transforms into CDS (for example, Corker 1998; Garland-Thomson 1997; Allan 1996; Tremain 2005; Sullivan 2005). What makes Foucault's ideas so useful to CDS is that they perform a radical de-familiarization of modern institutions and practices as caring and benevolent and reveal technologies and procedures that classify, normalize, manage, and control anomalous body-subjects (Foucault 1978; Burchell et al. 1991). While certainly disability studies was partially founded on its critique of institutional perspectives on disability (such as medicine and economics), the terms of critique had remained for the most part materialistic and adversarial. Disability studies in Foucauldian terms was operating with a juridical conception of power. Foucault (1978), however, posits a much more encompassing view of power relations in modernity—that is, the emergence of biopower as a set of procedures and

practices that objectivize and attempt to measure, predict, and manage phenomena and processes having to do with the life of the human species (such as reproduction and death) and its individual variances in terms of a norm. Rapid spread of these normalizing procedures and practices throughout modern institutions was enabled by governmentality, which is "any form of activity that aims to shape, guide or affect . . . conduct [in terms of] one's relation to oneself, interpersonal relations that involve some form of control or guidance, and relations within social institutions and communities" (Tremain 2005, 8). The important point to remember is that this understanding includes not only legitimate and overt forms of control, but also a micropolitics of power in which modern human beings are complicit with their subjection.

Beginning in the late 1990s, disability theorists began incorporating Foucault's thinking into analyses of institutional management of disabled people's lives (Allan 1996, 1999; Shildrick 1997; Levinson 2005). The publication of Tremain's (2005) edited volume has provided additional impetus for employing Foucauldian critiques of institutions that administer to disabled people. We think it is important to maintain a self-critical view with the employment of any critical notion, but especially with those terms that Foucault (re)formulated. It needs to be acknowledged that the very institutions and practices on the receiving end of his critique have often enabled disabled people to survive serious trauma and to re-enter society. Nevertheless, the extent to which these institutional discourses pervade social structures and cultural meanings to constitute the disabled subject is worthy of continual critique. As Sullivan (2005, 30) notes with respect to the rehabilitation of spinal-cord-injured persons:

If the paralysed body were not invested with specific techniques and knowledge, it would quickly deteriorate and die. If, however, Foucault is correct,...then it would be reasonable to expect that, during the process of rehabilitation, the body of the spinal-cord-injured individual would be objectivised as paralysed, the individual would be subjectivised as paraplegic, and the subject would come to know itself in these terms. Others would also come to "know" the spinal-cord individual in these terms.

Foucault's work also includes a complex conceptualization of resistance that is still being interpreted in diverse ways. In fact, Gabel and Peters (2004), acknowledging the influence of Foucault, argue that disability studies is increasingly moving towards resistance theories of disability (for example, Allan 1999; Kafer 2003; Gabel 2006). These authors perceive the concept of resistance as "offering a way to understand the complex relationships and negotiations between divergent ideas like discourse, the material body, socio-political systems and processes, power relations, cultural contexts of disability, impairment, and so on" (586). Gabel and Peters's focus on resistance is ultimately employed for critical and praxis purposes: "While the 'strong social model' has not recognized individual agency, resistance theory recognizes agency in the sense that individual resistance operates across the individual and collective levels and is enacted through critical self-reflection coupled with action" (93–94). While, to a large extent, Foucault viewed resistance as entrapped within the same logic as power, some interpreters perceive his later move (1997) from resistance to a focus on practices of the self as a possible space for personal and social transformation (for example, Rabinow 1997), and this notion has also been picked up by several disability scholars (Shuttleworth 2000, 2002; Reeve 2002; Allan 2005).

Feminism and the Gendered World of Disability

Feminism has been extremely important in the development of critical theory. Feminists, in particular, maintain critical self-reflexivity about their praxis, as evidenced by the number of theoretical "waves." A broad feminist critique of disability studies emerged in the 1980s. Many disabled feminist activists in the northern hemisphere had been active in the women's movement and were sensitive both to the construction of a male agenda in disability studies and to male control of the disability movement. Disabled women wanted to find their voice in the emerging discipline and in the movement. They identified their socioeconomic status as lower than that of disabled men. In every sphere of contemporary and social life, disabled women were faring worse, thus leading to the concept of "multiple disadvantage," a term not really adequate to understand the complex layering of meanings involved in the disability and gendered experience. These "competing" identities and lack of theoretical sophistication in analyzing multiple disadvantage led to the development of the concept of intersectionality (see below).

Disability studies engaged with feminism at a time when distinct groups were being marginalized on account of their race, class, or sexuality. The "essential" woman of the second wave was exposed as a myth. Women in more powerful and oppressive positions over less powerful women became an issue in feminist discourse, especially in issues of race. For disabled women, this was significant and brought to the fore issues such as care and abuse, and the right to reproduce and parent. It became clear that, for disabled women, issues about control of the agenda by disabled men constituted only part of the picture.

Women in their various roles as carers, parents, and professionals were making major decisions about the lives of disabled women and men and were often guilty of, and responsible for, abuse and neglect. Moreover, disabled women took exception to an analysis of care as "women's burden" (Morris 1991). A further and important critique of the social model of disability emerged from feminists who considered that the impaired body had been neglected (Crow 1996; Meekosha 1998; Thomas 2004). Feminist disability studies addressed questions of representation and difference and engaged with issues of identity, subjectivity, the body, sexuality, and language. For example, stereotypical representation of disabled women in public imagery and the media contributes to their second-class status. Moreover, the social relations of disability are often experienced as endangering the psychoemotional well-being of the individual (Reeve 2002; Thomas 1999; Soldatic 2007).

Garland-Thomson argued that feminist disability studies engages with critical theory in a number of ways: representation structures reality, the margins define the center, gender (or disability) is a way of signifying relationships of power, human identity is multiple and unstable, and analysis and evaluation have political implications (2002, 6). These engagements accord with some of the principles outlined earlier, but do not acknowledge that feminist disability studies should engage with dialogue among cultures. This failure, as we will elucidate later, is the most salient area that has been absent from what we term CDS.

Critical theory insists on revealing power dynamics. Disabled feminist scholars similarly insist on examining the power dynamics and hierarchical social relations of gendered disability. For example, being both a feminist and a disability activist can cause tensions and confrontations with disabled men and nondisabled feminists. These confrontations often emerge from a lack of understanding of the female

disability experience. Disabled women have a different experience and understanding of issues such as prenatal testing, reproductive rights, sterilization, abortion, and the right to parent. Thus, the body can no longer be understood as simply biological or bounded, it embodies oppressive social relations (Hughes and Paterson 1997; Corker and Shakespeare 2002; Wendell 1996; Meekosha 1998; Michalko 1998). Donna Haraway's "Cyborg Manifesto" (1990) enables us to examine the social relations of technology and disability in a transgressive way, where the boundaries between body and machine are blurred, thus further problematizing the dichotomous relationship between disability/ability and normal/abnormal. The possibility that we could reconstitute our bodies, both as mechanical and as organic, with the aid of prostheses and other mechanical devices means that we can embrace new technologies with positive identities rather than feeling victims of inadequate functioning.

In addition, Judith Butler's work on the body, on "abjected bodies" and "performativity" (Butler 1990, 1993), has remarkable applicability to disability studies, although as Samuels (2002) points out, Butler's work had largely been ignored by disability scholars. One of the reasons for ignoring Butler may well have been because she neglects to include any debate on disability, especially in *Bodies that Matter*. Yet Samuels (2002, 72) cautions against adopting Butler's work uncritically, and suggests that:

> merely inserting disability into the mix without thoroughly examining the meaning and implications of the new ideas we create is not only inaccurate, but falls short of pushing Butler's work the necessary next step to fully account for the not-always-able-body.

Recent disability studies scholarship is beginning to critically apply Butler's ideas (for example, McRuer 2006; Shildrick 2007b).

The challenge of feminism to the nature/culture and gender/sex divide has helped challenge the impairment/disability binary and has opened up the debate on the viability of the concepts of disability and ability and of a unified disability politics. Postmodern feminism has pointed to the importance of subjectivity and embodied lives within disability. Feminism is committed to improving the lives of women, so too is CDS. The integration between feminism and CDS remains a work in progress.

Considering and Reconsidering Identity

As Anthias (2006, 20) states: "It is increasingly important to think of a sense of belonging in terms of preconditions for quality of life, and not purely in terms of cultural initiation or cultural identity." A significant outcome of feminism, critical race theory, queer theory, and postmodern thought in general has been an increasing problematization of static and singular conceptions of identity and a turn to a more fluid and contextual understanding. One of the ways forward has been the introduction of the concept of intersectionality (see below). Rejecting simple us/them dichotomies and recognizing intra-group differences, these perspectives have questioned the usefulness of identity and have argued that identity politics may reinforce oppressive structures in society. Much has been discussed about disability identity, but the concept remains under-theorized. A sense of collective identity brought about by exclusion and discrimination is not necessarily the route to change—it may increase victimhood. Similarly, while identity because of shared pride in achievements by disabled people improves self-esteem, it may also

be problematic, as there is always a tendency to produce heroes. Many disabled people would prefer to find a "cure" and do *not* want to belong to this identity group. They might prefer to "pass" in an able-bodied world or live without the pain and frustration that impairment may bring. Or they might even, as do the US amputees in Kurzman's (2003) research, choose the identity of impaired but not disabled. Then again, it is often necessary for them to belong in order to access benefits and services provided by the state.

While there is much to be gained from conceiving of impairment–disability identities as contextual, fluid, multiple, and intersecting, this conceptual move should not mean a carte blanche to dilute the processes and structures of oppression that stigmatize and devalue people with certain kinds of impairments—that in fact constitute disabling responses. Implying that everyone has, or will acquire with age, some kind of impairment or is disabled, as some scholars do (see, for example, Davis 2003; Shakespeare and Watson 2001), can often obscure hierarchies of difference and oppressive social processes and social relations (Shuttleworth 2006; Hughes 2007). Indeed, post-positive realism has made us aware of the continuing significance of social location in social analysis (Moya and Hames-Garcia 2000), and thus the continuing relevance of the social model of disability in the lived experience of disabled people. It also seems fruitful, as Corker suggests (1999) to hold in "dialogic relation" the terms "impairment" and "disability," rather than universalize or dissolve one or both of them.

Intersectionality and Matrices of Domination

Intersectionality emerged out of the writings of black feminists in the US attempting to work out how the structures of race and gender intersect, and as an attempt to move beyond the notion of a single or multiple identity—the approach that adds the experiences of racial oppression to gender oppression (Collins 1990; Crenshaw 1991). Intersectionality has been important in critiquing these rather simplistic approaches to identity, and politically it assists in the process of building coalitions. The framework—as a normative concept, as a method in research (Hancock 2007, 63) and to describe social process—has become adopted in contemporary feminism theory, human rights debates, and critical race theory. It is often used along with metaphors of intermeshing, crossroads, and matrices of domination (Collins 2000, 21).[4]

In disability theory, the multiplier/additive model has been used to attempt to understand and describe the racialized, gendered, or aged disability experience (for example, Deegan and Brooks 1985; Stuart 1992). More recently, intersectional perspectives have been adopted by some scholars in CDS (for example, Erevelles 2000; Moser 2006; Dossa and Fraser 2007; Meekosha 2006). Nirmala Erevelles examines the intersectionality of race, class, gender, and disability, and argues that disability has been used in a much wider sense to allow the capitalist classes to accumulate wealth. Here disability has been used to "support separate regular and special education programs that assign students oppressively marked by race and class and gender to lower tracks within the educational matrix" (2000, 43).

One result of this increasing focus on intersectionality is the articulation of theoretical and/or political alliances between CDS and other emancipatory discourses, such as feminism and critical race theory. Robert McRuer's (2006) recent work exemplifies this trend in his engagement of CDS and queer theory. In his work, McRuer employs the critical self-reflexivity that is a hallmark of critical social theory. An implication of his argument for a "crip" theory

that would crip disability studies, similar to the way queer theory queers gay and lesbian studies, is a critique of the normalizing tendency that underpins the structural critique of society espoused by previous sociopolitical models of disability. Similar to the post-structural approach of Judith Butler and the critical social theorist Margrit Shildrick, McRuer perceives a normalizing orientation as necessarily entailing a demarcation of boundaries, of inclusion–exclusion and of "othering." McRuer clearly articulates the ways in which crip theory and queer theory implicate each other and can thus inform each other. While he is for the most part careful not to show priority to either crip theory or queer theory, there is always the danger that in application to the micropolitics of everyday life, this kind of approach may subordinate one to the other.

The question remains as to whether intersectionality will become a useful tool for CDS and whether it will contribute to in fact overcoming much of the marginalization and discrimination of disabled people. Perhaps even more concerning is whether intersectionality scholars remain attached to the conventional mantra of race, gender, sexuality, and class and continue to exclude other groups, such as disability and age.

The Global Majority: Colonialism, Post-colonialism and Globalization

A significant development in critical theory emerged from scholars writing from the perspective of the colonized. Their work connects most directly with our fourth principle of critical theory, that it should engage in dialogue among cultures. Most notably, Franz Fanon (1970) dealt with the dehumanization by colonialism of both the colonizers and the colonized and, in particular, described how the colonized internalized their oppression. Central to maintaining colonized peoples in a subordinate role has been the process whereby hegemonic ideologies of the dominant groups are transferred and internalized by the dominated.[5] Fanon's work speaks particularly to the disability experience in terms of internalized oppression. Disabled people experience alienation from their own bodies, from their sexuality, and from others in society (Charlton 2000, 74).

Post-colonialist theorists have been concerned with the cultural impact of colonialism. The deconstruction of Western literature, film, and philosophy from a standpoint of race and colonialism has revealed the ethnocentric foundations of the Western canon. From a disability standpoint, scholars in the humanities have similarly examined media and literature. Rosemary Garland-Thomson's work on imagery and the disabled body is one such example. She uses the concept of the "normate" for those who can present themselves as definitive or superior human beings. She argues that the normate can assume authority and wield power because of their bodily configuration and cultural capital (Garland-Thomson 1997, 8).

Another leading post-colonial theorist, Edward Said, has argued in his seminal work *Orientalism* (1978) that Western society depends on the construction of the Arab and the peoples of the "Orient" as different and threatening. In a similar vein, Lennard Davis has argued that the construction of what is normal relies on the existence of the disabled body for its legitimacy (1995, 158):

> the notion of normalcy...makes the idea of disability as well as the ideas of race, class and gender possible...I have been trying to show how deeply tied to the normalised body are the assumptions we make about art, language, literature and culture in general...Normalcy continues its hegemony even in progressive areas such as cultural studies.

Said argues that the West romanticized people of the Orient at the same time as "Orientalism" carried negative connotations. As is evident through studies in film and literature, disabled people's lives are also romanticized as well as being negatively construed. Here, romanticization often consists of the able-bodied hero "curing" the disabled person (Mitchell and Snyder 2001; Norden 1994).

Yet, despite the use of post-colonial approaches in disability literature, art, and film, we have not witnessed an extension, beyond the deconstruction of the text, to an investigation of the production of disability by the colonial enterprise and the exploitative and damaging effects embedded in the economic and material relations between the metropolis and the periphery. Although living in a world where race, racism, nationalism, and globalization are dominant forces, disability studies largely avoids these issues (see, however, McRuer 2006). Disability theory remains ethnocentric, with the global north dominating the agenda. CDS, on the other hand, can be self-conscious about its historicity by revealing the impact of colonialism and post-colonialism on those outside the metropolis who become disabled through invasion, dispossession, war, and the hegemonic processes of normalcy (Sherry 2007; Meekosha 2008).

Disabled people in the majority world have been marginalized often as a result of colonization, colonial rule, and post-colonialism; these cases constitute 80 percent of the 650 million disabled people in the world. The UN reports that for every child killed in warfare, three are injured and permanently disabled (UN 2006). Invasion, war, nuclear testing, mining, the export of pollution, and the militarization of the globe have all contributed to the increasing number of disabled people in the global south. The leading suppliers of arms remain the US and UK companies, with China and Russia also becoming major players, with the consequence a massive increase in the number of amputees and disabled people in the global south. There is much discussion on the rights of disabled people with the new UN convention, but little on the responsibilities of those profiting out of the production of disability.

EMPLOYING THE CRITICAL ATTITUDE IN DISABILITY STUDIES

Thompson (2003), in a penetrating discussion of Foucault's genealogy of the critical attitude, adeptly shows the transformations that occurred in his thinking of what constitutes critique. The critical attitude will, of course, always remain a utopian stance taken towards the current social organization of a society. But the lesson of Foucault's shifts in critical thinking for CDS, beyond the notion that the terms of engagement in a society change over time, is a reminder that our understanding of what constitutes the modes of critical analyses we employ is not set in stone. In this sense, CDS must continuously re-evaluate our analyses as both process and product. Autonomy and social participation can serve as beacons, but the contours of these concepts must remain flexible and amenable to the vicissitudes of history and critical thought itself. This radical reflexivity must of necessity also remain receptive to new theoretical perspectives to shed light on the changing structures and meanings that define and restrict emancipation. The task is always to balance the activist's cry for accessible conceptualization with the scholar's understanding of the complex, interwoven but continually changing fabric of human societies.

We claim that knowledge is power and theory development is integral to power. While being the latest marginalized group with a political agenda to connect with critical social theory in its present form, CDS intends to build an alternative body of work that will of necessity be subversive. As argued in this article, a combination of factors has led to the emergence of CDS. While there is some work on disability that is employing the principles and ideas from the range of current critical social theories, we hope that by making this development explicit we can once again bring some of the challenges faced by disabled people to the forefront of public discourse. The disability movement's struggle was not just about ramps: human rights issues—such as forced sterilization of minors, violence and abuse, poverty, unemployment, citizenship, the disabling effects of war and sexual exclusion, and the myriad issues of disabled people in the global south—must be included in the new CDS.

By making strategies of critique applied to disability issues explicit, CDS can also contribute important conceptual and empirical scholarship to critical theory's development. How societies divide "normal" and "abnormal" bodies is central to the production and sustenance of what it means to be human in society. It defines access to nations and communities. It determines choice and participation in civic life. It determines what constitutes "rational" men and women and who should have the right to be part of society and who should not.

CONCLUSION

CDS is guided by unique interdisciplinarities and productive debates on a range of issues and solutions. What unites CDS theorists is an agreement that disabled people are undervalued and discriminated against and this cannot be changed simply through liberal or neoliberal legislation and policy.

CDS will necessarily be eclectic and will continue to include materialist analyses, such as the political economy of disability. It will inevitably build on the work of the early pioneers in disability studies and continue to employ relevant aspects of social models of disability. The politics inherent in disabled people's lived experience and the multiple sociocultural factors that can constrain their agency, so difficult to theorize in terms of a strict materialism, constitute a central area for CDS. Likewise, the conceptual interface between chronic illness, impairment, and disability is no more understood now than it was during the heyday of the social model, despite Thomas's (2007) recent attempt to show the usefulness of the sociology of health and illness to disability studies (and vice versa). Then again, in terms of the social model, conditions that did not easily fit within its narrow conceptual framework, such as chronic illness and learning disability, were usually deemed anomalous or simply ignored. If CDS wants to contribute to theory and politics on a global level, we certainly need to listen to theories of emancipation and social participation emerging from the global south. It is hoped that with the acknowledgment that disabling social relations and cultural meanings can be critiqued from diverse theoretical perspectives, a wide range of issues and discourses will become more visible.

At the beginning of this article, we asked the question of whether the growing tendency of disability scholars to employ the term "CDS" represents a paradigm shift or a maturing of the discipline. Mairian Corker perhaps provided the best answer to our question 10 years ago, before the current nomenclature began to emerge. Corker envisioned a mature disability studies opening up to diverse theoretical strands of enquiry, but with the social model as a part of its historical development. Investigating difficult problems that disability studies tended to shy away from and opening up new lines of critical enquiry to elucidate these issues will be beneficial to the study of disability and contribute to an expanded understanding of disabled people's place in the world.

NOTES

1. On this account, see the article by Susan Magasi (2008) on integrating a disability studies perspective into rehabilitation practice.
2. Castoriadis (1987) provides an illustrative example. Like the Frankfurt School, he criticizes Western society's overvaluing of instrumental rationality, but posits that the West's obsession with instrumentalism ironically indicates a cultural imaginary that has been divested of a raison d'être. Function thus simply stands for itself and rationality loses its relation to critique, which obscures our relation to autonomy—that is, our ability to perceive ourselves as self-instituting beings and society.
3. For example, Herdt and Stoller (1990) criticize Foucault's claim that sexuality becomes central to self-constitution in Western society with cross-cultural evidence that "sex talk" relating to the self occurs in many societies.
4. Patricia Hill Collins in *Black Feminist Thought: Knowledge, Consciousness, and the Politics of Empowerment* (2009) uses the concept of "matrices of domination" to describe interconnections of oppression.
5. This is not to suggest that colonized peoples cannot be agents in their own right, in the same way as disabled people are also active subjects. Neither can we easily and meaningfully distinguish between the colonizers and the colonized.

REFERENCES

Agger B (1998) *Critical Social Theories: An Introduction* Westview Press, Boulder, CO.

Allan J (1996) "Foucault and special educational needs: a 'box of tools' for analysing children's experiences of mainstreaming" 11(2) *Disability & Society* pp 219–34.

Allan J (1999) "I don't need this: acts of transgression by students with special educational needs in Scotland" in K Ballard (ed.) *Inclusive Education: International Voices on Disability and Justice* Open University Press, Buckingham.

Allan J (2005) "Inclusion as an ethical project" in S Tremain (ed.) *Foucault and the Government of Disability* University of Michigan Press, Ann Arbor pp 281–97.

Anthias F (2006) "Belongings in a globalising and unequal world: rethinking translocations" in N Yuval-Davis and K Kannabiran (eds) *The Situated Politics of Belonging* Sage, London.

Ariotti L (1999) "Social construction of Anangu disability" 7 *Australian Journal of Rural Health* pp 216–22.

Burchell G, Gordon C and Miller P (eds) (1991) *The Foucault Effect: Studies in Governmentality* University of Chicago Press, Chicago.

Butler J (1990) *Gender Trouble: Feminism and the Subversion of Identity* Routledge, New York.

Butler J (1993) *Bodies that Matter: On the Discursive Limits of "Sex"* Routledge, New York.

Calhoun C (1995) *Critical Social Theory* Blackwell, Oxford.

Campbell F (2008) "Exploring internalized Ableism using critical race theory" 23(2) *Disability and Society* pp 151–62.

Castoriadis C (1987) *The Imaginary Institution of Society* K Blamey (trans.) MIT Press, Cambridge.

Castoriadis C (1997) "The Greek and the modern political imaginary" in *World in Fragments: Writings on Politics, Society, Psychoanalysis, and the Imagination* Stanford University Press, Stanford, CA, pp 84–107.

Charlton J (2000) *Nothing About Us Without Us: Disability, Oppression and Empowerment* University of California Press, Berkeley.

Collins P H (1990) *Black Feminist Thought: Knowledge Consciousness, and the Politics of Empowerment* Routledge, New York.

Collins P H (2000) *Black Feminist Thought: Knowledge Consciousness, and the Politics of Empowerment* (2nd edn) Routledge, London.

Collins P H (2009) *Black Feminist Thought: Knowledge Consciousness, and the Politics of Empowerment* (Routledge Classics) Routledge, London.

Corker M (1998) "Disability discourse in a postmodern world" in T Shakespeare (ed.) *The Disability Reader: Social Science Perspectives* Cassell, New York pp 221–33.

Corker M (1999) "Differences, conflations and foundations: the limits to "accurate" theoretical representation of disabled people's experience?" 14(5) *Disability and Society* pp 627–42.

Corker M and Shakespeare T (2002) "Mapping the terrain" in M Corker and T Shakespeare (eds) *Disability/Postmodernity: Embodying Disability Theory* Cassell, New York pp 1–17.

Crenshaw K (1991) "Demarginalizing the intersection of race and sex: a black feminist critique of anti-discrimination doctrine" 139(3) *Feminist Theory and Antiracist Politics* pp 139–67.

Crow L (1996) "Including all of our lives: renewing the social model of disability" in C Barnes and G Mercer (eds) *Exploring the Divide: Illness and Disability* Disability Press, Leeds pp 55–73.

Davis J (2000) "Disability studies as ethnographic research and text: research strategies and roles for promoting social change?" 15(2) *Disability and Society* pp 191–206.

Davis L (1995) *Enforcing Normalcy: Disability, Deafness and the Body* Verso: London.

Davis L (ed.) (1997) *The Disability Studies Reader* Routledge, London.

Davis L (2003) *Bending Over Backwards: Disability, Dismodernism & Other Difficult Positions* New York University Press, New York.

Deegan M and Brooks N (1985) *Women and Disability: The Double Handicap* Transaction Books, Oxford.

Dixson A and Rousseau C (eds) (2006) *Introduction in Critical Race Theory in Education: All God's Children Got a Song* Routledge, London.

Dossa P and Fraser S (2007) "Disability, marginality and the nation state—negotiating social markers of difference: Fahimeh's story" 21(4) *Disability & Society* pp 345–58.

Erevelles N (2000) "Educating unruly bodies: critical pedagogy, disability studies and the politics of schooling" 50(1) *Educational Theory* pp 25–47.

Erevelles N (2005) "Understanding curriculum as normalizing text: disability studies meet curriculum theory" 37(4) *Journal of Curriculum Studies* pp 421–29.

Fanon F (1970) *Black Skins White Masks* Paladin, London.

Finkelstein V (1980) *Attitudes and Disabled People* World Health Organization, Geneva.

Foucault M (1978) *The History of Sexuality, Volume I: An Introduction*, trans. R Hurley, Pantheon Books, New York.

Foucault M (1997) *Ethics: Subjectivity and Truth*, ed. Paul Rabinow, New Press, New York.

Gabel S (2006) "An aesthetic of disability" in S Gabel (ed.) *Disability Studies in Education: Readings in Theory and Method* Peter Lang, New York pp 21–36.

Gabel S and Peters S (2004) "Presage of a paradigm shift? Beyond the social model of disability toward resistance theories of disability" 19(6) *Disability & Society* pp 585–600.

Garland-Thomson R (1997) *Extraordinary Bodies: Figuring Physical Disability in American Culture and Literature* Columbia University Press, New York.

Garland-Thomson R (2002) "The politics of staring: visual rhetoric of disability in popular photography" in S L Snyder, B J Brueggemann and G R Thomson (eds) *Disability Studies: Enabling the Humanities* Modern Language Association of America, New York.

Ghai A (2002) "Disability in the Indian context: postcolonial perspectives" in M Corker and T Shakespeare (eds) *Disability/Postmodernity* Continuum, London pp 88–100.

Goodley D and Lawthom R (eds) (2005) *Disability and Psychology: Critical Introductions and Reflections* (1st edn) Palgrave Macmillan, New York.

Gustafson K (2007) "Parallel disciplines: critical race theory, disability studies, and the disciplinary gap between them," paper presented at the Annual Meeting of the Law and Society Association, TBA, Berlin, July.

Habermas J (1973) *Knowledge and Human Interests* Beacon Press, Boston.

Hancock A (2007) "When multiplication doesn't equal quick addition: examining intersectionality as a research paradigm" 5(1) *Perspectives on Politics* pp 63–79.

Haraway D (1990) "A manifesto for cyborgs: science, technology and socialist feminism in the 1980s" in L Nicholson (ed.) *Feminism/Postmodernism* Routledge, New York pp 190–233.

Held D (1980) *Introduction to Critical Theory: Horkheimer to Habermas* University of California Press, Berkeley.

Herdt G and Stoller R (1990) *Intimate Communications: Erotics and the Study of Culture* Columbia University Press, New York.

Horkheimer M (1974) *Critique of Instrumental Reason* Seabury Press, New York.

Horkheimer M (1986) *Critical Theory: Selected Essays* Continuum, New York.

Horkheimer M and Adorno T (1972) *Dialectic of Enlightenment* Herder and Herder, New York.

Hosking D (2008) "Critical disability theory," paper presented at the 4th Biennial Disability Studies Conference, Lancaster University, 2–4 September.

Hughes B (2007) "Being disabled: towards a critical ontology for disability studies" 22(7) *Disability and Society* pp 673–84.

Hughes B and Paterson K (1997) "The social model of disability and the disappearing body: towards a sociology of impairment" 12(3) *Disability & Society* pp 325–40.

Ingstad B and Reynolds Whyte S (eds) (2007) *Disability in Local and Global Worlds* University of California Press, Berkeley.

Kafer A (2003) "Compulsory bodies: reflections on heterosexuality and ablebodiedness" 15(3) *Journal of Women's History* pp 77–89.

Kalyvas A (2001) "The politics of autonomy and the challenge of deliberation: Castoriadis contra Habermas" 64(1) *Thesis Eleven* pp 1–19.

Kurzman S (2003) *Performing Able-Bodiedness: Amputees and Prosthetics in America,* unpublished doctoral dissertation, University of California, Santa Cruz.

Levinson J (2005) "The group home workplace and the work of know-how" 28 *Human Studies* pp 57–85.

Linton S (1998) *Claiming Disability: Knowledge and Identity* New York University Press, New York.

Longmore P (2003) *Why I Burned My Book and Other Essays on Disability* Temple University Press, Philadelphia.

Lorenzo T, Mzoliula T and Priestley M (2006) "Developing a disability studies programme: engaging activism and academia for social change" in B Watermeyer, L Swartz, T Lorenzo, M Schneider and M Priestley (eds) *Disability and Social Change: A South African Agenda* Human Science Research Council, Cape Town.

McRuer R (2006) *Crip Theory: Cultural Signs of Queerness and Disability* New York University Press, New York.

Magasi S (2008) "Disability studies in practice: a work in progress" 15(6) *Topics in Stroke Rehabilitation* pp 611–17.

Marcuse H (1965) "The concept of essence" in *Negations: Essays in Critical Theory* Beacon Press, Boston pp 43–88 (originally published in German in *Zeitschrift für Sozialforschung* vol. V, 1936).

Meekosha H (1998) "Body battles: bodies, gender and disability" in T Shakespeare (ed.) *The Disability Reader: Social Science Perspectives* Cassell, London.

Meekosha H (2004) "Drifting down the Gulf Stream: navigating the cultures of disability studies" 19(7) *Disability & Society* pp 721–34.

Meekosha H (2006) "What the hell are you? An intercategorical analysis of race, ethnicity, gender and disability" 8(2) *Australian Body Politic Scandinavian Journal of Disability Research* pp 161–76.

Meekosha H (2008) "Contextualizing disability: developing southern/global theory," keynote paper presented to 4th Biennial Disability Studies Conference, Lancaster University, 2–4 September.

Meekosha H and Dowse L (2007) "Integrating critical disability studies into social work" 19(3) *Practice Social Work in Action* pp 169–83.

Meekosha H and Green D (2004) *Disability Studies in Australian Universities: A Preliminary Audit of Subjects and Programs that Include the Social Dimensions of Disability* (1st edn) Disability Studies and Research Institute, University of New South Wales, School of Social Work, Sydney.

Mercer G (2004) "From critique to practice: emancipatory disability research" in C Barnes and G Mercer (eds) *Implementing the Social Model of Disability: Theory and Research* Disability Press, Leeds.

Michalko R (1998) *The Mystery of the Eye and the Shadow of Blindness* University of Toronto Press, Toronto.

Mitchell D and Snyder S (2001) "Representation and its discontents—the uneasy home of disability in literature and film" in G Albrecht (ed.) *Handbook of Disability Studies* Sage, Thousand Oaks, CA.

Morris J (1991) *Pride Against Prejudice* Women's Press, London.

Moser I (2006) "Sociotechnical practices and difference on the interferences between disability, gender, and class" 31(5) *Science, Technology, & Human Values* pp 537–64.

Moya P and Hames-Garcia M (eds) (2000) *Reclaiming Identity: Realist Theory and the Predicament of Postmodernism* University of California Press, Berkeley.

Norden M (1994) *The Cinema of Isolation: A History of Physical Disability in the Movies* Rutgers University Press, New Brunswick, NJ.

Oliver M (1990) *The Politics of Disablement* Macmillan, London.

Oliver M (1992) "Changing the social relations of research production?" 7(2) *Disability & Society* pp 101–14.

Paterson K and Hughes B (1999) "Disability studies and phenomenology: the carnal politics of everyday life" 14(5) *Disability & Society* pp 597–610.

Pfeiffer D (2003) "The disability studies paradigm" in P Devlieger, F Rusch and D Pfeiffer (eds) *Rethinking Anthropology: The Emergence of New Definitions, Concepts and Communities* Garant, Antwerp, Belgium.

Pothier D and Devlin R (2006) *Critical Disability Theory: Essays in Philosophy, Politics, Policy, and Law* UBC Press, Toronto.

Rabinow P (1997) "Introduction" in M Foucault *Ethics: Subjectivity and Truth,* ed. P Rabinow, New Press, New York.

Reeve D (2002) "Negotiating psycho-emotional dimensions of disability and their influence on identity constructions" 17(5) *Disability & Society* pp 493–508.

Roets G and Goodley D A (2008) "Disability, citizenship and uncivilized society: the smooth and nomadic qualities of self-advocacy" 28(4) *Disability Studies.*

Quarterly [Online] Available: <www.dsq-sds.org/article/view/131/131> [2009, June 1].

Said E (1978) *Orientalism* Peregrine, London.

Samuels E (2002) "Critical divides: Judith Butler's body theory and the question of disability" 14(3) *NWSA Journal* pp 58–77.

Shakespeare T (1994) "Cultural representation of disabled people: dustbins for disavowal" 9(3) *Disability & Society* pp 283–99.

Shakespeare T (2006) *Disability Rights and Wrongs* Routledge, Abingdon.

Shakespeare T and Watson N (2001) "The social model of disability: an outdated ideology?" 2 *Research in Social Science and Disability* pp 9–28.

Sherry M (2007) "(Post) colonising disability" 4 *Wagadu: A Journal of Transnational Women's and Gender Studies—Intersecting Gender and Disability Perspectives in Rethinking Postcolonial Identities* pp 10–22.

Shildrick M (1997) *Leaky Bodies and Boundaries: Feminism, Postmodernism and (Bio) Ethics* Routledge, London.

Shildrick M (2007a) "Contested pleasures: the sociopolitical economy of disability and sexuality" 4(1) *Sexuality Research and Social Policy* pp 53–66.

Shildrick M (2007b) "Dangerous discourses: anxiety, desire, and disability" 8(3) *Studies in Gender and Sexuality* pp 221–44.

Shuttleworth R (2000) *The Pursuit of Sexual Intimacy for Men with Cerebral Palsy,* unpublished doctoral dissertation, University of California San Francisco and Berkeley.

Shuttleworth R (2002) "Defusing the adverse context of disability and desirability as a practice of the self for men with cerebral palsy" in M Corker and T Shakespeare (eds) *Disability/Postmodernity: Embodying Disability Theory* Continuum, New York.

Shuttleworth R (2004) "Disability/difference" in C Ember and M Ember (eds) *The Encyclopedia of Medical Anthropology: Health and Illness in the World's Cultures* (3 vols) Kluwer/Plenum, New York pp 360–73.

Shuttleworth R (2006) "Critically engaging disability studies and anthropological research on impairment-disability," invited presentation, School of Psychology, Psychiatry and Psychological Medicine, Monash University, Melbourne.

Shuttleworth R (2007) "Introduction to the special issue: critical research and policy debates in disability and sexuality studies" 4(1) *Sexuality Research and Social Policy* pp 1–14.

Society for Disability Studies (SDS) (2009) *2009 Guidelines for Disability Studies Programs* [Online] Available: <www.disstudies.org/guidelines_for_disabilitystudies_programs> [2009, May 10].

Soldatic K (2007) "Disgust and the moral economy of disability," paper presented at the Australian Sociological Association/Sociological Association of Aotearoa New Zealand, Auckland, 4–7 December.

Soldatic K and Biyanwila J (2006) "Disability and development: a critical southern standpoint on able-bodied masculinity," paper presented at the TASA Conference, Murdoch University and University of Western Australia, December.

Stone E and Priestley M (1996) "Parasites, pawns and partners: disability researchers and the role of non-disabled researchers" 47 *British Journal of Sociology* pp 699–716.

Stuart O (1992) "Race and disability: just a double oppression?" 7(2) *Disability, Handicap and Society* pp 177–88.

Sullivan M (2005) "Subjected bodies: paraplegia, rehabilitation, and the politics of movement" in S Tremain (ed.) *Foucault and the Government of Disability* University of Michigan Press, Ann Arbor pp 27–44.

Thomas C (1999) *Female Forms: Experiencing and Understanding Disability* Open University Press, Buckingham.

Thomas C (2004) "How is disability understood?: an examination of sociological processes" 19(6) *Disability & Society* pp 569–83.

Thomas C (2007) *Sociologies of Disability and Illness* Palgrave Macmillan, Houndmills.

Thompson K (2003) "Forms of resistance: Foucault on tactical reversal and self-formation" 36 *Continental Philosophy Review* pp 113–38.

Torney S and Townshend J (2006) *Key Thinkers from Critical Theory to Post-Marxism* Sage Publications, London.

Tremain S (2005) "Foucault, governmentality and critical disability theory: an introduction" in S Tremain (ed.) *Foucault and the Government of Disability* University of Michigan Press, Ann Arbor pp 1–26.

United Nations (UN) (2006) "Some facts about persons with disabilities" [Online] Available: <www.un.org/disabilities/convention/facts.html> [2009, May 19].

Watermeyer B, Swartz L, Lorenzo T, Schneider M and Priestley M (eds) (2006) *Disability and Social Change: A South African Agenda* Human Science Research Council Press, Cape Town.

Wendell S (1996) *The Rejected Body: Feminist Philosophical Reflections on Disability* Routledge, London.

CHAPTER 13

The Social Model of Disability

Tom Shakespeare

SUMMARY

In this essay, Tom Shakespeare outlines how the social model of disability differs from the over-medicalized or individualistic accounts of disability that preceded it. The social model requires understanding some key dichotomies, the first of which is that an individual impairment differs from the social construction of disability that might surround that impairment. The earlier medical models tended to focus on disability as an individual deficit to be cured, but the social model identifies disability as a culturally and historically specific phenomenon. Additionally, the social model distinguishes between disabled people as an oppressed group and the non-disabled people that are the causes or contributors to that oppression.

Shakespeare highlights some political strengths of the social model, including its ability to unite disabled people for political action and its practicality in identifying public barriers to justice The social model shifts the blame away from disabled individuals and to society. But critics have also pointed out some of the model's weaknesses, as the social model's simplicity limits its viability as an academic account of disability. The social model also neglects impairment as part of many disabled people's lived experiences, and it is difficult to separate impairment from disability in researching everyday life. Because the social model conceives of disability as oppression, it becomes logically impossible to find disabled people who are not oppressed. And although the social model is useful for identifying barriers in the built environment, it also implicitly aims for a barrier-free utopia that is impossible to realize. Although Shakespeare compares disability activism to other identity groups, he points out that the comparisons are limited. There is nothing intrinsically problematic about being a woman, for example, but disabled people face intrinsic limitations. If disabled people are to be emancipated, society needs to provide resources to overcome these limitations rather than merely limiting discrimination. For these reasons and more, Shakespeare calls for more sophisticated and complex ways of theorizing disability while also acknowledging the social model as "indispensable."

INTRODUCTION

In many countries of the world, disabled people and their allies have organised over the last three decades to challenge the historical oppression and exclusion of disabled people (Driedger, 1989; Campbell and Oliver, 1996; Charlton, 1998). Key to these struggles has been the challenge to over-medicalised and individualist accounts of disability. While the problems of disabled people have been explained historically in terms of divine punishment, karma, or moral failing, and post-Enlightenment in terms of biological deficit, the disability movement has focused attention onto social oppression, cultural discourse, and environmental barriers.

The global politics of disability rights and deinstitutionalisation has launched a family of social explanations of disability. In North America, these have usually been framed using the terminology of minority groups and civil rights (Hahn, 1988). In the Nordic countries, the dominant conceptualisation has been the relational model (Gustavsson et al., 2005). In many countries, the idea of normalisation and social role valorisation has been inspirational, particularly amongst those working with people with learning difficulties (Wolfensberger, 1972). In Britain, it has been the social model of disability which has provided the structural analysis of disabled people's social exclusion (Hasler, 1993).

The social model emerged from the intellectual and political arguments of the Union of Physically Impaired Against Segregation (UPIAS). This network had been formed after Paul Hunt, a former resident of the Lee Court Cheshire Home, wrote to *The Guardian* newspaper in 1971, proposing the creation of a consumer group of disabled residents of institutions. In forming the organisation and developing its ideology, Hunt worked closely with Vic Finkelstein, a South African psychologist, who had come to Britain in 1968 after being expelled for his anti-apartheid activities. UPIAS was a small, hardcore group of disabled people, inspired by Marxism, who rejected the liberal and reformist campaigns of more mainstream disability organisations such as the Disablement Income Group and the Disability Alliance. According to their policy statement (adopted December 1974), the aim of UPIAS was to replace segregated facilities with opportunities for people with impairments to participate fully in society, to live independently, to undertake productive work, and to have full control over their own lives. The policy statement

defined disabled people as an oppressed group and highlighted barriers:

> We find ourselves isolated and excluded by such things as flights of steps, inadequate public and personal transport, unsuitable housing, rigid work routines in factories and offices, and a lack of up-to-date aids and equipment.
>
> (UPIAS Aims paragraph 1)

Even in Britain, the social model of disability was not the only political ideology on offer to the first generation of activists (Campbell and Oliver, 1996). Other disabled-led activist groups had emerged, including the Liberation Network of People with Disabilities. Their draft Liberation Policy, published in 1981, argued that while the basis of social divisions in society was economic, these divisions were sustained by psychological beliefs in inherent superiority or inferiority. Crucially, the Liberation Network argued that people with disabilities, unlike other groups, suffered inherent problems because of their disabilities. Their strategy for liberation included: developing connections with other disabled people and creating an inclusive disability community for mutual support; exploring social conditioning and positive self-awareness; the abolition of all segregation; seeking control over media representation; working out a just economic policy; encouraging the formation of groups of people with disabilities.

However, the organisation which dominated and set the tone for the subsequent development of the British disability movement, and of disability studies in Britain, was UPIAS. Where the Liberation Network was dialogic, inclusive, and feminist, UPIAS was hard-line, male-dominated, and determined. The British Council of Organisations of Disabled People (BCODP), set up as a coalition of disabled-led groups in 1981, adopted the UPIAS approach to disability. Vic Finkelstein and the other BCODP delegates to the first Disabled People's International World Congress in Singapore later that year, worked hard to have their definitions of disability adopted on the global stage (Driedger, 1989). At the same time, Vic Finkelstein, John Swain, and others were working with the Open University to create an academic course which would promote and develop disability politics (Finkelstein, 1998). Joining the team was Mike Oliver, who quickly adopted the structural approach to understanding disability, and was to coin the term "social model of disability" in 1983.

WHAT IS THE SOCIAL MODEL OF DISABILITY?

While the first UPIAS Statement of Aims had talked of social problems as an added burden faced by people with impairment, the Fundamental Principles of Disability discussion document, recording their disagreements with the reformist Disability Alliance, went further:

> In our view, it is society which disables physically impaired people. Disability is something imposed on top of our impairments, by the way we are unnecessarily isolated and excluded from full participation in society. Disabled people are therefore an oppressed group in society.
>
> (UPIAS, 1975)

Here and in the later development of UPIAS thinking are the key elements of the social model: the distinction between disability (social exclusion) and impairment (physical limitation) and the claim that disabled people are an oppressed group. Disability is now defined, not in functional terms, but as

> the disadvantage or restriction of activity caused by a contemporary social organisation which takes little or no account of people who have physical impairments and

thus excludes them from participation in the mainstream of social activities.

(UPIAS, 1975)

This redefinition of disability itself is what sets the British social model apart from all other socio-political approaches to disability, and what paradoxically gives the social model both its strengths and its weaknesses.

Key to social model thinking is a series of dichotomies:

1. Impairment is distinguished from disability. The former is individual and private, the latter is structural and public. While doctors and professions allied to medicine seek to remedy impairment, the real priority is to accept impairment and to remove disability. Here there is an analogy with feminism, and the distinction between biological sex (male and female) and social gender (masculine and feminine) (Oakley, 1972). Like gender, disability is a culturally and historically specific phenomenon, not a universal and unchanging essence.

2. The social model is distinguished from the medical or individual model. Whereas the former defines disability as a social creation—a relationship between people with impairment and a disabling society—the latter defines disability in terms of individual deficit. Mike Oliver writes:

> Models are ways of translating ideas into practice and the idea underpinning the individual model was that of personal tragedy, while the idea underpinning the social model was that of externally imposed restriction.
>
> (Oliver, 2004, 19)

Medical model thinking is enshrined in the liberal term "people with disabilities," and in approaches which seek to count the numbers of people with impairment, or which reduce the complex problems of disabled people to issues of medical prevention, cure, or rehabilitation. Social model thinking mandates barrier removal, anti-discrimination legislation, independent living, and other responses to social oppression. From a disability rights perspective, social model approaches are progressive, medical model approaches are reactionary.

3. Disabled people are distinguished from non-disabled people. Disabled people are an oppressed group, and often non-disabled people and organisations—such as professionals and charities—are the causes or contributors to that oppression. Civil rights, rather than charity or pity, are the way to solve the disability problem. Organisations and services controlled and run by disabled people provide the most appropriate solutions. Research accountable to, and preferably done by, disabled people offers the best insights.

For more than ten years, a debate has raged in Britain about the value and applicability of the social model (Morris, 1991; Crow, 1992; French, 1993; Williams, 1999; Shakespeare and Watson 2002). In response to critiques, academics and activists maintain that the social model has been misunderstood, misapplied, or even wrongly viewed as a social theory. Many leading advocates of the social model approach maintain that the essential insights developed by UPIAS in the 1970s still remain accurate and valid three decades later.

STRENGTHS OF THE SOCIAL MODEL

As demonstrated internationally, disability activism and civil rights are possible without adopting social model ideology. Yet the British social model is arguably the most powerful form which social approaches to disability have taken. The social model is simple, memorable, and effective, each of which is a key requirement of a political slogan or ideology. The benefits of the social model have been shown in three main areas.

First, the social model, which has been called "the big idea" of the British disability

movement (Hasler, 1993), has been effective *politically* in building the social movement of disabled people. It is easily explained and understood, and it generates a clear agenda for social change. The social model offers a straightforward way of distinguishing allies from enemies. At its most basic, this reduces to the terminology people use: "disabled people" signals a social model approach, whereas "people with disabilities" signals a mainstream approach.

Second, by identifying social barriers which should be removed, the social model has been effective *instrumentally* in the liberation of disabled people. Michael Oliver argues that the social model is a "practical tool, not a theory, an idea or a concept" (2004, 30). The social model demonstrates that the problems disabled people face are the result of social oppression and exclusion, not their individual deficits. This places the moral responsibility on society to remove the burdens which have been imposed, and to enable disabled people to participate. In Britain, campaigners used the social model philosophy to name the various forms of discrimination which disabled people (Barnes, 1991), and used this evidence as the argument by which to achieve the 1995 Disability Discrimination Act. In the subsequent decade, services, buildings, and public transport have been required to be accessible to disabled people, and most statutory and voluntary organisations have adopted the social model approach.

Third, the social model has been effective *psychologically* in improving the self-esteem of disabled people and building a positive sense of collective identity. In traditional accounts of disability, people with impairments feel that they are at fault. Language such as "invalid" reinforces a sense of personal deficit and failure. The focus is on the individual, and on her limitations of body and brain. Lack of self-esteem and self-confidence is a major obstacle to disabled people participating in society. The social model has the power to change the perception of disabled people. The problem of disability is relocated from the individual, to the barriers and attitudes which disable her. It is not the disabled person who is to blame, but society. She does not have to change, society does. Rather than feeling self-pity, she can feel anger and pride.

WEAKNESSES OF THE SOCIAL MODEL

The simplicity which is the hallmark of the social model is also its fatal flaw. The social model's benefits as a slogan and political ideology are its drawbacks as an academic account of disability. Another problem is its authorship by a small group of activists, the majority of whom had spinal injury or other physical impairments and were white heterosexual men. Arguably, had UPIAS included people with learning difficulties, mental health problems, or with more complex physical impairments, or more representative of different experiences, it could not have produced such a narrow understanding of disability.

Among the weaknesses of the social model are:

1. The neglect of impairment as an important aspect of many disabled people's lives. Feminists Jenny Morris (1991), Sally French (1993), and Liz Crow (1992) were pioneers in this criticism of the social model neglect of individual experience of impairment:

> As individuals, most of us simply cannot pretend with any conviction that our impairments are irrelevant because they influence every aspect of our lives. We must find a way to integrate them into our whole experience and identity for the sake of our physical and emotional well-being, and, subsequently, for our capacity to work against Disability.
>
> (Crow, 1992, 7)

The social model so strongly disowns individual and medical approaches, that it risks implying that impairment is not a problem. Whereas other socio-political accounts of disability have developed the important insight that people with impairments are disabled by society as well as by their bodies, the social model suggests that people are disabled by society not by their bodies. Rather than simply opposing medicalisation, it can be interpreted as rejecting medical prevention, rehabilitation, or cure of impairment, even if this is not what either UPIAS, Finkelstein, Oliver, or Barnes intended. For individuals with static impairments, which do not degenerate or cause medical complications, it may be possible to regard disability as entirely socially created. For those who have degenerative conditions which may cause premature death, or any condition which involves pain and discomfort, it is harder to ignore the negative aspects of impairment. As Simon Williams has argued, "endorsement of disability solely as social oppression is really only an option, and an erroneous one at that, for those spared the ravages of chronic illness" (1999, 812).

Carol Thomas (1999) has tried to develop the social model to include what she calls "impairment effects," in order to account for the limitations and difficulties of medical conditions. Subsequently, she suggested that a relational interpretation of the social model enables disabling aspects to be attributed to impairment, as well as social oppression:

> once the term "disability" is ring-fenced to mean forms of oppressive social reactions visited upon people with impairments, there is no need to deny that impairment and illness cause some restrictions of activity, or that in many situations both disability and impairment effects interact to place limits on activity.
>
> (Thomas, 2004, 29)

One curious consequence of the ingenious reformulation is that only people with impairment who face oppression can be called disabled people. This relates to another problem:

2. The social model assumes what it needs to prove: that disabled people are oppressed. The sex/gender distinction defines gender as a social dimension, not as oppression. Feminists claimed that gender relations *involved* oppression, but did not define gender relations *as* oppression. However, the social model defines disability as oppression. In other words, the question is not whether disabled people are oppressed in a particular situation, but only the extent to which they are oppressed. A circularity enters into disability research: it is logically impossible for a qualitative researcher to find disabled people who are not oppressed.

3. The analogy with feminist debates about sex and gender highlights another problem: the crude distinction between impairment (medical) and disability (social). Any researcher who does qualitative research with disabled people immediately discovers that in everyday life it is very hard to distinguish clearly between the impact of impairment, and the impact of social barriers (see for example Watson, 2002; Sherry, 2002). In practice, it is the interaction of individual bodies and social environments which produces disability. For example, steps only become an obstacle if someone has a mobility impairment: each element is necessary but not sufficient for the individual to be disabled. If a person with multiple sclerosis is depressed, how easy is it to make a causal separation between the effect of the impairment itself; her reaction to having an impairment; her reaction to being oppressed and excluded on the basis of having an impairment; other, unrelated reasons for her to be depressed? In practice, social and individual aspects are almost inextricable in the complexity of the lived experience of disability.

Moreover, feminists have now abandoned the sex/gender distinction, because it implies that sex is not a social concept. Judith Butler (1990) and others show that what we think of as sexual difference is always viewed through the lens of gender. Shelley Tremain (2002) has claimed similarly that the social model treats impairment as an unsocialised and universal concept, whereas, like sex, impairment is always already social.

4. The concept of the barrier-free utopia. The idea of the enabling environment, in which all socially imposed barriers are removed, is usually implicit rather than explicit in social model thinking, although it does form the title of a major academic collection (Swain et al., 1993). Vic Finkelstein (1981) also wrote a simple parable of a village designed for wheelchair users to illustrate the way that social model thinking turned the problem of disability on its head. Yet despite the value of approaches such as Universal Design, the concept of a world in which people with impairments were free of environmental barriers is hard to operationalise.

For example, many parts of the natural world will remain inaccessible to many disabled people: mountains, bogs, beaches are almost impossible for wheelchair users to traverse, while sunsets, birdsong, and other aspects of nature are difficult for those lacking sight or hearing to experience. In urban settings, many barriers can be mitigated, although historic buildings often cannot easily be adapted. However, accommodations are sometimes incompatible because people with different impairments may require different solutions: blind people prefer steps and defined curbs and indented paving, while wheelchair users need ramps, dropped curbs, and smooth surfaces. Sometimes, people with the same impairment require different solutions: some visually impaired people access text in Braille, others in large print, audio tape or electronic files.

Practicality and resource constraints make it unfeasible to overcome every barrier: for example, the New York subway and London Underground systems would require huge investment to make every line and station accessible to wheelchair users. A copyright library of five million books could never afford to provide all these texts in all the different formats which visually impaired users might potentially require. In these situations, it seems more practical to make other arrangements to overcome the problems: for example, Transport for London have an almost totally accessible fleet of buses, to compensate those who cannot use the tube, while libraries increasingly have arrangements to make particular books accessible on demand, given notice.

Moreover, physical and sensory impairments are in many senses the easiest to accommodate. What would it mean to create a barrier-free utopia for people with learning difficulties? Reading and writing and other cognitive abilities are required for full participation in many areas of contemporary life in developed nations. What about people on the autistic spectrum, who may find social contact difficult to cope with: a barrier-free utopia might be a place where they did not have to meet, communicate with, or have to interpret other people. With many solutions to the disability problem, the concept of addressing special needs seems more coherent than the concept of the barrier-free utopia. Barrier-free enclaves are possible, but not a barrier-free world.

While environments and services can and should be adapted wherever possible, there remains disadvantage associated with having many impairments which no amount of environmental change could entirely eliminate. People who rely on wheelchairs, or personal assistance, or other provision are more vulnerable and have fewer choices than the majority of able-bodied people. When Michael Oliver claims that "An aeroplane is a mobility aid for non-flyers in

exactly the same way as a wheelchair is a mobility aid for non-walkers" (1996, 108) his suggestion is amusing and thought provoking, but cannot be taken seriously. As Michael Bury has argued,

> It is difficult to imagine any modern industrial society (however organised) in which, for example, a severe loss of mobility or dexterity, or sensory impairments, would not be "disabling" in the sense of restricting activity to some degree. The reduction of barriers to participation does not amount to abolishing disability as a whole.
>
> (Bury, 1997, 137)

Drawing together these weaknesses, a final and important distinction needs to be made. The disability movement has often drawn analogies with other forms of identity politics, as I have done in this paper. The disability rights struggle has even been called the "Last Liberation Movement" (Driedger, 1989). Yet while disabled people do face discrimination and prejudice, like women, gay and lesbian people, and minority ethnic communities, and while the disability rights movement does resemble in its forms and activities many of these other movements, there is a central and important difference. There is nothing intrinsically problematic about being female or having a different sexual orientation, or a different skin pigmentation or body shape. These other experiences are about wrongful limitation of negative freedom. Remove the social discrimination, and women and people of colour and gay and lesbian people will be able to flourish and participate. But disabled people face both discrimination and intrinsic limitations. This claim has three implications. First, even if social barriers are removed as far as practically possible, it will remain disadvantageous to have many forms of impairment. Second, it is harder to celebrate disability than it is to celebrate Blackness, or Gay Pride, or being a woman. "Disability pride" is problematic, because disability is difficult to recuperate as a concept, as it refers either to limitation and incapacity, or else to oppression and exclusion, or else to both dimensions. Third, if disabled people are to be emancipated, then society will have to provide extra resources to meet the needs and overcome the disadvantage which arises from impairment, not just work to minimise discrimination (Bickenbach et al., 1999).

BEYOND THE SOCIAL MODEL?

In this chapter, I have tried to offer a balanced assessment of the strengths and weaknesses of the British social model of disability. While acknowledging the benefits of the social model in launching the disability movement, promoting a positive disability identity, and mandating civil rights legislation and barrier removal, it is my belief that the social model has now become a barrier to further progress.

As a researcher, I find the social model unhelpful in understanding the complex interplay of individual and environmental factors in the lives of disabled people. In policy terms, it seems to me that the social model is a blunt instrument for explaining and combating the social exclusion that disabled people face, and the complexity of our needs. Politically, the social model has generated a form of identity politics which has become inward looking and separatist.

A social approach to disability is indispensable. The medicalisation of disability is inappropriate and an obstacle to effective analysis and policy. But the social model is only one of the available options for theorising disability. More sophisticated and complex approaches are needed, perhaps building on the WHO initiative to create the International Classification of Functioning, Disability and Health. One strength of this approach is the recognition that disability is a complex phenomenon, requiring different levels of analysis and intervention, ranging from the medical to the sociopolitical. Another is the insight that disability is not a minority issue, affecting only those people defined as disabled people. As Irving Zola (1989) maintained, disability is a universal experience of humanity.

BIBLIOGRAPHY

Barnes, C. (1991) *Disabled People in Britain and Discrimination*. London: Hurst and Co.

Bickenbach, J. E., Chatterji, S., Badley, E. M., and Ustun, T. B. (1999) Models of disablement, universalism and the international classification of impairments, disabilities and handicaps. *Social Science and Medicine* 48: 1173–1187.

Butler, J. (1990) *Gender Trouble: Feminism and the Subversion of Identity*. New York: Routledge.

Bury, M. (1997) *Health and Illness in a Changing Society*. London: Routledge.

Campbell, J. and Oliver, M. (1996) *Disability Politics: Understanding Our Past, Changing Our Future*. London: Routledge.

Charlton, J. (1998) *Nothing About Us Without Us: Disability, Oppression and Empowerment*. Berkeley: University of California Press.

Crow, L. (1992) Renewing the social model of disability. *Coalition* July: 5–9.

Driedger, D. (1989) *The Last Civil Rights Movement*. London: Hurst.

Finkelstein, V. (1981) To deny or not to deny disability. In A. Brechin et al. *(eds) Handicap in a Social World*. Sevenoaks: Open University/Hodder and Stoughton.

Finkelstein, V. (1998) Emancipating disability studies. In T. Shakespeare (ed.) *The Disability Reader: Social Science Perspectives*. London: Cassell.

French, S. (1993) Disability, impairment or something in between. In J. Swain *et al.* (eds) *Disabling Barriers, Enabling Environments*. London: Sage, 17–25.

Gustavsson, A., Sandvin, J., Traustadóttir, R., and Tossebrø, J. (2005) *Resistance, Reflection and Change: Nordic Disability Research*. Lund, Sweden: Studentlitteratur.

Hahn, H. (1988) The politics of physical differences: disability and discrimination. *Journal of Social Issues* 44 (1): 39–47.

Hasler, F. (1993) Developments in the disabled people's movement. In J. Swain *et al.* (eds) *Disabling Barriers, Enabling Environments*. London: Sage.

Morris, J. (1991) *Pride Against Prejudice*. London: Women's Press.

Oakley, A. (1972) *Sex, Gender and Society*, London: Maurice Temple Smith.

Oliver, M. (1996) *Understanding Disability: From Theory to Practice.* Basingstoke: Macmillan.

Oliver, M. (2004) The social model in action: if I had a hammer. In C. Barnes and G. Mercer (eds) *Implementing the Social Model of Disability: Theory and Research.* Leeds: The Disability Press.

Shakespeare, T. and Watson, N. (2001) The social model of disability: an outdated ideology? In S. Barnarrt and B. M. Altman (eds) *Exploring Theories and Expanding Methodologies: Where Are We and Where Do We Need to Go? Research in Social Science and Disability volume 2.* Amsterdam: JAI.

Sherry, M. (2002) *If only I had a brain.* Unpublished PhD dissertation, University of Queensland.

Swain, J., Finkelstein, V., French, S., and Oliver, M. (eds) (1993) *Disabling Barriers, Enabling Environments.* London: Sage.

Thomas, C. (1999) *Female Forms.* Buckingham: Open University Press.

Thomas, C. (2004) Developing the social relational in the social model of disability: a theoretical agenda. In C. Barnes and G. Mercer (eds) *Implementing the Social Model of Disability: Theory and Research.* Leeds: The Disability Press.

Tremain, S. (2002) On the subject of impairment. In M. Corker and T. Shakespeare (eds) *Disability/ Postmodernity: Embodying Disability Theory.* London: Continuum, 32–47.

Union of the Physically Impaired Against Segregation (UPIAS) (1974/5) *Policy Statement,* www.leeds. ac.uk/disability-studies/archiveuk/archframe.htm (consulted August 10, 2005).

Union of the Physically Impaired Against Segregation (UPIAS) (1975) *Fundamental Principles,* www. leeds.ac.uk/disability-studies/archiveuk/archframe. htm (consulted August 10, 2005).

Watson, N. (2002) Well, I know this is going to sound very strange to you, but I don't see myself as a disabled person: identity and disability. *Disability and Society* 17 (5): 509–528

Williams, S. J. (1999) Is anybody there? Critical realism, chronic illness, and the disability debate. *Sociology of Health and Illness* 21 (6): 797–819.

Wolfensberger, W. (1972) *The Principle of Normalization in Human Services.* Toronto: National Institute on Mental Retardation.

Zola, I. K. (1989) Towards the necessary universalizing of a disability policy. *Milbank Quarterly* 67, suppl. 2, Pt. 2: 401–428.

CHAPTER 14

Narrative Prosthesis

David Mitchell and Sharon Snyder

SUMMARY

Just as cultures view disability as a problem in need of a solution, literary representations also cast disability as a crisis that needs to be solved by the text. In this introduction to *Narrative Prosthesis*, David Mitchell and Sharon Snyder argue that when a literary work uses a disabled character as the opportunity for metaphor, the story relies on disability as a sort of prosthesis for the function of the narrative.

Disability serves as an interruption to cultural truisms, and so the representation of a disabled body acts as a metaphor and example of the body's resistance to normalcy. Even though disability challenges ideals of a "normal" body, it also operates as a textual obstacle that causes a "stumbling" in the narrative's potential open-endedness. Instead of inviting multiple meanings, disability used as a narrative prosthesis closes down these possibilities. Disabled characters end up bound to a programmatic identity that uses disability to explain "either everything or nothing" about them as embodied beings.

The authors initially apply this framework to a children's story, *The Steadfast Tin Soldier*, about a group of toy soldiers in which one soldier is missing a leg. The story moves forward from that imperfection by establishing the exceptionality of the disabled soldier, but then the plot must make sure the disability is either left behind or punished for its lack of conformity. Examples such as this demonstrate that literary representation overdetermines the symbolic surface of the disabled body, allowing it to mean something crucial to the function of the narrative.

LITERATURE AND THE UNDISCIPLINED BODY OF DISABILITY

This chapter prefaces the close readings to come [in *Narrative Prosthesis*] by deepening our theory of narrative prosthesis as shared characteristics in the literary representation of disability. We demonstrate one of a variety of approaches in disability studies to the "problem" that disability and disabled populations pose to all cultures. Nearly every culture views disability as a problem in need of a solution, and this belief establishes one of the major modes of historical address directed toward people with disabilities. The necessity for developing various kinds of cultural accommodations to handle the "problem" of corporeal difference (through charitable organizations, modifications of physical architecture, welfare doles, quarantine, genocide, euthanasia programs, etc.) situates people with disabilities in a profoundly ambivalent relationship to the cultures and stories they inhabit. The perception of a "crisis" or a "special situation" has made disabled people the subject of not only governmental policies and social programs but also a primary object of literary representation.

Our thesis centers not simply upon the fact that people with disabilities have been the object of representational treatments, but rather that their function in literary discourse is primarily twofold: disability pervades literary narrative, first, as a stock feature of characterization and, second, as an opportunistic metaphorical device. We term this perpetual discursive dependency upon disability *narrative prosthesis*. Disability lends a distinctive idiosyncrasy to any character that differentiates the character from the anonymous background of the "norm." To exemplify this phenomenon, the opening half of this chapter analyzes the Victorian children's story *The Steadfast Tin Soldier* in order to demonstrate that disability serves as a primary impetus of the storyteller's efforts. In the second instance, disability also serves as a metaphorical signifier of social and individual collapse. Physical and cognitive anomalies promise to lend a "tangible" body to textual abstractions; we term this metaphorical use of disability the *materiality of metaphor* and analyze its workings as narrative prosthesis in our concluding discussion of Sophocles' drama *Oedipus the King*. We contend that disability's centrality to these two principal representational strategies establishes a conundrum: while stories rely upon the potency of disability as a symbolic figure, they rarely take up disability as an experience of social or political dimensions.

While each of the chapters that follow [in *Narrative Prosthesis*] set out some of the key cultural components and specific historical contexts that inform this history of disabled representations, our main objective addresses the development of a representational or "literary" history. By "literary" we mean to suggest a form of writing that explicitly values the production of what narrative theorists such as Barthes, Blanchot, and Chambers have referred to as "open-ended" narrative.[1] The identification of the open-ended narrative differentiates a distinctively "literary" component of particular kinds of storytelling: those texts that not only deploy but explicitly foreground the "play" of multiple meanings as a facet of their discursive production. While this definition does not overlook the fact that all texts are inherently "open" to a multiplicity of interpretations, our notion of literary narrative identifies works that *stage* the arbitrariness of linguistic sign systems as a characterizing feature of their plots and commentaries. Not only do the artistic and philosophical works under discussion here present themselves as available to a multiplicity of readings, they openly perform their textual *inexhaustibility*. Each shares a literary objective of destabilizing sedimented cultural meanings that accrue around ideas of bodily "deviance." Thus, we approach the writings of Montaigne, Nietzsche, Shakespeare, Melville, Anderson, Dunn, and an array of post-1945 American authors as writers who interrogate the objectives of narrative in general and the corporeal body in particular as discursive products. Their narratives all share a self-reflexive mode of address about their own textual production of disabled bodies.

This textual performance of ever-shifting and unstable meanings is critical in our interpretive approach to the representation of disability. The close readings that follow hinge upon the identification of disability as an ambivalent and mutable category of cultural and literary investment. Within literary narratives, disability serves as an interruptive force that confronts cultural truisms. The inherent vulnerability and variability of bodies serves literary narratives as a metonym for that which refuses to conform to the mind's desire for order and rationality. Within this schema, disability acts as a metaphor and fleshly example of the body's unruly resistance to the cultural desire to "enforce normalcy."[2] The literary narratives we discuss all deploy the mutable or "deviant" body as an "unbearable weight" (to use Susan Bordo's phrase) in order to counterbalance the "meaning-laden" and ethereal projections of the mind. The body's weighty materiality functions as a textual and cultural other—an object with its own undisciplined language that exceeds the text's ability to control it.

As many theorists have pointed out, this representational split between body and mind/text has been inherited from Descartes (although we demonstrate that disability has been entrenched in these assumptions throughout history). Keeping in mind that the perception of disability shifts from one epoch to another, and sometimes within decades and years, we want to argue that the disabled body has consistently held down a "privileged" position with respect to thematic variations on the mind/body split. Whether a culture approaches the body's materiality as a denigrated symbol of earthly contamination (such as in early Christian cultures), or as a perfectible *technē* of the self (as in ancient Athenian culture), or as an object of medical interpretation (as in Victorian culture), or as specular commodity in the age of electronic media (as is the case in postmodernism), disability perpetually serves as the symbolical symptom to be interpreted by discourses on the body. Whereas the "able" body has no definitional core (it poses as transparently "average" or "normal"), the disabled body surfaces as any body capable of being narrated as "outside the norm." Within such a representational schema, literary narratives revisit disabled bodies as a reminder of the "real" physical limits that "weigh down" transcendent ideals of the mind and knowledge-producing disciplines. In this sense, disability serves as the *hard kernel* or recalcitrant corporeal matter

that cannot be deconstructed away by the textual operations of even the most canny narratives or philosophical idealisms.[3]

For our purposes in [*Narrative Prosthesis*], the representation of disability has both allowed an interrogation of static beliefs about the body and also erupted as the unseemly *matter* of narrative that cannot be textually undone. We therefore forward readings of disability as a narrative device upon which the literary writer of "open-ended" narratives depends for his or her disruptive punch. Our phrase *narrative prosthesis* is meant to indicate that disability has been used throughout history as a crutch upon which literary narratives lean for their representational power, disruptive potentiality, and analytical insight. Bodies show up in stories as dynamic entities that resist or refuse the cultural scripts assigned to them. While we do not simply extol these literary approaches to the representation of the body (particularly in relation to recurring tropes of disability), we want to demonstrate that the disabled body represents a potent symbolic site of literary investment.

The reasons for this dependency upon disability as a device of characterization and interrogation are many, and our concept of narrative prosthesis establishes a variety of motivations that ground the narrative deployment of the "deviant" body. However, what surfaces as a theme throughout these chapters is the paradoxical impetus that makes disability into both a destabilizing sign of cultural prescriptions about the body *and* a deterministic vehicle of characterization for characters constructed as disabled. Thus, in works as artistically varied and culturally distinct as Shakespeare's *Richard III*, Montaigne's "Of Cripples," Melville's *Moby-Dick*, Nietzsche's *Thus Spoke Zarathustra*, Anderson's *Winesburg, Ohio*, Faulkner's *The Sound and the Fury*, Salinger's *The Catcher in the Rye*, Lee's *To Kill a Mockingbird*, Kesey's *One Flew Over the Cuckoo's Nest*, Dunn's *Geek Love*, Powers's

Operation Wandering Soul, and Egoyan's *The Sweet Hereafter*, the meaning of the relationship between having a physical disability and the nature of a character's identity come under scrutiny. Disability recurs in these works as a potent force that challenges cultural ideals of the "normal" or "whole" body. *At the same time, disability also operates as the textual obstacle that causes the literary operation of open-endedness to close down or stumble.*

This "closing down" of an otherwise permeable and dynamic narrative form demonstrates the historical conundrum of disability. Characters such as Montaigne's "les boiteaux," Shakespeare's "hunchback'd king," Melville's "crippled" captain, Nietzsche's interlocutory "throng of cripples," Anderson's storied "grotesques," Faulkner's "tale told by an idiot," Salinger's fantasized commune of deaf-mutes, Lee's racial and cognitive outsiders, Kesey's ward of acutes and chronics, Dunn's chemically altered freaks, and Power's postapocalyptic wandering children provide powerful counterpoints to their respective cultures' normalizing Truths about the construction of deviance in particular, and the fixity of knowledge systems in general. Yet each of these characterizations also evidences that the artifice of disability binds disabled characters to a programmatic (even deterministic) identity. Disability may provide an explanation for the origins of a character's identity, but its deployment usually proves either too programmatic or unerringly "deep" and mysterious. In each work analyzed in [*Narrative Prosthesis*], disability is used to underscore, in the words of Richard Powers, adapting the theories of Lacan, that the body functions "like a language" as a dynamic network of misfirings and arbitrary adaptations (*Goldbug* 545). Yet, this defining corporeal unruliness consistently produces characters who are indentured to their biological programming in the most essentializing manner. Their

disabilities surface to explain everything or nothing with respect to their portraits as embodied beings.

All of the above examples help to demonstrate one of the central assumptions undergirding [*Narrative Prosthesis*]: *disability is foundational to both cultural definition and to the literary narratives that challenge normalizing prescriptive ideals.* By contrasting and comparing the depiction of disability across cultures and histories, one realizes that disability provides an important barometer by which to assess shifting values and norms imposed upon the body. Our approach in the chapters that follow [in *Narrative Prosthesis*] is to treat disability as a narrative device—an artistic prosthesis—that reveals the pervasive dependency of artistic, cultural, and philosophical discourses upon the powerful alterity assigned to people with disabilities. In short, disability characterization can be understood as a prosthetic contrivance upon which so many of our cultural and literary narratives rely.

THE (IN)VISIBILITY OF PROSTHESIS

The hypothesis of this *discursive dependency* upon disability strikes most scholars and readers at first glance as relatively insubstantial. During a recent conference of the Herman Melville Society in Völös, Greece, we met a scholar from Japan interested in representations of disability in American literature. When asked if Japanese literature made use of disabled characters to the same extent as American and European literatures, he honestly replied that he had never encountered any. Upon further reflection, he listed several examples and laughingly added that of course the Nobel Prize winner Kenzaburo Oë wrote almost exclusively about the subject. This "surprise" about the pervasive nature of disabled images in national literatures catches even the most knowledgeable scholars unaware.

Without developed models for analyzing the purpose and function of representational strategies of disability, readers tend to filter a multitude of disability figures absently through their imaginations.

For film scholarship, Paul Longmore has perceptively formulated this paradox, asking why we screen so many images of disability and simultaneously screen them out of our minds. In television and film portraits of disability, Longmore argues, this screening out occurs because we are trained to compartmentalize impairment as an isolated and individual condition of existence. Consequently, we rarely connect together stories of people with disabilities as evidence of a wider systemic predicament. This same phenomenon can be applied to other representational discourses.

As we discussed in our introduction to *The Body and Physical Difference*, our current models of minority representations tend to formulate this problem of literary/critical neglect in the obverse manner (5). One might expect to find the argument in the pages to come that disability is an ignored, overlooked, or marginal experience in literary narrative, that its absence marks an ominous silence in the literary repertoire of human experiences. In pursuing such an argument one could rightly redress, castigate, or bemoan the neglect of this essential life experience within discourses that might have seen fit to take up the important task of exploring disability in serious terms. Within such an approach, disability would prove to be an unarticulated subject whose real-life counterparts could then charge that their own social marginality was the result of an attendant representational erasure outside of medical discourses. Such a methodology would theorize that disability's absence proves evidence of a profound cultural repression to escape the reality of biological and cognitive differences.

However, what we hope to demonstrate in [*Narrative Prosthesis*] is that disability has an unusual literary history. Between the social marginality of people with disabilities and their corresponding representational milieus, disability undergoes a different representational fate. While racial, sexual, and ethnic criticisms have often founded their critiques upon a pervasive absence of their images in the dominant culture's literature, we argue that images of disabled people abound in history.[4] Even if we disregard the fact that entire fields of study have been devoted to the assessment, cataloging, taxonomization, pathologization, objectification, and rehabilitation of disabled people, one is struck by disability's prevalence in discourses outside of medicine and the hard sciences. Once a reader begins to seek out representations of disability in our literatures, it is difficult to avoid their proliferation in texts with which one believed oneself to be utterly familiar. Consequently, as in the discussion of images of disability in Japanese literature mentioned above, the representational prevalence of people with disabilities is far from absent or tangential. As we discuss in *Narrative Prosthesis*, scholarship in the humanities study of disability has sought to pursue previously unexplored questions of the utility of disability to numerous discursive modes, including literature. Our hypothesis in *Narrative Prosthesis* is a paradoxical one: disabled peoples' social invisibility has occurred in the wake of their perpetual circulation throughout print history. This question is not simply a matter of stereotypes or "bad objects," to borrow Naomi Schor's phrase.[5] Rather, the interpretation of representations of disability strikes at the very core of cultural definitions and values. What is the significance of the fact that the earliest known cuneiform tablets catalog 120 omens interpreted from the "deformities" of Sumerian fetuses and irregularly shaped sheep's and calf's livers? How does one explain the disabled gods, such as the blind Hod, the one-eyed Odin, the one-armed Tyr, who are central to Norse myths, or Hephaestus, the "crook-footed god," in Greek literature? What do these modes of representation reveal about cultures as they forward or suppress physical differences? Why does the "visual" spectacle of so many disabilities become a predominating trope in the nonvisual textual mediums of literary narratives?

SUPPLEMENTING THE VOID

What calls stories into being, and what does disability have to do with this most basic preoccupation of narrative? Narrative prosthesis (or the dependency of literary narratives upon disability) forwards the notion that all narratives operate out of a desire to compensate for a limitation or to reign in excess. This narrative approach to difference identifies the literary object par excellence as that which has become extraordinary—a deviation from a widely accepted norm. Literary narratives begin a process of explanatory compensation wherein perceived "aberrancies" can be rescued from ignorance, neglect, or misunderstanding for their readerships. As Michel de Certeau explains in his well-known essay "The Savage 'I,'" the new world travel narrative in the fifteenth and sixteenth centuries provides a model for thinking about the movement of all narrative. A narrative is inaugurated "by the search for the strange, which is presumed different from the place assigned it in the beginning by the discourse of the culture" from which it originates (69). The very need for a story is called into being when something has gone amiss with the known world and, thus, the language of a tale seeks to comprehend that which has stepped out of line. In this sense, stories compensate for an unknown or unnatural deviance that begs an explanation.

Our notion of narrative prosthesis evolves out of this specific recognition: a narrative issues to resolve or correct—to "prostheticize" in David Wills's sense of the term—a deviance marked as improper to a social context. A simple schematic of narrative structure might run thus: first, a deviance or marked difference is exposed to a reader; second, a narrative consolidates the need for its own existence by calling for an explanation of the deviation's origins and formative consequences; third, the deviance is brought from the periphery of concerns to the center of the story to come; and fourth, the remainder of the story rehabilitates or fixes the deviance in some manner. This fourth step of the repair of deviance may involve an obliteration of the difference through a "cure," the rescue of the despised object from social censure, the extermination of the deviant as a purification of the social body, or the revaluation of an alternative mode of being. Since what we now call disability has been historically narrated as that which characterizes a body as deviant from shared norms of bodily appearance and ability, disability has functioned throughout history as one of the most marked and remarked upon differences that originates the act of storytelling. Narratives turn signs of cultural deviance into textually marked bodies.

In one of our 6-year-old son's books entitled *The Steadfast Tin Soldier,* this prosthetic relation of narrative to physical difference is exemplified. The story opens with a child receiving a box of tin soldiers as a birthday gift. The 25 soldiers stand erect and uniform in every way, for they "had all been made from the same tin spoon" (Campbell 1). Each of the soldiers comes equipped with a rifle and bayonet, a blue and red outfit signifying membership in the same regiment, black boots, and a stern military visage. The limited omniscient narrator inaugurates the conflict that will propel the story by pointing out a lack in one soldier that mars the uniformity of the gift: "All of the soldiers were exactly alike, with the exception of one, who differed from the rest in having only one leg" (2). This unfortunate blemish, which mars the otherwise flawless ideal of the soldiers standing in unison, becomes the springboard for the story that ensues. The incomplete leg becomes a locus for attention, and from this imperfection a story issues forth. The 24 perfect soldiers are quickly left behind in the box for the reason of their very perfection and uniformity—the "ideal" or "intended" soldier's form promises no story. As Barbara Maria Stafford points out, "there [is] only a single way of being healthy and lovely, but an infinity of ways of being sick and wretched" (284). This infinity of ways helps to explain the pervasive dependency of literary narratives upon the trope of disability. Narrative interest solidifies only in the identification and pursuit of an anomaly that inaugurates the exceptional tale or the tale of exception.

The story of *The Steadfast Tin Soldier* stands in a prosthetic relation to the missing leg of the titular protagonist. The narrative in question (and narrative in a general sense) rehabilitates or compensates for its "lesser" subject by demonstrating that the outward flaw "attracts" the storyteller's—and by extension the reader's—interest. The act of characterization is such that narrative must establish the exceptionality of its subject matter to justify the telling of a story. A subject demands a story only in relation to the degree that it can establish its own extraordinary circumstances.[6] The normal, routine, average, and familiar (by definition) fail to mobilize the storytelling effort because they fall short of the litmus test of exceptionality. The anonymity of normalcy is no story at all. Deviance serves as the basis and common denominator of all narrative. In this sense, the missing leg presents the aberrant soldier as the story's focus, for his physical difference exiles him from the rank and file of the uniform and physically undifferentiated troop. Whereas a sociality might reject, isolate, institutionalize, reprimand,

or obliterate this liability of a single leg, narrative embraces the opportunity that such a "lack" provides—in fact, wills it into existence—as the impetus that calls a story into being. Such a paradox underscores the ironic promise of disability to all narrative.

Display demands difference. The arrival of a narrative must be attended by the "unsightly" eruption of the anomalous (often physical in nature) within the social field of vision. The (re)mark upon disability begins with a stare, a gesture of disgust, a slander or derisive comment upon bodily ignominy, a note of gossip about a rare or unsightly presence, a comment upon the unsuitability of deformity for the appetites of polite society, or a sentiment about the unfortunate circumstances that bring disabilities into being. This ruling out-of-bounds of the socially anomalous subject engenders an act of violence that stories seek to "rescue" or "reclaim" as worthy of narrative attention. Stories always perform a compensatory function in their efforts to renew interest in a previously denigrated object. While there exist myriad inroads to the identification of the anomalous— femininity, race, class, sexuality—disability services this narrative appetite for difference as often as any other constructed category of deviance.

The politics of this recourse to disability as a device of narrative characterization demonstrates the importance of disability to storytelling itself. Literary narratives support our appetites for the exotic by posing disability as an "alien" terrain that promises the revelation of a previously uncomprehended experience. Literature borrows the potency of the lure of difference that a socially stigmatized condition provides. Yet the reliance upon disability in narrative rarely develops into a means of identifying people with disabilities as a disenfranchised cultural constituency. The ascription of absolute singularity to disability performs a contradictory operation: a character "stands out" as a result of an attributed blemish, but this exceptionality divorces him or her from a shared social identity. As in the story of *The Steadfast Tin Soldier,* a narrative disability establishes the uniqueness of an individual character and is quickly left behind as a purely biological fact. Disability marks a character as "unlike" the rest of a fiction's cast, and once singled out, the character becomes a case of special interest who retains originality to the detriment of all other characteristics. Disability cannot be accommodated within the ranks of the norm(als), and, thus, the options for dealing with the difference that drives the story's plot is twofold: a disability is either left behind or punished for its lack of conformity.

In the story of *The Steadfast Tin Soldier* we witness the exercise of both operations on the visible difference that the protagonist's disability poses. Once the soldier's incomplete leg is identified, its difference is quickly nullified. Nowhere in the story does the narrator call attention to a difficult negotiation that must be attempted as a result of the missing appendage. In fact, like the adventurer of de Certeau's paradigmatic travel narrative, the tin figure undergoes a series of epic encounters without further reference to his limitation: after he falls out of a window, his bayonet gets stuck in a crack; a storm rages over him later that night; two boys find the figure, place him into a newspaper boat, and sail him down the gutter into a street drain; he is accosted by a street rat who poses as gatekeeper to the underworld; the newspaper boat sinks in a canal where the soldier is swallowed by a large fish; and finally he is returned to his home of origin when the family purchases the fish for dinner and discovers the one-legged figure in the belly. The series of dangerous encounters recalls the epic adventure of the physically able Odysseus on his way home from Troy; likewise, the tin soldier endures the physically taxing experience without further remark upon the incomplete leg in the course of the tale. The journey and ultimate return home embody the cyclical nature of all narrative (and the story of disability in particular)—the deficiency inaugurates the need for a story but is quickly forgotten once the difference is established.

However, a marred appearance cannot ultimately be allowed to return home unscathed. Near the end of the story the significance of the missing leg returns when the tin soldier is reintroduced to his love— the paper maiden who pirouettes upon one leg. Because the soldier mistakes the dancer as possessing only one leg like himself, the story's conclusion hinges upon the irony of an argument about human attraction based upon shared likeness. If the maiden shares the fate of one-leggedness, then, the soldier reasons, she must be meant for him. However, in a narrative twist of deus ex machina the blemished soldier is inexplicably thrown into the fire by a boy right at the moment of his imagined reconciliation with the "one-legged" maiden. One can read this ending as a punishment for his willingness to desire someone physically perfect and therefore unlike himself. Shelley's story of Frankenstein (discussed in chapter 5 [of *Narrative Prosthesis*]) ends in the monster's anticipated obliteration on his own funeral pyre in the wake of his misinterpretation as monstrous, and the tin soldier's fable reaches its conclusion in a similar manner. Disability inaugurates narrative, but narrative inevitably punishes its own prurient interests by overseeing the extermination of the object of its fascination.

THE PHYSIOGNOMY OF DISABILITY

What is the significance of disability as a pervasive category of narrative interest? Why do the convolutions, distortions, and ruptures that mark the disabled body's surface prove seductive to literary representation? What is the relationship of the external evidence of disability's perceived deviances and the core of the disabled subject's being? The disabled body occupies a crossroads in the age-old literary debate about the relationship of form to content. Whereas the "unmarred" surface enjoys its cultural anonymity and promises little more than a confirmation of the adage of a "healthy" mind in a "healthy" body, disability signifies a more variegated and sordid series of assumptions and experiences. Its unruliness must be tamed by multiple mappings of the surface. If form leads to content or "embodies" meaning, then disability's disruption of acculturated bodily norms also suggests a corresponding misalignment of subjectivity itself.

In *Volatile Bodies* Elizabeth Grosz argues that philosophy has often reduced the body to a "fundamental continuity with brute, inorganic matter" (8). Instead of this reductive tendency, Grosz calls for a more complex engagement with our theorizations of the body: "the body provides a point of mediation between what is perceived as purely internal and accessible only to the subject and what is external and publicly observable, a point from which to rethink the opposition between the inside and the outside" (20). Approaching the body as a mediating force between the outside world and internal subjectivity would allow a more thoroughgoing theory of subjectivity's relationship to materiality. In this way, Grosz argues that the body should not be understood as a receptacle or package for the contents of subjectivity, but rather plays an important role in the formation of psychic identity itself.

Disability will play a crucial role in the reformulation of the opposition between interior and exterior because physical differences have so often served as an example of bodily form following function or vice versa. The mutability of bodies causes them to change over time (both individually and historically), and yet the disabled body is sedimented within an ongoing narrative of breakdown and abnormality. However, while we situate our argument in opposition to reading physical disability as a one-to-one correspondence with subjecthood, we do not deny its role as a foundational aspect of identity. The disabled subject's navigation of social attitudes toward people with disabilities, medical pathologies, the management of embodiment itself, and daily encounters with "perfected" physicalities in the media demonstrates that the disabled body has a substantial impact upon subjectivity as a whole. The study of disability must understand the impact of the experience of disability upon subjectivity *without simultaneously situating the internal and external body within a strict mirroring relationship to one another.*

In literature this mediating role of the external body with respect to internal subjectivity is often represented as a relation of strict correspondence. Either the "deviant" body deforms subjectivity, or "deviant" subjectivity violently erupts upon the surface of its bodily container. In either instance the corporeal body of disability is represented as manifesting its own internal symptoms. Such an approach places the body in an automatic physiognomic relation to the subjectivity it harbors. As Barbara Maria Stafford has demonstrated, practices of interpreting the significance of bodily appearances since the eighteenth century have depended upon variations of the physiognomic method.

> Physiognomics was body criticism. As corporeal connoisseurship, it diagnosed unseen spiritual qualities by scrutinizing visible traits. Since its adherents claimed privileged powers of detection, it was a somewhat sinister capability . . . . The master eighteenth-century physiognomist, Lavater, noted that men formed conjectures "by reasoning from the exterior to the interior." He continued: "What is universal nature but physiognomy. Is not everything surface and contents?

Body and soul? External effect and internal faculty? Invisible principle and visible end?"
(84)

For cultures that operated upon models of bodily interpretation prior to the development of internal imaging techniques, the corporeal surface was freighted with significance. Physiognomy became a paradigm of access to the ephemeral and intangible workings of the interior body. Speculative qualities such as moral integrity, honesty, trustworthiness, criminality, fortitude, cynicism, sanity, and so forth, suddenly became available for scrutiny by virtue of the "irregularities" of the body that enveloped them. For the physiognomist, the body allowed meaning to be inferred from the outside in; such a speculative practice resulted in the ability to anticipate intangible qualities of one's personhood without having to await the "proof" of actions or the intimacy of a relationship developed over time. By "reasoning from the exterior to the interior," the trained physiognomist extracted the meaning of the soul without the permission or participation of the interpreted.

If the "external effect" led directly to a knowledge of the "internal faculty," then those who inhabited bodies deemed "outside the norm" proved most ripe for a scrutiny of their moral or intellectual content. Since disabled people by definition embodied a form that was identified as "outside" the normal or permissible, their visages and bodily outlines became the physiognomist's (and later the pathologist's) object par excellence. Yet, the "sinister capability" of physiognomy proves more complex than just the exclusivity of interpretive authority that Stafford suggests. If the body would offer a surface manifestation of internal symptomatology, then disability and deformity automatically preface an equally irregular subjectivity. Physiognomy proves a deadly practice to a

population already existing on the fringes of social interaction and "humanity." While the "authorized" physiognomist was officially sanctioned to interpret the symbology of the bodily surface, the disabled person became every person's Rorschach test. While physiognomists discerned the nuances of facial countenances and phrenologists surveyed protuberances of the skull, the extreme examples offered by those with physical disabilities and deformities invited the armchair psychology of the literary practitioner to participate in the symbolic manipulation of bodily exteriors.

Novelists, dramatists, philosophers, poets, essayists, painters, and moralists all flocked to the site of a physiognomic circus from the eighteenth century on. "Irregular" bodies became a fertile field for symbolists of all stripes. Disability and deformity retained their fascination for would-be interpreters because their "despoiled" visages commanded a rationale that narrative (textual or visual) promised to decipher. Because disability represents that which goes awry in the normalizing bodily schema, narratives sought to unravel the riddle of anomaly's origins. Such a riddle was inherently social in its making. The physiognomic corollary seemed to provide a way in to the secrets of identity itself. The chapters that follow [in *Narrative Prosthesis*] demonstrate that the problem of the representation of disability is not the search for a more "positive" story of disability, as it has often been formulated in disability studies, *but rather a thoroughgoing challenge to the undergirding authorization to interpret that disability invites.* There is a politics at stake in the fact that disability inaugurates an explanatory need that the unmarked body eludes by virtue of its physical anonymity. To participate in an ideological system of bodily norms that promotes some kinds of bodies while devaluing others is to ignore the malleability of bodies and their definitively mutant natures.

Stafford's argument notwithstanding, the body's manipulation by physiognomic practices did not develop as an exclusively eighteenth century phenomenon. Our own research demonstrates that while physiognomics came to be consolidated as a scientific ideology in the eighteenth and nineteenth centuries, people with disabilities and deformities have always been subject to varieties of this interpretive practice. Elizabeth Cornelia Evans argues that physiognomic beliefs can be traced back as far as ancient Greece. She cites Aristotle as promoting physiognomic reasoning when he proclaims, "It is possible to infer character from physique, if it is granted that body and soul change together in all natural affections...For if a peculiar affection applies to any individual class, e.g., courage to lions, there must be some corresponding sign for it; for it has been assumed that body and soul are affected together" (7). In fact, one might argue that physiognomics came to be consolidated out of a general historical practice applied to the bodies of disabled peoples. If the extreme evidence of marked physical differences provided a catalog of reliable signs, then perhaps more minute bodily differentiations could also be cataloged and interpreted. In this sense, people with disabilities ironically served as the historical locus for the invention of physiognomy.

As we pointed out earlier, the oldest surviving tablets found along the Tigris River in Mesopotamia and dated from 3000 to 2000 B.C. deployed a physiognomic method to prognosticate from deformed fetuses and irregular animal livers. The evidence of bodily anomalies allowed royalty and high priests to forecast harvest cycles, geographic conditions, the outcomes of impending wars, and the future of city-states. The symbolic prediction of larger cultural conditions from physical differences suggests one of the primary differences between the ancient and modern periods: physical anomalies metamorphosed from a symbolic interpretation of worldly meanings to a primarily individualized locus of information. The movement of disability from a macro to a micro level of prediction underscores our point that disability has served as a foundational category of cultural interpretation. The longstanding practice of physiognomic readings demonstrates that disability and deformity serve as the impetus to analyze an otherwise obscured meaning or pattern at the individual level. In either case the overdetermined symbolism ascribed to disabled bodies obscured the more complex and banal reality of those who inhabited them.

THE MATERIALITY OF METAPHOR

Like Oedipus (another renowned disabled fictional creation), cultures thrive upon solving the riddle of disability's rhyme and reason. When the limping Greek protagonist overcomes the Sphinx by answering "man who walks with a cane" as the concluding answer to her three-part query, we must assume that his own disability served as an experiential source for this insight. The master riddle solver in effect trumps the Sphinx's feminine otherness with knowledge gleaned from his own experience of inhabiting an alien body. In doing so, Oedipus taps into the cultural reservoir of disability's myriad symbolic associations as an interpretive source for his own riddle-solving methodology. Whereas disability usually provides the riddle in need of a narrative solution, in this instance the experience of disability momentarily serves as the source of Oedipus's interpretive mastery. Yet, Sophocles' willingness to represent disability as a mode of experience-based knowledge proves a rare literary occasion and a fleeting moment in the play's dramatic structure.

While Oedipus solves the Sphinx's riddle in the wake of his own physical experience as a lame interpreter and an interpreter of lameness, his disability remains inconsequential to the myth's plot. Oedipus's disability—the result of Laius's pinning of his infant son's ankles as he sends him off to die of exposure—"marks" his character as distinctive and worthy of the exceptional tale. Beyond this physical fact, Sophocles neglects to explore the relationship of the body's mediating function with respect to Oedipus's kingly subjectivity. Either his "crippling" results in an insignificant physical difference, or the detailing of his difference can be understood to embody a vaguely remembered history of childhood violence enacted against him by his father. The disability remains a physical fact of his character that the text literally overlooks once this difference is established as a remnant of his repressed childhood. Perhaps those who share the stage with Oedipus either have learned to look away from his disability or have imbibed the injunction of polite society to refuse commentary upon the existence of the protagonist's physical difference.

However, without the pinning of Oedipus's ankles and his resulting lameness two important aspects of the plot would be compromised. First, Oedipus might have faltered at the riddle of the Sphinx like others before him and fallen prey to the voracious appetite of the she-beast; second, Sophocles' protagonist would lose the physical sign that literally connects him to an otherwise inscrutable past. In this sense, Oedipus's physical difference secures key components of the plot that allow the riddle of his identity to be unraveled. At the same time, his disability serves as the source of little substantive commentary in the course of the drama itself. Oedipus as a "lame interpreter" establishes the literal source of his ability to solve the baffling riddle and allows the dramatist to metaphorize humanity's incapacity to fathom the dictums of the gods. This movement exemplifies the literary oscillation between micro and macro levels of metaphorical meaning supplied by disability. Sophocles later moves to Oedipus's self-blinding as a further example of how the physical body provides a corporeal correlative to the ability of dramatic myth to bridge personal and public symbology.

What is of interest for us in this ancient text is the way in which one can read its representational strategy as a paradigm for literary approaches to disability. The ability of disabled characters to allow authors the metaphorical "play" between macro and micro registers of meaning-making establishes the role of the body in literature as a liminal point in the representational process. In his study of editorial cartoonings and caricatures of the body leading up to the French Revolution, Antoine de Baecque argues that the corporeal metaphor provided a means of giving the abstractions of political ideals an "embodied" power. To "know oneself" and provide a visual correlative to a political commentary, French cartoonists and essayists deployed the body as a metaphor because the body "succeeds in *connecting* narrative and knowledge, meaning and knowing" most viscerally (5). This form of textual embodiment concretizes an otherwise ephemeral concept within a corporeal essence. To give an abstraction a body allows the idea to simulate a foothold in the material world that it would otherwise fail to procure.

Whereas an ideal such as democracy imparts a weak and abstracted notion of governmental and economic reform, for example, the embodied caricature of a hunchbacked monarch overshadowed by a physically superior democratic citizen proved more powerful than any ideological argument. Instead of political harangue, the body offers an illusion of fixity to a textual effect:

> [Body] metaphors were able simultaneously to describe the event and to make the description

attain the level of the imaginary. The deployment of these bodily *topoi*—the degeneracy of the nobility, the impotence of the king the herculean strength of the citizenry, the goddesses of politics appearing naked like Truth, the congenital deformity of the aristocrats, the bleeding wound of the martyrs—allowed political society to represent itself at a pivotal moment of its history. ... One must pass through the [bodily] forms of a narrative in order to reach knowledge.

(de Baecque 4–5)

Such a process of giving body to belief exemplifies the corporeal seduction of the body to textual mediums. The desire to access the seeming solidity of the body's materiality offers representational literatures a way of grasping that which is most unavailable to them. For de Baecque, representing a body in its specificity as the bearer of an otherwise intangible concept grounds the reality of an ideological meaning. The passage through a bodily form helps secure a knowledge that would otherwise drift away of its own insubstantiality. The corporeal metaphor offers narrative the one thing it cannot possess—an anchor in materiality. Such a process embodies the materiality of metaphor; and literature is the writing that aims to concretize theory through its ability to provide an embodied account of physical, sensory life.

While de Baecque's theory of the material metaphor argues that the attempt to harness the body to a specific ideological program provides the text with an illusory opportunity to embody Truth, he overlooks the fact that the same process embeds the body within a limiting array of symbolic meanings: crippling conditions equate with monarchical immobility, corpulence evidences tyrannical greed, deformity represents malevolent motivation, and so on. Delineating his corporeal catalog, the historian bestows upon the body an elusive, general character while depending for his

readings almost exclusively upon the potent symbolism of disabled bodies in particular. Visible degeneracy, impotency, congenital deformity, festering ulcerations, and bleeding wounds in the passage previously quoted provide the contrastive bodily coordinates to the muscular, aesthetic, and symmetrical bodies of the healthy citizenry. One cannot narrate the story of a healthy body or national reform movement without the contrastive device of disability to bear out the symbolic potency of the message. The materiality of metaphor via disabled bodies gives all bodies a tangible essence in that the "healthy" corporeal surface fails to achieve its symbolic effect without its disabled counterpart.

As George Canguilhem has pointed out, the body only calls attention to itself in the midst of its breakdown or disrepair (209). The representation of the process of breakdown or incapacity is fraught with political and ideological significance. To make the body speak essential truths, one must give a language to it. Elaine Scarry argues that "there is ordinarily no language for [the body in] pain" (13). However, we would argue that the body itself has no language, since language is something foreign to its nonlinguistic materiality. It must be spoken for if its meanings are to prove narratable. The narration of the disabled body allows a textual body to *mean* through its long-standing historical representation as an overdetermined symbolic surface; the disabled body also offers narrative the illusion of grounding abstract knowledge within a bodily materiality. *If the body is the Other of text, then textual representation seeks access to that which it is least able to grasp.* If the nondysfunctional body proves too uninteresting to narrate, the disabled body becomes a paramount device of characterization. Narrative prosthesis, or the dependency upon the disabled body, proves essential to (even the essence of) the stories analyzed in the chapters to come [in *Narrative Prosthesis*].

NOTES

1. Many critics have designated a distinctive space for "the literary" by identifying those works whose meaning is inherently elastic and multiple. Maurice Blanchot identifies literary narrative as that which refuses closure and readerly mastery—"to write [literature] is to surrender to the interminable" (27). In his study of Balzac's *Sarrasine*, Roland Barthes characterizes the "plural text" as that which is allied with a literary value whose "networks are many and interact, without any one of them being able to surpass the rest; the text is a galaxy of signifiers, not a structure of signifieds; it has no beginning; it is reversible; we gain access to it by several entrances, none of which can be authoritatively declared to be the main one" (5). Ross Chambers's analysis of oppositionality argues that literature strategically deploys the "play" or "leeway" in discursive systems as a means of disturbing the restrictive prescriptions of authoritative regimes (iv). As our study develops, we demonstrate that the strategic "open-endedness" of literary narrative is paralleled by the multiplicity of meanings bequeathed to people with disabilities in history. In doing so, we argue not only that the open-endedness of literature challenges sedimented historical truths, but that disability has been one of the primary weapons in literature's disruptive agenda.

2. In his important study *Enforcing Normalcy*, Lennard Davis theorizes the "normal" body as an ideological construct that tyrannizes over those bodies that fail to conform. Accordingly, while all bodies feel insubstantial when compared to our abstract ideals of the body, disabled people experience a form of subjugation or oppression as a result of this phenomenon. Within such a system, we will argue in tandem with Davis that disability provides the contrastive term against which the concepts health, beauty, and ability are determined: "Just as the conceptualization of race, class, and gender shapes the lives of those who are not black, poor, or female, so the concept of disability regulates the bodies of those who are 'normal.' In fact, the very concept of normalcy by which most people (by definition) shape their existence is in fact tied inexorably to the concept of disability, or rather, the concept of disability is a function of a concept of normalcy. Normalcy and disability are part of the same system" (2).

3. Following the theories of Lacan, Slavoj Žižek in *The Sublime Object of Ideology* extracts the notion of the "hard kernel" of ideology. For Žižek, it represents the underlying core of belief that refuses to be deconstructed away by even the most radical operations of political critique. More than merely a rational component of ideological identification, the "hard kernel" represents the irrationality behind belief that secures the interpellated subject's "illogical" participation in a linguistically permeable system.

4. There is an equivalent problem to the representation of disability in literary narratives within our own critical rubrics of the body. The disabled body continues to fall outside of critical categories that identify bodies as the product of cultural constructions. While challenging a generic notion of white, male body as ideological proves desirable in our own moment within the realms of race, gender, sexuality, and class, there has been a more pernicious history of literary and critical approaches to the disabled body. In our introduction to *The Body and Physical Difference*, we argue that minority discourses in the humanities tend to deploy the evidence of "corporeal aberrancy" as a means of identifying the invention of an ideologically encoded body: "While physical aberrancy is often recognized as constructed and historically variable it is rarely remarked upon as its own legitimated or politically fraught identity" (5).

5. For Naomi Schor the phrase "bad objects" implies a discursive object that has been ruled out of bounds by the prevailing academic politics of the day, or one that represents a "critical perversion" (xv). Our use of the phrase implies both of these definitions in relation to disability. The literary object of disability has been almost entirely neglected by literary criticism in general until the past few years, when disability studies in the humanities has developed; and "disability" as a topic of investigation still strikes many as a "perverse" interest for academic contemplation. To these two definitions we would also add that the labeling of disability as a "bad object" nonetheless overlooks the fact that disabilities fill the pages of literary interest. The reasons for overabundance of images of disability in literature is the subject of [*Narrative Prosthesis*].

6. The title of Garland-Thomson's *Extraordinary Bodies: Figuring Disability in American Culture and Literature* forwards the term extraordinary in order to play off of its multiple nuances. It can suggest the powerful sentimentality of overcoming narratives so often attached to stories about disabled people. It can also suggest those whose bodies are the products of overdetermined social meaning that exaggerate physical differences or perform them as a way of enhancing their exoticness. In addition, we share with Garland-Thomson the belief that disabled bodies prove extraordinary in the ways in which they expose the variety and mutable nature of physicality itself.

WORKS CITED

Baecque, Antoine de. *The Body Politic: Corporeal Metaphor in Revolutionary France, 1770-1800.* Stanford, CA: Stanford University Press, 1997.

Blanchot, Maurice. *The Space of Literature.* 1955. Trans. Ann Smock. Lincoln: University of Nebraska Press, 1982.

Campbell, Katie. *The Steadfast Tin Soldier.* Morris Plains, NJ: Unicorn, 1990.

Chambers, Ross. *Room for Maneuver: Reading the Oppositional in Narrative.* Chicago: University of Chicago Press, 1991.

Davis, Lennard. *Enforcing Normalcy: Disability, Deafness, and the Body.* New York: Verso, 1995.

Garland-Thomson, Rosemarie. *Extraordinary Bodies: Figuring Disability in American Culture and Literature.* New York: Columbia University Press, 1997.

Grosz, Elizabeth A. *Volatile Bodies: Toward A Corporeal Feminism.* Bloomington: Indiana University Press, 1994.

Mitchell, David and Snyder, Susan (eds.) *The Body and Physical Difference: Discourses of Disability.* Ann Arbor: University of Michigan Press, 1997.

Scarry, Elaine. *The Body in Pain: The Making and Unmaking of the World.* New York: Oxford University Press, 1985.

Schor, Naomi. *Bad Objects: Essays Popular and Unpopular.* Durham, NC: Duke University Press, 1995.

Stafford, Barbara Maria. *Body Criticism: Imaging the Unseen in Enlightenment Art and Medicine.* Cambridge, MA: MIT Press, 1994.

Žižek, Slavoj. *The Sublime Object of Ideology.* New York: Verso, 1999.

CHAPTER 15

Aesthetic Nervousness

Ato Quayson

SUMMARY

Writing about the representation of disability in literature, Ato Quayson suggests that the presence of disability prompts a "short-circuiting" between a text's routine protocols and the reader. The reader's "aesthetic nervousness" in these moments overlaps with social biases of disability, and examining these moments can help shed light on encounters with disability in the real world.

Quayson writes that aesthetic nervousness is a form of the "anxiety"—based on normative assumptions of meaning—that occurs in encounters with disability. When the interpretive "frame" of a situation is disrupted by disability, whether in the real world or in literature, disability elicits a narrative explanation. But it also frustrates a complete comprehension of the disability, and this tension can structure a literary narrative on multiple levels. For example, Toni Morrison's disabled female characters are portrayed as empowered, but the narratorial perspective and symbolic implications of their disabilities contradict or complicate that representation of strength. The disabled characters in the work of Samuel Beckett, on the other hand, are rarely read as disabled because the narrative structure undercuts such a reading.

Although Quayson clarifies that the aesthetic nervousness around disabled literary figures cannot be equated to the real-life emotions of disabled people, he maintains that understanding the former can help illuminate interactions with the latter.

WHAT IS AESTHETIC NERVOUSNESS?

Let me begin formulaically: Aesthetic nervousness is seen when the dominant protocols of representation within the literary text are short-circuited in relation to disability. The primary level in which it may be discerned is in the interaction between a disabled and nondisabled character, where a variety of tensions may be identified. However, in most texts aesthetic nervousness is hardly ever limited to this primary level, but is augmented by tensions refracted across other levels of the text such as the disposition of symbols and motifs, the overall narrative or dramatic perspective, the constitution and reversals of plot structure, and so on. The final dimension of aesthetic nervousness is that between the reader and the text. The reader's status within a given text is a function of the several interacting elements such as the identification with the vicissitudes of the life of a particular character, or the alignment between the reader and the shifting positions of the narrator, or the necessary reformulations of the reader's perspective enjoined by the modulations of various plot elements and so on. As I shall show throughout this study, in works where disability plays a prominent role, the reader's perspective is also affected by the short-circuiting of the dominant protocols governing the text—a short-circuit triggered by the representation of disability. For the reader, aesthetic nervousness overlaps social attitudes to disability that themselves often remain unexamined in their prejudices and biases. The reader in this account is predominantly a nondisabled reader, but the insights about aesthetic nervousness are also pertinent to readers with disabilities, since it is the construction of a universe of apparent corporeal normativity both within the literary text and outside it whose basis requires examination and challenge that is generally at issue in this study. The various dimensions of aesthetic nervousness will be dealt with both individually and as parts of larger textual configurations in the works of Samuel Beckett, Toni Morrison, Wole Soyinka, and J. M. Coetzee. The final chapter, on the history of disability on Robben Island in South Africa, will be used to refocus attention from the literary-aesthetic domain to that of the historical intersection between disability, colonialism, and apartheid. This will help us see what extensions might be possible for the concept of aesthetic nervousness beyond the literary-aesthetic field.

There are two main sources for the notion of aesthetic nervousness that I want to elaborate here. One is Rosemarie Garland Thomson's highly suggestive concept of the normate, which we have already touched on briefly, and the other is drawn from Lennard Davis's and Mitchell and Snyder's reformulations of literary history from a disability studies perspective. As Thomson (1997) argues in a stimulating extension of some of Erving Goffman's (1959) insights about stigma, first-time social encounters between the nondisabled and people with disabilities are often short-circuited by the

ways in which impairments are interpreted. She puts the matter in this way:

> In a first encounter with another person, a tremendous amount of information must be organized and interpreted simultaneously: each participant probes the explicit for the implicit, determines what is significant for particular purposes, and prepares a response that is guided by many cues, both subtle and obvious. When one person has a visible disability, however, it almost always dominates and skews the normate's process of sorting out perceptions and forming a reaction. The interaction is usually strained because the nondisabled person may feel fear, pity, fascination, repulsion, or merely surprise, none of which is expressible according to social protocol. Besides the discomforting dissonance between experienced and expressed reaction, a nondisabled person often does not know how to act toward a disabled person: how or whether to offer assistance; whether to acknowledge the disability; what words, gestures, or expectations to use or avoid. Perhaps most destructive to the potential for continuing relations is the normate's frequent assumption that a disability cancels out other qualities, reducing the complex person to a single attribute.
> (Thomson 1997, 12)

To this we should quickly recall Mitchell and Snyder's remark concerning the degree to which Brueghel's paintings succeeded in disrupting and variegating the visual encounter between bodies in painting. Clearly, disruption and variegation are also features of real-world encounters between the nondisabled and persons with disabilities. Thomson proposes the notion of the "normate" to explicate the cluster of attitudes that govern the nondisabled's perception of themselves and their relations to the various "others" of corporeal normativity. As she persuasively shows, there are complex processes by which forms of corporeal diversity acquire cultural meanings that in their turn undergird a perceived hierarchy of bodily traits determining the distribution of privilege, status, and power. In other words, corporeal difference is part of a structure of power, and its meanings are governed by the unmarked regularities of the normate. However, as the paragraph quoted above shows, there are various elements of this complex relationship that do not disclose themselves as elements of power as such, but rather as forms of anxiety, dissonance, and disorder. The common impulse toward categorization in interpersonal encounters is itself part of an ideal of order that is assumed as implicit in the universe, making the probing of the explicit for the implicit part of the quest for an order that is thought to lie elsewhere. It is this, as we noted in the previous section, that persistently leads to the idea that the disabled body is somehow a cipher of metaphysical or divine significance. Yet the impairment is often taken to be the physical manifestation of the exact opposite of order, thus forcing a revaluation of that impulse, and indeed, of what it means to be human in a world governed by a radical contingency. The causes of impairment can never be fully anticipated or indeed prepared for. Every/body is subject to chance and contingent events. The recognition of this radical contingency produces features of a primal scene of extreme anxiety whose roots lie in barely acknowledged vertiginous fears of loss of control over the body itself (Grosz 1996; Wasserman 2001; Lacan 1948, 1949).[1] The corporeal body, to echo the sonnet "Death Be Not Proud" by John Donne, is victim to "Fate, chance, kings, and desperate men" and subject to "poison, warre, and sicknesse" as well. The dissonance and anxiety that cannot be properly articulated via available social protocols then define the affective and emotional economy of the recognition of contingency. In other words, the sudden recognition of contingency is not solely a philosophical one—in fact, it hardly ever is at the moment of the social

encounter itself—but is also and perhaps primarily an emotional and affective one. The usefulness of the social model of disability is precisely the fact that it now forces the subliminal cultural assumptions about the disabled out into the open for examination, thus holding out the possibility that the nondisabled may ultimately be brought to recognize the sources of the constructedness of the normate and the prejudices that flow from it.

Since the world is structured with a particular notion of unmarked normativity in mind, people with disabilities themselves also have to confront some of these ideas about contingency in trying to articulate their own deeply felt sense of being (Murphy 1990, 96–115). At a practical and material level, there are also the problems of adjustment to a largely indifferent world. As Wood and Bradley (1978, 149) put it: "On a material plane the disabled individual is...less able to adapt to the demands of his environment: he has reduced power to insulate himself from the assaults of an essentially hostile milieu. However, the disadvantage he experiences is likely to differ in relation to the nature of the society in which he finds himself." Contradictory emotions arise precisely because the disabled are continually located within multiple and contradictory frames of significance within which they, on the one hand, are materially disadvantaged, and, on the other, have to cope with the culturally regulated gaze of the normate. My use of the word "frames" in this context is not idle. Going back to the Scope poster, it is useful to think of such frames in the light of physical coordinates, as if thinking of a picture frame. The frames within which the disabled are continually placed by the normate are ones in which a variety of concepts of wholeness, beauty, and economic competitiveness structure persons with disability and place them at the center of a peculiar conjuncture of conceptions.

Thomson's notion of the relations between the normate and the disabled derives ultimately from a symbolic inter-actionism model. To put it simply, a symbolic interactionism model of inter-pretation operates on the assumption that "people do not respond to the world directly, but instead place social meanings on it, organize it, and respond to it on the basis of these meanings" (Albrecht 2001, 27). The idea of symbolic interactionism is pertin-ent to the discussion of literary texts that will follow because not only do the characters organize their perceptions of one another on the basis of given symbolic assumptions, but as fictional characters they are themselves also woven out of a network of symbols and interact through a symbolic relay of signs. Furthermore, as I shall show incrementally in different chapters and in a more situated form in the chapter on J. M. Coetzee (chapter 6 [original volume]), symbolic interaction-ism also implies the presence of an implied interlocutor with whom the character or indeed real-life person enters into a series of dialogical relationships, thus helping to shape a horizon of expectations against which versions of the self are rehearsed. Following Thomson's lead, the first aspect of aesthetic nervousness that I want to specify is that it is triggered by the implicit disruption of the frames within which the disabled are located as subjects of symbolic notions of wholeness and normativity. Disability returns the aesthetic domain to an active ethical core that serves to disrupt the surface of representation. Read from a perspective of disability studies, this active ethical core becomes manifest because the disability representation is seen as having a direct effect on social views of people with disability in a way that representations of other literary details, tropes, and motifs do not offer. In other words, the represen-tation of disability has an efficaciousness that ultimately transcends the literary domain and refuses to be assimilated to it. This does not mean that disability in literature can be read solely via an instru-mentalist dimension of interpretation; any intervention that might be adduced for it is not inserted into an inert and stable disability "reality" that lies out there. For, as we have noted, disability in the real world already incites interpretation in and of itself. Nevertheless, an instrumentalist dimension cannot be easily suspended either. To put the matter somewhat for-mulaically: the representation of disability oscillates uneasily between the aesthetic and the ethical domains, in such a way as to force a reading of the aesthetic fields in which the disabled are represented as always having an ethical dimension that cannot be easily subsumed under the aesthetic structure. Ultimately, aesthetic nervousness has to be seen as coextensive with the nervousness regarding the dis-abled in the real world. The embarrass-ment, fear, and confusion that attend the disabled in their everyday reality is trans-lated in literature and the aesthetic field into a series of structural devices that betray themselves when the disability representation is seen predominantly from the perspective of the disabled rather than from the normative position of the nondisabled.

In his essay entitled "Who Put the *The* in The Novel?" Lennard Davis (2002) explores the links that have largely been taken for granted in literary history between the novel form, an *English* nation, and the vari-ous destabilizations of the social status of character that help to define the essential structure of the novel in the eighteenth and nineteenth centuries. The realist novels of the two centuries were based on the con-struction of the "average" citizen. This aver-age citizen was nonheroic and middle class. But the average citizen was also linked to the concept of "virtue." As Davis notes, "Vir-tue implied that there was a specific and knowable moral path and stance that a character could and should take. In other words, a normative set of behaviours was demanded of characters in novels" (94). Entangled with these dual notions of the average citizen and of virtue were implicit ideas of wholeness, with no major protagonist in the entire period marked by a physical disability. Undergirding the novel's rise then is a binary opposition between normal/abnormal, with this binary generating a series of plots. Essentially, the key element of such plots is the initial destabilization of the character's social circumstances, followed by their efforts to rectify their loss and return, perhaps chastened, to their former position. Crucially, however, as the nineteenth century progresses the negative or immoral gets somatized and represented as a disability (95–98). One of the conclusions Davis draws from his discussion is that plot functions in the eighteenth and nineteenth centuries "by temporarily deforming or disabling the fantasy of nation, social class, and gender behaviors that are constructed norms" (97).

In taking forward Davis's argument, there are a number of qualifications I want to register. Distinctive in his account is the link he persuasively establishes between nation, the average citizen, virtue, and specific forms of novelistic emplotment. That cannot be questioned. However, it is not entirely accurate that the binary of normal/abnormal starts with the eighteenth- and nineteenth-century novels or indeed that they inaugurate the plots of the deformation of social status. On the contrary, as can be shown from an examination of folktales from all over the world, the plot of physical and/or social deformation is actually one of the commonest starting points of most story plots (see Propp 1958; Zipes 1979), so much so that it is almost as if the deformation of physical and/or social status becomes the universal starting point for the generation of narrative emplotment

as such. As Davis points out, in agreement with established scholarship on the novel, the crucial term that is introduced in the eighteenth and nineteenth century is "realism," the notion that somehow the novelistic form refracts a verisimilar world outside of its framework. But realism is itself a cultural construction, since for the Greeks their myths were also a form of realism. What needs to be taken from Davis's account is the effect that the collocation of the social imaginary of the nation and the production of a specific form of bodily and sexual realism had on the way the novel was taken to represent reality. In each instance, the assumed representation of reality depended upon unacknowledged views of social order deriving not just from an understanding of class relations but from an implicit hierarchization of corporeal differences. Even though Davis is not the only one to have noted the peculiar place of the disabled in the eighteenth- and nineteenth-century novel (see Holmes 2000, for example), it is in clarifying the status of the disabled body as *structurally constitutive* to the maintenance of the novel's realism that he makes a distinctive contribution to literary history.

However, in trying to extend the significance of the constitutive function of deformation from the novel to other literary forms, we also have to note that "deformation" can no longer be limited solely to that of social or class position, as Davis suggests in his discussion. From the novels of the early twentieth century onward, the deformations emerge from the intersection of a variety of vectors including gender, ethnicity, sexuality, urban identity, and particularly disability, these providing a variety of *constitutive points for the process of emplotment*. Indeed, Davis himself notes in another context the reiteration of disability in the works of Conrad. A similar view can be expressed of the work of Joyce (*Ulysses, Finnegan's Wake*), Virginia Woolf

(*Mrs. Dalloway*), Thomas Mann (*The Magic Mountain*), and T. S. Eliot's "The Waste Land," among others. I choose the phrase "constitutive points" as opposed to "starting points" to signal the fact that the social deformation does not always show itself at the beginning of the plot. In much of the work we will look at, from Beckett and Soyinka through Morrison and Coetzee, there are various articulations of a sense of social deformation. However, the deformation is not always necessarily revealed as inaugural or indeed placed at the starting point of the action or narrative as such. It is often revealed progressively or in fragments in the minds of the characters, or even as flashbacks that serve to reorder the salience of events within the plot. The varied disclosures of social deformation are also ultimately linked to the status of disability as a trigger or mechanism for such plot review and disclosure. In that sense, the range of literary texts we shall be exploring is not undergirded exclusively by the binary opposition of normal/abnormal, but by the *dialectical interplay* between unacknowledged social assumptions and the reminders of contingency as reflected in the body of the person with disability.

The notion of dialectical interplay is crucial to my model of interpretation, because one of the points I will repeat throughout the study is that a dialectical interplay can be shown to affect all levels of the literary text, from the perspectival modulations of the narrator (whether first or third person) and the characters to the temporal sequencing and ordering of leitmotifs and symbolic discourses that come together to structure the plotlines. Even though, as Davis rightly notes, the plots of social deformation dominated the eighteenth- and nineteenth-century novel, this view cannot be limited solely to novelistic discourse. Following the point I made a moment ago about the near universality of such plots, I want to suggest

that we consider the plot of social deformation as it is tied to some form of physical or mental deformation to be relevant for the discussion of *all* literary texts. This is a potentially controversial point, but given the ubiquity of the role of the disabled in texts from a range of cultures and periods it is difficult to shake off the view that disability is a marker of the aesthetic field as such. Disability teases us out of thought, to echo Keats, not because it resists representation, but because in being represented it automatically restores an ethical core to the literary-aesthetic domain while also invoking the boundary between the real and the metaphysical or otherworldly. Along with the category of the sublime, it inaugurates and constitutes the aesthetic field as such. And like the sublime, disability elicits language and narrativity even while resisting or frustrating complete comprehension and representation and placing itself on the boundary between the real and the metaphysical. When I state that disability "inaugurates" the aesthetic domain, it is not to privilege the "firstness" or "primariness" of first-time encounters between the disabled and nondisabled characters, even though this has been implied in my reliance on Thomson. Rather, I intend the term "inaugurate" in the sense of the setting of the contours of the interlocking vectors of representation, particularly in narrative and drama, which are the two literary forms that will feature mainly in this study. My position overlaps with Davis's but extends his insights to accommodate a more variegated methodology for understanding the status of disability in literary writing.

The analogy between the inaugural status of the sublime and of disability serves to open up a number of ways in which the structurally constitutive function of disability to literary form might be explored. In the *Critique of Judgment*, Kant follows his discussion of the beautiful and its relation to purposelessness or autonomy with the discussion of the sublime and its inherent link to the principle of disorder. For Kant, "*Beauty* is an object's form of purposiveness insofar as it is perceived in the object *without the presentation of purpose*" (1987, 31), the idea here being that only the lack of a determinate or instrumental end allows the subjective feeling of beauty to occur. The sublime, on the other hand, is an aspect of understanding in confrontation with something ineffable that appears to resist delimitation or organization. It exposes the struggle between Imagination and Reason: "[What happens is that] our imagination strives to progress toward infinity, while our reason demands absolute totality as a real idea, and so [the imagination,] our power of estimating the magnitude of things in the world of sense, is inadequate to that idea. Yet this inadequacy itself is the arousal in us of the feeling that we have within us a supersensible power" (108; translator's brackets). Even while generative of representation, the sublime transcends the imaginative capacity to represent it. As Crockett (2001, 75) notes in glossing the nature of this struggle, "the sublime is contra-purposive, because it conflicts with one's purposeful ability to represent it." The implicit dichotomy in the *Critique of Judgment* between the sublime and the beautiful has been explored in different directions by scholars in the intervening 350 years since its formulation, but what has generally been agreed upon is the idea of the resistance of the sublime to complete representation, even if this resistance is then incorporated into a motivation for representation as such.[2] What the representation of disability suggests, which both overlaps and distinguishes itself from the sublime as a conceptual category, is that even while also producing a contradictory semiotics of inarticulacy and articulation, it is quite directly and specifically tied to forms of social hierarchization. For disability, the semiotics

of articulation/inarticulation that may be perceived within the literary domain reflect difficulties regarding its salience for the nondisabled world. This, as can be gleaned from the Ingstad and Whyte collection already referred to, cuts across cultures. Thus even if the ambivalent status of disability for literary representation is likened to that of the sublime, it must always be remembered that, unlike the effects of the sublime on literary discourse, disability's ambivalence manifests itself within the real world in socially mediated forms of closure. We might then say that disability is an analogue of the sublime in literary-aesthetic representation (ineffability/articulation) yet engenders attempts at social hierarchization and closure within the real world.

Disability might also be productively thought of as being on a continuum with the sublime in terms of its oscillation between a pure abstraction and a set of material circumstances and conditions. Considered in this way, we can think of the sublime as occupying one end of the spectrum (being a pure abstraction despite generating certain psychological effects of judgment and the impulse to represent it in material forms) and disability occupying the other end and being defined by a different kind of oscillation between the abstract and the material. For unlike the sublime, disability oscillates between a pure process of abstraction (via a series of discursive framings, metaphysical transpositions, and socially constituted modalities of [non] response, and so forth) and a set of material conditions (such as impairment, accessibility and mobility difficulties, and economic considerations). It is not to be discounted also that many impairments also involve living with different levels of pain, such that the categories of pain and disability not infrequently imply each other. It is disability's rapid oscillation between a pure process of abstraction and a set of material conditions that ensures that the ethical core of its representation is never allowed to be completely assimilated to the literary-aesthetic domain as such. Disability serves then to close the gap between representation and ethics, making visible the aesthetic field's relationship to the social situation of persons with disability in the real world. This does not necessarily mean that we must always read the literary representation in a directly instrumental way. As noted earlier, the intervention of the literary representation is an intervention into a world that already situates disability within insistent framings and interpretations. The literary domain rather helps us to understand the complex *processes* of such framings and the ethical implications that derive from such processes.

Finally, it is to Mitchell and Snyder's book *Narrative Prosthesis* (2001) that I wish to turn in elaborating what I mean by aesthetic nervousness. Mitchell and Snyder follow David Wills (1995) in trying to define literary discourse as essentially performing certain prosthetic functions. Among these prosthetic functions are the obvious ones of using the disabled as a signal of moral disorder such that the nondisabled may glean an ethical value from their encounter with persons with disabilities. Since Mitchell and Snyder are also keen to situate narrative prosthesis as having significance for the lived experience of disability, they also assign an inherently pragmatic orientation to what they describe as textual prosthesis: "Whereas an actual prosthesis is always somewhat discomforting, a textual prosthesis alleviates discomfort by removing the unsightly from view. ... [T]he erasure of disability via a 'quick fix' of an impaired physicality or intellect removes an audience's need for concern or continuing vigilance" (8). They make these particular remarks in the context of films and narratives in which persons with disabilities somehow manage to overcome their difficulties and live a happy life within the realm of art. In such instances, the rep-

resentation of disability serves a pragmatic/cathartic function for the audience and the reader. More significantly, however, they also note that even while disability recurs in various works as a potent force to challenge cultural ideas about the normal and the whole, it also *"operates as the textual obstacle that causes the literary operation of open-endedness to close down or stumble"* (50).

This last observation brings their discussion of narrative prosthesis very close to my own notion of aesthetic nervousness, except that they proceed to expound upon this blocking function in what can only be nonaesthetic terms. This is how they put it:

> This "closing down" of an otherwise permeable and dynamic narrative form demonstrates the historical conundrum of disability. [Various disabled characters from literature] provide powerful counterpoints to their respective cultures' normalizing Truths about the construction of deviance in particular, and the fixity of knowledge systems in general. Yet each of these characterizations also evidences that the artifice of disability binds disabled characters to a programmatic (even deterministic) identity.
>
> (Mitchell and Snyder 2001, 50)

Thus Mitchell and Snyder's idea of the shutting down or stumbling of the literary operation is extrinsic to the literary field itself and is to be determined by setting the literary representations of disability against sociocultural understandings. While agreeing with them that the ultimate test of the salience of a disability representation are the various social and cultural contexts within which they might be thought to have an effect, I want to focus my attention on the devices of aesthetic collapse that occur within the literary frameworks themselves. Also, I would like to disagree with them on their view of the programmatic identity assigned to the disabled, because, as I will try to show by reading the disabled character within the wider discursive structure of relations among different levels of the text, we find that even if programmatic roles were originally assigned, these roles can shift quite suddenly, thus leading to the "stumbling" they speak of. I choose to elaborate the textual "stumbling" in terms of aesthetic nervousness.

When it comes to their specific style of reading, Mitchell and Snyder are inspired by Wills to elaborate the following provisional typology:

> Our notion of narrative prosthesis evolves out of this specific recognition: a narrative issues to resolve or correct—to "prostheticize" in David Wills's sense of the term—a deviance marked as improper to a social context. A simple schematic of narrative structure might run thus: first, a deviance or marked difference is exposed to the reader; second, a narrative consolidates the need for its own existence by calling for an explanation of the deviation's origins and formative consequences; third, the deviance is brought from the periphery of concerns to the center of the story to come; and fourth, the remainder of the story rehabilitates or fixes the deviance in some manner. The fourth step of the repair of the deviance may involve an obliteration of the difference through a "cure," the rescue of the despised object from social censure, the extermination of the deviant as a purification of the social body, or the revaluation of an alternative mode of being.... Narratives turn signs of cultural deviance into textually marked bodies.
>
> (53–54)

Again, their method is defined by an assumption of narrative pragmatism or instrumentalism; that is to say, the literary text aims solely to resolve or correct a deviance that is thought to be improper to a social context. Unlike them, I will be trying to show that this prostheticizing function is bound to fail, not because of the difficulties in erasing the effects of disability in the real world,

but because the aesthetic domain itself is short-circuited upon the encounter with disability. As mentioned earlier, disability joins the sublime as marking the constitutive points of aesthetic representation. Aesthetic nervousness is what ensues and can be discerned in the suspension, collapse, or general short-circuiting of the hitherto dominant protocols of representation that may have governed the text. To my mind, in this paragraph Mitchell and Snyder are attempting to define processes of representation that may occur separately (i.e., across individual and distinguishable texts) as well as serialized within a particular text. One of my central points is precisely the fact that even when the disabled character appears to be represented programmatically, the restless dialectic of representation may unmoor her from the programmatic location and place her elsewhere as the dominant aesthetic protocols governing the representation are short-circuited.

To establish the central parameters of aesthetic nervousness, then, a number of things have to be kept in mind. First is that in literature, the disabled are fictional characters created out of language. This point is not made in order to sidestep the responsibility to acknowledge language's social efficaciousness. Rather, I want to stress that as linguistic creations, the disabled in literature may trade a series of features with the nondisabled, thus transferring some of their significations to the nondisabled and vice versa. Furthermore, I want to suggest that when the various references to disability and to disability representation are seen within the broad range of an individual writer's work, it helps to foreground hitherto unacknowledged dimensions of their writing and, in certain cases, this can even lead to a complete revaluation of critical emphasis. Consider in this regard Shakespeare's *Richard III*, for instance, which is of course very widely discussed in disability studies. However, in Shakespeare disability also acts as a metaphor to mark anomalous social states such as those involving half-brothers and bastards. Indeed, there is a studied pattern in Shakespeare where bastards are considered to be internally deformed and villainous, their bastardy being directly correlated to a presumed moral deficit. And so we have the elemental and almost homicidal competition between half-brothers that reappears in conflicts between Robert Falconbridge and his bastard brother Philip in *King John,* between Don John and Don Pedro in *Much Ado About Nothing,* between Edmund and Edgar in *King Lear,* and between Richard III and Edward in *Richard III.* This last play is of course grounded on the resonance of jealousy and brotherhood, as well as on the Machiavellianism of a deformed protagonist. There the disability is placed at the foreground of the action from the beginning and brings together various threads that serve to focalize the question of whether Richard's deformity is an insignia of or indeed the cause of his villainy.[3] Thus to understand Richard III properly, we would have to attend equally to his disability and his bastardy in the wider scheme of Shakespeare's work. Once this is done, we find that our interpretation of the character has to be more complicated than just recognizing his villainy, which of course is the dominant invitation proffered by the play. The choice of Beckett, Soyinka, Morrison, and Coetzee is partly meant to serve this function of establishing the interrelations between disability and other vectors of representation among the wide oeuvre of each writer. However, comparisons and contrasts within the work of individual writers or indeed between them will not be made chronologically or with the suggestion of evolution and change in the representation of disability. Rather, I shall be focusing on thematic clusterings and on making links between apparently unrelated characters and scenes across the various texts to show how the parameters of aesthetic nervousness operate within individual texts as well as across various representations. Also, the writers will be used as nodal points from which to make connections to the work of other writers. Thus each chapter, though focusing predominantly on the individual writer in question, will also provide a gateway for connecting these writers to various others that have had something to say about disability. Each chapter is conceived of as comparative both in terms of the relations among the works of the main writers in the study and between these and the many other representations of disability that will be touched upon over the course of the discussions.

I want to emphasize my view that to properly establish the contours of aesthetic nervousness, we have to understand disability's resonance on a multiplicity of levels simultaneously; disability acts as a threshold or focal point from which various vectors of the text may be examined. Thus, as we shall see with respect to Toni Morrison, though her physically disabled female characters seem to be strong and empowered, there is often a contradiction between the levels of narratorial perspective, symbolic implication, and the determinants of the interactions among the characters themselves that ends up unsettling the unquestioned sense of strength that we might get from just focusing on what the disabled women in her texts do or do not do. With Beckett, on the other hand, we find that as he proliferates devices by which to undermine the stability of ontological categories, he ends up also undermining the means by which the many disabilities that he frequently represents in his texts may be interpreted. As can be seen from the vast scholarship on Beckett, it is very rare that his impaired characters are read as disabled, even though their disabilities are blatant and should be impossible to ignore. Rather, the characters are routinely assimilated by critics to philosophical categories and read off as such. This is due to the peculiarly self-undermining structures of his works, both the novels and the plays. Beckett is also unusual among the writers in this study in that he seems to fulfill a central feature of what Sandblom (1997) describes as the inextricable link between disease and creativity. Pertinent to the discussion of Beckett's work is that he himself suffered endless illnesses ranging from an arrhythmic heartbeat and night sweats to cysts and abscesses on his fingers, the palm of his left hand, the top of his palate, his scrotum and, most painfully later in life, his left lung. Often these cysts and abscesses had to be lanced or operated upon, leading to great and regular discomfort. It is not for nothing then that the deteriorating and impaired body held a special fascination for him. He used the disabled, maimed, and decaying body as a multiple referent for a variety of ideas that seem to have been at least partially triggered by encounters with others and his own personal experience of pain and temporary disability. This is something that has passed largely unremarked in the critical writings on Beckett, and. I propose to center on it to discuss the peculiar status he assigns to disability and pain in works such as *Endgame* and *Molloy*, both of which should to all intents and purposes be "painfull" but are not.

In a way, Wole Soyinka's work is quite different from that of the other three in the study. His writing focuses more securely on a set of ritual dispositions drawn from a traditional Yoruba and African cultural sensibility. This sensibility is then combined with an intense political consciousness, such that each of his plays may be read as partial allegories of the Nigerian and African postcolonial condition. The combination of the ritualistic with the political is something for which Soyinka has become notably famous. What I shall show with regard to his work are the ways in which disability acts as a marker of both ritual and the political,

but in ways that interrupt the two domains and force us to rethink the conceptual movement between the two. The final chapter, on Robben Island, will be used to bring to conclusion a particular vector of interpretation that will have been suggested in the chapter on Beckett, given further elaboration in the discussions of Morrison and Soyinka, and picked up and intensified in the one on Coetzee. I shall discuss this in various guises, but they will all come together under the conceptual rubric of the *structure of skeptical interlocution*. In essence, the idea derives from Bakhtin's proposition of the inherent dialogism of speech acts, that anticipation of an interlocutor even when the context of communication does not seem to explicitly denominate one. The choice of the plays of Beckett and Soyinka allows a certain salience to the idea of the (skeptical) interlocutor, since as dramatic texts they incorporate dialogue as an explicit feature of dialogism. But what I have in mind in relation to the structure of skeptical interlocution is a little bit more complicated than can be captured solely in dramatic texts. Rather, I mean to suggest that there is always an anticipation of doubt within the perceptual and imagined horizon of the disabled character in literature, and that this doubt is incorporated into their representation. This is so whether the character is represented in the first person, as we see in Beckett's Molloy, or in the third person, as we see in Coetzee's *Life and Times of Michael K.* The chapter on Coetzee will be used to focus on the difference between speech and the elective silence of autistic characters and on the ways in which these raise peculiar problems for the status of the skeptical interlocutor in literary writing. Autism features in that chapter not just as a dimension of disability but as a theoretical paradigm for raising questions about narrativity as such. However, it is when we come to the chapter on Robben Island that the structure of skeptical interlocution will be allowed to take life (literally and metaphorically, as will be demonstrated). The structure of interlocution with regard to the history of Robben Island will help to shed light on how aesthetic nervousness might be extended from discussions of the literary-aesthetic domain to an analysis of historical personages and real-life events.

I should like to address a point of potential confusion that may have arisen in this introduction. So far I have proceeded as though the literary representation of disabled persons and the aesthetic nervousness that attends such representation can be taken as an analogue to the real-life responses toward people with disabilities by society at large. This fusion of levels is only partially intended. For, as I noted earlier, there is no doubt that literary representation of disability somewhat subtends real-life treatment of disabled people in a variety of ways. However, I also want to note that the aesthetic nervousness of the literary-aesthetic domain cannot by any means be said to be equivalent to the responses to disabled persons in reality. To say that the literary model provides an analogue to reality does not mean that it is the same as that reality. The epistemological effect of representation is quite different from the emotional effects of misunderstanding and stereotyping in the real world. Thus the first may be used to illuminate aspects of the second but must not be taken to have exhausted or replaced it. Our commitment must ultimately be to changing the world and not merely reading and commenting on it.

It is important also to state at the outset that central to the ways in which I propose to establish the parameters of aesthetic nervousness is the device of close reading. This seems to me necessary in order to be able to do full justice to the subtle cues by which the literary text "stumbles" (to return to Mitchell and Snyder) and by which the literary representation reveals the parameters of aesthetic nervousness. Apart from Morrison, none of the writers in this study has previously been read from the perspective of disability studies. Part of my task will involve the rather boring process of taxonomizing the disability representations we find in the works in question. This will be done to provide a map of the varied uses to which the writers put the disabled in order to allow us to discern patterns that are elaborated upon or repeated across the works. It is a happy coincidence that all four writers are Nobel Prize winners and thus likely to be widely taken up in literary curricula. My choice of them was not informed by this fact, however (in fact, Coetzee was part of my study long before his Nobel Prize). I settle on them because of my years of teaching and thinking about their work in different contexts and the fact that they enable us to see a full range of discourses regarding disability and other details of literary representation. I wish to see students and other readers being able to pay close attention to all the subtle details of literary representation well beyond the focus on disability, even if that is their starting point. The focus on disability is thus meant to achieve two related effects: One is to make more prominent the active ethical core that is necessarily related to disability and that hopefully helps to restore a fully ethical reading to literature. The other is that from using disability to open up the possibility of close reading, I hope to encourage us to lift our eyes from the reading of literature to attend more closely to the implications of the social universe around us.

NOTES

1. On first considering this point about the vertiginous fears of the nondisabled regarding disability I focused primarily on Lacan's discussion of the mirror phase and his exploration of the *imagos* of dismemberment that come up for people under psychic stress. From this, I elaborated what I termed

the primal scene of the encounter between the disabled and the nondisabled, which, as I argued, was riven by constitutive emotional ambiguities. Even though I still find that perspective persuasive, in the current discussion I want to leave the contours of the psychoanalytic interpretation to one side and instead invoke the work of philosophers and disability writers who have thought and written about this matter. For my earlier argument, see "Disability and Contingency" in *Calibrations: Reading for the Social* (2003). At any rate, though I didn't know it then, the argument about Lacan and the primal scene of disability had already been quite persuasively put by Lennard Davis (1995, 140–142) and so will not be reprised here.

2. For the discussions of the sublime and the beautiful that I have drawn upon, see Allison (2001), Crockett (2001), Ashfield and de Bolla (1996), Caruth (1988), and de Man (1990). The issue of whether the sublime triggers an ethical recognition or not is a contentious one and not yet settled on either side, but Ashfield and de Bolla provide a good account of how the ethical debates on the sublime have unfolded in British literary history from the eighteenth century onward.

3. For particularly insightful readings of *Richard III* from a disability studies perspective, see Mitchell and Snyder (2001, 95–118) and Lennard Davis.

WORKS CITED

Albrecht, Gary L., Katherine D. Sleeman, and Michael Bury, eds. 2001. *Handbook of Disability Studies*. London: Sage.

Allison, Henry E. 2001. *Kant's Theory of Taste: A Reading of the Critique of Aesthetic Judgment*. Cambridge: Cambridge University Press.

Ashfield, Andrew, and Peter de Bolla. 1996. *The Sublime: A Reader in British Eighteenth-Century Aesthetic Theory*. Cambridge: Cambridge University Press.

Caruth, Cathy. 1988. "The Force of Example: Kant's Symbols." *Yale French Studies* 74: 17–37.

Crockett, Clayton. 2001. *A Theology of the Sublime*. London: Routledge.

Davis, Lennard J. 1995. *Enforcing Normalcy: Disability, Deafness, and the Body*. London: Verso.

——. 2002. "Who Put the *The* in The Novel?" In *Bending Over Backwards: Disability, Dismodernism, and other Difficult Positions*, 79–101. New York: New York University Press.

De Man, Paul. 1990. "Phenomenality and Materiality in Kant." In *The Textual Sublime*, ed. H. Silverman and G. Aylesworth, 87–108. Albany, NY: SUNY Press.

Goffman, Erving. 1959. *Stigma: Notes on the Management of Spoiled Identity*. New York: Simon and Schuster.

Grosz, Elizabeth. 1996. "Intolerable Ambiguity: Freaks as/at the Limit." In *Freakery: Cultural Spectacles of the Extraordinary Body*, ed. R. Thomson, 55–66. New York: New York University Press.

Holmes, Martha Stoddard. 2000. *Fictions of Affliction: Physical Disabilities in Victorian Culture*. Ann Arbor: University of Michigan Press.

Ingstad, Benedicte, and Susan Reynolds Whyte, eds. 1995. *Disability and Culture*. Berkeley: University of California Press.

Kant, Immanuel. 1987. *Critique of Judgment*. Trans. Werner Pluhar. Indianapolis: Hackett.

Lacan, Jacques. 1948. "Aggressivity in Psychoanalysis." In *Écrits*, trans. Alan Sheridan. London: Routledge, 1995.

——. 1949. "The Mirror Stage as Formative of the Function of the I as Revealed in Psychoanalytic Experience." In *Écrits*, trans. Alan Sheridan. London: Routledge, 1995.

Mitchell, David T., and Sharon L. Snyder. 2001. *Narrative Prosthesis: Disability and the Dependencies of Discourse*. Ann Arbor: University of Michigan Press.

Murphy, Robert. 1990. *The Body Silent*. New York: Norton.

Propp, Vladimir. 1958. *Morphology of the Folktale*. Trans. Laurence Scott. Bloomington: Indiana University Press.

Quayson, Ato. 2003. *Calibrations: Reading for the Social*. Minneapolis: Minnesota University Press.

Sandblom, Philip. 1997. *Creativity and Disease: How Illness Affects Literature, Art, and Music*. New York: Marion Boyars.

Thomson, Rosemarie Garland. 1997. *Extraordinary Bodies: Figuring Physical Disability in American Culture and Literature*. New York: Columbia University Press.

Wasserman, David. 2001. "Philosophical Issues in the Definition and Social Response to Disability." In *Handbook of Disability Studies*, ed. G. Albrecht et al., 219–251. London: Sage.

Wills, David. 1995. *Prosthesis*. Stanford, CA: Stanford University Press.

Wood, P., and N. Bradley. 1978. "An Epidemiological Appraisal of Disablement." In *Recent Advances in Community Medicine, No. 1*, ed. A. E. Bennett, 149–174. London: Heinemann.

Zipes, Jack. 1979. *Breaking the Magic Spell: Radical Theories of Folk and Fairy Tales*. Austin: University of Texas Press.

CHAPTER 16

The Unexceptional Schizophrenic:
A Post-Postmodern Introduction

Catherine Prendergast

SUMMARY

Catherine Prendergast contends that postmodern theory has used the figure of the schizophrenic—with all the legal, social, and rhetorical consequences of this diagnosis—to locate the boundaries of postmodernism. Even though postmodern theory has been crucial for challenging normativity and destabilizing narratives of progress, it achieves these ends by holding one identity stable: that of the schizophrenic.

For example, Frederic Jameson analogizes the postmodern condition to the breakdown of the signifying chain associated with schizophrenic thought, and Jean Baudrillard compares the experience of postmodern reality to the experience of schizophrenia. These figures and other postmodern theorists propose to liberate people at the same time that postmodern theory unwittingly casts the identity of the schizophrenic outside the social order—making schizophrenics always "exceptional" rather than integrated in civic life.

The tendency toward exceptionality is partly based, Prendergast suggests, on the fact that postmodern theory takes a few, rather exceptional schizophrenics from history as a model for the condition. She offers recent schizophrenic writings as a contrast; when these authors self-disclose schizophrenia, they invest the term with new meaning. Daniel Frey, for instance, suggests moving toward a focus on the masses of unexceptional schizophrenics with everyday lives. This means giving up the stability of schizophrenia as used by postmodern theorists and instead acknowledging the ability of schizophrenic people to participate in, as well as critique, late capitalism.

Postmodern theory has been indispensable to disability studies because it has challenged normativity and destabilized narratives of national progress, social order, and identity. The essay nevertheless contends that crucial texts of postmodern theory have only achieved such destabilizations by holding one identity stable: that of the schizophrenic. These texts base their understanding of schizophrenia (and, by extension, the post-modern condition) on the writing of a few, distinctly exceptional, schizophrenics. An explosion of civic writing in the mid-1990s by writers who mark themselves specifically as non-exceptional schizophrenics, how-ever, interrogates the desire for the stable schizophrenic, easy to recognize and there-fore incarcerate, or celebrate, as the occasion demands. Attention to such writing reveals schizophrenics to be an active and growing constituency arguing for their rights in the public sphere. The essay concludes that recognition of this constituency and the multitude of voices it represents could greatly inform future theoretical programs that invoke "the schizophrenic."

Wasn't it because they didn't go far enough in listening to the insane that the great observers who drew up the first classifications impoverished the material they were given—to such an extent it appeared problematic and fragmentary to them?

(Jacques Lacan)

Postmodern theory owes a great debt to schizophrenics—and to cyborgs, border-crossers, and other figures culturally designated as hybrid. But most belatedly, and most significantly to disability studies, the debt is owed to schizophrenics, those people who bear the diagnosis of schizophrenia, along with its legal, social, and rhetorical consequences. Without schizophrenics, postmodernity would struggle to limn its boundaries, for the schizophrenic in postmodern theory marks the point of departure from the modern, the Oedipal, the referential, the old. Postmodern theory has been indispensable to disability studies because it has allowed not only for a challenge to normativity, but also for the destabilizing of narratives of national progress, social order, and identity (Corker and Shakespeare). However crucial texts of postmodern theory have only achieved these destabilizations by holding one identity stable: that of the schizophrenic.

"Someone asked us if we had seen a schizophrenic—no, no, we have never seen one," Deleuze and Guattari assert in the final pages of *Anti-Oedipus: Capitalism and Schizophrenia* (380). While this claim, on its face, is somewhat unlikely for at least Guattari, the more immediate question is, how do they know? The schizophrenic is imagined here to be immediately recognizable with a disorder visible, and yet, because not seen, at the same time invisible and outside the social order. So distanced from the public domain, the schizophrenic is ripe for appropriation by Deleuze and Guattari who find in this figure their anti-Oedipus. It's a peculiarly honorary position the schizophrenic seems to hold: "The schizophrenic is closest to the beating heart of reality" (87), "the possessor of the most touchingly meager capital" (12). Rosi Braidotti, writing for *The Deleuze Dictionary*, aptly summarizes the importance of the schizophrenic to the anti-Oedipal project: "[T]he image of thought implied by liberal individualism and classical humanism is disrupted in favour of a multi-layered dynamic subject. On this level schizophrenia acts as an alternative to how the art of thinking can be practiced" (239). And yet this dynamic subject, always seemingly in motion, ever demonstrating this new mode of thinking, is nonetheless in Deleuze and Guattari's work to be sharply differentiated from "the schizo," reduced by hospitalization, "deaf, dumb and blind," cut off from reality, "occupying the void" (88). By *A Thousand Plateaus*, the schizophrenic has disappeared almost entirely, metaphorically consumed by the rhizome.

It is probable, that when Deleuze and Guattari proclaimed that "no, no," they had never seen a schizophrenic, they were not expecting to be taken literally. As active readers we might try a thought experiment of our own and replace "schizophrenic" in that phrase with "woman," or the designation for an individual of any racialized group. Such a statement would be so much less likely, because at the time *Anti-Oedipus* was published (originally in 1972, in French), the civil rights movement and the burgeoning women's rights movements would have drained the resulting expression of any ironic value. In the wake of a formerly disadvantaged group's clear entrée into the civic sphere, no purchase can be gained through claiming—even facetiously—never to have met a member of that group. That Deleuze and Guattari can make the claim to mediate schizophrenic experience while never having met a schizophrenic says a great deal about the lack of self-identifying schizophrenics in the public sphere one generation ago.

Deleuze and Guattari are hardly the only postmodern theorists to ground their analysis of the late capitalist order in a stereotypical portrayal of the schizophrenic. Frederic Jameson also delineates the position of the schizophrenic, analogizing the postmodern condition to the breakdown of the signifying chain that characterizes schizophrenic thought: "[T]he schizophrenic is reduced to an experience of pure material signifiers, or, in other words, a series of pure and unrelated presents in time" (27). Jean Baudrillard, similarly, analogizes the experience of postmodern reality to the experience of schizophrenia, correcting modernist notions of the schizophrenic as he does so: "The schizophrenic is not, as generally claimed, characterized by his loss of touch with reality, but by the absolute proximity to and total instantaneousness with things, this overexposure to the transparency of the world" (27). Reality is thus accessible to postmodern theory through the thought patterns of the schizophrenic. What is common in these moments of access is the certitude with which schizophrenics are discussed; the schizophrenic is allowed no change in position or in thinking, and no agenda of her or his own. In the wake of this certainty regarding how schizophrenics think and how they act, Petra Kuppers's comment on her viewing of the work of artist and schizophrenic Martín Ramírez is very refreshing: "I can't know Ramírez—that is the only firm knowledge I can take away from the images and their history of making, storing, display, and criticism" (189).

Postmodern theory has many roots, and in discussing Jameson, Baudrillard, and Deleuze and Guattari, those who have specifically drawn upon schizophrenia to elucidate postmodernity, I am not limiting postmodernism to those entities. Nor do I find reason to challenge the central insights of postmodern theory and their utility to much of disability studies. I do, however, believe that it is productive to consider postmodern attempts to ground the shared postmodern condition in the unshared position of the schizophrenic, and interrogate those attempts within the context of the disability rights and specifically mental disability rights movements. My examination of how one theoretical program can propose to liberate at the same time as it (certainly unwittingly) casts certain identities outside the social order—whether in celebratory fashion, as in Deleuze and Guattari or Jameson, or in pathologizing fashion, as in Baudrillard—draws inspiration from David T. Mitchell and Sharon L. Snyder's recollection in *Narrative Prosthesis* that the identity work conducted by race and sexuality studies historically involved distancing people of color and women from the "real" abnormalities with which they had long been metaphorically associated:

> As feminist, race, and sexuality studies sought to unmoor their identities from debilitating physical and cognitive associations, they inevitably positioned disability as the "real" limitation from which they must escape. … Formerly denigrated identities are "rescued" by understanding gendered, racial, and sexual differences as textually produced, distancing them from the "real" of physical or cognitive aberrancy projected onto their figures.
>
> (2–3)

Following Mitchell and Snyder, it is interesting to note that Deleuze and Guattari, to launch their critique of late capitalism, have to distance schizoanalysis from the "real" schizo, stuck in the void. This central displacement is necessary to allow for the metaphorizing of schizophrenia along the exclusively positive channels Deleuze and Guattari allow. However positive, this metaphorizing enacts what Susan Sontag would call a "rhetorical ownership" over schizo-phrenia. Sontag suggests that the "meta-phorical trappings" that attach to diagnoses have very real consequences, in terms of how people seek treatment, or don't, including what kind of treatment they seek. She writes: "it is highly desirable for a specific dreaded illness to come to be seen as ordinary. . . . Much in the way of individual experience and social policy depends on the struggle for rhetorical ownership of the illness: how it is possessed, assimilated in argument and in cliché" (93–94).

Clichés are, by definition, metaphors that have become too stable. The appropriation of the schizophrenic by postmodern theory is a cliché, one that posits continually the rhetorical exceptionalism of schizophre-nics. This stability mirrors the medicalized investment, which, as Snyder and Mitchell have observed in "Disability Haunting in American Poetics," finds disability to be "an organic predicament based on the common sense notion that disability status cannot be altered" (2). As a result of this common sense notion, Snyder and Mitchell argue, the disabled are not allowed to enter the history of U.S. social conflict as an active constituency arguing for their rights within the public sphere. Postmodern theory values schizophrenics precisely because it imagines them insulated from civic life. They are to remain the "exceptional, private citizenry" that Snyder and Mitchell identify as typical of the role given to the disabled. There is, however, an increasingly public citizenry of schizophrenics who claim the following: to speak publicly, particularly on issues that affect their lives; to self-identify as schizophrenic without having to embrace the stigma associated with the term nor undersign any medicalized invest-ment; to found and use their own press organs to further their causes (in this way, very much the "bodies with organs"); to be considered in public addresses, and finally, to enjoy a rhetorical position and a life that

is not predicated on complete absence of impairment. In short, they claim the right to unexceptional instability, which is not something postmodern theory has readily granted them.

THE MODEL SCHIZOPHRENIC

It is not surprising that the postmodern theory I have reviewed should hold the identity of schizophrenics so constant, because much of it is based on a few, rather exceptional schizophrenics. The history of perhaps the most exceptional I will turn to here: Judge Daniel Paul Schreber. As Rose-mary Dinnage observes, Schreber's 1903 *Memoirs of My Nervous Illness*, something of a self-report, is "the most written-about document in all psychiatric literature. . . . Everyone has had something to say about Schreber" (xi). Schreber's writings cannot help but come to us as metaphor, saturated with the resonances of his commentators: Freud, Jung, Lacan, and Deleuze and Guat-tari, chief among them. Equally exceptional as the reception of his work were Schreber's life and the course of his illness. A prominent German judge, Schreber was the son of Moritz Schreber, an immensely influential though controversial German authority on child-rearing. That Moritz Schreber's sys-tems for parenting stressed nearly sadistic obedience and control is a fact about which analyzers of Daniel Schreber's path-ology make some hay.[1] Also well-noted is that Schreber's schizophrenia did not manifest until he was in his forties in the midst of his career.[2] He recovered from his first breakdown only to be incarcerated for nearly a decade when he was in his fifties. While in the asylum, he recorded his obser-vations of his body and his religious con-ceptions including those supernatural matters "which cannot be expressed in human language; they exceed human understanding" (Schreber 16). Schreber was keen to publish his manuscript (his family, fearing embarrassment, not so very keen), however, inmates of asylums were not permitted by law to publish their work. In 1902, after a protracted legal battle, Schreber secured his release entering into the public sphere physically and, soon after, rhetorically. His *Memoirs*, published the following year, were quickly recognized as a critical account of psychosis. He had become fully exceptional. Lacan, who analyzed Schreber through his *Memoirs,* wrote: "That Schreber was *exceptionally gifted,* as he himself puts it, at observing phenomena of which he is the center and at searching for their truth, makes his testimony incomparably valuable" (233, emphasis Lacan's).

Undeniably, however, what made Judge Schreber most exceptional to modern commentators including Lacan was Freud's 1911 analysis of the Schreber case. Schreber might at first seem an unusual subject for Freud to analyze given that Freud considered schizophrenics unfit subjects for the talking cure. Colin McCabe records, "Any psychotic patient that presented him or herself in Freud's consulting rooms would, by the very nature of their condition, swiftly either refuse treatment or be referred on to a hospital" (ix). McCabe puzzles why Freud did not read Schreber's *Memoirs* until seven years after its publication, even though it had been a topic of great discussion in psychiatric circles. That Freud did eventually turn his attention to the Schreber case McCabe credits to Freud's fear that psychoanalysis, particularly its tenets grounding the relationship between the unconscious and the conscious in sexuality, faced threats from competing biological and social theories of the psyche. Schreber, to Freud, then, was also exceptional; Freud's location of Schreber's psychosis in repressed homosexuality was to be the exception that proved his rule of neurosis.

Freud's defensive and unconvincing analysis of Schreber through the *Memoirs* ("very unsatisfactory" Jung would deem it)[3]

made Schreber the perfect platform from which Deleuze and Guattari could launch their assault on psychoanalytic theory's complicity with the capitalist order. Judge Schreber, along with the also exceptional Antonin Artaud, became their model schizophrenics. But it was Schreber who allowed for the most direct attack on Freud. Deleuze and Guattari declared that Freud had done Schreber a great disservice in his reading of *Memoirs,* cutting off Schreber rhetorically at the kneecaps. "Not one word is retained," they complained, of Schreber's original work in Freud's treatment. Schreber, they wryly remarked, was not only sodomized by rays from heaven (as Schreber in his *Memoirs* describes), but was "posthumously oedipalized by Freud," who, they point out, never met his "patient" *in vivo* (57).

The concern Deleuze and Guattari have for Schreber seems to be one of recuperating his rhetorical position; Schreber, thus rhetorically enabled, can become the agent who can trick Freud in the session that never occurred, breaking through "the simplistic terms and functions of the Oedipal triangle" (14). However, Deleuze and Guattari themselves evince less than total confidence in Schreber's self-account. Their remark, "if we are to believe Judge Schreber's doctrine" (19) suggests that Schreber occupies only a qualified rhetorical position in *Anti-Oedipus,* one that is valuable, but provisional, even on the subject of Schreber's own experience. Deleuze and Guattari find in Schreber's memoirs the seeds of the break from representation, but they can only access it through an act of representation, one that grants Schreber no firmer rhetorical ground than he enjoyed through Freud's text.

Where Deleuze and Guattari find Schreber through Freud, Jameson finds him through Lacan: "I have found Lacan's account of schizophrenia useful here not because I have any way of knowing whether it has clinical accuracy but chiefly because—as description rather than diagnosis—it seems to me to offer a suggestive aesthetic model" (26). Through Jameson's formulation of Schreber's condition, we can understand schizophrenia as that state which enacts disruptions of temporality. Jameson cites as further examples of such disruption the work of John Cage and Samuel Beckett, neither of whom were diagnosed schizophrenics. Cage and Beckett quickly, however, become metaphors of schizophrenia through Jameson's analysis. In the end Jameson leaves us with an aestheticization of the schizophrenic experience. Schizophrenia is always/already artistic, always/already literary, always/already metaphorical. What might usefully rescue schizophrenia from these metaphoric entrapments is a shift in focus toward a rhetorical exploration, one that examines the circumstances of publication of schizophrenic writing, situating that writing within, as Snyder and Mitchell have suggested, histories of conflict over who may take up space in the public sphere.

NEWS FROM THE VOID

Two publications by schizophrenics entering the public sphere in 1995 form an interesting juxtaposition in this regard. One will be familiar and widely recognizable as exceptional: the publication of Ted Kaczynski's "Industrial Society and its Future" [commonly known as the "Unabomber manifesto"] in *The New York Times*, a 36,000 word rant against modernity Kaczynski would go so far as to kill to see published. The other publication is much less well known. In 1995 Editor-in-Chief Ken Steele released the inaugural edition of *New York City Voices: A Consumer Journal for Mental Health*. To appreciate the profundity of this publication, a short biography of Steele is appropriate. Steele began hearing voices in 1962 when he was 14 years old. The voices urged him repeatedly to kill himself. After a few failed attempts to follow their

orders, Steele ran away from home, and was shortly afterward diagnosed with schizophrenia by a physician. At age 17 he took off for New York City and was quickly ushered into the world of male hustling. Over the next 30 years he would be homeless, raped, shuttled between several psychiatric hospitals, and he would attempt to end his life several more times. In 1995, then under treatment with a new medication, Ken Steele's voices stopped. Five years later, Steele died of a heart attack, possibly related to obesity that has since been identified as a common side effect of the medication he had been taking.

Significantly, Steele had actually begun engaging in advocacy slightly before the end of his voices. In order to fulfill the mandated "structured activity" as part of his care, he decided to found a voter registration project for the mentally ill. He had become alarmed at growing threats to Social Security Disability and proposed cutbacks to a range of other services the mentally ill rely on: housing, mental health clinics, and research. While he was still coping with his voices, he took a folding table and voter registration cards to homeless shelters and mental health clinics to register mentally ill voters of any party. After his voices stopped, however, he decided not only to help the mentally ill enter the polity via the vote, but also to use rhetoric as a tool to increase their civic presence. He founded *New York City Voices* primarily as a journal to inform about legislative issues, but writing the journal itself served its own enfranchising purposes.

A typical example of a story from *New York City Voices*, written by Steele himself in the July/August 1999 issue, is not rhetorically exceptional in any of the ways postmodern theorists might expect:

> Did you know that only one-half of one percent of those Americans with disabilities presently receiving Social Security Disability

Insurance (SSDI) or Supplemental Security Income (SSI) are employed? How many more of us do you think would like to work but cannot, because we would lose cash benefits if we earn over $500 a month and Medicare and Medicaid health coverage if we work more than three years?

What follows is a plea to support the Ticket to Work and Self-Sufficiency Program. There is nothing distinctly disorganized about this opening of rhetorical questions, which lays out the false choice Steele sees between accepting work and accepting health coverage. I would even venture to say that were it not for Steele's self-identification as mentally ill throughout the article (and his invocation of an audience of the mentally ill), there would be nothing to mark Steele as schizophrenic.

Another writer for the journal, Lisa Gibson, in an article advocating for insurance parity in the January/February 2000 issue, writes that her manic depression has been the most crucial element of her life, exceeding the force of other social categories to which she also belongs. She begins by describing the importance of narrative in self-identification:

> Charles Dickens began his book David Copperfield with the words "I am born." If I were to write an autobiography, I would begin with the words "I am born with manic-depression," for this illness has been the single most defining factor of my life and my personality. No other factor—being female, being southern, being the middle child—has had such an impact on me as this disease.

As Steele notes in *The Day the Voices Stopped*:

> Most striking about *New York City Voices* has been the inclusion of personal stories by people with mental illness, written in our own words and under our own bylines (often accompanied by a photograph of the contributor). A bold but necessary move, self-disclosure is a first step toward successfully addressing the stigma associated with being mentally ill.

(221)

This self-disclosure is a defining feature of a rhetoric self-conscious of the usual position of the schizophrenic rhetor; typically schizophrenics are considered beings with speech, but speech that is generally treated as an index of sanity or insanity, with referentiality only to diagnostic criteria, and without referentiality to the civic world. Self-disclosure is thus a necessary component of civic rhetoric for these authors, involving the investiture of the previously stigmatizing moniker *schizophrenic* with new meaning. These writers appropriate the term *schizophrenic* in much the same way as the gay community successfully appropriated the previously denigrating term *queer*.

Snyder and Mitchell have identified the 1970s as the moment disability memoirs began to be published *en masse*: "These first person stories interrupted several hundred years of inaccurate disability representation by interested professionals in medicine, rehabilitation, and other caring professions" (9). When we look back at the mid-1990s from a vantage point 30 years hence, we will see it as the moment mental disability narratives began appearing *en masse*—which explains why the most blatant appropriations of the schizophrenic seem to end in the late 1980s. There is little getting around the fact that the explosion of civic rhetoric by schizophrenics corresponds with the advent of atypical antipsychotic medications in the 1990s. The first mass-market magazine authored primarily by schizophrenics, *Schizophrenia Digest*, began in 1994, for example, and continues to this day to chronicle schizophrenics' struggles with social discrimination, limited treatment options, and those medications that may have allowed for certain forms of expression, but with troubling and sometimes life-threatening side-effects. Within the *Digest*'s pages, schizophrenics write of the need to speak in order to break through the assumption of the normative audience that informs most published material. As Vicky Yeung writes of her experience reading personal finance books written from a normative perspective:

> [T]he author assumes I'm not limited by my mind's matter as to how much money I conceivably can make. These writers give tips that are unhelpful for me, like increasing my income through investing in mutual funds, working at several jobs, etc., as if I could do any of those things. Really, they're writing for the "normal healthy mind" audience.
>
> (47)

In this passage Yeung elucidates her exclusion from the normative processes of late capitalism, incapable as those processes are of incorporating a non-incarcerated, non-revenue producing, non-exceptional subject. Her quotation marks around "normal healthy mind" indicate that she does not consider herself "exceptional," except that normativity makes her so.

As Daniel Frey, successor to Steele as Editor-in-Chief of *New York City Voices* has observed of the erasure of this non-exceptional subject through the exceptionalizing of schizophrenics:

> The extremes of schizophrenia get the most publicity, like the genius John Nash on the one hand and the subway killer Gary Goldstein on the other. Every day people like me get overlooked even though we compose the vast majority of schizophrenics. The mental health consumer movement is the last great civil rights movement in this country.

Frey asks here for a move away from both pathologized and vaulted genius/artist versions of schizophrenics; he suggests

movement toward the vast middle ground of schizophrenics who hold unexceptional jobs, or move through multiple hospitalizations without either killing anyone or winning Nobel prizes. Frey's speech does not ask for leaps of interpretation, does not mark itself as any more "everyday" than he marks himself. He simply heralds the end of the exemplar schizophrenic. He asks that schizophrenics be able to participate in, as well as critique, late capitalism; one wonders what Deleuze and Guattari would have made of schizophrenic Bill MacPhee, publisher of *Schizophrenia Digest* in which Vicky Yeung's critique of capitalism appears, who affirmed that his life was changed in 1994 by the book *101 Ways to Start a Business with Little or No Capital*. His business? A magazine for schizophrenics.

To see the "ordinary" schizophrenic is, in short, to give up the stable schizophrenic. The identity of being a schizophrenic, because it is tied to a history of having been diagnosed with the condition, may remain constant, but impairments fluctuate in time. As Kuppers notes, "Mental health is a contested terrain: on the one hand, mental normalcy is a problematic concept given the malleability and changing nature of human mental and emotional states. On the other hand, certain permutations of mentality are severely policed and bracketed off into deviancy" (59). The public seemingly only desires the stable schizophrenic, easy to incarcerate, or easy to celebrate as the occasion requires. The public does not want to allow for fluctuation between states, and even less for the possibility that both states exist at once. A genuinely postmodern perspective would not insist that schizophrenic rhetoric be fixed, but rather would allow for Bill MacPhee, Lisa Gibson, Vicki Yeung, and Daniel Frey to continue to engage in civic rhetoric, while being schizophrenic. It would allow them to occupy the contested public sphere, bringing to it the force of their narratives.

The narrative power of fluctuations between mental states is perhaps best captured by Richard MacLean's memoir *Recovered, Not Cured*. MacLean begins the work on a past moment of impairment, set off in space and time: "Another World, August 1994. I am crouching in an alleyway. They can't see me here, so for a moment I am safe. There must be hundreds of loudspeakers projecting secret messages, and umpteen video cameras tracking every move I make" (xi). The book ends in "The Present":

> Nowadays, I say that I am recovered, not cured. I have a job as a graphic designer and illustrator, I have a band in which I do vocals and guitar, I have my friends and my family. I pay my taxes and do the dishes; I'm independent. I have achieved a sense of normality and live with the knowledge that a couple of pills a day will keep me slightly lethargic yet "sane" at the same time. I can live with that.
> (174)

The actual structure of MacLean's text belies the sense of progression that these two time points imply. Interspersed through MacLean's narrative are his own illustrations, many created "years ago," as well as numerous emails from schizophrenics he has received since beginning a life of public advocacy. This structure enacts a merging of all states in the present, a time when "sane" appears only in quotation marks. MacLean acknowledges in a section entitled "A Kind of Closure":

> If I had my way, of course, all this would never have happened. However, I hoped that by writing about it I might be able to seal off all the chaos I had experienced; seal it up with sealing wax, put it in a cupboard or throw it to the sea. It hasn't worked out quite so simply. To this day, although my illness is at a manageable level, I am residually delusional and sometimes read odd meanings into things.
> (172)

There is, MacLean asserts, no definitive closure for him.

I would like to return, in only provisional closing then, to the quote from Lacan I selected for the epigraph, a reflection on schizophrenic voice: "Wasn't it because they didn't go far enough in listening to the insane that the great observers who drew up the first classifications impoverished the material they were given—to such an extent it appeared problematic and fragmentary to them?" Lacan suggests that schizophrenics had not been listened to except metaphorically. The problem according to Lacan is that these great observers thought that what schizophrenics were saying could not really be what they were actually saying. It would have to be something else. Lacan was, ironically, talking about the much-observed Schreber, who died in an asylum four years after the publication of the *Memoirs*. Let us change Lacan's "it," though, so it no longer stands simply for the utterances of one schizophrenic at one moment in time. Let us have "it" stand in for all schizophrenic utterances at all points in time. That "it" should appear problematic. It should appear fragmentary. But it should appear, and once appearing, be considered unexceptional.[4]

NOTES

1. See, for example, *Soul Murder* by Schatzman.
2. Schreber was not diagnosed schizophrenic during his life (the diagnosis not then being in use), however, Deleuze and Guattari, typical of his modern commentators, ascribe him that condition.
3. Jung's response quoted in Dinnage, and further elaborated in McCabe.
4. Many thanks to the JLD reviewers for their invaluable comments on an earlier version of this essay.

WORKS CITED

Baudrillard, Jean. *The Ecstasy of Communication.* Trans. Bernard Schutze and Caroline Schutze. New York: Semiotext(e), 1988.

Braidotti, Rosi. "Schizophrenia." *The Deleuze Dictionary*. Ed. Adrian Parr. New York: Columbia University Press, 2005, 237–40.

Corker, Mairian and Tom Shakespeare, ed. *Disability/Postmodernity: Embodying Disability Theory*. New York: Continuum, 2002.

Deleuze, Gilles and Félix Guattari. *A Thousand Plateaus: Capitalism and Schizophrenia*. Trans. Brian Massumi. Minneapolis: University of Minnesota Press, 1987.

——. *Anti-Oedipus: Capitalism and Schizophrenia*. Trans. Robert Hurley, Mark Seem, and Helen R. Lane. Minneapolis: University of Minnesota Press, 2000.

Dinnage, Rosemary. Introduction. In *Memoirs of My Nervous Illness by Daniel Paul Schreber*, eds. Ida Macalpine and Richard A. Hunter, xi–xxiv. New York: New York Review of Books, 2000.

Freud, Sigmund. *The Schreber Case*. Trans. Andrew Webber. New York: Penguin, 2002.

Frey, Daniel. "First Break: Three Years Later." *New York City Voices*, www.nycvoices.org, posted 2002.

Gibson, Lisa. "Parity Matters to Me." *New York City Voices*, www.nyvoices.org, posted 2000.

Jameson, Frederic. *Postmodernism, or, the Cultural Logic of Late Capitalism*. Durham, NC: Duke University Press, 1992.

Kuppers, Petra. *The Scar of Visibility: Medical Performance and Contemporary Art*. Minneapolis: University of Minnesota Press, 2007.

Lacan, Jacques. *The Seminar of Jacques Lacan Book III: The Psychoses 1955–1956*. Trans. Russell Grigg. Ed. Jacques-Alain Miller. New York: Norton, 1997.

McCabe, Colin. Introduction. *The Schreber Case*. By Sigmund Freud, trans. Andrew Webber, vi–xxii. New York: Penguin, 2002.

MacLean, Richard. *Recovered, Not Cured: A Journey through Schizophrenia*. Crows Nest, Australia: Allen & Unwin, 2003.

Mitchell, David T. and Sharon L. Snyder. *Narrative Prosthesis: Disability and the Dependencies of Discourse*. Ann Arbor: University of Michigan Press, 2001.

Schatzman, Morton. *Soul Murder: Persecution in the Family*. New York: Random House, 1973.

Schreber, Daniel Paul. *Memoirs of My Nervous Illness*. Trans. Ida Macalpine and Richard A. Hunter. New York: New York Review of Books, 2000.

Snyder, Sharon L. and David T. Mitchell. "Disability Haunting in American Poetics." *Journal of Literary Disability* 1.1 (2007): 1–12.

Sontag, Susan. *Aids and Its Metaphors*. New York: Farrar, Strauss, and Giroux, 1988.

——. *Illness as Metaphor*. New York: Farrar, Strauss and Giroux, 1978.

Steele, Ken and Claire Berman. *The Day the Voices Stopped*. New York: Basic Books, 2002.

Yeung, Vicky. "Born with a Gift and a Purpose." *Schizophrenia Digest* 5.3 (2007): 47.

CHAPTER 17

Deaf Studies in the 21st Century: "Deaf-Gain" and the Future of Human Diversity

H-Dirksen L. Bauman and Joseph J. Murray

SUMMARY

By rethinking "hearing loss" as "gaining Deafness," H-Dirksen L. Bauman and Joseph J. Murray make the case for preserving Deaf communities from normalizing influences in order to protect the diversity— cultural, creative, and cognitive—accessible through deaf people and their signed languages. Deaf Studies might be well served by taking the position that all individuals would be enriched by becoming "a bit more Deaf." This essay presents a variety of ways Deaf communities have intrinsic and extrinsic value.

Acknowledging "Deaf-gain" allows us to see that much of what we know about the complexity of language is indebted to decades of research into sign languages. Using sign language has been linked to advanced visuospatial abilities and potential to learn visually for both deaf and hearing people. Because of its visuospatial aspects, scholars might one day use sign languages to more accurately represent mental images in their explanations.

Research still remains to be done in order to show how benefits might emerge from the work of Deaf filmmakers, and further work by groups like the Deaf Space Project will reveal the ways that sign language users can revitalize architecture and community planning. "Deaf-gain" can also help us reconsider the world of literature, as sign poetry extends both performance and visual traditions into new literary forms.

Rather than being hemmed in by cultural boundaries, Deaf Studies has begun to encompass a transnational perspective while also deepening analyses of how deaf people are integrated in their particular national contexts. For instance, use of International Sign has allowed Deaf travelers to communicate across linguistic boundaries with much more success than auditory language users. The authors of this essay suggest that in an era marked by dissolution of communities, the Deaf cultural community can provide models for restoring collectivity.

DEAF-GAIN: COGNITIVE, CULTURAL, AND CREATIVE DIVERSITY

Given the threats posed to the signing Deaf community by the medical and educational institutions of normalization, the Deaf community and Deaf Studies scholars find themselves cornered into the fundamental existential question: Why should deaf people continue to exist? Indeed, on what grounds can one argue for the preservation of what most consider a disability? As Burke (2006) notes, such bioethical arguments hinge on the demonstration of the intrinsic and extrinsic value of Deaf communities and their languages. Intrinsic arguments seek to prove the worth of deaf people and sign languages for their own good, whereas extrinsic arguments demonstrate the useful contributions of deaf people and their languages for the greater good of humanity. Although intrinsic arguments have long been made (i.e., Deaf culture and sign languages should be preserved because they are as valid as other cultures and languages), extrinsic arguments have not yet been fully developed or understood. Future directions in the field of Deaf Studies may be thought of as the vigorous exploration and demonstration of the important extrinsic value of Deaf communities and their languages.

While having to argue for the most basic right of all—the right to exist—Deaf Studies is put on the defensive. However, scholars are beginning to recognize that the most vigorous response would be to cease arguing against medical and educational institutions of normalization, and instead, go on the offensive by reframing representations of deafness from sensory lack to a form of sensory and cognitive diversity that offers vital contributions to human diversity. Within the frame of human diversity, Deaf Studies scholars are inquiring into the insights that may be gleaned from deaf people whose highly visual, spatial, and kinetic structures of thought and language may shed light into the blindspots of hearing ways of knowing.

The overarching extrinsic value of Deaf communities and their languages, then, may best be explained by the emerging discipline of biocultural diversity, a field that has arisen as an area of transdisciplinary research concerned with investigating the links between the world's linguistic, cultural, and biological diversity as manifestations of the diversity of life. The impetus for the emergence of this field came from the observation that all three diversities are under threat by some of the same forces, and from the perception that loss of diversity at all levels spells dramatic consequences for humanity and the earth (Maffi, 2005). A body of research has begun to link the decreases in biocultural and linguistic diversity, noting that when an indigenous language dies, the unique knowledge of the local environment, developed over centuries, dies with it (Harmon, 2002; Maffi, 2005; Skutnabb-Kangas, 2000). Most predictions suggest that within the next century, half of the world's 6,000 spoken languages will disappear, which is at the rate of a language death every two weeks (Crystal, 2002). There are currently no statistics about the number of signed languages in the world, and clearly, when a signed language dies, there may not be the same amount of biological and environmental knowledge lost with it. However, in the same vein, Deaf Studies scholars may begin to add to the notions of linguistic and biodiversity new categories of diversity foregrounded by signed languages—namely, cognitive, cultural, and creative diversity.

Once we place Deaf communities and their languages within the framework of biocultural diversity, a new frame emerges. The task of Deaf Studies in the new century is to ask a fundamental question: How does being Deaf reorganize what it means to be human? Indeed, what dramatic consequences would arise from the (neo)eugenic drive toward normalization? Embracing deaf people and their languages will invariably lead toward a deeper understanding of the human proclivity for adaptation. In the face of sensory loss, we may better appreciate the dynamic and pliable nature of the mind and the human will to communicate and to form community. In this light, deafness is not so much defined by a fundamental lack, as in *hearing loss*, but as its opposite, as a means to understand the plenitude of human being, as *Deaf-gain*.[1]

Deaf-gain, as we explore later, is the notion that the unique sensory orientation of Deaf people leads to a sophisticated form of visual–spatial language that provides opportunities for exploration into the human character. In this spirit, the Gallaudet University's Vision Statement commits to promoting "the recognition that deaf people and their sign languages are vast resources with significant contributions to the cognitive, creative, and cultural dimensions of human diversity" (www.gallaudet.edu/mission.xml). In what follows, contemporary and future directions for each of these forms of human diversity and "Deaf-gain" will be discussed as emerging and future trajectories of the field of Deaf Studies that collectively demonstrate the value of Deaf Studies to the academy and Deaf communities to humanity.

COGNITIVE DIVERSITY AND DEAF-GAIN: REDEFINING THE NATURE OF LANGUAGE

The prime example of the extrinsic value of deaf people and their languages is the wholesale redefinition of language that has come about as a result of sign language studies. Just as we once thought the flat Earth to be at the center of the universe, we once assumed that language could only take the form of speech. Now that we know the brain may just as easily develop a signed as a spoken language, we must reconfigure our understanding of language, in all its complexities. Four decades of sign language research has now deepened our awareness of the nature of language—from language acquisition, structure, and more. We now know that the fundamental character of the brain is plasticity and flexibility (Petitto, Zatorre, Gauna, Nikelski, Dostie, & Evans, 2000). This redefining would not have come about without the study of signed languages, and may be seen as the initial instance of Deaf-gain. Due to the existence of signing communities, linguists and anthropologists have been able to peer into the development of language, revealing insights into the debates over the innateness or social origins of language acquisition (Sandler, Meir, Padden, & Aronoff, 2005). In addition, sign languages have also provided insight into new and revived theories of the origins of language (Armstrong, 2002; Armstrong & Wilcox, 2007; Armstrong, Wilcox, & Stokoe, 1995; Corballis, 2003; Stokoe, 2001). The implications of these discoveries extend into the core of what it means to be human, but have yet to be applied to Deaf education. As Stokoe (2001, p. 16) wrote, "the status of deaf people, their education, their opportunities in life, and the utilization of their potential—all these could be much enhanced if we understood the way deaf people still make language may be the way the whole human race became human." As a result of the natural human proclivity to sign, hearing parents are increasingly using sign language, with results that suggest increased linguistic, cognitive, and social development.

COGNITIVE DIVERSITY AND DEAF-GAIN: VISUAL LANGUAGE/VISUAL LEARNING

Another significant area of future research in the area of Deaf-gain is the particular, highly developed visual ways of being in the world brought about by the unique sensory orientation of deaf individuals and communities (Bahan, 2008; Marschark, 2003). The link between enhanced visuospatial abilities and use of sign languages has been documented in studies of speed in generating mental images (Emmorey & Kosslyn, 1996; Emmorey, Kosslyn, & Bellugi, 1993), mental rotation skills (Emmorey, Klima, & Hicock, 1998), increased facial recognition skills (Bettger, Emmorey, McCullough, & Bellugi, 1997), increased peripheral recognition skills (Bavelier et al., 2000), and increased spatial cognition (Bellugi, O'Grady, Lillio-Martin, O'Grady Hynes, Van Hoek, & Corina, 1989; see also Chapter 30 [original volume]). We may take these indications of increased visual–spatial cognition and develop them into future research into practices of visual learning for all sighted individuals. The benefits may be far-reaching, for as Stokoe recognized, "vision may have an advantage, for it is neurologically a richer and more complex physiological system than hearing. Sight makes use of much more of the brain's capacity than does hearing" (p. 20). Given the drive to diversify education along the lines of "multiple intelligences" (Gardner, 1993), it would only makes sense that the most visually oriented of all humans would take the lead toward future experimentation in visual learning.

As testimony to the promises of the field of visual language and visual learning, the National Science foundation recently funded a Science of Learning Center at Gallaudet University to "gain a greater understanding of the biological, cognitive, linguistic, sociocultural, and pedagogical conditions that influence the acquisition of language and knowledge through the visual modality" (VL2, 2008; http://vl2. gallaudet.edu/). Given the immense amount of information processed visually[2] (for sighted people), it is not surprising that learning may be enhanced when pedagogies focus on transmitting visual information (Gardner, 1993; Moore & Dwyer, 1994). This project goes beyond the Deaf education model of addressing alternative (read: remedial) ways of teaching deaf people, to ask how deaf people's visual orientation to the world may be able to offer hearing people new ways of learning, even in fields traditionally dominated by an auditory/phonetic orientation, such as literacy development. Indeed, as textuality in the 21st century is becoming increasingly visual and digital, there is a trend away from traditional print-based texts to video and multimedia texts. Insights from the world's most visually acute people may provide insights on how we may all process information visually.

If this is the case, then future directions of Deaf Studies and Deaf education may have less to do with audiological loss than Deaf-gain—that is, a bilingual, visual learning environment could be so rich in processing information in multiple channels that hearing parents would want their children to go to sign language schools. In this scenario, Deaf education would give way to dual-language education, open to all who desire such a learning environment. Two examples of these types of bilingual sign language schools are P.S. 47: The American Sign Language (ASL)–English Bilingual School in New York City and The Cassato School, near Torino, Italy. Indeed, before such a paradigm shift were to take root in a systematic way, the status of sign languages as academic languages would have to be reconceived.

COGNITIVE DIVERSITY AND DEAF-GAIN: SIGN LANGUAGES AND ACADEMIC DISCOURSE

Traditionally, signed languages have been seen as, essentially "oral" languages as they have no written form.[3] Common wisdom holds that writing is an essential element to the development of literacy, as essential as water is to swimming. The word "literacy," after all, derives from the Greek *littere,* or "written letter." However, as Kuntze (2008) has suggested, just as definitions of language have changed in the wake of the validation of sign languages, so may the definition of literacy. Kuntze shows how one may demonstrate characteristics of literate thought in written, signed, and visual modalities. One such characteristic, notes Kuntze, is inference making. Whether the information that an individual receives "is expressed in written language or in a different language such as ASL or in a different mode like film, the act of inference making will be necessary if one is to achieve a richer interpretation of the content" (p. 150). Clearly, one may exercise inference and other critical thinking strategies using a nonwritten language such as ASL or through watching silent films.

Evolving definitions of literacy are happening in tandem with emerging video technologies that allow greater ease of producing academic texts in ASL. Once video journals such as the *Deaf Studies Digital Journal* (dsdj.gallaudet.edu) mature, standards for academic publishing in signed languages will develop. The significance of academic discourse in ASL may be most prominent if the visual, spatial, and kinetic dimensions of the language are explored for their greatest rhetorical power. For example, imagine how precisely an ASL-fluent biology professor would describe the process of cell mitosis, using ASL's rich classifier system to indicate pairs of chromosomes splitting and cell walls dividing, so that students may witness the linguistic reenactment of a physical process, or the precise description of the French philosopher Michel Foucault's notion of the "microphysics of power," which would be shown as a dispersion of multiple sites of power throughout society, rather than a more traditional top-down model of power. The point here is that sign languages are rich in what Taub (2001) calls "metaphoric iconicity," in which complex ideas are demonstrated through visual–spatial metaphors. Such a language does not lack in abstraction, but gains in clarity of the concrete representation of complex ideas.

This unique advantage of sign languages was originally articulated by the early 19th-century teacher of the deaf, Auguste Bebian, who believed that "sign language has a superior capacity for expressing mental operations" (1984, p. 151). The difference, Bebian explains, is that spoken language is fundamentally arbitrary, but discourse in sign language, would "frequently acquire a self-evident certainty or become a manifest absurdity to all" (p. 151). Indeed, the speaking biology student could say, "the

chromosomes split," whereas the signing biology student would reveal the internal mental images of her conception of how the chromosomes split visually and spatially. Similarly, the philosophy student would reveal the degree of precision of his understanding of Foucault's unique conception of "power" through the spatial arrangement of his description. Clearly, the validity of such observations about the unique qualities of intellectual discourse in sign language now lay before the fields of Deaf education, Deaf Studies, and linguistics to explore this vein of potential Deaf-gain.

CREATIVE DIVERSITY AND DEAF-GAIN: FILM LANGUAGE/ SIGN LANGUAGE

Comparisons have often been made between the film language and sign languages (Bahan, 2006; Bauman, 2006; Sacks, 1990). In addition to a traditional linguistic means of describing sign languages through phonology, morphology, and syntax, one may also see fluent signers as everyday filmmakers, a skill that is heightened in the literary and dramatic uses of sign language. Indeed, when seen through lens of film grammar (Arijon, 1991), sign languages present a constant tableau of close-up and distant shots, replete with camera movements and editing techniques. Given such an intimate, cognitive relationship with cinematic grammar, we must wonder what innovations might emerge if we were to invest in the cinematic education of the next generation of deaf children. Again, no research has been conducted to this point about the potential innovations that would emerge from Deaf filmmakers, but such exploration is clearly an important trajectory for Deaf Studies to explore the potential of Deaf-gain in this area. A rigorous educational film program in deaf schools would have the added benefit of inserting a deaf public voice into popular media.

CREATIVE DIVERSITY AND DEAF-GAIN: DEAF SPACE AND THE BUILT ENVIRONMENT

Although Deaf Studies is inherently inter-disciplinary, one may not immediately think of architecture as an important area of creative exchange. However, in 2005, Gallaudet University hosted a two-day "Deaf Space" workshop, which resulted in what has grown into a series of Deaf Studies courses, the Gallaudet University Deaf Space Design Guide (H. Bauman, in press), and the incorporation of some key Deaf Space principles in the Sorenson Language and Communication Center at Gallaudet.

The Deaf Space project does not focus on issues of accommodation, but rather on Deaf cultural aesthetics that are embodied in the built environment. In the original workshop in 2005, a common aesthetic emerged that was described as organic, curvilinear, and bathed in light. Since that time, students and faculty have researched core issues, such as the qualities of lighting, proxemics of signers, and the tension between open, visually accessible spaces and privacy. Although the notion of Deaf space generates from designing the optimal environment for Deaf signers, the basic precept is that Deaf space principles would create exceptional buildings for everyone, regardless of audiological status.

Further study of Deaf space and planning in the future of Deaf Studies may also lead toward an understanding of the urgency that Deaf communities may be strength-ened by gaining control over the spaces where deaf individuals live. As deaf individ-uals are born into a dispersion among hearing families, they are subject to a diasporic condition from the onset (Allen, 2007). Indeed, one of the primary differ-ences between the linguistic minority of sign language users and other language groups is that deaf people have never occupied a homeland. They may have congregated at residential schools, but these spaces were designed on 19th-century asylum architec-ture—hardly the autochthonous creation of a group with deep ties to the land. From schools to Deaf clubs, Deaf spaces have generally reflected the design of hearing architects. On a personal level, however, deaf people have a long tradition of home renovations that bear similarities—such as increasing the visual reach throughout a house—that permit greater visual com-munication, as well as a sense of connection (Malzkuhn, 2007). The cultural significance of home renovations and the deaf relation-ship to place cannot be underestimated, for as Findley (2005, p. 5) notes, "not having control of the space one is occupying is in some way demoralizing." For this reason, Deaf people have always felt the need to dream of a homeland, from Jacob Flour-noy's 19th-century proposals for a Deaf state (Krentz, 2000) to the recent proposal for Laurent, South Dakota (Willard, n.d.) as just such a homeland. Indeed, as Le Corbusier wrote, "the occupation of space is the first proof of existence" (Findley, 2005, p. 5). As such, Deaf people may find architecture and community planning an integral element to linguistic and cultural revitaliza-tion. Such a future exploration would result in diversity of the design and qualities of living spaces.

DEAF-GAIN AND CREATIVE DIVERSITY: SIGN LANGUAGE LITERATURE

Just as the validation of sign language revolutionized the study of language, so too must the nature of literature be reconsidered from the ground up. The unique visual and spatial properties of sign language make it a particularly rich medium for poetic image and metaphor (Bauman, 2008a; Bauman, Nelson, & Rose, 2006; Davidson, 2008; Taub, 2001; Wilcox, 2000). For centuries, writers have been seeking to extend both the visual and performative aspects of literature, resulting in various experimental forms, from the unity of painting and poetry in the works of William Blake to concrete poetry, slam, and performance poetry. Sign poetry extends both the performative and visual traditions of literature into new forms. Sign language poetic practice has become increasingly innovative in its use of visual textual forms, as sign language poets have experimented with the interaction of the components of film language—camera movement, editing, visual prosody, *mise en scene*—and sign language. Ella Mae Lentz's collaboration with Lynette Taylor (Lentz, 1996), and Dutch poets Wim Emmerik and Giselle Meyer's collaboration with Anja Hiddinga and Lendeert Pot (Hiddinga et al., 2005) represent the creative potential of blending cinematic techniques with sign language poetry. In addition to experimentation with visual textuality, sign language poetry extends the embodied, performative tradition, exemplified by the Beat generation's spoken word poetry. Allen Ginsberg, for one, recognized the enormous potential of sign language performance when he participated in a gathering of Deaf and hearing poets in Rochester, New York. When he asked Deaf poets to translate the phrase "hydrogen jukebox" from his poem, "Howl," Patrick Graybill responded with a translation that led Ginsberg to exclaim, "that is exactly it, what I have been trying to convey, the hard clear image of it" (Cohn, 1999; Cook, 2006).

Similarly, the history of theater reveals an enduring human desire for nonverbal, visual spectacle. The history of mime and theatrical tableau, and explorations in experimental visual theater by directors and writers like Antonin Artaud and Robert Wilson, indicate that theater yearns to draw particular attention to the spatial and kinetic modalities. Golden (2009) suggests that Deaf/sign language theater and the practice of visual theater engage in an exchange to the mutual benefit of each practice. Clearly, the highly visual nature of Deaf theater, Golden suggests, may enhance the genre of visual theater.

CULTURAL DIVERSITY AND DEAF-GAIN: TRANSNATIONAL DEAF COMMUNITY

The tools of cultural studies that have served Deaf Studies so well in earlier eras have now also changed. Scholars have called into question the old anthropology of culture, with its language of bounded cultural entities, cultural contact, and cross-cultural communication. The dangers of essentialism have gained increasing urgency, especially among scholars of South Asia, who see the results of religious essentialism in the violent clashes on the Indian subcontinent (Appadurai, 2006). Deaf Studies has begun to encompass a cosmopolitan, transnational perspective that moves outside the phase of legitimization of the category of Deaf and into a critical inquiry into the nature of being deaf, how ways of understanding and living as deaf have shaped the material and ideological worlds of Deaf and hearing people. In fact, the very trope of "Deaf worlds" and "hearing worlds" is being understood as a product of a particular set of historical conditions (Murray, 2007).

There is a small, but growing, body of work that explores how deaf people interact across national boundaries (Breivik, Haualand, & Solvang, 2002; Murray, 2007; Nakamura, 2006). Transnational contact between deaf people existed since the early 19th century, emerging at a series of Parisian Deaf-mute banquets, and a transnational Deaf public sphere developed alongside a series of international congresses of Deaf people from 1873 onward (Ladd, 2003; Murray, 2007). This sphere created a shared discursive field in which deaf people could articulate common strategies on living as visual minorities in societies governed by auditory principles. Taking a transnational orientation to deaf people's lives foregrounds the commonality of Deaf ways of being, but paradoxically also heightens our understanding of deaf people as intimately tied to local discursive constructions of nation and society. The physical assemblage of large numbers of deaf people often brings with it a reorganization of physical space according to Deaf norms, as deaf people temporarily colonize portions of a city at large-scale quadrennial events such as World Federation of the Deaf Congresses or Deaflympic sporting competitions. A complete understanding of the spatial reorganization that occurs and its implication in terms of "Deaf-gain" have yet to be realized. However, by viewing deaf peoples' lives in different national contexts, we also understand how integrated deaf people are into their national and social contexts. There are many ways to be Deaf, because deaf people are not isolated from the societies in which they live (Monaghan, Schmaling, Nakamura, & Turner, 2003).

An expanded frame of reference will naturally include the global South, which will have an increasingly prominent role in transnational Deaf communities of the future, especially if current demographic analyses regarding developed countries trend as predicted (Johnston, 2006). Economic disparities between the North and South have resulted in lesser rates of cochlear implantation, less use of genetic testing, and hindrances in the prevention of childhood illnesses, all of which have the result of expanding the population of deaf children and potential native signers. These factors will likely not persist, but what they mean for the present generation of deaf people is that the demographic imbalance between deaf people in developing and developed countries will likely become

even more prominent, with the rate of sign language use presumably shifting to developing countries as well. The central loci of Deaf Studies may well shift from Western countries to the global South, from discretely bounded national communities to a more fluid array of affinitive networks of various sizes and forms, existing in both physical and virtual space (Breivik, 2007; Kusters, 2007).

CULTURAL DIVERSITY AND DEAF-GAIN: INTERNATIONAL SIGN AND SIGNED LANGUAGES

Communication at international meetings of Deaf individuals often occurs in International Sign (IS), a form of cross-national communication that emerges when signers from different signed languages come into contact. Most research on IS to date has studied its linguistic properties. Although this research is still developing, early conclusions indicate that IS has more language-like properties than pidgins, another form of communication that emerges when two or more languages come into contact (Supalla & Webb, 1995). There is evidence of IS being used as far back as the early 19th century (Ladd, 2003), when it was used for political discourse at international meetings, as well as in informal interactions between Deaf travelers (Murray, 2007). The ability of signing deaf people to meet and interact across linguistic boundaries—without sharing a common language beforehand—has existed for at least two centuries. Some of this is no doubt due to the common experience of being Deaf in nondeaf societies. One author attributes this ease of understanding to a shared theory of mind among Deaf people, the term referring to the ability to "inhabit and intuit" another person's consciousness (Fox, 2008, pp. 80–81). Fox notes that semantically related signs for mental processes (think, decide, believe) are located at or near the head in ASL and European signed languages (Fox, 2008, p. 82), thus possibly assisting users of one signed language in understanding another signed language. The study of IS is still in its early stages and questions remain. If international signed communication has existed for two centuries, has there been continuity in lexical or other structural properties of IS in this period? Can we characterize "it" as an "it," or were there many versions of IS throughout the decades? A community of users has existed, but was there generational transmission and, if so, what does this tell us about the language-like properties of IS? Beyond a focus on IS as a distinct entity are questions IS raises by its very existence. At the very least, IS calls into question the inevitability of linguistic dissimilarities, with its apparatus of interpretation, and raises larger questions on the histories and modalities of communication between linguistically distinct groups of people.

The study of IS is part of a body of work going beyond the study of sign languages under national markers—ASL, Danish Sign Language—to a realization that signing exists in a diverse array of situations and communities. Scholars have seen a sign language being born in Nicaragua (Senghas, 1995, 2003) and are studying the use of signing among a Bedouin community in Israel (Fox, 2007; Sandler et al., 2005), one of many communities around the world where both hearing and deaf people sign (Groce, 1985; Johnson, 1994; Marsaja, 2008; see Chapter 18 [original volume]). There are obvious benefits to scholars in seeing linguistic phenomena take place in the field: scholars have never witnessed a spoken language being created, and the study of Nicaraguan sign language allows linguists the opportunity to see if their theories are correct. Think of astrophysicists being able to witness the Big Bang. Beyond this, the existence—and persistence—of sign languages allows us to understand the diversity of human ways of being and communicating, and offers a direct challenge to conceptions of normalcy that would peg all humans into a phonocentric square hole.

CULTURAL DIVERSITY AND DEAF-GAIN: DEAF COLLECTIVIST CULTURE AND THE FUTURE OF COMMUNITY

A growing body of research points toward the dissolution of a sense of community and civic engagement. Robert Putnam's *Bowling Alone: The Collapse and Revival of American Community* (2000) points to the factors of work, television, computers, suburban life, and family structures as having contributed to this decline. Other studies confirm Putnam's observations, noting that social networks and people's sense of connectedness have taken a precipitous decline in the past three decades (McPherson, Smith-Lovin, & Brashears, 2006). As a culture that exhibits a high degree of collectivism (Mindess, 2006), Deaf cultural relations may offer insights and examples to understand, if not emulate. The circular proxemics of deaf people as they align themselves to be seen are the structural embodiment of non-hierarchical relations. Although Derrida (1973) has highlighted the significance of "hearing oneself speak" as a prime source of deriving a sense of presence, deaf individuals can neither hear themselves speak nor fully see themselves sign (Bauman, 2008b). Granted that signers may see their own hand movements from their vantage, they will never be able to see their own faces, which are so vital to the linguistic and emotional content of sign language expression. The sense of presence conveyed through the system of hearing oneself speak is radically altered through the self-awareness of one's own signing. The sense of presence for signers, then, is derived through the presence of the *other*. This constant confirmation of presence through the face of the other may partially explain the prevalence of collectivism of Deaf cultures. Although the significance of prolonged face-to-face engagement and eye contact over a lifetime cannot be underestimated, little research has been done to understand the psychological implications of Deaf ways of being together.

One study is currently under way to examine the nature of human contact in the example of the "Deaf walk" as opposed to the hearing walk (Sirvage, forthcoming). As two hearing individuals engage in discussion while walking, they simply need to ensure that they are close enough and speak loudly enough for the other to hear. There is no need for eye contact. Significantly, when deaf people walk, however, they engage in constant eye contact, and more significantly, they must take care of the other person, extending their peripheral vision to ensure that the other person does not walk into any objects. Although this may seem a minor point, there is a larger lesson about the nature of Deaf collectivist relations. Signers take care of each other, whether strangers or intimate friends, when engaged in a peripatetic conversation. Future studies should inquire into expanding the notion of the Deaf walk to larger cultural ways of being that may have lessons for an increasingly isolated society.

SUMMARY AND CONCLUSIONS: MEDIA PRODUCTION AND THE DEAF PUBLIC VOICE

This brief discussion of human diversity and Deaf-gain has little to do with a critique of audism, or any other defensive posture that has largely characterized late 20th-century and early 21st-century Deaf Studies. The critique of power relations that forms a principal activity of all cultural studies is implicit in pointing out what has been lost in the oversight of sign languages and Deaf communities as having intrinsic and extrinsic value to human diversity. By taking advantage of the unique Deaf ways of being, forms of cultural production may provide new areas of experimentation and insight, left hidden in the phonocentric blindspots within the ways that cultural practices and disciplines have evolved.

Commerson (2008) suggested that such a reframing of human diversity and Deaf Studies would be more likely to take place if there is a strong visual presence in media. If deafness is reframed from lack to gain, then the sense of gain may be embodied through characters in film, television, video, Internet sites, newspapers, and other forms of public discourse. Given the existential threats to Deaf communities and their languages, the 21st-century practice of Deaf Studies must move from a defensive posture to one that actively seeks to redefine public perception—and do so quickly.

As 21st-century Deaf Studies argues for both intrinsic and extrinsic value, it must be careful to make the point that this argument is not simply for the preservation of deaf people and sign languages for the sake of scientific exploration of the human character. Instead, Deaf Studies may want to take the counterintuitive position that all individuals would be enriched by become a bit more Deaf. By that we mean society would do well to become more acutely aware of the nuances of communication, more engaged with eye contact and tactile relations, more fluent in a language rich in embodied metaphor, more aware of the role of being a member of close-knit communities, and if nothing else, more appreciative of human diversity, so that we are constantly reminded that the bedrock of reality may be just as diaphanous as any other social construction. As Sandel (2007) argues in *The Case Against Perfection*, human diversity teaches us the value of moving from an ethic of molding individuals to beholding them in their extraordinarily rich ways of being.

NOTES

1. The notion of "Deaf-gain" was originally articulated by the British performance artist, Aaron Williamson, who, when presenting to Dirksen Bauman's graduate class, "Enforcing Normalcy," stated that while all his doctors told him that he was losing his hearing, not one told him that he was gaining his deafness.

2. As Stokoe (2001) described, "The nerves connecting eyes and brain outnumber by far all the brain connections to the other sensory organs, the ears included. Visual processing involves so much of the brain that a visual field may convey an enormous amount of information simultaneously, whereas language sounds have to reach the ear sequentially, one by one, until the whole message is received and can be interpreted."

3. Despite no widely accepted written form, there have been many attempts throughout history. One of the earliest is August Bebian's Mimography (Renard, 2004), the most well-known is probably Sign Writing (www.signwriting.org/), and a promising new form is being developed by Arnold (2007).

BIBLIOGRAPHY

Akamatsu, C. T., Musselman, C., & Zweibel, A. (2000). Nature versus nurture in the development of cognition in deaf people. In P. Spencer, C. Erting, & M. Marschark (Eds.), *The deaf child in the family and at school.* (pp. 255–274). Mahwah, NJ: Lawrence Erlbaum.

Allen, S. (2007). *A deaf diaspora: Exploring underlying cultural yearnings for a deaf home.* Master's thesis, Gallaudet University, Washington, DC.

Appadurai, A. (2006). *Fear of small numbers: An essay on the geography of anger.* Durham, NC: Duke University Press.

Arijon, D. (1991). *Grammar of the film language.* Los Angeles: Silman-James Press.

Armstrong, D. (2002). *Original signs: Gesture, sign, and the sources of language.* Washington, DC: Gallaudet University Press.

Armstrong, D., & Wilcox, S. (2007). *The gestural origins of language.* Cambridge: Cambridge University Press.

Armstrong, D., Wilcox, S., & Stokoe, W. (1995). *Gesture and the nature of language.* Cambridge: Cambridge University Press.

Arnold, R. (2007). *Proposal for a written form of American Sign Language.* Unpublished Master's thesis, Gallaudet University, Washington, DC.

Arnos, K. (2003). The implications of genetic testing for deafness. *Ear and Hearing, 24,* 324–331.

Bahan, B. (2006). Face-to-face tradition in the American deaf community: Dynamics of the teller, the tale and the audience. In Bauman, H.-D., Nelson, J., & Rose, H. (Eds.), *Signing the body poetic: Essays on American Sign Language literature.* (pp. 21–50). Berkeley: University of California Press

Bahan, B. (2008). On the formation of a visual variety of the human race. In Bauman, H.-D., (Ed.), *Open your eyes: Deaf studies talking.* (pp. 83–99). Minneapolis: University of Minnesota Press.

Bauman, H.-D. (2006). Getting out of line: Toward a visual and cinematic poetics of ASL. In Bauman, H.-D., Nelson, J., & Rose, H. (Eds.), *Signing the body poetic: Essays on American Sign Language literature.* (pp. 95–117). Berkeley: University of California Press.

Bauman, H.-D. (2008a). Body/text: Sign language poetics and spatial form in literature. In K. Lindgren, D. DeLuca, & D. J. Napoli (Eds.), *Signs and voices: Deaf culture, language, identity, and arts.* (pp. 163–176). Washington, DC: Gallaudet University Press.

Bauman, H.-D. (2008b). Listening to phonocentrism with deaf eyes: Derrida's mute philosophy of (sign) language. *Essays in Philosophy, 9*(1). Retrieved October 22, 2009 from www.humboldt.edu/~essays/bauman.html

Bauman, H.-D (in press). *Gallaudet university deaf and diverse campus design guide.* Washington, DC: Gallaudet University institutional document.

Bauman, H.-D., Nelson, J., & Rose, H. (Eds.) (2006). *Signing the body poetic: Essays on American Sign Language literature.* Berkeley: University of California Press.

Bavelier, D., Tomann, A., Hutton, C., Mitchell, T. V., Corina, D. P., Liu, G., & Neville, H. J. (2000). Visual attention to the periphery is enhanced in congenitally deaf individuals. *Journal of Neuroscience, 20,* 1–6.

Baynton, D. C. (1996). *Forbidden signs: American culture and the campaign against sign language.* Chicago: University of Chicago Press.

Baynton, D. C. (2000). Disability and the justification of inequality in American history. In P. Longmore & L. Umansky (Eds.), *The new disability history: American perspectives.* (pp. 33–57). New York: New York University Press.

Bebian, A. (1984). Essay on the deaf and natural language, or introduction to a natural classification of ideas with their proper signs. In H. Lane (Ed.), *The Deaf experience: Classics in language and education.* [Trans. Philip, F.] Cambridge, MA: Harvard University Press.

Bell, A. G. (1883). *Memoir upon the formation of a deaf variety of the human race.* Washington, DC: Volta Bureau.

Bellugi, U., O'Grady, L., Lillio-Martin, D., O'Grady Hynes, M., Van Hoek, K., & Corina, D. (1989).

In V. Volterra & C. Erting (Eds.), *Enhancement of spatial cognition in deaf children. Gesture to language in hearing children.* (pp. 278–298). New York: Springer-Verlag.

Bettger, J. G., Emmorey, K., McCullough, S. H., & Bellugi, U. (1997). Enhanced facial discrimination: Effects of experience with American Sign Language. *Journal of Deaf Studies and Deaf Education, 2,* 223–233.

Biesold, H. (1999). *Crying hands: Eugenics and deaf people in Nazi Germany.* Washington, DC: Gallaudet University Press.

Breivik, J. K. (2007). *Døv identitet i endring-lokale livglobale bevegelser.* Oslo: Universitetsforlaget.

Breivik, J. K., Haualand, H., & Solvang, P. (2002). *Rome—a temporary deaf city!* Deaflympics 2001. Bergen, Norway: Rokkansentret Working Paper 2–2003.

Brownstein, Z., & Avraham, K. B. (2006). Future trends and potential for treatment of sensorineural hearing loss. *Seminars in Hearing, Genetics and Hearing Loss, 27*(3), 193–204.

Bryan, A. (November 22, 2007). Parliament: Deaf embryo selection to be made illegal. [Blog entry]. Retrieved November 20, 2008, from www.grumpyoldeafies.com/2007/11/parliament_deaf_embroyo_select.html

Burch, S. (2002). *Signs of resistance: American Deaf cultural history, 1900 to World War II.* New York: New York University Press.

Burke, T. B. (2006). Bioethics and the deaf community. In K. Lindgren, D. DeLuca, & D. J. Napoli (Eds.), *Signs and voices: Deaf culture, identity, language, and arts.* (pp. 63–74). Washington, DC: Gallaudet University Press.

Burke, T. B. (December 5, 2007). British bioethics and the human fertilisation and embryology bill. [Blog entry]. Retrieved November 20, 2008, from www.deafdc.com/blog/teresa-blankmeyer-burke/2007-l2-05/british-bioethics-and-the-human-fertilisation-and-embryology-bill/

Carty, B. (2006). Comments on "W(h)ither the deaf community?" *Sign Language Studies, 6*(2), 18l–l89.

Chorost, M. (2005). *Rebuilt: How becoming part computer made me more human.* Boston: Houghton Mifflin Harcourt.

Cohn, J. (1999). *Sign mind: Studies in American Sign Language poetics.* Boulder, CO: Museum of American Poetics Publications.

Commerson, R. (2008). *Media, power and ideology: Re-presenting DEAF.* Master's thesis, Gallaudet University, Washington, DC. Retrieved from http://mosinternational.com/

Cook, P. (Author and Signer). (2006). Hydrogen jukebox [ASL story on DVD]. In Bauman, H.-D., Nelson, J., & Rose, H. (Eds.), *Signing the body poetic: Essays in American sign language literature.* Berkeley: University of California Press.

Corballis, M. (2003). *From hand to mouth: On the origins of language.* Princeton, NJ: Princeton University Press.

Cripps, J., & Small, A. (2004). *Case report re: Provincial service delivery gaps for deaf children 0–5 years of age.* Mississauga: Ontario Cultural Society of the Deaf.

Crystal, D. (2002). *Language death.* Cambridge: Cambridge University Press.

Davidson, M. (2008). Tree-tangled in tree: Re-siting poetry through ASL. In K. Lindgren, D. DeLuca, & D. J. Napoli (Eds.), *Signs and voices: Deaf culture, identity, language and arts.* (pp. 177–188). Washington, DC: Gallaudet University Press.

Davis, L. (1995). *Enforcing normalcy: Deafness, disability and the body.* London: Verso.

Davis, L. (2006). Constructing normalcy: The bell curve, the novel, and the invention of the disabled body in the nineteenth century. In L. Davis (Ed.), *The disability studies reader* 2nd ed. (pp. 3–16). New York: Taylor and Francis.

Derrida, J. (1973). Of grammatology. Trans. Spivak, G. Baltimore: Johns Hopkins University Press.

Emmorey, K., Klima, S. L., & Hickok, G. (1998) Mental rotation within linguistic and nonlinguistic domains in users of American Sign Language. *Cognition, 68,* 221–226.

Emmorey, K., & Kosslyn, S. (1996). Enhanced image generation abilities in deaf signers: A right hemisphere effect. *Brain and Cognition, 32,* 28–44.

Emmorey, K., Kosslyn, S., & Bellugi, U. (1993). Visual imagery and visual-spatial language: Enhanced visual imagery abilities in deaf and hearing ASL signers. *Cognition, 46,* 139–181.

Erting, C. J., Johnson, R. C., Smith, D. L., & Snider, B. C. (1993). *The deaf way: Perspectives from the international conference on deaf culture.* Washington DC: Gallaudet University Press.

Findley, L. (2005). *Building change: Architecture, politics and cultural agency.* New York: Routledge.

Foucault, M. (1990). *History of sexuality Vol. 1. The will to knowledge.* New York: Vintage Press.

Fox, M. (2008). *Talking hands: What sign language reveals about the mind.* New York: Simon & Schuster.

Frontrunners Weekly Reports. (2005, September 30). Interviews on genocide. *Frontrunners.* Retrieved November 29, 2008, from http://frl.frontrunners.dk/Weekly%20Reports/weeklyreports.htm

Furman, N., Goldberg, D., & Lusin, N. (November 13, 2007). Foreign language enrollments in United States institutions of higher education, fall 2006. *Modern Language Association.* Retrieved November 23, 2009, from www.mla.org/2006_flenrollmentsurvey

Gardner, H. (1993). *Frames of mind: The theory of multiple intelligences.* New York: Basic Books.

Generic Evaluation of Congenital Hearing Loss Expert Panel. (2002). Genetics evaluation guidelines for the etiologic diagnosis of congenital hearing loss. *Genetics of Medicine*, 4(3), 162–171.

Golden, J. (2009). *Deaf ASL, and visual theatre: Connections and opportunities.* Unpublished Master's thesis, Gallaudet University, Washington, DC.

Gray, R. (2008, April 13). Couples could win right to select deaf baby. *Telegraph.co.uk.* Retrieved (November 29, 2008, from www.telegraph.co.uk/news/uknews/1584948/Couples-could-win-right-to-select-deaf-baby.html (Reader comments at: www.telegraph.co.uk/news/yourview/1584973/How-far-should-embryo-selection-go.html)

Groce, N. (1985). *Everyone here spoke sign language: Hereditary deafness on Martha's Vineyard.* Cambridge, MA: Harvard University Press.

Hall, S. (1973). *Encoding and decoding in television discourse.* Birmingham, AL: Birmingham Centre for Cultural Studies.

Harmon, D. (2002). *In light of our differences: How diversity in nature and culture makes us human.* Washington, DC: Smithsonian Institution Press.

Haualand, H. (Writer), & Otterstedt, L. (Director). (2007). *Arven etter frankenstein.* [Theatrical Production]. Oslo, Norway: Theater Manu.

Hiddinga, A., Pot, L. (Filmmakers); Emmerik, W., & Meyer, G. (Poets). (2005). *Motioning.* Amsterdam: Geelprodukt Productions.

Hoggart, R. (1957). *The uses of literacy in everyday life.* London: Chatto & Windus.

Hyde, M., Power, D. J., & Lloyd, K. (2006). Comments on "W(h)ither the deaf community?" *Sign Language Studies*, 6(2), 190–201.

Johannsen, K. (2008). Electronic mail communication received December 29, 2008.

Johnson, R. (1994). *Sign language and. the concept of deafness in a traditional Yucatec Mayan village.* In C. Erting, R. Johnson, D. Smith, & B. Sniden (Eds.), *The deaf way: Perspectives from the international conference on deaf culture.* (pp. 102–109). Washington, DC: Gallaudet University Press.

Johnston, T. (2004). W(h)ither the deaf community? Population, genetics, and the future of Australian Sign Language. *American Annals of the Deaf*, 148(5). Reprinted in (2006) *Sign Language Studies*, 6(2), 137–173.

Kochhar, A., Hildebrand, M. S., & Smith, R. J. (2007). Clinical aspects of hereditary hearing loss. *Genetics in Medicine*, 9(7), 393–408.

Krentz, C. (2000). *A mighty change: An anthology of deaf American writing, 1816–1864.* Washington, DC: Gallaudet University Press.

Kuntze, M. (2008). Turning literacy on its head. In H.-D. Bauman (Ed.), *Open your eyes: Deaf studies talking.* Minneapolis: University of Minnesota Press.

Kusters, A. (2007). *"Reserved for the handicapped?" Deafhood on the lifeline of Mumbai.* Unpublished Master's thesis, University of Bristol.

Ladd, P. (2003). *Understanding deaf culture: In search of deafhood.* Clevedon, UK: Multicultural Matters.

Lane, H. (1984). *When the mind hears: A history of the deaf.* New York: Random House.

Lane, H. (1992). *The mask of benevolence: Disabling the deaf community.* New York: Alfred A. Knopf.

Lane, H., & Fischer, R. (1993). Looking back: A reader on the history of deaf communities and their sign languages. *International Studies on Sign Language and Communication of the Deaf,* 20. Hamburg: Signum Verlag.

Lane, H., Hoffmeister, R., & Bahan, B. (1996). *Journey into the deaf world.* San Diego, CA: Dawn Sign Press.

Lentz, E. (Poet), & Taylor, L. (Filmmaker). (1996). *The treasure* [Signed Poetry]. Berkeley, CA: InMotion Press.

McPherson, M., Smith-Lovin, L., & Brashears, M. E. (2006). Social isolation in America: Changes in core discussion networks over two decades. *American Sociological Review*, 71, 353–375.

Maffi, L. (2005). Linguistic, cultural, and biological diversity. *Annual Review of Anthropology*, 34, 599–617.

Malzkuhn, M. (2007). *Home customization: Understanding deaf ways of being.* Unpublished Master's thesis, Gallaudet University, Washington, DC.

Marsaja, I. G. (2008). *Desa Kolok: A deaf village and its sign language in Bali, Indonesia.* Nijmegen, the Netherlands: Ishara Press.

Marschark, M. (2003). Cognitive functioning in deaf adults and children. In Marschark, M., & Spencer, P. (Eds.), *Oxford handbook of deaf studies, language, and education.* Oxford: Oxford University Press.

Mindess, A. (2006). *Reading between the signs. Intercultural communication for sign language interpreters,* 2nd ed. Boston: Intercultural Press.

Monaghan, L., Schmaling, C., Nakamura, K., & Turner, G. H. (2003). *Many ways to be deaf: International variation in deaf communities.* Washington, DC: Gallaudet University Press.

Moore, D., & Dwyer, F. (1994). *Visual literacy: A spectrum of visual learning.* Englewood Cliffs, NJ: Educational Technology Publications.

Morton, C. C., & Nance, W. E. (2006). Newborn hearing screening—a silent revolution. *New England Journal of Medicine*, 354(20), 2151–2164.

Mundy, L. (2002, March 31). A world of their own. *The Washington Post*, pp. W22.

Murray, J. (2002). True love and sympathy: The deaf–deaf marriages debate in transatlantic perspective. In J. V. Van Cleve (Ed.), *Genetics, disability, and deafness.* (pp.42–71). Washington, DC: Gallaudet University Press.

Murray, J. (2006). Genetics: A future peril facing the global deaf community. In H. Goodstein (Ed.), *The Deaf way II reader: Perspectives from the Second International Conference on Deaf Culture.* (pp. 351–356). Washington, DC: Gallaudet University Press.

Murray, J. (2007). *A touch of nature makes the whole world kin: The transnational lives of deaf Americans.* Unpublished doctoral dissertation, University of Iowa.

Nakamura, K. (2006). *Deaf in Japan: Signing and the politics of identity.* Ithaca, NY: Cornell University Press.

Noble, T. (2003, July 11). Deafness-test embryo fails to take. *The Age.* Retrieved November 23, 2009, from www.theage.com.au/articles/2003/07/10/1057783282446.html

Office of Public Sector Information. (2008). *The National Archives.* Retrieved January 2009, from www.opsi.gov.uk/acts/acts2008/ukpga_20080022_en_2#ptl-pb5-1lgl4

Padden, C., & Humphries, T. (1988). *Deaf in America: Voices from a culture.* Cambridge, MA: Harvard University Press.

Petitto, L. A., Zatorre, R., Gauna, K., Nikelski, E. J., Dostie, D., & Evans, A. (2000, December 5). Speech-like cerebral activity in profoundly deaf people while processing signed languages: Implications for the neural basis of human language. *Proceedings of the National Academy of Sciences,* 97(25), 13961–13966.

Putnam, R. (2000). *Bowling alone: The collapse and revival of American community.* New York: Simon & Schuster.

Renard, M. (2004). *Ecrire les signes. La mimographie d'Auguste Bébian et les notations contemporaines. [Escribir las señas. La Mimografía de Auguste Bébian y las notaciones contemporáneas].* Paris: Editions du Fox.

Sacks, O. (1990). *Seeing voices: Journey into the deaf world.* Berkeley: University of California Press.

Salmi, E., & Laakso, M. (2005). *Maahan lämpimäänn: Suomen viittomakielisten historia.* Helsinki: Kuurojen Liittory.

Sandel, M. (2007). *The case against perfection: Ethics in the age of genetic engineering.* Cambridge, MA: Harvard University Press.

Sandler, W., Meir, I., Padden, C., & Aronoff, M. (2005). The emergence of grammar in a new sign language. *Proceedings of the National Academy of Sciences,* 102(7), 2661–2665.

Senghas, A. (1995). Conventionalization in the first generation: A community acquires a language. *USD Journal of Contemporary Legal Issues,* 6, Spring.

Senghas, A. (2003). Intergenerational influence and ontogenetic development in the emergence of spatial grammar in Nicaraguan Sign Language. *Cognitive Development,* 18, 511–531.

Sirvage, R. (forthcoming). *Walking signers: An investigation on proxemics.* Unpublished Master's thesis. Gallaudet University, Washington, DC.

Skutnabb-Kangas, T. (2000). *Linguistic genocide in education—or worldwide diversity and human rights?* Mahwah, NJ: Lawrence Erlbaum.

Snoddon, K. (2008). American Sign Language and early intervention. *Canadian Modern Language Review,* 64(4), 581–604.

Stokoe, W. (2001). *Language in hand: Why sign came before speech.* Washington, DC: Gallaudet University Press.

Supalla, T., & Webb, R. (1995). The grammar of international sign: A new look at pidgin languages. In K. Emmorey & J. S. Reilly (Eds.), *Language, gesture, and space.* (pp. 333–351). Hillsdale, NJ: Lawrence Erlbaum.

Sutton, V. (2008). Retrieved November 20, 2008 from www.signwriting.org

Taub, S. (2001). *Language from the body: Iconicity and metaphor in American Sign Language.* Cambridge: University of Cambridge Press.

Van Cleve, J. V. (1993). *Deaf history unveiled: Interpretations from the new scholarship.* Washington, DC: Gallaudet University Press.

Van Cleve, J. V., & Crouch, B. A. (1989). *A place of their own: Creating the deaf community in America.* Washington, DC: Gallaudet University Press.

VL2. (2008). Visual language and visual learning website introduction. Retrieved November 20, 2008, from http://vl2.gallaudet.edu/

Wallvik, B. (1997) ... *ett folk uten land* ... Borgå: Finland: Döva och hörselskadade barns stödforening r.f.

Welles, E. B. (2004). Foreign language enrollments in United States institutions of higher education. *ADFL Bulletin,* 35(2–3).

Wilcox, P. (2000). *Metaphor in American Sign Language.* Washington, DC: Gallaudet University Press.

Willard, T. (n.d.). Special Report: Laurent, SD in Deafweekly. Deafweekly electronic mailing list. Retrieved November 20, 2008, from www.deafweekly.com/backissues/laurent.htm

Williams, R. (1958). *Culture and society, 1780–1950.* New York: Columbia University Press.

Williams, R. (1961). *The long revolution.* New York: Columbia University Press.

CHAPTER 18

Aesthetic Blindness: Symbolism, Realism, and Reality

David Bolt

SUMMARY

Encapsulated in the term *aesthetic blindness* are two erroneous yet commonplace preconceptions: first, that blindness is synonymous with ignorance; and, second, that aesthetic qualities are perceived by exclusively visual means. For David Bolt, understanding aesthetics can be important in revealing the principles that socially disqualify and oppress disabled people. In this essay he argues that aesthetic blindness produces an ocularcentric social aesthetic—an aesthetic that disqualifies disabled people.

Bolt focuses on aesthetic works and theories of the 1890s, an era in which beauty was typically rendered as perceivable by visual means. This assumption meant a greater emphasis on vision, and by extension, blindness. Maurice Maeterlinck's 1890 play, *The Blind*, features blind characters but is premised on sightedness. Information about the setting and even the time of day is communicated by visual means, as the characters are made to focus on their inability to see the sun rather than other sensory information to which they do have access. The blind characters are understood as incapable of forming meaningful relationships or knowing the truth because they cannot see.

These and other such representations of blindness are sometimes defended in the name of symbolism, Bolt writes, but these defenses are problematic when considering the embodied experience of visually impaired people. Aesthetic blindness depends on erroneous stereotypes of visually impaired people as lost or bewildered rather than a comprehensive understanding of embodiment; the fiction is created despite the facts. Bolt admits that the audiences of the 1890s might have been more familiar with these depictions of blindness and that he critiques *The Blind* from a contemporary sensibility. But he also insists that even though ableism was more present in the past, it has never been right.

As a representation of blindness, Maurice Maeterlinck's *The Blind* is highly problematic and becomes more so if we fail to engage with its social implications. This essay teases out these issues, compares their representation with contemporaneous works of realism, and illustrates the play's twenty-first-century relevance on the basis of visually impaired embodiment.

The critical term *aesthetic blindness* designates the highly problematic epistemological myth of blindness to aesthetic qualities. Encapsulated in the term are two erroneous yet commonplace preconceptions: first, that blindness is synonymous with ignorance; and, second, that aesthetic qualities are perceived by exclusively visual means. The representational problem that justifies this coinage is that blindness and aesthetics—like blindness and knowledge—are often constructed so that the one is remote from the other, in accordance with an ocularcentric aesthetic, and thus incompatible with visually impaired embodiment. When "conducted according to visual criteria," as David Feeney puts it, "imaginative affirmations" of blindness frequently serve to isolate people who have visual impairments from "their natural resources of aesthetic receptivity" (85). This point is exemplified in work from the 1890s, the era of the aesthete from which several blind characters sprang. Based on predominantly visual renderings of beauty and, by extension, knowledge, many such representations focus on sight, which means that the ontological status of the characters becomes diminished as they take on a ghostly form, an existence within yet without human society.

Any new work on disability aesthetics is bound to acknowledge a debt to Tobin Siebers's definitive monograph on the subject. Of particular interest to me is the way in which he explores the significance of aesthetics in relation to Sharon Snyder and David Mitchell's suggestion that disability is the "master trope of human disqualification" (125). The aesthetics of human disqualification are resonant throughout this essay, but where Siebers explores the way that some bodies make other bodies feel, I concentrate on the normative means of such perception. For Michael Davidson, disability aesthetics emphasizes the "extent to which the body becomes thinkable when its totality can no longer be taken for granted, when the social meanings attached to sensory and cognitive values cannot be assumed" (4). I take an approach that complicates the visual premise about these matters, but agree with Siebers and demonstrate that understandings of aesthetics are crucial because they reveal principles of disqualification used in the oppression of

minorities. One aspect of the master trope of human disqualification is, I argue, the ocularcentric social aesthetic that derives from the myth of aesthetic blindness.

Because my focus is on ocularcentric constructs of aesthetics and blindness, the nineteenth century in general offers a fruitful source of material. I make this assertion because the Victorians were "fascinated with the act of seeing, with the question of the reliability—or otherwise—of the human eye" (Flint 1). This fascination became manifest in many ways, one of which was the conception of what might be called beauty for the beholder's sake. For example, as psychologist Nancy Etcoff's *Survival of the Prettiest* points out, "some theologians believed that flowers were made beautiful as a divine gift for man's enjoyment" (70). The fascination with vision also became manifest in the surge of blind characters such as Charles Dickens's Stagg and Bertha, in *Barnaby Rudge* and *The Cricket on the Hearth*, respectively; Charlotte Brontë's Rochester, in *Jane Eyre*; Victor Hugo's Dea, in *The Man Who Laughs*; Robert Louis Stevenson's Pew and Duncan, in *Treasure Island* and *Kidnapped*; and so on. Indeed, as illustrated in the critical work of Elisabeth Gitter, among others, bittersweet blind figures or, more specifically, the bitter blind man and the sweet blind girl, were stock characters for many writers of the era.

While the Victorian age in general is of interest here, the 1890s are particularly relevant because of their great historical significance in relation to aestheticism. General definitions of the word *aesthetics* refer us to the "branch of philosophy dealing with the study of aesthetic values such as the beautiful and the sublime," the "study of the rules and principles of art," and, most notably in relation to visually impaired embodiment, "how something looks, especially when considered in terms of how pleasing it is" (*Encarta World English Dictionary*). These values were particularly prominent in what has been called the "self-proclaimed 'Aesthetic movement' of England's yellow 1890s" (Gates Jr. 233). For example, Oscar Wilde, that most famous of all aesthetes, marked the start of the decade with *The Picture of Dorian Gray*, a novel striking at least in part because the malevolence of the eponymous character becomes visually perceptible in his portrait but not in his face. This scenario is striking precisely because, according to Etcoff, minds are "not designed to disentangle surface and substance easily: deep down, few people believe that the relation between the two is accidental or arbitrary" (40). Wilde's novel draws on this lookism in an exploration of the social aesthetic, of how good looks can be deceiving and thus easily exploited on an interpersonal level.

Characterized by the aesthete and art for art's sake, by decadence and the dandy, the aesthetic movement of the 1890s was spearheaded and documented by a number of new periodicals, of which the most characteristic and prominent was *The Yellow Book*. With reference to this publication, the 1890s have been referred to as "the most colourful decade" of the century, spawning, as they did, magazines that "played a large part in creating that iridescent picture ranging from stark black-and-white Aubrey Beardsley drawings, to the heavenly blue of the Savoy and the dark pink of the Pageant" (Claes and Demoor 133). The eponymous color of the magazine was said to reflect the influence that the decadent French novel had on the aesthetic movement. For instance, French authors and dandies, such as Charles Baudelaire, had a great impact on Wilde's work (see Ramert). In *The Picture of Dorian Gray*, this influence is explicit when the protagonist becomes "absorbed" by the yellow book that Lord Henry sends him (100) and implicit when the recurrent motif of the color yellow signifies summer and beauty, for we are referred to "sulphur-yellow roses" (76), "huge sunlight" that

"flamed like a monstrous dahlia with petals of yellow fire" (66), laburnum that "will be as yellow next June as it is now" (22), and so on. Indeed, when incarcerated in April 1895, Wilde carried a yellow-backed French novel under his arm, which the people who infamously gathered at the Bow Street police station assumed was a copy of *The Yellow Book* (Nelson 67)—in fact, though embodying the aesthetic movement in many ways, Wilde's relationship with this periodical was not a good one; his work was explicitly pertinent, yet conspicuously absent from its pages.

Given that beauty is typically rendered as something perceived primarily, if not necessarily, by visual means, the focus on aestheticism in the 1890s resulted in a greater focus on vision and, by extension, blindness. In the year of Wilde's *The Picture of Dorian Gray* alone, the year on which I concentrate, the reading populace was presented with Maurice Maeterlinck's *The Blind*, Rudyard Kipling's *The Light That Failed*, and George Gissing's *New Grub Street*, all of which contained blind characters whom I consider in this essay. Other relevant noted works of the decade include Henry James's "The Glasses," Rabindranath Tagore's "The Gift of Sight," and Charles Kingsley's *Westward Ho!* The decade ended with the publication of Sigmund Freud's *The Interpretation of Dreams*, the most influential work of psychoanalysis that famously revisited the ancient myth in which Oedipus, upon discovering that his lover was also his mother, symbolically castrated himself by gouging out his own eyes.

Before starting the close reading at the heart of this essay, I must note a few contextual points about some of these authors. One link with aestheticism is clear because—unlike Wilde—Gissing and James both contributed to *The Yellow Book*. Also, Maeterlinck wrote in French and Tagore in Bengali, but their translation into English and, more specifically, their application of aesthetic blindness renders them relevant to the study. Indeed, in Theodor Adorno's *Aesthetic Theory*, Maeterlinck is explicitly likened to Wilde as an aesthete and precursor of the culture industry (Freedman xx).

Given that my reading rests on visually impaired embodiment, whereby ocular-centric assumptions are problematized if not dismissed, another thing to note about these authors is that none had a visual impairment, which may explain why their blind characters are generally blinded rather than born blind. Gissing's Alfred Yule goes blind in a way that proves fatal to his literary career; Kipling's Dick Heldar's artistic endeavors are ended by the onset of blindness; Tagore's Kusum is blinded due to the gross negligence of her husband; Kingsley's Amyas Leigh is transformed by a blinding flash of lightning; and so on. Even the Freudian framing of mental life features blindness as a consequence, a response to inappropriate desire. Granted, an exception to the rule can be found in the play on which I now focus, Maeterlinck's *The Blind*, for the dramatis personae includes three men born blind. But this name sets these three characters apart from the oldest blind man, the fifth blind man, the sixth blind man, three old blind women, the oldest blind woman, a young blind girl, and a mad blind woman. In other words, in Maeterlinck's play, as in its literary counterparts, blind characters generally begin their lives as sighted characters—they are premised on sightedness.

Even before Maeterlinck's *The Blind* commences, judging by its abundance and variety of blind characters, not to mention its title, we might infer that blindness is the main concern. But this impression soon diminishes in a reading informed by visually impaired embodiment. Set—as those of us familiar with literary blindness may have come to expect—in the *extraordinary darkness* of an ancient forest, the play begins with the corpse of a sighted priest

holding center stage, on the right of whom there are six blind men seated on stones, tree stumps, and dead leaves; on the left, separated from the men by more stones and a fallen tree, there are six blind women and a sighted baby. The gripping quality of this predicament, according to Maya Slater's late twentieth-century introduction to the play, rests in its very simplicity: "The blind depend on the priest to see them to safety; the audience can see the priest is dead, though the blind cannot; so the blind are without succor, although they do not know it" (xv). There is little in the way of action, but dramatic tension results from the audience seeing what the characters cannot see, engaging in a version of what Gitter calls "a teasing game of blindman's buff" with the characters "stranded in sightlessness" (679). As readers of Rosemarie Garland-Thomson's *Extraordinary Bodies* might put it, the drama both shores up and depends on the "normate" subject position of a sighted audience (8). This privileging of sightedness is introduced in the exposition and expressed by the characters throughout the play.

Bolstering, and bolstered by, the centrality of the dead sighted character, the play's preoccupation with not blindness but sight flies in the face of visually impaired embodiment. The preoccupation becomes manifest in, for instance, a number of references to the aesthetic quality of the sun. Like the planets of our solar system, the conversation circles around the sun whose heat is nonetheless ignored in favor of its light. That is to say, the ocularcentric aesthetic of that most colorful decade is betrayed by the way that, notwithstanding their non-visual means of perception, the characters think of the sun in purely visual terms. The young blind girl reminisces about the fact that she has "seen the sun" (22) and both the oldest blind man and the oldest blind woman say that they have "seen the sun" when they were "very young," whereas the third man born blind complains that he has "never seen the sun" (17). Indeed, by so modifying the verb *seen* with the adverb *never*, the third man born blind evokes a perplexingly profound sense of aesthetic exclusion, much as when the first man born blind dredges up the fact that they have "never been able to see" (16) and the oldest blind man predicts, "We'll never see each other" (31). The same exclusion is evoked when the young blind girl says that she has "never seen" herself (24) and that she will "never see" herself (31). Emphasized by repetition, the play's fixation on what has never been seen is indicative of the notion that aesthetic qualities are perceived by exclusively visual means and as such has epistemological implications.

Seeing is believing, according to one epistemological maxim, and this has long since been interpreted to mean that seeing is necessary rather than merely sufficient. Accordingly, Maeterlinck's characters have been referred to as "feeble, puerile, unadventurous people, with an obvious handicap preventing them from seeing the realities of life" (Slater xvii). This charge works on the assumption that reality is a visual experience, a commonplace confusion between seeing and knowing that is increasingly problematized in our own century (see Kövecses; Vidali), though explored fruitfully in Garland-Thomson's epistemological slant on the act of staring, to which I return in a moment. The characters in *The Blind* understand the sense of sight in terms of epistemology on a number of levels, one of which pertains to the time of day. The sixth blind man explains that when he is in the sunshine he can see a blue line under his eyelids, inferring that it must be very dark when he can see nothing. The third man born blind responds to this inference by saying, "Look up at the sky; maybe you'll see something." The point that a reader informed by visually impaired embodiment will note is that not the sixth

blind man alone follows this suggestion; it is only the three men born blind who "go on looking down at the ground" (14). In other words, nine of the twelve blind characters endeavor to see in order to work out the time of day. This ocularcentric conception of time is bolstered when the third man born blind rather grudgingly refers to the priest by saying, "Why does he want us to go out every time the sun shows its face? Which of us can tell the difference? When I'm out for a walk, I never know if it's midday or midnight" (17). The supposed irrelevance of the heat, sounds, smells, and emotions brought by sunrise has not only aesthetic but also epistemological implications, as knowing the difference between midday and midnight comes to require the sense of sight.

The knowledge of place as well as time is gained by solely visual means. The sixth blind man posits sightedness as a necessary condition for establishing the group's location when he asks, "Does anyone remember seeing the Island in the past, and can they tell us where we are?" (16). It is apparent that the blind characters are oblivious to everything about their journey, despite the fact that it has been described to them by the priest. The sensory information of the blind characters is completely irrelevant. That it has not been supplemented by verbal information, moreover, implies a lack of both communication and learning. This lack is also illustrated by the response of the young blind girl when the first man born blind asks from where she originates: "I couldn't say. How could I explain? It's too far from here, way across the sea. I come from a big country... I could only show you by making signs; but we can't see any more" (22). The implication that clashes with visually impaired embodiment is that sight is a necessity when it comes to learning about location, the full profundity of which becomes apparent as place merges with time and results in an empty form of ontology. This scenario invokes what Jacques Derrida refers to as hauntology, a neologistic variant on the word *ontology* that describes the paradoxical state of neither being nor non-being. It is not, writes Slater, that the characters' "life-stories are omitted, or that we do not bother with them," but that "there seem to be no details to give—the blind have come from nowhere in particular, they have no roots, they are lost souls" (xv). Indeed, the ocularcentric rendering of place negates not only the past but also the present when the oldest blind man asserts, "We've never seen the house we live in; it's all very well to run our hands over the walls and the windows, we don't know where we live!" Instead of being where the heart is (as we might expect), home is predicated on the sense of sight.

The ocularcentric epistemology of aesthetic blindness permeates the capacity for interpersonal relationships. The oldest blind man says, "We've never seen each other. We ask each other questions, and we answer them; we live together, we're always together, but we don't know what we are! . . . It's all very well to touch each other with our two hands, eyes can see better than hands" (24). Rather than conversation, shared experience, smell, sound, taste, touch, and so on, sight is the sole means by which he believes people get to know each other, a belief further illustrated when he adds, "We've been together for years and years, and we've never had a sight of each other! It's as if we're always on our own" (25). In these profoundly ocularcentric terms, sight is required to validate the very existence of Self and Other and thus fundamental to any connection between the two, to the formation and function of human society.

This relational problem raises issues of compassion and community that are opposed to visually impaired embodiment, for the blindness of Maeterlinck's characters "strikes at the very heart of their being— it prevents them not only from seeing each other, but also from feeling for each other, from understanding each other, from loving each other" (Slater xvi). Thus, following Snyder and Mitchell, via Siebers, we might say that the aesthetic blindness results in a form of human disqualification. For instance, referring to the fact that prior to the priest's death he had been crying for several days, the young blind girl says, "I don't know why, but it made me cry too, though I couldn't see him" (10). Her empathy is rendered mysterious because it is assumed that only sighted people are able to identify with another's feelings. Accordingly, the oldest blind man makes another link between sight and epistemology when referring to the death of the priest: "We didn't know a thing. . . . We've never seen him. . . . When have we ever known what's in front of our poor dead eyes?" (40). Perpetuated by the claim that one must "see to cry" (28), this assumption of emotional deficiency is taken to its extreme when the oldest blind man goes so far as to assert, "You can't love someone without seeing them" (25), the dehumanizing implication being that sightedness is a necessary condition of love.

These and other such problematic representations are sometimes defended in the name of symbolism. After all, as acknowledged by reviewer David Kornhaber, Maeterlinck's play made a "revolutionary advance in the theatre; its emphasis on mood and ambiance over plot and character helped in part to give rise to the surrealist and the symbolist movements." The "reality and the details of what blindness is really like are not a central point of interest," asserts Slater (thereby troubling any suggestion that the audience's enforced staring is epistemologically charged), for the "innovative" Maeterlinck rejects realism in favor of the "symbolic blindness" of, for example, Sophocles' *Oedipus Rex* (xx). Slater's use of the word *innovative* may seem rather misplaced in relation to Sophocles, but we should remember that, if only by a few years, Maeterlinck's play did precede the Freudian theory that elicited a proliferation of Oedipal allusions and references in creative and critical work. In these terms, the blind characters are symbolically castrated, the dead priest on whose knowledge they depend and the sun whose beauty they covet represent the father and mother, respectively—a psychoanalytic reading that I continue in a moment, with allusion to what Georgina Kleege's *Sight Unseen* terms the "shadow" of Oedipus (67). Alternatively, given that the dramatis personae consists of a priest and twelve blind people, the same number as Christ and the disciples, it is "up to us whether we see the blind as representing mankind, whether the priest is seen as symbolizing religion" (Slater xvii). Indeed, according to the British Broadcasting Company's Disability Affairs Correspondent Peter White, the blindness is symbolic of the "human condition: the bulk of us led astray, deceived, puzzled and abandoned by powerful political establishments." The inferences go on and on, the symbolism takes us in many directions, the persistent defense being that the dramatic rendition of blindness is not meant to represent visual impairment and so is without real implication for people who have visual impairments.

When informed by visually impaired embodiment, however, the symbolist defense is problematic in many ways. Embodiment is defined by Tanya Titchkosky as "all the many and various ways that we (self and other) accomplish relations to being in possession of the bodies that we are" (13). The trouble is that the tenor of symbolic blindness relies on the stereotypical assumptions of its vehicle, meaning that, far from being in possession of the bodies that they/we are, people who have visual impairments must be identified as likely to be lost in order to represent the metaphysical bewilderment of humanity. The characters may well be "portrayed as sightless in order to make a philosophical point," says former National Federation of the Blind president Kenneth Jernigan, but "what emerges on the stage is a ridiculous tableau of groping, groaning, and grasping at the air"; it "reinforces every negative stereotype of blindness," adds White, for the "group is lost, fearful, querulous, indecisive, ill-informed." Indeed, to represent people who have visual impairments as the blind, as a homogenous group, in semiotic terms, as a signifier, is to separate us/them from the humanity that is being signified. In effect, we have people symbolizing people, an example of metonymy at best, meaning that under scrutiny the parallel breaks down, for a section of the humanity represented by the blind will be in fact registered or otherwise regarded as blind.

This disregard for the experience of people who have visual impairments in the literary application of aesthetic blindness creates a form of narrative prosthesis, whereby disability becomes what Mitchell and Snyder famously call the "crutch" on which narratives "lean for their representational power, disruptive potentiality, and analytical insight" (49). A "common recent criticism among disability scholars" is, as Davidson points out, that "metaphoric treatments of impairment seldom confront the material conditions of actual disabled persons" (1). The fiction, we might say, is created in spite of the facts. For example, if the symbolism of the Oedipal reading is to work, we must accept that visual perception is not only paramount when it comes to aesthetics but also a necessary condition of desire. Yet Etcoff's work on the science of beauty outlines, first, a Freudian position by claiming that "seeing is ultimately derived from touching" and, second, a zoological stance by stating that flawless skin is the "most universally desired human feature" and that "flowing, healthy hair runs close behind" (91). From a feminist perspective there is much to be raised about these qualities, but the fact that they can be perceived by haptic as well as visual means begins to reveal the lie of the Oedipal position and its construction of symbolic castration.

Notably, although the representational problems with Maeterlinck's *The Blind* are often excused by (or at least put down to) symbolism, aesthetic blindness is also found in contemporaneously published works of realism such as Kipling's *The Light That Failed*. This novel tells the story of Dick Heldar, a painter who loses his sight as a result of a head injury sustained during his time as a war correspondent in Sudan. Prior to losing his sight he just manages to complete his magnum opus, an oil painting called *The Melancholia*, which unbeknown to him is almost immediately defaced by its subject, Bessie Broke. This means that, as in Wilde's *The Picture of Dorian Gray*, the subject takes control over the art to which the artist thereby becomes oblivious. After all, Dick's idea of what is on the canvas in which he takes so much pride is manifestly erroneous. This example of aesthetic blindness is disrupted from time to time in the novel, such as when Dick is presented with some modeling wax, but, as Kleege's "Dialogues with the Blind" points out, he "rejects the tacit suggestion that he might switch from painting to sculpture because he is certain that switching from vision to touch will take too long" (4). In other words, the novel contains some recognition that aesthetic qualities may be perceived by haptic means, but vision remains paramount overall. The haptic aspect of aesthetics is dismissed by the artistic protagonist whose life thereby becomes meaningless; he is effectively a ghost of his former self.

The writing or at least reading of Oedipus into *The Light That Failed* invokes revealing parallels with Maeterlinck's *The Blind*. Rather than a priest, though, it is Dick's friend Torpenhow who frequently fulfills the paternal role: "Dick had been sent to bed—blind men are ever under the orders of those who can see—and since he had returned from the Park had fluently sworn at Torpenhow because he was alive, and all the world because it was alive and could see, while he, Dick, was dead in the death of the blind, who, at the best, are only burdens upon their associates" (142). This jealousy of the father figure is complemented, in terms of an Oedipal reading, by several levels of symbolic castration. Though not as dramatic as Maeterlinck's congenitally blind characters, Kipling's Dick Heldar reflects on his life in comparably visual ways and so inevitably emerges wanting. He thinks, "at length, with imagery and all manner of reminiscences," of his would-be lover Maisie and "past success, reckless travels by land and sea, the glory of doing work and feeling that it was good," and of "all that might have happened had the eyes only been faithful to their duty" (167). Moreover, much as the preoccupation with sight becomes manifest in Maeterlinck's references to the sun, the moon becomes the object of desire in *The Light That Failed*. During the long journey to Sudan, Dick asks his companion if there is a moon, is informed that "she" is near "her" setting, and wishes that he could "see her" (206). These anthropomorphic applications of the feminine pronoun bolster the Oedipal reading elicited when Maisie deems Dick symbolically castrated, "down and done for—masterful no longer, but rather a little abject; neither an artist stronger than she, nor a man to be looked up to—only some blind one that sat in a chair and seemed on the point of crying." Indeed, "filled with pity most startlingly distinct from love," Maisie is "more sorry" for Dick than she has "ever been for anyone in her life" (159). This reading reveals issues of jealousy, parasitic dependency, and sexual inadequacy—amounting to a variant if not an illustration of what Ato Quayson calls a "primary scene of extreme anxiety" (17) or, more overtly, aesthetic nervousness—from which it becomes apparent that the ocularcentric aesthetic deters interpersonal relationships with the blind character.

Though ultimately pejorative, the construction of blindness in *The Light That Failed* is not as ocularcentric as Maeterlinck's *The Blind*. Granted, like Maeterlinck's blind characters, Kipling's Dick Heldar does come to confuse day and night, "dropping to sleep through sheer weariness at mid-day, and rising restless in the chill of the dawn." So confused about the time, however, he would "grope along the corridors of the chambers till he heard someone snore. Then he would know that the day had not yet come" (167). In other words, Dick's epistemology is informed by auditory as well as visual means, a multidimensional perspective that also has an aesthetic impact on his life. When longing for the sight of the moon, for example, he pauses to "hear the desert talk" (206). The novel contains several such departures from aesthetic blindness, although a reader informed by visually impaired embodiment cannot ignore the overall idea that the light fails, soon to be followed by love, respect, art, beauty, and life itself. This pejorative representation is epitomized as the story ends with Dick returning to the battlefield and, as anticipated within and without the novel, getting killed.

A comparable but less prominent blind character is provided in Gissing's *New Grub Street*. Chiming on many levels with *The Yellow Book*, speaking very much of its time, this novel tells the story of a group of writers, editors, journalists, scholars, and other such literary folk. The group is said to be caught in a cultural crisis that hits Britain as universal education, popular journalism, and mass communication begin to have an impact on the literary community. Alfred Yule is of primary interest to us, but his daughter Marian Yule, as Stephen Severn suggests, is the "only completely admirable character" (157). She works selflessly as a researcher and ghostwriter for her father

until he loses his sight and thus his ability to be productive as an editor. Marian then takes financial responsibility for their family and works to the point of nervous breakdown, thereby reminding us of the central role played by Maeterlinck's dead sighted character. So instead of a priest (or a friend) fulfilling the paternal role, in *New Grub Street* it is effectively the daughter.

Like Maeterlinck's blind characters and Kipling's Dick Heldar, Gissing's Alfred Yule comes to endure an existence that is not only empty but also deemed burdensome. We are informed that, with blindness, there "fell upon" Alfred the "debility of premature old age" (414), that he "might as well go home" and "take his place meekly by the fireside," for he "was beaten," soon to be a "useless old man, a burden and annoyance to whosoever had pity on him" (335). This is the ocularcentric ontology, indeed hauntology, also portrayed by Kipling, for Dick is "dead in the death of the blind, who, at the best, are only burdens upon their associates" (142). Because of the ocularcentric social aesthetic, both characters are judged parasitic. Their professional lives end because they have nothing left to give. Dick's life is "nothing better than death" (167) and Alfred's is "over" and "wasted" (335). Indeed, when blind, Alfred becomes so insubstantial in relation to his former self that, as Severn points out, even his death is not narrated directly, but merely mentioned in passing at the dinner party with which *New Grub Street* closes: "He died in the country somewhere, blind and fallen on evil days, poor old fellow" (420). This bleak end vividly illustrates the level of human disqualification that results from aesthetic blindness.

That works of realism published at the same time as Maeterlinck's *The Blind* contain similarly problematic motifs clearly troubles the symbolist defense of aesthetic blindness, but a reading informed by visually impaired embodiment is also likely to face charges of anachronism. For an audience with "contemporary sensibilities," writes one critic, the play is "highly problematic: It depends for its effect on the utter helplessness of the blind characters," who, though sightless from birth, all seem unable to "function" (Kornhaber). Along similar lines, actor Gerard McDermott says, "Don't go and watch this with your 1980s disability-activist hat on. You're likely to take offence" (quoted in White). That is not to say that the play's scenario is now irrelevant. Well within living memory, for instance, White recalls his time at a boarding school for children who had visual impairments, being "taken out in a crocodile" with his classmates, "all holding onto each other," and completely uninformed about where they were going. This state of affairs and the resulting disorientation clearly resonates with Maeterlinck's *The Blind*. But the anticipated contention is that in Maeterlinck's day "blind people would have been in institutions" and "led out on ropes" (White), so for us to engage with the representation on the basis of twenty-first-century disability studies is anachronistic. Indeed, I once endeavored to write a short article on ocularcentric symbolism in Maeterlinck's *The Blind* that, on these very grounds, was rejected, deemed too "short sighted" for publication by an anonymous reviewer, a supposed criticism that I could only assume was meant to be humorous and/or ironic.

So perhaps those of us who have visual impairments and impairments more generally, not to mention those of us who are disability activists, advocates, academics, and so on, need, as is sometimes said, to lighten up, to develop a thicker skin or a greater sense of humor. After all, Maeterlinck's *The Blind* undoubtedly provides a ridiculous idea of visual impairment, so to take it seriously more than a century on from the original publication may seem, at best, pointless and, at worst, foolish. But I

am reminded of the classic postcolonial work of Frantz Fanon that reflects on a social encounter in which the author is objectified on racial grounds: he is overtly and repeatedly insulted by a manifestly fearful young child: "Mama, see the Negro! I'm frightened!" Chiming on one level with Quayson's concept of aesthetic nervousness, this fear is profoundly disturbing, absolutely ridiculous, and thus on another level quite hilarious, yet Fanon arrives at the point where he can "no longer laugh" because he knows that there are "legends, stories, history, and above all historicity" (112). The thing is that historicity may help to explain but does not excuse prejudicial representations. Racism was more prominent in the past but it has never been right, of course, and the same can be said of prejudice against people who have visual impairments. To have a severe visual impairment in the nineteenth century was to have one's bodily experience habitually described as "afflicted," "deprived," or even "defective," writes Martha Stoddard Holmes, so how could one "build a life of economic stability, much less develop a satisfying sense of self?" (27). The burden of uncriticized cultural representation should be neither underestimated nor dismissed—a matter to which I return in my conclusion.

The point about economic stability brings us to another consequence of aesthetic blindness. Although the dramatis personae consist of blind characters only, Maeterlinck's *The Blind* has traditionally been played by actors who do not have visual impairments. Even in 2005, more than a century on from the original staging of the play, Kornhaber's review of Kristjan Thorgeirsson's contemporary version recognizes many radical changes, but notes that the actors perform "wearing opaque contact lenses such that their vision is entirely obscured," or put differently, that they engage in an ableist equivalent of the outmoded racist practice known as "blacking up." On the plus side, when Jack McNamara's version of the play opened at London's Arcola Theatre in 2008, it was possible for White's review to state that, in "an intriguing twist," it was "performed by an all-blind cast." But the foregrounded exceptionality of this state of affairs indicates the persistence of the representational problem.

I should add that Maeterlinck's *The Blind* remains relevant not only because it is still being staged and studied, but also because of the surrounding discourse, the symbolist defense that is rehearsed, for example, in relation to José Saramago's novel *Blindness*. As well as sharing ocularcentric epistemology, both Saramago's *Blindness* and Maeterlinck's *The Blind* bring together a group of characters whose lack of sight equates with a lack of history and results in despair. Reminding us of the abundance of unnamed blind characters in Maeterlinck's play, Saramago's novel begins with a nameless man who loses his sight as he waits in his car for the traffic lights to change, and an epidemic of blindness ensues. Reminiscent, too, of the fact that home for Maeterlinck's characters is "an asylum of sorts" (Kornhaber), the response of the government in Saramago's novel is to quarantine all newly blinded people in an unused mental institution. Insofar as we are presented with what Davidson calls "a world no longer dependent on sight," where people "begin to rely on other senses for communication, location, locomotion, and survival" (17), there is an apparent departure from ocularcentrism. But given that the resultant community is essentially dystopian, starvation, squalor, rape, and other violence soon become commonplace, Fernando Meirelles's filmic adaptation has been met with much protest from disability activists. This reaction against what is meant as an allegory that depicts a "blindness of rationality" is deemed "misguided" by Saramago (quoted in CBC), a normate defense that, alas, depends on those of us who have visual impairments being rendered as irrational, and those of us who do not, as rational.

Epitomized by the use of extraordinary darkness in a product of the sunny yellow decade, the irony of Maeterlinck's *The Blind* is clear. Blindness is explicit in the title, not to mention the dramatis personae, but a reading informed by visually impaired embodiment, and disability studies more generally, reveals and problematizes the fact that sightedness is the actual focus of the play. According to Slater, the audience is "made to concentrate on one particular aspect of blindness—the helplessness that it induces in sufferers, and their resulting feelings of anxiety and distress" (xix). But in fact the audience is immersed in aesthetic blindness and thus made to concentrate on the value (if not to imagine the necessity) of sight in a social setting. Rendered in accordance with this aesthetic, the characters are burdensome, unproductive, devoid of empathy, and deficient in terms of both epistemology and ontology. These motifs are supposed to be symbolic in the play and yet recur in contemporaneous works of realism. If Wilde's *The Picture of Dorian Gray* horrifically explores how looks and looking can be exploited on an interpersonal level, Kipling and Gissing provide realist depictions of how the notion of aesthetic blindness results in an ocularcentric social aesthetic that is indicative of human disqualification.

This critique of aesthetic blindness raises a number of questions about the possibility for representational progress. Should Maeterlinck's *The Blind* be staged no longer? Should it be reinterpreted for a new audience? Should we find a new way to depict human subjectivity and the lack of morality that does not stigmatize people who have visual impairments? Should we focus on why the tropes of blindness are so persistent? These are some of the probing and provocative questions already posed by readers of this essay and in each case I could surely answer in the affirmative. But in the first instance I am compelled to stress the importance of a far more basic response that is both academic and activist. Part of the response is demonstrable in this essay's very challenge to critical avoidance—that is, the "general lack of informed tropological criticism in the humanities," the "absence of critical readings that are appreciative of disability" (Bolt 292). Any such response is important because without visually impaired embodiment the representational problematics of aesthetic blindness are far more likely to extend beyond the page. Matters of aesthetics are, as Davidson argues, "deeply implicated in social attitudes toward disabled persons" (7). It is, therefore, important that we enter into the spirit of James Charlton's *Nothing About Us Without Us*—and, more recently, Lizzy Clark's "Don't Play Me Pay Me" campaign, which seeks to remove the barriers that disabled actors face in finding work and, more broadly, to encourage disabled people to follow their chosen creative careers. After all, if aesthetic blindness is only meant to be symbolic in Maeterlinck's *The Blind*, the effect is nonetheless demonstrable in the casting of most versions, be it in the nineteenth, twentieth, or twenty-first century. Indeed, although contemporaneous with McNamara's progressive version of the play, Meirelles's film adaptation of *Blindness* does not employ actors who have visual impairments. This means that, like their fictional counterparts Kipling's Dick Heldar and Gissing's Alfred Yule, actors who have visual impairments have been and still are disqualified on account of an ocularcentric social aesthetic, illustrating that, irrespective of symbolism, the effect of aesthetic blindness remains a lived reality for many people.

WORKS CITED

Bolt, David. "Social Encounters, Cultural Representation, and Critical Avoidance." *Routledge Handbook of Disability Studies*. Ed. Nick Watson, Alan Roulstone, and Carol Thomas. London: Routledge, 2012, 287–97.

CBC News. "Author Decries Blindness Protests as Misguided." *CBC News*. 4 October 2008: n.p. Web. 16 January 2012.

Claes, Koenraad, and Marysa Demoor. "The Little Magazine in the 1890s: Towards a 'Total Work of Art.'" *English Studies* 91.2 (2010): 133–49.

Davidson, Michael. *Concerto for the Left Hand: Disability and the Defamiliar Body*. Ann Arbor: University of Michigan Press, 2008.

Etcoff, Nancy. *Survival of the Prettiest: The Science of Beauty*. London: Brown, 1999.

Fanon, Frantz. *Black Skin, White Masks*. 1952. Trans. Charles Lam Markmann. London: Pluto, 1986.

Feeney, David. "Sighted Renderings of a Non-Visual Aesthetics: Exploring the Interface between Drama and Disability Theory." *Journal of Literary & Cultural Disability Studies* 3.1 (2009): 85–100.

Flint, Kate. *The Victorians and the Visual Imagination*. Cambridge: Cambridge University Press, 2000.

Freedman, Jonathan. *Professions of Taste: Henry James, British Aestheticism and Commodity Culture*. Stanford, CA: Stanford University Press, 1990.

Garland-Thomson, Rosemarie. *Extraordinary Bodies: Figuring Physical Disability in American Culture and Literature*. New York: Columbia University Press, 1997.

Gates Jr., Henry Louis. "The Black Man's Burden." *Fear of a Queer Planet: Queer Politics and Social Theory*. Ed. Michael Warner. Minneapolis: University of Minnesota Press, 1993. 230–38.

Gissing, George. *New Grub Street*. 1891. Ware, Herts: Wordsworth, 1996.

Gitter, Elisabeth G. "The Blind Daughter in Charles Dickens's 'Cricket on the Hearth.'" *Studies in English Literature, 1500–1900* 39.4 (1999): 675–89.

Holmes, Martha Stoddard. "Working (with) the Rhetoric of Affliction: Autobiographical Narratives of Victorians with Physical Disabilities." *Embodied Rhetorics: Disability in Language and Culture*. Ed. James C. Wilson and Cynthia Lewiecki-Wilson. Carbondale: Southern Illinois University Press, 2001, 27–44.

Jernigan, Kenneth. "Blindness: Is Literature Against Us?" Presented to the National Federation of the Blind Annual Convention. Chicago, 3 July 1974.

Kipling, Rudyard. *The Light That Failed*. 1891. London: Penguin, 1988.

Kleege, Georgina. "Dialogues with the Blind: Literary Depictions of Blindness and Visual Art." *Journal of Literary & Cultural Disability Studies* 4.1 (2010): 1–16.

——. *Sight Unseen*. New Haven, CT: Yale University Press, 1999.

Kornhaber, David. *"The Blind." Disability Studies Quarterly* 25.3 (2005): n.p. Web. 14 December 2011.

Kövecses, Zoltán. *Metaphor: A Practical Introduction.* Oxford: Oxford University Press, 2002.

Maeterlinck, Maurice. *The Blind.* 1891. *Three Pre-Surrealist Plays.* Trans. Maya Slater. Oxford: Oxford University Press, 1997, 2–48.

Mitchell, David T., and Sharon L. Snyder. *Narrative Prosthesis: Disability and the Dependencies of Discourse.* Ann Arbor: University of Michigan Press, 2003.

Nelson, James G. *Publisher to the Decadents: Leonard Smithers in the Careers of Beardsley, Wilde, Dowson.* University Park: Penn State University Press, 2000.

Quayson, Ato. *Aesthetic Nervousness: Disability and the Crisis of Representation.* New York: Columbia University Press, 2007.

Ramert, Lynn. "A Century Apart: The Personality Performances of Oscar Wilde in the 1890s and U2's Bono in the 1990s." *Popular Music and Society* 32. 4 (2009): 447–60.

Severn, Stephen E. "Quasi-Professional Culture, Conservative Ideology, and the Narrative Structure of George Gissing's *New Grub Street.*" *Journal of Narrative Theory* 40.2 (2010): 156–88.

Siebers, Tobin. *Disability Aesthetics.* Ann Arbor: University of Michigan Press, 2010.

Slater, Maya. Introduction. *Three Pre-Surrealist Plays.* Oxford: Oxford University Press, 1997, ix–xlii.

Snyder, Sharon L., and David T. Mitchell. *Cultural Locations of Disability.* Chicago: University of Chicago Press, 2006.

Titchkosky, Tanya. *Reading and Writing Disability Differently: The Textured Life of Embodiment.* Toronto: University of Toronto Press, 2007.

Vidali, Amy. "Seeing What We Know: Disability and Theories of Metaphor." *Journal of Literary & Cultural Disability Studies* 4.1 (2010): 33–54.

White, Peter. "Lost in the Woods." *Guardian* 5 February 2008: n.p. Web. 9 January 2012.

Wilde, Oscar. *The Picture of Dorian Gray.* 1891. Ware, Herts: Wordsworth, 1992.

CHAPTER 19

Life with Dead Metaphors: Impairment Rhetoric in Social Justice Praxis

Tanya Titchkosky

SUMMARY

Tanya Titchkosky points out that many scholars who work for social justice still repeatedly use terminology, such as being "color blind" or "deaf to the call of justice," that relies on ableism. In this chapter, she seeks to understand how socially aware people and their movements seem to need impairment rhetoric to drive social justice. The real relationships between disability and injustice are assumed but not actually addressed by seemingly convenient impairment rhetoric.

The rhetorical use of impairment, Titchkosky says, is an intoxicatingly easy way to diagnose a historical moment of injustice. For example, terms like "colonial amnesia" are often used among postcolonial scholars to describe social situations without any fidelity to the organic, embodied situation of a person with a brain injury. The medicalized term is used to express the problematic "mindset" of privileged whiteness and its domination of land and people. Similarly, political ideas are often described as being "legless" or "lame," a description that emphasizes (and assumes) amputation as dysfunctionality.

Titchkosky resists the urge to label these examples as merely ableist slip-ups, and she focuses instead on these bits of rhetoric as an opportunity to understand disability in the context of oppressed human lives. These metaphors of disability are a form of social action; they give meaning to people and events by expressing them in relation to each other through a comparison. These words not only have their common meanings but also have the potential for unexpected new meanings.

When impairment rhetoric is repeated as diagnosis of social injustice, it gives up its critical impulse in exchange for a certainty about highlighting what's wrong. But that doesn't mean disability rhetoric has no place in social justice. Instead of ignoring the diagnostic potential of disability metaphors, Titchkosky makes the case for investigating how such rhetoric might articulate the conditions of bodies under historical injustice. If social justice scholars can frame disability as a way of being in the world, they can incite greater critical imaginations.

The article examines the ubiquitous use of impairment rhetoric within scholarly endeavors oriented by the call of social justice. However, rather than pointing out disableism, the article seeks to reveal some of the life and death relations that tie disability with race through impairment rhetoric. It shows how such ties were part of the founding of "disability studies" and are still accomplished today, reconstituting a version of the nature–culture divide that borrows its power from a medical sounding act of diagnosis that declares that injustice is disabling. The discussion turns to the creative potential of *metaphor* when engaged through a hermeneutic understanding that seeks a more life-filled relation to otherwise deadening uses of impairment rhetoric. The conclusion is that disability can open the imagination to the possibility of new worlds since it is more than a diagnostic signifier of already dead ones.

INTRODUCTION

Still we say *color blind, deaf to the call of justice, suffering from historical amnesia; blind to structural oppression, limping under the weight of inequality; an amputated self, simply crazy, subject to colonial aphasia, agnosia, even alexia; nothing but a deformed autonomy made to fit a crippled economy—devastatingly disabled*. What compels such impairment rhetoric? It is obviously steeped in ableism punctuated with medical overtones. These rhetorical expressions also *include* disability as a devalued and excludable type. And yet, is there something not so obvious that we should notice here?

This article explores the *not-so-obvious* by suggesting that something more than disableism is driving the rhetorical use of disability metaphor; and that something more than a dismissive diagnosis of cultural disablement can be found when metaphor is engaged in a non-rhetorical fashion. I want neither to "overlook," nor "forgive," but rather to "understand" how it is that otherwise politically astute and socially aware people and/or movements want and seemingly need impairment rhetoric to drive their social justice endeavors (Arendt 308).

Informed by disability studies, my examination traces the ubiquity of the interest that generates the use of impairment rhetoric within social justice praxis. I show how this interest is tied to a history of the genesis of disability studies itself. I also demonstrate that impairment rhetoric reproduces a nature–culture divide (Linton 8; Michalko 30). Rhetorical uses of this taken-for-granted divide configure disability as the edge of

human life by (re)producing a conception of the human steeped in its own inhumanity. Consequently, social justice praxis forestalls the possibility of social change but not simply because of the presence of prejudicial rhetoric. Instead, such rhetoric diminishes a radical engagement with abnormality by transmogrifying disability into a dead metaphor that people use only to diagnose injustice. Finally, working through Frantz Fanon's metaphor of "amputation," I demonstrate how disability can open the imagination to the possibility of new worlds since it can be more than a signifier of already dead ones.

Overall, my work aims to join those critical orientations that attempt to "reverse the hegemony of the normal," as Lennard Davis puts it, by seeking "alternative ways of thinking about the abnormal" (49). This is why I conclude with a demonstration of how to put the brakes on impairment rhetoric by re-engaging the meaningfulness of disability through the complicated relation of hermeneutics of metaphor as a living potentiality or, as Paul Ricoeur claims, "the main problem" of language (134). My aim is to show how a non-rhetorical relation to disability offers an imaginative way to re-approach social justice praxis while simultaneously reconsidering the urge to re-trace the edges of the discard-able human (Bauman).

PURSUING JUSTICE VIA IMPAIRMENT RHETORIC

First, we might consider the ubiquity of the common practice of rhetorically deploying impairment metaphor. There are, for example, about 1 million Google hits for "colonial amnesia," referring to the incapacity to remember the "historical stages of coloniality" or the "coloniality of power intrinsic to modernity" (Mignolo 426). Recently, impairment rhetoric has found its expression in less commonly known yet equally medicalized terms, such as "colonial aphasia," a loss of words so profound that colonialism is not addressed since it is not conceptualized. Colonial aphasia, despite its specialized medical tone, has significant global reach. For example, in a talk given in New York, Toronto, Tel Aviv, Utrecht, and Los Angeles, Ann Laura Stoler makes extensive use of "aphasia" and it serves as the title and frame for her subsequent publication, "Colonial Aphasia: Race and Disabled Histories in France." Stoler is dissatisfied with "amnesia" as a rhetorical trope to understand the ramifications of colonial history (122). She argues that aphasia emphasizes "both loss of access and active dissociation. In aphasia, an occlusion of knowledge is the issue . . . and, most important, a difficulty comprehending what is spoken" (125), leading to a "disabled history" for France.

A related development in the use of impairment rhetoric is that of "agnosia," as in to be without knowledge (*gnosis*) itself. Agnosia, according to the medical realm from which the term arises, is the result of brain injury. We might consider the title of Jodi Byrd's talk, "Silence Will Fall: The Cultural Politics of Colonial Agnosia." This shows, according to a poster advertising the talk, that the "colonization of American Indian nations depends upon a colonial agnosia that is unable to attach meaning, significance, or temporality to the everyday signs and structures that underwrite colonialism". Byrd also makes use of agnosia at the Oak Lake writer's retreat, where she borrows:

> from neurological science, a form of blindness in which one's eyes can see but one cannot comprehend what one sees . . . Again, agnosia: Colonial violence and history—even what one sees before one's eyes—cannot be comprehended. Overall, I think our writers found this a useful analytical intervention.
>
> (quoted in Tallbear)

Amnesia, aphasia, agnosia—none of these terms, say the scholars who use them, are meant to be used with any organic fidelity—thus "brain damage" has only rhetorical status—but through their sophisticated medical tonality they seem to transcend the schoolyard nastiness of the term *retard*. Still, *amnesia, aphasia,* and *agnosia*—all medical terms indicative of conditions following brain injury—are being used to rhetorically express the problematic "mindset" of privileged whiteness and its domination of land and people. Through such rhetoric a nature–culture divide is posited between perception and comprehension: the rhetoric suggests that the Real of cultural organization fails to be adequately comprehended due to impaired perception generated by racism, and this is expressed in medical terms. Regardless of an intention to use impairment terms with organic fidelity or not, positing this nature–culture divide risks re-inscribing a belief in a true, right, strong, and free perceptual awareness and its diseased or impaired other.

Still, impairment rhetoric abounds. There are, for example, over 12 million Google hits for "colonial blindness." The blindness of colonialism became a popular title and framework in the 1950s and remains so today. For instance, it has been asserted that "Blindness is a structural component of colonialism; the colonial master sees Africa but not the Africans, Palestine but not the Palestinians, Iraq but not the Iraqis" (Al-Barghouti 1). While the social organization of ordinary seeing seems a more likely culprit than blindness, the "normal" operation of perception is not the point. We can also find social justice praxis making use of blindness and deafness simultaneously, as in "Organizational Theory: Blind and Deaf to Gender." As a framework for unraveling patriarchy and sexism, the rhetorical trope is expressed by the call to overcome "male pattern blindness," the political blind spots that conceal sexism; or by noting that we are deaf to gender distortions, "forced to limp along like a one eyed man" (Minnich, frontispiece) under the blinding weight of patriarchy. Or, expressing male indifference toward feminist pursuits, it has been said, "We can hardly fail to welcome male feminist criticism when we have so long lamented the blindness, the deafness and the indifference of the male critical establishment towards our work" (Showalter 131).[1]

A more recent expression of impairment rhetoric includes conceiving of culture itself as "autistic." This has been used to suggest a widespread inability to attend to environmental degradation and economic exploitation, and to express concerns regarding the war on terror. For example, there is the "central problem of the liberal hawk school when it comes to the War on Terror: an indifference verging on autism towards the views of the Muslim world in general, and the Arab world in particular" (Lieven and Hulsman 72). Again, the culprit might be non-neurodiverse forms of attention, but this is not "normally" attended to.

Along with intellectual, emotional, and sensory based impairment rhetoric, there is also rhetoric that relies on physical impairments, which goes well beyond the quick dismissal achieved by calling an argument "lame," or a political action "legless." A common yet complicated rhetorical device involves amputation: amputation of self from self, amputation of self from history or land, and amputation of history from culture. Even Fanon's provocative suggestion to resist amputation (which I explore later) is sometimes made to mean little beyond a rhetorical flourish that notes that amputation is *dysfunctional* and *not good.* Amputation sometimes appears in social justice praxis as *an empty nothingness* against which is configured the fullness of being of the complete and proper body of the anti-colonialist, pre-contact peoples, or the body of work produced by a feminist or anti-patriarchy *stance.*

In the end, it is all pretty "crazy."

WORKING THE IMPAIRMENT DRIVE

What animates the common desire to drive social justice discourse under the influence of impairment rhetoric? Perhaps there is something intoxicating about the clarity of disability as an obviously devalued and excludable type but, still, is there not more? At times, it is casually slipped into the analysis, such as when people quickly dismiss an event by calling it crazy, paralyzed, or blind, but impairment rhetoric also appears as title and frame for critique itself. As a casual slip, or as methodic application, impairment rhetoric is present within critical social justice work today. The "Focus on the body," in Seemanthini Niranjana's words, is a "symbolic one where the body is perceived as a sign or code important to the extent that it is speaking about a social reality other than itself" (quoted in Ghai 302) and, I would add, speaking about a reality other to social justice praxis. The forms of life of disability and injustice are not addressed but assumed by impairment rhetoric. The terms of impairment are a convenient means to speak about the devastating and deadly social reality of injustice. Moreover, the rhetorical use of impairment is an intoxicatingly easy way to gear into a diagnostic moment.

There is a problem.
What is wrong?
History and Culture are disabled.
Ah, crazy.

Still, there must be something behind this common diagnostic practice.

Respecting the rhetorical drive *as a* symbolic arena forged between reader and writer permits us to notice a perplexing phenomenon that hovers at the borders of any desire for social change. However we articulate and work on oppression, the words and deeds generated by such work are inhabited by the terms and conditions of the same world from which they spring and which we wish to change. Our words are part of, made from, and flow back into the same world we want to make different.

I am going to work *with* the perplexity in which we are essentially embedded, given our emersion in the terms and conditions of a world ordered by colonial oppression and its post-colonial dispersions, even as we work to re-imagine the tragedies of this world. Ricoeur's work on metaphor suggests a way to work with, instead of against, this perplexity. The metaphorical expression of human tragedy, says Ricoeur,

> includes all the paradoxes of reference. On the one hand, it expresses a world of human action which is already there; tragedy is bound to express human reality, the tragedy of life. But, on the other hand, *mimesis* does not mean duplication of reality; *mimesis* is *poiesis*, that is, fabrication, construction, creation.
>
> (147)

Every expression of the need for social change is bound to the duplication of the tragedies of the world that have not changed but nonetheless have created the need for change. How then are we to find, let alone nurture, *poiesis* in *mimesis*, or creativity in the banal reproduction of "what is"? Perhaps, we can nurture this potential by attending to the "paradox of reference" within the historical imbrications of race, gender, and disability where these terms may repeat the tragedies from which they spring even as we try to re-make colonial history. Given the welter of impairment references in social justice praxis, this paradox of reference invites a consideration of how "disability studies" itself has grown from this colonial history. In the next section, I turn to a brief historical account of disability studies in order to show the tensions between disability and social justice praxis. This account is a way to return to the question of addressing impairment rhetoric in order to open meanings other than

the obvious duplication of charges such as "ableism," "racism," and "sexism." While I do not want to deny the importance of making such charges, it is still my hope that there is more substance here since metaphors, even dead ones, contain the promise of creativity; a *poiesis* in *mimeses*; the potential of creation within duplication.

IMBRICATIONS OF DISABILITY AND RACE

There is a complex relation between disability and race as it appears through the genesis of what today is called disability studies since both race and disability can be read as the result of the colonial organization of the terms and conditions of life and death, and the conceptions of the human that lie between (Bhabha 54–56; Goodley et al.). Both disability and race can be understood as terms used against their bearers for the sake of profit and control by the powers that be; both can be understood as the effects of inequality. To be disabled, to be racialized, or to be one against, yet within, the other (drapetomania; dependency complex; crazy; amputated) is to be positioned on the borders of what has come to be regarded as human. The terms *disability* and *race* are used to point out the act of dehumanization within the social political orders of the day, *and* are also used for the ongoing accomplishment of dehumanization.

Studying current formations of the human/nonhuman via disability studies does not have a very long history. Still, we might consider the imbrication of race and disability just prior to there being such a thing as disability studies in academia. Disability was included in the 1948 Universal Declaration of Human Rights (and other charters), not as a form of human distinction, but as an *event* against which others should not discriminate (UN UDHR 1948, article 25).[2] Nonetheless, the 1960s witnessed a particular political and scholarly attention toward disability and, once again, the tie between disability and race came to the fore. For example, with the advent of deviance studies in sociology in the USA, 1963 marks the publication of Goffman's *Stigma*. In this book, Goffman documents how a stigmatized person is constituted through interaction as the "not quite human person" (5–7). This not quite human person, produced through a special relation between "attribute and stereotype," takes three major forms: stigma, in Goffman's words, is generated in relation to "blemishes of character"; "tribal" factors (e.g., race, nation, religion); and through "abominations of the body" (5). While the majority of the examples come from the realm of what today is called disability, the tie to race is established since both, according to Goffman, are constituted via stigmatized interaction between attribute and stereotype.

Three years later, in 1966, another book entitled *Stigma* appears, edited by Paul Hunt, but this time written by disabled people about the experience of disability in the UK—with no mention of Goffman's work (Schweik). Most of the authors were living in institutional settings with little control over when they ate; whom they could visit, be friends with, or kiss; or when they might sit in a chair or be left in bed. They are all white, or so it is implied. This is the context in 1966 when Hunt writes in his chapter, "Disability as a Critical Condition":

> Maybe it is invidious to compare our situation with that of racial minorities in any way. The injustice and brutality suffered by so many because of racial tension makes our troubles as disabled people look very small. But I think there is a connection somewhere, since all prejudice springs from the same roots. And there stirs in me a little of the same anger as the Negro writer James Baldwin reveals in the *Fire Next Time* when I remember the countless times I have seen disabled people hurt, treated as less than people, told what to do and how to behave by those whose only claim to do this came from prejudice and their power over them.
>
> (11)

Along with Hunt's anger, there comes his reader's anger too, but not always mirroring his. In my graduate classes, for example, students sometimes express anger that Hunt dared to compare race and disability; at other times, students are angry at Hunt for forging a separation between race and disability; at still other times, the anger comes from somewhere else altogether. Between reader and writer, a point of contact is made and noticed between race and disability, and there is an unexpected disruption. To what do we owe the consistent response that comes with this particular touch of corporeal dissonance?

Joining Hunt, in what would become the development of a UK version of disability studies a few years later, Vic Finkelstein tells of how he was jailed in South Africa for participating in the fight against apartheid. Ironically, it is in jail that Finkelstein, a white man, is accommodated and has access for the first time in his wheelchair-using life. Released from jail but with a series of banning orders regarding where he can move and with whom he can associate, he finds that this punishment is in fact the reality he already lives. Everything he is banned from doing, is already denied him because of the inaccessible character of the built environment in South Africa.

Finkelstein's story of the development of disability studies in the UK includes a reference to Nelson Mandela's 1963 Speech at the Rivonia Trial:

> Above all, we want equal political rights, because without them our disabilities will be permanent. I know this sounds revolutionary to the whites of this country, because the majority of voters will be Africans. This makes the white man fear democracy.
>
> (Mandela 41–42)

To this, Finkelstein (having since moved to the UK) responds:

> Well, you could say all the same things about people who have impairments. But what does it mean if you say that without equal political rights identified by Nelson Mandela "our [African] disabilities will be permanent"? Does it mean that it's not OK if anyone is disabled by social restrictions *except* people with impairments? For us (people who have impairments) is it OK if our disabilities are permanent?
>
> (Finkelstein, addition his own)

By drawing out this race–disability connection, or conflict, Finkelstein aims to question the naturalness of excluding disability from "equal political rights." The sense that it is not nature that grounds the exclusion of people with impairments provoked the forging of the social model of disability in the UK. This model, articulated by the Union of the Physically Impaired against Segregation (quoted in Oliver), says that it is society's failure to respond or its inappropriate responses that transforms people with impairments into disabled people—an unnecessarily oppressed and excluded people (who then claim the name *disabled people* and reject the term *people with disabilities*). An understanding of segregation as socially constituted leads to the possibility of examining individualized and medicalized conceptions of impairment as the cultural means through which permanent restrictions are imposed on disabled people. The social model of disability reflects this understanding.

Various imbrications of race and disability have played a significant role in forging something called "disability studies." Sometimes this forging of disability studies is done alongside race; at other times, against it; and sometimes disability studies empties disability of life, making it serve as nothing other than a symptom of societal dysfunction. This suggests that it is possible to read any manifestation of disability studies for its exemplification of a relation between disability and race, regardless of whether this relation is made explicit. This is true in as much as these modern ways of addressing human distinctions and events are borne of a colonial legacy from which they arise (Bhabha; Mignolo; Walcott). For example, the once dominant feminist distinction of a sex–gender divide was used to secure rights and inclusion, and this is mirrored in an impairment–disability divide by British work of the 1970s on the social model of disability that continues to this day. The divides between unjustly disabled and permanently disabled, as well as between sex and gender, or impairment and disability, reproduce a conception of "nature" that does not take into account its own social genesis. "Natural divides" are thus posited as a given in the face of which people have little agency.

Through these few examples, I depict disability studies as a field of inquiry that is tied to the racist histories of Western power and tied to scholarly, activist, and artistic attempts to change that history. To this day, disability studies connects and compares, yet also contrasts and distinguishes itself from anti-racism, race, and cultural studies, as well as gender, feminist, and queer studies. And the charge of empty or reductive analogy, even the charge of conflation (i.e., to deliver a blow via comparison) hovers at the borders of disability studies. This blow is based on disability and modernist conceptions of nature remaining tied together but unquestioned. For example, a key mechanism used to discount the abolitionists, the suffragettes, and the radical reformers was to deploy disability as a dismissive diagnostic for those who disrupt the natural order (Watts and Erevelles 276). Impairment rhetoric is used to deliver a blow to legitimacy since it (disability) is naturalized as an unwanted way of being and as devastatingly negative. Claims are made that race is not, or should not be, disability; or gender is not, or should not be, deformity. Still, disability studies' attempts to *be* via such comparisons (e.g., we are people too), combined with a hesitancy to assume any association with race, has provided the grounds for Chris Bell's charge of "white disability studies" (275) and his aim to change it (*Blackness and Disability*), and also grounds Corbett O'Toole's charge of "The sexist inheritance of the disability movement" (294). Such work demonstrates that disability studies has not faced the colonial legacy that inhabits the terms and conditions of its existence, even as such work is facing this history and is part of how the field emerged (Garland-Thomson). This paradox is, perhaps, a problem for all forms of critical inquiry insofar as no one has found a way to move into the land of milk and honey, equity or justice, without bringing with them a language that was made and inhabited by colonial history.

With this brief account of the imbrication of race and disability, I return to the phenomenon of impairment rhetoric. I do so as a way to further explore disability and race at the point of specific meaning making achieved through metaphoric engagement with impairment. Exploring the social meaning of metaphor, I then turn to a consideration of Fanon's invocation of the metaphor of amputation as a way to explicate the "fact of blackness."

OPENING THE RHETORICAL DRIVE

Resisting the diagnostic impulse to call the rhetorical use of impairment an ableist slip or straight-up offensive, we might treat impairment rhetoric in social justice praxis as a cultural arena in which to explore the meaning of disability within narratives of human life unjustly damaged. The use of impairment rhetoric can be conceived of as a cultural arena insofar as we recognize that metaphor is a

form of social action; it gives meaning to people and events by expressing them in relation to each other through a comparison. With the use of metaphor we open up a social arena where words come to mean what they do through referencing their common meanings, but in relation to something other or unexpected, potentially releasing new meanings (*poiesis*).

Ricoeur approaches metaphor in this way in his discussion of "Metaphor: The Main Problem of Language." Suggesting that language *is* metaphoric transposition, Ricoeur says:

> Allow me to conclude in a way which would be consistent with a theory of interpretation which lays the stress on "opening up a world." . . . On what? Maybe on the old problem of imagination, which I cautiously put aside. We are prepared to inquire into the power of imagination, no longer as the faculty of deriving "images" from sensory experiences, but as the capacity to let new worlds build our self-understanding.
>
> (148)

For Ricoeur, imagination is not best understood as what the mind does with input of a body-of-sensory-experience and, in this way, he distances metaphor from the physicality of "the senses" while highlighting it as an imaginative world–self *relation*. Imagination conceived of *as an en-worlded mind–body relation* allows us to turn to our embedded-ness as that which makes possible the "opening" of something new (Mitchell and Snyder 48). This making new through the use of what already exists (*poiesis* in *mimesis*) is the power Ricoeur finds in the life of metaphor.

Of particular importance to my discussion of impairment and rhetoric is the sense that, embedded in the terms fixed by history, neither the body-of-sensory-experience nor unexpected or abnormal bodies determines the limits of imagination. Instead, between sense and the sensible world lies the potential "metaphoric" engagement of the terms and conditions of our embedded-ness, through which we can share the possibility of opening worlds to the building of self-understanding. Sensory experience is not itself a communicative act; however, to imagine sensory experience *as* a worldly relation *is*. To regard metaphor as a place where we nurture the capacity to let new understandings arise is also a way to orient to the call in disability studies (Davis 49; Ghai 306; Goodley; Michalko) to reconsider the place and meaning of abnormalcy as an opening on the meaning of normalcy. Through a non-rhetorical relation to metaphor we can ask how we open the worlds that lie behind the rhetorical use of impairment metaphors prevalent in social justice praxis today. In order to pursue this question, I now turn to an exploration of the metaphoric use of "amputation."

Current uses of amputation within social justice praxis include colonized people amputated from their homeland, from mainstream thought, and from history; people amputated from learning, tradition, and indigenous knowledge; people amputated from Blackness, Aboriginality, and from others; and finally, and first, self amputated from self. The result of amputation via colonial power is assumed to be the paralysis of analysis, resulting in a crippled human capacity and the production of the not-quite-human human. Fanon's use of amputation in *Black Skin, White Masks* (1967) may have laid the ground for these various uses of amputation. However, recalling Ricoeur, we can imagine that our sense of Fanon is not limited to current uses of his words. Through the image of amputation, we can open those relations that are embedded in self, sense, and history, and such imagination may even be something that Fanon himself invites. We might consider the last lines of *Black Skin, White Masks*:

My final prayer:

O my body, make of me always a man who questions!

(232)

The body, understood not only as a straightforward series of senses and functions, but also as a prayer, that is, as a form of relationality, provokes the imaginative move toward amputation as opening new worlds of understanding. Fanon prays to his body, a body not regarded as "man" by others, to make (of) him a way to encounter the question of being a human body. With the body of this prayer for provocation, we might return to Fanon's original use of amputation.

Amputation appears in the chapter "The fact of blackness" as Fanon narrates the constitution of blackness under the racist gaze. He writes, "I came into the world imbued with the will to find a meaning in things, my spirit filled with the desire to attain the course of the world, and then I found that I was an object in the midst of other objects" (109). He was thus "Sealed into that crushing objecthood," but he "turned beseechingly to others" (109). In turning away from his objecthood and toward others, Fanon finds possibility but also something else:

> completely dislocated, unable to be abroad with the other, the white man, who unmercifully imprisoned me, I took myself far off from my own presence, far indeed, and made myself an object. What else could it be for me but an amputation, an excision, a haemorrhage, that spattered my whole body with black blood? But I did not want this revision, this thematization.
>
> (112)

Wanted or not, this amputation resulted in Fanon sensing, "I am over-determined from without. … I am *fixed*" (116). Further, he becomes a "Negro Rehabilitated 'standing before the bar'" (127).

In the crush of the amputation of self and humanness as the fact of blackness, Fanon ends his chapter as follows:

> The crippled veteran of the Pacific war says to my brother, "Resign yourself to your color the way I got used to my stump; we're both victims."
>
> Nevertheless with all my strength I refuse to accept that amputation. I feel in myself a soul as immense as the world, truly a soul as the deepest of rivers, my chest has the power to expand without limit. I am a master and I am advised to adopt the humility of the cripple. Yesterday, awakening to the world, I saw the sky turn upon itself utterly and wholly. I wanted to rise, but the disemboweled silence fell back upon me, its wings paralyzed. Without responsibility, straddling Nothingness and Infinity, I began to weep.
>
> (140)

To resign oneself to one's stump is, as they say in rehabilitation, to "come to terms" with it, to accept it, to re-encounter one's possibilities of entering normalcy, *such as it is*. Standing before the bar, prosthetic in hand, or on stump, we are to accept our changed and "normally" devalued selves, accommodate our body's possibilities in the realm of normalcy by rehabilitating, "fixing" ourselves, which means returning to a former state (Stiker 121; Michalko 66). "Resign yourself!" says the "crippled veteran of the Pacific war," who is depicted both in a play and then a film as facing racial slurs hurled at him till he gets up and walks (Fanon 140n29). Through the figure of the racialized veteran, disability is made into an image of potential conformity to the powers that be. The veteran symbolizes the one who conforms to the dominant understanding of amputation as the call of normalcy to stand before the bar, rehabilitate, re-adjust, and re-enter the world, such as it is. The veteran is configured as the one who attempts to guide Fanon to treat amputation as the object that the world imagines it to be, namely, pure disadvantage in need of remedial attention in order to re-enter the world, but again only such as it is.

This Fanon refuses: he refuses this way of relating to amputation and thus enables the embattled metaphor of amputation possibly to open imagination on the world. Such a non-rhetorical reading of Fanon's amputation metaphor is also suggested by Rinaldo Walcott's discussion of resisting amputation. Walcott says, "By resisting borders and boundaries, Black cultures refuse to accept what Frantz Fanon called 'amputation.' ... Acceptance of amputation leads to the imprisonment that accepts the boundaries and borders that state national policies can create" (76). To "resist amputation," he continues, "names the process that refuses to allow blackness to be pinned down to specific categories" (76). Walcott asks us to imagine what the targets of acceptance or resistance actually are and thus resist being imprisoned by taken-for-granted (un-theorized) relation to categories. Amputation, as a category that invites the consideration of the borders of understanding, means engaging the metaphors that contain people and in so doing to encounter something other than a rhetorical use of impairment for the quick intoxication that comes with the act of cultural diagnosis—"Ableist" or "Racist."

AMPUTATION AND IMAGINATION

What exactly is Fanon resisting, since he is not refusing the notion that he has been amputated? Amputation has happened. We might recall that he says, "completely dislocated ... What else could it be for me but an amputation, an excision. ... But I did not want this revision, this thematization." He did not want it, but struck and jammed by the terms of a colonized world, amputation occurred. What is refused is the crushing objectification that amputation typically, medically, normally means—he refuses the singular path that allows amputation to stand only for nothingness (i.e., inability, lack, something missing). Fanon refuses to accept the ordinary medicalized and individualized conception of amputation as "an inability to perform in a way considered normal for a human being" (WHO 28). Within this refusal, amputation becomes other than a diagnostic category. It becomes, instead, a call to respond since it is a place from which Fanon writes and engages his self and the world. He writes in and through amputation by refusing to accept this impairment condition as a sign of nothingness or death. But he is also refusing to accept the infinity of being that simply transcends its difference, regarding wounds as if they are no-thing and no-where. This is, as Katie Aubrecht suggests, to recognize that while colonial power "conditions our experiences of ourselves [this] is only the beginning. We need to continue to question the grounds of our commonalities and the meaning of our differences" (75).

Imagined as a breaking of boundaries, amputation is about being situated as both a whole and a part where we are invited to accept a kind of third space (Bhabha 54) between infinity and nothing; authentic and deformed; human and not. Fanon refuses to resign himself to understanding amputation as a demand only to stand before the bar, rehabilitate, and return to a former normal state albeit with the "humility of the cripple." His disemboweled silence and its paralysis invites him to straddle the fact that he is embedded in the terms and conditions of the colonial world and simultaneously to recognize that he has "truly a soul as the deepest of rivers, my chest has the power to expand without limit." Amputation marks the intertwined character of limit and possibility.

Fanon refuses the ordinary meaning of amputation as well as an unimaginative relation to taken-for-granted meanings of

the category. For Fanon, enjambment seems to be in order. This is not the whole human versus the half human; this is the human writ by culture needing to re-engage, perhaps re-write, what has become of him/her. It is an image of disability that exemplifies the paradox with which this article began and is expressed by Stiker ("We are always other than what society made us and believes us to be" [51]), and Ricoeur ("*mimesis* is *poiesis*" [147]). Amputation—to be missing a part of self *as something essentially a part of one's self*: this is an abnormality that Fanon does not hurl himself past in favor of entering the infinity of becoming normal. Instead, he straddles the normal, writes through this enjambment, maybe even engages it with his difference.

And, he weeps. He weeps since the normal, colonizing world has done this and then demands only that one stands before the bar and regard oneself as less than human. Fanon's text can be read as his tears opening imagination on new worlds.

Following this opening, we might consider the relation between "natural" disasters and amputation, such as the earthquake in Haiti (McRuer 327). These amputations are tied to the ongoing effects of the colonial organization and exploitation of that country. Or, in Canada, the ongoing result of taking land from First Nations people has simultaneously resulted in taking many limbs. With poverty, lack of health care, unfit places to live, there is much amputation that, as a living metaphor, might give rise to a provocation that cannot be contained by a conception of disability as not-life. Amputation has happened. To refuse to accept amputation is to resist bureaucratized, individualized, and medicalized definitions of the situation that suggest that disability is only an inability to do or be normal while also refusing to accept disability as only the aftershock of injustice.

If "amputation" is used within social justice praxis today as a diagnostic category of what colonial powers have done to colonized peoples, it will not open the world on the abnormal and there will be no disruption to the movement of normalizing-colonizing history. The same holds true when the diagnostic slur of "ableist!" is hurled back at such work. What is needed, instead, is a non-rhetorical engagement with metaphors of impairment in order to do something other than draw on the power of medicine and bureaucracy to characterize what is wrong, to diagnose, to contain and control. Used only to diagnose colonial settler violence, disability reproduces impairments (amputation, aphasia, amnesia) as deadly rhetoric and may, in fact, kill Fanon's prayer—Oh my body, make of me always a being who questions!

Enacting this prayer means engaging abnormality as something other than a call to return to the ordinary and the same. Impairment rhetoric, when fixed in the repetitive power of diagnosis, gives up its movement, its critical impulse, while gaining the pleasure of the certainty that comes with the act of highlighting what is wrong. Such highlighting does delimit the boundaries of human recognition; but beyond making the diagnostician seem more powerful, little changes. Though not exactly reckless, driving the social justice agenda forward under the influence of impairment rhetoric names a condition in order to belittle it, rehabilitate it, or kill it, and this may end only in forestalling change. To refuse to accept a normalizing conception of impairment rhetoric is to live differently with the terms and conditions of our bodies as living testimonies to the history they are made from and made to straddle. A new task for social justice praxis today is to stop killing the metaphors and to stop putting a lid on our capacity to imagine a different world. Perhaps it is time to refuse to shut down the world that disability metaphor is ready to open for us, and attempt to straddle disability by understanding it as a way of being that could incite a critical imagination.

NOTES

1. For recent reviews of the disabling character of impairment rhetoric see Schalk; Dolmage & Lewiecki-Wilson; Vidali. Gringley provocatively provides a creative rendering of blindness and deafness rhetoric in critical theoretical scholarship.

2. Article 25 of the Universal Declaration of Human Rights (UN, UDHR, 1948) includes disability: "the right to security in the event of unemployment, sickness, disability, widowhood, old age or other lack of livelihood in circumstances beyond his control." The fact that human rights for disabled people were initially framed not as belonging to the distinction of disability but, instead, to the event of a calamity, has been felt (but also unnoticed) through disability's absence from various government and workplace "non-discrimination" clauses—The University of Toronto being a case in point (Titchkosky, "Monitoring Disability," 121; *The Question of Access*, 97).

WORKS CITED

Al-Barghouti, Tamim. "Colonial Blindness: The Occupation of the Middle East is a Return to the Age of Classical Colonialism." 17 June 2004. Web. 15 December 2013.

Arendt, Hannah. *Arendt: Essays in Understanding: 1930–1954*. New York: Harcourt Brace, 1994.

Aubrecht, Katie. "Rereading the Ontario Review of the Roots of Youth Violence Report: The Relevance of Fanon for a Critical Disability Studies Perspective." *Fanon and Education: Thinking through Pedagogical Possibilities*. Ed. George J. Sefa Dei and Marlon Simmons. New York: Peter Lang, 2010. 55–78.

Bauman, Zygmunt. *Wasted Lives: Modernity and its Outcasts*. Cambridge: Polity, 2004.

Bell, Chris, ed. *Blackness and Disability: Critical Examinations and Cultural Interventions*. East Lansing: Michigan State University Press, 2011.

——. "Introducing White Disability Studies: A Modest Proposal." *The Disability Studies Reader*. Ed. Lennard J. Davis. New York: Routledge, 2006. 275–82.

Bhabha, Homi K. *The Location of Culture*. New York: Routledge, 1994.

Byrd, Jodi. "Silence Will Fall: The Cultural Politics of Colonial Agnosia." Presented to the Women and Gender Studies Institute, University of Toronto Public Talk. 23 October 2013.

Davis, Lennard J. *Enforcing Normalcy: Disability, Deafness, and the Body*. London: Verso, 1995.

Dolmage, Jay and Cynthia Lewiecki-Wilson. "Refiguring Rhetorica: Linking Feminist Rhetoric and Disability Studies." *Rhetorica in Motion: Feminist Rhetorical Methods and Methodologies.* Ed. Eileen E. Schell and Kelly Rawson. Pittsburgh, PA: University of Pittsburgh Press, 2010. 23–38.

Fanon, Frantz. *Black Skin, White Masks.* New York: Grove Press, 1967.

Finkelstein, Vic. "A Personal Journey into Disability Politics." Presented to the Leeds University Centre for Disability Studies. 7 February 2001.

Garland-Thomson, Rosemarie. "Disability Studies: A Field Emerged." *American Quarterly* 65.4 (2014): 915–26. Web. 13 November 2014.

Ghai, Anita. "Disabled Women: An Excluded Agenda of Indian Feminism." *Rethinking Normalcy: A Disability Studies Reader.* Ed. Tanya Titchkosky and Rod Michalko. Toronto: Canadian Scholars Press, 2009. 296–311.

Goffman, Erving. *Stigma: Notes on the Management of a Spoiled Identity.* Englewood Cliffs, NJ: Prentice Hall, 1963.

Goodley, Dan. *Dis/ability Studies: Theorising Disablism and Ableism.* London: Routledge, 2014.

Goodley, Dan, Rebecca Lawthom and Katherine Runswick Cole. "Posthuman Disability Studies." *Subjectivity* 7 (2014): 342–61.

Gringley, Joseph. "Blindness and Deafness as Metaphors: An Anthological Essay." *Journal of Visual Culture* 5.2 (2006): 227–41.

Hunt, Paul. "Disability as a Critical Condition." 1966. Web. 15 December 2013.

——. ed. *Stigma: The Experience of Disability.* London: Geoffrey Chapman, 1966.

Lieven, Anatol and John C. Hulsman. "Neo-Conservatives, Liberal Hawks, and the War on Terror: Lessons from the Cold War." *World Policy Journal* 23.3 (2006): 64–74.

Linton, Simi. *Claiming Disability: Knowledge and Identity.* New York: New York University Press, 1998.

McRuer, Robert. "Reflections on Disability in Haiti." *Journal of Literary & Cultural Disability Studies* 4.3 (2010): 327–32.

Mandela, Nelson. *Nelson Mandela: In His Own Words.* New York: Little, Brown, 2003.

Michalko, Rod. *The Mystery of the Eye and the Shadow of Blindness.* Toronto: University of Toronto Press, 1998.

Mignolo, Walter. "Coloniality of Power and Subalternity." *The Latin American Subaltern Studies Reader.* Ed. Ileana Rodriguez. Durham, NC: Duke University Press, 2001. 424–44.

Minnich, Elisabeth. *Transforming Knowledge.* Philadelphia: Temple University Press, 1990.

Mitchell, David T. and Sharon L. Snyder. *Narrative Prosthesis: Disability and the Dependencies of Discourse.* Ann Arbor: University of Michigan Press, 2000.

Oliver, Michael. *Understanding Disability: From Theory to Practice.* New York: St. Martin's Press, 1996.

O'Toole, Corbett. "The Sexist Inheritance of the Disability Movement." *Gendering Disability.* Ed. Bonnie G. Smith and Beth Hutchison. New Brunswick, NJ: Rutgers University Press, 2004. 294–300.

Ricoeur, Paul. *The Philosophy of Paul Ricoeur: An Anthology of his Work.* Ed. Charles E. Reagan and David Stewart. Boston: Beacon Press, 1978.

Schalk, Sami. "Metaphorically Speaking: Ableist Metaphors in Feminist Writing." *Disability Studies Quarterly* 33.4 (2013). Web. 13 November 2014.

Schweik, Susan. "Stigma Management." *Disability Studies Quarterly* 34.1 (2014). Web. 13 November 2014.

Showalter, Elaine. "Critical Cross-Dressing: Male Feminists and the Woman of the Year." *Raritan* 3.2 (1983): 130–49. Web. 13 November 2014.

Stiker, Henri Jacques. *The History of Disability.* Ann Arbor: University of Michigan Press, 1999.

Stoler, Ann Laura. "Colonial Aphasia: Race and Disabled Histories in France." *Public Culture* 23.1 (2011): 121–36.

Tallbear, Kimberly. Blog: Oak Lake Retreat, South Dakota State University. 8 August 2012. Web. 30 December 2013.

Titchkosky, Tanya. "Monitoring Disability: The Question of the 'Human' in Human Rights Projects." *Disability, Human Rights and the Limits of Humanitarianism.* Ed. Michael Gill and Cathy Schulund-Vials. London: Ashgate, 2014. 119–35.

——. *The Question of Access: Disability, Space, Meaning.* Toronto: University of Toronto Press, 2011.

United Nations (UN), *Universal Declaration of Human Rights.* 1948. Web. 30 December 2013.

Vidali, Amy. "Seeing What We Know: Disability and Theories of Metaphor." *Journal of Literary & Cultural Disability Studies* 4.1 (2010): 33–54.

Walcott, Rinaldo. "Voyage through the Multiverse: Contested Canadian Identities." *Conflict, Order and Action: Readings in Sociology.* Ed. Edward Ksenych and David Liu. Toronto: Canadian Scholars Press, 2001. 75–81.

Watts, Ivan Eugene and Nirmala Erevelles. "These Deadly Times: Reconceptualizing School Violence by Using Critical Race Theory and Disability Studies." *American Educational Research Journal* 41.2 (2004): 271–99.

World Health Organization (WHO). *International Classification of Impairment, Disability and Handicap (ICIDH).* Published in accordance with resolution WHA 29 35 of the 29th World Health Association, 1980.

CHAPTER 20

At the Same Time, Out of Time: Ashley X

Alison Kafer

SUMMARY

In this chapter Alison Kafer focuses on the well-publicized case of a girl named Ashley X who was given estrogen treatments and surgery to stop her growth into puberty. The case offers an illustration of how disability is often understood as a kind of disruption in time. Kafer argues that Ashley's parents and doctors justified her treatment by holding her imagined future body—one that they believed grew out of sync with Ashley's mind—against her.

Arresting Ashley's development was intended to help make it easy for her parents to carry her, and the removal of her reproductive organs also prevented her from being "sexualized" or, in the view of her parents, reaching an adulthood that would be out of alignment with her cognition. As Kafer points out, the temporal rhetoric around this "misalignment" has been used routinely to infantilize disabled people and deny them adulthood. Without the ability to reproduce, Ashley became labeled as a "pillow angel" incapable of both inhabiting an adult body and reproducing. Considered from a feminist perspective, the removal of Ashley's reproductive organs reinforces the centrality of reproduction to female bodies; doctors thought that because her breasts and uterus would not serve their purpose, they could be dismissed. Missing from the discussion about Ashley's quality of life is the possibility of pleasure, and Kafer calls out the assumption that a disabled female body is incapable of sensations other than pain.

Kafer argues that it makes no sense to think of the "Ashley Treatment" as a cure for her condition; it is only a curative response to disability. Furthermore, Ashley's case represents the trend of increasing privatization for caregiving and disability that makes decisions about disability seem like private concerns for parents rather than issues for public debate. Doctors argue that the treatment helps Ashley avoid institutionalization, a goal shared with the disability rights movement. But her parents' decision to attenuate Ashley's growth relies on judgments about her "quality of life" and cognitive infancy that anticipates a narrowed future for Ashley. Ashley has been misunderstood by feminists and disability activists as somehow exceptional, but Kafer urges us to "look for her" and to imagine a crip future that makes space for Ashley and other people like her.

The stories of women with disabilities must be told, not as stories of vulnerability, but as stories of injustice.

(Sherene Razack, "From Pity to Respect")

In thinking about crip futurity, I find myself haunted by Ashley X. Born in 1997, the girl known as Ashley X was diagnosed with "static encephalopathy" a few months after her birth. "In the ensuing years," doctors note, "her development never progressed beyond that of an infant," and her doctors held no hope that her cognitive or neurological baseline would improve.[1] "At the age of 6 years, she [could] not sit up, ambulate, or use language."[2] Concerned about their daughter's long-term future, Ashley's parents met with doctors in 2004 to discuss the potential effects of puberty and physical growth on their ability to care for her at home. Together they crafted a two-pronged plan: "attenuate" Ashley's growth by starting her on a high-dose estrogen regimen; and, prior to the estrogen treatment, remove Ashley's uterus and breast buds in order "to reduce the complications of puberty" and mitigate potential side effects of the estrogen treatment.[3] According to her parents and doctors, these interventions were necessary for Ashley's future quality of life: they would reduce her pain and discomfort (by removing the possibility of her menstruating or developing breasts) and would enable her parents to continue caring for her at home (by keeping her small enough to turn and lift easily). Her parents worried that, without the Treatment, Ashley would become too cumbersome for them to lift safely, and, as a result, her participation in social and recreational activities would decrease dramatically.[4] Ashley's doctors took this concern a step further, expressing fear that caring for her at home might eventually become "untenable" and that Ashley's parents would need to place her "in the hands of strangers."[5]

From the moment this case became public, in late 2006, it has garnered widespread attention. Both Ashley's doctors and Ashley's parents have written extensively about the case, carefully articulating their respective positions on the appropriateness of the Treatment. Bioethicists, disability rights activists, pediatric specialists, parents of disabled children, policy makers, disability studies scholars, legal experts, bloggers, and journalists have joined the fray, debating the ramifications of this case in particular and of growth attenuation/sterilization in general.[6] Critics of the Treatment have condemned the hospital for violating sterilization regulations, challenged the parents' presumption that they know what is best for their daughter, and debated the appropriateness of reshaping children's bodies without their consent. Supporters of the Treatment have stressed the difficulties of parenting severely disabled children, the noble intentions of the parents, and the alleged benefits of growth attenuation and sterilization. Rather than rehash that work here, parsing the legalities of the case or determining the proper decision-making authority or debating the moral permissibility of surgically shaping children, I want to take a different tack, rereading Ashley's case through the lens of time and futurity.

As becomes clear in both parental and medical justifications of the Treatment, the case of Ashley X offers a stark illustration of how disability is often understood as a kind of disruption in the temporal field.[7] Supporters of the Treatment frame Ashley's disability as a kind of temporal disjuncture; not only had she failed to grow and develop "normally," but her mind and body were developing at different speeds from each other. According to this logic, Ashley's body required intervention because her body was growing apart from her mind; physically, her body was developing rapidly, but mentally, her mind was failing to develop at all. As a result, she was embodied asynchrony; her mind and body were out of sync. By arresting the growth of Ashley's body, the Treatment could stop this gap between mind and body from growing any wider. In order to make this argument, Ashley's parents and doctors had to hold her future body—her *imagined* future body—against her, using it as a justification for the Treatment. Without intervention, the asynchrony between mind and body would only grow wider; Ashley's body would become more and more unbearable to her, to her parents, and to those encountering her in public. This future burden, brought on by the future Ashley, could only be avoided by arresting the present Ashley in time. Adding to the future framing of the case is the fact that both parents and doctors have offered the Treatment as a template for other children; they have expressed the hope that the Treatment will, in the future, become more widespread. The Ashley case, in other words, is shot through with temporal framings of the mind/body, especially the disabled mind/body, and with rhetoric about the future.

Before examining the temporal framing of the case, I will first present an overview of the Treatment and its legal aftermath, as well as a summary of how Ashley's parents and doctors explain and justify the Treatment. The bulk of the chapter reads the case through a temporal framing, focusing on the ways in which Ashley was cast, and cast as, out of time; from the beginning of the case, she has been represented as temporally disjointed, as an eternal child, and as threatened by her future self. In addition, I explore the gendered dimensions and assumptions of the Treatment, detailing how Ashley's femaleness, or future femaleness, rendered her atemporality particularly grotesque. As this story makes painfully clear, not all disability futures are desirable; in other words, the problem is not only the inclusion of disability in our futures but also the nature of that inclusion. I conclude the chapter, then, with a brief reflection about how to imagine desirably disabled futures.

A CASE HISTORY OF THE ASHLEY TREATMENT

Ashley's surgery took place under the direction of Dr. Daniel Gunther in July 2004, at Seattle Children's Hospital; the procedure, which was "uneventful," included a hysterectomy, a bilateral mastectomy, and an appendectomy.[8] For the next two and a half years, Ashley received high doses of estrogen in an attempt to stunt her growth. (Estrogen accelerates the "maturation of the epiphyseal growth plates," which means one's bone plates fuse quickly, arresting growth).[9] At the conclusion of the estrogen regimen, Ashley's size was about average for a 9-year-old girl: fifty-three inches tall and sixty-three pounds. Three years later, in January 2010, her parents reported that her size had remained virtually unchanged (fifty-three inches tall and sixty-five pounds). X-rays of her hands revealed that the gaps between her finger bones had fused, indicating that she had indeed reached her maximum height.[10] By her doctors' and her parents' measure, the Treatment was a success.[11]

For many disabled people and disability activists, however, the Treatment was nothing to celebrate. As the case became public, disability rights organizations, disability activists, and disability studies scholars spoke out against the hospital's actions, and the Washington Protection and Advocacy System (WPAS) launched an investigation in January 2007.[12] In May that year, reviewers from WPAS issued their report on the case, finding that "[t]he sterilization portion of the 'Ashley Treatment' was conducted in violation of Washington State law, resulting in violation of Ashley's constitutional and common law rights."[13] According to WPAS, the hospital should have sought a court order before moving forward with the sterilization; state regulations mandate judicial review prior to the sterilization of patients who do not or cannot consent.

Although the hospital's own ethics committee had noted in regard to the hysterectomy that "there is need for a court review of this aspect of [the] proposal," no such review took place.[14] Instead, after the ethics committee issued its report, Ashley's parents consulted with attorney Larry Jones about the sterilization. In a June 2004 letter to Ashley's father, Jones asserts, "It is not necessary to have a court hearing on sterilization when the object of the medical procedure is not sterilization, but to obtain another medically necessary benefit."[15] Rather, sterilization would be "merely a byproduct of surgery performed for other compelling medical reasons," namely the prevention of bleeding associated with estrogen therapy and the cessation of menstruation.[16] Since sterilization was not the main goal of the Treatment, Jones argued, a court order was unnecessary. Moreover, he explained, the sterilization policies were intended to protect those patients who might develop or regain the capacity to raise children; Ashley would never have the ability to make child-bearing decisions, so there was no need to protect her from the permanence of sterilization.[17] Ashley's father sent the letter to Ashley's doctors, who later told WPAS that they had accepted the letter as a form of "court review" and acted accordingly.[18]

The Washington Protection and Advocacy System disagreed with this logic, arguing not only that the parents' consultation with Jones did not qualify as judicial review, but that his legal opinion "is not supported by a reasonable interpretation of pertinent law."[19] They explained that existing policy clearly required the hospital to safeguard Ashley's interests through a thorough judicial review. Seattle Children's Hospital accepted the findings in the WPAS report, agreeing that they had acted inappropriately in not following their own ethics committee's push for a court review. According to a joint statement signed by both parties in May 2007:

> [Seattle] Children's [Hospital] agrees with the finding in the report that Ashley's sterilization proceeded without a court order in violation of Washington State law, resulting in violation of Ashley's constitutional and common law rights. Children's deeply regrets its failure to assure court review and a court order prior to allowing performance of the sterilization and

is dedicated to assuring full compliance with the law in any future case.[20]

Dr. David Fisher, the medical director of Seattle Children's Hospital, issued a statement supporting the WPAS findings, admitting "an internal miscommunication which resulted in a violation of the law" and taking "full responsibility."[21] In their joint statement with WPAS, Seattle Children's Hospital agreed to obtain a court order before permitting growth attenuation or sterilization procedures on other disabled children; they also pledged to develop stronger oversight and monitoring programs over their sterilization practices and policies. Finally, the hospital consented to the addition of a disability rights advocate to their ethics committee.

Although the case of Ashley X is "closed"—WPAS has released their findings; Seattle Children's Hospital has apologized and issued new guidelines per their agreement with WPAS—the Ashley Treatment remains an open question. Ashley's doctors and parents continue to write (separately) about the Treatment, presenting it as a viable course of action for other families. The University of Washington held symposia devoted to the case in 2007 and 2009; in late 2010, the Seattle Growth Attenuation and Ethics Working Group (SWG), an offshoot of the first symposium, published a position paper on growth attenuation.[22] In that report, they argue that "growth attenuation can be morally permissible under specific conditions and after thorough consideration"; one of those conditions is that the patient be neither ambulatory nor communicative.[23] Although most of the 20-person group were able to agree to this compromise position, two participants wrote brief dissents, spelling out continued points of disagreement among some members.[24] These points of dissension, combined with the report's call for additional research, suggest that more debates and reports lie ahead.

DOCUMENTING THE ASHLEY TREATMENT

The details of the Ashley Treatment became public almost two and a half years after her surgery. In October 2006, two doctors centrally involved in the case—Dr. Daniel Gunther, a pediatric endocrinologist, and Dr. Douglas Diekema, a pediatric bioethicist—published the results of the growth attenuation therapy in the *Archives of Pediatric and Adolescent Medicine.* Several months later, Ashley's parents launched a blog called *The "Ashley Treatment": Towards a Better Quality of Life for "Pillow Angels."* As these titles suggest, both texts took a future-oriented approach; they presented the Ashley Treatment as a new tool in the care of disabled children, one that other parents and doctors might choose to replicate. Before addressing this future-orientation, or analyzing the rhetoric deployed in each text, I first offer a brief summary of each document.

In their initial article, which focused primarily on the growth attenuation therapy, Gunther and Diekema argue that Ashley will benefit both physically and emotionally from her smaller size:

> A child who is easier to move will in all likelihood be moved more frequently. Being easier to move means more stimulation, fewer medical complications, and more social interaction. Personal contact between parent and child is likely to be more direct and personal without the need for hoisting apparatus or other devices. Being easier to move and transfer also makes it more likely that the child will be included in family activities and family outings.[25]

Gunther and Diekema frame the growth attenuation therapy as essential to Ashley's future quality of life; without it, they claim, her parents would eventually be unable to care for her at home or to include her in family events.

Gunther and Diekema's article is as interesting for what it excludes as for what it includes. While the WPAS report stressed the hysterectomy, discussing it at length, the two doctors limit discussion of the procedure and its ramifications to a single paragraph. "A word here about hysterectomy is probably appropriate," they concede, casting discussion about the hysterectomy—and, by extension, the hysterectomy itself—as a mere side issue to the more important topic of growth attenuation.[26] The hysterectomy is apparently so trivial, or so incidental, as not to merit extensive analysis on its own; they do not even use the word "sterilization" in regard to Ashley, thereby avoiding that conversation altogether. In downplaying the hysterectomy, Gunther and Diekema echo the stance of attorney Larry Jones: as Jones argued in his letter to the family, the hysterectomy and resultant sterilization were only by products of treatment done for other reasons. The hysterectomy was performed not in order to sterilize Ashley but to mitigate the risks of uterine bleeding (a side effect of the estrogen regimen) and the anxiety and discomfort of menstruation. Since Ashley would never develop the ability to raise children, preserving her reproductive health was not an issue; she had no need of her uterus, so there was no need to discuss it.

Effectively rendering Ashley's breasts as even more expendable than her uterus, Gunther and Diekema do not mention the bilateral mastectomy at all—nor does Diekema in an interview with CNN a few months later.[27] When eventually pressed about this silence, Gunther and Diekema argue that the mastectomy was irrelevant to growth attenuation and high-dose estrogen therapy; there was nothing to discuss.[28] Although Diekema has addressed the mastectomy in more recent articles, he seems to do so only in response to criticism, not because he sees the mastectomy as anything meriting attention in and of itself.[29]

Ashley's parents, however, understand the mastectomy differently, representing it on their blog as an essential component of "the Ashley Treatment"; for them, the hysterectomy, mastectomy, and estrogen regimen are all of a piece. The mastectomy, or, to use their language, "breast bud removal," was necessary for three reasons.[30] The primary reason for the "removal" was that any breast development was likely to cause Ashley pain and discomfort. Breasts would make lying down unpleasant for Ashley ("large breasts are uncomfortable lying down with a bra and even less comfortable without a bra") and would "impede securing Ashley in her wheelchair, stander, or bath chair, where straps across her chest are needed to support her body weight."[31] Those straps would then compress Ashley's breasts, causing further pain and confusion. Buttressing this rationale for the procedure were two "additional and incidental benefits": the bilateral mastectomy would eliminate the possibility of breast cancer or fibrocystic growth, two conditions present in the family; it would also prevent Ashley from being inappropriately "sexualized." According to Ashley's parents, the mastectomy "posed the biggest challenge to Ashley's doctors, and to the ethics committee," but the parents ultimately convinced them of the benefits of the procedure.[32]

Ashley's parents launched their blog on January 2, 2007, not long after Ashley completed her estrogen regimen, and it was this text that generated worldwide attention. Such attention seemed to be the parents' goal, as they started the blog "for two purposes: first, to help families who might bring similar benefits to their bedridden Pillow Angels; second, to address some misconceptions about the treatment and our motives for undertaking it."[33] The blog covers much of the same terrain as Gunther and Diekema's article, although more informally; it discusses Ashley's medical history and diagnosis, the details of the

Treatment, and a point-by-point justification for the procedures. These pieces are supplemented by family photographs of Ashley (with her parents' and siblings' faces blurred for privacy), "testimonies" from other parents of "pillow angels," letters of support, and excerpts from sympathetic editorials and commentaries.[34] The blog also offers definitions for two key terms that did not appear in the original article by Gunther and Diekema: "the Ashley Treatment" and "Pillow Angel." "The Ashley Treatment" refers to the combination of growth-attenuating estrogen regimen, hysterectomy, and "breast bud removal," while "Pillow Angel" signifies

> people with a cognitive and mental developmental level that will never exceed that of a 6-month old child as well as associated extreme physical limitations, so they will never be able to walk or talk or in some cases even hold up their head or change position in bed. Pillow Angels are entirely dependent on their caregivers.[35]

Given the intent of the blog, it is not surprising that Ashley's parents see the Treatment as an unmitigated success. As they told CNN in 2008, "Ashley did not grow in height or weight in the last year, she will always be flat-chested, and she will never suffer any menstrual pain, cramps, or bleeding."[36]

OUT OF LINE, OUT OF TIME

Always flat-chested, never menstruating, finished growing: for Ashley's parents, the Treatment was undeniably about arresting Ashley's development so that they might continue to lift and carry her without difficulty. Mention of Ashley's flat chest and hysterectomy, however, suggests that more than weight was at stake in their decision. They were also concerned about the developmental disjuncture taking place as her body, which was developing more typically, grew further away from her mind, which "stopped growing . . . when she was a few months old." They understood Ashley's body as en route to "adulthood," even though her mind was permanently mired in "childhood," and this disconnect required intervention. Doctors and bioethicists following the case echoed this concern; the Treatment was necessary to keep Ashley's cognitive self and physical self aligned. The Ashley Treatment thus enacted a circular temporal logic: Ashley's disabilities rendered her out of time, asynchronous, because of this developmental gap between mind and body; her development needed to be arrested to correct this mind/body misalignment; this arrested development then cast her further out of time, more befitting her permanent cognitive infancy.

From the beginning, the Treatment was described as a way to correct the disjuncture between Ashley's body and mind. "When you see Ashley," Dr. Diekema tells CNN, "it's like seeing a baby in a much larger body."[37] Without the Treatment, this disjuncture would only become more pronounced, as Ashley would eventually become not only a baby in a much larger body, but a baby in an *adult's* body. What was needed, as her parents put it, was to bring Ashley's "physical self closer to [her] cognitive self."[38] As John Jordan argues, "Despite her otherwise healthy prognosis, Ashley's body had to be articulated as 'wrong' in such a way that the Treatment could be recognized as the best way to make her 'right.'"[39] This "wrongness" was framed in terms of a temporal and developmental misalignment between mind and body, "the brain of a 6-month-old" in the body of one much older; to the extent possible, the Treatment corrects that disjuncture.[40]

In this desire for mind and body to align, what we see is a temporal framing of disability dovetailing with a developmental model of childhood. In classical child development theory, children move through a defined sequence of stages toward adulthood, a one-way and linear march "upward." Children can be seen in this framework as "unfinished" adults, or as people who have yet to move through the necessary stages of growth and development.[41] What this understanding of childhood often means is that disabled people, particularly those with intellectual disabilities (or "developmental" disabilities, as they are often known), are also cast as "unfinished" adults. Diekema's description of Ashley as a "baby in a much larger body" reflects an extension of this logic: regardless of how old Ashley is chronologically, she will always be a "baby" developmentally. (Similar logics are at work when Jerry Lewis refers to adults with multiple dystrophy as "kids" or when Christopher Reeve describes paralysis as having "suddenly transformed [him] into a forty-two-year-old infant."[42] Reeve aligns physical dependence with infancy, and Lewis frames disability as inherently infantilizing.)

The linkage of intellectual disabilities with childhood has a long history. Licia Carlson, explaining that people classified as "idiots" in the late nineteenth and early twentieth centuries were seen as "remain[ing] at an early stage of development," notes that superintendents of state institutions often referred to their wards as "man-baby," "woman-baby," and "child-baby."[43] Within this framework, there is no room for the adult with intellectual disabilities; if adulthood is about independence, autonomy, and productivity, then adulthood becomes both unachievable and inconceivable in relation to profound intellectual impairment like Ashley's.

In their initial defense of the Treatment, Gunther and Diekema stress that Ashley faces a future of no future: she is "an individual who will never be capable of holding a job, establishing a romantic relationship, or interacting as an adult."[44] Within the logics of normative time, adults work, marry, and live independently; but according to Gunther and Diekema, disability renders too many of such practices impossible. As a result, the interventions can do no harm; she is already prohibited by her disabilities from having romantic relationships (or children), so her breasts and uterus are easily removed.

Notice, too, in their description the conflation of adulthood with productivity; interacting as an adult is paralleled with holding a job. Disability, then, is defined as a lack of productivity; in a move that brings the word closer to its roots, being disabled means being unable to work. Bioethicist Norman Fost makes plain this perspective in his summary of the case: "It [the Ashley case] reminds [me] of the scandal some years ago when it was discovered that some Cadillacs had Chevrolet engines."[45] In positioning Ashley as "a Cadillac with a Chevrolet engine," Fost not only references the "deceptive" nature of her imagined future appearance—a child in an adult's body—but reveals the degree to which we view normal adulthood as a time of, and as defined by, productivity. We are all to be smoothly running engines, and disability renders us defective products. Ashley does not merit the protections offered adults or other children because she will never be an adult.

The term "pillow angel" both reflects and perpetuates this linking of disability with infancy and childhood. Ashley's parents explain that they "call her our Pillow Angel since she is so sweet and stays right where we place her—usually on a pillow."[46] This phrasing paints a picture of infant-like dependency and passivity; it makes it difficult to imagine Ashley as a teenager or a woman-to-be. Thus, much as the estrogen therapy and mastectomy make Ashley look like the permanent child she allegedly is, the "pillow angel" label names her as such. Within this schema, her body, mind, and identity all line up perfectly.

Such alignment is necessary not only to ensure that people treat Ashley "in ways that are more appropriate to [her] developmental age," but also to protect those around her from disruptions in their temporal fields.[47] Dr. Norman Fost, a bioethicist who has often written about the case, echoes Diekema's concerns about the problem of mind/body misalignment:

> [H]aving her size be more appropriate to her developmental level will make her less of a "freak." ... I have long thought that part of the discomfort we feel in looking at profoundly retarded adults is the aesthetic disconnect between their developmental status and their bodies. There is nothing repulsive about a 2 month old infant, despite its limited cognitive, motor, and social skills. But when the 2 month baby is put into a 20 year old body, the disconnect is jarring.[48]

In invoking the image of an adult body with a baby's brain, and assuming such an image prompts repulsion, Fost enters the realm of the grotesque. He positions Ashley as the embodiment of category confusion, of "matter out of place"; the imagined Ashley blurs infancy and adulthood together, troubling cultural understandings of the normative life course.[49] We are to imagine an adult that looks like "us" but can never function or think like us, and this collision of sameness and difference makes us uncomfortable. George Dvorsky, another bioethicist commenting on the case, makes explicit this link to the grotesque. Writing in support of the Treatment, he too praises its ability to "endow her with a body that more closely matches her cognitive state—both in terms of her physical size and bodily functioning." He then goes on to argue that the "estrogen treatment is not what is grotesque here. Rather, it is the prospect of having a full-grown and fertile woman endowed with the mind of a baby."[50] The disjuncture between mind and body is apparently all the more jarring, all the more *grotesque*, because of

Ashley's gender. Within this framework, Ashley's imagined future body is held against her present body and deemed excessive and inappropriate: too tall, too big-breasted, too fertile, too sexual, too *adult* for her true baby nature. The Treatment was thus necessary to prevent this imagined big and breasty body—this grotesque, fertile body—from coming into being. Dvorsky makes clear the unspoken reason why the growth attenuation had to be combined with a hysterectomy; without the latter, Ashley would remain grotesquely fertile.

The definitions that Ashley's parents provide on their blog reveal their own anxieties about the too-big, too-fertile body to come: they describe the hysterectomy as the "removal of *tiny* uterus" and the mastectomy as "breast bud removal: removal of *almond sized* glands."[51] Both procedures must be done quickly, they argue, before "rapid growth of breasts and uterus" begins.[52] Of course, any such "rapid growth" would be caused, at least in part, by the estrogen regimen itself, but the rhetoric has the effect of depicting Ashley's body as out-of-control; it is as if the imagined future Ashley, with her large breasts and uterus, is going to take over, to *consume*, the angelic pillow angel with her "almond sized breast buds." The Treatment is positioned as a cure for adult womanhood as much as adult disability.

Feminists have long challenged the reduction of women to their reproductive capacities, and the case of Ashley X reveals how disability both complicates and enables that reduction. On the one hand, despite the surgical focus on her reproductive organs, Ashley is understood to be completely removed from the realm of reproduction. What makes the bilateral mastectomy and hysterectomy permissible is the underlying conviction that Ashley will never need or use her breasts and uterus. Her parents explain that the only reason to

forgo the "breast-bud removal" is if childbearing and breastfeeding are in Ashley's future; since they are not, her breasts can be removed without any problem.[53] They present the hysterectomy in similar terms. In their diagram describing the treatment, the hysterectomy is placed next to the appendectomy, suggesting that for Ashley, her uterus is an appendix: useless, unnecessary, and expendable.[54] Thus, Ashley's disabilities prevent her from being reduced to her reproductive organs; unlike nondisabled women, she is not to be understood in those terms.

At the same time, however, the Treatment reveals the extent to which the female body is always and only framed as reproductive. Dvorsky's anxieties about Ashley's fertility suggest that disability only renders such fertility more threatening, more in need of containment and intervention. Furthermore, her parents' presentation of her breasts and uterus as irrelevant and unnecessary testifies to the persistence of a reproductive use-value understanding of female bodies. The only purpose of these body parts is reproductive; if reproduction is not in one's future, then these parts can be shed without ethical concern. The centrality of reproductive frameworks to our understanding of what constitutes a woman or a female is what made the mastectomy and hysterectomy possible or imaginable. Ashley's breasts and uterus were never going to serve their real purpose, so they could be dismissed.

Indeed, a dismissive attitude toward mastectomy and hysterectomy pervades Gunther and Diekema's original article. Their approach makes sense, in that to focus on the hysterectomy *qua* hysterectomy might prompt questions about state sterilization protections. But their discussion of the procedure makes clear that they had no real concerns about it; sterilizing someone like Ashley takes on the appearance of common sense. Indeed, they acknowledge concerns about forced sterilization only to brush them away:

> Hysterectomy in children, particularly in the disabled, is controversial and invariably associated with the negative connotations and history of forced "sterilization." But in these profoundly impaired children, with no realistic reproductive aspirations, prophylactic hysterectomy has several advantages as an adjunct to high-dose estrogen treatment.[55]

Placing "sterilization" in scare quotes suggests that Gunther and Diekema do not see it as a real concern, almost as if it were not an accurate description of a hysterectomy. The history of forced sterilization apparently has no bearing on cases of such profound impairment. Nor, apparently, do feminist critiques of sterilization, as the procedure is completely degendered in this passage. They describe hysterectomy in *children,* as if boys also have hysterectomies, as if there were no gendered dimension to such procedures.[56] Or, perhaps, the use of "children" is an indication that Diekema and Gunther do not recognize disabled children as gendered at all; they cannot be boys or girls because both categories presume an able-bodied/able-minded norm. The Treatment is thus a surgical manifestation of the conceptualization of Ashley as a permanent child. As a child, Ashley has no need of reproductive organs; as a disabled person, she has no sexuality. Maintaining her small size and keeping her flat-chested and infertile ensures that her physical appearance matches her cognitive functioning, and that both reflect the lack of sexuality befitting a disabled person/baby.

At first blush, it makes no sense to describe Ashley as cured or the Treatment as a kind of cure for her condition. The Treatment did not improve her cognitive or physical functioning nor was it intended to do so. Yet it is undoubtedly a curative

response to disability. Ashley had to be cured of her asynchrony, at least to the fullest extent possible. She also had to be freed of the specter of her future body, the full-sized, large-breasted, menstruating and fertile body to come. Ashley had her imagined body held against her, and held against her in both senses of the phrase: it was this imagined body that justified the Treatment, and it was this imagined body that became grotesque when compared to her present body.

"TOWARDS A BETTER QUALITY OF LIFE FOR 'PILLOW ANGELS'"

Ashley's parents and doctors are concerned not only about Ashley's future (and future body), both real and imagined, but also about the futures of other disabled children. The very fact of their writing proves as much, with each publication geared toward presenting the Treatment as effective, morally permissible, and ethically appropriate for others. Blogging enables Ashley's parents to communicate with other families worldwide and generates press coverage to further their message; publishing in medical journals is a way for Gunther and Diekema to gain peer validation, approval, and, ultimately, adoption of a new treatment beyond the featured case.

One need look no further than the title of Gunther and Diekema's article for proof that they see the growth-attenuating estrogen therapy as having an application beyond Ashley: "A New Approach to an Old Dilemma." The "old dilemma" is how best to care for children with severe disabilities, particularly how to keep them out of nursing homes and state institutions; the "new approach" to this problem is growth attenuation (and its accompanying surgeries).[57] Indeed, they frame their whole article in terms of the struggle against institutionalization. The first sentence of the article sets this tone, noting that the "American Academy of Pediatrics recently endorsed the goal of *Healthy People 2010* to reduce the number of children and youth with disabilities in congregate care facilities to zero by the year 2010."[58] For Gunther and Diekema, such an ambitious goal both requires and justifies bold new approaches such as growth attenuation; it also requires other doctors to take up the practice with their own patients.

Throughout the piece, Gunther and Diekema stress the efficacy of high-dose estrogen treatment in order to make the case for its use with other disabled children. Quite simply, their goal is to

> make an argument for the careful application of such a treatment strategy in nonambulatory, profoundly impaired children. We believe that foreshortening growth in these children could result in a positive benefit in the quality of life for both child and caregiver, and we propose that in situations in which parents request such an intervention, it is both medically feasible and ethically defensible.[59]

As this passage suggests, Gunther and Diekema see the Treatment as more appropriate for some children than others ("nonambulatory, profoundly impaired children"), but they refrain from setting out strict or definitive criteria, opening the door for even wider applicability. Aware that the Treatment might be controversial, they suggest the formation of a decision-making board to determine the appropriateness of the Treatment in particular cases; this recognition of the need for outside observers proves that they imagined the Treatment as having a life beyond Ashley.

Similarly, Ashley's parents imagine their blog as a resource for other parents seeking such treatments for their children; the subtitle of the blog makes this desire plain: "Towards a Better Quality of Life for 'Pillow Angels.'" The plural "angels" makes clear that they do not see Ashley as a unique case. "It is our hope," they explain, "that this treatment becomes well-accepted and available to such families, so they can bring its benefits to their special needs child if appropriate and at an optimal age in order to obtain the most benefits." They insist that the blog is not a defense or justification of the Treatment but rather a place to "share their learned lessons."[60] To that end, they offer a one-page summary of the Treatment—"The 'Ashley Treatment' for the wellbeing of 'Pillow Angels'"—that breaks down each component of the Treatment in terms of its primary and secondary benefits to Ashley. They urge other parents interested in the Treatment to contact them for advice and assistance, stressing that the Treatment is not limited to girls; in fact, they suggest, "it even makes more sense in [boys'] case, since boys tend to grow taller and bigger."[61]

Ashley's parents claim to have heard from "about a dozen" families who have successfully acquired the Treatment for their children (both boys and girls). Other families have apparently tried to do so, but without success; the blog mentions a family whose request was denied at the last minute, not by the ethics committee but because of "PR concerns."[62] More promisingly, from Ashley's parents' perspective, is the growing acceptance of growth attenuation by pediatric specialists. On their blog, they mention a packed session on growth attenuation at the 2008 Pediatric Academic Societies Meeting; according to a doctor present at the session, "half of the room said they had been approached by a family seeking growth attenuation, and about a dozen raised their hands when asked if they had offered it to a family."[63] Moreover, the recent report by the SWG proves that Ashley's parents and doctors have been successful in getting the medical and bioethics communities to take the Treatment seriously; the group's finding that growth attenuation is morally permissible under certain conditions and guidelines suggests that the practice may very well become more common.[64] Even when the

Treatment first made news, and the voices of critics were more prominent, many observers saw the procedures as acceptable. A 2007 MSNBC poll, for example, found that 59 percent of respondents supported the decisions by Ashley's parents.[65]

Reading the "testimonials" and "letters of support" posted on the parents' blog drives home how persuasive Ashley's parents and doctors have been in making their case. Countless medical professionals, caregivers, and parents of disabled children have written to voice their support and, often, their wish that the Treatment had been available to the people in their care. Many of these responses illustrate the slippery expansiveness of categories like "pillow angel" and "severely disabled." While Ashley's parents, her doctors, and ethicists have all offered guidelines for the degree of impairment required for the Treatment to be appropriate (the most common criteria are "nonambulatory" and "noncommunicative"), those parameters are not universally accepted.[66] One parent writes, for example,

> I am the father of a child (now 16) born with Spina Bifida. Whitley is paralyzed [sic] from the waist down. We were talking about your daughter and the treatment that you were giving Ashley. ... Whitley agrees with me that if she was much smaller the effort she would need to "get around" would be much easier. She weighs about 120 lbs and is 4'11" tall. She is a handful to lift. God bless you and Ashley and keep up the good work for her, God is guiding you in a good direction.[67]

Whitley and her father would perhaps not get their wish for the Treatment; not only is she likely too old to benefit, an ethics committee might not approve its use with someone of her level of impairment. She is able not merely to communicate, but to evaluate her situation and express her own desires; she may not be able to walk, but she is able to "get around." She is not impaired enough, in other words, to qualify for the

Treatment, at least according to the criteria recommended by the SWG. But, according to her father, she *is* sufficiently impaired. His comments reveal that the attempt to draw bright lines between classes of disability is rarely successful; one person's "severe" may be another's "moderate" or "mild." Supporters of the Treatment insist that it is to be used only in rare cases, cases of "profoundly impaired" children, and that concerns of its being expanded to cover ever-broader categories of disability are overblown. They may be right; yet, as Whitley's father makes clear, defining "profound" impairment constitutes contested, and slippery, terrain.

THE FUTURE WILL BE PRIVATIZED: THE ASHLEY CASE IN CONTEXT

Discourses surrounding the Ashley Treatment serve as a template not only for future medical interventions or standards of care but also for how to view the place of disability and caregiving in the early twenty-first century. The future invoked by the Ashley Treatment is a wholly privatized one: disability and disabled people belong in the private sphere, cared for by and within the nuclear family; and the nuclear family should be the sole arbiter of what happens within it. This is not to say that such cases have no bearing on the public sphere, but rather that the public sphere is to have little bearing on such cases. Even as the case is debated in public, it is repeatedly cast by supporters of the Treatment as a private matter. We can see traces of this position in the family's insistence that there was no need for judicial review in this case. In their response to the WPAS investigation, they go so far as to suggest that judicial oversight should never play a role in private, familial deliberations involving children like Ashley:

> While we support laws protecting vulnerable people against involuntary sterilization, the

law appears to be too broadly based to distinguish between people who are or can become capable of decision making and those who have a grave and unchanging medical condition such as Ashley, who will never become remotely capable of decision making. Requiring a court order for all hysterectomies performed on all disabled persons regardless of medical condition, complexity, severity, or prognosis puts an onerous burden on already over-burdened families of children with medical conditions as serious as Ashley's.[68]

This rejection of judicial oversight dovetails with long-standing cultural presumptions about the objectivity and authority of Western medicine. Within this framework, doctors and scientists are objective observers of the truth of the body, uniquely able to read, interpret, and understand the mind and body. Logically, then, medical experts are better able to evaluate and adjudicate questions of medical ethics because they can bracket their own political or emotional investments and focus only on the case at hand. They are able, as Donna Haraway puts it, to perform the "god trick of seeing everything from nowhere," making decisions free from bias or subjective opinion.[69] Dr. Diekema's response to the WPAS recommendations serves as a case in point. Challenging the WPAS demand for the addition of disability advocates to hospital ethics committees, Diekema asserts that "ethics committees are not for people with political agendas."[70] With this claim, Diekema positions people living with disability—family members, disability advocates, and disabled people, i.e., those constituting community members within the framework of the WPAS report—as political actors in ways that doctors and bioethicists are not. Such professionals apparently have no such "political agendas" and therefore are the only proper members of ethics committees. Families—such as Ashley's parents—play an integral role in medical decisions, but only in terms of their own families' cases; their agendas turn political if directed outward, beyond their individual situations. Noteworthy is Diekema's depoliticization not only of doctors and bioethicists but of the whole decision-making process. Both disability and decisions about disability are private concerns rather than political ones.

Thus, parents, with guidance from doctors, are the only ones with standing in such cases. As Ashley's parents explain on their blog, "In our opinion, only parents with special-needs children are in a position to fully relate to this topic. Unless you are living the experience, you are speculating and you have no clue what it is like to be the bedridden child or their caregivers."[71] Leaving aside for the moment their assumption that parents are always the best—indeed the only—spokespeople for disabled children, I want to focus on how their rhetoric excludes all other voices from this debate. Parents are not only the ultimate arbiters but also the only ones with any right to speak or reflect on the case; both decision making and debate belong only within the realm of the family. As a result, outside observers are invited to participate only within the terms of the parent–child relationship. Many editorials, commentaries, and blogs personalized and thereby privatized the debate by phrasing it exclusively in terms of familial questions: What would you do if this were your child? Who would you want caring for your child? How would you feel if the state/the medical establishment/disability activists took away your right to determine your child's care? What would you do if an ethics committee refused you access to a treatment you knew was in your family's best interest? The very phrasing of the questions reveals how pervasive this private framing is.

One of the main themes running throughout critiques of the Ashley Treatment is the need for more social support for parents of disabled children. Supporters of the Treatment counter that such services are currently unavailable and that to "abandon" Ashley's parents to "these harsh social and economic realities" would be cruel; "Ashley does not live in a utopian world," Sarah Shannon notes in *Pediatric Nursing,* and to focus on the need for accessible houses or in-home attendant care is a "utopian view of care."[72] Shannon's read of current realities is unfortunately accurate, but calling any and all talk of social supports as utopian and therefore unreasonable denies the possibility of different futures and different presents. As Adrienne Asch and Anna Stubblefield explain, there are already-existing practices and technologies that make home care easier, such as mechanized lifts that can assist with transfers. Moreover, many "full-size" adults live successfully in independent settings and receive care outside of institutions, even without the kind of growth-stunting interventions that the Treatment involves.[73] Completely brushing aside frank talk of social supports renders these kinds of options invisible, such that the Treatment appears as the only real choice parents can make for their children.

Thus the dilemma described by Ashley's doctors is a choice between the Treatment and institutionalization: if we let her imagined grotesque body come into being, then the only possible future that can await her is the one of the institution, or what Harriet McBryde Johnson calls the "disability gulag."[74] Ashley must be protected, then, from that future location and the future body that would put her there; the Treatment is her only hope for a future away from the institution. That this is a false choice—for surely these are not the only two options, and the Treatment by no means guarantees that she will never be institutionalized—does not take away from the rhetorical power of this justification for the Treatment.

Supporters of the Treatment make a compelling case, and its power is one of the reasons why this story is essential to an analysis of crip futures. The doctors involved in the case, Ashley's parents, their supporters: all draw on rhetoric and ideas nourished and developed from within disability rights movements, but to far different effects. In their initial article, for example, Gunther and Diekema stress the importance of moving as many disabled children as possible out of institutions and other long-term care facilities, keeping them with their families and in their communities. Ashley's parents and their supporters similarly tout the importance of keeping Ashley at home, allowing her to grow up with her siblings and surrounded by people who love her rather than isolated in an institution. (Indeed, they assert that they would never place Ashley in an institution, Treatment or not.) These are undoubtedly goals shared by, and long advocated by, disability rights and independent living movements.

The use of these arguments to justify growth attenuation, sterilization, and mastectomy—as if such practices were necessary to stave off institutionalization—requires those of us concerned and invested in these movements to challenge this appropriation of language and ideology. We need to be much more vigilant and aware of the risks inherent in touting the importance of family involvement and family care. Too easily, those calls can be reinterpreted to mean that the only care worth supporting is that provided by relatives, inadvertently demonizing and pathologizing the use of paid attendants. This is not to say that family members who provide attendant care for their disabled relatives should not themselves be compensated for their work; indeed, I support consumer-directed attendant services that allow disabled people to hire their own attendants, including family members. But, as Laura Hershey explains, seeing attendant care as something best provided by a family member too easily perpetuates the idea that disability is a private problem concerning the family that has no place in the public sphere. This attitude, in turn, leads to the continued devaluation of caregiving; abysmal wages and working conditions are justified on the basis that family members—almost always women—would be doing this work anyway and therefore any compensation, no matter how meager, is sufficient.[75] Moreover, casting disability as a private, familial problem, one properly confined to the home, makes it possible to remove caregiving—regardless of whether it is provided by a relative, regardless of whether it is compensated—from the political realm of public policy. This attitude suggests that the only thing that matters is having a loving relative by one's side, rather than attending to the resources, support, and training that a loved one might need to make such caregiving sustainable over the long term.[76]

UNKNOWN FUTURES, NARROWED FUTURES: MEASURING "QUALITY OF LIFE"

The Ashley Treatment has been presented as necessary to Ashley's quality of life. Ashley will be "better off" as the result of these interventions, the story goes; her parents and doctors had to intervene in order to protect her from future harms. "Quality of life" is a familiar refrain in discussions of disability, as the term has often been used as a measure of the worth of disabled people's lives. "Measure" is perhaps too precise a term, as the meaning or criteria of "quality" of life are often taken to be common sense. Many people, regardless of dis/ability, may use the term to examine their own experiences, but disabled people often find their own quality of life described by others as if it were self-evident in their appearance or diagnosis; such discussions almost always include descriptions of the disabled person's (assumed) level of function and pain.[77] Yet accurately evaluating

function is not as easy as it might seem. If a disabled person has never been given any kind of adaptive therapy or training, or if someone has no access to adaptive equipment (or only to substandard equipment), then one's function might be much lower than one's ability. Quality of life, then, is affected by one's access to resources and bodies of knowledge rather than a necessary fact of the body/mind. Indeed, descriptions of another's pain and suffering often rely more on assumption than fact, as do presumptions about what level of function is required for a good quality of life.[78]

As a result, analyses of other people's lives, ones intended to demonstrate a certain quality of life (or lack thereof), are often ambiguous and contradictory. Descriptions of Ashley are no different, rife with inconsistencies about the nature of her life. Ashley's doctors and parents describe her as having the cognitive functioning of an infant, but her parents also talk about her experiencing confusion, feeling boredom, and having musical preferences (she reportedly waves her arms along with music that she likes). Reading each of these reactions in relation to each other suggests that Ashley's cognitive abilities might be more advanced than justifications for the Treatment assert; or, perhaps, her family is reading more into her behaviors than others can see. In either case, the combination of observations suggests that function and quality of life are not as straightforward as some analyses might claim. Given someone like Ashley, who "cannot communicate," these questions of quality of life become all the more complicated; she cannot tell us what she thinks about her life.

The issue of communication is itself complicated. According to her parents and doctors, Ashley is unable to communicate and will always remain so. This lack of communication was one of the factors used to justify the Treatment (and one the SWG extended, casting "noncommunicative" as one of the criteria used to evaluate the appropriateness of growth attenuation). But, again, as I note above, if Ashley's parents are able to track boredom, confusion, and musical preferences in Ashley's reactions, then she does not sound completely non-communicative. Perhaps she could eventually develop a means of communicating with others; in their analysis of the Ashley case, Adrienne Asch and Anna Stubblefield remind us that "there is a long history of experts underestimating the cognitive abilities of people who appear to be profoundly intellectually impaired."[79] Some parents of children with "severe" or "profound" disabilities have reported seeing changes in behavior or capacity over time, despite the fact that their children were given static, unchanging prognoses. They report that their children changed in their ability to interact with the world even if the world remained unable to recognize their interactions as communication or intent.[80] Ashley may never develop the ability to speak or interact in a normative fashion, but perhaps her "reactions" could be extended or enhanced through technologies such as assisted communication. Assisted communication—which often involves an aide helping a disabled person point toward letters, words, symbols, or pictures on a communication board (or, increasingly, electronic device)—remains controversial, but it does at least raise the question of whether Ashley's noncommunicative status is permanent or complete. There certainly are examples of people who claim to have received similar diagnoses and yet eventually learned ways to communicate with others.[81] Given that possibility, why engage in such an extensive medical intervention based in part on the fact of her noncommunication? Is there not a possibility that new technologies could enable some form of communication in the not-too-distant future?

I cannot know the answer to that question, and asking it seems only to raise a whole other set of problems and complexities. Stressing that Ashley might "get better" either through technological interventions or therapy (or both) suggests that it is the "getting better" that renders the Treatment offensive or inappropriate. And if that is the case, then the Treatment is appropriate as long as we make sure we are getting the "right" children, the ones who do not have a chance of improving their function. But drawing lines between levels of impairment is notoriously difficult and, as Eva Kittay points out, suggests that some people are more deserving of ethical concern and consideration than others.[82]

Rather the key seems to be to focus on the unknowability inherent in the case.[83] There is no way to know for certain whether the Treatment improved Ashley's quality of life. We have no baseline of "quality" by which to measure, for Ashley or for any of us. Supporters of the Treatment claim medical evidence for their assertion that the Treatment had a positive effect, but they are extrapolating from other cases or other situations. Ashley's parents' long-term quality of life likely improved, given that Ashley will remain easier to lift, and Ashley's quality of life is bound up in her parents'; if they are doing well, the odds are higher that she is doing well. But, again, we cannot know, not for certain, whether the Treatment benefited Ashley's quality of life.

Were the interventions a success in terms of reducing Ashley's pain? I don't know; I can't know. The surgery itself likely resulted in pain both physical and psychological, but perhaps that pain has faded from Ashley's memory. Perhaps that pain, now passed, is less significant than the constant pain of compressed breasts or the recurring pain of menstrual cramps. Or perhaps not. We cannot know the answers to these questions, but they are presented in Treatment-supportive discourses as self-evident. The claim that the Treatment reduced Ashley's pain is taken as fact.

Missing from this discussion of Ashley's quality of life is the possibility of pleasure; how might the Treatment have foreclosed upon a range of potential sites and sources of pleasure? It is possible that Ashley would have developed the large breasts that reportedly run in her family, and it is possible that she would have experienced discomfort from them. It seems equally possible, however, that she would have experienced pleasure from those imagined large breasts: the sensation of her shirt moving against her skin, or of her skin moving against her sheets, or of her own arms brushing against her breasts. Even the tight chest straps holding her in her chair could have been sources of pleasure: perhaps she would enjoy the sensation of support, or take pleasure in the alternation between binding and release as she was moved in and out of her wheelchair. The inability or unwillingness to imagine these pleasures is a manifestation of cultural approaches to female sexuality and disability. It is seemingly inconceivable to imagine Ashley's body—her disabled female body—as the source of any sensation other than pain. We have few tools for recognizing female sexuality, particularly disabled female sexuality, as positive; nor can we recognize the potential for a self-generated and self-directed sexuality.

Ashley's parents see the mastectomy as offering an "additional benefit to Ashley" beyond its elimination of imagined future pain; according to them, the mastectomy will also prevent "sexualization towards [her] caregiver."[84] Their syntax is odd here. To what does the "towards" refer? Is it meant to imply the possibility of a caregiver taking sexual liberties with Ashley, so that the mastectomy prevents caregivers from sexualizing her? Or does it refer to the possibility that Ashley might feel sexual when touched by her caregiver? In either case, it is a troubling rationale for the surgical removal of her breast buds. A lack of breasts does not render one safe from sexual assault or abuse, and

many would argue that such assault is more the result of a desire for power and control than of sexualization.[85] Or, if their concern is more about Ashley feeling sexual (and it is profoundly unclear what they would imagine that to mean, given their positioning of her as a noncommunicative infant), then the surgery has been justified, in part, on the need to diminish Ashley's access to pleasurable sensations. Maybe Ashley experiences pleasure from being held or hugged, from being bathed in warm water or toweled off, from nestling into a fresh bed or feeling the sun on her face. And if we can recognize those physical sensations as human pleasures to which even the disabled are entitled, then why deny her the future possibility of feeling the sensations of her breasts?[86] The Treatment foreclosed on some of the ways Ashley might experience, or understand, or interact with her own body. Her inability to describe such interactions or even to understand them intellectually does not necessarily translate into an inability to feel them.

AT THE SAME TIME, OUT OF TIME; OR, LOOKING FOR ASHLEY AMONG CRIPS AND QUEERS

"Out of time": I choose this phrase for its multiple meanings. First, Ashley's being "frozen in time" is a casting out of time; the development of her female body has been arrested, removing her from expected patterns of female development and aging. Second, the use of Ashley as a "case study" only exacerbates this frozen-ness, as scholars and activists—including myself—continue to focus on what happened to Ashley in the past, as if the intervening years never happened, as if she weren't continuing to live beyond the dates of our analyses. Third, the Treatment itself was justified on the basis of Ashley's being always already out of time: her mind and body were so asynchronous that medical intervention was necessary to prevent her from falling further out of time. Finally,

Ashley has run out of time. We are too late to stop the Treatment, too late to interrupt this representation of her as endangered by her future self or as embodied asynchrony.

To return then to where I started: In thinking about crip futurity, I find myself haunted by Ashley X. Of course, Ashley is not the only one doing the haunting. Ashley's parents suggest that there have been other pillow angels who have undergone the Treatment, and, if so, their stories remain unknown; I am haunted by that unknown. I think also of those disabled children who were altered in more traditional but no less invasive ways, children whose stories have not been seen as worth remembering, let alone preserving or disseminating.[87] Perhaps the interventions in their bodies were considered a matter of course, a part of the standard of care, and therefore not prompting judicial review or public response; or maybe they were children who were seen not as figures in a sentimental narrative but as the inevitable and unremarkable casualties of poverty, violence, and inequality. Perhaps the details of their lives were unable to capture the public imagination in the same way a white pillow angel could. Sentimentality has historically and culturally been linked with white middle-class femininity, and Ashley's representation as a "pillow angel" calls to mind these racialized discourses of domesticity and passivity. As Patricia Williams points out, the "pillow angel" label held sway in public discussions of the case in no small part because of Ashley's race and class. Williams doubts, and with good reason, that "a poor black child would have been so easily romanticized as a 'pillow angel.'"[88] Williams uses the case as a reminder that we are more concerned with the quality of some lives than others (even as the steps ostensibly taken to "ensure" that quality reveal profound ableist and misogynist anxiety).

I draw on this language of haunting to mark the difficulty of this case, to recognize the power with which it hit. In the years since this story first broke, conversations about the Ashley case have repeated and repeated themselves, a citational frequency that reveals the emotional toll the case took—and continues to take—on disabled people. I know that I continue to feel a mixture of anger, shame, and betrayal about the Ashley case: betrayal that mainstream feminists largely kept silent about the case, perhaps seeing it as only a "disability" issue; anger that these medical and surgical interventions were allowed to happen and will likely happen again; and shame that we could not save her, that we cannot reach her.

Yet supporters of the Treatment argue that disability activists have no bearing on this case because Ashley is too severely disabled to be considered a disabled person.[89] Ashley's parents, for example, refer to her as "permanently unabled" in order to distinguish her from other disabled people; "unabled" is a "new category" that includes "less than 1% of children with disability."[90] Although she does not argue for this kind of new terminology, Anita J. Tarzian agrees that it might be a "misnomer" to call Ashley disabled. Both disability rights and people-first or self-advocacy movements are concerned with individuals who "have some level of cognitive capacity," she explains, which means that these movements do not have the tools or the rhetoric to address those with "severe neurological impairments."[91]

Predominant models of disability studies and activism too often *do* skim over such people, and Ashley's situation is not, and never has been, similar to most of us working in disability studies. How, then, are we to understand the differences between our experiences even as we name us all as disabled? Or, to move in the other direction, how might such an identification—we are all Ashley X—work to trouble the binaries of functional/nonfunctional, physical/developmental, or moderate/severe disability? What work are we enabled to do by placing Ashley in the center of disability scholarship and activism, or by positioning her as part of disability communities and movements? If crip theory and critical disability studies remind us to attend not only to the experiences of disabled people but also, and especially, to the ways in which disability and ability work in the world, then we need to contest this representation of some minds and bodies as beyond the reach of disability analysis and activism.

I want to caution, then, against viewing Ashley as exceptional or her case as a spectacular anomaly. After all, there remains a very real possibility that growth attenuation (and its attendant surgeries) will be performed on other disabled kids, which means that we cannot dismiss the case as a one-time event. More to the point, Ashley herself is *not* wholly unlike the other disabled people inhabiting the pages of this book [*Feminist Queer Crip* (2013)] or the movements and scholarship discussed here. To see her differently, to accept the representation of her as "unabled" rather than "disabled," is to accept an ableist logic that positions impairment—if "severe" enough—as inherently depoliticizing; "unability" becomes the category that allows "disability" to separate itself from those bodies/minds that remain in the margins.

We will remain haunted by the Ashley case, in other words, if we refuse to look for her among crips and queers, if we refuse to recognize her as part of our work. How might we imagine futures that hold space and possibility for those who communicate in ways we do not yet recognize as communication, let alone understand? Or futures that make room for diverse, unpredictable, and fundamentally unknowable experiences of pleasure? If, as I discussed in the previous chapter, queerness entails nonheteronormative approaches to temporality, then how might we learn to approach asynchronous bodies and minds as something other than

grotesque or pathological? Reading Ashley through the lens of temporality is likely going to require changes to both our theories of disability and our approaches to queer/crip futurity. As we intervene in the representation of Ashley as abnormally asynchronous or grotesquely fertile, as we interrupt the depiction of her as developmentally and temporally other, we must take care, as feminist disability scholars and crip theorists, not to write Ashley out of our own desirably disabled futures.

NOTES

1. D. F. Gunther and D. S. Diekema, "Attenuating Growth in Children with Profound Developmental Disability: A New Approach to an Old Dilemma," *Archives of Pediatrics and Adolescent Medicine* 160, no. 10 (2006): 1014.
2. Ibid., 1014.
3. Ibid.
4. Following Laura Hershey, I capitalize "treatment" to distinguish between the specific set of surgical and medical interventions used on Ashley (what her parents term "the Ashley Treatment") and the more abstract, general notion of "treatment" as any set of practices that attempt to solve a problem. As Hershey explains, referring to the interventions as a "treatment" accepts and perpetuates the notion that Ashley's body was sick or wrong and in need of a cure. Laura Hershey, "Stunting Ashley," *off our backs* 37, no. 1 (2007): 8.
5. Gunther and Diekema, "Attenuating Growth in Children," 1014.
6. Although bloggers, journalists, and disability rights activists have tended to examine the Treatment as a whole—addressing growth attenuation, breast bud removal, and hysterectomy all at once—some of the medical and bioethics texts have separated these procedures, focusing on either the growth attenuation or the sterilization. See, for example, John Lantos, "It's Not the Growth Attenuation, It's the Sterilization!" *American Journal of Bioethics* 10, no. 1 (2010): 45–46; and Benjamin S. Wilfond, Paul Steven Miller, Carolyn Korfatis, Douglas S. Diekema, Denise M. Dudzinski, Sara Goering, and the Seattle Growth Attenuation and Ethics Working Group, "Navigating Growth Attenuation in Children with Profound Disabilities: Children's Interests, Family Decision-Making, and Community Concerns," *Hastings Center Report* 40, no. 6 (2010): 27–40.

7. Lennard Davis describes disability as "a disruption in the visual, auditory, or perceptual field as it relates to the power of the gaze." As we will see, one of the lines of defense for the Treatment was that it would make it easier for people to see and interact with Ashley; the Treatment would alleviate the alleged visual asynchrony of Ashley's mind and body. Lennard J. Davis, *Enforcing Normalcy: Disability, Deafness, and the Body* (New York: Verso, 1995), 129.

8. Gunther was Ashley's endocrinologist; along with Dr. Douglas Diekema, he is one of the doctors most closely identified with the Ashley Treatment. Gunther committed suicide in September 2007, several months after an investigative report determined that the hospital had acted improperly in sterilizing Ashley. In the years since Gunther's death, Diekema has continued to write about the case, often with Dr. Norman Fost.

9. Gunther and Diekema, "Attenuating Growth in Children," 1013.

10. Ashley's Mom and Dad, *The "Ashley Treatment": Towards a Better Quality of Life for "Pillow Angels,"* March 25, 2007 http://pillowangel.org/Ashley%20Treatment%20v7.pdf; Wilfond et al., "Navigating Growth Attenuation in Children," 27.

11. The effect of the Treatment on Ashley's growth, however, is a matter of some debate. Gunther and Diekema explain that the Treatment had to be started quickly because Ashley had already begun to show signs of a growth spurt; what they do not mention is how much of her final height she had already achieved by the time the estrogen regimen began. As Rebecca Clarren reports, there is a possibility that Ashley was already approaching her maximum size; perhaps the Treatment had only a small effect. Rebecca Clarren, "Behind the Pillow Angel," *Salon,* February 9, 2007, www.salon.com/news/feature/2007/02/09/pillow_angel/index.html.

12. As described in the investigative report, "The Washington Protection and Advocacy System (WPAS) is the federally mandated protection and advocacy (P&A) agency for the state of Washington. The P&As, which exist in every state and territory, are 'watchdog' agencies with legal authority under federal statutes to investigate allegations of abuse and neglect of persons with disabilities and to advocate for their legal and human rights." WPAS changed its name to Disability Rights Washington in 2007 and is part of the National Disability Rights Network. Washington Protection and Advocacy System, "Executive Summary—Investigative Report Regarding the 'Ashley Treatment,'" *Disability Rights Washington,* 1, last modified October 1, 2010, www.disabilityrightswa.org/home/Executive_Summary_InvestigativeReportRegardingtheAshley Treatment.pdf/view?searchterm=ashley. See lso www.disabilityrightswa.org/.

13. Washington Protection and Advocacy System, "Executive Summary," 1.

14. The committee did, however, sign off on the other two pieces of the Ashley Treatment, the mastectomy and the growth attenuation regimen: "[I]t was the consensus of the Committee members that the potential long term benefit to Ashley herself outweighed the risks; and that the procedures/interventions would improve her quality of life, facilitate home care, and avoid institutionalization in the foreseeable future." As Clarren notes in her coverage of the case, there were deep divisions in the committee and at the hospital; many at Children's felt uncomfortable with the team's decisions. Washington Protection and Advocacy System, Exhibit L., "Special CHRMC Ethics Committee Meeting/Consultation," *Investigative Report Regarding the "Ashley Treatment,"* May 4, 2004, www.disabilityrightswa.org/home/Exhibits_K_T_InvestigativeReportRegardingtheAshleyTreatment.pdf, 1; Clarren, "Behind the Pillow Angel."

15. Washington Protection and Advocacy System, Exhibit O, "Letter from Larry Jones," *Investigative Report Regarding the "Ashley Treatment,"* June 10, 2004, www.disabilityrightswa.org/home/Exhibits_K_T_InvestigativeReportRegardingtheAshleyTreatment.pdf, 1.

16. Washington Protection and Advocacy System, "Letter from Larry Jones," 4.

17. Ibid.

18. David Carlson and Deborah Dorfman, "Full Report—Investigative Report Regarding the 'Ashley Treatment,'" Washington Protection and Advocacy System, May 8, 2007, www.disabilityrightswa.org/home/Full_Report_InvestigativeReportRegardingtheAshleyTreatment.pdf, 14.

19. Carlson and Dorfman, "Full Report," 14.

20. Washington Protection and Advocacy System, Exhibit T, "Agreement Between Children's Hospital and Regional Medical Center and the Washington Protection and Advocacy System (Disability Rights Washington) Promoting Protection of Individuals with Developmental Disabilities," *Investigative Report Regarding the "Ashley Treatment,"* May 1, 2007, www.disabilityrightswa.org/home/Exhibits_K_T_InvestigativeReportRegardingtheAshleyTreatment.pdf, 1–2.

21. Jessica Marshall, "Hysterectomy on Disabled US Girl Was Illegal," *New Scientist,* May 9, 2007, www.newscientist.com/article/dn11809–hysterectomy-on-disabled-us-girl-was-illegal.html.

22. Wilfond et al., "Navigating Growth Attenuation in Children."

23. The report does not define "communicative" or "ambulatory"; according to *Dorland's Illustrated Medical Dictionary*, "ambulatory" refers to someone "able to walk" (*Dorland's* offers no definition for "communicative"), *Dorland's Illustrated Medical Dictionary* (Philadelphia: W. B. Saunders, 1994), 54; Wilfond et al., "Navigating Growth Attenuation in Children," 29, 39.

24. Although he supported the group's decision, Norman Fost asserts that "too much deference has been given to the claims of third parties" in medical decision making. He disagrees with the working group's conclusions that the perspectives of disabled people and disability advocates should be included in the decision-making progress and that families contemplating such decisions should be given information about disability organizations and experiences. Eva Feder Kittay, on the other hand, insists that growth attenuation is never "ethically or medically appropriate," and that limiting the practice to "children with profound developmental and intellectual impairments" is itself abusive and discriminatory. "If growth attenuation should not be done on children without these impairments," she argues, "then it should not be done on any children. To do otherwise amounts to discrimination." Norman Fost, "Offense to Third Parties?" *Hastings Center Report* 40, no. 6 (2010): 30; Eva Feder Kittay, "Discrimination against Children with Cognitive Impairments?" *Hastings Center Report* 40, no. 6 (2010): 32.

25. Gunther and Diekema, "Attenuating Growth in Children," 1016.

26. Ibid., 1015.

27. Amy Burkholder, "Ethicist in Ashley Case Answers Questions," *CNN.com*, January 11, 2007.

28. Daniel Gunther and Douglas Diekema, letter in reply to Carole Marcus, "Only Half of the Story," *Archives of Pediatrics and Adolescent Medicine* 161 (June 2007): 616.

29. Douglas Diekema and Norman Fost, "Ashley Revisited: A Response to the Critics," *American Journal of Bioethics* 10, no. 1 (2010): 30–44.

30. The parents never refer to the procedure as a mastectomy, only as "breast bud removal," but the hospital billing report clearly lists it as "bilat simple mastectomy." Washington Protection and Advocacy System, Exhibit R, "Hospital Billing Report," *Investigative Report Regarding the "Ashley Treatment,"* March 28, 2007, www.disabilityrightswa.org/home/Exhibits_K_T_InvestigativeReportRegardingtheAshleyTreatment.pdf, 3.

31. Ashley's Mom and Dad, *"Ashley Treatment."*

32. This interpretation makes the absence of any mention of the mastectomy in the doctors' original piece all the more disturbing.

33. Ashley's Mom and Dad, *"Ashley Treatment."*

34. The photographs on the blog are quite remarkable, but not because of their depiction of Ashley. Seen lying on her bed, or strapped into her wheelchair/stroller, she looks like an average disabled kid. What is jarring are the images of her parents and siblings, each depicted with black boxes covering their eyes and faces. For the viewer familiar with medical images of deviant bodies, it is a phenomenal switch; I am accustomed to seeing black boxes over the faces of disabled people, "freaks," and patients, but not over the faces of the normate. Yet the effect is, surprisingly, the same. The disabled person is still clearly marked as other, as fundamentally unlike the other humans in the frame. She is marked as to-be-seen, while the other bodies are protected from gaze.

35. Ashley's Mom and Dad, *"Ashley Treatment."*

36. Amy Burkholder, "Disabled Girl's Parents Defend Growth-Stunting Treatment," *CNN.com*, March 12, 2008.

37. Burkholder, "Ethicist in Ashley Case."

38. Ashley's Parents, "AT Summary," last modified March 17, 2012, http://pillowangel.org/AT-Summary.pdf.

39. John W. Jordan, "Reshaping the 'Pillow Angel': Plastic Bodies and the Rhetoric of Normal Surgical Solutions," *Quarterly Journal of Speech* 95, no. 1 (February 2009): 25.

40. Burkholder, "Ethicist in Ashley Case Answers Questions."

41. Mark Priestley, *Disability: A Life Course Approach* (Cambridge: Polity Press, 2003), 67.

42. Christopher Reeve, *Nothing Is Impossible: Reflections on a New Life* (New York: Random House, 2002), 6.

43. Licia Carlson, *The Faces of Intellectual Disability* (Bloomington: Indiana University Press, 2010), 30.

44. Gunther and Diekema, "Attenuating Growth in Children," 1016.

45. Mims, "The Pillow Angel Case—Three Bioethicists Weigh In," *Scientific American,* January 5, 2007, http://tinyurl.com/9fycg2u.

46. Ashley's Mom and Dad, *"Ashley Treatment."*

47. Gunther and Diekema, "Attenuating Growth in Children," 1016.

48. Christopher Mims, "The Pillow Angel Case."

49. Mikhail Bakhtin describes the grotesque as a temporal category, casting a senile, pregnant hag as the perfect illustration of the grotesque for her blending of youth and old age. But, as Mary Russo argues, "for the feminist reader, this image of the pregnant hag is more than ambivalent. It is loaded with all of the connotations of fear and loathing around the biological processes of reproduction and of aging." Mikhail Bakhtin, *Rabelais and His World*, trans. Helene Iswolsky (Bloomington: Indiana University

Press, 1984), 24–27; Mary Russo, *The Female Grotesque: Risk, Excess, and Modernity* (New York: Routledge, 1994), 63. On "matter out of place," see Mary Douglas, *Purity and Danger: An Analysis of Concepts of Pollution and Taboo* (London: Routledge, 2002); on disability and the grotesque, see Rosemarie Garland-Thomson, *Extraordinary Bodies: Figuring Physical Disability in American Culture and Literature* (New York: Columbia University Press, 1997), 111–15; and Margrit Shildrick, *Embodying the Monster: Encounters with the Vulnerable Self* (London: Sage, 2002).

50. George Dvorsky, "Helping Families Care for the Helpless," Institute for Ethics and Emerging Technologies, November 6, 2006, http://ieet.org/index.php/IEET/more/809/.

51. Ashley's Parents, "AT Summary," emphasis mine. Ashley's parents draw the distinction between breasts and breast buds on their blog, describing reports of Ashley's breasts being removed as a media inaccuracy. They explain that "her almond-sized breast buds (not breasts) were removed." Ashley's Mom and Dad, "Updates on Ashley's Story," January 9, 2007, www.pillowangel.org/updates.htm.

52. Ashley's Parents, "AT Summary."

53. Ashley's Mom and Dad, *"Ashley Treatment,"* 9–10.

54. Ashley's Parents, "AT Summary."

55. Gunther and Diekema, "Attenuating Growth in Children," 1015.

56. As Patricia Williams notes, it is hard to imagine parents or doctors choosing to castrate a young boy because of fears that his penis or testicles might cause pain and discomfort. Patricia J. Williams, "Judge Not?" *Nation* (New York), March 26, 2007, 9.

57. If we view the hysterectomy as a key component of the Treatment, however, then their "new approach" isn't really all that new. Indeed, this phrasing is one of several moments in which justifications of the Treatment echo early eugenic arguments. Many eugenicists presented sterilization as a "humane" alternative to institutionalization; through sterilization, communities could be "protected" from the reproduction of the "feeble-minded," and the "feeble-minded" could be "allowed" to return to their home communities.

58. Gunther and Diekema, "Attenuating Growth in Children," 1013. This goal of deinstitutionalization has obviously not been met, and the rampant budget cutting underway on both the state and federal level makes progress seem unlikely. The more recent *Healthy People 2020* plan stakes out a similar goal but, like the earlier report, does not include a detailed plan for its achievement. See *Healthy People 2020*, accessed July 8, 2011, www.healthypeople.gov/2020/topicsobjectives2020/overview.aspx?topicid=9.

59. Gunther and Diekema, "Attenuating Growth in Children," 1014.

60. Indeed, they criticize media reports for depicting their blog as a defense of the Treatment; on the contrary, they assert, the blog was always intended as a way to share the Treatment with other families. Ashley's Mom and Dad, "Updates on Ashley's Story," January 9, 2007.

61. Ashley's Mom and Dad, *"Ashley Treatment."*

62. Ashley's Mom and Dad, "Third Anniversary Update," January 13, 2010, www.pillowangel.org/updates.htm. For the story of one family who, with assistance from Ashley's parents, successfully acquired the Treatment for their daughter, see Karen McVeigh, "The 'Ashley Treatment': Erica's Story," *Guardian* (UK), March 16, 2012, www.guardian.co.uk/society/2012/mar/16/ashley-treatment-ericas-story.

63. Ibid.

64. Indeed, according to a recent article in the *Guardian*, the Treatment is "on the rise." Ed Pilkington and Karen McVeigh, "'Ashley Treatment' On the Rise amid Concerns from Disability Rights Groups," *Guardian* (UK), March 15, 2012, www.guardian.co.uk/society/2012/mar/15/ashley-treatment-rise-amid-concerns.

65. Cited in Wilfond et al., "Navigating Growth Attenuation in Children," 27.

66. David Allen, Michael Kappy, Douglas Diekema, and Norman Fost, "Growth-Attenuation Therapy: Principles for Practice," *Pediatrics* 123, no. 6 (2009): 1556–61; Gunther and Diekema, "Attenuating Growth in Children"; and Wilfond et al., "Navigating Growth Attenuation in Children."

67. "Testimonies from Families and Caregivers with Direct Experience," *"Ashley Treatment,"* accessed March 2, 2012, www.pillowangel.org/testimonies.htm.

68. Ashley's Mom and Dad, "Updates on Ashley's Story," May 8, 2007, www.pillowangel.org/updates.htm.

69. Haraway distinguishes this traditional understanding of objectivity from the embodied feminist objectivity of partial perspectives and situated knowledges. Donna J. Haraway, *Simians, Cyborgs, and Women: The Reinvention of Nature* (New York: Routledge, 1991), 189.

70. Carol M. Ostrom, "Child's Hysterectomy Illegal, Hospital Agrees," *Seattle Times*, May 9, 2007, http://community.seattletimes.nwsource.com/archive/?date=20070509&slug=childrens09m.

71. Ashley's Mom and Dad, *"Ashley Treatment."*

72. Sarah E. Shannon and Teresa A. Savage, "The Ashley Treatment: Two Viewpoints," *Pediatric Nursing* 32, no. 2 (2007): 177.

73. Adrienne Asch and Anna Stubblefield, "Growth Attenuation: Good Intentions, Bad Decision," *American Journal of Bioethics* 10, no. 1 (2010): 46–48.

74. Harriet McBryde Johnson, "The Disability Gulag," *New York Times Magazine*, November 23, 2003, www.nytimes.com/2003/11/23/magazine/the-disability-gulag.html.

75. Laura Hershey, *Just Help*, 207–35. See also Eileen Boris and Rhacel Salazar Parreñas, eds., *Intimate Labors: Cultures, Technologies, and the Politics of Care* (Stanford, CA: Stanford University Press, 2010); and Evelyn Nakano Glenn, *Forced to Care: Coercion and Caregiving in America* (Cambridge, MA: Harvard University Press, 2010).

76. Reed Cooley, "Disabling Spectacles: Representations of Trig Palin and Cognitive Disability," *Journal of Literary and Cultural Disability Studies* 5, no. 3 (2011): 309.

77. For an insightful discussion of "the problem of projection" in determinations of another's quality of life, and especially of the prominence of "suffering" in such determinations, see Carlson, *Faces of Intellectual Disability.*

78. Moreover, as Susan Wendell explains, "function" is also determined by one's cultural and historical context. Susan Wendell, *The Rejected Body: Feminist Philosophical Reflections on Disability* (New York: Routledge, 1996).

79. Adrienne Asch and Anna Stubblefield, "Growth Attenuation: Good Intentions, Bad Decision," *American Journal of Bioethics* 10, no. 1 (2010): 47.

80. Sara Goering, "Revisiting the Relevance of the Social Model of Disability," *American Journal of Bioethics* 10, no. 1 (2010): 55. For one account of such shifts, see Eva Kittay and Jeffrey Kittay, "Whose Convenience? Whose Truth?" *Hastings Center Bioethics Forum,* February 28, 2007, www.thehastingscenter.org/Bioethicsforum/Post.aspx?id=350&blogid=140.

81. Anne McDonald describes herself as a former pillow angel; she spent most of her childhood in an institution where she was assumed to be fully, and permanently, noncommunicative. Anne McDonald, "The Other Story from a 'Pillow Angel,'" *Seattle Post-Intelligencer,* June 16, 2007, www.seattlepi.com/opinion/319702_noangel17.html. See also Jeremy L. Brunson and Mitchell E. Loeb, eds., "Mediated Communication," special issue of *DSQ: Disability Studies Quarterly* 31, no. 4 (2011); and Nirmala Erevelles, "Signs of Reason: Rivière, Facilitated Communication, and the Crisis of the Subject," in *Foucault and the Government of Disability,* ed. Shelley Tremain (Ann Arbor: University of Michigan Press, 2005): 45–64.

82. Kittay, "Discrimination against Children with Cognitive Impairments?" 32.

83. Asch and Stubblefield make a similar point, stressing that neither the supporters nor the critics of the Treatment can know for certain how the interventions have affected Ashley or what her experiences of them were. They explain, "Ashley's parents and doctors decided to proceed with her growth attenuation with good intentions in circumstances of uncertainty about how Ashley experiences herself and the world. Our objection to performing growth attenuation procedures on children like Ashley is also based on good intentions in identical circumstances of uncertainty. So the acceptability of this intervention cannot be decided based on which side has better intentions or on which side has more certain knowledge of what life is like for Ashley." Asch and Stubblefield, "Growth Attenuation," 46–47.

84. Ashley's Parents, "AT Summary."

85. For more on violence against people with disabilities, see, for example, Mark Sherry, *Disability Hate Crimes: Does Anyone Really Hate Disabled People?* (Burlington, VT: Ashgate, 2010); and Dick Sobsey, D. Wells, R. Lucardie, and S. Mansell, eds., *Violence and Disability: An Annotated Bibliography* (Baltimore, MD: Paul H. Brookes Publishing, 1995).

86. I refer here only to the kind of sensations I mentioned above: the binding and release of her seat belts; the feel of her clothes rubbing across her skin; warm bathwater. To be clear, I am not in any way condoning or encouraging sexual acts with someone unable to consent. Urging for a recognition that Ashley might feel pleasure in her body, through her skin, is significantly different from encouraging others to take pleasure (or power, or control) in her body.

87. Ashley is not the only child to have had her body medically and surgically altered through interventions that were cast as necessary to her quality of life. Children born intersexed or with "ambiguous" genitalia have faced all kinds of surgical interventions intended to normalize them without regard to their pain, sense of self, or relation to their bodies. Other children have endured limb-lengthening or limb-straightening procedures or have been made to wear braces and splints that often led to chronic pain and no real increase in function.

88. Williams, "Judge Not?" 9.

89. Anita J. Tarzian notes that a similar phenomenon and critique happened with the Terri Schiavo case: disability rights activists, organizations, and scholars treated the case as a disability issue (even as they disagreed about the proper course of action), while critics disputed the relevance of the case to disability rights. Anita J. Tarzian, "Disability and Slippery Slopes," *Hastings Center Report* 37, no. 5 (2007): C3.

90. Ashley's Parents, "AT Summary."

91. Tarzian, "Disability and Slippery Slopes," C3.

CHAPTER 21

Centering Justice on Dependency and Recovering Freedom

Eva Feder Kittay

SUMMARY

Eva Feder Kittay reveals how her relationship with her daughter has inspired questions about her philosophical beliefs of cognitive disability and personhood. In this essay, she asserts that it is necessary to reformulate any theory of social justice that would treat her daughter as a nonperson. Any adequate theory of justice must account for the interdependency that structures all human lives.

In Kittay's view, justice provides the fair terms of social life, given our mutual and inevitable dependency and our inextricable interdependency. The way to include disabled people is to focus on the vulnerability of all human beings. Although disabled people have made great strides to gain and acknowledge their independence, Kittay suggests that gaining employment or even mobility is not independence as such. Rather, disabled people gain independence from certain forms of oppression while remaining actually dependent on other conditions and social arrangements. That's why it is important to create a social structure that can meet the needs for many different forms of dependence.

Kittay proposes replacing the theoretical social contract with a covenant in which the responsibilities and constraints benefit not only the contracting parties but also those who are affected by their agreements. Such a covenant model offers justice to people with cognitive or other disabilities who are least able to offer a self-determination of their interests. It might also respond to the complicated relationship between disability and independence, in which the cost of living with a disability is unfairly shifted to the disabled person and his or her family. By focusing our concepts of justice on the inevitability of dependency, Kittay suggests, we can find a source of value and a place for connection.

[T]he loathing and disgust which many people have at the sight of an idiot is a feeling which, though having some foundation in human nature, is not necessarily attached to it in any virtuous degree, but is owing in a great measure to a false delicacy, and, if I may say it without rudeness, a certain want of comprehensiveness of thinking and feeling.

> (William Wordsworth, "Letter to John Wilson (on the poem *The Idiot Boy*)")

[T]here is a question about how the limits of the practicable are discerned and what the conditions of our social world in fact are; the problem here is that the limits of the possible are not given by the actual, for we can to a greater or lesser extent change political and social institutions, and much else.

> (John Rawls, "Justice as Fairness," s1.4)

INTRODUCTION

Starting with Sesha

In the summer of 2001, Anita Silvers and I co-directed the NEH Summer Institute on

Justice and Disability. There we began to exchange our very different views on what it means to include disability within theories of justice. Our work has developed in part in response to each other's thinking and writing. As we have responded to each other, we have learned from each other, and our views today are more compatible and less divergent than they were when we each started on our journeys. Yet we each come to the experience very differently, and this is reflected in our different approaches.

My relationship to disability began when I first became a mother in 1969. Shortly after my daughter Sesha's birth, my partner and I began to understand that she was not developing as other babies were and that she would have severe lifelong disabilities, primarily cognitive disabilities. This realization came while I was still a graduate student in philosophy. I have already written quite a bit about my daughter Sesha and the way in which she has had a profound impact on the way I thought about a number of philosophical issues. Some readers might be familiar with her from my writings or (more likely) from the writings of such notables as Martha Nussbaum, Anita Silvers and Leslie Francis, or William Kymlicka. (I tell her that she is much more famous and more frequently cited than her mother.) As I studied philosophy, and later taught and wrote, there was always a bracketed consideration that needed attention: namely, that the world as philosophy portrayed it had no room in it for people such as my daughter. She failed to fit the definition of "man" or "personhood" or "moral agent" or—most pertinent to this essay—a subject due justice. Yet I never treated her as anything but a person, and although I did not expect moral agency from her, she radiated sweetness and light, harmony and, dare I say it, goodness; that is, goodness in the sense of a lack of malice, anger, or any sort of viciousness. If and when she was slighted or mistreated or denied what was

due anyone else, I have reacted to these as injustices. There was no point of equilibrium I could reach between the theories espoused by philosophers and the reflected considerations that guided my interactions with and expectations concerning my daughter. Although I could not calibrate my relationship to my daughter by philosophical theories without diminishing her, and robbing myself of the fullness of motherhood, I continued to believe in the importance of theory, both as an intellectual project and in its influence on practice and social policy. So I have chosen to alter the theory rather than regard my daughter as a nonperson shut out from the protections and entitlements of justice. I have concluded that if a theory of justice could not accommodate my daughter, it failed a crucial criterion of adequacy.

TOWARD A MORE INCLUSIVE THEORY OF JUSTICE

To include people like my daughter, and to make a theory more amenable to other disabilities as well, it doesn't suffice to accept the Rawlsian view of justice as fair terms of social cooperation. Those we wish to include may not fit the model of the social cooperator without a lot of distortion, if at all. Yet the notion of fair terms has something to offer us. I propose an alternative: justice provides the *fair terms of social life given our mutual and inevitable dependency and our inextricable interdependency*. The way to include *all* people with disabilities is to focus on the nature of human beings as vulnerable to

inevitable dependency
the care of inevitable dependency, and
the inextricable interdependence of humans on one another.

In a still larger vision, one could argue that our interdependence on the nonhuman world of animals and our environment is similarly a matter of justice, but I will not attempt this here.

When battling imposed dependencies, the cry for "Independence!" can be valuable. A woman who asks for the right to enter the workplace so she can be economically independent is asking for the right to be recognized as a particular sort of efficacious, self-determining agent. A disabled person who demands workplace accommodation so that she can be independent is similarly asserting the right to such recognition. But workers are dependent on their bosses, entrepreneurs are dependent on their investors and their customers, and so on. Entering the workforce and being able to earn a living is not independence as such but independence from certain oppressive conditions, and a dependence on other conditions that are hopefully more respectful of our desire to be efficacious agents.

We are inextricably interdependent. The notion of social cooperation captures elements of this interdependence, but retains some of the fiction that as self-determining and self-sufficient agents we can take or leave this cooperative arrangement if we do not agree to the terms. To insist on our inextricable interdependence is to say that no matter what social arrangements we enter into on a voluntaristic basis, the fact is that we must be engaged in *some* social arrangements, some forms of dependence; interdependence is not a matter of voluntarism.

This is because a social structure needs to be in place to meet our needs as dependents, dependency workers, and in our role as providers of resources needed in our dependency and in our dependency work. The most ubiquitous of dependency relations, that of infant and caregiver, requires more than a dyadic relationship. Because human infants are as needy and helpless as they are, a single person alone can rarely succeed without social supports to care for that infant. For this reason, argues Sara Hrdy, humans could evolve into the sorts of creatures we are only because we (and we alone among apes) had to engage in shared caregiving, a sharing of responsibilities and resources that both depend upon and help develop social capacities such as trust and cooperation (Hrdy 2009). The complex social and political structures that characterize human societies, the liberal democratic structures that appear to many as requirements for a just society, would be impossible, perhaps even inconceivable, without the capacities that arise out of the necessity of dependency relationships, and to join with Anita Silvers and Leslie Francis, the *trust* that they require and engender (Silvers and Francis 2005).

Starting from this perspective, it is impossible to see how a theory of justice can be adequate if it leaves out the needs of disabled people. Caring for one another with our different needs and capacities is a fundamental reason human beings join together in social arrangements.

If we are to respect the critical nature of social arrangements for actual human beings, human beings "as they truly are" (to invoke J. S. Mill), we want a theory of justice that provides principles for the fair terms of social life given our inevitable dependence and our inextricable interdependence. This too is justice as based on fair terms, but the point of engagement and the nature of those involved and affected by the social interactions and institutions are not idealized and fictionally independent, normal, and fully cooperating agents. In their stead are the dependent and the disabled, the caregivers and the assistants. Independence, normalcy, and the ability to engage in social cooperation are not absolute terms with fixed meaning, but relative ones (we may be *relatively* independent at this moment in our lives). Their meanings are contingent on norms we have chosen (we are *normal* given *such and such* a norm), and social institutions and physical structures we have built (with *these* social supports in place and in *this* built environment I can function *relatively* independently).

A theory this inclusive cannot be thought of as a contract because those whose interests are most in need of protection are those least able to come to the table. Contract theory, however, does important work in political theory. Among other things, it provides a framework for what constitutes legitimate coercive state power. Alternatives to contract theory such as a capabilities approach fail to do this. The idea of a covenant can retain this function but include within its parameters those who are not able to be a party to a contract. The term *covenant* has many meanings and is sometimes used simply as a synonym or as a particular form of contract (cf. Silvers and Francis 2005). The way in which I wish to understand it is twofold: First, a covenant implies a preexisting entity, relationship, or agreement, which serves as a constraint and generates responsibilities. Second, these responsibilities and constraints are not *only* (or not at all) for the benefit of the contracting parties, but for all those affected by their agreements. For example, a group of landowners joins together and makes a covenant to protect the beauty of their individual and jointly held lands and the richness of its wildlife. They agree to the restrictions on the use of this land. That agreement protects *the land* from certain forms of exploitation, and it protects the interests of present and future owners in living with the undisturbed beauty of the land. A landowner is, however, free to sell her land. Now the contracting parties are the buyer and seller—but the restraints regarding the use of that land and the responsibilities entailed in the covenant constrain them both from engaging in an exchange that might otherwise prove to be more profitable for each of them. The land and the creatures who live on it (who cannot be a party to a contract), as well as the other members of the community, all are beneficiaries of the covenant, even though they are not part of the contract between buyer and seller.

As in the case of our example, where justice is concerned, we never start *de novo*. There is already an arrangement in place—otherwise the humans involved could not have survived to adulthood. Furthermore, all those affected by the social arrangements cannot be parties to an agreement as these include those who are in different stages or degrees of dependence and may be incapable of setting forward their own interests. A covenant protects their rights and interests as well as the rights and interests of those who engaged in contracting with one another and establishing (or consenting to) the principles by which they are to live. Individuals forging relationships of obligation to one another understand that they have obligations and responsibilities to others affected by their agreements. The covenant would seek to establish fair terms of social life given our inevitable dependencies and our inextricable interdependencies. This is only a start for thinking about an alternative to contractual theories and noncontractual ones such as capability theory. This short essay aims merely to introduce the idea.

However, as this approach to justice for people with disabilities assimilates the question of justice for people with disabilities to one that centers on dependency, it is important to offer some reflections on what is sometimes an uneasy relationship between disability and dependency.

THE RELATIONSHIP BETWEEN DISABILITY AND DEPENDENCY[1]

The main organs of the disability movement have insisted that justice for disabled people means allowing them to live independently and that justice requires that society be organized so that impairments do not lead to dependency. Justice for people with disabilities has been likened to other social movements such as justice for women or for people of color. These injustices, although they invoke bodily difference, are rectified not by altering the bodies but altering the circumstances that discriminate, oppress, and otherwise disadvantage people with those marked bodies. Disabled people have claimed that the injustice of disability is no less *social* than is racism or sexism or homophobia. In some cases, however, there are residual dependencies that remain even when we have modifications in the social and physical environment intended to allow people with disabilities to function "independently." It is these dependencies, not those that are altered by changed environments, that I focus on since extant theories of justice may well have the resources to deal with disability as construed entirely on the social model.

The uneasy relationship of some in the disability community toward matters of care and dependency is not shared by all. But we should recognize that the unease is sometimes warranted. The refusal to be labeled "dependent" is based, first, on the refusal to become an infantilized object of paternalistic concern, and second, on the supposition that the source of dependency is internal to the individual. Disabled people have preferred to redefine independence as including "the vast networks of assistance and provision that make modern life possible" (Davis 2007, 4), and thus, as literary and disability scholar Lennard Davis says, "the seeming state of exception of disability turns out to be the unexceptional state of existence" (4). In demanding the means by which to become independent, disability scholars and activists provided a counter-narrative (Lindemann 2001) to the narrative of the inevitability of their dependence. Many people with impairments feel justifiably that they have been *made* dependent, just as they have

been dis-abled, by a social environment not accommodated to their bodies.

However, sorting out the different senses of independence has not always been easy, even for the disabled individual himself. As medical sociologist and disability rights activist Irving Zola discovered, the independence to which he aspired was "the quality of life that [he] . . . could live *with help*" (De Jong 1983, 15; emphasis mine).

Although the call for independence has promoted the interests and improved the life prospects of people with physical disabilities, and has successfully been expanded to include some with cognitive disabilities, there are important limitations. First, some impairments affect the capacity for self-determination, just as some impairments affect mobility or sensory perception. Second, the call for the independence of the disabled, which has too frequently been taken up by public officials when it has been tied to savings for "the public purse," can have the effect of disadvantaging those least able to fend for themselves, shifting the cost and care to struggling families. Furthermore, it can backfire when that independence requires overall increased, not reduced, costs. Third, resources and policies intended to allow disabled people independence are sometimes justified because this enables disabled people to engage in "productive" work. Although arguments that bind independence to productivity are useful insofar as most people, disabled or not, desire meaningful work, for some, no amount of accommodation can make this possible. It is an especially punishing view for those whose capacities for productive labor diminish with age (Morris 2004, 2011). Finally, the demand for independence for disabled people relies heavily on the availability and compliance of caregivers. The hazard here is that the "independence" of the disabled person may render invisible the assistant enabling this "independence" (Rivas 2002).

Can one still protect the benefits to be gained by disabled people's demands for independence without re-stigmatizing those who do not benefit and without unduly subordinating the interests of dependency workers? What I hope my approach to dependency and to justice for the disabled contributes is the acknowledgment of dependency as a condition none of us escapes entirely. The neediness and necessity of dependency appears to doom it as a feature of human life that we wish to openly acknowledge; but other conditions to which we are subject are not necessarily viewed as unfortunate. We are compelled to breathe air, a fact we rarely rue and simply accept as a condition of being alive. Our need for food does not make it loathsome. Instead, the need is turned into occasions for sociality, artisanship—even artistry, cultural identification, and so forth.

It is not the necessity and neediness of dependency that repels us, it is the disadvantages that are a consequence of political, social, and economic arrangements. By centering a theory of justice on the inevitability of human dependency and the inextricable nature of our interdependence, we can then look at the fact of human dependency anew. We see it not as an impediment to living well, but as a source of value: a source of connection; an occasion for developing our capacities for thought, empathy, sensitivity, trust, ingenuity, and creativity; in short, as providing for us the conditions of our distinctive human freedom and dignity.

NOTE

This essay is part of a presentation I made at the Eastern APA Session for the Leibowitz Prize winners. I want to express my deep appreciation to the Leibowitz Family Foundation, APA and the Phi Beta Kappa society for this extraordinary recognition and opportunity to engage publicly with my very esteemed co-winner, Anita Silvers.

1. This section borrows heavily on Kittay 2015.

REFERENCES

Davis, Lennard J. 2007. Dependency and justice: A review of Martha Nussbaum's frontiers of justice. *Journal of Literary Disability* 1 (2): 1–4.

DeJong, G. 1983. Defining and implementing the independent living concept. In *Independent living for physically disabled people*, ed. Nancy Crew and Irving K. Zola. San Francisco: Jossey-Bass Publishers.

Hrdy, Sarah Blaffer. 2009. *Mothers and others: The evolutionary origins of mutual understanding.* Cambridge, MA: Belknap Press.

Kittay, Eva Feder. 2015. Dependency. In *Keywords in disability studies*, ed. Rachael Adams and Benjamin Reiss. New York: New York University Press.

Lindemann, Hilde. 2001. *Damaged identities: Narrative repair.* Ithaca, NY: Cornell University Press.

Morris, Jenny. 2004. Independent living and community care: A disempowering framework. *Disability and Society* 19 (5): 427–42.

——. 2011. "Rethinking disability policy." Posted on 15 November. https://www.jrf.org.uk/report/rethinking-disability-policy

Rawls, John. 2001. *Justice as fairness: A restatement*, ed. E. Kelly. Cambridge, MA: Harvard University Press.

Rivas, Lynn May. 2002. Invisible labors: Caring for the independent person. In *Global women: Nannies, maids, and sex workers in the global economy*, ed. Barbara Ehrenreich and Arlie Russell Hochchild. New York: Henry Holt.

Silvers, Anita, and Leslie Pickering Francis. 2005. Justice through trust: Disability and the "outlier problem" in social contract theory. *Ethics* 116 (1): 40–76.

PART V

*I*dentities and Intersectionalities

Disability and the Theory of Complex Embodiment: For Identity Politics in a New Register

Tobin Siebers

SUMMARY

In this chapter, Tobin Siebers critiques the ideology of ability that entails a preference for ablebodiedness and defines humanness by bodily measures. This ideology creates exclusionary social locations and labels them as disability. But, Siebers argues, the "invisible center" of disability identity can present a critical framework that disturbs ableism's ideological assumptions.

Identity is the means by which a person comes to join a social body—all the narratives, ideas, myths, and values that represent the individual's capacity to join a collective. Cultural theorists have long questioned the value of identity politics, but Siebers defends disability identity by claiming that experiences based on disability have the status of theory because they represent forms of embodiment from which dominant ideologies become visible.

For Siebers, it does little to conclude that an ideology about identity is socially constructed. Rather, we should locate that construction in a specific time and place and a complex form of embodiment. The theory of complex embodiment accounts for both the effects of a disabling environment and the lived experience of the body. The body and its representations mutually transform each other: what we think of a body is informed by the lived experience, and the experience of living with the body is informed by the social prejudices and ideologies that represent the body. The theory of complex embodiment promises to give disabled people greater control over their bodies where increased knowledge and control are possible. It also supports arguments about social construction, identity and the body that are better suited to the experiences of disabled people.

THE IDEOLOGY OF ABILITY

We seem caught as persons living finite lives between two sets of contradictory ideas about our status as human beings. The first contradiction targets our understanding of the body itself. On the one hand, bodies do not seem to matter to who we are. They contain or dress up the spirit, the soul, the mind, the self. I am, as Descartes explained, the thinking part. At best, the body is a vehicle, the means by which we convey who we are from place to place. At worst, the body is a fashion accessory. We are all playing at Dorian Gray, so confident that the self can be freed from the dead weight of the body, but we have forgotten somehow to read to the end of the novel. On the other hand, modern culture feels the urgent need to perfect the body. Whether medical scientists are working on a cure for the common cold or the elimination of all disease, a cure for cancer or the banishment of death, a cure for HIV/AIDS or control of the genetic code, their preposterous and yet rarely questioned goal is to give everyone a perfect body. We hardly ever consider how incongruous is this understanding of the body—that the body seems both inconsequential and perfectible.

A second but related contradiction targets the understanding of the human being in time. The briefest look at history reveals that human beings are fragile. Human life confronts the overwhelming reality of sickness, injury, disfigurement, enfeeblement, old age, and death. Natural disasters, accidents, warfare and violence, starvation, disease, and pollution of the natural environment attack human life on all fronts, and there are no survivors. This is not to say that life on this earth is wretched and happiness nonexistent. The point is simply that history reveals one unavoidable truth about human beings—whatever our destiny as a species, we are as individuals feeble and finite. And yet the vision of the future to which we often hold promises an existence that bears little or no resemblance to our history. The future obeys an entirely different imperative, one that commands our triumph over death and contradicts everything that history tells us about our lot in life. Many religions instruct that human beings will someday win eternal life. Science fiction fantasizes about aliens who have left behind their mortal sheath; they are superior to us, but we are evolving in their direction. Cybernetics treats human intelligence as software that can be moved from machine to machine. It promises a future where human beings might be downloaded into new hardware whenever their old hardware wears out. The reason given for exploring human cloning is to defeat disease and aging. Apparently, in some future epoch, a quick trip to the spare-parts depot will cure what ails us; people will look better, feel healthier, and live three times longer. Finally, the human genome project, like eugenics before it, places its faith in a future understanding of human genetics that will perfect human characteristics and extend human life indefinitely.

However stark these contradictions, however false in their extremes, they seem credible in relation to each other. We are capable of believing at once that the body does not matter and that it should be perfected. We believe at once that history charts the radical finitude of human life but that the future promises radical infinitude. That we embrace these contradictions without interrogating them reveals that our thinking is steeped in ideology. Ideology does not permit the thought of contradiction necessary to question it; it sutures together opposites, turning them into apparent complements of each other, smoothing over contradictions, and making almost unrecognizable any perspective that would offer a critique of it. In fact, some cultural theorists claim to believe that ideology is as impenetrable as the Freudian unconscious—that there is no outside to ideology, that it can contain any negative, and that it sprouts contradictions without suffering them (see Goodheart 1996; Siebers 1999). I argue another position: ideology creates, by virtue of its exclusionary nature, social locations outside of itself and therefore capable of making epistemological claims about it. The arguments that follow here are based on the contention that oppressed social locations create identities and perspectives, embodiments and feelings, histories and experiences that stand outside of and offer valuable knowledge about the powerful ideologies that seem to enclose us.

This book [*Disability Theory* (2008)] pursues a critique of one of these powerful ideologies—one I call the ideology of ability. The ideology of ability is at its simplest the preference for ablebodiedness. At its most radical, it defines the baseline by which humanness is determined, setting the measure of body and mind that gives or denies human status to individual persons. It affects nearly all of our judgments, definitions, and values about human beings, but because it is discriminatory and exclusionary, it creates social locations outside of and critical of its purview, most notably in this case, the perspective of disability. Disability defines the invisible center around which our contradictory ideology about human ability revolves. For the ideology of ability makes us fear disability, requiring that we imagine our bodies are of no consequence while dreaming at the same time that we might perfect them. It describes disability as what we flee in the past and hope to defeat in the future. Disability identity stands in uneasy relationship to the ideology of ability, presenting a critical framework that disturbs and critiques it.

One project of this book is to define the ideology of ability and to make its workings legible and familiar, despite how imbricated it may be in our thinking and practices, and despite how little we notice its patterns, authority, contradictions, and influence as a result. A second and more important project is to bring disability out of the shadow of the ideology of ability, to increase awareness about disability, and to illuminate its kinds, values, and realities. Disability creates theories of embodiment more complex than the ideology of ability allows, and these many embodiments are each crucial to the understanding of humanity and its variations, whether physical, mental, social, or historical. These two projects unfold slowly over the course of my argument for the simple reason that both involve dramatic changes in thinking. The level of literacy about disability is so low as to be nonexistent, and the ideology of ability is so much a part of every action, thought, judgment, and intention that its hold on us is difficult to root out. The sharp difference between disability and ability may be grasped superficially in the idea that disability is essentially a "medical matter," while ability concerns natural gifts, talents, intelligence, creativity, physical prowess, imagination, dedication, the eagerness to strive, including the capacity and desire to strive—in brief, the essence of the human spirit. It is easy to write a short list about disability, but the list concerning ability goes on and on, almost without end, revealing the fact that we are always dreaming about it but rarely thinking critically about why and how we are dreaming.

I resort at the outset to the modern convention of the bullet point to introduce the ideology of ability as simply as possible. The bullet points follow without the thought of being exhaustive or avoiding contradiction and without the full commentary that they deserve. Some of the bullets are intended to look like definitions; others describe ability or disability as operators; others still gather stereotypes and prejudices. The point is to begin the accumulation of ideas, narratives, myths, and stereotypes about disability whose theory this book seeks to advance, to provide a few small descriptions on which to build further discussion of ability as an ideology, and to start readers questioning their own feelings about ability and disability:

- Ability is the ideological baseline by which humanness is determined. The lesser the ability, the lesser the human being.
- The ideology of ability simultaneously banishes disability and turns it into a principle of exclusion.
- Ability is the supreme indicator of value when judging human actions, conditions, thoughts, goals, intentions, and desires.
- If one is able-bodied, one is not really aware of the body. One feels the body only when something goes wrong with it.
- The able body has a great capacity for self-transformation. It can be trained to do almost anything; it adjusts to new situations. The disabled body is limited in what it can do and what it can be trained to do. It experiences new situations as obstacles.

- Disability is always individual, a property of one body, not a feature common to all human beings, while ability defines a feature essential to the human species.
- Disability can be overcome through will power or acts of the imagination. It is not real but imaginary.
- "Disability's no big deal," as Mark O'Brien writes in his poem, "Walkers" (1997, 36).
- It is better to be dead than disabled.
- Nondisabled people have the right to choose when to be able-bodied. Disabled people must try to be as able-bodied as possible all the time.
- Overcoming a disability is an event to be celebrated. It is an ability in itself to be able to overcome disability.
- The value of a human life arises as a question only when a person is disabled. Disabled people are worth less than nondisabled people, and the difference is counted in dollars and cents.
- Disabilities are the gateway to special abilities. Turn disability to an advantage.
- Loss of ability translates into loss of sociability. People with disabilities are bitter, angry, self-pitying, or selfish. Because they cannot see beyond their own pain, they lose the ability to consider the feelings of other people. Disability makes narcissists of us all.
- People who wish to identify as disabled are psychologically damaged. If they could think of themselves as able-bodied, they would be healthier and happier.

To reverse the negative connotations of disability apparent in this list, it will be necessary to claim the value and variety of disability in ways that may seem strange to readers who have little experience with disability studies. But it is vital to show to what extent the ideology of ability collapses once we "claim disability" as a positive identity (Linton 1998). It is equally vital to understand that claiming disability, while a

significant political act, is not only political but also a practice that improves quality of life for disabled people. As documented in the case of other minority identities, individuals who identify positively rather than negatively with their disability status lead more productive and happier lives. Feminism, the black and red power movements, as well as gay and disability pride—to name only a few positive identity formations—win tangible benefits for their members, freeing them not only from the violence, hatred, and prejudice directed toward them but also providing them with both shared experiences to guide life choices and a community in which to prosper.

Some readers with a heightened sense of paradox may object that claiming disability as a positive identity merely turns disability into ability and so remains within its ideological horizon. But disability identity does not flounder on this paradox. Rather, the paradox demonstrates how difficult it is to think beyond the ideological horizon of ability and how crucial it is to make the attempt. For thinking of disability as ability, we will see, changes the meaning and usage of ability.

MINORITY IDENTITY AS THEORY

Identity is out of fashion as a category in critical and cultural theory. While it has been associated by the Right and Left with self-victimization, group think, and political correctness, these associations are not the real reason for its fall from grace. The real reason is that identity is seen as a crutch for the person who needs extra help, who is in pain, who cannot think independently. I use the word "crutch" on purpose because the attack on identity is best understood in the context of disability.

According to Linda Martin Alcoff's extensive and persuasive analysis in *Visible Identities*, the current rejection of identity has a particular philosophical lineage, one driven, I believe, by the ideology of ability (2006, 47–83). The line of descent begins with the Enlightenment theory of rational autonomy, which represents the inability to reason as the sign of inbuilt inferiority. Usually, the defense of reason attacked non-Europeans as intellectually defective, but because these racist theories relied on the idea of biological inferiority, they necessarily based themselves from the start on the exclusion of disability. "The norm of rational maturity," Alcoff makes clear, "required a core self stripped of its identity. Groups too immature to practice this kind of abstract thought or to transcend their ascribed cultural identities were deemed incapable of full autonomy, and their lack of maturity was often 'explained' via racist theories of the innate inferiority of non-European peoples" (2006, 22). The Enlightenment view then descends to two modern theories, each of which sees dependence on others as a form of weakness that leads to oppressive rather than cooperative behavior. The first theory belongs to Freud, for whom strong identity attachments relate to pathological psychology and figure as symptoms of ego dysfunction. In psychoanalysis, in effect, a lack lies at the heart of identity (2006, 74), and those unable to overcome this lack fall into patterns of dependence and aggression. Second, in Sartre's existential ontology, identity is alienated from the real self. Identity represents for Sartre a social role, linked to bad faith and motivated by moral failing and intellectual weakness, that tempts the self with inauthentic existence, that is, an existence insufficiently free from the influence of others (2006, 68).

Dossier No. 1 *The Nation* November 6, 2006

Show Him the Money

By Katha Pollitt

I wanted to admire *The Trouble with Diversity*, Walter Benn Michaels's much-discussed polemic against identity politics and economic inequality. Like him, I'm bothered by the extent to which symbolic politics has replaced class grievances on campus, and off it too: the obsessive cultivation of one's roots, the fetishizing of difference, the nitpicky moral one-upmanship over language. Call an argument "lame" on one academic-feminist list I'm on and you'll get—still!—an electronic earful about your insensitivity to the disabled. . . .

These two strains of thinking, despite their differences, support the contemporary distrust of identity. Thus, for Michel Foucault and Judith Butler—to name two of the most influential theorists on the scene today—identity represents a "social necessity that is also a social pathology" (Alcoff 2006, 66); there supposedly exists no form of identity not linked ultimately to subjugation by others. In short, contemporary theorists banish identity when they associate it with lack, pathology, dependence, and intellectual weakness. Identity in their eyes is not merely a liability but a disability.

Notice, however, that identity is thought defective only in the case of minorities, whereas it plays no role in the critique of majority identifications, even among theorists who assail them. For example, no one attacks Americanness specifically because it is an identity. It may be criticized as an example of nationalism, but identity receives little or no mention in the critique. Identity is attacked most frequently in the analysis of minority identity—only people of color, Jews, Muslims, gay, lesbian, bisexual, and transgendered people, women, and people with disabilities seem to possess unhealthy identities. It is as if identity itself occupied a minority position in present critical and cultural theory—for those who reject identity appear to do so only because of its minority status, a status linked again and again to disability.

Moreover, the rejection of minority identity repeats in nearly every case the same psychological scenario. The minority identity, a product of damage inflicted systematically on a people by a dominant culture, is rearticulated by the suffering group as self-affirming, but because the identity was born of suffering, it is supposedly unable to shed its pain, and this pain soon comes to justify feelings of selfishness, resentment, bitterness, and self-pity—all of which combine to justify the oppression of other people. Thus, J. C. Lester (2006) complains that "the disabled are in danger of being changed," because of disability studies, "from the proper object of decent voluntary help, where there is genuine need, into a privileged and growing interest group of oppressors of more ordinary people." Nancy Fraser also points out that identity politics "encourages the reification of group identities" and promotes "conformism, intolerance, and patriarchalism" (2000, 113, 112). Even if this tired scenario were credible—and it is not because it derives from false ideas about disability—it is amazing that so-called politically minded people are worried that a few minority groups might somehow, some day, gain the power to retaliate for injustice, when the wealthy, powerful, and wicked are actively plundering the globe in every conceivable manner: the decimation of nonindustrial countries by the industrial nations, arms trafficking, enforcement of poverty to maintain the circuit between cheap labor and robust consumerism, global warming, sexual trafficking of women, industrial pollution by the chemical and oil companies, inflation of costs for drugs necessary to fight epidemics, and the cynical failure by the wealthiest nations to feed their own poor, not to mention starving people outside their borders.

My argument here takes issue with those who believe that identity politics either springs from disability or disables people for viable political action. I offer a defense of identity politics and a counterargument to the idea, embraced by the Right and Left, that identity politics cannot be justified because it is linked to pain and suffering. The idea that suffering produces weak identities both enforces the ideology of ability and demonstrates a profound misunderstanding of disability: disability is not a pathological condition, only analyzable via individual psychology, but a social location complexly embodied. Identities, narratives, and experiences based on disability have the status of theory because they represent locations and forms of embodiment from which the dominant ideologies of society become visible and open to criticism. One of my specific tactics throughout this book is to tap this theoretical power by juxtaposing my argument with dossier entries detailing disability identities, narratives, images, and experiences. The dossier is compiled for the most part from news stories of the kind that appear in major newspapers across the country every day, although I have avoided the feel-good human-interest stories dominating the news that recount how their disabled protagonists overcome their disabilities to lead "normal" lives. Rather, the dossier tends to contain testimony about the oppression of disabled people, sometimes framed in their own language, sometimes framed in the anguage of their oppressors. At first, the dossier entries may have no particular meaning to those untutored in disability studies, but my hope is that they will grow stranger and stranger as the reader progresses, until they begin to invoke feelings of horror and disgust at the blatant and persistent prejudices directed against disabled people. The dossier represents a deliberate act of identity politics, and I offer no apology for it because identity politics remains in my view the most practical course of action by which to address social injustices against minority peoples and to apply the new ideas, narratives, and experiences discovered by them to the future of progressive, democratic society.

Identity is neither a liability nor a disability. Nor is it an ontological property or a state of being. Identity is, properly defined, an epistemological construction that contains a broad array of theories about navigating social environments. Manuel Castells calls identity a collective meaning, necessarily internalized by individuals for the purpose of social action (1997, 7), while Charles Taylor argues, "My identity is defined by the commitments and identifications which provide the frame or horizon within which I can try to determine from case to case what is good, or valuable, or what ought to be done, or what I endorse or oppose" (1987, 27). Alcoff explains that "identity is not merely that which is given to an individual or group, but is also a way of inhabiting, interpreting, and working through, both collectively and individually, an objective social location and group history" (2006, 42). We do well to follow these writers and to consider identity a theory-laden construction, rather than a mere social construction, in which knowledge for social living adheres—though not always and necessarily the best knowledge. Thus, identity is not the structure that creates a person's pristine individuality or inner essence but the structure by which that person identifies and becomes identified with a set of social narratives, ideas, myths, values, and types of knowledge of varying reliability, usefulness, and verifiability. It represents the means by which the person, qua individual, comes to join a particular social body. It also represents the capacity to belong to a collective on the basis not merely of biological tendencies but symbolic ones—the very capacity that distinguishes human beings from other animals.

While all identities contain social knowledge, mainstream identities are less critical, though not less effective for being so, because they are normative. Minority identities acquire the ability to make epistemological claims about the society in which they hold liminal positions, owing precisely to their liminality. The early work of Abdul JanMohamed and David Lloyd, for example, privileges the power of the minor as critique: "The study—and production—of minority discourse requires, as an inevitable consequence of its mode of existence, the transgression of the very disciplinary boundaries by which culture appears as a sublimated form with universal validity. This makes it virtually *the* privileged domain of cultural critique" (1987, 9). The critique offered by minority identity is necessarily historical because it relies on the temporal contingency of its marginal position. Different groups occupy minority positions at different times, but this does not mean that their social location is any less objective relative to their times. Nor does it suggest that structures of oppression differ in the case of every minority identity. If history has taught us anything, it is that those in power have the ability to manipulate the same oppressive structures, dependent upon the same prejudicial representations, for the exclusion of different groups. The experiences of contemporary minority people, once brought to light, resound backward in history, like a reverse echo effect, to comment on the experiences of past minority peoples, while at the same time these past experiences contribute, one hopes, to an accumulation of knowledge about how oppression works.

Minority identity discovers its theoretical force by representing the experiences of oppression and struggle lived by minority peoples separately but also precisely as minorities, for attention to the similarities between different minority identities exposes their relation to oppression as well as increases the chance of political solidarity. According to the definition of Gary and Rosalind Dworkin, minority identity has recognizable features that repeat across the spectrum of oppressed people. "We propose," Dworkin and Dworkin write, "that a minority group is a group characterized by four qualities: identifiability, differential power, differential and pejorative treatment, and group awareness" (1976, 17). These four features form the basis of my argument about minority identity as well, with one notable addition—that minority status also meets an ethical test judged both relative to society and universally. These features require, each one in turn, a brief discussion to grasp their collective simplicity and power and to arrive at a precise and universal definition of minority identity on which to base the elaboration of disability identity, to describe its relation to minority identity in general, and to defend identity politics as crucial to the future of minority peoples and their quest for social justice and inclusion.

1. *Identifiability* as a quality exists at the heart of identity itself because we must be able to distinguish a group before we can begin to imagine an identity. Often we conceive of identifiability as involving visible differences connected to the body, such as skin color, gender traits, gestures, affect, voice, and body shapes. These physical traits, however, are not universal with respect to different cultures, and there may be actions or cultural differences that also figure as the basis of identifiability. Note as well that identifiability exists in time, and time shifts its meaning. As a group is identified, it acquires certain representations, and the growth of representations connected to the group may then change how identifiability works. For example, the existence of a group called disabled people produces a general idea of the people in the group—although the existence of the group does not depend on every disabled person fitting into it—and it then becomes easier, first, to identify people with it and, second, to shift the meaning of the group definition. Fat people are not generally considered disabled at this moment, but there are signs that they may be in the

not too distant future (Kirkland 2006). Deaf and intersex people have resisted being described as disabled; their future relation to the identity of disabled people is not clear.

Two other obvious characteristics of identifiability need to be stressed. First, identifiability is tied powerfully to the representation of difference. In cases where an existing minority group is not easily identified and those in power want to isolate the group, techniques will be used to produce identifiability. For example, the Nazis required that Jews wear yellow armbands because they were not, despite Nazi racist mythology, identifiably different from Germans. Second, identity is social, and so is the quality of identifiability. There are many physical differences among human beings that simply do not count for identifiability. It is not the fact of physical difference that matters, then, but the representation attached to difference—what makes the difference identifiable. Representation is the difference that makes a difference. We might contend that there is no such thing as private identity in the same way that Wittgenstein claimed that private language does not exist. Identity must be representable and communicable to qualify as identifiable. Identity serves social purposes, and a form of identity not representable in society would be incomprehensible and ineffective for these purposes.

Of course, people may identify themselves. Especially in societies where groups are identified for differential and pejorative treatment, individuals belonging to these groups may internalize prejudices against themselves and do on their own the work of making themselves identifiable. Jim Crow laws in the American South counted on people policing themselves—not drinking at a white water fountain if they were black, for example. But the way in which individuals claim identifiability also changes as the history of the group changes. A group may be singled out for persecution, but as it grows more rebellious, it may work to preserve its identity, while transforming simultaneously the political values attached to it. The American military's policy, "Don't ask, don't tell" in the case of gay soldiers, tries to stymie the tendency of individuals to claim a positive minority identity for political reasons.

2. *Differential power* is a strong indicator of the difference between majority and minority identity; in fact, it may be the most important indicator because minority status relies on differential power rather than on numbers. The numerical majority is not necessarily the most powerful group. There are more women than men, and men hold more political power and have higher salaries for the same jobs. Numerical advantage is significant, but a better indicator is the presence of social power in one group over another. Dworkin and Dworkin mention the American South in the 1950s and South Africa under apartheid as good examples of differential power located in a nonnumerical majority (12). Minorities hold less power than majority groups.

3. A central question is whether the existence of *differential treatment* already implies pejorative treatment. Allowing that differential treatment may exist for legitimate reasons—and it is not at all certain that we should make this allowance—the addition of pejorative treatment as a quality of minority identity stresses the defining connection between oppression and minority status. Differential and pejorative treatment is what minority group members experience as a consequence of their minority position. It affects their economic standing, cultural prestige, educational opportunities, and civil rights, among other things. Discrimination as pejorative treatment often becomes the focus of identity politics, those concerted attempts by minorities to protest their inferior and unjust status by forming political action groups.

The emergence of identity politics, then, relies on a new epistemological claim. While it is not necessarily the case that a group will protest against discrimination, since there is a history of groups that accept inferior status and even fight to maintain it, the shift to a protest stance must involve claims different from those supporting the discriminatory behavior. A sense of inequity comes to pervade the consciousness of the minority identity, and individuals can find no reasonable justification for their differential treatment. Individuals in protest against unjust treatment begin to develop theories that oppose majority opinion not only about themselves but about the nature of the society that supports the pejorative behavior. They develop ways to represent the actions used to perpetuate the injustice against them, attacking stereotypes, use of violence and physical attack, and discrimination. Individuals begin to constitute themselves as a minority identity, moving from the form of consciousness called internal colonization to one characterized by a new group awareness.

4. *Group awareness* does not refer to group identifiability but to the perception of common goals pursued through cooperation, to the realization that differential and pejorative treatment is not justified by actual qualities of the minority group, and to the conviction that majority society is a disabling environment that must be transformed by recourse to social justice. In other words, awareness is not merely self-consciousness but an epistemology that adheres in group identity status. It is the identity that brings down injustice initially on the individual's head. This identity is constructed in such a way that it can be supported only by certain false claims and stereotypes. Resistance to these false claims is pursued and shared by members of the minority identity through counterarguments about, and criticism of, the existing state of knowledge. Thus, minority identity linked to group awareness achieves the status of a theoretical claim in itself, one in

conflict with the mainstream and a valuable source of meaningful diversity. Opponents of identity politics often argue that identity politics preserves the identities created by oppression: these identities are born of suffering, and embracing them supposedly represents a form of self-victimization. This argument does not understand that new epistemological claims are central to identity politics. For example, societies that oppress women often assert that they are irrational, morally depraved, and physically weak. The minority identity "woman," embraced by feminist identity politics, disputes these assertions and presents alternative, positive theories about women. Identity politics do not preserve the persecuted identities created by oppressors because the knowledge claims adhering in the new identities are completely different from those embraced by the persecuting groups.

Opponents of identity politics are not wrong, however, when they associate minority identity with suffering. They are wrong because they do not accept that pain and suffering may sometimes be resources for the epistemological insights of minority identity. This issue will arise whenever we consider disability identity, since it is the identity most associated with pain, and a great deal of discrimination against people with disabilities derives from the irrational fear of pain. It is not uncommon for disabled people to be told by complete strangers that they would kill themselves if they had such a disability. Doctors often withhold treatment of minor illnesses from disabled people because they believe they are better off dead—the doctors want to end the suffering of their patients, but these disabled people do not necessarily think of themselves as in pain, although they must suffer discriminatory attitudes (Gill 2000; Longmore 2003, 149–203). Nevertheless, people with disabilities are not the only people who suffer from prejudice. The epistemological claims of minority identity in general are often based on feelings of injustice that are painful. Wounds received in physical attacks may pale against the suffering experienced in the idea that one is being attacked because one is unjustly thought inferior—and yet suffering may have theoretical value for the person in pain. While there is a long history of describing pain and suffering as leading to egotism and narcissism—a metapsychology that plays, I argue in chapter 2 [in the original volume], an ancillary role in the evolution of the ideology of ability—we might consider that the strong focus given to the self in pain has epistemological value.[1] Suffering is a signal to the self at risk, and this signal applies equally to physical and social situations. The body signals with pain when a person is engaged in an activity that may do that person physical harm. Similarly, consciousness feels pain when the individual is in social danger. Suffering has a theoretical component because it draws attention to situations that jeopardize the future of the individual, and when individuals who suffer from oppression gather together to share their experiences, this theoretical component may be directed toward political ends.

By suggesting that suffering is theory-laden—that is, a sensation evaluative of states of reality—I am trying to track how and why minority identity makes epistemological claims about society. All identity is social theory. Identities are the theories that we use to fit into and travel through the social world. Our identities have a content that makes knowledge claims about the society in which they have evolved, and we adjust our identities, when we can, to different situations to improve our chances of success. But because mainstream identities so robustly mimic existing social norms, it is difficult to abstract their claims about society. Identities in conflict with society, however, have the ability to expose its norms. Minority identity gains the status of social critique once its content has been sufficiently developed by groups that unite to protest their unjust treatment by the society in which they live.

5. In addition to the four qualities proposed by Dworkin and Dworkin, groups claiming minority identity need to meet an *ethical test*. Minority identities make epistemological claims about the societies in which they hold liminal positions, but not all theories are equal in ethical content, especially relative to minority identity, since it begins as a product of oppression and acquires the status of social critique. While matters ethical are notoriously difficult to sort out, it is nevertheless worth pausing briefly over how ethics relates to minority identity because ethical content may serve to check fraudulent claims of minority status. For example, in South Africa of recent date, the ideology of apartheid represented the majority position because it held power, identified the nature of minority identity, and dictated differential and pejorative treatment of those in the minority. Today in South Africa, however, the apartheidists are no longer in the majority. Applying the theory of Dworkin and Dworkin, they might be construed as having a minority identity: they are identifiable, they have differential power, they are treated pejoratively, and they possess group awareness—that is, they present a set of claims that actively and consciously criticize majority society. They also believe themselves to be persecuted, and no doubt they feel suffering about their marginal position.

Why are the apartheidists not deserving of minority status? The answer is that the theories contained in apartheidist identity do not pass an ethical test. The contrast between its ethical claims and those of the majority are sufficiently striking to recognize. The apartheidists propose a racist society as the norm to which all South African citizens should adhere. Relative to South African social beliefs and those of many other countries, apartheid ideology is unacceptable on ethical grounds because it is biased, violent, and oppressive. Consequently, the apartheidists fail to persuade us with their claims, and we judge them not a minority group subject to oppression but a fringe group trying to gain unlawful advantage over others.

To summarize, the definition embraced here—and used to theorize disability identity—does not understand minority identity as statistical, fixed in time, or exclusively biological but as a politicized identity possessing the ability to offer social critiques. There are those who attack minority identities precisely because they are politicized, as if only minorities made political arguments based on identity and politicized identity in itself were a species of defective attachment. But many other examples of politicized identity exist on the current scene—Democrats, Republicans, Socialists, the Christian Coalition, the American Nazi Party, and so on. In fact, any group that forms a coalition to make arguments on its own behalf and on the behalf of others in the public forum takes on a politicized identity. Arguments to outlaw minority political action groups merely because they encourage politicized identities would have to abolish other political groups as well.

DISABILITY AND THE THEORY OF COMPLEX EMBODIMENT

Feminist philosophers have long argued that all knowledge is situated, that it adheres in social locations, that it is embodied, with the consequence that they have been able to claim that people in marginal social positions enjoy an epistemological privilege that allows them to theorize society differently from those in dominant social locations (Haraway 1991, 183–201; Harding 1986). Knowledge is situated, first of all, because it is based on perspective. There is a difference between the knowledge present in a view of the earth from the moon and a view of the earth from the perspective of an ant. We speak blandly of finding different perspectives on things, but different perspectives do in fact give varying conceptions of objects, especially social objects. Nevertheless, situated knowledge does not rely only on changing perspectives. Situated knowledge adheres in embodiment. The disposition of the body determines perspectives, but it also spices these perspectives with phenomenological knowledge—lifeworld experience—that affects the interpretation of perspective. To take a famous example from Iris Young, the fact that many women "throw like a girl" is not based on a physical difference. The female arm is as capable of throwing a baseball as the male arm. It is the representation of femininity in a given society that disables women, pressuring them to move their bodies in certain, similar ways, and once they become accustomed to moving in these certain, similar ways, it is difficult to retrain the body. "Women in sexist society are physically handicapped," Young explains. "Insofar as we learn to live out our existence in accordance with the definition that patriarchal culture assigns to us, we are physically inhibited, confined, positioned, and objectified" (2005, 171). It is possible to read the differential and pejorative treatment of women, as if it were a disability, on the surface of their skin, in muscle mass, in corporeal agility. This form of embodiment is also, however, a form of situated knowledge about the claims being made about and by women in a given society. To consider some positive examples, the particular embodiment of a woman means that she might, after experiencing childbirth, have a new and useful perception of physical pain. Women may also have, because of menstruation, a different knowledge of blood. Female gender identity is differently embodied because of women's role in reproductive labor. The presence of the body does not boil down only to perspective but to profound ideas and significant theories about the world.

Embodiment is, of course, central to the field of disability studies. In fact, a focus on disability makes it easier to understand that embodiment and social location are one and the same. Arguments for the specificity of disability identity tend to stress the critical nature of embodiment, and the tacit or embodied knowledge associated with particular disabilities often justifies their value to larger society. For example, George Lane's body, we will see in chapter 6 [in the original volume], incorporates a set of theoretical claims about architecture that the Supreme Court interprets in its ruling against the State of Tennessee, finding that Lane's inability to enter the Polk County Courthouse reveals a pattern of discrimination against people with disabilities found throughout the American court system. Chapter 5 [in the original volume] explores disability passing not as avoidance of social responsibility or manipulation for selfish interests but as a form of embodied knowledge—forced into usage by prejudices against disability—about the relationship between the social environment and human ability. The young deaf woman who tries to pass for hearing will succeed only if she possesses significant knowledge about the informational potential, manners, physical gestures, conversational rituals, and cultural activities that define hearing in her society. Disabled people who pass for able-bodied are neither cowards, cheats, nor con artists but skillful interpreters of the world from whom we all might learn.

Dossier No. 2 *New York Times Online* November 15, 2006

Officials Clash over Mentally Ill in Florida Jails

By Abby Goodnough

MIAMI, Nov. 14—For years, circuit judges here have ordered state officials to obey Florida law and promptly transfer severely mentally ill inmates from jails to state hospitals. But with few hospital beds available, Gov. Jeb Bush's administration began flouting those court orders in August. ... "This type of arrogant activity cannot be tolerated in an orderly society," Judge Crockett Farnell of Pinellas-Pasco Circuit Court wrote in an Oct. 11 ruling. State law requires that inmates found incompetent to stand trial be moved from county jails to psychiatric hospitals within 15 days of the state's receiving the commitment orders. Florida has broken that law for years, provoking some public defenders to seek court orders forcing swift compliance. ...

Two mentally ill inmates in the Escambia County Jail in Pensacola died over the last year and a half after being subdued by guards, according to news reports. And in the Pinellas County Jail in Clearwater, a schizophrenic inmate gouged out his eye after waiting weeks for a hospital bed, his lawyer said. ...

The problem is not unique to Florida, although it is especially severe in Miami-Dade County, which has one of the nation's largest percentages of mentally ill residents, according to the National Alliance for the Mentally Ill, an advocacy group. ...

In Miami, an average of 25 to 40 acutely psychotic people live in a unit of the main county jail that a lawyer for Human Rights Watch, Jennifer Daskal, described as squalid after visiting last month. ... Ms. Daskal said that some of the unit's 14 "suicide cells"—dim, bare and designed for one inmate—were holding two or three at a time, and that the inmates were kept in their cells 24 hours a day except to shower. ...

But embodiment also appears as a bone of contention in disability studies because it seems caught between competing models of disability. Briefly, the medical model defines disability as a property of the individual body that requires medical intervention. The medical model has a biological orientation, focusing almost exclusively on disability as embodiment. The social model opposes the medical model by defining disability relative to the social and built environment, arguing that disabling environments produce disability in bodies and require interventions at the level of social justice. Some scholars complain that the medical model pays too much attention to embodiment, while the social model leaves it out of the picture. Without returning to a medical model, which labels individuals as defective, the next step for disability studies is to develop a theory of complex embodiment that values disability as a form of human variation.

The theory of complex embodiment raises awareness of the effects of disabling environments on people's lived experience of the body, but it emphasizes as well that some factors affecting disability, such as chronic pain, secondary health effects, and aging, derive from the body. These last disabilities are neither less significant than disabilities caused by the environment nor to be considered defects or deviations merely because they are resistant to change. Rather, they belong to the spectrum of human variation, conceived both as variability between individuals and as variability within an individual's life cycle, and they need to be considered in tandem with social forces affecting disability.[2] The theory of complex embodiment views the economy between social representations and the body not as unidirectional as in the social model, or nonexistent as in the medical model, but as reciprocal. Complex embodiment theorizes the body and its representations as mutually transformative. Social representations obviously affect the experience of the body, as Young makes clear in her seminal essay, but the body possesses the ability to determine its social representation as well, and some situations exist where representation exerts no control over the life of the body.

As a living entity, the body is vital and chaotic, possessing complexity in equal share to that claimed today by critical and cultural theorists for linguistic systems. The association of the body with human mortality and fragility, however, forces a general distrust of the knowledge embodied in it. It is easier to imagine the body as a garment, vehicle, or burden than as a complex system that defines our humanity, any knowledge that we might possess, and our individual and collective futures. Disability gives even greater urgency to the fears and limitations associated with the body, tempting us to believe that the body can be changed as easily as changing clothes. The ideology of ability stands ready to attack any desire to know and to accept the disabled body in its current state. The more likely response to disability is to try to erase any signs of change, to wish to return the body magically to a past era of supposed perfection, to insist that the body has no value as human variation if it is not flawless.

Ideology and prejudice, of course, abound in all circles of human existence, labeling some groups and individuals as inferior or less than human: people of color, women, the poor, people with different sexual orientations, and the disabled confront the intolerance of society on a daily basis. In nearly no other sphere of existence, however, do people risk waking up one morning having become the persons whom they hated the day before. Imagine the white racist suddenly transformed into a black man, the anti-Semite into a Jew, the misogynist into a woman, and one might begin to approach the change in mental landscape demanded by the onset of disability. We require the stuff of science fiction to describe these scenarios, most often for comic effect or paltry moralizing. But no recourse to fiction is required to imagine an able-bodied person becoming disabled. It happens every minute of every day.

The young soldier who loses his arm on an Iraqi battlefield wakes up in bed having become the kind of person whom he has always feared and whom society names as contemptible (Corbett 2004). Given these circumstances, how might we expect him to embrace and to value his new identity? He is living his worst nightmare. He cannot sleep. He hates what he has become. He distances himself from his wife and family. He begins to drink too much. He tries to use a functional prosthetic, but he loathes being seen with a hook. The natural prosthetic offered to him by Army doctors does not really work, and he prefers to master tasks with his one good arm. He cannot stand the stares of those around him, the looks of pity and contempt as he tries to perform simple tasks in public, and he begins to look upon himself with disdain.

The soldier has little chance, despite the promise of prosthetic science, to return to his former state. What he is going through is completely understandable, but he needs to come to a different conception of himself, one based not on the past but on the present and the future. His body will continue to change with age, and he may have greater disabling conditions in the future. He is no different in this regard from any other human being. Some disabilities can be approached by demanding changes in how people with disabilities are perceived, others by changes in the built environment. Some can be treated through medical care. Other disabilities cannot be approached by changes in either the environment or the body. In almost every case, however, people with disabilities have a better chance of future happiness and health if they accept their disability as a positive identity and benefit from the knowledge embodied in it. The value of people with disabilities to themselves does not lie in finding a way to return through medical intervention to a former physical perfection, since that perfection is a myth, nor in trying to conceal from others and themselves that they are disabled. Rather, embodiment seen complexly understands disability as an epistemology that rejects the temptation to value the body as anything other than what it was and that embraces what the body has become and will become relative to the demands on it, whether environmental, representational, or corporeal.

INTERSECTIONAL IDENTITY COMPLEXLY EMBODIED

The ultimate purpose of complex embodiment as theory is to give disabled people greater knowledge of and control over their bodies in situations where increased knowledge and control are possible. But the theory has side benefits for at least two crucial debates raging on the current scene as well. First, complex embodiment makes a contribution to influential arguments about intersectionality—the idea that analyses of social oppression take account of overlapping identities based on race, gender, sexuality, class, and disability.[3] While theorists of intersectionality have never argued for a simple additive model in which oppressed identities are stacked one upon another, a notion of disability embodiment helps to resist the temptation of seeing some identities as more pathological than others, and it offers valuable advice about how to conceive the standpoint of others for the purpose of understanding the prejudices against them. This is not to suggest that the intersection of various identities produces the same results for all oppressed groups, since differences in the hierarchical organization of race, gender, sexuality, class, and disability do exist (Collins 2003, 212). Rather, it is to emphasize, first, that intersectionality as a theory references the tendency of identities to construct one another reciprocally (Collins 2003, 208); second, that identities are not merely standpoints where one may stand or try to stand but also complex embodiments; and, third, that the ideology of ability uses the language of pathology to justify labeling some identities as inferior to others.[4]

For example, theorists of intersectional identity might find useful the arguments in disability studies against disability simulation because they offer a view of complex embodiment that enlarges standpoint theory. The applied fields of occupational therapy and rehabilitation science sometimes recommend the use of disability simulations to raise the consciousness of therapists who treat people with disabilities. Instructors ask students to spend a day in a wheelchair or to try navigating classroom buildings blindfolded to get a better sense of the challenges faced by their patients. The idea is that students may stand for a time in the places occupied by disabled people and come to grasp their perspectives. Disability theorists have attacked the use of simulations for a variety of reasons, the most important being that they fail to give the student pretenders a sense of the embodied knowledge contained in disability identities. Disability simulations of this kind fail because they place students in a time-one position of disability, before knowledge about disability is acquired, usually resulting in emotions of loss, shock, and pity at how dreadful it is to be disabled. Students experience their body relative to their usual embodiment, and they become so preoccupied with sensations of bodily inadequacy that they cannot perceive the extent to which their "disability" results from social rather than physical causes. Notice that such games focus almost entirely on the phenomenology of the individual body. The pretender asks how his or her body would be changed, how his or her personhood would be changed, by disability. It is an act of individual imagination, then, not an act of cultural imagination. Moreover, simulations tempt students to play the game of "What is worse?" as they experiment with different simulations. Is it worse to be blind or deaf, worse to lose a leg or an arm, worse to be paralyzed or deaf, mute, and blind? The result is a thoroughly negative and unrealistic impression of disability.

The critique of disability simulation has applications in several areas of intersectional theory. First, the practice of peeling off minority identities from people to determine their place in the hierarchy of oppression is revealed to degrade all minority identities by giving a one-dimensional view of them. It also fails to understand the ways in which different identities constitute one another. Identities may trump one another in the hierarchy of oppression, but intersectional identity, because embodied complexly, produces not competition between minority identities but "outsider" theories about the lived experience of oppression (see Collins 1998). Additionally, coming to an understanding of intersecting minority identities demands that one imagine social location not only as perspective but also as complex embodiment, and complex embodiment combines social and corporeal factors. Rather than blindfolding students for an hour, then, it is preferable to send them off wearing sunglasses and carrying a white cane, in the company of a friend, to restaurants and department stores, where they may observe firsthand the spectacle of discrimination against blind people as passersby avoid and gawk at them, clerks refuse to wait on them or condescend to ask the friend what the student is looking for, and waiters request, usually at the top of their lungs and very slowly (since blind people must also be deaf and cognitively disabled), what the student would like to eat.[5]

It is crucial to resist playing the game of "What is worse?" when conceiving of intersectional identity, just as it is when imagining different disabilities. Asking whether it is worse to be a woman or a Latina, worse to be black or blind, worse to be gay or poor registers each identity as a form of ability that has greater or lesser powers to overcome social intolerance and prejudice. Although one may try to keep the focus on society and the question of whether it oppresses one identity more than another, the debate devolves all too soon and often to discussions of the comparative costs of changing society and making

accommodations, comparisons about quality of life, and speculations about whether social disadvantages are intrinsic or extrinsic to the group. The compelling issue for minority identity does not turn on the question of whether one group has the more arduous existence but on the fact that every minority group faces social discrimination, violence, and intolerance that exert toxic and unfair influence on the ability to live life to the fullest (see Asch 2001, 406–7).

SOCIAL CONSTRUCTION COMPLEXLY EMBODIED

Second, the theory of complex embodiment makes it possible to move forward arguments raging currently about social construction, identity, and the body. Aside from proposing a theory better suited to the experiences of disabled people, the goal is to advance questions in identity and body theory unresponsive to the social construction model. Chapters 3, 4, and 6 [original volume] make an explicit adjustment in social construction theory by focusing on the realism of identities and bodies. By "realism" I understand neither a positivistic claim about reality unmediated by social representations, nor a linguistic claim about reality unmediated by objects of representation, but a theory that describes reality as a mediation, no less real for being such, between representation and its social objects.[6] Rather than viewing representation as a pale shadow of the world or the world as a shadow world of representation, my claim is that both sides push back in the construction of reality. The hope is to advance discourse theory to the next stage by defining construction in a radical way, one that reveals constructions as possessing both social and physical form. While identities are socially constructed, they are nevertheless meaningful and real precisely because they are complexly embodied. The complex embodiment apparent in disability is an especially strong example to contemplate because the disabled body compels one to give concrete form to the theory of social construction and to take its metaphors literally.

Consider an introductory example of the way in which disability complexly embodied extends the social construction argument in the direction of realism. In August 2000 a controversy about access at the Galehead hut in the Appalachian Mountains came to a climax (Goldberg 2000). The Appalachian Mountain Club of New Hampshire had just constructed a rustic 38-bed lodge at an elevation of thirty-eight hundred feet. The United States Forest Service required that the hut comply with the Americans with Disabilities Act (ADA) and be accessible to people with disabilities, that it have a wheelchair ramp and grab bars in larger toilet stalls. The Appalachian Mountain Club had to pay an extra $30,000 to $50,000 for a building already costing $400,000 because the accessible features were late design changes. Its members ridiculed the idea that the building, which could be reached only by a super-rugged 4.6 mile trail, would ever be visited by wheelchair users, and the media tended to take their side.

At this point a group from Northeast Passage, a program at the University of New Hampshire that works with people with disabilities, decided to make a visit to the Galehead hut. Jill Gravink, the director of Northeast Passage, led a group of three hikers in wheelchairs and two on crutches on a 12-hour climb to the lodge, at the end of which they rolled happily up the ramp to its front door. A local television reporter on the scene asked why, if people in wheelchairs could drag themselves up the trail, they could not drag themselves up the steps into the hut, implying that the ramp was a waste of money. Gravink responded, "Why bother putting steps on the hut at all? Why not drag yourself in through a window?"

The design environment, Gravink suggests pointedly, determines who is able-bodied at the Galehead lodge. The distinction between the disabled and nondisabled is socially constructed, and it is a rather fine distinction at that. Those who are willing and able to climb stairs are considered able-bodied, while those who are not willing and able to climb stairs are disabled. However, those who do climb stairs but are not willing and able to enter the building through a window are not considered disabled. It is taken for granted that nondisabled people may choose when to be able-bodied. In fact, the built environment is full of technologies that make life easier for those people who possess the physical power to perform tasks without these technologies. Stairs, elevators, escalators, washing machines, leaf and snow blowers, eggbeaters, chainsaws, and other tools help to relax physical standards for performing certain tasks. These tools are nevertheless viewed as natural extensions of the body, and no one thinks twice about using them. The moment that individuals are marked as disabled or diseased, however, the expectation is that they will maintain the maximum standard of physical performance at every moment, and the technologies designed to make their life easier are viewed as expensive additions, unnecessary accommodations, and a burden on society.

The example of the Galehead hut exposes the ideology of ability—the ideology that uses ability to determine human status, demands that people with disabilities always present as able-bodied as possible, and measures the value of disabled people in dollars and cents. It reveals how constructed are our attitudes about identity and the body. This is a familiar point, and usually social analysis comes to a conclusion here, no doubt because the idea of construction is more metaphorical than real. The implication seems to be that knowledge of an object as socially constructed is sufficient to undo any of its negative effects. How many books and essays have been written in the last 10 years, whose authors are content with the conclusion that x, y, or z is socially constructed, as if the conclusion itself were a victory over oppression?

Far from being satisfied with this conclusion, my analysis here will always take it as a point of departure from which to move directly to the elucidation of embodied causes and effects. Oppression is driven not by individual, unconscious syndromes but by social ideologies that are embodied, and precisely because ideologies are embodied, their effects are readable, and must be read, in the construction and history of societies. When a Down syndrome citizen tries to enter a polling place and is turned away, a social construction is revealed and must be read. When wheelchair users are called selfish if they complain about the inaccessibility of public toilets, a social construction is revealed and must be read (Shapiro 1994, 126–27). When handicapped entrances to buildings are located in the rear, next to garbage cans, a social construction is revealed and must be read. When a cosmetic surgeon removes the thumb on a little boy's right hand because he was born with no thumb on his left hand, a social construction is revealed and must be read (Marks 1999, 67). What if we were to embrace the metaphor implied by social construction, if we required that the "construction" in social construction be understood as a building, as the Galehead hut for example, and that its blueprint be made available? Not only would this requirement stipulate that we elaborate claims about social construction in concrete terms, it would insist that we locate the construction in time and place as a form of complex embodiment.

Whenever anyone mentions the idea of social construction, we should ask on principle to see the blueprint—not to challenge the value of the idea but to put it to practical use—to map as many details about the construction as possible and to track its political, epistemological, and real effects in the world of human beings. To encourage this new requirement, I cite three familiar ideas about social construction, as currently theorized, from which flow—or at least should—three methodological principles. These three principles underlie the arguments to follow, suggesting how to look for blueprints and how to begin reading them:

- Knowledge is socially situated—which means that knowledge has an objective and verifiable relation to its social location.
- Identities are socially constructed—which means that identities contain complex theories about social reality.
- Some bodies are excluded by dominant social ideologies—which means that these bodies display the workings of ideology and expose it to critique and the demand for political change.

NOTES

1. The nature of pain and the methodology of its study are diverse because they involve the definition of emotion and consciousness. Aydede collects a strong sampling of contemporary views about pain; one of which, the perceptual theory, appeals to the idea that pain has the capacity to signal changes in states of reality (59–98).
2. Snyder and Mitchell express this view powerfully throughout *Cultural Locations of Disability*. For example: "As Darwin insisted in *On the Origin of Species*, variation serves the good of the species. The more variable a species is, the more flexible it is with respect to shifting environmental forces. Within this formulation, one that is central to disability studies, variations are features of biological elasticity rather than a discordant expression of a 'natural' process gone awry" (2006, 70).
3. The literature on intersectionality is now vast. Some key texts relating to disability include Barbee and Little; Beale; Butler and Parr; Fawcett; Hayman and Levit; Ikemoto; Jackson-Braboy and Williams; Martin; O'Toole (2004); and Tyjewski.

4. While not aware of disability studies per se, Johnny Williams provides an excellent intersectional analysis of stereotypical conflations of race and class, arguing that American society explains the social and economic failures of minority groups in terms of personal "inabilities," while maintaining the belief that "social arrangements are fundamentally just" (221).

5. Catherine Kudlick proposed, on the DS-HUM listserve, an exercise similar to this one to replace traditional and biased disability simulations often used by classroom instructors. I am indebted to her discussion.

6. Philosophical realism has a number of varieties. The particular lineage of interest to me focuses on Hilary Putnam in philosophy and Richard Boyd in the philosophy of science. Satya P. Mohanty imports Boyd's ideas into the humanities in general and critical theory in particular, putting the concept of realism in the service of minority studies in novel and convincing ways. Other important figures in philosophical realism working in the humanities include Linda Martin Alcoff, Michael Hames-Garcia, Paula M. L. Moya, and Sean Teuton.

BIBLIOGRAPHY

Alcoff, Linda Martin. *Real Knowing: New Versions of Coherence Theory*. Ithaca, NY: Cornell University Press, 1996.

——. "Who's Afraid of Identity Politics?" *Reclaiming Identity: Realist Theory and the Predicament of Postmodernism*. Ed. Paula M. L. Moya and Michael R. Hames-Garcia. Berkeley and Los Angeles: University of California Press, 2000. Pp. 312–44.

——. *Visible Identities: Race, Gender and the Self*. New York: Oxford University Press, 2006.

Alcoff, Linda Martin, Michael Hames-Garcia, Satya P. Mohanty, and Paula M. L. Moya, eds. *Identity Politics Reconsidered*. New York: Palgrave Macmillan, 2006.

Asch, Adrienne. "Critical Race Theory, Feminism, and Disability: Reflections on Social Justice and Personal Identity." *Ohio State Law Journal* 62.1 (2001): 391–423.

Asch, Adrienne, and Harilyn Rousso. "Therapists with Disabilities: Theoretical and Clinical Issues." *Psychiatry* 48 (1985): 1–12.

Asch, Adrienne, and Michelle Fine. *Women with Disabilities: Essays in Psychology, Culture, and Politics*. Philadelphia: Temple University Press, 1988.

Aydede, Murat. ed. *Pain: New Essays on Its Nature and Methodology of Its Study*. Cambridge: MIT Press, 2005.

Barbee, L. Evelyn, and Marilyn Little. "Health, Social Class and African-American Women." *Theorizing Black Feminisms: The Visionary Pragmatism of Black Women*. Ed. Stanlie M. James and Abena P. A. Busia. London: Routledge, 1993. Pp. 182–99.

Beale, Frances. "Double Jeopardy: To Be Black and Female." *Words of Fire: An Anthology of African-American Feminist Thought*. Ed. Beverley Guy-Sheftall. New York: New York Press, 1995. Pp. 146–55.

Boyd, Richard. "How to Be a Moral Realist." *Essays on Moral Realism*. Ed. Geoffrey Sayre-McCord. Ithaca, NY: Cornell University Press, 1988. Pp. 181–228.

Butler, Ruth, and Hester Parr, eds. *Mind and Body Spaces: Geographies of Illness, Impairment and Disability*. London: Routledge, 1999.

Castells, Manuel. *The Power of Identity*. 2nd ed. Oxford: Blackwell, 1997 (2004).

Collins, Patricia Hill. "Learning from the Outsider within Revisited." *Fighting Words: Black Women and the Search for Justice*. Minneapolis: University of Minnesota Press, 1998. Pp. 3–10.

——. "Some Group Matters: Intersectionality, Situated Standpoints, and Black Feminist Thought." *A Companion to African-American Philosophy*. Ed. Tommy L. Lott and John P. Pittman. Malden, MA: Blackwell, 2003. Pp. 205–29.

Corbett, Sara. "The Permanent Scars of Iraq." *New York Times Magazine*, 15 February 2004: 34–41, 58, 60, 66.

Dworkin, Anthony Gary, and Rosalind J. Dworkin, eds. *The Minority Report: An Introduction to Racial, Ethnic, and Gender Relations*. New York: Praeger, 1976.

Fawcett, Barbara. *Feminist Perspectives on Disability*. Harlow: Prentice Hall, 2000.

Fraser, Nancy. "Rethinking Recognition." *New Left Review* 3 (May–June 2000): 107–20.

Gill, Carol J. "Health Professionals, Disability, and Assisted Suicide: An Examination of Relevant Empirical Evidence and Reply to Batavia." *Psychology, Public Policy, and Law* 6.2 (2000): 526–45.

Goldberg, Carey. "For These Trailblazers, Wheelchairs Matter." *New York Times Online*, August 17, 2000. Available at http://query.nytimes.com/gst/fullpage.html.res9EoCE3DA173EF934A2575B-CoA9669C8B63&sec=health&spon=&pagewanted=all (accessed December 22, 2006).

Goodheart, Eugene. *The Reign of Ideology*. New York: Columbia University Press, 1996.

Haraway, Donna J. *Simians, Cyborgs, and Women: The Reinvention of Nature*. New York: Routledge, 1991.

Harding, Sandra. *The Science Question in Feminism*. Ithaca, NY: Cornell University Press, 1986.

Hayman, Robert L., Jr., and Nancy Levit. "Un-Natural Things: Construction of Race, Gender and Disability." *Crossroads, Directions, and a New Critical*

Race Theory. Ed. Francisco Valdes, Jerome McCristal Culp, and Angela P. Harris. Philadelphia: Temple University Press, 2002. Pp. 157–86.

Ikemeto, Lisa C. "Furthering the Inquiry: Race, Class, and Culture in the Forced Medical Treatment of Pregnant Women." *Critical Race Feminism: A Reader.* Ed. Katherine Adrien Wing. New York: New York University Press, 1997. Pp. 136–43.

Jackson-Braboy, Pamela and David R. Williams. "The Intersection of Race, Gender and SES: Health Paradoxes." *Gender, Race, Class, and Health: Intersectional Approaches.* Ed. Amy J. Schulz and Leith Mullings. San Francisco: Jossey-Bass, 2006. Pp. 131–62.

JanMohamed, Abdul, and David Lloyd. "Introduction: Minority Discourse—What Is to Be Done?" *Cultural Critique* 7 (1987): 5–17.

Kirkland, Anna. "What's at Stake in Fatness as a Disability?" *Disability Studies Quarterly* 26.1 (2006). Available at www.dsq-sds.org/_articles_htmlJ2006/winter/kirkland.asp (accessed November 17, 2006).

Lester, J. C. "The Disability Studies Industry." *Libertarian Alliance*, September 26, 2002. Available at www.la-articles.org.uk/dsi.htm (accessed November 11, 2006).

Linton, Simi. *Claiming Disability: Knowledge and Identity.* New York: New York University Press, 1998.

Linton, Simi, Susan Mello, and John O'Neill. "Disability Studies: Expanding the Parameters of Diversity." *Radical Teacher* 47 (1995): 4–10.

Longmore, Paul. *Why I Burned My Book and Other Essays on Disability.* Philadelphia: Temple University Press, 2003.

Marks, Deborah. *Disability: Controversial Debates and Psychosocial Perspectives.* London: Routledge, 1999.

Martin, Emily. "Moods and Representations of Social Inequality." *Gender, Race, Class, and Health: Intersectional Approaches.* Ed. Amy J. Schulz and Leith Mullings. San Francisco: Jossey-Bass, 2006. Pp. 60–88.

O'Brien, Mark. "On Seeing a Sex Surrogate." *The Sun* 174 (May), 1990. Available at www.pacificnews.org/marko/sex-surrogate.html (accessed April 29, 2005).

——. *The Man in the Iron Lung.* Berkeley, CA: Lemonade Factory, 1997.

——. n.d. "Questions I Feared the Journalist Would Ask." Mark O'Brien Papers, BANC MSS 99/247c. Bancroft Library, University of California, Berkeley.

O'Brien, Mark, with Gillian Kendall. *How I Became a Human Being: A Disabled Man's Quest for Independence.* Madison: University of Wisconsin Press, 2003.

O'Toole, Corbett Joan. "The Sexist Inheritance of the Disability Movement." *Gendering Disability.* Ed. Bonnie G. Smith and Beth Hutchison. New Brunswick, NJ: Rutgers University Press, 2004. Pp. 294–300.

Putnam, Hilary. *Realism with a Human Face.* Cambridge, MA: Harvard University Press, 1990.

Shapiro, Joseph. *No Pity: People with Disabilities Forging a New Civil Rights Movement.* New York: Three Rivers Press, 1994.

——. "Disability Policy and the Media: A Stealth Civil Rights Movement Bypasses the Press and Defies Conventional Wisdom." *Policy Studies Journal* 22.1 (1994): 123–32.

Siebers, Tobin. *Morals and Stories.* New York: Columbia University Press, 1992.

——. "Kant and the Politics of Beauty." *Philosophy and Literature* 22.1 (1998): 31–50.

——. "My Withered Limb." *Michigan Quarterly Review* 37.2 (1998): 196–205.

——. *The Subject and Other Subjects: On Ethical, Aesthetic, and Political Identity.* Ann Arbor: University of Michigan Press, 1998.

——. "*The Reign of Ideology* by Eugene Goodheart." *Modern Philology* 96.4 (1999): 560–63.

——. *The Mirror of Medusa.* Rev. ed. Christchurch, New Zealand: Cybereditions, 2000.

——. "What Can Disability Studies Learn from the Culture Wars?" *Cultural Critique* 55 (2003): 182–216.

Snyder, Sharon L., and David T. Mitchell. *Cultural Locations of Disability.* Chicago: University of Chicago Press, 2006.

Taylor, Charles. *Sources of the Self: The Making of Modern Identity.* Cambridge, MA: Harvard University Press, 1987.

Teuton, Sean. *Red Land, Red Power: Grounding Knowledge in the American Indian Novel.* Durham, NC: Duke University Press, 2008.

Tyjewski, Carolyn. "Hybrid Matters: The Mixing of Identity, the Law and Politics." *Politics and Culture* 3, 2003. aspen.conncoll.edu/politicsandculture/page.cfm?key=240 (accessed August 3, 2004).

Williams, Johnny E. "Race and Class: Why All the Confusion?" *Race and Racism in Theory and Practice.* Ed. Berel Lang. Lanham, MD: Rowman and Littlefield, 2000. Pp. 215–24.

Young, Iris. *On Female Body Experience: "Throwing Like a Girl" and Other Essays.* Cambridge, MA: Oxford University Press, 2005.

CHAPTER 23

Defining Mental Disability

Margaret Price

SUMMARY

Drawing on her own experiences with the mental health system, Margaret Price interrogates the language used to describe mental disability, including the terms psychiatric disability, mental illness, madness, and countless other words. Price points out that mental illness is understood as the complement to mental health, a term preferred by the medical and insurance communities, and the distinction is based on a wellness/unwellness paradigm that identifies mental illness as needing a definitive cure.

However, the term mental illness also facilitates conversations about the intersection of illness and disability with Disability Studies. In order to bridge the conceptual chasm between being "healthy disabled" and chronically ill, scholars must rework the social model of disability that separates impairment and disability. Price suggests that part of this reworking must acknowledge differences between physical and mental illness. The diagnosis of mental illness can mark a person as "permanently damaged" so that even a state of wellness can be considered evidence of a person's unwellness. Citing Bradley Lewis (Chapter 7 in this volume), Price writes that the psychiatric practice (and language) must change to become more democratic and less driven by pharmaceutical interests. Only then will it include the voices and concerns of all its stakeholders, whether they identify themselves as consumers, survivors, or (ex-) patients.

For Price, terminology matters in a pragmatic sense. Although some scholars have settled on terms of neurotypicality and neurodiversity, Price asks whether the optimism around diversity can "flatten individual difference." Reappropriating the term *psychosocial* could potentially challenge the boundaries between the psychic and social, but Price suggests that this word doesn't mean anything for many people in many social contexts. Thus the essay ends with a suggestion that the term mental disability can reassign meaning for disabled people while effectively describing cognitive, intellectual, and even physical disabilities of various kinds.

NAMING AND DEFINITION

Who am I talking about? So far I've used a variety of terms to denote impairments of the mind, and I haven't yet exhausted the list. Contemporary language available includes *psychiatric disability, mental illness, cognitive disability, intellectual disability, mental health service user* (or *consumer*), *neurodiversity, neuroatypical, psychiatric system survivor, crazy,* and *mad.* "No term in the history of madness is neutral," Geoffrey Reaume argues, "not *mental illness, madness,* or any other term" (182). Moreover, as Ian Hacking has pointed out, particular names may thrive in a particular "ecological niche"—for instance, the intersection of the diagnosis "neurasthenia" with nineteenth-century French stories of the "Wandering Jew" (2, 120) or the diagnosis "drapetomania," applied to African American slaves who attempted to escape (Jackson 4). Keeping this dynamism in mind, the following analysis does not aim to accept some terms and discard others. Rather, I want to clarify the different areas they map and show that each does particular kinds of cultural work in particular contexts. Although I use *mental disability* as my own term of choice, I continue to use others as needed, and my overall argument is for deployment of language in a way that operates as inclusively as possible, inviting coalition, while also attending to the specific texture of individual experiences. In doing so, I follow the urging of Tanya Titchkosky, who argues that the aim of analyzing language about disability should not be to mandate particular terms but rather "to examine what our current articulations of disability are saying in the here and now" ("Disability" 138). The problem of naming has always preoccupied DS scholars,[1] but acquires a particular urgency when considered in the context of disabilities of the mind, for often the very terms used to name persons with mental disabilities have explicitly foreclosed our status *as* persons. Aristotle's famous declaration that man is a rational animal (1253a; 1098a) gave rise to centuries of insistence that to be named mad was to lose one's personhood.

Mad is a term generally used in non-U.S. contexts, and has a long history of positive and person-centered discourses. MindFreedom International, a coalition of grassroots organizations, traces the beginning of the "Mad Movement" to the early 1970s, and reports on "Mad Pride" events that continue to take place in countries including Australia, Ghana, Canada, England, and the

United States. MindFreedom and other groups organize activist campaigns, sponsor exhibits and performances, and act as forums and support networks for their thousands of members. *Mad* is less recognizable in the United States, which can be to its advantage, since its infrequency helps detach it from implication in medical and psychiatric industries. In addition, *mad* achieves a broad historical sweep. Psychiatry, with its interest in brains, chemistry, and drugs, arose only in the last couple of centuries; however, writings on madness can be found in pre-Socratic discourse, and their historical progression through centuries spans medicine, philosophy, and literature, as Allen Thiher shows in *Revels in Madness: Insanity in Medicine and Literature*.

> The center of our discourses on madness has had many names: *thymos, anima,* soul, spirit, self, the unconscious, the subject, the person. Whatever be the accent given by the central concept, access to the entity afflicted with madness is obtained through a language game in which these concepts or names play a role, organizing our experience of the world even as the world vouchsafes criteria for correct use of these notions.
>
> (3)

Thiher does not discuss at length his choice of *mad,* but it is evident from the far-reaching scope of his study that this term achieves a flexibility that *mental illness* and *cognitive disability* do not: it unites notions of that "central concept" through time and across cultures. As with *queer,* the broad scope of *mad* carries the drawback of generality but also the power of mass.

Many persons in the mad movement identify as psychiatric system survivors. According to MindFreedom, psychiatric system survivors are "individuals who have personally experienced human rights violations in the mental health system." A more inclusive term is *consumer/survivor/*

ex-patient (*c/s/x*). Drawing upon the work of Linda J. Morrison, Bradley Lewis argues that this term "allows a coalition among people with diverse identification" while also indicating that the relationship between the three positions is neither exclusive nor linear (157). Lewis goes on to suggest that we might add *patient* as well, making the abbreviation into a quatrad (p/c/s/x), to represent the fact that some persons within the psychiatric system are forced into this objectified and passive role (157).

When I first encountered the term *survivor*, I felt hesitant. It seemed to have unsettling similarities to "cure": a survivor, I thought, implicitly had *had* a traumatic experience and come out the other side. This doesn't describe my experience. I make regular use of the psychiatric system, and I consider myself the agent and director of my treatments; for example, I interviewed and discarded psychiatrists until I found one who agrees with my approach to my bodymind.[2] However, there is no avoiding the fact that he, not I, wields the power of the prescription pad. In addition, I possess the economic and cultural privilege that permits me to try out and reject various caregivers, a privilege not open to many in the c/s/x group. And finally, like any "patient," I am subject to my caregivers' power over information. For example, when my psychiatrist and my therapist conferred and arrived at one of my diagnoses, they chose not to share that diagnosis with me until some months later (their stated reason being that I had been in the midst of a crisis and was not ready to process the information). As it happens, I think they made an appropriate decision, but the fact remains that regardless of what I thought, the outcome would have been the same; I had no say in the matter.

In her ethnographic study *Talking Back to Psychiatry*, Linda J. Morrison interviewed activists in the c/s/x movement, which she defines as "people who have been diagnosed as mentally ill and are engaged in different forms of 'talking back' to psychiatry and the mental health system," as well as allies including "dissident mental health professionals, lawyers, advocates, and family members" (ix). Morrison found that they made use of the term *survivor* in various ways, and that a "heroic survivor narrative" is deeply influential in the movement, both through published accounts (such as Kate Millett's *The Loony-Bin Trip*) and in individuals' processes of identity formation vis-à-vis psychiatric discourse (101). Participants' survivor narratives "exist in a range of intensity, from high drama to muted skeptical observations" (129), but the narrative as a whole, Morrison argues, plays a crucial role in the movement, helping to build solidarity and empower resistant voices. Significantly, this narrative, and the term *survivor,* have also been singled out for denigration by critics (Morrison 152–53).

My own thinking on *psychiatric system survivor* was deepened when I discussed it with my colleague Petra Kuppers. One evening at a conference, sitting on the bed in her hotel room and chewing over my thoughts, I said that I didn't feel I "survived" the psychiatric system so much as worked within it, negotiating and resisting as I went. "But," Petra said simply, "that *is* survival." Her insight has shifted my view of the term: rather than thinking of a survivor as one who has undergone and emerged from some traumatic experience (such as incarceration in a mental institution), it can also denote one who is actively and resistantly involved with the psychiatric system on an ongoing basis.

Mental illness introduces a discourse of wellness/unwellness into the notion of madness; its complement is *mental health,* the term of choice for the medical community as well as insurance companies and social support services. This well/unwell paradigm has many problems, particularly its implication that a mad person needs to be "cured" by some means. One material consequence of this view is that mental health insurance operates on a "cure" basis, demanding "progress" reports from therapists and social workers, and cutting off coverage when the patient is deemed to have achieved a sufficiently "well" state. For instance, although the American Psychiatric Association recommends that persons with my diagnoses remain in long-term talk therapy, my insurance company (CIGNA) determined in 2006 that I was "well enough" and terminated my mental-health coverage, except for brief pharmaceutical consultations with my psychiatrist. During a months-long battle with the "physician reviewer" employed by CIGNA, my therapist's and psychiatrist's requests for continued coverage (which, according to CIGNA's rules, I was not permitted to make directly) were repeatedly turned down. Ultimately, my therapist was informed that the decision would stand unless I "actually attempt[ed] suicide," at which point I would be deemed unwell enough to resume therapy. This "well/unwell" paradigm reflects the larger tendency of American medical systems to intervene in "problems" rather than practice a more holistic form of care.

However, an advantage of *mental illness* is that it can be allied with the substantial—and sometimes contentious—conversation within DS on the intersections between illness and disability. In a 2001 *Hypatia* article, "Unhealthy Disabled: Treating Chronic Illnesses as Disabilities," Susan Wendell points out that activists in the disability rights movement in the United States have often sought to "distinguish themselves from those who are ill" (18). This has led to a schism between those she calls the "healthy disabled," whose impairments "are relatively stable and predictable for the foreseeable future" (19), and those who are chronically ill. Because those with chronic illnesses are often exhausted, in pain, or experiencing mental confusion, their very identities as activists come into question:

> Fluctuating abilities and limitations can make people with chronic illnesses seem like unreliable activists, given the ways that political activity in both disability and feminist movements are structured. ... Commitment to a cause is usually equated to energy expended, even to pushing one's body and mind excessively, if not cruelly.
>
> (25)

Wendell acknowledges that "healthy disabled" and "unhealthy disabled" are blurry categories: a person with cerebral palsy, for example, may also experience exhaustion, pain, or mental confusion; indeed, a person with a physical impairment may also have a chronic illness. Usually, however, "disabled" implicitly means "healthy disabled," and full inclusion of the unhealthy disabled must involve "changes in the structure, culture, and traditions of political activism," with new attitudes toward "energy and commitment, pace and cooperation" (Wendell 26). As yet, such changes are largely unrealized. Consider the last conference you attended: did events run from 9:00 a.m. until late at night? Consider the "tenure clock," or activist efforts that call for attendance in public places for hours at a time: do such occasions assume each participant will have the ability to meet people, interact, and function for hours on end? Consider the persons who did not attend. Do you know who they are?

Andrea Nicki's theory of psychiatric disability picks up Wendell's point about energy and health, but reshapes it to critique the implicitly rational mind of the "good" disabled person—or, as Quintilian might have put it, the "good disabled person speaking well" (see Brueggemann, *Lend*). Not only must this person be of rational mind, Nicki argues; he must also adhere to a "cultural demand of cheerfulness," which is particularly insidious because in some cases—for a person with depression, for example—this would involve not just an attitude *toward* his illness but a direct erasure *of* his illness (94). Like Wendell, Nicki calls for redesign of our social and work environments, emphasizing the importance of interdependence as a means to achieve this goal. Anne Wilson and Peter Beresford have argued that the project will be difficult, and will involve not just surface-level changes, but a full reworking of the social model of disability (145).

One part of this reworking will be the acknowledgment that, although discursive alliances can be drawn between physical and mental illness, important differences exist as well. For example, while members of the disability rights movement, including myself, proudly call ourselves "disabled," many members of the c/s/x movement view the term *disabled* with more suspicion. In the view of the c/s/x movement, when psychiatry assigns a diagnosis of "mental illness" to a person, that person is marked as permanently damaged, and as one whose rights may be taken away—unless, of course, she complies with psychiatry's requirements for "care," which may include medication, incarceration, or electroshock. Morrison makes this point by contrasting psychiatric diagnosis with the diagnosis of a cold:

> In modern psychiatry, a person who has been diagnosed with a serious and persistent mental illness (SPMI) is rarely considered "cured" or completely free of illness. The implied expectation is that mental illnesses are chronic. They may remit but they are likely to recur. Compare, for example the yearly cold symptoms with congestion and cough that many people experience, followed by recovery to a "normal" state. In psychiatric illness, recovery from the symptoms would not be considered the end of the problem. The likelihood of a return to a symptomatic state, with resultant need for medical intervention,

> would be assumed...[A] former patient is always expected to become a future patient and the sick role is ongoing. In fact, if a patient believes otherwise, this can be considered a symptom of exacerbated illness.
>
> (5)

This paradox, in which belief of one's own wellness may *in itself* be considered evidence of unwellness, lies at the heart of psychiatric diagnosis. To accept the psychiatric profession's definition of oneself as sick is considered a key move toward getting well; the technical term for acceptance of a psychiatric label is "insight." Although members of the c/s/x movement occupy a range of perspectives, generally the movement resists psychiatry's efforts to place its "patients" into the "sick role." Like Deaf activists, c/s/x activists have much in common with disability activists, but strong differences as well—one of which is the issue of whether or not to self-identify as *disabled*.

One thing c/s/x and disability activists agree upon, however, is the deeply problematic nature of modern psychiatric discourse. Working in concert with the gigantic forces of for-profit insurance companies and the pharmaceutical industry, mainstream psychiatry places ever-increasing emphasis on a biological and positivist definition of mental illness, all while claiming to remain "theory-neutral" (Lewis 97). However, dissident voices can be heard within psychiatry as well. As Morrison shows, some medical professionals are members of the c/s/x movement. Groups that bring together critical psychologists and psychiatrists and the c/s/x movement have proliferated since the 1990s, and include the Critical Psychiatry Network; Psychology, Politics and Resistance; the Mental Health Alliance; and Radical Psychology Network. This resistant strain of psychiatry is sometimes called *postpsychiatry,* a theory/practice that views "mind" philosophically and socially as well as biologically.

Postpsychiatrist medical philosophers Patrick Bracken and Philip Thomas argue that, once Descartes had established the now-conventional body/mind split (as well as valorization of the individual subject), subsequent theories of mind continued to perpetuate this belief, extending into nineteenth- and twentieth-century psychiatry, which expanded its effects still further. Bracken and Thomas identify three outcomes of this philosophy: the beliefs that "madness is internal"; that madness can be explained neurologically and treated (solely) with pharmaceuticals; and that psychiatrists have the "right and responsibility" to coerce their patients ("Postpsychiatry" 725). Postpsychiatry offers an alternative path, Bracken and Thomas suggest, not by replacing old techniques with new ones, but rather by "open[ing] up spaces in which other perspectives can assume a validity previously denied them"—especially the perspectives of those labeled "mentally ill" ("Postpsychiatry" 727). In addition to centering the agency of mad people, Bracken and Thomas argue for replacing the conventional separation of body and mind with an emphasis on social context, ethical as well as technical (chemical) modes of care, and an end to the claim that coercive "treatments" are applied for "objective" or "scientific" reasons. In a later, briefer article, Bracken and Thomas clarify the relationship of Cartesian dualism to postpsychiatry: human mental life, they argue, is not "some sort of enclosed world residing inside the skull," but is constructed "by our very presence and through our physical bodies" ("Time to Move" 1434).

Bradley Lewis offers an in-depth account of postpsychiatry in *Moving Beyond Prozac, DSM, & the New Psychiatry: The Birth of Postpsychiatry*. Describing himself as a "hybrid academic," Lewis holds both an M.D. in psychiatry and a Ph.D. in interdisciplinary humanities (ix). From this unusual position, Lewis makes a call for postpsychiatry that is both pragmatic and theoretical: cyborg theory, neurophysiology, and the governing structure of the APA all occupy significant parts of his attention. *Moving Beyond Prozac* describes "a theorized postpsychiatry," which would "take seriously the role of language and power" as well as "work without the pseudo-foundations and pseudo-certainties of modernist science and reason" (17). Lewis does not wish to do away with psychiatrists and clinics, but rather to reform them. The reformed "clinical encounter," for example, would include "not only the modernist values of empirical diagnosis and rational therapeutics but also additional clinical values like ethics, aesthetics, humor, empathy, kindness and justice" (17; see also Lewis, "Narrative Psychiatry"). While pragmatic, Lewis's argument is not individualistic, but aimed at discourses and structures of power. Individual psychiatrists and practices do need to change, Lewis suggests, but the core project is revision of the psychiatric profession to become more democratic, less positivist, less capitalistic, and to include the voices and concerns of *all* its stakeholders, including the c/s/x group.

Neuroatypical and *neurodiverse* mark a broader territory than psychiatric discourse: these terms include all whose brains position them as being somehow different from the neurotypical run of the mill. *Neuroatypical* is most often used to indicate persons on the autism spectrum, including those with Asperger's syndrome (AS), but has also been used to refer to persons with bipolar disorder (Antonetta) and traumatic brain injuries (Vidali). In her "bipolar book" (13) *A Mind Apart*, Susanne Antonetta argues that neurodiversity acts a positive force in human evolution, enabling alternative and creative ways of thinking, knowing, and apprehending the world.

A potential problem with the rhetoric of neurodiversity is that it can read as overly chipper (like a "Celebrate Diversity!" bumper sticker); its optimism can flatten individual difference. However, it also carries a complement, *neurotypical* (or NT), which destabilizes assumptions about "normal" minds and can be used to transgressive effect (Brownlow). For example, Aspies For Freedom has used NT to parody the rhetoric of "cure" propagated by the organization Fighting Autism. Until very recently, Fighting Autism published and maintained a graphic called the "autism clock" which purported to record the "incidence" of autism for persons aged 3 to 22 and the supposed economic "cost" of this incidence.[3] In response, Aspies For Freedom published a parody of the autism clock, which pathologizes neurotypicals and suggests that for the onrush of diagnoses ("1 every minute"), there will be "2 to take them."

While Fighting Autism viewed autism as a disease that must be battled and cured, Aspies For Freedom takes the stance that autism is a form of neurodiversity, that is, of difference, not something that should be eradicated. Although public opinion of autism tends to be dominated by the disease/cure model, resistant voices of neurodiversity have proliferated, especially through web-based communities, blogs, and webtexts (see, for example, Yergeau, "Aut(hored)ism").

Some DS scholars, including Cynthia Lewiecki-Wilson, have called for a coalition of those with psychiatric and cognitive disabilities; she suggests that the term *mental disability* can be used to denote the rhetorical position of both groups:

> For the purposes of this paper, I group mental illness and severe mental retardation under the category *mental disabilities*. Despite the varieties of and differences among mental impairments, this collective category focuses attention on the problem of gaining rhetoricity

to the mentally disabled: that is, rhetoric's received tradition of emphasis on the individual rhetor who produces speech/writing, which in turn confirms the existence of a fixed, core self, imagined to be located in the mind.
>
> (157)

In other words, according to Lewiecki-Wilson, the notion that one's disability is located in one's mind unites this category, not because such a thing is inherently true, but because persons with these kinds of disabilities share common experiences of disempowerment as rhetors—a lack of what both Prendergast and Lewiecki-Wilson call "rhetoricity." My own struggles for adequate terminology follow Lewiecki-Wilson's call for coalition politics. Although it is important to note the differences between specific experiences, in general I believe we need *both* local specificity *and* broad coalitions for maximum advantage. Persons with impaired bodyminds have been segregated from one another enough.

For a while, I used the term *psychosocial disability*. I like its etymology, the fact that it bumps *psych* (soul) against social context; I like its ability to reach toward both mind and world. Its emphasis on social context calls attention to the fact that psychosocial disabilities can be vividly, and sometimes unpredictably, apparent in social contexts. Although it's common to describe psychosocial disabilities as "invisible," or "hidden," this is a misnomer. In fact, such disabilities may become vividly manifest in forms ranging from "odd" remarks to lack of eye contact to repetitive stimming.[4] Like queerness, psychosocial disability is not so much invisible as it is apparitional, and its "disclosure" has everything to do with the environment in which it dis/appears.[5] *Psychosocial disability* announces that it is deeply intertwined with social context, rather than buried in an individual's brain.

Although *psychosocial* has been used in narrow ways that comply with a medical model of disability, it also has considerable traction within disability studies. In her introduction to a 2002 special issue of *Disability Studies Quarterly*, Deborah Marks argues that a psychosocial perspective can "challenge the disciplinary boundary between psychological and social paradigms." Taking up her point, Patrick Durgin has amplified the term's radical possibilities:

> A "psycho-social formulation" is, in short, the none-of-the-above option in the diagnostic pantheon. It is the excluded middle or liminal space where impairment meets world to become disability. To use clinical language, it does not "present" clinically because it resists being given diagnostic surmise; and yet it won't "pass" as normal.
>
> (138)

Durgin goes on to argue that, although *psychosocial* may seem a kind of "golden mean" between medical and social paradigms, it too must undergo critical examination; not least, I would add, because this term can and has been used in medicalized and positivist projects. For example, in the third and fourth editions of the *Diagnostic and Statistical Manual of Mental Disorders,* the authors have made a great show of considering social factors in their new classification of "mental disorders," and also of having involved a broad base of patients and clinicians in developing the manual. Yet, as Lewis points out, that show is largely illusory; the central developers of the landmark DSM-III (and inventors of its categories) numbered just *five persons*, and the overarching rationale for the manual is increasingly positivist and biological. Despite this history, I value the potential of *psychosocial* for reappropriation. In a sense, Durgin is saying to the authors of the DSM, "You want social? We'll give you social."

My appreciation of *psychosocial* has been affirmed by philosopher Cal Montgomery, who pointed out its usefulness in terms of sensory as well as cognitive disabilities, saying, "I do think we need a way of talking inclusively about people for whom access to human interaction is problematic." (See chapter 6 [original volume] for elaboration of this point.) However, having spent the last couple of years trying this term out—on the page, in conference presentations, at dinner with friends—I've become increasingly uncomfortable with it, because in most cases if seems to provoke puzzlement rather than connection. Explaining my experiences to Cal, I wrote: "I've been using the term 'psychosocial disability' in various settings for over a year—at conferences, in casual conversations, in my writing, etc.—and it seems that, *unless* I'm writing an article where I can fully explain what I'm getting at, people just kind of go blank when I use the term. I have started to feel like, what's the point of using a term that no one gets but me?" Put simply, in most social contexts, *psychosocial* failed to *mean.*

So I have taken another tack. Following Lewiecki-Wilson, these days I'm using *mental disability.* As Lewiecki-Wilson argues, this term can include not only madness, but also cognitive and intellectual dis/abilities of various kinds. I would add that it might also include "physical" illnesses accompanied by mental effects (for example, the "brain fog" that attends many autoimmune diseases, chronic pain, and chronic fatigue). And, as Cal suggests, we should keep in mind its potential congruence with sensory and other kinds of disabilities—that is, its commonalities with "people for whom access to human interaction is problematic."

Finally, while I respect the concerns of those who reject the label *disabled,* I have chosen to use a term that includes *disability* explicitly. In my own experience, claiming disability has been a journey of community, power, and love. Over the last 20 years, I have migrated from being a person who spent a lot of time in hospitals, who was prescribed medications and prodded by doctors, to a person who inhabits a richly diverse, contentious, and affectionate disability community. Let me tell a story to explain this migration: On a December day in 2008, I arrived in a fluorescent-lit hotel room in San Francisco to listen to a panel of scholars talk about disability. I had recently made a long airplane journey and felt off-balance, frightened, and confused. I sat beside disability activist and writer Neil Marcus, and when he saw my face, he opened his arms and offered me a long, hard-muscled hug. That hug, with arms set at awkward angles so we could fit within his wheelchair, with chin digging into scalp and warm skin meeting skin—that, to me, is disability community. Neil may or may not know what it is like to wake with night terrors at age 40, I may or may not know what it feels like to struggle to form words, but the reaching across those spaces is what defines disability for me. We write, we question and disagree, we are disabled. Simi Linton has said of the term *disability* that "We have decided to reassign meaning rather than choose a new name" (31).

And so, in naming myself a crazy girl, neuroatypical, mentally disabled, psychosocially disabled—in acknowledging that I appear (as a colleague once told me) "healthy as a horse" yet walk with a mind that whispers in many voices—I am trying to reassign meaning. In the best of all possible worlds I would refuse to discard terms, refuse to say which is best. I believe in learning the terms, listening to others' voices, and naming myself pragmatically according to what the context requires. I believe that this is language.

NOTES

1. See Christensen; Dajani; Linton, chap. 2; Titchkosky, "Disability"; Trent, introduction; and Zola.
2. I use the term *bodymind* to emphasize that although "body" and "mind" usually occupy separate conceptual and linguistic territories, they

are deeply intertwined. This theory is drawn in part from Babette Rothschild's *The Body Remembers*. Although Rothschild's usage refers to persons who have experienced trauma, I believe it can be usefully applied to persons with mental disabilities of all kinds, for—as I argue throughout this book—our problems are in no sense "all in our minds." If it weren't so unwieldy, I would be tempted to use something like *psychobiosocialpoliticalbodymind*.

3. Just as this book was going to press, the autism clock was removed from the website. When I wrote to inquire, I received a notice that it has "been brought to our attention that the autism clock was offensive to some members of the autism community." In addition, the domain name of the website was changed from fightingautism.org to thoughtfulhouse.org. While limited, these measures indicate that the hard work of neurodiverse activists is being noticed.

4. *Stimming,* short for "self-stimulating," is a self-soothing repetitive activity that may be practiced by persons with a variety of disabilities, including autism, obsessive-compulsive disorder, or anxiety.

5. For more on the apparitional nature of mental disabilities, see Montgomery, "Critic of the Dawn" and "A Hard Look at Invisible Disability," and Samuels. For more on the apparitional nature of disability and illness generally, see Myers, "Coming Out" and Siebers, "Disability as Masquerade."

WORKS CITED

American Psychiatric Association. *Diagnostic and Statistical Manual of Mental Disorders*. Text revision. 4th ed. Arlington, VA: APA, 2000.

Antonetta, Susanne. *A Mind Apart: Travels in a Neurodiverse World*. New York: Penguin, 2005.

Aristotle. *The Complete Works of Aristotle*. Jonathan Barnes, ed. and trans. Bollingen Series LXXI: 1–2. Princeton, NJ: Princeton University Press, 1984.

Aristotle. *The Nicomachean Ethics*. Trans. J. A. K. Thomson. Rev. Hugh Tredennick. Intro. Jonathan Barnes. New York: Penguin, 2004.

Bracken, Patrick, and Philip Thomas. "Postpsychiatry: A New Direction for Mental Health." *British Medical Journal* 322 (2001): 724–27.

Bracken, Patrick, and Philip Thomas. "Time to Move Beyond the Mind–Body Split." *British Medical Journal* 325 (2002): 1433–34.

Brownlow, Charlotte. "Re-presenting Autism: The Construction of 'NT Syndrome.'" *Journal of Medical Humanities* 31 (2010): 243–55.

Brueggemann, Brenda Jo. *Lend Me Your Ear: Rhetorical Constructions of Deafness*. Washington, DC: Gallaudet Press, 1999.

Christensen, Carol. "Disabled, Handicapped or Disordered: What's in a Name?" *Disability and the Dilemmas of Education and Justice*. Ed. Carol Christensen and Fazal Rizvi. Buckingham: Open University Press. 63–77.

Dajani, Karen Finlon. "What's in a Name? Terms Used to Refer to People with Disabilities." *Disability Studies Quarterly* 21.3 (2001).

Durgin, Patrick F. "Psychosocial Disability and Post-Ableist Poetics: The 'Case' of Hannah Weiner's *Clairvoyant Journals*." *Contemporary Women's Writing* 2:2 (2008): 131–54.

Hacking, Ian. *Mad Travelers: Reflections on the Reality of Transient Mental Illness*. Cambridge, MA: Harvard University Press, 1998.

Jackson, Vanessa. "In Our Own Voice: African-American Stories of Oppression, Survival and Recovery in Mental Health Systems." MFI Portal. April 4, 2009. www.mindfreedom.org/kb/mental-healthabuse/Racism/InOurOwn-Voice/vie.

Lewiecki-Wilson, Cynthia. "Rethinking Rhetoric through Mental Disabilities." *Rhetoric Review* 22.2 (2003): 156–67.

Lewis, Bradley. *Moving Beyond Prozac, DSM, & the New Psychiatry*. Ann Arbor: University of Michigan Press, 2006.

Lewis, Bradley. "Narrative Psychiatry." *Comprehensive Textbook of Psychiatry*, 9th ed. Ed. Benjamin J. Saddock and Virginia A. Sadock. Philadelphia: Lippincott, 2009. 2934–39.

Linton, S. *Claiming Disability: Knowledge and Identity*. New York: New York University Press, 1998.

Marks, Deborah. "Introduction: Counselling, Therapy and Emancipatory Praxis." *Disability Studies Quarterly* 22.3 (2002).

Millet, Kate. *The Loony-Bin Trip*. New York: Simon and Schuster, 1990.

Montgomery, Cal. "Critic of the Dawn." *Ragged Edge Online* 22.3 (May 2001). www.ragged-edgemag.com/0501/0501cov.htm.

Montgomery, Cal. "A Hard Look at Invisible Disability." *Ragged Edge Online* 22.2 (March 2001). www.ragged-edge-mag.com/0301/0301ft1.htm.

Morrison, Linda J. *Talking Back to Psychiatry: The Psychiatric Consumer/Survivor/Ex-Patient Movement*. New York: Routledge, 2005.

Myers, Kimberly R. "Coming Out: Considering the Closet of Illness." *Journal of Medical Humanities* 25.4 (2004): 255–70.

Nicki, Andrea. "The Abused Mind: Feminist Theory, Psychiatric Disability, and Trauma." *Hypatia* 16.4 (2001): 80–104.

Prendergast, Catherine. "On the Rhetorics of Mental Disability." In *Embodied Rhetorics: Disability in Language and Culture*, ed. James C. Wilson and Cynthia Lewiecki-Wilson. Carbondale: Southern Illinois University Press, 2001. 45–60. Also in *Towards a Rhetoric of Everyday Life: New Directions in Research on Writing, Text, and Discourse*. Ed. Martin Nystrand and John Duffy. Madison: University of Wisconsin Press, 2003. 189–206.

Reaume, Geoffrey. "Mad People's History." *Radical History Review* 94 (2006): 170–82.

Rothschild, Babette. *The Body Remembers: The Psychophysiology of Trauma and Trauma Treatment*. New York: Norton, 2000.

Samuels, Ellen. "My Body, My Closet: Invisible Disability and the Limits of Coming-out Discourse." *GLQ* 9.1 (2003): 233–55.

Siebers, Tobin. "Disability as Masquerade." *Literature and Medicine* 23.1 (2004): 1–22.

Thiher, Allen. *Revels in Madness: Insanity in Medicine and Literature*. Ann Arbor: University of Michigan Press, 2004.

Titchkosky, Tanya. "Disability: A Rose by Any Other Name? 'People-First' Language in Canadian Society." *Canadian Review of Sociology and Anthropology* 38.2 (2001): 125–40.

Trent, James W. Jr. *Inventing the Feeble Mind: A History of Mental Retardation in the United States*. Berkeley: University of California Press, 1994.

Vidali, Amy. "Rhetorical Hiccups: Disability Disclosure in Letters of Recommendation." *Rhetoric Review* 28.2 (2009): 185–204.

Wendell, Susan. "Unhealthy Disabled: Treating Chronic Illnesses as Disabilities." *Hypatia* 16.4 (2001): 17–33.

Wilson, Anne, and Peter Beresford. "Madness, Distress and Postmodernity: Putting the Record Straight." In *Disability/Postmodernity: Embodying Disability Theory*, ed. M. Corker and T. Shakespeare. London: Continuum, 2002.

Yergeau, Melanie. "Aut(hored)ism." *Computers and Composition Online* (Spring 2009). www.bgsu.edu/cconline/dmac/index.html

Zola, Irving Kenneth. "Self, Identity and the Naming Question: Reflections on the Language of Disability." *Social Science and Medicine* 36.2 (1993): 167–73.

CHAPTER 24

My Body, My Closet: Invisible Disability and the Limits of Coming Out

Ellen Samuels

SUMMARY

How is the "coming out" process similar or different for people who identify as queer or disabled? Although there are inherent problems with analogizing social identities, Ellen Samuels suggests that employing analogies critically might yield greater results than avoiding these analogies. When a disability is not immediately signaled by a person's appearance, the disabled person experiences a kind of "coming out": both in revealing (and "proving") disability identity to family members and in experiencing the revelation of disability itself.

The perception persists that nonvisibly disabled people prefer to "pass" by minimizing the role of disabled identity. Samuels pointed out that passing conflates two separate dynamics: deliberately hiding a disability and passing by default because of nonvisibility. When a disabled person reveals a disability rather than attempting to pass, he or she is often met with a suspicion of fraud. The analogy of coming out as queer and coming out as disabled breaks down when comparing the meanings and consequences of these declarations.

Nevertheless, Samuels discusses how two identities—lesbian-femme and nonvisibly disabled—both cause a "category crisis" when visible appearance doesn't correlate to self-identification. Moreover, people with nonvisible disabilities can be marginalized within disability communities and the community at large when disabilities are unrecognized. Similarly, femme lesbians must negotiate queer identity when choices about personal appearance don't signal queer identity to a wider community. Samuels argues for analogizing identities (and queering disability studies) in order to find subversion at the meeting points between bodies and communities, between voices and resistant audiences of power.

THE LIMITS OF ANALOGY

A story: On a breezy afternoon one April I met with "Samantha," a student in an undergraduate course on literature and disability, to talk about her paper on cultural images of burn survivors. After showing me her draft, she remained, eager to talk about issues of disability and visibility, about her own experience as a person who appears "normal" until one looks closely enough to see the scars on her jaw and neck, the puckered skin that disappears under the neck of her T-shirt and reappears on her arm and wrist. Since I almost always look "normal" despite my disabling chronic illness, I sympathized with her struggle over how and when to come out about her disability identity. "My parents don't understand why I would call myself disabled," Samantha said matter-of-factly; then she added with a mischievous grin, "In fact, there are two basic things my family just doesn't want to accept: that my cousin is gay and that I'm disabled. So we're going to take a picture of ourselves at a gay pride march next month and send it to them."

The moral: I admire Samantha's wit and intelligence. I am also struck by the convergence of many themes in her story: the shifting and contested meanings of disability; the uneasy, often self-destroying tension between appearance and identity; the social scrutiny that refuses to accept statements of identity without "proof"; and, finally, the discursive and practical connections between coming out—in all the meanings of the term—as queer and as disabled. Thus I begin with Samantha's story to frame a discussion not only of analogies between queerness and disability but of the specifics of coming out in each context as a person whose bodily appearance does not immediately signal one's own sense of identity. In the first section of this essay I consider the complicated dynamics inherent in the analogizing of social identities, with specific reference to feminist, queer, and disability studies. In the second section I turn to the politics of visibility and invisibility, drawing on autobiographical narratives as well as social theory to explore constructions of coming out or passing in a number of social contexts. In the third section I further explore these issues through a focus on two "invisible" identities: lesbian-femme and nonvisible disability.[1] Thus each section seeks to "queer" disability in order to develop new paradigms of identity, representation, and social interaction.

A number of disability theorists suggest that disability has more in common with sexual orientation than with race, ethnicity, or gender—other categories often invoked analogically to support the social model of disability.[2] One argument for this connection is that most people with disabilities, like most queers, do not share their identity with immediate family members and often have difficulty accessing queer or

crip culture.[3] The history of an oppressive medical model for homosexuality and the nature–nurture and assimilation–transformation debates in the modern LGBT civil rights movement offer additional areas of potential common ground with disability activism. Haunting such arguments, however, is the vexed issue of analogy itself, which cannot be extracted from the tangled history of the use and misuse of such identity analogies in past liberation movements.

In particular, most current analogies between oppressed social identities draw in some fashion on the sex–race analogy that emerged from the women's liberation movement of the 1970s. This analogy was used primarily by white women to claim legitimacy for feminist political struggle by analogizing it to the struggle of African Americans for civil rights. The sex–race analogy has been extensively critiqued, most importantly by feminists of color, and has by now been renounced by most white feminists. The gist of such a critique is suggested by the title of Tina Grillo and Stephanie M. Wildman's article "Obscuring the Importance of Race: The Implications of Making Comparisons between Racism and Sexism (or Other Isms)," and is summarized by Lisa Maria Hogeland:

> First, in its use of *race,* it represents a fantastic vision of African-American identity, community, and politics—uncontested, uncontradictory, unproblematic—that is shaped by a simultaneous nostalgia for and forgetting of the Civil Rights Movement, as if identity, community, and politics had never been the subjects of struggle. Second, the analogy attempts to forge out of that nostalgia and forgetting an equally fantastic vision of a self-evident identity, community, and politics of *sex,* whether construed as gender or as sexuality. Third, implicit in the setting together of the two is a fantasy of coalition . . . [which] sidesteps the processes and practices that would make such coalition possible.[4]

Despite the validity of this critique, Hogeland observes that the sex–race analogy continues to function in feminist theory and has also emerged strongly in queer theory (45).

My own investigation of the analogies regarding disability, however, suggests that their use has transformed from a comparison between *similar* oppressions to a strategic *contrasting* of identities to elucidate a particular aspect of the primary identity under discussion. Such a transformation accords with the classic definition of analogy as based on "a similarity or resemblance of relations, in which the resemblance lies in the qualities of two or more objects that are essentially dissimilar."[5] In practice, such analogies often both create and rely on artificial dichotomies that not only produce inequality between the terms of comparison but exclude or elide anomalous experiences that do not fit easily within their terms.

For John Swain and Colin Cameron, strategic contrasting supports the claim that disability and sexual "preference" are both social labels that are "usually self-referent from only one side," so that, unlike dual or multiple labels such as male and female, and black, Asian, Latina, and white, the labels of nondisabled and heterosexuality are always already presumed "unless otherwise stated." Swain and Cameron conclude: "There is a coming out process for gay men and lesbian women which has no real equivalent in gender and race categorizations," and "there is a similar coming out process for disabled people."[6] In this argument, the identities of gayness and disability are stabilized and opposed to those of gender and race. Such an analogy not only relies on an overly restrictive, unilateral view of gender and race but implies false equations between the two identities on each side of the opposition (gay = disabled; gender = race), thereby invoking the original sex–race analogy in a renewed form. While this analogy claims for sexual oppression the same legitimacy as that (supposedly) achieved for racial oppression—my experience is *like* your experience—contrasting analogies such as that employed by Swain and Cameron claim for gay or disabled oppression a different valence than that of gender or race: my experience is *different* from yours. Yet both analogies have the same goal—to persuade the listener of the validity and urgency of the speaker's original experience—and thus both implicitly devalue the other term of comparison.

An important difference between the analogies of sex–race and sexual orientation–disability is that the former relates to oppressions, while the latter describes processes of liberation and self-actualization, in this case, "coming out." Perhaps analogies between liberatory practices are less problematic than those between oppressions, since they claim a sameness not of experience but of resistance. This argument has a certain logic; however, it does not address the deeper issue of the presumption of sameness that produces oversimplified "mapping analogies." As Eve Tavor Bannet explains, the mapping analogy represents a historical mutation of analogy that, by

> stressing resemblance over difference to make different entities more or less alike[,] transformed analogy into an equivalence—a rule of presumed resemblance, structural isomorphism, or homology between domains. The moment of essential difference which distinguishes analogy from identity, and different entities from each other, was flattened into a moment of proportional representation.[7]

Clearly, the sex–race analogy suffers from the endemic flaws of the mapping analogy itself, yet all language functions in a sense through analogy, and so it remains an inescapable part of the communicative realm. Certainly, the tendency to make analogies between identities and liberation movements is pervasive and often persuasive, and so I suggest not that we attempt to escape from analogy but that we seek to employ it more critically than in the past.

Bannet examines a particular means of destabilizing and evolving mapping analogies through her discussion of Wittgenstein, for whom

> analogy is not just an image, an extended simile, or the juxtaposition of objects of comparison. ... analogy in Wittgenstein's sense is a traditional method of reasoning from the known to the unknown, and from the visible to the speculative, by carrying familiar terms, paradigms, and images across into unfamiliar territory.[8]

I find this model of analogy especially useful, both because of its acknowledgment of the instability of its terms and because of its foregrounding of the issue of visibility as a key component of analogical language. Indeed, when we consider that "theories and practices of identity and subject formation in Western culture are largely structured around the logic of visibility, whether in the service of science (Victorian physiognomy), psychoanalysis (Lacan's mirror stage), or philosophy (Foucault's reading of the Panopticon)," it becomes apparent that the speculative or "invisible" has generally functioned as the subordinate term in analogical equations to this date.[9] Thus a central premise of this essay is that it behooves us to refocus our endeavors from the visible signs of these identities to their invisible manifestations. The focus on specularity and visible difference that permeates much disability theory creates a dilemma not only for nonvisibly disabled people who wish to enter the conversation but for the overarching concepts of disability and normalization themselves.[10] Passing, closeting, and coming out become vexed issues that strain at the limitations of the discourse meant to describe them.

THE LIMITS OF VISIBILITY

> Coming out, then, for disabled people, is a process of redefinition of one's personal identity through rejecting the tyranny of the *normate,* positive recognition of impairment and embracing disability as a valid social identity. Having come out, the disabled person no longer regards disability as a reason for self-disgust, or as something to be denied or hidden, but rather as an imposed oppressive social category to be challenged and broken down. ... Coming out, in our analysis, involves a political commitment. Acceptance of a medical model of disability and being categorized by others as disabled does not constitute coming out as disabled.
>
> (Swain and Cameron, "Unless Otherwise Stated")

One of the limitations of Swain and Cameron's analogy between coming out as gay or lesbian and coming out as disabled is their one-sided definition of coming out itself. For these writers, coming out refers specifically to accepting one's "true" identity and must entail identification with the political analysis of the marginalized group. In both queer and disabled contexts, however, coming out can entail a variety of meanings, acts, and commitments. The dual meanings most crucial to my argument can be signified grammatically: to "come out to" a person or group usually refers to a specific revelatory event, while to "come out" (without an object) usually refers to the time that one first realized and came to terms with one's own identity. When *coming out* is considered as a self-contained phrase, as in Swain and Cameron's article, we may grant some validity to the observation that "people with hidden impairments are sometimes less likely to 'come out' as disabled, and move to a positive acceptance of difference and a political identity, because it is easier to maintain a 'normal' identity."[11] However, when we add the preposition *to* to the phrase, the above statement becomes almost an oxymoron: the narratives of people with "hidden impairments," like those of people with other nonvisible social identities, are suffused with themes of coming out, passing, and the imperatives of identity.

Nor is coming out a static and singular event, as Swain and Cameron imply, an over-the-rainbow shift that divides one's life before and after the event. Certainly, there must be some people who experience such momentous comings out, but I believe that the majority of us find that, even after our own internal shift, and even after a dozen gay pride marches, we must still make decisions about coming out on a daily basis, in personal, professional, and political contexts. In *Dress Codes,* Noelle Howey's memoir about her father's transition from male to female, she describes four separate moments of her father's coming out: when he told her mother, when her mother told her, when the family threw a party for Noelle's father to come out as female to friends and coworkers, and when Noelle's father came out to her years later as a lesbian.[12] Eli Clare writes of coming out as a complex convergence of identities and desires: "My coming out wasn't as much about discovering sexual desire and knowledge as it was about dealing with gender identity. Simply put, the disabled, mixed-class tomboy who asked her mother, 'am I feminine?' didn't discover a sexuality among dykes but rather a definition of woman large enough to be comfortable for many years."[13]

When we look at narratives of disabled people about their own coming-out processes, we see that the language of coming out is used liberally but often carries very different meanings. While many of these stories emphasize connections with a disability community, much as Swain and Cameron suggest, they also demonstrate the various methods and implications that coming out entails for different individuals. Rosemarie Garland-Thomson, who calls her book *Extraordinary Bodies* "the consequence of a coming-out process," describes how she had long thought of her congenital disability as a "private matter" and did not identify with disability culture or disabled people, although she did feel a special connection with disabled characters in the literature she studied.[14] Deciding to focus her scholarly work on disability was both a cause and a consequence of her coming to identify with the disability community. Similarly, Nomy Lamm, born with one leg, did not come out as disabled until late in her teens, when, through her involvement in queer and feminist activism, she met two other "freaky crip girls" and transitioned fairly quickly from "I'm not really disabled, and even if I am, nobody notices" to "I am a foxy one-legged dyke, and you will love it, or else."[15]

Not all coming-out processes are so straightforward. Carolyn Gage writes: "Did I come out? Not at first. I told my friends I had CFIDS [chronic fatigue immune dysfunction syndrome], but I did not really tell them what that meant. ... When I did go places with friends, I passed for able-bodied as much as I could."[16] For Gage, coming out did not take place until nearly a decade after she first fell ill, and it took the form of a letter to her friends that explicitly spelled out her disability, her limitations, and what she needed in terms of accommodation and support. Perhaps because of the nonvisible, contingent, and fluctuating nature of chronic illness, as opposed to the disabilities of Garland-Thomson and Lamm, Gage's coming-out process was not primarily focused on claiming the label of "disability." Rather, it required her to construct a specific narrative explaining her body to a skeptical, ignorant, and somewhat hostile audience. Susan Wendell, who also has CFIDS, speaks of the difficulty of convincing people to take her word for it regarding her abilities: "Some people offer such acceptance readily, others greet every statement of limitation with skepticism, and most need to be reminded from time to time."[17]

What is notable in Gage's and Wendell's accounts is that coming out is primarily portrayed as the process of revealing or explaining one's disability *to* others, rather than as an act of self-acceptance facilitated by a disability community. I would suggest that the nonvisible nature of Gage's and Wendell's disabilities means that, for them, the primary meaning of coming out includes the term *to* and connotes the daily challenge of negotiating assumptions about bodily appearance and function. This dynamic is not limited to those with chronic illnesses but can also be found in narratives by people with a range of nonvisible disabilities, especially sensory disabilities.[18] Megan Jones, a deaf-blind woman, writes of her response to the ubiquitous question "So, how bad is your vision and hearing anyway? I mean, you seem to get around pretty good as far as I can tell."[19] Jones admits that she once felt obliged to respond with an extended narrative explaining exactly the permeability of her cornea and the sound frequencies she could detect. Georgina Kleege writes about her need "to identify [her] blindness in public," particularly in the classroom, so that her students will understand why she cannot see them raising their hands. Kleege also writes of situations in which she chooses *not* to mention her blindness, such as social settings and a previous job, largely to avoid patronizing reactions or the suspicion of fraud but also simply because her "blindness was an irrelevant fact that they did not need to know about me, like my religion or political affiliation."[20]

Kleege's account points to the flip side of having to come out to be recognized as disabled: the ability to pass. Like racial, gender, and queer passing, the option of passing as nondisabled provides both a certain level of privilege and a profound sense of misrecognition and internal dissonance. Kleege reflects ruefully on a circumstance in which, during a flight on which

nondisabled passengers and flight attendants were ignoring or complaining about a wheelchair-using passenger, she did not come out: "Because my disability was invisible to them, it allowed them to assume I felt about the disabled as they did, that I would have behaved as they had."[21] Even though Kleege and her husband were the only passengers who assisted the wheelchair user, and Kleege came out to *her* as blind, she still expresses profound guilt that she failed to identify herself as a member of the woman's community to the airline staff and other passengers.

This dilemma can be even more complicated for those with a disability whose symptoms and severity fluctuate widely. Wendell writes:

> Because my disability is no longer readily apparent, and because it is an illness whose symptoms vary greatly from day to day, I live between the world of the disabled and the nondisabled. I am often very aware of my differences from healthy, non-disabled people, and I often feel a great need to have my differences acknowledged when they are ignored. ... On the other hand, I am very aware of how my social, economic, and personal resources, and the fact that I can "pass" as non-disabled among strangers, allow me to live a highly assimilated life among the non-disabled.[22]

Wendell then emphasizes that, even when she herself passes as nondisabled, she makes a point of identifying herself with the disability community and working for disability rights. Thus she complicates the assumption of a direct relationship between visible impairment and political identification with disability rights, as well as crucially undermining the related claim that passing as "normal" is by definition a form of negative disability identity.[23]

Nevertheless, the perception persists that nonvisibly disabled people prefer to pass and that passing is a sign and product of assimilationist longings: "By passing as non-disabled, by minimizing the significance of their impairments within their own personal and social lives... people with hidden impairments often make an effort to avoid the perceived stigma ttached to a disabled identity." Even when passing is acknowledged as a valid strategy for negotiating certain situations, it is portrayed as an undesirable response: "If... disabled people pursue normalization too much, they risk denying limitations and pain for the comfort of others and may edge into the self-betrayal associated with 'passing.'"[24] I do not deny that some nonvisibly disabled people may wish to assimilate or choose to pass; however, I believe that such an overall negative perception of passing exceeds the reality and must be interpreted in the context of other forms of bodily passing in Euro-American culture. As Lisa Walker observes: "Traditionally, passing (for straight, for white) has been read as a conservative form of self-representation that the subject chooses in order to assume the privileges of the dominant identity. Passing is the sign of the sell out" and of the victim.[25]

Such condemnations of passing often conflate two dynamics: passing deliberately (as implied by the term *hidden)* and passing by default, as it were. I certainly do not make any effort to appear "heterosexual" or "nondisabled" when I leave the house in the morning; those are simply the identities usually derived from my appearance by onlookers. While there are a number of queer accoutrements, such as buttons, stickers, jewelry, and T-shirts, that I could (and often do) choose to wear to signal my lesbian identity, a very different cultural weight is placed on any attempt to signal a disabled identity, as suspicions of fraud attach to any visible sign of disability that is not functionally essential. The analogy between coming out as queer and coming out as disabled breaks down as the different meanings and consequences of such acts come into consideration.

My quandary is not unique, nor is my search for a nonverbal sign. Deborah Peifer observes that "I don't look blind, so strangers, sisters, don't realize that I'm not seeing them. After so many years of being defiantly out of the closet as a lesbian, I am, in some ways, passing as sighted. Other than wearing a 'Yes, I am legally blind' sign, I don't know of any way to provide that information to strangers." Jones became so frustrated with strangers not believing in her visual and hearing impairments, and so oppressed by their refusal to respect her assistance dog's status, that she began to use a white cane she did not need: "I find that when I use a cane people leave me alone. ... people go right into their Blind-Person-With-A-Cane-And-Guide-Dog Red Alert mode." Kleege also mentions that "I now carry a white cane as a nonverbal sign that I don't see as much as I seem to. But like a lot of blind people who carry canes and employ guide dogs, these signs are not always understood, and the word still needs to be spoken."[26] These writers each contend with cultural assumptions that the identity they wish to signal exists only as visible physical difference. Since race, in Euro-American culture, is also assumed to be immediately visible and intelligible, Toi Derricotte, a light-skinned African American woman, writes of wishing for "a cross, a star, some sign of gold to wear so that, before they wonder or ask, I can present a dignified response to the world's interrogations."[27] In this case, coming out as disabled appears to have more in common with racial discourses of coming out or passing than with queer discourse, since the contingent (non)visibility of queer identity has produced a variety of nonverbal and/or spoken means to signal that identity, while the assumed visibility of race and disability has produced an absence of nonverbal signs and a distrust of spoken claims to those identities.

In the absence of recognized nonverbal signs, we often resort to the "less dignified" response of claiming identity through speech.

The complex longing, fear of disbelief, and internal dissonance caused by coming out in this form resound through the narratives of all people who pass by default. Passing subjects must cope with a variety of external social contexts, few of which welcome or acknowledge spontaneous declarations of invisible identity. Derricotte writes that "for several years I wore my identity like a banner. 'Hello, I'm Toi Derricotte, I'm black.'" The awkwardness of such revelations is amplified in Peifer's account of how she chose to voice her lesbian identity after blindness prevented her from participating in the subtle visual signals with which queer people in public often acknowledge each other: "They now know at the grocery store ('As a lesbian, I wish to buy these peaches') and the drugstore ('As a lesbian, I wish to explain that the yeast infection for which I am purchasing this ointment was the result of taking antibiotics, not heterosexual intercourse')."[28] Clearly, simply voicing one's identity in any and all situations is a far-from-perfect solution to the dilemmas presented by invisibility. In addition, the general cultural prejudice against such statements means that embarrassment may be the least disturbing negative response they evoke.

Suspicions of fraud often greet declarations of nonvisible identity. As Amanda Hamilton writes, people with nonvisible disabilities "are in a sense forced to pass, and at the same time assumed to be liars." Adrian Piper, a light-skinned African American, also writes of the catch-22 of remaining silent versus speaking up: "For most of my life I did not understand that I needed to identify my racial identity publicly and that if I did not I would be inevitably mistaken for white. I simply didn't think about it. But since I also made no special effort to hide my racial identity, I often experienced the shocked and/or hostile reactions of whites who discovered it after the fact." Piper adds that "some whites simply can't take my avowed racial affiliation at face value, and

react to what they see rather than what I say."[29] It takes tremendous chutzpah for nonvisibly disabled people to assert our disabilities in public settings or to ask for accommodation; denial, mockery, and silent disapproval are some of the cultural mechanisms used to inhibit us. While nonvisibly disabled people are usually required to produce medical documentation of our impairments, people who pass racially, like Derricotte and Piper, face semantic battles, interrogations about their ancestry, and challenges to their dedication to the African American community.[30]

Derricotte's memoir, *The Black Notebooks*, is an expanded meditation on race, passing, and the self. In the chapter "Diaries at an Artist's Colony" she describes hearing a racist comment on her first night at the colony and not confronting the speaker. Later, in a section of that chapter called "Coming Out," she concedes that "I [was] afraid to come out as a black person, to bear that solitude, that hatred, that invisibility."[31] Here Derricotte locates invisibility *not* as equivalent to passing but as the alienating consequence of coming out in a hostile context. When she does come out later to a white woman, the woman's resistance ironically foregrounds the white colonists' own anxiety about race:

> She said, "There aren't any black people here. I haven't seen any." "Yes there are," I said, smiling.
> "Who?"
> "You're looking at one."
> "You're not really black. Just an eighth or something." . . .
> A woman at the table said, "Did you read that article in *The New York Times* that said if they were strict about genetics, sixty percent of the people in the United States would be classified as black?"
> I looked around the table; I was laughing. The others were not. They were worried about how black I was and they should have been worrying about how black *they* were.
>
> (145)

Derricotte's story can be read as a narrative enactment of Elaine Ginsberg's observation that "passing forces reconsideration of the cultural logic that the physical body is the site of identic intelligibility."[32] Derricotte reverses the terms of the racial dichotomy black/white to refocus racial anxiety onto whiteness as an artificial cultural construct, in a move that reflects Wittgenstein's reversal of analogy to lead us "from what we suppose *is* the case everywhere to what *might* happen otherwise in particular cases."[33] While Derricotte's coming out was necessary for the scene to unfold, her passing provided the foundational meaning of the exchange. Thus we see how passing can become a subversive practice and how the passing subject may be read not as an assimilationist victim but as a defiant figure who, by crossing the borders of identities, reveals their instability.[34]

THE LIMITS OF SUBVERSION

A story: When a friend of mine read the story of Samantha with which this essay opens, she asked why Samantha would identify as disabled. I did not have a concrete answer for her. Faced with that question, many of us might point to our Social Security status, our medical records, our neurological test results, or the signs of difference on our bodies. I cannot tell you where Samantha would point. I can only observe the pride with which she claims her identity, the eagerness with which she seeks to communicate it to others. I can only conclude that, for Samantha, "being disabled" means being not a victim, not a special case, but a member of a proud and fierce community.

Her attitude is refreshing. It demonstrates the usefulness of analogizing concepts of pride between queer and disability contexts. As I continue in this section to investigate the complex dynamics of passing and visibility by examining two contemporary identities—lesbian-femme and nonvisible disability—issues of pride, resistance, and subversion come to the fore. While I myself claim both identities, that is not the main reason I chose them. When reading about coming out and queer identity, I found that writings that questioned the politics of visibility largely focused on the controversial category of lesbian-femme. Similarly, in both the disability community and the field of disability studies, the question of nonvisible disability is emerging as a highly vexed, profoundly challenging concern. Embodying both identities as I do, I naturally notice connections between the experiences they produce; at the same time, I am also aware of the significant differences and contradictions between those experiences.[35] To begin with, we may briefly examine some of the interesting correspondences and contrasts between these identities. Considering Joan Nestle's suggestion that "if the butch deconstructs gender, the femme constructs gender," what useful trains of thought can we set into motion by analogizing *butch/femme* and *gender* to *visibly/nonvisibly disabled* and *ability,* and what are the inherent problems of such an analogy?[36]

Both femme lesbians and people with nonvisible disabilities present what Marjorie Garber calls a "category crisis."[37] In the dominant cultural discourse, as well as in lesbian and disability subcultures, certain assumptions about the correlation between appearance and identity have resulted in an often exclusive focus on visibility as both the basis of community and the means of enacting social change. Discourses of coming out and passing are central to visibility politics, in which coming out is generally valorized while passing is seen as assimilationist. Thus vigilant resistance to external stereotypes of disability and lesbianism has not kept our subcultures from enacting dynamics of exclusion and surveillance over their members. Nor does a challenge to those dynamics necessarily imply a wish on my part to discard visibility politics or a rejection of the value and importance of visibility for marginalized communities. As Walker observes:

> The impulse to privilege the visible often arises out of the need to reclaim signifiers of difference which dominant ideologies have used to define minority identities negatively. But while this strategy of reclamation is often affirming, it can also replicate the practices of the dominant ideologies which use visibility to create social categories on the basis of exclusion. The paradigm of visibility is totalizing when a signifier of difference becomes synonymous with the identity it signifies. In this situation, members of a given population who do not bear that signifier of difference or who bear visible signs of another identity are rendered invisible and are marginalized within an already marginalized community.[38]

Moreover, people with nonvisible disabilities not only are marginalized in disability communities but walk an uneasy line between those communities and the dominant culture, often facing significant discrimination because our identities are unrecognized or disbelieved.

The history of femme identity in Euro-American culture, much like that of nonvisible disabilities, is one of indeterminacy and ambiguity: "The femme woman has been the most ambiguous figure in lesbian history; she is often described as the nonlesbian lesbian, the duped wife of the passing woman, the lesbian who marries."[39] Extending Terry Castle's analysis of the "apparitional lesbian," Walker suggests that "the feminine lesbian . . . perhaps more than any other figure for same-sex desire, 'haunts the edges of the field of vision.'" The sexologists who first named lesbianism in the early twentieth century had difficulty describing femmes except as dupes of the masculine "inverts" on whom their theories centered, since "the feminine lesbian produces a collapse at the intersection of the systems of marking and visibility that underpin the theory of inversion."[40] During the rise of lesbian feminism in the 1970s and 1980s, femme lesbians were shunned for supposedly copying heterosexual roles and buying into misogynist beauty standards. In the early 1990s, with the publication of Nestle's groundbreaking anthology, *The Persistent Desire,* many femme writers and activists began to speak out in defense of their identities and to protest "the penalties we have had to pay because we look like 'women'—from straight men, from so-called radical feminists, and from some lesbian separatists who, because of their anger at the social construction of femininity, cannot allow us to even exist." Yet Rebecca Ann Rugg, a member of the generation following Nestle's, still describes facing "two constant problems for a nineties femme: invisibility as a dyke and how to authenticate herself as one despite doubt and rudeness from others."[41]

Rugg's comment also rings true for the experiences of many people with nonvisible disabilities, who face not only uneasy inclusion in the disability community but a daily struggle for accommodation and benefits that reflects the dominant culture's insistence on visible signs to legitimate impairment. The very diversity of nonvisible disabilities, which include a wide range of impairments, such as chronic and terminal illness, sensory impairment, learning and cognitive differences, mental illness, and repetitive strain injuries, presents a category crisis. While I do not claim to present a comprehensive range of impairments among the authors I cite, a reading of numerous narratives across impairments suggests a common experience structured by the disbelieving gaze of the normate (much as theorists such as Garland-Thomson and Lennard J. Davis argue that disability is constructed via the normate's stare confronted by people with visible disability).[42]

In an intriguing twist, Cal Montgomery rejects the distinction between visible and nonvisible disabilities and instead points to contradictions between "tools," behaviors, and social expectations:

> The person who uses a white cane when getting on the bus, but then pulls out a book to read while riding; the person who uses a wheelchair to get into the library stacks, but then stands up to reach a book on a high shelf; the person who uses a picture-board to discuss philosophy; the person who challenges the particular expectations of *disability* that other people have is suspect. "I can't see what's wrong with him," people say, meaning, "He's not acting the way I think he should." "She's invisibly disabled," they say, meaning, "I can't see what barriers she faces."[43]

Montgomery's examples illustrate the category crisis evoked by invisible and non-visible disabilities. These contradictions among appearance, behavior, and social expectations are, of course, embodied as well in the figure of the femme: "Women who look and act like girls and who desire girls. We're just the queerest of the queers."[44] Yet there are significant differences between nonvisible disability and femme identity. Nestle writes of the "bitter irony" that while "in the straight world, butches bear the brunt of the physical and verbal abuse for their difference, in the lesbian-feminist world, femmes have had to endure a deeper attack on their sense of self-worth."[45] This remark highlights an important distinction, for it appears that femme lesbians are marginalized primarily in lesbian subculture, while people with non-visible disabilities write more often of the frustration and discrimination they face in the dominant culture. Thus passing and coming out take on different valences with regard to these different identities. However, as we have seen, these different valences are translated into the theoretical fields based on those identities, that is, queer theory and disability studies, in intriguingly similar fashions.

The difficulty of circulating in the dominant culture as a femme is largely produced by unwanted attention from men and by the general assumption that one is heterosexual. Combined with denigration and misrecognition in the lesbian community, these dynamics can cause significant frustration and alienation for femmes: "Femme is *loquería* ['the crazies']. Having your identity constantly under question, who wouldn't risk losing their mind, and their identity along the way?"[46] Nevertheless, there appears to be a wide difference between that alienation and the harassment, discrimination, and economic repercussions experienced by nonvisibly disabled people in the culture at large. Many write of being denied benefits and accommodations because their nonvisible disabilities are perceived as minor or imaginary.[47] Nonvisibly disabled people who use disabled parking permits are routinely challenged and harassed by strangers.[48] Recently, a sympathetic nondisabled friend of mine told me that a colleague of hers had reported triumphantly her detection of someone using a disabled parking permit illegally. The colleague's conclusion was based on the fact that the woman she saw getting out of the car was young and "well-groomed" and had no sign of a limp. In addition, the colleague continued, she had followed the woman closely as they entered the building and had ascertained that she was breathing "normally" and so could have no respiratory impairments. Such constant and invasive surveillance of nonvisibly disabled bodies is the result of a convergence of complicated cultural discourses regarding independence, fraud, malingering, and entitlement; the form it takes almost always involves a perceived discontinuity between appearance, behavior, and identity.

It is useful here to consider Foucault's interpretation of the Panopticon as a cultural mechanism that, among its other uses, functions to "distinguish 'laziness and stubbornness'" and "to put beggars and idlers to work." Foucault invokes the Panopticon, a nineteenth-century prison design in which a central watchtower is surrounded by individual windowed cells, as the metaphoric basis for contemporary surveillance of and by individual members of society. The Panopticon's power is to "induce in the inmate a state of conscious and permanent visibility that assures the automatic functioning of power."[49] Thus the Panopticon-like surveillance promoted by cultural myths of fraud ensures that, just as "the Other named as invisible is unseen as an individual, while simultaneously [it is] hyper-visible as a stereotype," the nonvisibly disabled subject is rendered hypervisible through social scrutiny and surveillance.[50] Thus many nonvisibly disabled people may feel that our choice is between passing and performing the dominant culture's stereotypes of disability: "Many people are more comfortable relating to me and accommodating me if they can be absolutely certain that I am who I say I am, a deaf-blind person. And they are not absolutely certain that I am that person until I bump into a wall or shape my hands into what is to them an incomprehensible language. In other words, I must make myself completely alien to these people in order for them to feel that they understand me."[51]

In contrast to this general cultural reaction to nonvisible disability, the disability community, while still largely structured around visible disabilities, is increasingly cognizant and welcoming of nonvisibly disabled people. There are certainly exceptions, which often seem to arise in connection with questions of access to disability-centered events, such as conferences.[52] Nevertheless, a large body of writing criticizing the disability community for excluding those with nonvisible disabilities simply does not exist. In contrast, the vast majority of twentieth-century American writings on femme identity make some reference to

feeling excluded, ignored, or belittled in the larger lesbian community. I have already discussed the history of the lesbian feminist movement's rejection of femme identity, as well as the contemporary response. Both Rugg and Walker suggest that queer theory, which challenges categories of gender and desire, may have indirectly contributed an epistemological basis for the latest devaluing of femme identity: Rugg writes that "femme circulates as a term of derision" in many dyke spaces, particularly in the "pomo dyke scene," which emphasizes gender bending and androgyny.[53] Similarly, I would suggest that, while disability studies has presented profound challenges to dominant cultural conceptions of the body, social identity, and independence, it has not provided the theoretical basis on which to critique and transform the equation of appearance with ability. Instead, its focus on the visual continues to render nonvisible disabilities *invisible* while reinforcing the exact cultural reliance on visibility that oppresses all of us.

Walker suggests that "the femme can be read as the 'blind spot' in [Judith] Butler's notion of gender as a performance."[54] I have often felt a similar gap in disability studies texts, even as I have benefited hugely from many of their insights. Their focus on visuality and the "gaze" sometimes leads me to question if my extremely limiting and life-changing health condition really qualifies as a disability according to the social model. Such anxieties open up larger questions regarding the shifting definition of disability and the need to resist hierarchies of oppression.

In a phrase that echoes the experiences of people with nonvisible disabilities, Rugg observes that "daily lives lived femme constantly require negotiating problems of visibility," but she subverts the victimizing potential of this observation with its conclusion: "Thus, there are innumerable examples of radical and subversive performances of femme in every imaginable context."[55] Mykel Johnson also argues for an interpretation of femme as subversive performance:

> It seems to me that femme dykes, as well as butch dykes, fuck with gender. We are not passing as straight women. Lesbian femme is not the same as "feminine." . . . a femme dyke is not trying to be discreet. There is something in femme, in fact, that is about creating a display. A femme dyke displays the erotic power of her beauty. She is bold enough to claim that power in a culture that has maintained a tyranny of "beauty norms" that may or may not include her. . . . A femme dyke is not domesticated but wild.[56]

It is challenging, however, to imagine nonvisible disability as a subversive display. While many markers of femme identity carry erotic significance and are linked to a fundamental discourse of desire, markers of nonvisible disability tend to carry medical significance and be linked to fundamental discourses of illness. However, it is possible for nonvisibly disabled people, like femme lesbians, to choose to ally ourselves with individuals visibly marked by their shared identity; as Rugg insists, "Those of us perceived as acceptable by an assimilationist politics must constantly show our alliance to people marked as stereotypical."[57]

Furthermore, some clues may be given for the possibility of such subversive performance from the narratives of people with multiple identities, including femme and disabled. Mary Frances Platt writes of her struggle to reclaim femme identity after becoming disabled as an adult:

> The more disabled I became, the more I mourned the ways my sexual femme self had manifested through the nondisabled me. . . . It's been five years now since I began using a wheelchair. I am just awakening to a new reclamation of femme. . . . An outrageous, loud-mouthed femme who's learning to dress, dance, cook, *and* seduce on wheels;

finding new ways to be gloriously fucked by handsome butches and aggressive femmes. I hang out more with the sexual outlaws now— you know, the motorcycle lesbians who see wheels and chrome between your legs as something exciting, the leather women whose vision of passion and sexuality doesn't exclude fat, disabled me.[58]

Like Platt, Sharon Wachsler found a new source of "femmeness" in herself after being forced to relinquish many external signifiers and behaviors of femme:

> Because of my chemical sensitivities, I had to throw out all my personal-care products, including perfume, hair-styling aids and cosmetics. . . . Now that I could no longer attend those [queer] events or wear the clothing, makeup and accessories that went with them, was I still femme? Where is the meaning in being femme if I'm absent from the queer women's community and have lost the markers of femme identity?

Since becoming disabled, Wachsler has learned to value aspects of herself that she once considered "too femme," such as accepting help from others. By creating accessible spaces in which to enact her new femme identity, Wachsler has reconnected with its meaning: "I carry my femmeness inside me like a red satin cushion. It comforts me. It gives me a place to rest. It sets me aglow with color. And I know that when it can, my femme flare will emerge glittering."[59]

Platt's and Wachsler's transformations indicate a merging of femme and disability identities that produces a third identity, "disabled femme," one intriguing example of "disability queered." This identity can be understood as well through Gloria Anzaldúa's concept of *"mestiza* consciousness": "The work of *mestiza* consciousness is to break down the subject–object duality that keeps her [the *mestiza*] a prisoner and to show in the flesh and through the images in her work how duality is transcended."[60] Gaby Sandoval, a Chicana nondisabled femme, draws on Anzaldúa's work when she revises passing into a positive strategy by suggesting that her experience as a Chicana who grew up "passing the border" between the United States and Mexico gave her the skills to negotiate the ambiguities of mixed-race and femme identity: "I am at home in my discomfort. I am a queer child; never quite fitting in, but always passing. I am a femme who exploits the confines of gender perceptions. . . . These abilities are definitely telling of a life lived on the border, with all of its contradictions and confusions."[61] Similarly, Willy Wilkinson, a disabled Asian American transperson, writes of a merging of border identities that inform and empower one another:

> The thing about mixed [race] people is that, like transgendered people, we are stealth. You don't always see us coming, and you can't be so sure about what you're dealing with. . . . I'm accustomed to cultural conflict and surprise with the same intimacy that I know the terrain of my features and the hues of my skin. . . . How fitting to become disabled with an illness [CFIDS] rife with ambiguity and complexity, one whose very realness is questioned. It's the story of my life.[62]

In each of these cases, *mestiza* consciousness emerges not simply as a combination of factors but as a praxis of embodied identities that occupies the border as homeland. Femme identity and nonvisible disability can both benefit from such examples, which urge us to find subversion at the meeting points between our bodies and our chosen communities, between our voices and the resistant audiences of power. In addition, by queering disability in these ways, we offer the larger fields of queer and disability studies new possibilities beyond simple analogizing as we explore "unfamiliar territory" together.

The moral: Recently, I met with Samantha to show her a draft of this essay, to see if my memory and representation of our encounter matched her own recollection. After reading my words, she showed me prints of the photo-essay she is constructing for her senior thesis: black-and-white shots of the gnarled skin of her hands juxtaposed against other landscapes: cypress bark, deep-sea sponges, the surface of San Francisco Bay. These images will be juxtaposed with head shots of disabled and nondisabled people covering their faces with their hands, hiding their identities behind their smooth skin. In a way, Samantha is my opposite: her disability lives on the skin, while mine hides beneath it. But as we work toward one another, I begin to believe that the skin, the boundary between us, can be our homeland, our shared definition.

NOTES

For feedback and support through several versions of this essay, I am grateful to Alison Kafer, Robert McRuer, Meagan Rosser, Susan Schweik, Stefanie Stroup, and Abby L. Wilkerson.

1. In current disability discourse, the terms *invisible disability* and *nonvisible disability* are often used interchangeably. Yet while the term *invisible* may be used in a literal sense to signify an unmarked social identity, the metaphor of invisibility has long been used to indicate the marginality or oppression of a social group. Thus disability discourse (like queer theory and other liberatory movements) also employs metaphorics of visibility that are unmoored from any question of marked or unmarked bodies. To minimize confusion in this essay, I employ *nonvisible* to indicate the condition of unmarked identity and *invisible* to indicate social oppression and marginality. However, I also seek to investigate how the two meanings and conditions intersect, since nonvisible disabilities remain largely invisible, both in disability discourse and in the culture at large.

2. For a prominent example of the disability/sexual orientation analogy see John Swain and Colin Cameron, "Unless Otherwise Stated: Discourses of Labelling and Identity in Coming Out," in *Disability Discourse*, ed. Mairian Corker and Sally French (Philadelphia: Open University Press, 1999), 68–78.

Tom Shakespeare analogizes disability to gender, sexual orientation, and race in "Disability, Identity, and Difference," in *Exploring the Divide: Illness and Disability,* ed. Colin Barnes and Geof Mercer (Leeds: Disability, 1996), 94–113. Rosemarie Garland-Thomson and Susan Wendell both make frequent analogies between disability and gender. See Garland-Thomson, *Extraordinary Bodies: Figuring Physical Disability in American Culture and Literature* (New York: Columbia University Press, 1997); and Wendell, *The Rejected Body: Feminist Philosophical Reflections on Disability* (New York: Routledge, 1996). Garland-Thomson also argues for a view of disability as ethnicity, but she invokes sexual orientation only with regard to nonvisible disability, which, "much like a homosexual identity, always presents the dilemma of whether or when to come out or to pass" (14). Lennard J. Davis, however, defines disability both in analogies to race, gender, and class and in contrast to them in *Enforcing Normalcy: Disability, Deafness, and the Body* (London: Verso, 1995), xvi, 2.

3. See Shakespeare, "Disability, Identity, and Difference," 105; and Wendell, *Rejected Body,* 82.

4. Tina Grillo and Stephanie M. Wildman, "Obscuring the Importance of Race: The Implications of Making Comparisons between Racism and Sexism (or Other Isms)," in *Critical White Studies: Looking behind the Mirror,* ed. Richard Delgado and Jean Stefancic (Philadelphia: Temple University Press, 1997), 619–26; Lisa Maria Hogeland, "*Invisible Man* and Invisible Women: The Sex/Race Analogy of the 1970s," *Women's History Review* 5 (1996): 46.

5. Nilli Diengott, "Analogy As a Critical Term: A Survey and Some Comments," *Style* 19 (1985): 228.

6. Swain and Cameron, "Unless Otherwise Stated," 68. The example of "black, Asian, Latina, and white" is one that I have extrapolated from Swain and Cameron's article rather than one that they themselves offer.

7. Eve Tavor Bannet, "Analogy As Translation: Wittgenstein, Derrida, and the Law of Language," *New Literary History* 28 (1997): 658.

8. Ibid., 655.

9. Linda Schlossberg, introduction to *Passing: Identity and Interpretation in Sexuality, Race, and Religion,* ed. María Carla Sánchez and Linda Schlossberg (New York: New York University Press, 2001), 1.

10. Davis writes that "disability is a specular moment" and argues that all disability, even mental illness, "shows up as a disruption in the visual field" (*Enforcing Normalcy,* xvi, 11–15, 129–42). Garland-Thomson also focuses on the "stare" that constructs the category of disability (*Extraordinary Bodies,* 26); Kenny Fries uses a similar focus (*Staring*

Back: The Disability Experience from the Inside Out [New York: Plume, 1997], 1).

11. Tom Shakespeare, Kath Gillespie-Sells, and Dominic Davies, *The Sexual Politics of Disability: Untold Desires* (New York: Cassell, 1996), 55. These authors clearly share Swain and Cameron's definition of coming out, as seen in their summary on page 58.

12. From a private conversation with Noelle Howey, July 2001. Howey further discusses her experiences in *Dress Codes: Of Three Girlhoods—My Mother's, My Father's, and Mine* (New York: Picador, 2002).

13. Eli Clare, *Exile and Pride: Disability, Queerness, and Liberation* (Cambridge, MA: South End, 1999), 133.

14. Garland-Thomson, *Extraordinary Bodies,* ix.

15. Nomy Lamm, "Private Dancer: Evolution of a Freak," in *Restricted Access: Lesbians on Disability,* ed. Victoria A. Brownworth and Susan Raffo (Seattle: Seal, 1999), 160–61.

16. Carolyn Gage, "Hidden Disability: A Coming Out Story," in Brownworth and Russo, *Restricted Access,* 203. CFIDS is a debilitating systemic illness that primarily affects the neurological, immune, and muscular systems. It is also known as myalgic encephalomyelitis. For more detail see Peggy Munson, ed., *Stricken: Voices from the Hidden Epidemic of Chronic Fatigue Syndrome* (New York: Haworth, 2000).

17. Wendell, *Rejected Body,* 4.

18. This dynamic can be found as well in the writings of people with visible disabilities who ponder whether to "come out" textually, thus revealing their absent bodies much as nonvisibly disabled people who come out are revealing some aspect of their health or mental status. As Nancy Mairs reflects in *Waist-High in the World: A Life among the Nondisabled* (Boston: Beacon, 1996), "I might have chosen to write in such a way as to disregard or deny or disguise the fact that I have MS" (10).

19. Megan Jones, "'Gee, You Don't *Look* Handicapped ...': Why I Use a White Cane to Tell People That I'm Deaf," *Electric Edge,* July–August 1997, accessed on 10 July 2002 at www.ragged-edge-mag.com/archive/look.htm.

20. Georgina Kleege, *Sight Unseen* (New Haven, CT: Yale University Press, 1999), 11–12.

21. Ibid., 38–39.

22. Wendell, *Rejected Body,* 76.

23. See Shakespeare, "Disability, Identity, and Difference," 100.

24. Swain and Cameron, "Unless Otherwise Stated," 76; Garland-Thomson, *Extraordinary Bodies,* 13.

25. Lisa Walker, *Looking Like What You Are: Sexual Style, Race, and Lesbian Identity* (New York: New York University Press, 2001), 8.

26. Deborah Peifer, "Seeing Is Be(liev)ing," in Brownworth and Russo, *Restricted Access*, 34; Jones, "'Gee, You Don't *Look* Handicapped ...'"; Kleege, *Sight Unseen*, 39.

27. Toi Derricotte, *The Black Notebooks. An Interior Journey* (New York: Norton, 1997), 112.

28. Ibid., 111; Peifer, "Seeing Is Be(lieve)ing," 34.

29. Amanda Hamilton, "Oh the Joys of Invisibility!" letter to the editor, *Electric Edge*, July–August 1997, accessed on 10 July 2002 at www.ragged-edge-mag.com/archive/look.htm; Adrian Piper, "Passing for White, Passing for Black," in *Passing and the Fictions of Identity*, ed. Elaine K. Ginsberg (Durham, NC: Duke University Press, 1996), 256–57, 266.

30. Derricotte, *Black Notebooks*, 145, 160, 182; Piper, "Passing for White, Passing for Black," 234–38, 256–57, 262–64.

31. Derricotte, *Black Notebooks*, 142.

32. Ginsberg, *Passing*, 4.

33. Bannet, "Analogy As Translation," 663.

34. This dynamic may also be observed from the role of passing in transgender contexts, in which the ability to pass for a new or different gender, or to present an ambiguous gender, is often experienced as a validation of radical identity rather than as assimilation or misrecognition.

35. To locate myself in my analysis, I refer to both femmes and people with nonvisible disabilities with the pronoun *we* throughout this section; however, I do not mean to imply that I speak for all femmes or all nonvisibly disabled people or that all people who share these identities think alike.

36. Joan Nestle, ed., *The Persistent Desire: A Femme-Butch Reader* (Boston: Alyson, 1992), 16.

37. Cited in Ginsberg, *Passing*, 8.

38. Walker, *Looking Like What You Are*, 209–10.

39. Nestle, *Persistent Desire*, 15–16.

40. Walker, *Looking Like What You Are*, 11, 5.

41. Nestle, *Persistent Desire*, 18; Rebecca Ann Rugg, "How Does She Look?" in *Femme: Feminists, Lesbians, and Bad Girls*, ed. Laura Harris and Elizabeth Crocker (New York: Routledge, 1997), 175.

42. See the pages referenced in note 10 for a discussion of this argument. One further distinction to be made here, however, is that the disbelieving gaze structuring the experience of the nonvisibly disabled subject may come not only from the normate but also from other disabled subjects. See Cal Montgomery, "A Hard Look at Invisible Disability," *Ragged Edge*, no. 2 (2001): 16.

43. Ibid., 16.

44. Madeline Davis, "Epilogue: Nine Years Later," in Nestle, *Persistent Desire*, 270.

45. Nestle, *Persistent Desire*, 15.

46. Gaby Sandoval, "Passing *Loquería*," in Harris and Crocker, *Femme*, 173. Sandoval adapts Gloria Anzaldúa's description of being a lesbian of color as making for *"loquería*, the crazies" (*Borderlands*, 2d ed. [San Francisco: Aunt Lute, 1999], 19).

47. Jones, a graduate student, once received a letter from her university, responding to her request for funds for assistance, "which essentially said, 'We do not understand what you mean when you refer to yourself as "deaf-blind." When you were in the office the other day you seemed to function just fine'" ("'Gee, You Don't *Look* Handicapped ...'"). It took Jones a year of procuring letters from every authority imaginable to receive the necessary funding. This dynamic is not unusual, but it is brought up frequently in conversations among people with nonvisible disabilities. As Hamilton observes, responding to Jones's story, many students with nonvisible disabilities are forced to "'pass' as 'normal' students, making sophisticated compensation strategies in order to complete our requirements and research, at which point, when we hit barriers ... sure enough, we aren't disabled enough—thanks to the success of previous compensation efforts" ("Oh the Joys of Invisibility!").

48. I have experienced this harassment many times, as has every nonvisibly disabled person with a parking permit I have asked about it.

49. Michel Foucault, *Discipline and Punish: The Birth of the Prison*, trans. Alan Sheridan (New York: Vintage, 1995), 203–5, 201.

50. Hogeland, "*Invisible Man* and Invisible Women," 36.

51. Jones, "'Gee, You Don't *Look* Handicapped ...'"

52. Montgomery observes that "although [the disability community] may understand disability differently than others do, we have not, as a group, abandoned the suspicion of people who may not be 'really' disabled, who may be 'slacking' or 'faking' or encroaching on 'our' movement and 'our' successes. And we respond to people who challenge *our* ideas of what disabled people are 'really like' just as nondisabled people do: with suspicion" ("Hard Look at Invisible Disability," 16).

53. Rugg, "How Does She Look?" 176.

54. Walker, *Looking Like What You Are*, 203. Furthermore, "Butler's genealogy rests on deconstructing the normative paradigm that figures a correspondence between sex, gender, and sexuality. In turn, this rests on an inner/outer distinction that 'stabilizes and consolidates the coherent subject.' This binary locates the 'self' within the body and reads the body as reflection of the 'truth' of that self. ... In a strategy of destabilization which relies on the visual performance of difference, the fact that no distinction between 'inner' and 'outer' identities is made visible on the surface of the femme's body as

it is on the drag queen's and the butch's bodies marginalizes the femme" (204–5). For more on Butler's original claims see Judith Butler, *Bodies That Matter: On the Discursive Limits of "Sex"* (New York: Routledge, 1993).

55. Rugg, "How Does She Look?" 176.

56. Mykel Johnson, "Butchy Femme," in Nestle, *Persistent Desire,* 397–98.

57. Rugg, "How Does She Look?" 180.

58. Mary Frances Platt, "Reclaiming Femme . . . Again," in Nestle, *Persistent Desire,* 388–89.

59. Sharon Wachsler, "Still Femme," in Brownworth and Russo, *Restricted Access,* 111–12, 114.

60. Anzaldúa, *Borderlands,* 102. I use the term *mestiza* with acute awareness of its racial and cultural references. While many of the authors I refer to are white or Anglo, Anzaldúa's term appears to be an appropriate and accurate description of the consciousness that they reveal, and the application of her theoretical terms to disability seems a logical extension of her own compelling interest in the "magical," boundary-crossing potential of "abnormality and so-called deformity" (41).

61. Sandoval, "Passing *Loquería*," 170–71.

62. Willy Wilkinson, "Stealth," in Munson, *Stricken,* 81.

CHAPTER 25

Integrating Disability, Transforming Feminist Theory

Rosemarie Garland-Thomson

SUMMARY

Rosemarie Garland-Thomson points out that when disabilities scholars try to address new problems in their own discipline, they are often focusing on "issues that feminist theory has been grappling with for years." At the same time, feminist theory has often overlooked disability in analysis of a wide variety of problems. Thus Garland-Thomson calls for a mutually beneficial integration and transformation of the two disciplines.

Feminist theory, defined here as an investigation into "how culture saturates the particularities of bodies with meanings," has always scrutinized the ways that various forms of identity affect one another. By including the understanding of disability, feminist theory can address more broad issues about the status of the body and cultures of normalcy. Just as feminists understand the way that gender permeates all aspects of culture, disability theorists identify the role of ability and disability in structuring identities, institutions, and practices. Garland-Thomson writes that "disability, like femaleness, is not a natural state of corporeal inferiority. . . . Rather, disability is a culturally fabricated narrative of the body, similar to what we understand as the fictions of race and gender."

This essay applies Garland-Thomson's vision of a feminist disability to four fundamental domains. First, feminist disability theory can shed light on the way systems of representation mark certain bodies as expendable or redundant. Disability analysis can also illuminate the ways that feminists investigate the materiality and politics of embodiment, and this domain of the body can be better understood by discussing the normalization of bodies. Garland-Thomson also suggests the domain of identity, and its identity category of woman, can be productively disrupted by disability theory. Finally, the essay discusses activism, a domain in which feminist progress can benefit from considering disability theory's persistent critique of normalization.

DISABILITY STUDIES AND FEMINIST STUDIES

Over the last several years, disability studies has moved out of the applied fields of medicine, social work, and rehabilitation to become a vibrant new field of inquiry within the critical genre of identity studies that has developed so productively in the humanities over the last 20 or so years. Charged with the residual fervor of the civil rights movement, women's studies and race studies established a model in the academy for identity-based critical enterprises that followed, such as gender studies, queer studies, disability studies, and a proliferation of ethnic studies, all of which have enriched and complicated our understandings of social justice, subject formation, subjugated knowledges, and collective action.

Even though disability studies is now flourishing in disciplines such as history, literature, religion, theater, and philosophy in precisely the same way feminist studies did 25 years ago, many of its practitioners do not recognize that disability studies is part of this larger undertaking that can be called identity studies. Indeed, I must wearily conclude that much of current disability studies does a great deal of wheel reinventing. This is largely due to the fact that many disability studies scholars simply don't know either feminist theory or the institutional history of women's studies. All too often the pronouncements in disability studies of what we need to start addressing are precisely issues that feminist theory has been grappling with for years. This is not to say that feminist theory can be transferred wholly and in tact over to the study of disability studies, but it is to suggest that feminist theory can offer profound insights, methods, and perspectives that would deepen disability studies.

Conversely, feminist theories all too often do not recognize disability in their litanies of identities that inflect the category of woman. Repeatedly feminist issues that are intricately entangled with disability—such as reproductive technology, the place of bodily differences, the particularities of oppression, the ethics of care, the construction of the subject—are discussed without any reference to disability. Like disability studies practitioners unaware of feminism, feminist scholars are often simply unacquainted with disability studies perspectives. The most sophisticated and nuanced analyses of disability, in my view, come from scholars conversant with feminist theory. And the most compelling and complex analyses of gender intersectionality take into consideration what I call the ability/disability system—along with race, ethnicity, sexuality, and class.

I want to give the omissions I am describing here the most generous interpretation I can. The archive, Foucault has shown us, determines what we can know. There has been no archive, no template for understanding disability as a category of analysis and knowledge, as a cultural trope and a historical community. So just as the now widely recognized centrality of gender and race analyses to all knowledge was unthinkable 30 years ago, disability is still not an icon on many critical desktops now. I think, however, that feminist theory's omission of disability differs from disability studies' ignorance of feminist theory. I find feminist theory and those familiar with it quick to grasp the broad outlines of disability theory and eager to consider its implications. This, of course, is because feminist theory itself has undertaken internal critiques and proved to be porous and flexible. Disability studies is news, but feminist theory is not. Nevertheless, feminist theory is still resisted for exactly the same reasons that scholars might resist disability studies: the assumption that it is narrow, particular, and has little to do with the mainstream of academic practice and knowledge (or with themselves). This reductive notion that identity studies are intellectual ghettos limited to a narrow constituency demanding special pleading is the persistent obstacle that both feminist theory and disability studies must surmount.

Disability studies can benefit from feminist theory and feminist theory can benefit from disability studies. Both feminism and disability studies are comparative and concurrent academic enterprises. Just as feminism has expanded the lexicon of what we imagine as womanly, has sought to understand and destigmatize what we call the subject position of woman, so has disability studies examined the identity disability in the service of integrating disabled people more fully into our society. As such, both are insurgencies that are becoming institutionalized underpinning inquiries outside and inside the academy.

A feminist disability theory builds on the strengths of both.

FEMINIST DISABILITY THEORY

My title here, "Integrating Disability, Transforming Feminist Theory," invokes and links two notions, integration and transformation, both of which are fundamental to the feminist project and to the larger civil rights movement that informed it. Integration suggests achieving parity by fully including that which has been excluded and subordinated. Transformation suggests reimagining established knowledge and the order of things. By alluding to integration and transformation, I set my own modest project of integrating disability into feminist theory in the politicized context of the civil rights movement in order to gesture toward the explicit relation that feminism supposes between intellectual work and a commitment to creating a more just, equitable, and integrated society.

This essay aims to amplify feminist theory by articulating and fostering feminist disability theory. In naming feminist disability studies here as an academic field of inquiry, I am sometimes describing work that is already underway, some of which explicitly addresses disability and some which gestures implicitly to the topic. At other times, I am calling for study that needs to be done to better illuminate feminist thought. In other words, this essay in part sets an agenda for future work in feminist disability theory. Most fundamentally, though, the goal of feminist disability theory, as I lay it out in this essay, is to augment the terms and confront the limits of the ways we understand human diversity, the materiality of the body, multiculturalism, and the social formations that interpret bodily differences. The fundamental point I will make here is that integrating disability as a category of analysis and a system of representation deepens, expands, and challenges feminist theory.

Academic feminism is a complex and contradictory matrix of theories, strategies, pedagogies and practices. One way to think about feminist theory is to say that it investigates how culture saturates the particularities of bodies with meanings and probes the consequences of those meanings. Feminist theory is a collaborative, interdisciplinary inquiry and a self-conscious cultural critique that interrogates how subjects are multiply interpellated: in other words, how the representational systems of gender, race, ethnicity, ability, sexuality, and class mutually produce, inflect, and contradict one another. These systems intersect to produce and sustain ascribed, achieved, and acquired identities, both those that claim us and those that we claim for ourselves. A feminist disability theory introduces the ability/disability system as a category of analysis into this diverse and diffuse enterprise. It aims to extend current notions of cultural diversity and to more fully integrate the academy and the larger world it helps shape.

A feminist disability approach fosters more complex understandings of the cultural history of the body. By considering the ability/disability system, feminist disability theory goes beyond explicit disability topics such as illness, health, beauty, genetics, eugenics, aging, reproductive technologies, prosthetics, and access issues. Feminist disability theory addresses such broad feminist concerns as the unity of the category "woman," the status of the lived body, the politics of appearance, the medicalization of the body, the privilege of normalcy, multiculturalism, sexuality, the social construction of identity, and the commitment to integration. To borrow Toni Morrison's notion that blackness is an idea that permeates American culture, disability too is a pervasive, often unarticulated, ideology informing our cultural notions of self and other (*Playing in the Dark* 19). Disability—like gender—is a concept that pervades all aspects of culture: its structuring institutions, social identities, cultural practices, political positions, historical communities, and the shared human experience of embodiment.

Integrating disability into feminist theory is generative, broadening our collective inquiries, questioning our assumptions, and contributing to feminism's multiculturalism. Introducing a disability analysis does not narrow the inquiry, limit the focus to only women with disabilities, or preclude engaging other manifestations of feminisms. Indeed, the multiplicity of foci we now call feminisms is not a group of fragmented, competing subfields, but rather a vibrant, complex conversation. In talking about "feminist disability theory," I am not proposing yet another discrete "feminism," but suggesting instead some ways that thinking about disability transforms feminist theory. Integrating disability does not obscure our critical focus on the registers of race, sexuality, ethnicity, or gender, nor is it additive (to use Gerda Lerner's famous idea). Rather, considering disability shifts the conceptual framework to strengthen our understanding of how these multiple systems intertwine, redefine, and mutually constitute one another. Integrating disability clarifies how this aggregate of systems operate together, yet distinctly, to support an imaginary norm and structure the relations that grant power, privilege, and status to that norm. Indeed, the cultural function of the disabled figure is to act as a synecdoche for all forms that culture deems non-normative.

We need to study disability in a feminist context to direct our highly honed critical skills toward the dual scholarly tasks of unmasking and reimagining disability, not only for people with disabilities but for everyone. As Simi Linton puts it, studying disability is "a prism through which one can gain a broader understanding of society and human experience" (1998, 118). It deepens the understanding of gender and sexuality, individualism and equality, minority group definitions, autonomy, wholeness, independence, dependence, health, physical appearance, aesthetics, the integrity of the body, community, and ideas of progress and perfection in every aspect of culture. A feminist disability theory introduces what Eve Sedgwick has called a "universalizing view" of disability that will replace an often persisting "minoritizing view." Such a view will cast disability as "an issue of continuing, determinative importance in the lives of people across the spectrum" (1990, 1). In other words, understanding how disability operates as an identity category and cultural concept will enhance how we understand what it is to be human, our relationships with one another, and the experience of embodiment. The constituency for a feminist disability theory is all of us, not only women with disabilities: disability is the most human of experiences, touching every family and—if we live long enough—touching us all.

THE ABILITY/DISABILITY SYSTEM

Feminist disability theory's radical critique hinges on a broad understanding of disability as a pervasive cultural system that stigmatizes certain kinds of bodily variations. At the same time, this system has the potential to incite a critical politics. The informing premise of feminist disability theory is that disability, like femaleness, is not a natural state of corporeal inferiority, inadequacy, excess, or a stroke of misfortune. Rather, disability is a culturally fabricated narrative of the body, similar to what we understand as the fictions of race and gender. The disability/ability system produces subjects by differentiating and marking bodies. Although this comparison of bodies is ideological rather than biological, it nevertheless penetrates into the formation of culture, legitimating an unequal distribution of resources, status, and power within a biased social and architectural environment. As such, disability has four aspects: first, it is a system for interpreting and disciplining bodily variations; second, it is a relationship between bodies and their environments; third, it is a set of practices that produce both the able-bodied and the disabled; fourth, it is a way of describing the inherent instability of the embodied self. The disability system excludes the kinds of bodily forms, functions, impairments, changes, or ambiguities that call into question our cultural fantasy of the body as a neutral, compliant instrument of some transcendent will. Moreover, disability is a broad term within which cluster ideological categories as varied as sick, deformed, abnormal, crazy, ugly, old, feebleminded, maimed, afflicted, mad, or debilitated—all of which disadvantage people by devaluing bodies that do not conform to cultural standards. Thus the disability system functions to preserve and validate such privileged designations as beautiful, healthy, normal, fit, competent, intelligent—all of which provide cultural capital to those who can claim such status, who can reside within these subject positions. It is, then, the various interactions between bodies and world that materialize disability from the stuff of human variation and precariousness.

A feminist disability theory denaturalizes disability by unseating the dominant assumption that disability is something that is wrong with someone. By this I mean, of course, that it mobilizes feminism's highly developed and complex critique of gender, class, race, ethnicity, and sexuality as exclusionary and oppressive systems rather than as the natural and appropriate order of things. To do this, feminist disability theory engages several of the fundamental premises of critical theory: (1) that representation structures reality; (2) that the margins define the center; (3) that gender (or disability) is a way of signifying relationships of power; (4) that human identity is multiple and unstable; (5) that all analysis and evaluation have political implications.

In order to elaborate on these premises, I discuss here four fundamental and inter-penetrating domains of feminist theory and suggest some of the kinds of critical inquiries that considering disability can generate within these theoretical arenas. These domains are: (1) representation; (2) the body; (3) identity; (4) activism. While I have disentangled these domains here for the purposes of setting up a schematic organization for my analysis, these domains are, of course, not discrete in either concept or practice, but rather tend to be synchronous.

REPRESENTATION

The first domain of feminist theory that can be deepened by a disability analysis is representation. Western thought has long conflated femaleness and disability, understanding both as defective departures from a valued standard. Aristotle, for example, defined women as "mutilated males." Women, for Aristotle, have "improper form;" we are "monstrosit[ies]" (1944, 27–8; 8–9). As what Nancy Tuana calls "misbegotten men," women thus become the primal freaks in western history, envisioned as what we might now call congenitally deformed as a result of their what we might now term a genetic disability (1993, 18). More recently, feminist theorists have argued that female embodiment is a disabling condition in sexist culture. Iris Marion Young, for instance, examines how enforced feminine comportment delimits women's sense of embodied agency, restricting them to "throwing like a girl" (1990b, 141). Young asserts that, "Women in a sexist society are physically handicapped" (1990b, 153). Even the general American public associates femininity and disability. A recent study on stereotyping showed that housewives, disabled people, blind people, so-called retarded people, and the elderly were judged as being similarly incompetent. Such a study suggests that intensely normatively feminine positions—such as a housewife—are aligned with negative attitudes about people with disabilities (Fiske 2001).[1]

Recognizing how the concept of disability has been used to cast the form and functioning of female bodies as non-normative can extend feminist critiques. Take, for example, the exploitation of Saartje Bartmann, the African woman exhibited as a freak in nineteenth-century Europe (Fausto Sterling 1995; Gilman 1985). Known as the Hottentot Venus, Bartmann's treatment has come to represent the most egregious form of racial and gendered degradation. What goes unremarked in studies of Bartmann's display, however, is the ways that the language and assumptions of the ability/disability system were implemented to pathologize and exoticize Bartmann. Her display invoked disability by presenting as deformities or abnormalities the characteristics that marked her as raced and gendered. I am not suggesting that Bartmann was disabled, but rather that the concepts of disability discourse framed her presentation to the western eye. Using disability as a category of analysis allows us to see that what was normative embodiment in her native context became abnormal to the western mind. More important, rather than simply supposing that being labeled as a freak is a slander, a disability analysis presses our critique further by challenging the premise that unusual embodiment is inherently inferior. The feminist interrogation of gender since Simone de Beauvoir has revealed how women are assigned a cluster of ascriptions, like Aristotle's, that mark us as Other. What is less widely recognized, however, is that this collection of interrelated characterizations is precisely the same set of supposed attributes affixed to people with disabilities.

The gender, race, and ability systems intertwine further in representing subjugated people as being pure body, unredeemed by mind or spirit. This sentence of embodiment is conceived of as either a lack or an excess. Women, for example, are considered castrated, or—to use Marge Piercey's wonderful term—"penis-poor" (1969). They are thought to be hysterical, or have overactive hormones. Women have been cast as alternately having insatiable appetite in some eras and as pathologically self-denying in other times. Similarly, disabled people supposedly have extra chromosomes or limb deficiencies. The differences of disability are cast as atrophy, meaning degeneration, a hypertrophy, meaning enlargement. People with disabilities are described as having aplasia, meaning absence or failure of formation, or hypoplasia, meaning underdevelopment. All these terms police variation and reference a hidden norm from which the bodies of people with disabilities and women are imagined to depart.

Female, disabled, and dark bodies are supposed to be dependent, incomplete, vulnerable, and incompetent bodies. Femininity and race are the performance of disability. Women and the disabled are portrayed as helpless, dependent, weak, vulnerable, and incapable bodies. Women, the disabled, and people of color are always ready occasions for the aggrandizement of benevolent rescuers, whether strong males, distinguished doctors, abolitionists, or Jerry Lewis hosting his Telethons. For example, an 1885 medical illustration of a pathologically "love deficient" woman who fits the cultural stereotype of the ugly woman or perhaps the lesbian suggests how sexuality and appearance slide into the terms of disability. This illustration shows the language of deficiency and abnormality used to simultaneously devalue women who depart from the mandates of femininity by equating them with disabled bodies. Such an interpretive move economically invokes the subjugating effect of one oppressive system to deprecate people marked by another system of representation.

Subjugated bodies are pictured as either deficient or as profligate For instance, what Susan Bordo describes as the too-muchness of women also haunts disability and racial discourses, marking subjugated bodies as ungovernable, intemperate, or threatening (1993). The historical figure of the monster, as well, invokes disability, often to serve racism and sexism. Although the term has expanded to encompass all forms of social and corporeal aberration, *monster* originally described people with congenital impairments. As departures from the normatively human, monsters were seen as category violations or grotesque hybrids. The semantics of monstrosity are recruited to explain gender violations such as Julia Pastrana, for example, the Mexican Indian "bearded woman," whose body was displayed in nineteenth-century freak shows both during her lifetime and after her death. Pastrana's live and later embalmed body spectacularly confused and transgressed established cultural categories. Race, gender, disability, and sexuality augmented one another in Pastrana's display to produce a spectacle of embodied otherness that is simultaneously sensational, sentimental, and pathological (Garland-Thomson 1999). Furthermore much current feminist work theorizes figures of hybridity and excess such as monsters, grotesques, and cyborgs to suggest their transgressive potential for a feminist politics (Haraway 1991; Braidotti, 1994; Russo, 1994). However, this metaphorical invocation seldom acknowledges that these figures often refer to the actual bodies of people with disabilities. Erasing real disabled bodies from the history of these terms compromises the very critique they intend to launch and misses an opportunity to use disability as a feminist critical category.

Such representations ultimately portray subjugated bodies not only as inadequate or unrestrained but at the same time as redundant and expendable. Bodies marked and selected by such systems are targeted for elimination by varying historical and cross-cultural practices. Women, people with disabilities or appearance impairments, ethnic others, gays and lesbians, and people of color are variously the objects of infanticide, selective abortion, eugenic programs, hate crimes, mercy killing, assisted suicide, lynching, bride burning, honor killings, forced conversion, coercive rehabilitation, domestic violence, genocide, normalizing surgical procedures, racial profiling, and neglect. All these discriminatory practices are legitimated by systems of representation, by collective cultural stories that shape the material world, underwrite exclusionary attitudes, inform human relations, and mold our senses of who we are. Understanding how disability functions along with other systems of representation clarifies how all the systems intersect and mutually constitute one another.

THE BODY

The second domain of feminist theory that a disability analysis can illuminate is the investigation of the body: its materiality, its politics, its lived experience, and its relation to subjectivity and identity. Confronting issues of representation is certainly crucial to the cultural critique of feminist disability theory. But we should not focus exclusively on the discursive realm. What distinguishes a feminist disability theory from other critical paradigms is that it scrutinizes a wide range of material practices involving the lived body. Perhaps because women and the disabled are cultural signifiers for the body, their actual bodies have been subjected relentlessly to what Michel Foucault calls "discipline" (1979). Together, the gender, race, ethnicity, sexuality, class, and ability systems exert tremendous social pressures to shape, regulate, and normalize subjugated bodies. Such disciplining is enacted primarily through the two interrelated cultural discourses of medicine and appearance.

Feminist disability theory offers a particularly trenchant analysis of the ways that the female body has been medicalized in modernity. As I have already suggested, both women and the disabled have been imagined as medically abnormal—as the quintessential "sick" ones. Sickness is gendered feminine. This gendering of illness has entailed distinct consequences in everything from epidemiology and diagnosis to prophylaxis and therapeutics.

Perhaps feminist disability theory's most incisive critique is revealing the intersections between the politics of appearance and the medicalization of subjugated bodies. Appearance norms have a long history in western culture, as is witnessed by the anthropometric composite figures of ideal male and female bodies made by Dudley Sargent in 1893. The classical ideal was to be worshiped rather than imitated, but increasingly in modernity the ideal has migrated to become the paradigm which is to be attained. As many feminist critics have pointed out, the standardization of the female body that the beauty system mandates has become a goal to be achieved through self-regulation and consumerism (Wolf 1991; Haiken 1997). Feminist disability theory suggests that appearance and health norms often have similar disciplinary goals. For example, the body braces developed in the 1930s to "correct" scoliosis, discipline the body to conform to the dictates of both the gender and the ability systems by enforcing standardized female form similarly to the nineteenth-century corset, which, ironically, often disabled female bodies. Although both devices normalize bodies, the brace is part of medical discourse while the corset is cast as a fashion practice.

Similarly, a feminist disability theory calls into question the separation of reconstructive and cosmetic surgery, recognizing their essentially normalizing function as what Sander L. Gilman calls "aesthetic surgery" (1998). Cosmetic surgery, driven by gender ideology and market forces, now enforces feminine body standards and standardizes female bodies toward what I have called the "normate"—the corporeal incarnation of culture's collective, unmarked, normative characteristics (1997, 8). Cosmetic surgery's twin, reconstructive surgery, eliminates disability and enforces the ideals of what might be thought of as the normalcy system. Both cosmetic and reconstructive procedures commodify the body and parade mutilations as enhancements that correct flaws so as to improve the psychological well-being of the patient. The conception of the body as what Susan Bordo terms "cultural plastic" increasingly through surgical and medical interventions pressures people with disabilities or appearance impairments to become what Michel Foucault calls "docile bodies." (1979, 135). The twin ideologies of normalcy and beauty posit female and disabled bodies, particularly, as not only spectacles to be looked at, but as pliable bodies to be shaped infinitely so as to conform to a set of standards called "normal" and "beautiful."

Normal has inflected beautiful in modernity. What is imagined as excess body fat, the effects of aging, marks of ethnicity such as "jewish" noses, bodily particularities thought of as blemishes or deformities, and marks of history such as scarring and impairments are now expected to be surgically erased to produce an unmarked body. This visually unobtrusive body may then pass unnoticed within the milieu of anonymity that is the hallmark of social relations beyond the personal in modernity. The point of aesthetic surgery, as well as the costuming of power, is not to appear unique—or to "be yourself," as the ads endlessly promise—but rather not to be conspicuous, not to look different.

This flight from the nonconforming body translates into individual efforts to look normal, neutral, unmarked, to *not* look disabled, queer, ugly, fat, ethnic, or raced. For example, beauty is set out comparatively and supposedly self-evidently in an 1889 treatise called *The New Physiognomy* which juxtaposed a white, upper-class English face called "Princess Alexandra" with a stereotypical face of an Irish immigrant, called "Sally Muggins" in a class and ethnic-based binary of apparently self-evident beauty and ugliness. Beauty, then, dictates corporeal standards that create not distinction but utter conformity to a bland look that is at the same time unachievable so as to leash us to consumer practices that promise to deliver such sameness. In the language of contemporary cosmetic surgery, the unreconstructed female body is persistently cast as having abnormalities that can be corrected by surgical procedures which supposedly improve one's appearance by producing ostensibly natural looking noses, thighs, breasts, chins, and so on. Thus, our unmodified bodies are presented as unnatural and abnormal while the surgically altered bodies are portrayed as normal and natural. The beautiful woman of the twenty-first century is sculpted surgically from top to bottom, generically neutral, all irregularities regularized, all particularities expunged. She is thus nondisabled, deracialized, and de-ethnicized.

In addition, the politics of prosthetics enters the purview of feminism when we consider the contested use of breast implants and prostheses for breast cancer survivors. The famous 1993 *New York Times* cover photo of the fashion model, Matushka, baring her mastectomy scar or Audre Lorde's account of breast cancer in *The Cancer Journals* (1980) challenge the sexist assumption that the amputated breast must always pass for the normative, sexualized one either through concealment or prosthetics. A vibrant feminist conversation has emerged

about the politics of the surgically altered, the disabled, breast. Diane Price Herndl challenges Audre Lorde's refusal of a breast prosthesis after mastectomy and Iris Marion Young's classic essay "Breasted Experience" queries the cultural meanings of breasts under the knife (2002; 1990a).

Another entanglement of appearance and medicine involves the spectacle of the female breast, both normative and disabled. In January 2000, the San Francisco-based Breast Cancer Fund mounted "Obsessed with Breasts," a public awareness poster campaign showing women boldly displaying mastectomy scars. The posters parodied familiar commercial media sites—a Calvin Klein perfume ad, a Cosmopolitan magazine cover, and a Victoria Secret catalog cover—that routinely parade women's breasts as upscale soft porn. The posters replace the now unremarkable eroticized breast with the forbidden image of the amputated breast. In doing so, they disrupt the visual convention of the female breast as sexualized object for male appropriation and pleasure. The posters thus produce a powerful visual violation by exchanging the spectacle of the eroticized breast, which has been desensationalized by its endless circulation, with the medicalized image of the scarred breast, which has been concealed from public view. The Breast Cancer Fund used these remarkable images to challenge both sexism in medical research and treatment for breast cancer as well as the oppressive representational practices that make everyday erotic spectacles of women's breasts while erasing the fact of the amputated breast.

Feminist disability theory can press far its critique of the pervasive will-to-normalize the non-standard body. Take two related examples: first, the surgical separation of conjoined twins and, second, the surgical assignment of gender for the intersexed, people with ambiguous genitalia and gender characteristics. Both these forms of embodiment are regularly—if infrequently—occurring, congenital bodily variations that spectacularly violate sacred ideologies of western culture. Conjoined twins contradict our notion of the individual as discrete and autonomous—actually, quite similarly to the way pregnancy does. Intersexed infants challenge our insistence that biological gender is unequivocally binary. So threatening to the order of things is the natural embodiment of conjoined twins and intersexed people that they are almost always surgically normalized through amputation and mutilation immediately after birth (Clark and Myser 1996; Dreger 1998a; Kessler 1990; Fausto-Sterling 2000). Not infrequently, one conjoined twin is sacrificed to save the other from the supposed abnormality of their embodiment. Such mutilations are justified as preventing suffering and creating well-adjusted individuals. So intolerable is their insult to dominant ideologies about who patriarchal culture insists that we are that the testimonies of adults with these forms of embodiment who say that they do not want to be separated is routinely ignored in establishing the rationale for "medical treatment" (Dreger 1998b). In truth, these procedures benefit not the affected individuals, but rather they expunge the kinds of corporeal human variations that contradict the ideologies the dominant order depends upon to anchor truths it insists are unequivocally encoded in bodies.

I do not want to oversimplify here by suggesting that women and disabled people should not use modern medicine to improve their lives or help their bodies function more fully. But the critical issues are complex and provocative. A feminist disability theory should illuminate and explain, not become ideological policing or set orthodoxy. The kinds of critical analyses I'm discussing here offer a counter logic to the overdetermined cultural mandates to comply with normal and beautiful at any cost. The medical commitment to healing, when coupled with modernity's faith in technology and interventions that control outcomes, has increasingly shifted toward an aggressive intent to fix, regulate, or eradicate ostensibly deviant bodies. Such a program of elimination has often been at the expense of creating a more accessible environment or providing better support services for people with disabilities. The privileging of medical technology over less ambitious programs such as rehabilitation has encouraged the cultural conviction that disability can be extirpated, inviting the belief that life with a disability is intolerable. As charity campaigns and telethons repeatedly affirm, cure rather than adjustment or accommodation is the overdetermined cultural response to disability (Longmore 1997). For instance, a 1949 March of Dimes poster shows an appealing little girl stepping out of her wheelchair into the supposed redemption of walking: "Look, I Can Walk Again!" the text proclaims while at once charging the viewers with the responsibility of assuring her future ambulation. Nowhere do we find posters suggesting that life as a wheelchair user might be full and satisfying, as many people who actually use them find their lives to be. This ideology of cure is not isolated in medical texts or charity campaigns, but in fact permeates the entire cultural conversation about disability and illness. Take, for example, the discourse of cure in get well cards. A 1950 card, for instance, urges its recipient to "snap out of it." Fusing racist, sexist, and ableist discourses, the card recruits the Mammy figure to insist on cure. The stereotypical racist figure asks, "Is you sick, Honey?" and then exhorts the recipient of her care to "jes hoodoo all dat illness out o you."

The ideology of cure directed at disabled people focuses on changing bodies imagined as abnormal and dysfunctional rather than on exclusionary attitudinal, environmental, and economic barriers. The emphasis on cure reduces the cultural tolerance for human variation and vulnerability by locating disability in bodies imagined as flawed rather than social systems in need of fixing. A feminist disability studies would draw an important distinction between prevention and elimination. Preventing illness, suffering, and injury is a humane social objective. Eliminating the range of unacceptable and devalued bodily forms and functions the dominant order calls disability is, on the other hand, a eugenic undertaking. The ostensibly progressive socio-medical project of eradicating disability all too often is enacted as a program to eliminate people with disabilities through such practices as forced sterilization, so-called physician-assisted suicide and mercy killing, selective abortion, institutionalization, and segregation policies.

A feminist disability theory extends its critique of the normalization of bodies and the medicalization of appearance to challenge some widely held assumptions about reproductive issues as well. The cultural mandate to eliminate the variations in form and function that we think of as disabilities has undergirded the reproductive practices of genetic testing and selective abortion (Saxton 1998; Parens and Asch 2000; Rapp 1999). Some disability activists argue that the "choice" to abort fetuses with disabilities is a coercive form of genocide against the disabled (Hubbard 1990). A more nuanced argument against selective abortion comes from Adrienne Asch and Gail Geller, who wish to preserve a woman's right choose whether to bear a child, but who at the same time objects to the ethics of selectively aborting a wanted fetus because it will become a person with a disability (1996). Asch and Geller counter the quality-of-life and prevention-of-suffering arguments so readily invoked to justify selective abortion, as well as physician-assisted suicide, by pointing out that we cannot predict or—more precisely—control in advance such equivocal human states as happiness, suffering, or success. Neither is any amount of prenatal engineering going to produce the life that any of us desire and value. Indeed, both hubris and a lack of imagination characterize the prejudicial and reductive assumption that having a disability ruins lives. A vague notion of suffering and its potential deterrence drives much of the logic of elimination that rationalizes selective abortion (Kittay 2000). Life chances and quality are simply far too contingent to justify prenatal prediction.

Similarly, genetic testing and applications of the Human Genome Project as the key to expunging disability are often critiqued as enactments of eugenic ideology, what the feminist biologist Evelyn Fox Keller calls a "eugenics of normalcy" (1992). The popular utopian notion that all forms of disability can be eliminated through prophylactic manipulation of genetics will only serve to intensify the prejudice against those who inevitably will acquire disabilities through aging and encounters with the environment. In the popular celebrations of the Human Genome Project as the quixotic pinnacle of technological progress, seldom do we hear a cautionary logic about the eugenic implications of this drive toward what Priscilla Wald calls "Future Perfect" (2000, 1). Disability scholars have entered the debate over so-called physician-assisted suicide, as well, by arguing that oppressive attitudes toward disability distort the possibility of unbiased free choice (Battin et al. 1998). The practices of genetic and prenatal testing as well as physician-administered euthanasia, then, become potentially eugenic practices within the context of a culture deeply intolerant of disability. Both the rhetoric and the enactment of this kind of disability discrimination create a hostile and exclusionary environment for people with disabilities that perhaps exceeds the less virulent architectural barriers that keep them out of the workforce and the public sphere.

Integrating disability into feminism's conversation about the place of the body in the equality and difference debates produces fresh insights as well. Whereas liberal feminism emphasizes sameness, choice, and autonomy, cultural feminism critiques the premises of liberalism. Out of cultural feminism's insistence on difference and its positive interpretation of feminine culture comes the affirmation of a feminist ethic of care. This ethic of care contends that care giving is a moral benefit for its practitioners and for humankind. A feminist disability studies complicates both the feminist ethic of care and liberal feminism in regard to the politics of care and dependency.

A disability perspective nuances feminist theory's consideration of the ethics of care by examining the power relations between the givers and receivers of care. Anita Silvers has argued strongly that being the object of care precludes the equality that a liberal democracy depends upon and undermines the claim to justice as equality that undergirds a civil rights approach used to counter discrimination (1995). Eva Kittay, on the other hand, formulates a "dependency critique of equality" (1999, 4), which asserts that the ideal of equality under liberalism repudiates the fact of human dependency, the need for mutual care, and the asymmetries of care relations. Similarly, Barbara Hillyer has called attention to dependency in order to critique a liberal tendency in the rhetoric of disability rights (1993). Disability itself demands that human interdependence and the universal need for assistance be figured into our dialogues about rights and subjectivity.

IDENTITY

The third domain of feminist theory that a disability analysis complicates is identity. Feminist theory has productively and rigorously critiqued the identity category of woman, on which the entire feminist enter-

prise seemed to rest. Feminism increasingly recognizes that no woman is ever *only* a woman, that she occupies multiple subject positions and is claimed by several cultural identity categories (Spelman 1988). This complication of *woman* compelled feminist theory to turn from an exclusively male/female focus to look more fully at the exclusionary, essentialist, oppressive, and binary aspects of the category woman itself. Disability is one such identity vector that disrupts the unity of the classification woman and challenges the primacy of gender as a monolithic category.

Disabled women are, of course, a marked and excluded—albeit quite varied—group within the larger social class of women. The relative privileges of normative femininity are often denied to disabled women (Fine and Asch 1988). Cultural stereotypes imagine disabled women as asexual, unfit to reproduce, overly dependent, unattractive—as generally removed from the sphere of true womanhood and feminine beauty. Woman with disabilities must often struggle to have their sexuality and rights to bear children recognized (Finger 1990). Disability thus both intensifies and attenuates the cultural scripts of femininity. Aging is a form of disablement that disqualifies older women from the limited power allotted females who are young and meet the criteria for attracting men. Depression, anorexia, and agoraphobia are female-dominant, psychophysical disabilities that exaggerate normative gendered roles. Feminine cultural practices such as foot binding, clitorectomies, and corseting, as well as their less hyperbolic costuming rituals such as stiletto high heels, girdles, and chastity belts—impair women's bodies and restrict their physical agency, imposing disability on them.

Banishment from femininity can be both a liability and a benefit. Let me offer—with some irony—an instructive example from popular culture. Barbie, that cultural icon of femininity, offers a disability analysis that clarifies both how multiple identity and diversity is commodified and how the commercial realm might offer politically useful feminist counter images. Perhaps the measure of a group's arrival into the mainstream of multiculturalism is to be represented in the Barbie pantheon. While Barbie herself still identifies as able-bodied—despite her severely deformed body—we now have several incarnations of Barbie's "friend," Share-A-Smile Becky. One Becky uses a cool hot pink wheelchair; another is Paralympic Champion Becky, brought out for the 2000 Sydney Olympics in a chic red-white-and-blue warm-up suit with matching chair. Most interesting however is Becky, the school photographer, clad in a preppy outfit, complete with camera and red high-top sneakers. As she perkily gazes at an alluring Barbie in her camera's viewfinder, this Becky may be the incarnation of what one scholar has called "Barbie's queer accessories" (Rand 1995).

A disabled, queer Becky is certainly a provocative and subversive fusion of stigmatized identities, but more important is that Becky challenges notions of normalcy in feminist ways. The disabled Becky, for example, wears comfortable clothes: pants with elastic-waists no doubt, sensible shoes, and roomy shirts. Becky is also one of the few dolls who has flat feet and legs that bend at the knee. The disabled Becky is dressed and poised for agency, action, and creative engagement with the world. In contrast, the prototypical Barbie performs excessive femininity in her restrictive sequined gowns, crowns, and push-up bras. So while Becky implies on the one hand that disabled girls are purged from the feminine economy, on the other hand Becky also suggests that disabled girls might be liberated from those oppressive and debilitating scripts. The last word on Barbies comes from a disability activist who quipped that he'd like to outfit a disabled doll with a power wheelchair chair and a briefcase to make her a civil rights lawyer who enforces the Americans with Disabilities Act. He wants to call her "Sue-Your-Ass-Becky."[2] I think she'd make a very good role model.

The paradox of Barbie and Becky, of course, is that the ultra-feminized Barbie is a target for sexual appropriation both by men and beauty practices while the disabled Becky escapes such sexual objectification at the potential cost of losing her sense of identity as a feminine sexual being. Some disabled women negotiate this possible identity crisis by developing alternate sexualities, such as lesbianism (Brownworth and Raffo 1999). However, what Harlan Hahn calls the "asexual objectification" of people with disabilities complicates the feminist critique of normative sexual objectification (1988). Consider the 1987 *Playboy* magazine photos of the paraplegic actress Ellen Stohl. After becoming disabled, Stohl wrote to editor Hugh Hefner that she wanted to pose nude for *Playboy* because "sexuality is the hardest thing for disabled persons to hold onto" ("Meet Ellen Stohl," 68). For Stohl, it would seem that the performance of excessive feminine sexuality was necessary to counter the social interpretation that disability cancels out sexuality. This confirmation of normative heterosexuality was then for Stohl no Butlerian parody, but rather was the affirmation she needed as a disabled woman to be sexual at all.

Ellen Stohl's presentation by way of the sexist conventions of the porn magazine illuminates the relation between identity and the body, an aspect of subject formation that disability analysis can offer. Although binary identities are conferred from outside through social relations, these identities are nevertheless inscribed on the body as either manifest or incipient visual traces. Identity's social meaning turns on this play of visibility. The photos of Stohl in *Playboy* both refuse and insist on marking her impairment. The centerfold spread—so to speak—of Stohl nude and masturbating erases her impairment to conform to the sexualized conventions of the centerfold. This photo expunges her wheelchair and any other visual clues to her impairment. In other words, to avoid the cultural contradiction of a sexual disabled woman, the pornographic photos must offer up Stohl as visually nondisabled. But to appeal to the cultural narrative of overcoming disability that sells so well, seems novel, and capitalizes on sentimental interest, Stohl must be visually dramatized as disabled at the same time. So *Playboy* includes several shots of Stohl that mark her as disabled by picturing her in her wheelchair, entirely without the typical porn conventions. In fact, the photos of her using her wheelchair invoke the asexual poster child. Thus, the affirmation of Stohl's sexuality she sought by posing nude in the porn magazine came at the expense of denying through the powerful visual register her identity as a woman with a disability, even while she attempted to claim that identity textually.

Another aspect of subject formation that disability confirms is that identity is always in transition. Disability reminds us that the body is, as Denise Riley asserts, "an unsteady mark, scarred in its long decay" (1999, 224). As Caroline Walker Bynum's intriguing work on werewolf narratives suggests, the body is in a perpetual state of transformation (1999). Caring for her father for over 20 years of Alzheimer's disease prompted Bynum to investigate how we can understand individual identity as continuous even though both body and mind can and do change dramatically, certainly over a lifetime and sometimes quite suddenly. Disability invites us to query what the continuity of the self might depend upon if the body perpetually metamorphoses. We envision our racial, gender, or ethnic identities as tethered to bodily traits that are relatively secure. Disability and sexual identity, however, seem more fluid, although sexual mutability is imagined as elective

where disability is seldom conceived of as a choice. Disability is an identity category that anyone can enter at any time, and we will all join it if live long enough. As such, disability reveals the essential dynamism of identity. Thus, disability attenuates the cherished cultural belief that the body is the unchanging anchor of identity. Moreover, it undermines our fantasies of stable, enduring identities in ways that may illuminate the fluidity of all identity.

Disability's clarification of the body's corporeal truths suggests as well that the body/self materializes—in Judith Butler's sense—not so much through discourse, but through history (1993). The self materializes in response to an embodied engagement with its environment, both social and concrete. The disabled body is a body whose variations or transformations have rendered it out of sync with its environment, both the physical and the attitudinal environments. In other words, the body becomes disabled when it is incongruent both in space and the milieu of expectations. Furthermore, a feminist disability theory presses us to ask what kinds of knowledge might be produced through having a body radically marked by its own particularity, a body that materializes at the ends of the curve of human variation. For example, an alternative epistemology that emerges from the lived experience of disability is nicely summed up in Nancy Mairs's book title, *Waist High in the World*, which she irreverently considered calling "cock high in the world." What perspectives or politics arise from encountering the world from such an atypical position? Perhaps Mairs's epistemology can offer us a critical positionality called sitpoint theory, a neologism I can offer that interrogates the ableist assumptions underlying the notion of standpoint theory (Harstock 1983).

Our collective cultural consciousness emphatically denies the knowledge of bodily vulnerability, contingency, and mortality. Disability insists otherwise, contradicting such phallic ideology. I would argue that disability is perhaps the essential characteristic of being human. The body is dynamic, constantly interactive with history and environment. We evolve into disability. Our bodies need care; we all need assistance to live. An equality model of feminist theory sometimes prizes individualistic autonomy as the key to women's liberation. A feminist disability theory, however, suggests that we are better off learning to individually and collectively accommodate the body's limits and evolutions than trying to eliminate or deny them.

Identity formation is at the center of feminist theory. Disability can complicate feminist theory often quite succinctly by invoking established theoretical paradigms. This kind of theoretical intertextuality inflects familiar feminist concepts with new resonance. Let me offer several examples: the idea of "compulsory ablebodiedness," which Robert McRuer (1999) has coined, extends Adrienne Rich's famous analysis of "compulsory heterosexuality" (2001, 1986). Joan Wallach Scott's germinal work on gender is recruited when we discuss disability as "a useful category of analysis" (1988, 1). The feminist elaboration of the gender system informs my use of the disability system. Lennard Davis suggests that the term *normalcy studies* supplant the name *disability studies*, in the way that *gender studies* sometimes succeeds *feminism* (1995). The oft invoked distinction between sex and gender clarifies a differentiation between impairment and disability, even though both binaries are fraught. The concept of performing disability, cites (as it were) Judith Butler's vigorous critique of essentialism (1990). Reading disabled bodies as exemplary instances of "docile bodies" invokes Foucault (1979). To suggest that identity is lodged in the body, I propose that the body haunts the subject, alluding to Susan Bordo's notion regarding masculinity that "the penis haunts the phallus"

(1994, 1). My own work has complicated the familiar discourse of the gaze to theorize what I call the stare, which I argue produces disability identity. Such theoretical shorthand impels us to reconsider the ways that identity categories cut across and redefine one another, pressuring both the terms *woman* and *disabled*.

A feminist disability theory can also highlight intersections and convergences with other identity-based critical perspectives such as queer and ethnic studies. Disability coming out stories, for example, borrow from gay and lesbian identity narratives to expose what previously was hidden, privatized, medicalized in order to enter into a political community. The politicized sphere into which many scholars come out is feminist disability studies, which enables critique, claims disability identity, and creates affirming counter narratives. Disability coming out narratives raise questions about the body's role in identity by asking how markers so conspicuous as crutches, wheelchairs, hearing aids, guide dogs, white canes, or empty sleeves be closeted.

Passing as nondisabled complicates ethnic and queer studies' analyses of how this seductive but psychically estranging access to privilege operates. Some of my friends, for example, have measured their regard for me by saying, "But I don't think of you as disabled." What they point to in such a compliment is the contradiction they find between their perception of me as a valuable, capable, lovable person and the cultural figure of the disabled person whom they take to be precisely my opposite: worthless, incapable, and unlovable. People with disabilities themselves routinely announce that they don't consider themselves as disabled. Although they are often repudiating the literal meaning of the word *disabled*, their words nevertheless serve to disassociate them from the identity group of the disabled. Our culture offers profound disincentives and few rewards to identifying as disabled. The trouble, of course, with such statements is that they leave intact without challenge the oppressive stereotypes that permit, among other things, the unexamined use of disability terms such as *crippled, lame, dumb, idiot, moron* as verbal gestures of derision. The refusal to claim disability identity is in part due to a lack of ways to understand or talk about disability that are not oppressive. People with disabilities and those who care about them flee from the language of *crippled* or *deformed* and have no other alternatives. Yet, the civil rights movement and the accompanying Black-is-beautiful identity politics have generally shown white culture what is problematic with saying to Black friends, "I don't think of you as Black." Nonetheless, by disavowing disability identity, many of us learned to save ourselves from devaluation by a complicity that perpetuates oppressive notions about ostensibly "real" disabled people. Thus, together we help make the alternately menacing and pathetic cultural figures who rattle tin cups or rave on street corners, ones we with impairments often flee from more surely than those who imagine themselves as nondisabled.

ACTIVISM

The final domain of feminist theory that a disability analysis expands is activism. There are many arenas of what can be seen as feminist disability activism: marches, protests, the Breast Cancer Fund poster campaign I discussed above, action groups such as the Intersex Society of North America (ISNA), and Not Dead Yet, who oppose physician-assisted suicide, or the American Disabled for Accessible Public Transit (ADAPT). What counts as activism cuts a wide swath through U.S. society and the academy. I want to suggest here two unlikely, even quirky, cultural practices that function in activist ways but are seldom considered as potentially transformative. One practice is

disabled fashion modeling and the other is academic tolerance. Both are different genres of activism from the more traditional marching-on-Washington or chaining-yourself-to-a-bus modes. Both are less theatrical, but perhaps fresher and more interestingly controversial ways to change the social landscape and to promote equality, which I take to be the goal of activism.

The theologian and sociologist, Nancy Eiseland, has argued that in addition to legislative, economic, and social changes, achieving equality for people with disabilities depends upon cultural "resymbolization" (1994, 98). Eiseland asserts that the way we imagine disability and disabled people must shift in order for real social change to occur. Whereas Eiseland's work resymbolizes our conceptions of disability in religious iconography, my own examinations of disabled fashion models do similar cultural work in the popular sphere, introducing some interesting complications into her notion of resymbolization.

Images of disabled fashion models in the media can shake up established categories and expectations. Because commercial visual media are the most widespread and commanding source of images in modern, image-saturated culture, they have great potential for shaping public consciousness—as feminist cultural critics are well aware. Fashion imagery is the visual distillation of the normative, gilded with the chic and the luxurious to render it desirable. The commercial sphere is completely amoral, driven as it is by the single logic of the bottom line. As we know, it sweeps through culture seizing with alarming neutrality anything it senses will sell. This value-free aspect of advertising produces a kind of pliable potency that sometimes can yield unexpected results.

Take, for example, a shot from the monthly fashion feature in *WE Magazine*, a *Cosmopolitan* knock-off targeted toward the disabled consumer market. In this conventional, stylized, high fashion shot, a typical female model—slender, white, blond, clad in a black evening gown—is accompanied by her service dog. My argument is that public images such as this are radical because they fuse two previously antithetical visual discourses—the chic high fashion shot and the earnest charity campaign. Public representations of disability have traditionally been contained within the conventions of sentimental charity images, exotic freak show portraits, medical illustrations, or sensational and forbidden pictures. Indeed, people with disabilities have been excluded most fully from the dominant, public world of the marketplace. Before the civil rights initiatives of the mid-twentieth century began to transform the public architectural and institutional environment, disabled people were segregated to the private and the medical spheres. Until recently, the only available public image of a woman with a service dog that shaped the public imagination was a street-corner beggar or a charity poster. By juxtaposing the elite body of a visually normative fashion model with the mark of disability, this image shakes up our assumptions about the normal and the abnormal, the public and the private, the chic and the desolate, the compelling and the repelling. Introducing a service dog—a standard prop of indigents and poster children—into the conventional composition of an upscale fashion photo forces the viewer to reconfigure assumptions about what constitutes the attractive and the desirable.

I am arguing that the emergence of disabled fashion models is inadvertent activism without any legitimate agent for positive social change. Their appearance is simply a result of market forces. This both troubling and empowering form of entry into democratic capitalism produces a kind of instrumental form of equality: the freedom to be appropriated by consumer culture. In a democracy, to reject this paradoxical liberty is one thing; not to be granted it is another. Ever straining for novelty and capitalizing on titillation, the fashion advertising world promptly appropriated the power of disabled figures to provoke responses. Diversity appeals to an upscale liberal sensibility these days, making consumers feel good about buying from companies that are charitable toward the traditionally disadvantaged. More important, the disability market is burgeoning. At 54 million people and growing fast as the baby boomers age, their spending power was estimated to have reached the trillion-dollar mark in 2000 (Williams 1999).

For the most part, commercial advertising that features disabled models are presented the same as nondisabled models, simply because all models look essentially the same. The physical markings of gender, race, ethnicity, and disability are muted to the level of gesture, subordinated to the overall normativity of the models' appearance. Thus commercial visual media cast disabled consumers as simply one of many variations that compose the market to which they appeal. Such routinization of disability imagery—however stylized and unrealistic it may be—nevertheless brings disability as a human experience out of the closet and into the normative public sphere. Images of disabled fashion models enable people with disabilities, especially those who acquire impairments as adults, to imagine themselves as a part of the ordinary, albeit consumerist, world rather than as in a special class of excluded untouchables and unviewables. Images of impairment as a familiar, even mundane, experience in the lives of seemingly successful, happy, well-adjusted people can reduce the identifying against oneself that is the overwhelming effect of oppressive and discriminatory attitudes toward people with disabilities. Such images, then, are at once liberatory and oppressive. They do the cultural work of integrating a previously excluded group into the dominant order—for better or worse—much like the inclusion of women in the military.

This form of popular resymbolization produces counter images that have activist potential. A clearer example of disability activism might be Aimee Mullins, who is a fashion model, celebrity, champion runner, a Georgetown University student, and double amputee. Mullins was also one of *People Magazine*'s 50 Most Beautiful people of 1999. An icon of disability pride and equality, Mullins exposes—in fact calls attention to—the mark of her disability in most photos, refusing to normalize or hide her disability in order to pass for nondisabled. Indeed, her public version of her career is that her disability has been a benefit: she has several sets of legs, both cosmetic and functional, and so is able to choose how tall she wants to be. Photographed in her prosthetic legs, she embodies the sexualized jock look that demands women be both slender and fit. In her cosmetic legs, she captures the look of the high fashion beauty in the controversial shoot by Nick Knight called "Accessible," showcasing outfits created by designers such as Alexander McQueen. But this is high fashion with a difference. In the jock shot her functional legs are brazenly displayed, and even in the voguishly costumed shot, the knee joints of her artificial legs are exposed. Never is there an attempt to disguise her prosthetic legs; rather the entire photos thematically echo her prostheses and render the whole image chic. Mullins's prosthetic legs—whether cosmetic or functional—parody, indeed proudly mock, the fantasy of the perfect body that is the mark of fashion, even while the rest of her body conforms precisely to fashion's impossible standards. So rather than concealing, normalizing, or erasing disability, these photos use the hyperbole and stigmata traditionally associated with disability to quench postmodernity's perpetual search for the new

and arresting image. Such a narrative of advantage works against oppressive narratives and practices usually invoked about disabilities. First, Mullins counters the insistent narrative that one must overcome an impairment rather than incorporating it into one's life and self, even perhaps as a benefit. Second, Mullins counters the practice of passing for nondisabled that people with disabilities are often obliged to enact in the public sphere. So Mullins uses her conformity with beauty standards to assert her disability's violation of those very standards. As legless and beautiful, she is an embodied paradox, asserting an inherently disruptive potential.

What my analysis of these images reveals is that feminist cultural critiques are complex. On the one hand, feminists have rightly unmasked consumer capitalism's appropriation of women as sexual objects for male gratification. On the other hand, these images imply that the same capitalist system in its drive to harvest new markets can produce politically progressive counter images and counter narratives, however fraught they may be in their entanglement with consumer culture. Images of disabled fashion models are both complicit and critical of the beauty system that oppresses all women. Nevertheless, they suggest that consumer culture can provide the raw material for its own critique.

The concluding version of activism I offer is less controversial and more subtle than glitzy fashion spreads. It is what I call academic activism—the activism of integrating education—in the very broadest sense of that term. The academy is no ivory tower but rather it is the grass roots of the educational enterprise. Scholars and teachers shape the communal knowledge and the archive that is disseminated from kindergarten to the university. Academic activism is most self-consciously vibrant in the aggregate of interdisciplinary identity studies—of which women's studies is exemplary—that strive to expose the workings of oppression, examine subject formation, and offer counter narratives for subjugated groups. Their cultural work is building an archive through historical and textual retrieval, canon reformation, role modeling, mentoring, curricular reform, and course and program development.

A specific form of feminist academic activism I elaborate here can be deepened through the complication of a disability analysis. I call it the methodology of intellectual tolerance. By this I don't mean tolerance in the more usual sense of tolerating each other—although that would be useful as well. What I mean is the intellectual position of tolerating what has previously been thought of as incoherence. As feminism has embraced the paradoxes that have emerged from its challenge to the gender system, it has not collapsed into chaos, but rather it developed a methodology that tolerates internal conflict and contradiction. This method asks difficult questions, but accepts provisional answers. This method recognizes the power of identity, at the same time that it reveals identity as a fiction. This method both seeks equality and it claims difference. This method allows us to teach with authority at the same time that we reject notions of pedagogical mastery. This method establishes institutional presences even while it acknowledges the limitations of institutions. This method validates the personal but implements disinterested inquiry. This method both writes new stories and recovers traditional ones. Considering disability as a vector of identity that intersects gender is one more internal challenge that threatens the coherence of woman, of course. But feminism can accommodate such complication and the contradictions it cultivates. Indeed the intellectual tolerance I am arguing for espouses the partial, the provisional, the particular. Such an intellectual habit can be informed by disability experience and

acceptance. To embrace the supposedly flawed body of disability is to critique the normalizing, phallic fantasies of wholeness, unity, coherence, and completeness. The disabled body is contradiction, ambiguity, and partiality incarnate.

My claim here has been that integrating disability as a category of analysis, a historical community, set of material practices, a social identity, a political position, and a representational system into the content of feminist—indeed into all inquiry—can strengthen the critique that is feminism. Disability, like gender and race, is everywhere, once we know how to look for it. Integrating disability analyses will enrich and deepen all our teaching and scholarship. Moreover, such critical intellectual work facilitates a fuller integration of the sociopolitical world—for the benefit of everyone. As with gender, race, sexuality, and class: to understand how disability operates is to understand what it is to be fully human.

NOTES

1. Interestingly, in Fiske's study, feminists, business women, Asians, Northerners, and Black professionals were stereotyped as highly competent, thus envied. In addition to having very low competence, housewives, disabled people, blind people, so-called retarded people, and the elderly were rated as warm, thus pitied.
2. Personal conversation with Paul Longmore, San Francisco, CA, June 2000.

WORKS CITED

Americans with Disabilities Act of 1990. Retrieved 15 August 2002, from www.usdoj.gov/crt/ada/pubs/ada.txt.

Aristotle. 1944. *Generation of Animals*. Trans. A. L. Peck. Cambridge, MA: Harvard University Press.

Asch, Adrienne, and Gail Geller. 1996. "Feminism, Bioethics and Genetics." In *Feminism, Bioethics: Beyond Reproduction*, ed. S. M. Wolf, 318–50. Oxford: Oxford University Press.

Battin, Margaret P., Rosamond Rhodes, and Anita Silvers, eds. 1998. *Physician Assisted Suicide: Expanding the Debate*. New York: Routledge.

Bordo, Susan. 1994. "Reading the Male Body." In *The Male Body*, ed. Laurence Goldstein, 265–306. Ann Arbor: University of Michigan Press.

——. 1993. *Unbearable Weight: Feminism, Western Culture and the Body*. Berkeley: University of California Press.

Braidotti, Rosi. 1994. *Nomadic Subjects: Embodiment and Sexual Difference in Contemporary Feminist Thought*. New York: Columbia University Press.

Brownsworth, Victoria A., and Susan Raffo, eds. 1999. *Restricted Access: Lesbians on Disability*. Seattle, WA: Seal Press.

Butler, Judith. 1993. *Bodies That Matter*. New York: Routledge.

——. 1990. *Gender Trouble*. New York: Routledge.

Bynum, Caroline Walker. 1999. "Shape and Story: Metamorphosis in the Western Tradition." Paper presented at NEH Jefferson Lecture. 22 March, Washington, DC.

Clark, David L., and Catherine Myser. 1996. "Being Humaned: Medical Documentaries and the Hyperrealization of Conjoined Twins." In *Freakery: Cultural Spectacles of the Extraordinary Body*, ed. Rosemarie Garland-Thomson, 338–55. New York: New York University Press.

Davis, Lennard. 1995. *Enforcing Normalcy: Disability, Deafness, and the Body*. New York: Verso.

De Beauvoir, Simone. (1952) 1974. *The Second Sex*. Trans. H. M. Parshley. New York: Vintage Press.

Dreger, Alice Domurat. 1998a. *Hermaphrodites and the Medical Invention of Sex*. Cambridge, MA: Harvard University Press.

——. 1998b. "The Limits of the Individuality: Ritual and Sacrifice in the Lives and Medical Treatment of Conjoined Twins." In *Freakery: Cultural Spectacles of the Extraordinary Body*, ed. Rosemarie Garland-Thomson, 338–55. New York: New York University Press.

Eiesland, Nancy. 1994. *The Disabled God: Toward a Liberatory Theology of Disability*. Nashville, TN: Abingdon Press.

Fausto-Sterling, Anne. 2000. *Sexing the Body: Gender Politics and the Construction of Sexuality*. New York: Basic Books.

——. 1995. "Gender, Race, and Nation: The Comparative Anatomy of Hottentot Women in Europe, 1815–1817." In *Deviant Bodies: Cultural Perspectives in Science and Popular Culture*, eds. Jennifer Terry and Jacqueline Urla, 19–48. Bloomington: Indiana University Press.

Fine, Michelle, and Adrienne Asch, eds. 1988. *Women with Disabilities: Essays in Psychology, Culture, and Politics*. Philadelphia: Temple University Press.

Finger, Anne. 1990. *Past Due: A Story of Disability, Pregnancy, and Birth*. Seattle, WA: Seal Press.

Fiske, Susan T., Amy J. C. Cuddy, and Peter Glick. 2001. "A Model of (Often Mixed) Stereotype Content: Competence and Warmth Respectively Follow from Perceived Status and Competition." Unpublished study.

Foucault, Michel. 1979. *Discipline and Punish: The Birth of the Prison*. Trans. Alan M. Sheridan-Smith. New York: Vintage Books.

Garland-Thomson, Rosemarie. 1999. "Narratives of Deviance and Delight: Staring at Julia Pastrana, 'The Extraordinary Lady.'" In *Beyond the Binary*, ed. Timothy Powell, 81–106. New Brunswick, NJ: Rutgers University Press.

——. 1997. *Extraordinary Bodies: Figuring Physical Disability in American Culture and Literature*. New York: Columbia University Press.

Gilman, Sander L. 1999. *Making the Body Beautiful*. Princeton, NJ: Princeton University Press.

——. 1998. *Creating Beauty to Cure the Soul*. Durham, NC: Duke University Press.

——. 1985. *Difference and Pathology: Stereotypes of Sexuality, Race, and Madness*. Ithaca, NY: Cornell University Press.

Hahn, Harlan. 1988. "Can Disability Be Beautiful?" *Social Policy* 18 (Winter): 26–31.

Haiken, Elizabeth. 1997. *Venus Envy: A History of Cosmetic Surgery*. Baltimore, MD: Johns Hopkins University Press.

Haraway, Donna. 1991. *Simians, Cyborgs, and Women*. New York: Routledge.

Harstock, Nancy. 1983. "The Feminist Standpoint: Developing the Ground for a Specifically Feminist Historical Materialism." In *Discovering Reality*, eds. Sandra Harding and Merrell Hintikka, 283–305. Dortrecht, Holland: Reidel Publishing.

Herndl, Diane Price. 2002. "Reconstructing the Posthuman Feminist Body: Twenty Years after Audre Lorde's Cancer Journals." In *Disability Studies: Enabling the Humanities*, eds. Sharon Snyder, Brenda Brueggemann, and Rosemarie Garland-Thomson, 144–55. New York: MLA Press.

Hillyer, Barbara. 1993. *Feminism and Disability*. Norman: University of Oklahoma Press.

Hubbard, Ruth. 1990. "Who Should and Who Should Not Inhabit the World?" In *The Politics of Women's Biology*, 179–98. New Brunswick, NJ: Rutgers University Press.

Keller, Evelyn Fox. 1992. "Nature, Nurture and the Human Genome Project." In *The Code of Codes: Scientific and Social Issues in the Human Genome Project*, eds. Daniel J. Kevles and Leroy Hood, 281–99. Cambridge, MA: Harvard University Press.

Kessler, Suzanne J. 1990. *Lessons from the Intersexed*. New Brunswick, NJ: Rutgers University Press.

Kittay, Eva Feder. 1999. *Love's Labor: Essays on Women, Equality, and Dependency*. New York: Routledge.

Kittay, Eva, with Leo Kittay. 2000. "On the Expressivity and Ethics of Selective Abortion for Disability: Conversations with My Son." In *Prenatal Testing and Disability Rights*, eds. Erik Parens and Adrienne Asch, 165–95. Washington, DC: Georgetown University Press.

Linton, Simi. 1998. *Claiming Disability: Knowledge and Identity*. New York: New York University Press.

Longmore, Paul K. 1997. "Conspicuous Contribution and American Cultural Dilemmas: Telethon Rituals of Cleansing and Renewal." In *The Body and Physical Difference: Discourses of Disability*, eds. David Mitchell and Sharon Snyder, 134–58. Ann Arbor: University of Michigan Press.

Lorde, Audre. 1980. *The Cancer Journals*. San Francisco: Spinsters Ink.

Mairs, Nancy. 1996. *Waist High in the World: A Life Among the Disabled*. Boston: Beacon Press.

McRuer, Robert. 1999. "Compulsory Able-Bodiedness and Queer/Disabled Existence." Paper presented at MLA Convention, 28 December, Chicago, IL.

"Meet Ellen Stohl." 1987. *Playboy*. July: 68–74.

Morrison, Toni. 1992. *Playing in the Dark: Whiteness and the Literary Imagination*. Cambridge, MA: Harvard University Press.

Parens, Erik, and Adrienn Asch. 2000. *Prenatal Testing and Disability Rights*. Washington, DC: Georgetown University Press.

Piercy, Marge. 1969. "Unlearning Not to Speak." In *Circles on Water*, 97. New York: Doubleday.

Rand, Erica. 1995. *Barbie's Queer Accessories*. Durham, NC: Duke University Press.

Rapp, Rayna. 1999. *Testing Women, Testing the Fetus: The Social Impact of Amniocentesis in America*. New York: Routledge.

Rich, Adrienne. 2001. *Arts of the Possible: Essays and Conversations*. New York: W.W. Norton.

——. 1986. "Compulsory Heterosexuality and Lesbian Existence." In *Blood, Bread, and Poetry*, 23–75. New York: Norton.

Riley, Denise. 1999. "Bodies, Identities, Feminisms." In *Feminist Theory and the Body: A Reader*, eds.

Janet Price and Margrit Shildrick, 220–6. Edinburgh: Edinburgh University Press.

Russo, Mary. 1994. *The Female Grotesque: Risk, Excess, and Modernity*. New York: Routledge.

Saxton, Marsha. 1998. "Disability Rights and Selective Abortion." In *Abortion Wars: A Half Century of Struggle (1950–2000)*, ed. Ricky Solinger, 374–93. Berkeley: University of California Press.

Scott, Joan Wallach. 1988. "Gender as Useful Category of Analysis." In *Gender and the Politics of History*, 29–50. New York: Columbia University Press.

Sedgwick, Eve Kosofsky. 1990. *Epistemology of the Closet*. Berkeley: University of California Press.

Silvers, Anita. 1995. "Reconciling Equality to Difference: Caring (f)or Justice for People with Disabilities." *Hypatia* 10(1): 30–55.

Spelman, Elizabeth V. 1988. *Inessential Woman: Problems of Exclusion in Feminist Thought*. Boston: Beacon Press.

Tuana, Nancy. 1993. *The Less Noble Sex: Scientific, Religious and Philosophical Conceptions of Woman's Nature*. Indianapolis: Indiana University Press.

Wald, Priscilla. 2000. "Future Perfect: Grammar, Genes, and Geography." *New Literary History* 31(4): 681–708.

Williams, John M. 1999. "And Here's the Pitch: Madison Avenue Discovers the 'Invisible Consumer.'" *WE Magazine*, July/August: 28–31.

Wolf, Naomi. 1991. *The Beauty Myth: How Images of Beauty Are Used Against Women*. New York: William Morrow.

Young, Iris Marion. 2002. *Throwing Like a Girl and Other Essays in Feminist Philosophy and Social Theory*. Ann Arbor, MI: UMI Books on Demand.

——. 1990a. "Breasted Experience." In *Throwing Like a Girl and Other Essays in Feminist Philosophy and Social Theory*, 189–209. Bloomington: Indiana University Press.

——. 1990b. "Throwing Like a Girl." In *Throwing Like a Girl and Other Essays in Feminist Philosophy and Social Theory*, 141–59. Bloomington: Indiana University Press.

CHAPTER 26

Unspeakable Offenses: Untangling Race and Disability in Discourses of Intersectionality

Nirmala Erevelles and Andrea Minear

SUMMARY

Individuals located at the intersections of race, class, gender, and disability are constituted as non-citizens and (no)bodies by the very social institutions designed to protect, nurture, and empower them. In this essay, Nirmala Erevelles and Andrea Minear demonstrate how the omission of disability in discussions of intersectionality has dangerous consequences for disabled people of color. Considering that the intersection of race and disability is more than simply adding one kind of difference to another, disability scholars have argued that disability is constitutive of most social differences, particularly race.

Erevelles and Minear present the "unspeakable life" of Junius Wilson, who was born in North Carolina in 1908 and became deaf as a toddler. At school, Wilson learned "Raleigh signs," which were specific to the school and contributed to his later isolation from both the deaf and the black communities. Wilson was incarcerated and eventually castrated, as the intersection of disability and race culminated his being labeled "feeble-minded" and dangerous in court.

The case of Cassie Smith and her mother, Aliya Smith, provides a contemporary example of intersectionality. The 5-year-old Cassie faced "imprisonment" at an institution that was supposed to be a haven for kids with emotional and behavioral problems, and later attempts to integrate in other educational settings proved frustrating and ineffective. Repeated labels of mental retardation, learning disability, and attention disorders were used as justification for isolating Cassie. Erevelles and Minear point out that in the case of both the Smiths and Wilson, the intersection of oppressed identities can cohere to place disabled people beyond the pale of intervention by the institutions designed to serve them. In such narratives of intersectionality, disability serves as the ideological force that organizes social hierarchies in their historical contexts.

The Literature of Critical Race Feminist Theory approaches disability as an expression of intersectional identity wherein devalued social characteristics compound stigma resulting in so-called spirit murder. Three diverging practices of intersectionality are identified as guiding scholarship on the constitutive features of multiply minoritizing identities: (1) anticategorical frameworks that insist on race, class, and gender as social constructs/fictions; (2) intracategorical frameworks that critique merely additive approaches to differences as layered stigmas; and (3) constitutive frameworks that describe the structural conditions within which social categories in the above models are constructed by (and intermeshed with) each other in specific historical contexts. In being true to Critical Race Feminist Theory approaches, the article draws on two other narratives, one historical and one contemporary, to describe how individuals located perilously at the intersections of race, class, gender, *and* disability are constituted as non-citizens and (no)bodies by the very social institutions (legal, educational, and rehabilitational) that are designed to protect, nurture, and empower them.

> On October 29, 1984, Eleanor Bumpurs, a 270 pound, arthritic, sixty-seven year old woman was shot to death while resisting eviction from her apartment in the Bronx. She was $98.85, or one month, behind in her rent. New York City mayor Ed Koch and police commissioner Benjamin Ward described the struggle preceding her demise as involving two officers with plastic shields, one officer with a restraining hook, another officer with a shotgun, and at least one supervising officer. All the officers also carried service revolvers. According to Commissioner Ward, during the course of the attempted eviction Eleanor Bumpurs escaped from the restraining hook twice and wielded a knife that Commissioner Ward said was "bent" on one of the plastic shields. At some point, Officer Stephen Sullivan, the officer positioned furthest away from her aimed and fired his shotgun. It is alleged that the blast removed half of her hand so that, according to the Bronx district attorney's office, "it was anatomically impossible for her to hold the knife." The officer pumped his gun and shot again, making his mark completely the second time around.
> (Williams, 271)

In her essay, "Spirit Murdering the Messenger," Critical Race Feminist (CRF) Patricia Williams describes the brutal murder of a poor, elderly, overweight, disabled, black woman by several heavily armed police officers. Trapped at the intersections of multiple oppressive contexts, Eleanor Bumpurs's tattered body was quite literally torn apart by her multiple selves—being raced, classed, gendered, *and* disabled. In the essay, Williams reads this murder as an unambiguous example of "racism [experienced] as . . . an offense so painful and assaultive as to constitute . . . 'spirit murder'" (230). Toward the end of the essay Williams struggles to fathom why the officer who fired the fatal shots saw such an "'immediate threat and endangerment to life'. . . . [that he] could not allay his need to kill a sick old lady fighting off hallucinations with a knife" (234). In this quote, Williams recognizes Eleanor Bumpurs's disability when invoking her arthritis and possible mental illness. However, Williams deploys disability merely as a descriptor, a difference that is a matter of "magnitude" or "context," what another CRF scholar, Angela Harris, has described as "nuance theory" (14). According to Harris, "nuance theory constitutes black women's oppression as only an intensified example of (white) women's oppression" and is therefore used as the "ultimate example of how bad things [really] are" for all women (15).

While we agree with the critique of nuance theory in feminist analyses that ignore the real experiences of black women, we argue that CRF scholars deploy a similar analytical tactic through their unconscious non-analysis of disability as it intersects with race, class, and gender oppression. Disability, like race, offers not just a "nuance" to any analysis of difference. For example, one could argue that the outrage emanating from a heaving, black body wielding a knife sent a nervous (and racist) police officer into panic when confronted by his own racialized terror of otherness. But what about the other ideological terrors that loomed large in this encounter? Could the perception of Eleanor Bumpurs as a dangerous, obese, irrational, black woman also have contributed to her construction as criminally "insane" (disability) because her reaction to a "mere" legal matter of eviction (class) was murderous rage? And did our socially sanctioned fears of the mentally ill and our social devaluation of disabled (arthritic and elderly) bodies of color justify the volley of shots fired almost instinctively to protect the public from the deviant, the dangerous, and the disposable? We, therefore, argue that in the violent annihilation of Eleanor Bumpurs's being, disability as it intersects with race, class, and gender served more than just a "context" or "magnifier" to analyze the oppressive conditions that caused this murder.

In this article, we demonstrate how the omission of disability as a critical category in discussions of intersectionality has disastrous and sometimes deadly consequences for disabled people of color caught at the violent interstices of multiple differences. In the first section, we will theorize intersectionality as first proposed by Crenshaw and explore the different ways in which it can be utilized by both Critical Race Theory and Disability Studies to analyze the experiences of people located at the interstices of multiple differences. Next, true to CRT tradition, we draw on two other narratives, one historical and one contemporary, to describe how individuals located perilously at the interstices of race, class, gender, *and* disability are constituted as non-citizens and (no) bodies by the very social institutions (legal, educational, and rehabilitational) that are designed to protect, nurture, and empower them.

INTERSECTIONALITY AT THE CROSSROADS: THEORIZING MULTIPLICATIVE DIFFERENCES

With the deconstruction of essentialism, the challenge of how to theorize identity in all its complex multiplicity has preoccupied feminist scholars of color.[1] Kimberlé Crenshaw, one of the key proponents of the theory of intersectionality, has argued that "many of the experiences black women face are not subsumed within the traditional boundaries of race or gender oppression as these boundaries are currently understood" (358). Part of the problem of "relying on a static and singular notion of being or of

identity" (Pastrana, 75) is that the single characteristic that is foregrounded (e.g. female or black) is expected to explain all of the other life experiences of the individual or the group. Additionally, Crenshaw points out that social movements based on a single identity politics (e.g. the Feminist Movement, Black Power Movement, GLBT, and the Disability Rights Movement) have historically conflated or ignored intragroup differences and this has sometimes resulted in growing tensions between the social movements themselves.

Feminists of color have, therefore, had the difficult task of attempting to theorize oppression faced at the multiple fronts of race, class, gender, sexuality, and disability.[2] Thus, if one is poor, black, elderly, disabled, and lesbian, must these differences be organized into a hierarchy such that some differences gain prominence over others? What if some differences coalesce to create a more abject form of oppression (e.g. being poor, black, and disabled) or if some differences support both privilege/invisibility within the same oppressed community (e.g. being black, wealthy, and gay)? What happens if we use "race" as a stable register of oppression against which other discriminations gain validity through their similarity and difference from that register? (Arondekar).

In the face of this theoretical challenge, intersectionality has been set up as the most appropriate analytical intervention expected to accomplish the formidable task of mediating multiple differences. For example, Patricia Hill Collins writes that "[a]s opposed to examining gender, race, class, and nation as separate systems of oppression, intersectionality explores how these systems mutually construct one another" (63). CRF Adrien Wing writes:

> We, as black women, can no longer afford to think of ourselves as merely the sum of separate parts that can be added together or subtracted from, until a white male or female

stands before you. The actuality of our experience is multiplicative. Multiply each of my parts together, WE X WE X WE X WE X I, and you have *one* indivisible being. If you divide one of these parts from one you still have one.

(31)

But this is all much easier said than done. Attempts to deploy intersectionality as an analytical tool in academic research have taken on different forms with varying analytical outcomes—some more useful than others. McCall, in an overview of how intersectionality has been utilized in women studies' scholarship, has identified three different modes of theorizing intersectionality. The first mode uses an *anticategorical* framework based on the poststructuralist argument that social categories like race, gender, sexuality, and disability are merely social constructions/fictions. CRF scholars are, however, unwilling to completely do away with the social categories that constitute identity in the first place. As Crenshaw explains:

> To say that a category such as race and gender is socially constructed is not to say that the category has no significance in our world. On the contrary, a large and continuing project for subordinated people . . . is thinking about the way in which power is clustered around certain categories and is exercised against others.
>
> (375)

As a result, feminists of color are more apt to use an *intracategorical* framework that focuses on "particular social groups at neglected points of intersection of multiple master categories" (McCall, 2005). As Crenshaw explains:

> [I]ntersectionality provides a basis for reconceptualizing race as a coalition between men and women of color. . . . Intersectionality may provide the means for dealing with other marginalizations as well. For example,

race can also be a coalition of straight and gay people of color, and thus serve as a basis for critique of churches and other cultural institutions that reproduce heterosexism.

(377)

The intracategorical framework is especially promising to CRF scholars because it validates the reality of racism as it intersects with sexism and other social categories of difference (e.g. heterosexism; classism) in the everyday lives of women of color. However, Yuval-Davis, while producing a list of possible differences (potentially incomplete) that includes "'race'/skin color; ethnicity; nation/state; class, culture; ability; age; sedentariness/origin; wealth; North–South; religion, stage of social development" (202), asks if it is even conceivable to address all these possible social categories intersecting with a common master category (e.g. race or gender) at any given time? Do some differences acquire greater prominence than others (e.g. sexuality)? Are some "other" differences just added on to merely complicate and "nuance" this intersectional analysis (e.g. disability)?

If the intracategorical framework rejects merely tacking on another difference to its litany of categories (e.g. disability), it would have to, in effect, reject the additive approach to multiple differences and instead utilize what Yuval-Davis has described as the constitutive approach to multiple differences. This approach, while foregrounding the actual experiences of women of color at the intersection of multiple social categories, also describes the structural conditions within which these social categories are constructed by, and intermeshed with each other in specific historical contexts. McCall calls this third approach to theorizing intersectionality the *intercategorical* framework. Yuval-Davis explains:

> The point of intersectional analysis is not to find "several identities under one." . . . This

would reinscribe the fragmented, additive model of oppression and essentialize specific social identities. Instead the point is to analyse the differential ways by which social divisions are concretely enmeshed and constructed by each other and how they relate to political and subjective constructions of identities.

(205)

Therefore, rather than merely adding disability to nuance an intersectional analysis, we will foreground the historical contexts and structural conditions within which the identity categories of race and disability intersect.

POINTS OF CONTACT: AT THE INTERSECTION OF CRT AND DISABILITY STUDIES

In educational contexts, the association of race with disability has resulted in large numbers of students of color (particularly African American and Latino males) being subjected to segregation in so-called special-education classrooms through sorting practices such as tracking and/or through labels such as mild mental retardation and/or emotional disturbance.[3] The PBS film, *Beyond Brown: Pursuing the Promise* (Haddad, Readdean, and Valadez) substantiates these claims with the following statistics.

- Black children constitute 17 percent of the total school enrollment, but 33 percent of those labeled "mentally retarded."
- During the 1998–1999 school year more than 2.2 million children of color in U.S. schools were served by special education. Post-high school outcomes for these students were striking. Among high school youth with disabilities, about 75 percent of African Americans, compared to 39 percent of whites, are still not employed three to five years out of

school. In this same time period, the arrest rate for African Americans with disabilities is 40 percent, compared to 27 percent for whites.
- States with a history of legal school segregation account for five of the seven states with the highest overrepresentation of African Americans labeled mentally retarded. They are Mississippi, South Carolina, North Carolina, Florida, and Alabama.
- Among Latino students, identification for special education varies significantly from state to state. Large urban schools districts in California exhibit disproportionately large numbers of Latino English-language learners represented in special education classes in secondary schools.
- Some 20 percent of Latino students in grades 7 through 12 had been suspended from school according to statistics from 1999 compared with 15 percent of white students and 35 percent of African American students.

The association of race with disability has been extremely detrimental to people of color in the U.S.—not just in education, but also historically where associations of race with disability have been used to justify the brutality of slavery, colonialism, and neocolonialism. Unfortunately, rather than nurturing an alliance between race and disability, CRT scholars (like other radical scholars) have mistakenly conceived of disability as a biological category, as an immutable and pathological abnormality rooted in the "medical language of symptoms and diagnostic categories" (Linton, 8). Disability studies scholars, on the other hand, have critiqued this "deficit" model of disability and have described disability as a socially constructed category that derives meaning and social (in)significance from the historical, cultural, political, and economic structures that frame social life.

Thus, at the first point of contact, both CRT and disability scholars begin with the critical assumption that race and disability are, in fact, social constructs. Thus, Haney Lopez explains "Biological race is an illusion. ... Social race, however, is not. ... Race has its genesis and maintains its vigorous strength in the realm of social beliefs" (172). Similarly, Garland-Thomson describes disability as "the attribution of corporeal deviance—not so much a property of bodies [but rather] ... a product of cultural rules about what bodies should be or do" (6). At their second point of contact, race and disability are both theorized as relational concepts. Thus, CRT scholars argue that "[r]aces are constructed relationally against one another, rather than in isolation" (Haney Lopez, 168) such that the privileges that whites enjoy are linked to the subordination of people of color (Harris). Similarly, Lennard Davis points out that "our construction of the normal world is based on a radical repression of disability" (22) because "without the monstrous body to demarcate the borders of the generic ... and without the pathological to give form to the normal, the taxonomies of bodily value that underlie political, social and economic arrangements would collapse" (Garland-Thomson, 20). Finally, at the third point of contact, both perspectives use stories and first-person accounts to foreground the perspectives of those who have experienced victimization by racism and ableism first-hand (Espinoza and Harris; Angela Harris; Ladson-Billings and Tate IV; Parker, Deyhle, and Villenas; Linton; Connor).

In building on these alliance possibilities, disability-studies scholars have argued that disability is, in fact, constitutive of most social differences, particularly race (Baynton; Erevelles 1996; James and Wu). One example to support the above claim lies in the historical narrative of eugenics as a program of selective breeding to prevent the degeneration of the human species. Colonial ideologies conceiving of the colonized races as intrinsically degenerate sought to bring these "bodies" under control via segregation and/or destruction. Such control was regarded as necessary for the public good. The association of degeneracy and disease with racial difference also translated into an attribution of diminished cognitive and rational capacities of non-white populations. Disability related labels such as feeble-mindedness and mental illness were often seen as synonymous with bodies marked oppressively by race (Baynton; Gould). Fearing that such characteristics could be passed down from generation to generation and further pose a threat to the dominant white race, "protective" practices such as forced sterilizations, rigid miscegenation laws, residential segregation in ghettoes, barrios, reservations and other state institutions, and sometimes even genocide (e.g. the Holocaust) were brought to bear on non-white populations under the protected guise of eugenics. However, constructing the degenerate "other" was not just an ideological intervention to support colonialism. In the more contemporary context of transnational capitalism, Erevelles argues that:

> the 'ideology' of disability is essential to the capitalist enterprise because it is able to regulate and control the unequal distribution of surplus through invoking biological difference as the 'natural' cause of all inequality, thereby successfully justifying the social and economic inequality that maintains social hierarchies ... [D]isability ... is [therefore] the organizing grounding principle in the construction of the categories of gender, race, class, and sexual orientation.
>
> (526)

It is easy to dismiss eugenics as a relic of a bygone era, but the continued association of race and disability in debilitating ways necessitates that we examine how eugenic practices continue to reconstitute social hierarchies in contemporary contexts via the deployment of a hegemonic ideology of disability that have real material effects on people located at the intersections of difference. To illustrate the argument, we will now draw on the narratives of two protagonists, Junius Wilson and Cassie Smith.

THE "UNSPEAKABLE" LIFE OF JUNIUS WILSON

The first narrative, the story of Junius Wilson, poignantly told in Susan Burch and Hannah Joyner's book, *Unspeakable: The Life of Junius Wilson*, occurred at the intersection of disability, race, gender, and class. Born in 1908 to Sidney and Mary Wilson in the predominantly African American community of Castle Hayne on the outskirts of Wilmington, North Carolina, Junius Wilson became deaf as a toddler. The tensions of raising a deaf child in poverty conditions within a political context of racial violence caused Sidney Wilson to desert his family, forcing his wife Mary to send the young Wilson to the residential North Carolina School for the Colored Blind and Deaf in Raleigh. In the segregated school in Raleigh, Wilson was initiated into a "black deaf community" and "Raleigh signs" that were specific to the school and that had almost no currency elsewhere—a fact that would later contribute to Wilson's social isolation in both the deaf and the black communities. Additionally, in line with racist ideologies of African American students' low mental capacities, the school encouraged vocational work over traditional classroom work, so while Wilson could write his name out, he was unable to read and write anything else. Then, in 1924, Wilson was expelled from the school because of a minor infraction and forced to return home.

Returning home from Raleigh, Wilson's habits of "touching or holding people, stamping feet and waving arms" (33) constructed him as a threatening figure in a society ruled by Jim Crow laws—habits that could compromise the safety of himself, his family, and his community. It was perhaps for all these reasons and in an effort to protect his family and his community that Arthur Smith, the family friend, accused the 17-year-old Junius Wilson of assaulting and attempting to rape his young wife, Lizzie. Thus, in August 1925, Junius Wilson was arrested and taken to New Hanover County jail. Unable to communicate with Wilson, the court held a lunacy hearing where it was concluded that Wilson was both "feeble-minded" and dangerous, and was therefore committed to the criminal ward of the North Carolina State Hospital for the Colored Insane in Goldsboro that housed epileptics, "idiots," and other "mental defectives" and exerted institutional control rather than practices of healing.

With eugenic ideologies dominant in the early twentieth century, one means of social control was castration, the surgical removal of the testicles. Thus, in 1932, Wilson was castrated and henceforth was no longer perceived as a danger because he became "a submissive black man . . . [with] eyes downcast, silent, and reserved . . . a gentle childlike patient" (49). Seen now as a potentially useful worker, Wilson was sent to work in the Farm Colony (the farm attached to the hospital) and was leased to private farmers till his retirement in 1970, where he was transferred to a geriatric ward. Even though all charges against him were dropped by then, he continued to be incarcerated for another 20 years because it was conceived of as "the most benevolent course of action" (1).

In the 1970s, in response to the Civil Rights of Institutionalized Persons Act, Carolina Legal Assistance (CLA), a group of attorneys in Raleigh, found scores of African American men and women "dumped in hospitals, abandoned by communities, and otherwise mislabeled as feebleminded" (124), one of whom was Junius Wilson. After several years of lawsuits and the involvement of advocates and family members, Wilson was moved out to a cottage on the grounds of the hospital on February 4, 1994. He died on March 17, 2001. Hovering precipitously at the boundaries of race, class, gender, *and* disability, Wilson had been held in the isolating confines of the institution for more than three quarters of his life. Overwhelmed by the enormity of the crime committed against Wilson, Burch and Joyner (2007) ask, "How should a society— indeed, how can a society—make amends for past misdeeds?" (3).

But society seldom makes amends for past misdeeds. On the contrary, it is often apt to repeat them. Junius Wilson's story took place in the early twentieth century. Our second narrative, Cassie Smith's story, takes place in the present, almost a century later. The terrifying aspect of Cassie's story is that it continues Wilson's narrative, in effect becoming its sequel by once again foregrounding the violence that lies at the intersection of race, class, gender, *and* disability.

HER TIME IS UP! CASSIE GOTTA GO!: EXCLUSION AT THE INTERSECTIONS

One of the authors of this article, Andrea, had met Cassie two years ago at the home school cooperative, DAWN, which she ran for students like Cassie who did not seem to "fit" in public school. Cassie's mother, Aliya Smith, a single mother on disability for the last 15 years, lives in public housing with her daughter Cassie and her 6-year-old son Charles in a small southern town. Cassie's father lives close by but has been mostly absent from her life. She had been very close to her grandmother who passed away a year ago.

On her first day at DAWN, Cassie tried desperately to fit in with the other eight adolescent girls at the school. She was dressed neatly. But she had severe eczema on her skin and was eyed suspiciously by the other girls as if her rash was contagious. Her hair was braided stylishly, but her braids were already loosening and falling out because she picked at her head continuously. Her big toothy grin gave way to raucous laughter, much louder than the children in the small school were used to. She tried so hard to be friendly, but she was met with wariness.

After barely less than a day of observation and evaluation, Andrea realized that Cassie could not read—a fact that she had successfully hidden from even her closest friends. When asked to write a journal entry, her sentences contained a string of three letter words that made little sense such as "pig as you as zoo cat by as no as dog pig as zoo no by you as zoo as cat red." Cassie "pretended" very well, opening her book, following along, and even reading "along with" someone, saying a word immediately after the other person began the word. Because she did not read, she had limited knowledge of other subject areas. She could barely add and could not subtract. She recognized some coins, but could not figure money. Andrea realized with dismay that 12-year-old Cassie was functionally illiterate.

When we interviewed Cassie and her mother, her turbulent and tragic educational history was slowly revealed. We learned to our horror that Cassie had been bounced around to a different school every year of her school life; two schools in some years. As a toddler, Cassie spent a lot of time with her grandmother because of Aliya's poor health. At age 4, Cassie started out in a private preschool program at the Holy Trinity Baptist School. Without the benefit of records or first-hand knowledge, we wonder whether the fact that Cassie was an economically disadvantaged black child in an all-white school caused her to appear "behind" and uncontrollable. Aliya recalls,

"She used to get temper tantrums and they told me if I couldn't get her straightened up, she gotta go!" Aliya moved Cassie to the Head Start program and then to her neighborhood school for kindergarten:

> And then they [the school personnel] said that she needed help (Cassie interjects: "No, I don't!"). So we had to go through evaluations, meetings, and stuff. They tried to say that she was mentally retarded. (Cassie interjects, "I am not MR!") . . . [Aliya continues in response to Cassie] But she was then. So they sent her to Sally's Corner.

In this small southern town, Sally's Corner was touted as the haven for kids with severe emotional and behavioral problems. In its mission statement the school claimed to offer treatment based on "an interdisciplinary approach with psychology, education, nursing, psychiatry, social work and counseling comprising the professions that impact each client's treatment." The website also included several testimonials from parents and one child that described Sally's Corner very positively. Cassie's memories of Sally's Corner, however, were very dark:

> [Sally's Corner] is like a bad place. They put you there when you get in trouble. They restrain you. They put your arms like this . . . sit on you kinda and put you in a room where no windows at and a little time out room by yourself. . . . And they come and look at you. And I say, "Let me out" and kick the door. . . .
>
> NE: What is it that that gets you really angry?
> Cassie: When somebody tries to fight with me and pull my hair
> NE: But the teachers don't try to fight with you, do they?
> Cassie: Oh I'll still fight you the big ole fat ole . . . sit on me . . . Half ton white folks.

By Cassie's own admission, we can understand that she was no easy client, and it is reasonable to assume that Cassie was in need of some kind of program that would help manage her fits of rage so she could also learn. And surely, they had all that expertise from the multidisciplinary team to do something for her. But again, we do not really know what happened there except for this explanation from Aliya about why she wanted Cassie to leave Sally's Corner after only a couple of months there:

> They locked you up all the time. They had this jail cell. She had spit on the wall while she was in there. They called my mama [Cassie's grandmother]. I was sick at that time. My mama and my sister-in-law went. My mama was so mad when she went out there. She told them, "Open the door. Let that child outta there!" My mama did not understand. Actually she did not care. Like she [Cassie] was being treated like a dog or something. . . . And then they said that before she left she had to scrub the room. My mama said, "Get that child outta there!" And they said she could not leave before she did that. So my mom told Cassie what were the spots that she spit at. And to clean just them. They wanted her to clean the whole room! Then she got to get ready to go. . . . It was time for her to go. . . . Kept on trying to get her out. . . . They finally agreed and I got her to go to Woodberry Gardens.

Once again, while we acknowledge that we have only one side of the story, there are aspects that still puzzle us. Surely "a model treatment program" had more options for a small, angry 5-year-old African American girl with anger-management issues than being thrown into a "jail cell"? What was it about that tiny enraged black body that terrified the staff so much that they threw all their knowledge out of the window, opting instead for the behavioral strategy of "imprisonment"?

This was the educational legacy that Cassie would carry forward with her as she moved into the first grade at her new elementary school, Woodberry Gardens.

After two good years she was inexplicably moved to Spartan elementary and once again to Nottingham. Each time, as Aliya put it, they told her that "It was time for her to leave there. ... Her time was up."

Apparently, at this time, Cassie no longer held the label "mental retardation." Still, when asked, her mother just says, "She acted crazy!" She was now thrown into a regular program at Nottingham with no supports. Once again her academic and behavioral problems were exacerbated. Once again she was teased and called names by her peers. Once again she fought back—she cut a classmate's hair. And once again she suffered the consequences of her negative behavior. Less than two months before her graduation from elementary school, Cassie was transferred to her eighth school, Athena. Aliya was livid:

> You talking about somebody was mad. No! I could never understand why they sent her to Athena. I went over there and met with the teacher. ... It had something to do with her learning. There was a month and half to graduate and they sent her to Athena. Then that teacher was up there ill-treating her. ... They wanted her to graduate with her Athena [special education] class. And I said, "I didn't spend all that money and time at Nottingham for this. I was so mad. I told them that I would have her out of school if they would not let me take her out [of Athena]. Then they listened. When they figured out that I was not playing with them, they got those papers. Like they couldn't get them fast enough. They just moved them in the office. And I took her to Nottingham and she was there for three days so that she could graduate with her class. And they did it [the graduation ceremony] in such a way, that she had to be escorted. Like she was such a bad child. Like she was coming from prison. Her last two teachers had to walk with her side by side. She was the last one to walk.

Thus, after being in eight schools in eight years, Cassie came to DAWN, the home-school cooperative, as a sixth grader with a plethora of problems. In this supportive context, Cassie made great leaps in her social behavior and even made some academic headway. However, Andrea was forced to close DAWN at the end of the year for financial reasons, and so Cassie prepared to re-enter public school in the next fall.

Eager to learn, but receiving very little help in school, Cassie soon got frustrated and into fights again. She was sent to the Alternative School which ironically she actually liked because of the structure and individual attention. But then, even this realm of contentment vanished one day— the day of the "incident." One spring day, six students (four boys and two girls) were left without supervision in a classroom for a few minutes while one of the teachers walked a student to his car to speak to his mother. The boys teased and taunted the girls making rude, sometimes vulgar, suggestions and then laughing them off. One of the boys told Cassie, "So-and-so thinks you're pretty. He wants you to suck his dick." And so she went behind the cubbies and obliged.

By the next day, word spread all over the school. As the rumor gathered momentum, more and more people became aware, including the school counselor and the assistant principal. However, neither the classroom teacher, nor the parents of the perpetrators were notified for nearly two or three weeks. According to the assistant principal, there was an ongoing investigation and then a meeting was called with the Building Based Special Team (BBST) and the parent to discuss what they called a "manifestation determination." The question of the day: Was it Cassie's "learning disability" that caused her to have oral sex with a boy in her class or was this done on her own volition? Following "procedure" each member concurred that her "learning disability" could not have caused her to perform oral sex. She knew what she was doing. Therefore she was GUILTY. Under the zero-tolerance policy, this called for expulsion.

Not once did the committee even bother to look at Cassie's painful history of exclusion, segregation, incarceration, and negation. It was lucky that Andrea was there. Aliya was a poor advocate for her child. Intimidated, angry, confused, and defensive, she often ended up blaming her daughter for the "stupid thing she did." It was Andrea who saved the day. Drawing on her experiences as a former special education teacher, Andrea brought up Cassie's educational history of social isolation and low self-esteem that were the by-products of her "learning disability" and that may have influenced her decision to perform a sexual act that garnered her some form of warped recognition/respect/visibility among her peers. In addition, Andrea had to spell out the possible legal ramifications of leaving students unsupervised in a locked and isolated classroom for even a short period of time. We believe that it was the last statement that sealed the deal. It was not the history of educational abuse, but the threat of legal ramifications that made the committee decide that they would not recommend expulsion. Cassie would have another chance at school. But whether she would have the support that she needed to make it through another school year was still an open question.

The process of narrating Cassie's educational history during the interviews inadvertently produced an unpredictable benefit for Aliya. In a marked difference from the "professionals" who were reviewing Cassie's case, it was Aliya, confused, angry, troubled, and yet still hopeful, who was able to see how the different disruptive, demeaning, and punitive experiences that began early in Cassie's life were now responsible for the risky, sullen, and disorderly behaviors of her teenage daughter. Now with the gift of hindsight, and therefore conscious of her own disempowerment in the process, Aliya poignantly reflected:

> If I had known the system better, I would not have put her there [Sally's Corner]. But at that time I did not know the system. It seemed that they were trying to hurt me, rather than help me.

"UNSPEAKABLE OFFENSES": AN INTERCATEGORICAL ANALYSIS OF INTERSECTIONALITY

Just like Junius Wilson, Cassie is also located at the boundaries of race, class, gender, *and* disability. Each of their stories brings to the forefront several questions: How does racism in its interaction with the inauspicious combination of class, gender, *and* disability oppression cohere to locate Wilson and the Smiths beyond the pale of appropriate interventions by the very institutions (legal, rehabilitative, and educational) that were designed to nurture and empower them? At which point did disability trump race? When did class become the critical influential factor? At what point did gender become the only perceivable threat? In each of the stories, it is very difficult to unravel and isolate the strands that played an integral part in weaving the violent tapestry of their broken lives.

For Junius Wilson, it was the sociopolitical context of racial terror and abject poverty in the Jim Crow South that constituted his deafness as "dangerous" difference that could only be contained within the institutional confines of a segregated residential school for the "Colored" deaf. Ironically, this confinement provided Wilson with a cultural community of other deaf students of color while it at the same time alienated him from his community outside the school. Additionally, unlike white deaf students, being black and deaf located him at the lowest rungs of the social hierarchy of the time, providing him with an inferior education that would also play a part in his continued social isolation. On returning home, his disability cast a shadow on his race and gender and contributed to his construction as the dangerously virile young black male—images that led to the false accusation of sexual assault, his incarceration, and ultimately to the final violent act of his castration. During that time, he was put to work in the farm colony as part of the surplus population being utilized to produce profits for the institution. Without financial resources and other social supports, his family could do little to intervene on his behalf, which resulted in him languishing in an institution for 76 years. The institution's refusal to release him even after all charges were dropped against him was justified under a mantle of benevolence. It was this same benevolence that allowed the institution to justify the unequal and oppressive conditions in the institution by arguing that "the lack of facilities are not due to racial biases but the fact [that] Negro patients are willing to accept what is provided to them, 'which is more than they have at home'" (Burch and Joyner, 74).

In an earlier section of this article, we wrote that Cassie Smith provided Junius Wilson's story with its unwelcome sequel. At first glance, this assertion may seem far-fetched in the contemporary historical context of the New South where Jim Crow (re)appears as only a distant and shameful memory. Yet, Cassie's story foregrounds an interesting twist to the continuing saga of racial segregation in the New South. In place of Jim Crow, Cassie's ever-changing labels of mental retardation (MR), learning disability (LD), and attention deficit hyperactivity disorder (ADHD) were used as the justification for her continued segregation in an effort to protect the mainstream from a dangerous racialized Other—the economically disadvantaged disabled African American girl. Here, class and race also played a significant role in maintaining this

segregation. As educators, we have known privileged white students with similar behavioral problems whose parents were able to corral the school's best resources, were able to access professional help outside the school, and, in the worst case scenario, were able to transfer their child to a private school. Aliya Smith's economic and social disadvantages did not permit her these luxuries. Instead, her disadvantages proved to be a further liability, a signal to the school professionals that there was really no need to "fight" for her daughter Cassie. As a result, even though Cassie had an Individualized Education Program (IEP) replete with individualized goals to improve both her behavior and her learning, she never met most of those goals, and nobody cared. This was apparent in her seventh grade report card that listed her as earning As and Bs, even though she was still functionally illiterate and still had little behavior control.

Finally, perhaps most telling is how disability as a "social" not a "clinical" condition was used to establish the benevolence of the special education bureaucracy and in doing so masked the violence that became an inextricable part of Cassie's educational career. Cassie was first MR, then ADHD, and then LD—labels that ebbed and flowed with the passing tides in different contexts. Clearly, given its temporality, "mental retardation" cannot be a robust category. So, could it then be that the educational gatekeepers, when confronted with an allegedly undisciplined, economically disadvantaged, African American girl, fearfully sought the protection of the label "mental retardation"—a label that would justify her incarceration at the tender age of 5 years old and continue to support her social isolation as it made its punitive march on the successive legs of her young educational career?

We argue here that an intercategorical analysis of intersectionality enables us to foreground the structural context where the social categories of race, class, gender, *and* disability are (re) constituted within the two narratives of Junius Wilson and Cassie Smith. First, we identify disability as the organizing ideological force that is deployed in both narratives as the means to organize the social hierarchies in their respective historical contexts. Here, we describe disability as the very embodiment of the disruption of normativity that is, in turn, symbolic of efficient and profitable individualism and the efficient economic appropriation of those profits produced within capitalist societies. In the early twentieth century, Jim Crow and eugenics served as the two principal mechanisms that patrolled the boundaries of society in order to identify those individuals/communities who were seen as a threat to the normative social order (the status quo) within an incipient capitalist society. The New South replaced those outmoded mechanisms of segregation with more modern systems that were more appropriately in keeping with the times. Thus, for example, in educational contexts the special education bureaucracy with its complex machinery of pseudo-medical evaluations, confusing legal discourses, and overwhelming paperwork administered by a body of intimidating professionals now performs tasks that are not very different from Jim Crow and eugenic ideologies. To put it more simply, special education, instead of being used to individualize education programs to meet the special needs of students, is instead used to segregate students who disrupt the "normal" functioning of schools. Moreover, on the few occasions when Cassie's mother sought to confront them, they invoked their complicated bureaucracy (e.g. using phrases like *manifestation determination*) to further confuse and intimidate her. While we do not deny that Cassie did have significant problems, we argue that the only intervention that was sought by the special education bureaucracy as the most effective was segregation and ultimately incarceration

(alternative school and later a very real possibility of prison). Cassie is, no doubt, difficult to manage and perhaps even challenging to care about enough to help her conquer her barriers. But it is her *right* that she *not* be made dispensable.

"SPIRIT MURDER" AND THE "NEW" EUGENICS: CRITICAL RACE THEORY MEETS DISABILITY STUDIES

The three stories of Eleanor Bumpurs, Junius Wilson, and Cassie and Aliya Smith, however poignant they may appear to be, are not unique. Police brutality, false imprisonment, and educational negligence are commonplace in the lives of people of color—especially those who are located at the margins of multiple identity categories. So common are these practices that CRF scholar Patricia Williams has argued that these kinds of assaults should not be dismissed as the "odd mistake" but rather be given a name that associates them with criminality. Her term for such assaults on an individual's personhood is "spirit murder," which she describes as the equivalent of body murder.

> One of the reasons I fear what I call spirit murder, or disregard for others whose lives qualitatively depend on our regard, is that its product is a system of formalized distortions of thought. It produces social structures centered around fear and hate, it provides a timorous outlet for feelings elsewhere unexpressed. ... We need to see it as a cultural cancer; we need to open our eyes to the spiritual genocide it is wreaking on blacks, whites, and the abandoned and abused of all races and ages. We need to eradicate its numbing pathology before it wipes out what precious little humanity we have left.
>
> (234)

Clearly, in our educational institutions there are millions of students of color, mostly economically disadvantaged and disabled, for whom spirit murder is the most significant experience in their educational lives. In fact, it is this recognition of spirit murder in the everyday lives of disabled students of color that forges a critical link between disability studies and CRT/F through the intercategorical analysis of intersectionality. In other words, utilizing an intercategorical analysis from the critical standpoint of disability studies will foreground the structural forces in place that constitute certain students as a surplus population that is of little value in both social and economic terms. That most of these students are poor, disabled, and of color is critical to recognize from within a CRT/F perspective. By failing to undertake such an analysis, we could miss several political opportunities for transformative action.

NOTES

1. See e.g. bell hooks; Angela Davis; Audre Lorde; Gloria Anzaldúa; Gloria Hull, Patricia Bell Scott, and Barbara Smith.
2. For examples, consult Gloria Anzaldúa; Kimberlé Crenshaw; Angela Harris; Adrien Wing; and Audre Lorde.
3. Artiles; Artiles, Harry, Reschly, and Chinn; Connor and Ferri; Reid and Knight; Watts and Erevelles.

WORKS CITED

Anzaldúa, Gloria. *Making Face Making Soul: Haciendo Caras: Creative and Critical Perspectives of Women of Color*. San Francisco: Aunt Lute Books, 1990.

Arondekar, Anjali. "Border/Line Sex: Queer Positionalities, or How Race Matters Outside the United States." *Interventions* 7.2 (2005): 236–50.

Artiles, Alfredo J. "The Dilemma of Difference: Enriching the Disproportionality Discourse with Theory and Content." *Journal of Special Education* 32.1 (1998): 32–7.

Artiles, Alfredo J., Beth Harry, Daniel J. Reschly, and Philip C. Chinn. "Over-Identification of Students of Color in Special Education: A Critical Overview." *Multicultural Perspectives* 4.1 (2002): 3–10.

Baynton, Douglas. "Disability in History." *Perspectives* 44.9 (2006): 5–7.

Beyond Brown: Pursuing the Promise. Dir. Lulie Haddad, Cyndee Readdean and John J. Valadez. PBS, 2004.

Burch, Susan and Hannah Joyner. *Unspeakable: The Life of Junius Wilson*. Chapel Hill: University of North Carolina Press, 2007.

Connor, David J. *Urban Narratives: Portraits in Progress—Life at the Intersections of Learning Disability, Race, and Class*. New York: Peter Lang, 2007.

Connor, David J. and Beth. A. Ferri. "Integration and Inclusion—A Troubling Nexus: Race, Disability, and Special Education." *Journal of African American History* 90.1/2 (2005): 107–27.

Crenshaw, Kimberlé. "Mapping the Margins: Intersectionality, Identity Politics, and Violence against Women." *Critical Race Theory: The Key Writings that formed the Movement*. Ed. Kimberlé Crenshaw, Neil Gotanda, Gary Pellar, and Kendall Thomas. New York: New Press, 1996. 357–83.

Davis, Angela. Y. *Women, Race, and Class*. New York: Vintage, 1983.

Davis, Lennard J. *Enforcing Normalcy: Disability, Deafness, and the Body*. New York: Verso, 1995.

Erevelles, Nirmala. "(Im)Material Citizens: Cognitive Disability, Race and the Politics of Citizenship." *Disability, Culture, and Education* 1.1 (2002): 5–25.

Erevelles, Nirmala. "Disability and the Dialectics of Difference." *Disability and Society* 11.4 (1996): 519–37.

Espinoza, Leslie and Angela. P. Harris. "Afterword: Embracing the Tar-Baby—LatCrit Theory and the Stick Mess of Race." *California Law Review* 88.5 (1997): 499–559.

Garland-Thomson, Rosemarie. *Extraordinary Bodies: Figuring Physical Disability in American Culture and Literature*. New York: Columbia University Press, 1997.

Gould, Stephen. J. *The Mismeasure of Man*. New York: Norton, 1981.

Haney Lopez, Ian. F. "The Social Construction of Race." *Critical Race Theory: The Cutting Edge*. Ed. Richard Delgado and Jean Stefancic. Philadelphia: Temple University Press, 2007. 163–75.

Harris, Angela. "Race and Essentialism in Feminist Legal Theory." *Critical Race Feminism*. Ed. Adrien. K. Wing. New York: New York University Press, 1997. 11–26.

Harris, Cheryl I. "Whiteness as Property." *Critical Race Theory: Key Writings that Formed the Movement*. Ed. Kimberlé Crenshaw, Neil Gotanda, Gary Pellar, and Kendall Thomas. New York: New Press, 1995. 276–91.

Hill Collins, Patricia. "It's All in the Family: Intersections of Gender, Race, and Nation." *Hypatia* 13.3 (1998): 62–82.

Hooks, bell. *Feminist Theory: From Margin to Center.* Cambridge, MA: South End Press, 1985.

Hull, Gloria. T., Patricia Bell Scott, and Barbara Smith. *All the Women are White, All the Men are Black, But some of Us are Brave.* New York: The Feminist Press at CUNY, 1982.

James, Jennifer. C. and Cynthia Wu. "Editors' Introduction: Race, Ethnicity, Disability, and Literature: Intersections and Interventions." *MELUS* 31. 3 (2003): 3–13.

Ladson-Billings, Gloria and William F. Tate IV. "Toward a Critical Race Theory of Education." *Teachers College Record* 97.1 (1995): 47–68.

Linton, Simi. *Claiming Disability: Knowledge and Identity.* New York: New York University Press, 1998.

Lorde, Audre. *Sister Outside: Essays and Speeches.* Berkeley, CA: The Crossing Press Feminist Series, 1984.

McCall, Leslie. "The Complexity of Intersectionality." *Signs: Journal of Women in Culture and Society* 30. 3 (2005): 1771–1800.

Parker, Laurence, Donna Deyhle, and Sofia Villenas. *Race is…Race isn't: Critical Race Theory and Qualitative Studies in Education.* Boulder, CO: Westview Press, 1999.

Pastrana, Antonio. "Black Identity Constructions: Inserting Intersectionality, Bisexuality, and (Afro-) Latinidad into Black Studies." *Journal of African American Studies* 8.1–2 (2004): 74–89.

Reid, D. Kim and Michelle G. Knight. "Disability Justifies Exclusion of Minority Students: A Critical History Grounded in Disability Studies." *Educational Researcher* 35.6 (2006): 18–33.

Watts, Ivan and Nirmala Erevelles. "These Deadly Times: Reconceptualizing School Violence by Using Critical Race Theory and Disability Studies." *American Educational Research Association* 41.2 (2004): 271–99.

Williams, Patricia. J. "Spirit Murdering the Messenger: The Discourse of Fingerpointing as the Law's Response to Racism." *Critical Race Feminism: A Class Reader.* Ed. Adrien. K. Wing. New York: New York University Press, 1997. 229–42.

Wing, Adrien. "Brief Reflections toward a Multiplicative Theory and Praxis of Being." *Critical Race Feminism: A Reader.* Ed. Adrien K. Wing. New York: New York University Press, 1997. 27–34.

Yuval-Davis, Nira. "Intersectionality and Feminist Politics." *European Journal of Women's Studies* 13.3 (2006): 193–203.

Compulsory Able-Bodiedness and Queer/Disabled Existence

Robert McRuer

SUMMARY

When lesbian existence is imagined as a marginal alternative to the centrality of heterosexuality, it reinforces the notion that heterosexuality is naturally dominant. In this essay, Robert McRuer applies Adrienne Rich's idea about lesbian identity to disability studies. If thinking about lesbian existence reveals "compulsory heterosexuality," so too can we analyze "compulsory able-bodiedness" from the perspective of disability.

Queer and feminist theorists have long critiqued the definition of heterosexuality as "normal relations between sexes" and insisted that homosexuality is subordinated because of the standard of normalcy. Disability studies also draws on critiques of normalcy, as demonstrated by Lennard Davis, and McRuer suggests that able-bodiedness is seen as even more "natural" than heterosexuality. Because able-bodiedness is considered a "normal" requirement for life in the industrial capitalist system, having an "able body" becomes compulsory. Like heterosexuality, able-bodied identity is defined by its repeated performances, and McRuer points out that many cultural institutions are dedicated to showcasing these bodily performances.

There is a constant need to affirm able-bodied identity because able-bodied norms are in reality impossible to embody, and even the status of being able-bodied is only a temporary part of a human life. Since both queerness and disability have the potential to disrupt the performance of able-bodied heterosexuality, both must be contained and embodied by queer/disabled figures that "can be tolerated" in popular imagination. McRuer argues that like being "critically queer," being "severely disabled" can foster a sharp critique of compulsory able-bodiedness. He suggests that the commonly marginalized bodies are the best positioned to refuse the "mere toleration" that keeps those bodies at the margins.

CONTEXTUALIZING DISABILITY

In her famous critique of compulsory heterosexuality Adrienne Rich opens with the suggestion that lesbian existence has often been "simply rendered invisible" (178), but the bulk of her analysis belies that rendering. In fact, throughout "Compulsory Heterosexuality and Lesbian Existence," one of Rich's points seems to be that compulsory heterosexuality depends as much on the ways in which lesbian identities are made visible (or, we might say, comprehensible) as on the ways in which they are made invisible or incomprehensible. She writes:

Any theory of cultural/political creation that treats lesbian existence as a marginal or less "natural" phenomenon, as mere "sexual preference," or as the mirror image of either heterosexual or male homosexual relations is profoundly weakened thereby, whatever its other contributions. Feminist theory can no longer afford merely to voice a toleration of "lesbianism" as an "alternative life-style," or make token allusion to lesbians. A feminist critique of compulsory heterosexual orientation for women is long overdue.

(178)

The critique that Rich calls for proceeds not through a simple recognition or even valuation of "lesbian existence" but rather through an interrogation of how the system of compulsory heterosexuality utilizes that existence. Indeed, I would extract from her suspicion of mere "toleration" confirmation for the idea that one of the ways in which heterosexuality is currently constituted or founded, established as the foundational sexual identity for women, is precisely through the deployment of lesbian existence as always and everywhere supplementary— the margin to heterosexuality's center, the mere reflection of (straight and gay) patriarchal realities. Compulsory heterosexuality's casting of some identities as alternatives ironically buttresses the ideological notion that dominant identities are not really alternatives but rather the natural order of things.[1]

More than 20 years after it was initially published, Rich's critique of compulsory heterosexuality is indispensable, the criticisms of her ahistorical notion of a "lesbian continuum" notwithstanding.[2] Despite its continued relevance, however, the realm of compulsory heterosexuality might seem to be an unlikely place to begin contextualizing disability.[3] I want to challenge that by considering what might be gained by understanding "compulsory heterosexuality" as a key concept in disability studies. Through a reading of compulsory heterosexuality, I want to put forward a theory of what I call compulsory able-bodiedness. The Latin root for *contextualize* denotes the act of weaving together, interweaving, joining together, or composing. This chapter thus

contextualizes disability in the root sense of the word, because I argue that the system of compulsory able-bodiedness that produces disability is thoroughly interwoven with the system of compulsory heterosexuality that produces queerness, that—in fact—compulsory heterosexuality is contingent on compulsory able-bodiedness and vice versa. And, although I reiterate it in my conclusion, I want to make it clear at the outset that this particular contextualizing of disability is offered as part of a much larger and collective project of unraveling and decomposing both systems.[4]

The idea of imbricated systems is of course not new—Rich's own analysis repeatedly stresses the imbrication of compulsory heterosexuality and patriarchy. I would argue, however, as others have, that feminist and queer theories (and cultural theories generally) are not yet accustomed to figuring ability/disability into the equation, and thus this theory of compulsory able-bodiedness is offered as a preliminary contribution to that much-needed conversation.[5]

ABLE-BODIED HETEROSEXUALITY

In his introduction to *Keywords: A Vocabulary of Culture and Society*, Raymond Williams describes his project as

> the record of an inquiry into a *vocabulary*: a shared body of words and meanings in our most general discussions, in English, of the practices and institutions which we group as *culture* and *society*. Every word which I have included has at some time, in the course of some argument, virtually forced itself on my attention because the problems of its meaning seemed to me inextricably bound up with the problems it was being used to discuss.
>
> (15)

Although Williams is not particularly concerned in *Keywords* with feminism or gay and lesbian liberation, the processes he describes should be recognizable to feminists and queer theorists, as well as to scholars and activists in other contemporary movements, such as African American studies or critical race theory. As these movements have developed, increasing numbers of words have indeed forced themselves on our attention, so that an inquiry into not just the marginalized identity but also the dominant identity has become necessary. The problem of the meaning of masculinity (or even maleness), of whiteness, of heterosexuality has increasingly been understood as inextricably bound up with the problems the term is being used to discuss.

One need go no further than the *Oxford English Dictionary* to locate problems with the meaning of heterosexuality. In 1971 the *OED Supplement* defined *heterosexual* as "pertaining to or characterized by the normal relations of the sexes; opp. to *homosexual*." At this point, of course, a few decades of critical work by feminists and queer theorists have made it possible to acknowledge quite readily that heterosexual and homosexual are in fact not equal and opposite identities. Rather, the ongoing subordination of homosexuality (and bisexuality) to heterosexuality allows for heterosexuality to be institutionalized as "the normal relations of the sexes," while the institutionalization of heterosexuality as the "normal relations of the sexes" allows for homosexuality (and bisexuality) to be subordinated. And, as queer theory continues to demonstrate, it is precisely the introduction of normalcy into the system that introduces compulsion: "Nearly everyone," Michael Warner writes in *The Trouble with Normal: Sex, Politics, and the Ethics of Queer Life*, "wants to be normal. And who can blame them, if the alternative is being abnormal, or deviant, or not being one of the rest of us? Put in those terms, there doesn't seem to be a choice at all. Especially in America where [being] normal probably outranks all other social aspirations" (53).

Compulsion is here produced and covered over, with the appearance of choice (sexual preference) mystifying a system in which there actually is no choice.

A critique of normalcy has similarly been central to the disability rights movement and to disability studies, with—for example—Lennard Davis's overview and critique of the historical emergence of normalcy or Rosemarie Garland-Thomson's introduction of the concept of the "normate" (Davis 23–49; Garland-Thomson 8–9). Such scholarly and activist work positions us to locate the problems of able-bodied identity, to see the problem of the meaning of able-bodiedness as bound up with the problems it is being used to discuss. Arguably, able-bodied identity is at this juncture even more naturalized than heterosexual identity. At the very least, many people not sympathetic to queer theory will concede that ways of being heterosexual are culturally produced and culturally variable, even if and even as they understood heterosexual identity itself to be entirely natural. The same cannot be said, on the whole, for able-bodied identity. An extreme example that nonetheless encapsulates currently hegemonic thought on ability and disability is a notorious *Salon* article attacking disability studies that appeared online in the summer of 1999. Norah Vincent writes, "It's hard to deny that something called normalcy exists. The human body is a machine, after all—one that has evolved functional parts: lungs for breathing, legs for walking, eyes for seeing, ears for hearing, a tongue for speaking and most crucially for all the academics concerned, a brain for thinking. This is science, not culture."[6] In a nutshell, you either have an able body, or you don't.

Yet the desire for definitional clarity might unleash more problems than it contains; if it's hard to deny that something called normalcy exists, it's even harder to pinpoint what that something is. The *OED* defines *able-bodied* redundantly and negatively as "having an able body, i.e. one free from physical disability, and capable of the physical exertions required of it; in bodily health; robust." Able-bodiedness, in turn, is defined vaguely as "soundness of health; ability to work; robustness." The parallel structure of the definitions of ability and sexuality is quite striking: first, to be able-bodied is to be "free from physical disability," just as to be heterosexual is to be "the opposite of homosexual." Second, even though the language of "the normal relations" expected of human beings is not present in the definition of able-bodied, the sense of "normal relations" is, especially with the emphasis on work: being able-bodied means being capable of the normal physical exertions required in a particular system of labor. It is here, in fact, that both able-bodied identity and the *Oxford English Dictionary* betray their origins in the nineteenth century and the rise of industrial capitalism. It is here as well that we can begin to understand the compulsory nature of able-bodiedness: in the emergent industrial capitalist system, free to sell one's labor but not free to do anything else effectively meant free to have an able body but not particularly free to have anything else.

Like compulsory heterosexuality, then, compulsory able-bodiedness functions by covering over, with the appearance of choice, a system in which there actually is no choice. I would not locate this compulsion, moreover, solely in the past, with the rise of industrial capitalism. Just as the origins of heterosexual/homosexual identity are now obscured for most people so that compulsory heterosexuality functions as a disciplinary formation seemingly emanating from everywhere and nowhere, so too are the origins of able-bodied/disabled identity obscured, allowing what Susan Wendell calls "the disciplines of normality" (87) to cohere in a system of compulsory able-bodiedness that similarly emanates

from everywhere and nowhere. Able-bodied dilutions and misunderstandings of the minority thesis put forward in the disability rights movement and disability studies have even, in some ways, strengthened the system: the dutiful (or docile) able-bodied subject now recognizes that some groups of people have chosen to adjust to or even take pride in their "condition," but that recognition, and the tolerance that undergirds it, covers over the compulsory nature of the able-bodied subject's own identity.[7]

Michael Bérubé's memoir about his son Jamie, who has Down syndrome, helps exemplify some of the ideological demands currently sustaining compulsory able-bodiedness. Bérubé writes of how he "sometimes feel[s] cornered by talking about Jamie's intelligence, as if the burden of proof is on me, official spokesman on his behalf." The subtext of these encounters always seems to be the same: "*In the end, aren't you disappointed to have a retarded child? . . . Do we really have to give this person our full attention?*" (180). Bérubé's excavation of this subtext pinpoints an important common experience that links all people with disabilities under a system of compulsory able-bodiedness—the experience of the able-bodied need for an agreed-on common ground. I can imagine that answers might be incredibly varied to similar questions—"In the end, wouldn't you rather be hearing?" and "In the end, wouldn't you rather not be HIV positive?" would seem, after all, to be very different questions, the first (with its thinly veiled desire for Deafness not to exist) more obviously genocidal than the second. But they are not really different questions, in that their constant repetition (or their presence as ongoing subtexts) reveals more about the able-bodied culture doing the asking than about the bodies being interrogated. The culture asking such questions assumes in advance that we all agree: able-bodied identities, able-bodied perspectives are preferable and what we all, collectively, are aiming for. A system of compulsory able-bodiedness repeatedly demands that people with disabilities embody for others an affirmative answer to the unspoken question, Yes, but in the end, wouldn't you rather be more like me?

It is with this repetition that we can begin to locate both the ways in which compulsory able-bodiedness and compulsory heterosexuality are interwoven and the ways in which they might be contested. In queer theory, Judith Butler is most famous for identifying the repetitions required to maintain heterosexual hegemony:

> The "reality" of heterosexual identities is performatively constituted through an imitation that sets itself up as the origin and the ground of all imitations. In other words, heterosexuality is always in the process of imitating and approximating its own phantasmatic idealization of itself—*and failing*. Precisely because it is bound to fail, and yet endeavors to succeed, the project of heterosexual identity is propelled into an endless repetition of itself.
>
> ("Imitation" 21)

If anything, the emphasis on identities that are constituted through repetitive performances is even more central to compulsory able-bodiedness—think, after all, of how many institutions in our culture are showcases for able-bodied performance. Moreover, as with heterosexuality, this repetition is bound to fail, as the ideal able-bodied identity can never, once and for all, be achieved. Able-bodied identity and heterosexual identity are linked in their mutual impossibility and in their mutual incomprehensibility—they are incomprehensible in that each is an identity that is simultaneously the ground on which all identities supposedly rest and an impressive achievement that is always deferred and thus never really guaranteed. Hence Butler's queer theories of gender performativity could be easily extended to disability studies, as this

slightly paraphrased excerpt from *Gender Trouble* might suggest (I substitute, by bracketing, terms having to do literally with embodiment for Butler's terms of gender and sexuality):

> [Able-bodiedness] offers normative . . . positions that are intrinsically impossible to embody, and the persistent failure to identify fully and without incoherence with these positions reveals [able-bodiedness] itself not only as a compulsory law, but as an inevitable comedy. Indeed, I would offer this insight into [able-bodied identity] as both a compulsory system and an intrinsic comedy, a constant parody of itself, as an alternative [disabled] perspective.
>
> (122)

In short, Butler's theory of gender trouble might be resignified in the context of queer/disability studies to highlight what we could call "ability trouble"—meaning not the so-called problem of disability but the inevitable impossibility, even as it is made compulsory, of an able-bodied identity.

QUEER/DISABLED EXISTENCE

The cultural management of the endemic crises surrounding the performance of heterosexual and able-bodied identity effects a panicked consolidation of hegemonic identities. The most successful heterosexual subject is the one whose sexuality is not compromised by disability (metaphorized as queerness); the most successful able-bodied subject is the one whose ability is not compromised by queerness (metaphorized as disability). This consolidation occurs through complex processes of conflation and stereotype: people with disabilities are often understood as somehow queer (as paradoxical stereotypes of the asexual or oversexual person with disabilities would suggest), while queers are often understood as somehow disabled (as ongoing medicalization of identity, similar to what people with disabilities more generally encounter, would suggest). Once these conflations are available in the popular imagination, queer/disabled figures can be tolerated and, in fact, utilized in order to maintain the fiction that able-bodied heterosexuality is not in crisis. As lesbian existence is deployed, in Rich's analysis, to reflect back heterosexual and patriarchal "realities," queer/disabled existence can be deployed to buttress compulsory able-bodiedness. Since queerness and disability both have the potential to disrupt the performance of able-bodied heterosexuality, both must be safely contained—embodied—in such figures.

In the 1997 film *As Good As It Gets*, for example, although Melvin Udall (Jack Nicholson), who is diagnosed in the film as obsessive-compulsive, is represented visually in many ways that initially position him in what Martin F. Norden calls "the cinema of isolation" (i.e., Melvin is represented in ways that link him to other representations of people with disabilities), the trajectory of the film is toward able-bodied heterosexuality. To effect the consolidation of heterosexual and able-bodied norms, disability and queerness in the film are visibly located elsewhere, in the gay character Simon Bishop (Greg Kinnear). Over the course of the film, Melvin progressively sheds his own sense of inhabiting an anomalous body, and disability is firmly located in the non-heterosexual character, who is initially represented as able-bodied, but who ends up, after he is attacked and beaten by a group of burglars, using a wheelchair and cane for most of the film. More important, the disabled/queer figure, as in many other contemporary cultural representations, facilitates the heterosexual romance: Melvin first learns to accept the differences Simon comes to embody, and Simon then encourages Melvin to reconcile with his girlfriend, Carol Connelly (Helen Hunt). Having served their purpose, Simon, disability, and queerness are all hustled offstage together. The film concludes with a fairly traditional romantic reunion between the (able-bodied) male and female leads.[8]

CRITICALLY QUEER, SEVERELY DISABLED

The crisis surrounding heterosexual identity and able-bodied identity does not automatically lead to their undoing. Indeed, as this brief consideration of *As Good As It Gets* should suggest, this crisis and the anxieties that accompany it can be invoked in a wide range of cultural texts precisely to be (temporarily) resolved or alleviated. Neither gender trouble nor ability trouble is sufficient in and of itself to unravel compulsory heterosexuality or compulsory able-bodiedness. Butler acknowledges this problem: "This failure to approximate the norm . . . is not the same as the subversion of the norm. There is no promise that subversion will follow from the reiteration of constitutive norms; there is no guarantee that exposing the naturalized status of heterosexuality will lead to its subversion" ("Critically Queer" 22; quoted in Warner, "Normal and Normaller" 168–169, n. 87). For Warner, this acknowledgment in Butler locates a potential gap in her theory, "let us say, between virtually queer and critically queer" (Warner, "Normal and Normaller" 168–169, n. 87). In contrast to a virtually queer identity, which would be experienced by anyone who failed to perform heterosexuality without contradiction and incoherence (i.e., everyone), a critically queer perspective could presumably mobilize the inevitable failure to approximate the norm, collectively "working the weakness in the norm," to use Butler's phrase ("Critically Queer" 26).[9]

A similar gap could be located if we appropriate Butler's theories for disability studies. Everyone is virtually disabled, both in the sense that able-bodied norms are "intrinsically impossible to embody" fully, and in the sense that able-bodied status is always temporary, disability being the one identity category that all people will embody if they live long enough. What we might call a critically disabled position, however, would differ from such a virtually disabled position; it would call attention to the ways in which the disability rights movement and disability studies have resisted the demands of compulsory able-bodiedness and have demanded access to a newly imagined and newly configured public sphere where full participation is not contingent on an able body.

We might, in fact, extend the concept and see such a perspective not as critically disabled but rather as severely disabled, with *severe* performing work similar to the critically queer work of *fabulous*. Tony Kushner writes:

> *Fabulous* became a popular word in the queer community—well, it was never *un*popular, but for a while it became a battle cry of a new queer politics, carnival and camp, aggressively fruity, celebratory and tough like a streetwise drag queen: *"FAAAAABULOUS!"* ... *Fabulous* is one of those words that provide a measure of the degree to which a person or event manifests a particular, usually oppressed, subculture's most distinctive, invigorating features.
>
> (vii)

Severe, though less common than *fabulous*, has a similar queer history: a severe critique is a fierce critique, a defiant critique, one that thoroughly and carefully reads a situation— and I mean reading in the street sense of loudly calling out the inadequacies of a given situation, person, text, or ideology. "Severely disabled," according to such a queer conception, would reverse the able-bodied understanding of severely disabled bodies as the most marginalized, the most excluded from a privileged and always elusive normalcy, and would instead suggest that it is precisely those bodies that are best

positioned to refuse "mere toleration" and to call out the inadequacies of compulsory able-bodiedness. Whether it is the "army of one-breasted women" Audre Lorde imagines descending on the Capitol; the Rolling Quads, whose resistance sparked the independent living movement in Berkeley, California; Deaf students shutting down Gallaudet University in the Deaf President Now action; or ACT UP storming the National Institutes of Health or the Food and Drug Administration, severely disabled/critically queer bodies have already generated ability trouble that remaps the public sphere and reimagines and reshapes the limited forms of embodiment and desire proffered by the systems that would contain us all.[10]

Compulsory heterosexuality is intertwined with compulsory able-bodiedness; both systems work to (re)produce the able body and heterosexuality. But precisely because these systems depend on a queer/ disabled existence that can never quite be contained, able-bodied heterosexuality's hegemony is always in danger of being disrupted. I draw attention to critically queer, severely disabled possibilities to further an incorporation of the two fields, queer theory and disability studies, in the hope that such a collaboration (which in some cases is already occurring, even when it is not acknowledged or explicitly named as such) will exacerbate, in more productive ways, the crisis of authority that currently besets heterosexual/able-bodied norms. Instead of invoking the crisis in order to resolve it (as in a film like *As Good As It Gets*), I would argue that a queer/disability studies (in productive conversations with disabled/ queer movements outside the academy) can continuously invoke, in order to further the crisis, the inadequate resolutions that compulsory heterosexuality and compulsory able-bodiedness offer us. And in contrast to an able-bodied culture that holds out the promise of a substantive (but paradoxically always elusive) ideal, a queer/disabled perspective would resist delimiting the kinds of bodies and abilities that are acceptable or that will bring about change. Ideally, a queer/disability studies—like the term *queer* itself—might function "oppositionally and relationally but not necessarily substantively, not as a positivity but as a positionality, not as a thing, but as a resistance to the norm" (Halperin 66). Of course, in calling for a queer/disability studies without a necessary substance, I hope it is clear that I do not mean to deny thc materiality of queer/disabled bodies, as it is precisely those material bodies that have populated the movements and brought about the changes detailed above. Rather, I mean to argue that critical queerness and severe disability are about collectively transforming (in ways that cannot necessarily be predicted in advance) the substantive uses to which queer/disabled existence has been put by a system of compulsory able-bodiedness, about insisting that such a system is never as good as it gets, and about imagining bodies and desires otherwise.

NOTES

1. In 1976, the Brussels Tribunal on Crimes against Women identified "compulsory heterosexuality" as one such crime (Katz 26). A year earlier, in her important article "The Traffic in Women: Notes on the 'Political Economy' of Sex," Gayle Rubin examined the ways in which "obligatory heterosexuality" and "compulsory heterosexuality" function in what she theorized as a larger sex/gender system (179, 198; cited in Katz 132). Rich's 1980 article, which has been widely cited and reproduced since its initial publication, was one of the most extensive analyses of compulsory heterosexuality in feminism. I agree with Jonathan Ned Katz's insistence that the concept is redundant because "any society split between heterosexual and homosexual is compulsory" (164), but I also acknowledge the historical and critical usefulness of the phrase. It is easier to understand the ways in which a society split between heterosexual and homosexual is compulsory precisely because of feminist deployments of the redundancy of compulsory heterosexuality. I would also suggest that popular queer

theorizing outside of the academy (from drag performances to activist street theater) has often employed redundancy performatively to make a critical point.

2. In an effort to forge a political connection between all women, Rich uses the terms "lesbian" and "lesbian continuum" to describe a vast array of sexual and affectional connections throughout history, many of which emerge from historical and cultural conditions quite different from those that have made possible the identity of lesbian (192–199). Moreover, by using "lesbian continuum" to affirm the connection between lesbian and heterosexual women, Rich effaces the cultural and sexual specificity of contemporary lesbian existence.

3. The incorporation of queer theory and disability studies that I argue for here is still in its infancy. It is in cultural activism and cultural theory about AIDS (such as John Nguyet Erni's *Unstable Frontiers* or Cindy Patton's *Fatal Advice*) that a collaboration between queer theory and disability studies is already proceeding and has been for some time, even though it is not yet acknowledged or explicitly named as such. Michael Davidson's "Strange Blood: Hemophobia and the Unexplored Boundaries of Queer Nation" is one of the finest analyses to date of the connections between disability studies and queer theory.

4. The collective projects that I refer to are, of course, the projects of gay liberation and queer studies in the academy and the disability rights movement and disability studies in the academy. This chapter is part of my own contribution to these projects and is part of my longer work in progress, titled *De-Composing Bodies: Cultural Signs of Queerness and Disability.*

5. David Mitchell and Sharon Snyder are in line with many scholars working in disability studies when they point out the "ominous silence in the humanities" on the subject of disability (1). See, for other examples, Simi Linton's discussion of the "divided curriculum" (71–116), and assertions by Rosemarie Garland-Thomson and by Lennard Davis about the necessity of examining disability alongside other categories of difference such as race, class, gender, and sexuality (Garland-Thomson 5; Davis xi).

6. Disability studies is not the only field Vincent has attacked in the mainstream media; see her article "The Future of Queer: Wedded to Orthodoxy," which mocks academic queer theory. Neither being disabled nor being gay or lesbian in and of itself guarantees the critical consciousness generated in the disability rights or queer movements, or in queer theory or disability studies: Vincent herself is a lesbian journalist, but her writing clearly supports both able-bodied and heterosexual norms.

Instead of a stigmaphilic response to queer/disabled existence, finding "a commonality with those who suffer from stigma, and in this alternative realm [learning] to value the very things the rest of the world despises" (Warner, *Trouble* 43), Vincent reproduces the dominant culture's stigmaphobic response. See Warner's discussion of Erving Goffman's concepts of stigmaphobe and stigmaphile (41–45).

7. Michel Foucault's discussion of "docile bodies" and his theories of disciplinary practices are in the background of much of my analysis here (135–169).

8. The consolidation of able-bodied and heterosexuality identity is probably most common in mainstream films and television movies about AIDS, even—or perhaps especially—when those films are marketed as "new and daring." The 1997 Christopher Reeve-directed HBO film *In the Gloaming* is an example. In the film, the disabled/queer character (yet again, in a tradition that reaches back to *An Early Frost* [1985]), is eliminated at the end but not before effecting a healing of the heteronormative family. As Simon Watney writes about *An Early Frost*, "The closing shot . . . shows a 'family album' picture. . . . A traumatic episode is over. The family closes ranks, with the problem son conveniently dispatched, and life getting back to normal" (114). I am focusing on a non-AIDS-related film about disability and homosexuality, because I think the processes I theorize here have a much wider currency and can be found in many cultural texts that attempt to represent queerness or disability. There is not space here to analyze *As Good As It Gets* fully; for a more comprehensive close reading of how heterosexual/able-bodied consolidation works in the film and other cultural texts, see my article "As Good As It Gets: Queer Theory and Critical Disability." I do not, incidentally, think that these processes are unique to fictional texts: the MLA's annual *Job Information List*, for instance, provides evidence of other locations where heterosexual and able-bodied norms support each other while ostensibly allowing for tolerance of queerness and disability. The recent high visibility of queer studies and disability studies on university press lists, conference proceedings, and even syllabi has not necessarily translated into more jobs for disabled/queer scholars.

9. See my discussion of Butler, Gloria Anzaldúa, and critical queerness in *The Queer Renaissance: Contemporary American Literature and the Reinvention of Lesbian and Gay Identities* (149–153).

10. On the history of the AIDS Coalition to Unleash Power (ACT UP), see Douglas Crimp and Adam Rolston's *AIDS DemoGraphics*. Lorde recounts her experiences with breast cancer and imagines a movement of one-breasted women in *The Cancer Journals*. Joseph P. Shapiro recounts both the history of the Rolling Quads and the Independent Living Movement and the Deaf President Now action in *No Pity: People with Disabilities Forging a New Civil Rights Movement* (41–58, 74–85). Deaf activists have insisted for some time that deafness should not be understood as a disability and that people living with deafness, instead, should be seen as having a distinct language and culture. As the disability rights movement has matured, however, some Deaf activists and scholars in Deaf studies have rethought this position and have claimed disability (that is, disability revalued by a disability rights movement and disability studies) in an attempt to affirm a coalition with other people with disabilities. It is precisely such a reclaiming of disability that I want to stress here with my emphasis on severe disability.

WORKS CITED

As Good As It Gets. Dir. James L. Brooks. Perf. Jack Nicholson, Helen Hunt, and Greg Kinnear. TriStar, 1997.

Bérubé, Michael. *Life As We Know It: A Father, a Family, and an Exceptional Child*. New York: Vintage-Random House, 1996.

Butler, Judith. "Critically Queer." *GLQ: A Journal of Lesbian and Gay Studies* 1.1 (1993): 17–32.

——. *Gender Trouble: Feminism and the Subversion of Identity*. New York: Routledge, 1990.

——. "Imitation and Gender Insubordination." *Inside/Out: Lesbian Theories, Gay Theories*. Ed. Diana Fuss. New York: Routledge, 1991. 13–31.

Crimp, Douglas and Adam Rolston. *AIDS DemoGraphics*. Seattle: Bay Press, 1990.

Davidson, Michael. "Strange Blood: Hemophobia and the Unexplored Boundaries of Queer Nation." *Beyond the Binary: Reconstructing Cultural Identity in a Multicultural Context*. Ed. Timothy Powell. New Brunswick, NJ: Rutgers University Press, 1999. 39–60.

Davis, Lennard J. *Enforcing Normalcy: Disability, Deafness, and the Body*. London: Verso, 1995.

Erni, John Nguyet. *Unstable Frontiers: Technomedicine and the Cultural Politics of "Curing" AIDS*. Minneapolis: University of Minnesota Press, 1994.

Foucault, Michel. *Discipline and Punish: The Birth of the Prison*. Trans. Alan Sheridan. New York: Vintage-Random House, 1977.

Garland-Thomson, Rosemarie. *Extraordinary Bodies: Figuring Physical Disability in American Culture and Literature*. New York: Columbia University Press, 1997.

Halperin, David, *Saint Foucault: Toward a Gay Historiography,* Oxford: Oxford University Press, 1995.

In the Gloaming. Dir. Christopher Reeve. Perf. Glenn Close, Robert Sean Leonard, and David Strathairn. HBO, 1997.

Katz, Jonathan Ned. *The Invention of Heterosexuality.* New York: Dutton, 1995.

Kushner, Tony. "Foreword: Notes Toward a Theater of the Fabulous." *Staging Lives: An Anthology of Contemporary Gay Theater.* Ed. John M. Clum. Boulder, CO: Westview Press, 1996. vii–ix.

Linton, Simi. *Claiming Disability: Knowledge and Identity.* New York: NYU Press, 1998.

Lorde, Audre. *The Cancer Journals.* San Francisco: Aunt Lute Books, 1980.

McRuer, Robert. "As Good As It Gets: Queer Theory and Critical Disability." *GLQ: A Journal of Lesbian and Gay Studies* 9.1–2 (2003): 79–105.

——. *The Queer Renaissance: Contemporary American Literature and the Reinvention of Lesbian and Gay Identities.* New York: NYU Press, 1997.

Mitchell, David T. and Sharon L. Snyder. "Introduction: Disability Studies and the Double Bind of Representation." *The Body and Physical Difference: Discourses of Disability.* Ed. Mitchell and Snyder. Ann Arbor: University of Michigan Press, 1997. 1–31.

Norden, Martin F. *The Cinema of Isolation: A History of Physical Disability in the Movies.* New Brunswick, NJ: Rutgers University Press, 1994.

Patton, Cindy. *Fatal Advice: How Safe-Sex Education Went Wrong.* Durham, NC: Duke University Press, 1997.

Rich, Adrienne. "Compulsory Heterosexuality and Lesbian Existence." *Powers of Desire: The Politics of Sexuality.* Ed. Ann Snitow, Christine Stansell, and Sharon Thompson. New York: Monthly Review Press, 1983. 177–205.

Rubin, Gayle. "The Traffic in Women: Notes on the 'Political Economy' of Sex." *Toward an Anthropology of Women.* Ed. Rayna R. Reiter. New York: Monthly Review Press, 1975. 157–210.

Shapiro, Joseph P. *No Pity: People with Disabilities Forging a New Civil Rights Movement.* New York: Times Books-Random House, 1993.

Vincent, Norah. "Enabling Disabled Scholarship." *Salon.* 18 August 1999. <www.salon.com/books/it/1999/08/18/disability>.

——. "The Future of Queer: Wedded to Orthodoxy." *The Village Voice* 22 February 2000: 16.

Warner, Michael. "Normal and Normaller: Beyond Gay Marriage." *GLQ: A Journal of Lesbian and Gay Studies* 5.2 (1999): 119–171.

——. *The Trouble with Normal: Sex, Politics, and the Ethics of Queer Life.* New York: Free Press, 1999.

Watney, Simon. *Policing Desire: Pornography, AIDS, and the Media.* 2nd ed. Minneapolis: University of Minnesota Press, 1989.

Wendell, Susan. *The Rejected Body: Feminist Philosophical Reflections on Disability.* New York: Routledge, 1996.

Williams, Raymond. *Keywords: A Vocabulary of Culture and Society.* Rev. ed. New York: Oxford University Press, 1983.

CHAPTER 28

Is Disability Studies Actually White Disability Studies?

Chris Bell

SUMMARY

Does the field of Disability Studies "whitewash" disability history, ontology, and phenomenology? In this essay, Chris Bell proposes that the field is better labeled as White Disability Studies because of its failure to engage issues of race and ethnicity in a substantive capacity. Bell admits his relabeling will strike scholars as hyperbolic or counterintuitive, but his message can't be dismissed only because of its unpopularity. Even though disability scholars think of their exclusionary tendencies as innocently done and difficult to remedy, the field has entrenched whiteness as its constitutive underpinning.

To illustrate his point, Bell gives an overview of various cornerstone works in Disability Studies to reveal their tendency to take whiteness as a norm. For instance, he points out that when Joseph Shapiro calls disabled people the U.S.'s "largest minority community," he inherently imagines that community as a monolithic one without the divisions of race and ethnicity. Personal accounts of disability are most often white ones, and this has created a dearth of writing about and for disabled people of color.

In the satirical mode of Jonathon Swift's "Modest Proposal," Bell moves on to a 10-point plan of keeping whiteness at the center of Disability Studies. Among the suggestions is to avoid analyzing a number of texts, such as W.E.B. DuBois's *The Souls of Black Folk* or Ralph Ellison's *Invisible Man*, for intersections between race and disability. Bell's list both begins and ends with the imperative to "not change a thing," which suggests that without a concerted and meaningful intervention, the field of Disability Studies will remain White Disability Studies.

My modest proposal is inspired by a popular television program airing on the Chicago PBS affiliate. "Check, Please!" gathers three "ordinary" residents who, after selecting their favorite restaurant, anonymously dine at all three establishments, then gather in a studio to debate the relative merits and shortfalls of each culinary venue. During one episode, the trio included a self-styled *bon vivant* whom I will call Dorian Gray. Dorian, while sharing his observations about a Chinese restaurant in a south Chicago suburb, expressed his unadulterated amazement at the composition of one particular entrée. "The shrimp were *artificial!*" he bemoaned, dread contorting his facial features into an expression of unrecoverable distress. The individual selecting said restaurant as his favorite—I'll call him Bubba Gump—blinked nary an eye at this revelation. Instead, Bubba stoically intoned, "If it looks like a shrimp, and it smells and tastes like a shrimp, it's a shrimp."

Bubba Gump's matter-of-fact rejoinder to Dorian Gray is, I think, indicative of the whiteness of Disability Studies in its present incarnation. The fact that Disability Studies is marketed as such when it is in actuality an artificial (read: limited and limiting) version of the field does nothing to prevent it from being understood as Disability Studies, which is what Bubba, by extension, apprised Dorian of. I contend that it is disingenuous to keep up the pretense that the field is an inclusive one when it is not. On that score, I would like to concede the failure of Disability Studies to engage issues of race and ethnicity in a substantive capacity, thereby entrenching whiteness as its constitutive underpinning. In short, I want to call a shrimp a shrimp and acknowledge Disability Studies for what it is, White Disability Studies.

In contradistinction to Disability Studies, White Disability Studies recognizes its tendency to whitewash disability history, ontology, and phenomenology. White Disability Studies, while not wholeheartedly excluding people of color from its critique,[1] by and large focuses on the work of white individuals and is itself largely produced by a corps of white scholars and activists. White Disability Studies envisions nothing ill-advised with this leaning because it is innocently done and far too difficult to remedy. A synoptic review of some of the literature and related aspects of Disability Studies bears this out.

Vital Signs: Crip Culture Talks Back

This documentary was filmed during a conference on Disability and the Arts on the campus of the University of Michigan. The film is distressing because of its absence of non-white individuals. Given the absence of people of color, I suggest that a significant number of myths and misconceptions about who/what is constitutive of disability or "crip" culture are bolstered and reinforced in the film.

No Pity: People with Disabilities Forging a New Civil Rights Movement

In his introduction, author Joseph Shapiro refers to the disabled community as the largest minority community in the United States, with more members than communities tallied by race, ethnicity, or sexual orientation amongst other socially constructed identity categories (7). What interests me is Shapiro's obfuscation of divisions within this ostensibly largest minority community and his insinuation that the disabled community is a monolithic one, struggling against the same oppressors, striving for identical degrees of dignity, recognition, and cultural representation. Such a characterization is a limited one that does not consider or address the rich diversity within disability communities—racial and ethnic diversity, for example.

A Matter of Dignity: Changing the Lives of the Disabled

Comprised of a series of interviews with disabled people from various life strata, the dearth of people of color in the text is as undeniable as it is flagrant. In order to prevent this text from surprising the unexpecting reader, it might be a good idea to acknowledge that whiteness is positioned as its center. Doing so would make for a much more accurate description of who/what is represented.

Claiming Disability: Knowledge and Identity

In her well-known text, Simi Linton describes Disability Studies by stating, "The field explores the critical divisions our society makes in creating the normal versus the pathological, the insider versus the outsider, or the competent citizen versus the ward of the state"(2). The reader should recognize the dichotomous line of thought here, the binary fashion with which Linton makes her critique. At the very least, it should be understood that many white disabled people have cultural capital by virtue of their race and are, therefore, more on the inside than they are on the outside. As an insider, Linton appears unaware of her positioning, and it is that unawareness that is one of the hallmarks of White Disability Studies.

Enforcing Normalcy: Disability, Deafness, and the Body
Throughout this text, Davis takes whiteness as a norm. From his discussion of the desirability of the Venus de Milo to his examination of the protagonist in *Born on the Fourth of July*, Davis's emphasis on whiteness is undeniable. There is, to be sure, nothing wrong with this focus (aside from being egregiously misleading with regard to which communities and subjectivities are constitutive of "disability"). I only wish Davis had broadened his source materials, or at the very least opted for a more accurate title e.g., *Enforcing Normalcy: Disability, Deafness, and the White Body*. Moreover, it matters that an excerpt from this text is reprinted in *The Norton Anthology of Theory and Criticism*, the ostensible Bible of literary studies. Those readers coming across this excerpt will necessarily receive a distorted view of Disability Studies as a result of Davis's focus on whiteness.

Queer Disability Conference
Near the conclusion of the first day of this conference that convened in San Francisco in June 2002, I met with approximately 13 other self-identified queer and disabled people of color during a caucus session. Our conversation focused on our individual and collective sense of exclusion based on race and ethnicity.[2] We could not fathom how the conference organizers—every one of them a white person—could publicize this conference in numerous international contexts and venues—drawing participants from Finland, Australia, and the United Kingdom among other nations—but fail to devise and implement an outreach plan that would attract people of color and other marginalized groups within the queer and disabled communities in the local Bay Area. We also could not understand the overarching mentality of many of the attendees, perhaps best expressed by a remark made in a breakout session: "Being disabled is just like being black, so society should stop hating us and give us our rights."

Society for Disability Studies Annual Conference, 2005
During the business meeting at the conference's conclusion, the people of color caucus presented a list of action items to the membership in an effort to shore up the marginal presence race and ethnicity had at the conference (despite the fact that the conference was themed "Conversations and Connections Across Race and Disability"). Although the hour-long conversation that ensued was collegial and productive, I cannot help wondering, drawing on my experience at the Queer Disability Conference,[3] how many times these questions of inclusion and exclusion have to be raised by people of color to white individuals? As I averred during the business meeting, "I'm tired of being one of the few to point out what should be obvious."

Modern Language Association (MLA) Conference on Disability Studies and the University.

Convened on the campus of Emory University March 5–7, 2004, the conference is notable at the outset for the sheer whiteness of those who presented. A quick glance down the list of presenters (as published in *PMLA* in 2005)[4] bears this out. An additional concern is the content of what was shared during this conference.

In his address, "Disability: The Next Wave or Twilight of the Gods?," Lennard Davis, thankfully, speaks to the white nature of Disability Studies: "Disability studies has by and large been carried out by white people" (530). He is grossly incorrect, however, in the follow-up assertion that the field will benefit from "the disability studies book about the African American experience of disability" (ibid.). To be sure, there is no singular, structuralist African American experience of disability and it is imprudent to advocate for one. Davis is further incorrect when he insists that said text must incorporate the recent "post-race" debate. Placing strictures on a text is foolish, especially when the strictures themselves lack intellectual value and integrity.[5]

In "What Is Disability Studies?," Simi Linton includes an instructive albeit telling example to illustrate the difficulty of answering the titular question:

A few years ago, a controversy about the golfer Casey Martin and the golf cart captured a great deal of attention. Martin petitioned the PGA—the Professional Golfers' Association—for permission to ride a golf cart in pro tournaments as an accommodation for a mobility impairment. When the PGA turned him down, Martin took the case to court. It was eventually deliberated in the Supreme Court, where Martin prevailed. The most significant outcome of the debate, I think, is that the discussion came down to the question, What *is* the game of golf? Some people said, If he rides a cart, that's not golf. I'd like to know, then, what golf is and who has decided.

(519)

As I mentioned, the example is instructive, but also rather telling: GOLF?! Come

on! I challenge the reader to name one non-white golfer—Okay, now name one non-white golfer *besides* Tiger and Vijay.

On a more serious note, as I read through the collection of essays and presentations from the Emory conference I am concerned with how often each scholar cites the other, revealing an uncomfortable incestuousness about Disability Studies. These individuals seem unwilling to step aside even briefly and let someone else have the (proverbial) microphone for a moment. Granted, if the MLA calls, there is appeal in the form of professional legitimacy. But I also suggest that there is appeal in giving someone else a chance to speak to the issues embedded in and examined by Disability Studies, in asking who will be there and figuring out who *should* be there, as well as who has not been asked and why. The failure to do so practically ensures that the silences, namely those concerning race and ethnicity, will not be addressed and will continue.

* * * * *

If Disability Studies as a field had taken a reflexive look at itself at some point, particularly with regard to its failings in examining issues of race and ethnicity, there might not be such a glaring dearth of disability-related scholarship by and about disabled people of color. As it stands, Disability Studies has a tenuous relationship with race and ethnicity: while the field readily acknowledges its debt to and inspiration by inquiries such as Black Studies, its efforts at addressing intersections between disability, race, and ethnicity are, at best, wanting. Disability Studies claims to examine the experiences of a vast number of disabled people, yet the form that representation takes is, far too often, a white one. This is by no means a sporadic occurrence. Quite the contrary, the slights occur habitually and, as the preceding examples prove, in various contexts, from published works to conferences. I think it is essential to illuminate the fragile relationship between disability, race, and ethnicity in extant Disability Studies, arguing not so much for a sea-change in this formulation, rather for a more definitive and accurate identification of the happening.

What follows then is my 10-point scheme (*pace,* Mr. Letterman) on how to keep White Disability Studies in vogue and instantiated as disability praxis. Given the fact that well-intentioned individuals are inclined to ask what can be done to "make things more diverse," I have purposely crafted the following as a series of "do nots." By doing so, I hope to shore up how presumptuous it is to position the subaltern as the all-knowing savant insofar as issues of diversity; requesting definitive answers from that person when the answers might best come from within, following an extended period of rumination.

10. **Do not change a thing.** Let's keep doing what we're doing. Let's remain firmly rooted in *this* wave of disability, consciously opting not to move to the next. Let's continue to acknowledge white individuals as the Disability Studies core constituency.[6] Do not outreach to communities of color or participate in their events when the opportunity to forge connections arises. Do not solicit for a themed issue of *Disability Studies Quarterly* on race, ethnicity, and disability[7] and if by chance said issue should be produced, make sure that it occurs only once; that there are no efforts to ensure that these intersections are spoken to throughout future iterations of the journal in a non-"special issue" context. In sum, do not change a thing. Continue to fetishize and exoticize people of color as subalterns by constantly focusing on *their* race and ethnicity, but not that of the white subject.

9. **Do not address ethnicity, rather continually focus on race.** Many Disability Studies scholars—and people in general—are unwilling or unable to pick up on the cultural significance of ethnicity in contraposition to what some are (erroneously) convinced is the biological foundation of race. Regardless of where the two concepts spring from, the fact is that they are distinct. It becomes problematic then when all that comprises ethnicity gets collapsed under the umbrella term of race. As a field White Disability Studies has no stake in this process and therefore should do nothing to address it.

8. **Do not consider that, as Stuart Hall has explained, "Cultural identity is not an essence but a positioning"** (229). Generally speaking, the same people who hold power in the community of scholars known as Disability Studies are a mimetic rendering of those holding power in non-disabled communities: white people. Despite the fact that people of color outnumber white people in the world, white people harbor hegemony and cultural capital. Whether or not disabled people of color outnumber disabled white individuals—or whether people of color interested in Disability Studies outnumber whites interested in the same—the fact is Disability Studies is conceived of as a white field (recall Davis's comments from the Emory conference). White Disability Studies should pay no attention to this, doing nothing to change this conception, this positioning. It does not matter that whiteness is not an essentialist prerequisite for a disability identity. We can just pretend that it is.

7. **Pay no attention to Ann duCille's recognition that "[O]ne of the dangers of standing at an intersection ... is the likelihood of being run over"** (593). When you come across a non-white disabled person, focus on the disability, eliding the race and ethnicity, letting them be run over, forgotten. Do not consider how the intersection

in which this subject lives influences her actions and the way she is seen. Choose not to see that intersection and quickly move on down the road of disability, away from the "perpendicular" roads of race and ethnicity. The fact that the intersection exists is not your fault. It is a prime example of poor engineering.

6. **Disregard Evelynn Hammonds's idea that "visibility in and of itself does not erase a history of silence nor does it challenge the structure of power and domination, symbolic and material, that determines what can and cannot be seen"** (141). Do not forgot to revel in the idea that as more and more disabled people enter the mainstream, all disabled people, irrespective of their racial and ethnic subjectivity, occupy the same place at the table. Equate visibility with inclusivity. Sit back and be satisfied, and do not allow yourself to be troubled by those who carp about their invisibility within disability communities.

5. **Ignore Horkheimer and Adorno's augury that failure to conform to the culture industry results in the individual being "left behind"** (37). The two theorists warn of the perils of living in a culture industry whereby one must subscribe to the right magazines and watch the correct films in order to be accepted in the culture. White Disability Studies is nothing like this; there is nothing even remotely similar to a "disability industry." Thus, it is not true that if you make a film about "crip culture" and you populate that film with only white people, you will be left behind. Quite the contrary, you will receive awards and plaudits, kudos and huzzahs, for this. It is not true that if you enter a room that purports to gather together those interested and engaged in Disability Studies and see not a single person of color present, those people have been left behind or otherwise disinvited. Be still; speak not. Do not draw attention to their absence. Let them be

remaindered out. They always have been, and besides, they have probably chosen not to enter the space.

4. **Make no allowances for liminality and hybridity.** Instead, continue the pretense of normality, the idea that everything's just fine and that the disability community is one happy family with no diversity, no multivalence, only a collective sameness. Do not conceive of the silences that are imbricated in extant Disability Studies. Likewise, do not conceive of the concerted efforts to counter those silences, to advocate for liminality and hybridity, as described, in a different context, in Abena Busia's "Silencing Sycorax: On African Colonial Discourse and the Unvoiced Female":

> The systematic refusal to hear our [African American females] speech is not the same thing as our silence. That we have hitherto been spoken of as absent or silenced does not mean we have been so. ... The systematic refusal to hear our speech which colonial literature mirrors, though it has historically removed us from the nexus of certain kinds of power, does not and never actually could render us silent. In unmasking the dispossessions of the silences of fiction and the fictions of silence, we (re) construct self-understanding. Furthermore, for women, "Narrative" is not always and only, or even necessarily a speech act. We women signify: we have many modes of (re)dress.
>
> (103–4)

Do not consider how minority discourse from within a minority discourse is in and of itself counter-hegemonic. Do not encourage the proliferation of that discourse even though it is resistive and liberating. As we all know, the presence of too many voices results in senseless cacophony and what good is that?

3. **Do whatever you can *not* to discuss those texts rife with possibilities insofar**

as parsing out intersections between disability, race, and ethnicity, namely:

The Souls of Black Folk

In 1903, W.E.B. DuBois introduced his concept of double consciousness that speaks to the black American's irreconcilable sense of self as "an African" and "an American." Since there is nothing to be gained by applying this theory to black disabled subjects (triple consciousness?), it is best not to consider this text as having any bearing on Disability Studies.

Up From Slavery

Published around the same time as DuBois's text, *Up From Slavery* is frequently taught alongside *The Souls of Black Folk*. Washington takes a much more assimilationist approach to black subjectivity in contraposition to DuBois. Perhaps a Disability Studies scholar might draw parallels between the Washington/DuBois ideas of black subjectivity and the difference between those disabled subjects who want to advocate for peaceful resistance and mainstreaming in juxtaposition to those who take a more activist, resistant stance. But then again, that would be an utter waste of the scholar's time.

Invisible Man

> *I am an invisible man . . . I am invisible, understand, simply because people refuse to see me.*
>
> (3)

The first lines of Ellison's text speak to the difficulty of black ontology in the United States. Ellison's protagonist, of course, is not speaking of a literal invisibility so much as he is drawing light to how it is that others (read: whites with hegemonic power) choose not to see him in totality. If this characterization does not seem applicable to Disability Studies—wherein the racialized subaltern is remembered and considered solely as a matter of convenience more often than not—I don't know what would be. Yet it would be foolish to illuminate this text's applicability to Disability Studies, or, furthermore, to consider the prophetic final lines of the novel—"who know but that, on the lower frequencies, I speak for you?" (581)—wherein the protagonist considers the complexities of representing and/or embodying communal univocality. I do not recommend examining this.

Roots

A Disability Studies scholar might examine aspects of disability throughout the text, namely those that are linked to racial positioning, e.g., the causes and effects of Kunta Kinte's "crippling." Then again, she might not.

"Beauty: When the Other Dancer Is the Self"

This widely anthologized personal narrative describes Alice Walker's sense of self as a disabled subject after she is blinded as a child. "I didn't pray for sight," she writes, "I prayed for beauty." Any Disability Studies scholar worth her salt should immediately discern the implications of this statement, but that does not mean that she must act upon it in her scholarship. Likewise, the scholar might pay attention to Walker's intentional use of language, e.g., the allusion to Stevie Wonder towards the end of the narrative. Alas, she might pay attention to it, but there is absolutely nothing to be gained from explicating it.

"The Cure"

Ginu Kamani's short story is set in contemporary India. The protagonist must deal with living in a culture that has deemed her "too-tall." What is interesting is that the reader never learns just how tall she is, evidentiary of a societal code that is unspoken and yet accepted. Unfortunately, since the story is set in India, where whites are the minority, it cannot be of interest to a Disability Studies scholar.

The Adventures of Felix

Race is usually considered a black and white issue. This film complicates that assessment. The protagonist, the titular Felix, is a multiracial French gay man with HIV who sets out to find the father he never knew. Although many critics and individuals familiar with AIDS narratives herald the film for its portrayal of a person with AIDS who is effortlessly "handling" his disease, a disability theorist might pay particular attention to how easily AIDS is removed from the narrative in favor of other concerns. But I doubt that would ever happen.

Birth of a Nation, or The Clansman

Long before *Triumph of the Will* was unleashed on the populace, this legendary slice of propaganda was released and heralded. The issues of performativity at play here are rife for discussion, as are their implications insofar as who gets to represent race and/or disability. A Disability Studies scholar might link the use of blackface in this film with the use of non-disabled actors to play disabled figures in contemporary films. But, again, I doubt that would ever happen.

In sum, continue thinking that these texts are too long (e.g., *Invisible Man*) and that the disability perspective is too tangential (e.g., *The Adventures of Felix*) to warrant devoting time to. Do not select key scenes to analyze and discuss. Ignore the texts altogether. Continue to herald the overt elisions and missed opportunities.

2. **Do not note how odd "White Disability Studies" looks on this page,** how much effort it requires (or does it?) to contort one's tongue in order to articulate it. Do not take into account how foreign a phrase it seems (although just because something is foreign doesn't necessarily mean that it is incomprehensible . . .).

1. **Do not change a thing.** Keep doing what *you're* doing. Do so because what you're doing is fine, more than enough to keep White Disability Studies firmly instantiated as the norm. Make no effort to be more inclusive in your scholarship. Do not start today, do not start tomorrow. Wait for someone else to do inclusive work. Wait for however long it takes.

* * * * *

By way of conclusion, I want to stress that Disability Studies is not the only field of inquiry wherein individuals of color are treated as second-class citizens. If anything, Disability Studies is merely aping the ideology of the vast majority of academic disciplines and ways of thinking that preceded it and which it now sits alongside of. While I could have devoted this modest proposal to advocating for a more hybrid Disability Studies, a liminal version, the fact is I am not certain that advocating for such an idea is a worthwhile undertaking. I deem it far more instructive to acknowledge that we are positioned in the realm of "White Disability Studies" and continue along with the truth of this positioning in mind.

Moreover, offering White Disability Studies, even in the form of a tongue-in-cheek modest proposal, is bound to unnerve many of the individuals who consider themselves engaged in Disability Studies. White Disability Studies will most likely strike these individuals as a hyperbolic and counterintuitive claim. Perhaps my actions might be deemed impolitic and offensive. That is the point. I think it is tactless to dismiss a message solely because of its ostensible unpopularity or because the individual bearing the message seems undesirable. Such a process is itself counterintuitive, intended to draw attention away from a message that, while perhaps unpopular, might contain more than a modicum of validity. Because Disability Studies in its current incarnation *is* White Disability Studies, proposing we honor that creates no crisis of conscience for me. If anything, I take heart in remembering what Bubba Gump declared to Dorian Gray on "Check, Please!": "If it looks like a shrimp, and it smells and tastes like a shrimp, it's a shrimp."

NOTES

1. Far from excluding people of color, White Disability Studies treats people of color as if they were white people; as if there are no critical exigencies involved in being people of color that might necessitate these individuals understanding and negotiating disability in a different way from their white counterparts.
2. Reader: If you think it odd that our feelings of solidarity were premised on disinvitation, realize that this is a reality of many people of color engaged in White Disability Studies.
3. Coincidentally, the people of color caucuses at both conferences presented their list of action items in the exact same space, the Mary Ward Hall at San Francisco State University.
4. The pagination to follow is from this issue of *PMLA*.
5. Briefly, the "post-race debate" argues that race is no longer a valid social construct or marker. By that light, the culture as a whole should move on and focus on other, purportedly more pressing issues, e.g., class. I can deconstruct the entire post-race argument by simply pointing out that in a culture where racism exists and is pervasive, the casual dismissal of race is specious.
6. I offer AIDS as a precedent here. From the early 1980s until fairly recently, the conception of the AIDS afflicted subject was a gay white man. Indeed, the legacy still retains purchase on mainstream cultural consciousness. Of course, if there were only a few overtures to assess how the disease was impacting women and people of color—and when you think

about the history of AIDS, you realize that up until quite recently this was the case—then it becomes obvious how gay white men became equated with AIDS. It is difficult to offer a counternarrative when the structures of power determining which identities comprise a subject are unyielding in their conception.
7. A cursory glance of the past few years of *DSQ*'s topical issues is rather enlightening in this regard. There is an abundance of special topics, none of which verge on what is, to me, one of the more obvious absences in the discourse.

WORKS CITED

The Adventures of Felix. Dir. Olivier Ducastel and Jacques Martineau. DVD. Perf. Sami Bouajila. Fox Lorber, 2000.

Birth of a Nation, or The Clansman. Dir. D.W. Griffiths. 1915. DVD. Perf. Lillian Gish. Image Entertainment, 2002.

Busia, Abena P. A. "Silencing Sycorax: On African Colonial Discourse and the Unvoiced Female." *Cultural Critique* 14 (1989–90): 81–104.

Du Bois, W.E.B. *The Souls of Black Folk*. 1903. New York: Penguin, 1996.

duCille, Ann. "The Occult of True Black Womanhood: Critical Demeanor and Black Feminist Studies." *Signs* 19, 3 (1994): 591–629.

Davis, Lennard. "Disability: The Next Wave or Twilight of the Gods?" Conference on Disability Studies and the University. *PMLA* 120, 2 (2005): 527–532.

——. *Enforcing Disability: Disability, Deafness, and the Body*. London: Verso, 1995.

Ellison, Ralph. *Invisible Man*. New York: Random House, 1952.

Haley, Alex. *Roots*. New York: Doubleday, 1976.

Hall, Stuart. "Cultural Studies and Its Theoretical Legacies." In *Cultural Studies*, edited by Lawrence Grossberg, Cary Nelson, and Paula Treichler *et al.*, 227–234. New York: Routledge, 1992.

Hammonds, Evelynn. "Black (W)holes and the Geometry of Black Female Sexuality." *differences* 6, 2–3 (1994): 126–145.

Horkheimer, Max, and Theodor Adorno. "The Culture Industry: Enlightenment as Mass Deception." *The Dialectic of Enlightenment* (originally published as *Dialektik der Aufklarung*, 1944). New York: Continuum, 1993.

Kamani, Ginu. "The Cure." *Junglee Girl*. San Francisco: Aunt Lute, 1995.

Leitch, Vincent *et al*. *The Norton Anthology of Theory and Criticism*. New York: W.W. Norton, 2001.

Linton, Simi. *Claiming Disability: Knowledge and Identity*. New York: NYU Press, 1998.

———. "What Is Disability Studies?" Conference on Disability Studies and the University. *PMLA*. 120, 2 (2005): 518–522.

Potok, Andrew. *A Matter of Dignity: Changing the Lives of the Disabled*. New York: Bantam, 2003.

Shapiro, Joseph. *No Pity: People with Disabilities Forging a New Civil Rights Movement*. New York: Times Books, 1993.

Vital Signs: Crip Culture Talks Back. Dir. David Mitchell and Sharon Snyder. DVD. Brace Yourselves Productions, 1996.

Walker, Alice. "Beauty: When the Other Dancer Is the Self." *In Search of Our Mother's Gardens: Womanist Prose*, 361–370. New York: Harcourt, Brace and Jovanovich, 1983.

Washington, Booker T. *Up From Slavery*. 1900. New York: Dover, 1995. 283.

CHAPTER 29

Token of Approval

Harilyn Rousso

SUMMARY

In this chapter from *Don't Call Me Inspirational: A Disabled Feminist Talks Back*, Harilyn Rousso describes her experiences working in a feminist group while also trying to represent the disability rights community. Rousso writes that even though the social justice community made improvements in accessibility and inclusion for disabled people through the 1970s and 1980s, her interpersonal reactions with feminist leaders were often as problematic as they were outside the feminist world. In "Token of Approval" Rousso suggests that women's organizations and others like them become truly inclusive of disability only very slowly—if at all.

In 1992, Rousso began a six-year period of service on the board of directors for a prominent women's fund. From the first meeting, she noted that the 20 million disabled American women weren't on the group's radar. Rousso admits that she was willing to play the "token crip" role initially so that she could parlay her contacts and influence into substantial gains for disabled women, the same way that women of color had once forced their way into the (white) women's movement. When the organization began to focus more on fund-raising than programming, Rousso left and became hesitant to accept invitations to other organizations that would make her the first and only disabled member. Even though there were some victories for disabled women in feminist organizations, Rousso tells us that the welcome mat is not yet out.

I was a feminist before I was a disability activist. In the early 1970s, I joined a women's consciousness-raising group, where I discovered my commonalities with other women. I was amazed to find out that the other women in the group hated parts of their bodies and doubted their womanliness like I did. Together we learned that our self-doubts were grounded in society's sexist attitudes, not in our personal defects, enabling us to develop a political consciousness and claim our own strengths. Through that group I found a sense of community after a lifetime of being an outsider; my disability was not a barrier to sisterhood. When I became a disability activist in the late 1970s, I was eager to bring my disability consciousness into the women's movement, expecting feminists to welcome me and my disabled sisters as I had been welcomed by that group.

At first, there was no welcome mat; rather, the entry door was slammed shut. Women's conferences were held in inaccessible locations, and conference organizers showed little interest in including issues of disabled women on the program. But gradually, conference sites became more accessible, and one or two workshops on disabled women began appearing. I led some of those early workshops, only to discover that few if any nondisabled feminists attended them. By the late 1980s, disabled women were invited to present at workshops on not only disability but also mainstream women's issues, such as salary inequities in the workplace and sexual harassment, and occasionally they were invited to give keynote speeches. As a result, more and more nondisabled feminists began to hear about disability issues, whether they wanted to or not.

But they still didn't quite get what we were saying. Many of the responses to our presentations were of the "You're so inspirational" variety. We rarely got invitations to join in informal activities during the conference, such as evening networking sessions at the hotel bar, or to sit on conference planning committees, much less on the governing boards of the women's organizations spearheading these conferences. I was deeply disturbed and perplexed by the distance that I felt from the women's community. Feminists understood oppression based on sexism. And they seemed to understand the multiple forms of bias that African American women, poor women, lesbians, and other "minority" groups of women faced (although I would later discover that their understanding of these groups was less comprehensive than I had thought and that what they had learned was only in response to pressure from these groups). Why didn't they grasp the double whammy of sexism and disability bias? Why were they reacting to me and other disabled women in the same negative ways as the politically unsophisticated world did?

So I had not expected that phone call in the spring of 1992. "Would you like to join our board of directors?" Claudia asked. Claudia was the executive director of a prominent women's fund in the Midwest— one of the first of many throughout the country that had been established specifically to fund projects by and for women and girls. After immediately answering, "Yes," I thought, "Ah, disabled women have finally arrived in the women's movement." "You won't have an easy job," she went on to say. "You'll be the first disabled woman on the board. Our fund has become wonderfully diverse in recent years. But when it comes to disabled women . . . Well, for us, that's been the last and hardest group to include." "Don't worry," I said assuredly. "We'll figure out together how to do it."

I had met Claudia at a human rights conference in which one of the speakers made some sexist comments and we both went at him. We immediately bonded, and over lunch she mentioned a small research project her fund was undertaking on how young women in their twenties make career choices. I explained to her that the issue for disabled women was not so much what type of work they would choose but whether they would be able to work at all given the barriers they faced. Claudia seemed very interested. "You know," she said somewhat apologetically, "we haven't included any disabled women in the study so far. We have so little money for the study." I wasn't going to let lack of funds stop her, so I offered to convene a group of my disabled women friends for a conference call with her researcher. She was delighted with the offer.

On the conference call, as my friends and I exchanged experiences, the fund's researcher took copious notes, which she incorporated into her report. When the report was published, I had every disabled woman activist I know call Claudia to thank her for being inclusive. A few months later, she was on the phone inviting me to join the board.

And so began a very ambivalent six-year period in my life. I had high hopes of transforming the organization into one that was totally inclusive of disabled women's issues in every aspect of its work. Such naivety. Such unrealistic expectations, given my previous years of frustration with the women's movement. I did some good while I was there, such as facilitating the funding of some projects for disabled women and girls. And I personally benefited by meeting some extraordinary women on the board who facilitated my career as an activist and an artist. A few, by sharing their personal, often limited resources to help other women move forward, were good role models and inspired me to do the same.

In hindsight, perhaps the greatest benefit to me (although it did not feel like a benefit at the time) was an up-close and personal glimpse into the way that women's and other organizations—and political movements—change to become more inclusive of any group: slowly and with difficulty, if at all.

I remember in great detail that first board meeting. Famous feminists whom I was accustomed to seeing on TV or conference podiums were now sitting across the table. They were warm and welcoming, even when I spilled an entire cup of coffee while carrying it from the buffet to my seat. After that incident I had many people volunteering to carry for me anything and everything. There were several other new board members, women representing various racial and ethnic groups, at that meeting, so the first order of business was to fill us in on the fund's history, mission, goals, and programs. When we were handed the mission statement, which included a commitment to address and redress the various types of bias that women face, I hit the first speed bump. The more than 20 million women with disabilities in America had not yet shown up on the fund's radar screen. I immediately drew their attention to this serious omission. Claudia and some of the old-timers on the board appeared somewhat embarrassed, and fairly quickly the board voted to amend the mission statement to include disability bias. That was a victory, one that my disabled sisters around the country immediately appreciated. But as I would discover, mission statements, like laws, were not always enforced.

We next reviewed the docket of grant proposals under consideration for funding. The board's job was to vote on the projects after the staff had carefully screened and approved the proposals. We were not a rubber stamp; we rejected some proposals that the staff had accepted. I have to confess to enjoying a heady sense of power. After applying for so many grants and feeling at the mercy of funders, I was gratified to be on the other side, to be a decision maker for a change. But even stronger than the feeling of power was my fascination with the kinds of programs and projects women's groups were developing. They gave me ideas about programs that might benefit disabled women.

But why weren't there programs for disabled women of any type already on the grants docket? Claudia explained that they simply didn't receive many proposals involving disabled women, maybe one or two a year, and that this quarter they had received none. I wasn't completely surprised. Given the architectural, transportation, communication, financial, and other barriers that disabled women faced, many had a hard enough time getting out into the community to do the basics of daily life much less to develop programs. Nonetheless, I knew there were at least a number of disabled women's projects around the country, so there should have been more proposals than Claudia described. I offered to beat the bushes to get more proposal submissions; Claudia and the board were appreciative.

I didn't negotiate the board's postmeeting ritual nearly as smoothly. It was customary after meetings for everyone to dine together and, after dinner, to engage in group discussions of a personal, if not intimate, nature, greatly facilitated by a few glasses of wine. For me, that discussion was initiation by fire. "So what was your wildest, weirdest sexual encounter during adolescence?" was the topic that emerged that night. I found myself thinking, "Can we get back to talking about program proposals? Please!" Having had an asexual adolescence, I knew I was in big trouble. I initially decided to concoct a story, but as I heard some of the other women's outrageous accounts of sexual acts I had never conceived of, I knew my imagination was not up to the task. "I was a virginal good girl," I confessed when my turn came. Then, when the laughter died down, I heard "Me, too" emerge from the mouth of another board member. "Me three," said yet another. "Well, my dears," said one of the women who had told a particularly lewd story, "You three are entitled to a totally risqué middle age. Don't let the rest of us down. We expect to hear stories. And soon!" I could see I was going to learn more from my sisters on the board than I had realized.

Between meetings I networked with as many disabled women as I could, encouraging them to submit proposals to the fund. At the next meeting the head of development proudly showed me the invitation for the fund-raising event that the entire board was scheduled to attend that night after the meeting. She wanted to make sure I had noticed the disability access symbol, the by-now-familiar small, stylized image of a wheelchair, on the lower corner of the invitation. She explained that Claudia and the staff had decided that from now on, all of the fund's events would be held in accessible sites, and all notices about events would bear the access symbol. I thanked her but was less ecstatic and effusive than she might have expected. By then I had already encountered too many women's organizations that demonstrated their commitment to disabled women by providing ramps and sign-language interpreters at their programs—and not doing anything else. By 1993 we should have gone beyond the realm of symbolism. I was waiting to see some substance.

Sure enough, on the docket of potential grants there were still no proposals focused on disabled women. The fund had, in fact, received two related to disability, but, I was told, neither was quite right: One was in too early a stage of development; the other was in a topic area not typically covered by the fund. "Maybe we need to be a bit more creative or flexible if we want to support disabled women's projects," I said to Claudia and the rest of the board. "Perhaps we need to give some planning or start-up grants. Or consider supporting projects even if they are not exactly in the areas we typically fund." "Maybe," Claudia said. "But you know, we have such a limited grant-making budget. I'd hate to dilute our focus. We can't bend over backward to meet the needs of every group." But they already had "bent over backward" for groups of women that they considered "priorities," including women of color and poor women. Of course, racism and poverty had severe consequences for women, but I could never quite make sense of this notion of the hierarchy of oppressions. How can we say that one group of oppressed women has suffered more than another? Besides, what about disabled women of color or, better yet, poor disabled women of color (a group I knew well from my work with the mentoring project for disabled girls)? Where do they fit in? But I held my tongue and my questions. I was still learning the ropes and trying to find my place. I didn't want to make trouble.

And then the conversation shifted. "So what type of gown is everyone wearing to tonight's fund-raising event?" one of the longtime board members asked. "Gowns?" I had thought that my simple black cocktail dress would do. Even that was a stretch for me. I had given up wearing dresses or even skirts some time ago. "And just how feminist is it to be comparing gowns?" I wondered. Quite feminist, I discovered, as each of the strong, powerful, politically savvy women sitting around the table began to describe in great detail the gown she was planning to wear. I had to tell them that I had misjudged the dress code and had brought from home, several hundred miles away, only a plain black sheath. "Not to worry," said one of the women. "I have a fabulous gown you can borrow; it's just your size." "And if that doesn't work," said another woman, "there's a darling dress shop right around the corner from here. I'll help you pick something that's just right." It was my first experience with feminists as fashionistas. Live and learn.

The fund-raising event itself was a who's who of feminism, including founders of some of the other women's funds and, of course, a lot of very wealthy women (and men). Claudia made it a point to introduce me to everyone who was anyone. Maybe she was eager to show off her token "crip," but frankly, I didn't care. I kept thinking, "If I make a few or even one of these big-shot people aware of the issues of disabled women, that will be an achievement." I was hopeful that some of the contacts I made at this event would lead to opportunities to promote my work and, to be honest, myself. I wasn't disappointed. People that I met at this fund-raising event and others would lead to a host of speaking engagements, invitations to join the board of directors of other women's organizations, some honors for my work, and even the sale of a few of my paintings.

Ego stroking aside, with each successive board meeting, I was seeing little evidence of disabled women benefiting from my participation on the board. "So what's the story?" my disabled women friends would ask. "Any more dollars from that fund of yours going to disabled women?" "No," I had to confess. "They're not receiving too many proposals from disabled women." "Oh, please. I'll bet that's just the kind of excuse they used to use to keep out African American women from knocking on their door," said one of my more outspoken friends. "Oh, no," I said. "Women of color

have a great deal of power in that fund." "And how about ten years ago? Or even five? Did they have power then, or were they tokens like you?" she asked. I didn't know, but of course she was right. The fund had been started by white, middle-class women, as had the larger women's movement. Women of color had to scream, yell, pressure, threaten, boycott, and fight their way into both the fund and the movement to lessen if not fully overcome the racism they encountered. Other minorities didn't have a much easier time. A chance encounter a few years into my tenure on the board told the tale. I met a Native American woman and a Latina who had joined the board when I had, but each had dropped out within the first year, claiming too many other responsibilities. But they both told me they had left because they found the fund unresponsive to their community's needs. And later on, after I had left the organization, I met a woman who was one of "the first and only" African American women on the board. She, too, had departed early and could barely describe her experiences without becoming enraged.

I regret that I hadn't paid closer attention to my friend's comment—or hadn't met those women earlier. Then I might have seen the resistance to including disabled women that I was beginning to encounter in a larger context of the organization's resistance to change.

The fund continued to receive few if any proposals involving disabled women that fit its criteria, and I didn't push the planning/start-up grant suggestion. Without Claudia's support, I didn't think that idea would stand a chance. I do believe that if there had been a will, that group of women on the board would have found a way. For example, they could have mandated that all community groups receiving funds must make an effort to include disabled women in their projects. Or they could have provided a financial incentive, maybe a few thousand dollars extra, to groups that included disabled women in their programs.

Eventually, by pushing and shoving, I got a few results for my efforts. For example, a special initiative to promote the career development of young women included a project for disabled women that got a fair amount of press. But there were not nearly enough grants to show a strong, clear commitment to disabled women.

The funding of projects with specific disability content wasn't the only way the fund fell short. The presence of disabled women in programs designed to raise awareness of general women's issues was, from my perspective, limited. For example, there was a big "women's right to choose" campaign that included a survey of women's attitudes and a blitz in the media. I encouraged the inclusion of disabled women in the survey, reminding Claudia that they might have some different attitudes toward choice than nondisabled women, particularly regarding when and how disability is used to justify abortion. "We already know about the attitudes of disabled women," Claudia told me. And I suppose she did, because unlike some other media campaigns on choice that I had seen, there was nothing in the materials about aborting disabled fetuses. But I would have preferred to have the voices of disabled women included in a more direct way. Also, in a poster promoting the fund's young women's career project that included images of a diverse group of young women, there were no women with visible disabilities. When I expressed my concern to one of the department heads of the fund, who was Latina, she said, "Well, there are no Latina women portrayed in the poster either." And I thought to myself, "Just because you are a poor advocate for your community, I should be one too?"

Increasingly over time, I felt like a one-song Suzie, constantly repeating the question, "What about disabled women?" I grew to hate my own ineffective voice among these women, raging at myself as much as at them. I kept thinking if only I were a better activist, if only I screamed louder, if only I weren't so eager to fit in, if only I were a better conversationalist and could sweet-talk some of the other board members into supporting my issue, if only, if only. Not all my rants against myself were unwarranted. I was not the ideal "first and only" disabled woman for this organization. I was not willing enough to go out on a limb for what I believed in and run the risk of being rejected by this group of feminists that I was so eager to be part of. Although I had been "out of the closet" as disabled for more than 15 years, I was still a bifurcated woman, struggling between and straddling the disabled and nondisabled worlds. I wanted to belong somewhere but wasn't at home anywhere. I was afraid to make waves, ambivalent about power, and hence too often kept quiet to keep the peace, to find my place at the table. In fact, part of the problem was that I was trying to create change by myself, a Lone Ranger who really needed to be part of a posse.

In the midst of my disillusionment, Claudia began moving the fund in a new direction. Thanks to a huge donation from a private donor, she was transforming the organization into a much larger, stronger, and more powerful resource, voice, and presence for women. The move would have a price, one that made my goal of including disabled women even more difficult to achieve. The transformation started with a change in board functions. The board would no longer review and approve grants but would focus instead on "higher-level" tasks like setting overall fund policies and building a substantial endowment. Claudia must have known that I would be upset by the board's loss of its right to review the grants docket because she called me before the meeting to let me know that a vote on this issue was on the agenda. Of course, I was upset. This was the only modicum of control

I had over the fund's grant making with regard to disabled women, paltry though it was. I voted no at the meeting, but most of the rest of the board voted yes, so I was overruled. Later on, a few other board members said they wanted to vote no also but felt it was pointless. They knew Claudia would ultimately have her way.

The new emphasis on fund-raising finally led me to leave before the end of my second term. Requiring board members to raise money was not unique to this women's fund; it became increasingly common among most women's organizations. While I understood that this was essential for survival, I was disturbed by its effects on the board and the organization. "We need to invite some women of wealth—or at least women who know some women of wealth to join our board," Claudia had remarked. "I thought board members are supposed to represent the diverse communities of women that our fund serves," one of my sister board members responded. "We know enough about diversity. Now we need money," Claudia explained. And at that moment, I felt corporate America descending on us. Over time, we did have increasing numbers of women of wealth and women who held prominent positions in large corporations join our board or in other ways become involved with the fund, in some ways shifting it in a more conservative direction. I felt increasingly impotent since I was by no means a woman of wealth, had no connections to wealthy people, and represented a constituency of women who were among the poorest of the poor and hence were not potential donors.

After I quit the board, I became temporarily preoccupied with my lack of effectiveness. I felt that, overall, I hadn't done much for the fund—a few grants here, a few programs there; mainly I felt like a thorn in the fund's, and particularly the executive director's, side. But as other women who had been through similar experiences would later reassure me, the first and only of any group who joins a mainstream organization never does much. My presence was just a beginning, a baby step. I don't regret the six years I spent there. I learned a great deal about the slow pace of progress and the need for patience, perseverance, and most important, realistic expectations.

Being on that board also gave me a higher level of credibility in the women's community. Now I was associated with not only a mentoring project for disabled adolescent girls but also a well-known, highly respected women's fund. The connection with that fund led to invitations to join the boards of other women's organizations, also as the first and only disabled woman. "What? Again? Didn't I learn from experience?" I would ask myself each time I accepted another invitation. Actually, I did. While I didn't have a major impact on any of these organizations, I was less frustrated and depressed because I didn't expect to make a big dent. By then, I was pleased to have any impact, even if all I did was open the door a bit. There were some considerable achievements: a number of grants for disabled women's projects from the second women's fund I joined; a heightened awareness of accessibility when another women's group whose board I served on was purchasing a new building; and, one of my most exciting moments, a congressional hearing on the issues of young disabled women, orchestrated by a third group. I have to acknowledge that those hearings were not my idea. They were the brainchild of the president, who had been advocating for the rights of disabled women, not exclusively, but as part of her work on behalf of all women, for more years than I had, even though she had never before invited a disabled woman to join her board. My presence on the board served as a catalyst to further her work on behalf of disabled women and girls, but I didn't have to do much advocacy. My tenure on that board demonstrated how much easier it is to promote inclusion when the leader of an organization has some knowledge and experience with disability rights issues; then change, while not necessarily easy, can be much smoother and less disruptive. But such people are hard to find.

To this day I still wonder about Claudia's notion that disability was the hardest issue for her organization to address. I regret not pushing her for an explanation. Maybe I thought I knew at least some of the reasons, such as that for this or any group of feminists invested in seeing themselves as strong, competent, and independent, disabled women, stereotypically viewed as needy and dependent, stirred up anxieties about their own dependency needs, especially as they age. Or perhaps they felt resentful that they would have to take care of their disabled sisters, as they have had to care for sick, aging, or otherwise dependent family members. Or maybe the presence of disabled women precipitated these women's doubts about the intactness of their own bodies or their fears of vulnerability or reinforced stereotypes of women as victims. Or, more mundanely, perhaps they were afraid that accommodating disabled women would be expensive, draining limited funds and resources.

Now, some 15 years later (and 30-plus years since I first began pushing my way into the women's movement), feminists have become more inclusive. Virtually every women's conference addresses disabled women's issues in at least a few sessions, and a small number of well-known women's organizations have sponsored entire conferences on disability. Yet few disabled women serve on governing boards or in leadership positions in mainstream women's groups, and those who do are often "the first and only." Even today, disabled women are more likely to be included out of obligation than out of appreciation of the contribution they can make. They are not seen as a rich source of diversity. The welcome mat is not yet out.

PART VI

*D*isability and Culture

Sculpting Body Ideals: *Alison Lapper Pregnant* and the Public Display of Disability

Ann Millett-Gallant

SUMMARY

In 2005, artists Alison Lapper and Marc Quinn unveiled *Alison Lapper Pregnant*, an 11.5-foot tall, 13-ton sculpture installed in Trafalgar Square. Lapper, who was born without arms and with shortened legs, was cast in the nude at seven months pregnant. Lapper has been called a heroine of cultural diversity, but critics have also accused Quinn of using the sculpture as a publicity stunt. In this essay, Ann Millett-Gallant argues that *Alison Lapper Pregnant* is a public statement about a disabled woman's right to be represented as a productive social subject and a reproductive sexual being. The sculpture recycles the representation of disability as both freakish and heroic.

As a work of public art, *Alison Lapper Pregnant* raises issues of social and artistic representation in a public space traditionally filled with monuments to able-bodied, white and male figures. The pregnant statue acknowledges bodies (female, disabled, pregnant) that have been socially devalued or excluded from notions of the public. The fact that the figure is pregnant provokes the fear that a "broken" body will reproduce a "damaged" child, which calls into question mainstream values about reproductive rights. By using classical technique and materials—and by placing the sculpture alongside those of traditional male British heroes—Quinn produces confusion between the ideal and anti-ideal in order to make stereotypes about disability visible and open to public debate.

Millett-Gallant provides an overview of works by both Quinn and Lapper, and she points out the way that Lapper publicly mediates the reception of *Alison Lapper Pregnant*. Lapper's presence in public debate and her collaboration with Quinn show how perspective of disability is necessary for any productive dialogue about disability. Such dialogues can forge fresh images of disability in the public eye and can potentially sculpt liberating body ideals for the public.

In 2005, artist Alison Lapper was thrust into fame when her 11.5-foot tall, 13-ton sculptural portrait, *Alison Lapper Pregnant*, was unveiled on the fourth plinth of Trafalgar Square. Lapper agreed to being cast in the nude by British artist Marc Quinn when she was seven months pregnant and to be placed on public display; many have called the piece a collaboration. The controversial sculpture has brought widespread attention to the model's body and her life story. Lapper, born without arms and with shortened legs, is an alumnus of British institutions for disabled children and programs for disabled artists, a now single mother, and an artist who makes work about her embodied experiences as a disabled woman. Carved from precious Italian marble and placed on a pedestal among statues of naval captains, Lapper has been called a contemporary heroine of cultural diversity, while the work has also been regarded as a tasteless publicity stunt for Quinn. The exposure of Lapper's body transcends the fact that she is nude, for Lapper grew up in insolated environments of public institutions and had limited interactions with public life; for Lapper, the work is a true coming out. *Alison Lapper Pregnant* makes a public statement about this disabled woman's right to be represented as a productive social subject *and* a reproductive sexual being and her right to represent others.

This essay will interrogate the sculpture's representation of disability within the contexts of Trafalgar Square, the genre of Public Art, as well as in comparisons with Quinn's previous series of sculptural amputees, *The Complete Marbles* (2002), and, foremost, with Lapper's self-representations. I will argue that *Alison Lapper Pregnant* significantly responds to, as well as transforms the history of, its particular space and interacts with the populations who inhabit that space. Rather than displaying trite political correctness or simple shock value, as much of its criticism wages, the work plays monumental roles in the histories of both disability representation and art. As a public spectacle, it recycles, and I will argue contemporizes, the representation of disability as both heroic and freakish. Further, Lapper's photography and her recently published memoir are key components of such discussions, as they provide perspectives by and a voice to the disabled subject on display. By weaving together these contexts of and reactions to Quinn's and Lapper's works, this essay underscores the necessity of placing the works of disabled and non-disabled artists in dialogues with one another and with larger histories of visual culture.

Public art raises issues of social and artistic representation and the visibility and invisibility of certain members of society. Public space and its monuments have been gendered male and raced white traditionally, and public space is largely ableist in attitude, not to mention accessibility (or lack thereof). Public art, when the most effective, creates dialogues about the role of art in society and whom is included and excluded in the notion of the "public." By honoring individuals marginalized and erased by dominant values and the structures which personify them, many more contemporary public art projects have explicitly protested the status quo. These public art forms, in which I contextualize *Alison Lapper Pregnant*, embody cultural battles for and of representation.

The sculpture produces Lapper as a representative of the historically underrepresented. Lapper has positioned the work at the forefront of such initiatives, stating: "I regard it as a modern tribute to femininity, disability and motherhood. ... The sculpture makes the ultimate statement about disability—that it can be as beautiful and valid a form of being as any other." She acknowledges how her body becomes a monument to bodies and identities that have been socially devalued, shamed, and excluded from public life historically. Lapper goes on to note: "It is so rare to see disability in everyday life—let alone naked, pregnant and proud. The sculpture makes the ultimate statement about disability—that it can be as beautiful and valid a form of being as any other."[1] Here, she characterizes her body as a form of anti-monument, for it represents the "other" to traditional subjects of public monuments, as well as an anti-ideal. Positive feedback about the sculpture also champions it as a liberating anti-ideal.[2] The work may function to force the viewer to question their perceptions of the "ideal," while also questioning whose ideals Lapper is purported to represent.

The work functions visually on confusions between the ideal and anti-ideal. Quinn's work is specifically a quotation of eighteenth- and nineteenth-century Neo-classicism. Neoclassical figurative painting, sculpture, and architectural programs taught lessons on heroism and moral virtue, often by depicting the deeds of great and powerful men.[3] In Western culture from the Renaissance to today, this Neoclassical form is characteristically employed for public statutes of religious and political heroes. Neoclassicism and its Classical heritage communicate philosophical and political ideals through mathematically constructed aesthetics, specifically, in "whole" bodies.

Quinn subverts the signification of Neo-classical form as the ideal "whole" in *Alison Lapper Pregnant* (2005) and in his series of life size, marble sculptures of amputees, *The Complete Marbles* (2002), which adopt par-ticularly Roman qualities of portrait like-ness. By using many high profile disabled models, such as artist Peter Hull and the confrontational "freak" performer and punk rock musician, Matt Fraser, Quinn produces depictions of recognizable sub-jects and celebrities. Titled with the sub-jects' proper names, these works challenge how the viewer perceives the body in art, as well as in everyday life, as whole and/or bro-ken.[4] Quinn titled this series *The Complete Marbles* strategically. *The Elgin Marbles* are precious Classical sculptures appropriated from the Parthenon in Greece (produced c. 438–423 BCE). *The Elgin Marbles*, many bro-ken and missing limbs and heads, were amputated from their architectural base (the Parthenon); they are fragments of pro-foundly aesthetic "wholes," for the Parthe-non remains a cultural icon today for its integrated, carefully orchestrated balance and proportion and its intense, methodical control of aesthetics. Extracted from the Temple to Athena, the marbles both frag-ment and "stand" (or symbolize) one of the greatest symbols of power and wealth in Western history—specifically one famous for its ideal wholeness. Quinn's title for the series, *The Complete Marbles*, places

contemporary disabled bodies in these his-torical legacies, and they are designated as "whole" by their own counter-conventional body standards and disarming beauty.

Quinn's artistic procedures and materials are central to the significances of his works. Like all of the pieces in *The Complete Marbles*, *Alison Lapper Pregnant* was sculpted in Quinn's studio in Pietrasenta, Italy, the center for Carrara marble—the same marble sought by Michelangelo and many Neoclassical sculptors. *Alison Lapper Pregnant* took 10 months to craft from the stubborn substance, which contains exalted histories and symbolic significances. Quinn is quite particular about the material, as he literally goes out of his way to use it, and he prefers this marble for its "intrinsic and metaphoric content."[5] Carrara marble provides a luminosity that makes his ampu-tees shine and radiate, like works from the Greek Hellenistic period.

Many critics deem Quinn's art historical references as subversive, specifically because he focuses on disabled bodies. For example, art writer for the *Sunday Times*, Waldemar Januszczak, states the following about *Alison Lapper Pregnant*:

> By carving Alison Lapper out of pristine marble, Quinn is *taking on* the Greeks; he is *disputing* with Phidias, with Michelangelo, with Sir Joshua Reynolds, with every author-itarian with imagination that has ever insisted upon a standard shape for the human in art; he is contradicting 2,000 years of creative *misrep-resentation* of what being human means; and he is giving Alison Lapper the same amount of artistic attention that Canova gave the Empress Josephine. As if that were not enough, Quinn is also cheekily rhyming his sculptures with the broken remnants of classical art—the armless Venus, the legless Apollo—that are the staple diet of all collections of the antique. These are serious achievements.[6]
>
> (emphasis mine)

My italics here underscore how Januszczak describes Quinn's use of amputees in art historical, specifically Classical and Neoclassical images, as confrontational and revisionist, as if the works are affronts to these traditions because of the amputees featured. This comment suggests that certain social prejudices against amputees function in critical interpretations of Quinn's work. The form of the Lapper sculpture has been the target of much criticism; however, criticisms against the artistic value of *Alison Lapper Pregnant* (the work) may suggest simultaneous rejection of Alison Lapper pregnant (as an embodiment and social subject). Many have charged Quinn with capitalizing on the shock value and taboo nature of disabled bodies in public spaces.[7] The work functions to make such stereotypes visible and open to public debate.

On the other hand (or stump), positive evaluations of the *Alison Lapper Pregnant* further complicate how the sculpture represents disability in the public eye, as they purport Lapper to be a hero. This idea recalls the stereotype of a disabled hero that is premised on sentimentalization of and low expectations for disabled people in society. What kind of hero is Lapper in these descriptions, one who dismantles notions of appropriate versus shocking bodies? Or one who rehashes the stereotype of "overcoming," which functions to ignore social constructs of disability and is based on the problematic notion of disability as an individual "problem"? Framed as the representation of a hero, the sculpture celebrates Lapper's impairments and perhaps also de-politicizes, or literally aestheticizes disability, as a marginalizing social construct, for the public. Or perhaps it redefines our ideas about heroism and makes a disabled figure a role model, in a positive light.

Lapper's heroism may also be problematically tied to her pregnancy, such that motherhood becomes a means for Lapper to "overcome" disability by conforming to standards for women's roles in society, a point which Kim Q. Hall has interrogated. Hall quotes Quinn: "For me, *Alison Lapper Pregnant* is a monument to the future possibilities of the human race as well as the resilience of the human spirit."[8] Hall frames this comment within political propaganda that has imposed the duty upon women historically to reproduce the nation; such dogma is similar to that expressed throughout Trafalgar Square by the national heroes depicted. Hall argues that the sculpture is championed by Quinn and many others because it confounds the taboo nature of disabled bodies in public spaces, as well as patriarchal and heterosexual values that assert that reproduction validates women. Yet, Hall's persuasive arguments reframe how Lapper's presence in the square plays upon traditional gender roles and disability stereotypes only tangentially, for the sculpture's and Lapper's own consistent divergence from convention affirms the work's adamant non-conformity to "family values." Mainstream discourses that breed women for motherhood suggest that a productive female member of the society is a *reproductive* one, specifically within the institution of marriage. Far from glorifying a nuclear family, Lapper was born to a single, working class mother and is herself an unmarried mother, who has benefited from public programs for disabled artists. Many may view Lapper's choices as amoral and her subsistence as a public burden, therefore she hardly acts in the legacy of national heroes.

Lapper's maternal situation defies ideals of both society and of art for women's bodies. Pregnant bodies, seen most often in art history as fertility figures and virginal Madonnas, occupy a liminal status, as both an ideal state of the female motherhood, yet one that contrasts with the conventions for the sexualized nude, particularly for twenty-first-century eyes. Popular representations have tended to idealize pregnancy socially, yet they also veil the pregnant female body, reinstating its preferred existence within the proverbial home. Pregnancy is glorified and yet stigmatized and indeed often considered a disability. However, images of pregnant women have become trendy lately, particularly among the elite, with the celebrity "baby boom" displayed in the aesthetic "bumps" on otherwise perfect bodies and within the romanticized unions of the Brangelinas and Tom-Kats of the world; Demi Moore, Melania Trump, and most recently, Brittany Spears have been featured by mainstream women's magazines as so-called liberated covergirls and centerfolds, revealing their scantily clad and fashionable pregnant bodies. Again, these pregnant bodies are framed specifically within dominant social ideals and values (with perhaps the exception of Spears and the notorious "Fed-Ex"), values to which Alison Lapper could never conform. *Alison Lapper Pregnant* confuses perceptions of the body in art history and popular culture, ultimately because, for many, the work assertively provokes the fear that the disabled body will reproduce another "damaged" child—from a "broken" body and a "broken" home. The work advocates controversial reproductive rights for disabled women and for single women more broadly. Further, any attempt on Lapper's part to fulfill her role to reproduce the next generation may produce a disabled one, which remains a horror rather than a triumph, according to mainstream values and exclusive social standards for quality of life. Lapper's maternal "acts" poignantly fail to service social ideals, as the sculpture becomes pregnant with ambivalent meanings.

Viewers' reactions to the work as shocking and/or inspiring seem polarized, and yet both connote, to varying degrees, the desire to make a lesson out of the disabled body, in order to justify its display. Many who critique the work and Quinn's *The Complete Marbles*

series demand explanation about the cause of the models' impairments and the usefulness of such displays to society. Januszczak has also stated: "With a subject as serious as the loss of human limbs, or the birth of a child to a deformed mother, it is absolutely incumbent upon the gallery to cease playing aesthetic games and to make clearer the artist's intentions."[9] This quote expresses viewers' desire for medical diagnosis to make the works more palatable and less sensationalistic. However, the sculpture also provokes some viewers to question their own desires to know "what happened" to the body and assumptions that the disabled body necessarily connotes accident or victimization.

The notion of making the disabled body into a lesson is relevant to the realm of public art specifically, within which the body becomes a monument to instruct, for public art has a duty, in the eyes of many, to educate and inform. The origin of the word "monument" derives from Latin *nomere*, meaning "to remind," "to admonish," "warn," "advise," and "instruct."[10] Poignantly, this word origin emerges also in the word "monster," as scholars of the freak show have pointed out, explaining how the disabled body has historically been seen as an indicator of either supernatural foreshadowing or scientific mistake. The use of the disabled body as a lesson has included public exploitation of so-called medical anomalies, practices which have reinforced medical models, crossed genres into freak shows, and staged the disabled body as an instructional object for the non-disabled viewers. The nineteenth- and early twentieth-century freak show entertained and affirmed middle class spectators' senses of "normalcy," which was constructed specifically in binary opposition to the strikingly "abnormal" spectacle.

The freak show is another relevant comparison for considering the role of Lapper's body in a public space, particularly one that serves as a tourist attraction[11]: "She is presented 'like some 19th-century fairground exhibit,'" one critic stated.[12] In the freak show, the disabled and other extraordinary (exotic, minority) bodies were eroticized, the nudity of the sculpture, to which some take offense, is intrinsic to its unashamed display of the pregnant disabled body and its Neoclassical form; it places the work in both a history of art and a history of displaying the body as spectacle, in the freak show, pornography, and other voyeuristic venues. This context raises a key question: does the sculpture exploit Alison Lapper?

Lapper is benefiting from the attention the work has drawn to her own art and her life, as she recently published a memoir (2005). In it, she relates Quinn's sculpture to her own self-portrait nude photography, with which she expresses comfort in her own skin and challenges her personal history of being considered physically defective and sexually unattractive. Addressing the controversy regarding the nudity of the statue, Lapper has written:

In most societies, even in Britain today, pregnant women are not considered to have a beautiful shape. On top of that, short people, who are missing both arms, are generally considered even less beautiful. I was someone who currently combined both disadvantages. How could Marc possibly think I was a suitable subject for a sculpture that people would want to look at? Statues are created and exhibited to give pleasure, to be admired. Would anybody be able to admire the statue of a naked, pregnant, disabled woman?[13]

She attributes the controversy of the sculpture to a society that is prudish to nudity in general, as well as to pregnancy and to disability specifically. Many may deem the work amoral, and therefore in direct opposition to Neoclassical, moralistic traditions, and yet, as Lapper articulates, moral judgments are subjective to the eyes of the beholders.

Lapper does not express feeling exploited. Describing her decision to pose, Lapper writes:

It was January 1999 when I received a phone call from an artist called Marc Quinn. ... I was extremely suspicious. I thought he might be just another one in the long line of people who have exploited disability and used it for its curiosity and value. However, when we talked, I realised Marc wasn't interested in disability in the way most people wanted to depict it. He wasn't pitying or moralising—I knew it wasn't a freak show or some kind of weird sexual focus that he was aiming at.[14]

Lapper here recognizes the problematic tropes of representing disabled bodies as sentimentalized heroes or freakish spectacles, both of which make the disabled body into a symbol and lesson to be learned by the so-called normal. Poignantly, she ties these tropes together. Yet by collaborating with Quinn, Lapper makes a statement about the need for public education and exposure of/to disability in contemporary society in order to overturn the stereotypes and the status quo.

Trafalgar Square is an ideal place to raise and interrogate these issues. The modern city, and public squares like Trafalgar especially, were built for tourist gazing, urban surveillance, and commercial spectatorship.[15] Trafalgar Square, designed by John Nash and built by Sir Charles Barry in the 1820s and 1830s to commemorate British naval captain and famous imperialist Admiral Horatio Nelson (1758–1805), was named after the Spanish Cape Trafalgar where Nelson's last battle was won. Characteristic of nineteenth-century Roman revival in Britain, the square's architecture and statuary is specifically Neoclassical to portray political ideals. A monument to Lord Nelson (1758–1805) became the central vision of the square. This Neoclassical likeness of Nelson stands on a 185-foot tall column, overseeing the public—a tradition which continues today. Nelson's monument, modeled after the triumphant Roman Column of Trajan, and its surroundings place modern Britain in the traditions of Roman imperialism. Surrounding Nelson are other monuments to British military heroes, represented in idealizing Neoclassical forms.[16] Like the design of the square, the Neoclassical monuments display a particular side of British history and society, one whose power depends on the subordination of those rendered invisible.

With her marble, feminine curves and serene posture, *Alison Lapper Pregnant* would seem out of place in such a paternalistic environment[17]—the freakish anti-hero. And yet others see the sculpture as right at home with the other monuments. She has been compared symbolically and corporeally with Admiral Nelson himself, as the work reinterprets notions of disabled and non-disabled heroes and spectacles. For example, in letters to the editor, Michael Gallagher calls Lapper: "A great Briton in the truest sense of the word. I am sure that Nelson would have recognised her as a kindred spirit," and Jeanette Hart notes: "Nelson only had one arm, and was blind in one eye, and he was just known as a great man; no one labelled him."[18] Nelson was indeed blinded in one eye during the capture of Corsica from French troops in 1794 and lost his arm in a 1797 capture of the Canary Islands. He continued to lead troops with these impairments until his death at the Battle of Trafalgar in 1805, an act which has augmented his status as a national hero. The column is topped by a statue of Nelson posed with his uniform coat sleeve draped along his chest and tucked into his suitcoat, in a conventional pose for leaders, yet his sleeve is empty. This view is not perceptible for the viewer below. Quinn's public display of Alison Lapper and its comparisons to Nelson's Column have illuminated for some that the disabled body is always

already present in an existing vision of heroism. Viewing Lapper as a hero reinterprets or expands the image of a heroic body, and perhaps this designation does not simply rehash stereotypes of overcoming, but rather describes the meaning of her body as a public image within a specific location and historical context.

Alison Lapper Pregnant follows in multiple histories of public art that are celebratory of or in protest to their context—a simultaneous monument and anti-monument. All of the submissions for the Fourth Plinth project competition since 1990 have been consciously critical of the square's aristocratic, nationalistic, and paternalistic traditions, both in content and form. As art critic Paul Usherwood describes it, Lapper carries on this contemporary trend of mocking the square's: "macho triumphalism and formality."[19] Lapper's Neo- or post-Classical form embodies also a breaching of boundaries between convention and subversion. And by embodying contradictions, Lapper once again fits right into Trafalgar Square and translates its history to contemporary debates over civil and human rights. The controversial debates surrounding the work continue a long-standing history of Trafalgar Square, which has been wrought with conflict historically (as evidenced by the background stories on the lives of the men honored there). Trafalgar Square has served as the city's most popular rallying point and the site of: public executions; political, economic, and religious protests; interventions of military law; class battles; protests for freedom of speech and rights to assemble, for women's suffrage, and for civil rights, liberties, and decolonization; and pro- and anti-war, pro- and anti-Fascism and Semitism, and pro- and anti-communism rallies.[20] Poignantly, all these displays of activism represent multiple and opposing sides of social and political issues since the nineteenth century, and, significant, most of these demonstrations have centered on the base of Nelson's Column, because of its physical prominence and its symbolic significance. The monuments of Nelson and Lapper both embody multiple significances contextually and over time and have been witnesses to multiplicities of perspectives. Both Nelson's and Lapper's bodies in Trafalgar Square pay tribute to the necessity of public debate.

The sculpture of Alison Lapper and its social and symbolic meanings must be considered within its specific context. The work embodies, transforms, and contemporizes the history of its space. *Alison Lapper Pregnant* carries on the square's traditions by provoking debate and dissent. The controversy and many opposing opinions expressed publicly about the sculpture enact its social work. Lapper's body on display has provoked constructive investigation about the role of art in society and the roles of disabled bodies as heroes and spectacles. It asks us to interrogate our assumptions about what forms of bodies should or should not appear in public spaces and how. The dubious representations of disability the work evokes are both liberating and stereotypical, which is necessary to provoke debate. That Lapper herself has been so vocal in the discussions is key, for her collaboration with Quinn and her public mediation of the work shows how perspectives *of* disability, not just *about* them, are necessary for any productive dialogue.

Comparisons of Quinn's work with Lapper's own body art, which self-narrates her experiences as a disabled woman artist, provide significant dialogues about disability and visual representation. Born in 1965, Lapper grew up in institutional settings and art schools. Although she was always skilled at making art, Lapper remarks on having to prove herself repeatedly to non-disabled people, intellectually, artistically, and sexually, due to assumptions about her so-called "lacking" anatomy. She moved to London at age 19, where she lived independently for the first time and attended the University of Brighton, graduated with a degree in fine art at age 20, purchased a home in Southwick, and began her work as an artist. Lapper has been the focus of the BBC1 series *Child of Our Time* program, to which she has returned for annual appearances, and an hour long documentary by Milton Media for Denmark's TV2, titled *Alison's Baby*, which has been broadcast in many countries and won the Prix Italia and the Prix Leonardo. In 2003, Lapper won the MBE award for service to the arts. Since graduation from Brighton, she has worked fulltime for the Mouth and Foot Painting Artists' Association of England (MFPA). Funding for this program comes from the artists' production of decorative images for card designs, marketed by the MFPA, and Lapper writes that she still enjoys producing such genre scenes and landscapes, along with her self-portrait work.

Lapper's self-portrait body art, in the forms of photography, sculpture, and installation, marks a continuous process of self discovery. At the University of Brighton, an opinionated viewer challenged the nature of Lapper's figurative work of non-disabled bodies, by suggesting that perhaps Lapper had not fully accepted her own body. This moment became a turning point for Lapper, as she began envisioning her own body as a work of art. Inspired by a photograph of the armless or "broken" Greek statue, the *Venus de Milo*, in which she saw her own likeness, Lapper began casting her body in plaster and photographing herself in Venus-like poses. Like arm-free performance artist Mary Duffy, who delivers impassioned speech about her experiences of being medically and socially objectified, while posing in the nude, Lapper adopted the Venus de Milo as her body image. Lapper's graduation exhibit featured an installation the viewer had to enter on hands and knees, at the height of

Lapper herself, in order to see photographs and sculpted casts of her full body and body parts. This installation created an environment that removed the viewer from their own comfort zone physically and perceptually. Other disabled artists also employ their embodied perspectives in their work, such as little person Ricardo Gil. Gil photographs his wife and daughter, both little people, from the perspectives at which he views them—literally, in terms of his height, and figuratively, as intimate close-ups that establish affectionate, familial relationships between the subject and the camera's gaze. In *Johann's Kiss*, 1999, Gil features his smiling wife centered in the frame, embraced by an average-sized, kneeling man, whose head is cropped at the top of the photograph. Figures in the background are cut off at mid torso; however, these are not mistakes of an amateur. Here, "normal" size people don't fit in the little woman's privileged, compositional space or in Gil's proud gaze. Lapper's installation, like Gil's photographs, explored the relationships between the viewer's versus the artist's own acts of looking at, judging, and experiencing the disabled body.[21]

Lapper's self-portrait work and her personifications specifically of the armless Venus de Milo (a cultural icon of artistic and feminine beauty), like Duffy's, explore the complicated interactions of disability and sexuality, particularly for women. Lapper's shameless public exposure in a public art display (*Alison Lapper Pregnant*) takes root in a longer artistic and personal process of "coming out" as a sexual, and indeed reproductive woman. In contrast with the mainstream vision of Lapper's often assumed a-sexuality, a bold and seductive body image emerges in Lapper's work. Lapper's *Untitled* (2000) features three views of her nude body in Venus-like, s-curve poses. The photographic media articulates her musculature, flesh, and curve of the breast, while aestheticizing equally her upper-arm

"stumps." The strong contrasts of the black background with the marble whiteness of her skin create a photographic sculpture in the round. The photograph, like Duffy's performance and Quinn's *The Complete Marbles* series, plays with the viewer's recognition of Classical statuary (particularly a goddess of love and fertility) and the disabled flesh, as well as perceptions of "whole" versus "deficient" bodies. Carving a sculpture "in the round" refers specifically to Classical and Neoclassical methods of producing balanced, proportional "wholes." This symbolic practice was quoted also by feminist performance artist Eleanor Antin in *Carving: A Traditional Sculpture* (July 15, 1972–August 21, 1972), in which Antin documented her body from all sides daily, as it gradually reduced during a crash diet. Antin's photographs are formally clinical in their starkness, referring to the "before" and "after" photographs quite familiar in our makeover-obsessed contemporary culture, while her body becomes a piece of sculpture in characteristic practices of performance art. Particularly to twenty-first-century eyes, Antin's images refer to eating disorders and the extents to which women will go to "perfect" their bodies, according to increasingly narrow and impossible social standards for beauty. Lapper's and Antin's photographic sculptures in the round, like Quinn's sculptures, expose the notion of the "ideal" as fabricated. Lapper's work especially presents a certain disruption between artistic and social visions of the ideal and anti-ideal female body.

Art has provided a means for Lapper to interrogate others' and her own images of her body and to reinvent her image in the public eye. These themes continued in a 2000 exhibit at the Fabrica Gallery in Brighton, featuring sculptural works and photographs of Lapper from childhood to adulthood. The photographic collection intentionally crossed genres, by including artistic self-portraits, snapshots taken by friends at key moments in Lapper's life, and early childhood medical photographs, which questioned viewers' assumptions about seeing her body in different visual contexts. The inclusion of medical photographs in particular was meant to disarm the viewer and incorporate, as well as intervene on, Lapper's experiences of feeling like a medical spectacle and specimen. Indeed, Lapper's unique medical history, chronicled in her memoir as a series of objectifying and shameful displays of her body by doctors to "instruct" their peers on deformity and anomaly, connects intimately in the process of her work; Lapper remarks on her extensive history of being measured and cast in plaster particularly, in both medical and artistic contexts. Other works in the show featured Lapper's face in the vintage black-and-white style of classic Hollywood photographs. These images were strategically placed in a frame on the floor and covered in salt crystals. The viewer had to kneel down and brush aside the crystals to see Lapper's face, portrayed in a photographic softness reminiscent of glamor shots and intended to offset the hard-edge format of the medical images. The demand for viewer interaction with these works, as well at their themes of veiling, revealing, and concealing the body, make them performative—another public display of the disabled body.

Lapper strives in this work to showcase the disabled body as artistic and worthy of aestheticized display. She also makes photographic collages with elements such as flowers and angel wings to symbolize her biographical and artistic journeys. In *Angel* (1999), Lapper's head and nude torso, shot in black-and-white film, project from the right edge of the painted frame. She bears wings and her body thrusts upward, soaring, like the winged messenger god Hermes, or the confident, yet tragic Icarus, to unforeseen heights of knowledge and to personal vistas. Winged figures, from Classical mythology to contemporary fantasy, transverse the heavens and the earth—the realms

of the gods and mortals; they are figures with extraordinary bodies and supernatural abilities for travel. Lapper here incarnates goddess imagery, enacting a re-vision of art history and resurgence of the disabled body in shameless, empowered self display. She appropriates allegorical bodies to present her own body image. In this frame, *Angel* invokes also the winged Nike, the mythical personification of victory, who is sometimes depicted bearing wings in the place of arms (as in the monumental, *Nike of Samothrace*, c.190 CE). Believed to once stand at the helm of a ship, the headless and armless Greek Hellenistic Nike is now a grand attraction at the Louvre Museum in Paris and a relic of Western culture. The Nike form is poignantly a derivative of Athena, the goddess known for her protection of the city of Athens and who is venerated still today at the Parthenon, the original home of the *Elgin Marbles*. Athena, or Minerva as she was known by the Romans, was a single mother and the goddess of wisdom, women's deeds, and the arts—a quite fitting allegory for Lapper to embody. Further, as Marina Warner (1985) describes, Athena shape-shifted to a number of personas and bodies in order to invoke powers and enact deeds. These performative masquerades of the goddess included her strategic exposure and concealment of her body and identity. Like Athena's performances, Lapper's self-portrait works reveal and conceal her body in multiplying references and significances; similarly to *Alison Lapper Pregnant*, Lapper's body work is pregnant with meaning.

Lapper's works, like Quinn's, juxtapose the portrayal of the body as symbolic allegory and as a portrait subject. As an allegorical figure, *Alison Lapper Pregnant* follows in a tradition of staging the female body particularly as a symbol of heroic, virtuous, and largely patriarchal social values. Justice, Prudence, Fortitude, and Temperance, for example, are values embodied by the female allegory of British history, Britannia, a Neoclassical figure derived from the Roman Minerva (Athena) and featured most prominently in Neoclassical design on Roman-inspired British coins. Classical Roman revival in Britain, which inspired the architecture and figurative program of Trafalgar Square, appealed to traditions of piety, austerity, and humility in British society, social ideals upheld still today across much of Britain's political landscape. *Alison Lapper Pregnant*, as a Neoclassical sculpture in the round, brings to life the corporeal reality of metaphysical, bodily allegories. Lapper's arch defiance of such long-standing conservative ideals, however, radiates from the sparkling surface of her body and tells "other" stories of British citizenship. She both conforms to and reforms stereotypes of disability, as well as of the British "public." Lapper's self-portrait photographs present additionally graphic portrayals of her particularized experiences, while co-opting the powers of infamous female beings. Britannia follows in the legacy of Minerva as the civic goddess and as a symbol of law-abiding chastity; as a reincarnation of these goddesses, Lapper gives birth to new histories of the square and the British nation, both by posing for the statue and by producing self-representations.

Lapper's role in the mediation of *Alison Lapper Pregnant* has brought a voice to its depiction of a pregnant amputee woman, as well as of a contemporary artist; Lapper's own work, which has experienced more attention, albeit slowly, contributes to significant dialogues and representations of disability in visual culture, both today and historically. Quinn's and Lapper's images cause the viewer to do a double-take and to perceive bodies on display in different lights and with frameworks outside of the strict conventions of social ideals. These artists call into question the integrity of Neoclassicism and other idealizing and/or disfiguring traditions for displaying the body in art, as well as in everyday life. These juxtapositions also emphasize the necessity of placing the works of disabled and non-disabled artists in dialogues with each other and with larger visual contexts, in order to see art through new eyes and from the perspective *of* disability. In collaboration, such dialogues can forge fresh, multidimensional images of disability in the public eye, and potentially, can sculpt new, liberating body ideals for the public.

NOTES

1. Alison Lapper (with Guy Feldman), *My Life in My Hands* (London: Simon & Schuster, 2005), 236.
2. For example, Bert Massie, the chairman of the commission, was quoted in *The Guardian* newspaper as stating: "Congratulations to Marc for realising that disabled bodies have a power and beauty rarely recognised in an age where youth and 'perfection' are idolised." This article also states that the Disability Rights Commission welcomed the statue as a source of pride and a blow against the cult of perfection that effectively disables bodies who don't conform to the norm. Others have suggested, like Lapper, that the work's depiction of a specific embodiment largely underrepresented in visual life, at least in a positive way, broadens and humanizes notions of beauty, as well as humanizes certain socially stigmatized individuals. For example, see: Adrian Searle, "Arresting, strange and beautiful," *The Guardian*, September 16, 2005.
3. Some of the better known artists of this style are the French painter Jacques-Louis David, as well as British painters Joshua Reynolds and Benjamin West, and the sculptors Antonio Canova and Bertel Thorvaldson. By reviving Classical figures, Neoclassical artists sought to portray eternal beauty and cultural idealism, in balanced, symmetrical, and "able," or extra-able bodies. In Classical traditions, on which Neoclassicism was based, figures were composed from the most idyllic features of different individuals and mathematically derived proportions in order to create a composite "whole" body ideal.
4. One the few works in *The Complete Marbles* that is not titled with the models' names, *Kiss*, 2002, refers specifically to Impressionist sculptor Auguste Rodin's canonical work *The Kiss*. Quinn's *Kiss* features two life-size amputees cast from live models, standing on one leg and leaning against one another

(rather than seated, as in Rodin's original), to embrace passionately. Quinn here showcases a disabled couple in an allegory of romantic love and as contemporary sexual beings, which challenges popular stereotypes of disability as sexually undesirable. *Kiss* and other works in *The Complete Marbles* series are portraits that call for re-visions of art history and social ideals.

5. Preece.

6. Waldemar Januszczak, "Matter of life and death—Art—Profile—Marc Quinn," *The Sunday Times*, December 10, 2000.

7. Quinn has a certain reputation as a "bad boy" among art critics, exacerbated by inclusion in the controversial exhibit of 1991, in which he debuted one of his most famous pieces, *Self* (1991), a self-portrait bust made from nine pints of Quinn's blood frozen. Some have connected *Alison Lapper Pregnant* with a longer interest in birth in Quinn's work, as exemplified by *Birth* or *Lucas* (2001), a frozen representation of his son Lucas's head made from real placenta, three days old. His work has many bodily and biological themes; has worked with DNA imaging (*DNA Garden* (2002), grid of 77 Petri dishes), test tubes, and silicon preservation. Examples of Quinn's other works that use body fluids and forms are: *Yellow Cut Nervous Breakdown*, *Invisible Man*, *No Invisible Means of Escape XI* (formed from cast white rubber resembling flesh), *The Great Escape* (a cast of his body inside pod), *Continuous Present* (2000) (which features a skull that rotates around a reflective cylinder), *Shit Paintings* and *Shit Head* (1997), *Incarnate* (a boiled sausage form with his blood), *Eternal Spring* I and II (1998) (a series featuring Calla lilies suspended in water), and *Garden* (2000) (a glass walled installation of flora and fauna that was deceptively composed of frozen units of silicon). As exemplified by these examples, Quinn's work has repeatedly used blood, placenta, excrement, ice, and flowers. He chooses materials because of their corporeality and symbolic connotations.

8. Kim Q. Hall, "Pregnancy, Disability and Gendered Embodiment: Rethinking Alison Lapper Pregnant," lecture delivered at the Society for Disability Studies Conference, Bethesda, MD, June 17, 2006.

9. Januszczak.

10. Charles L. Griswold, "The Vietnam Veterans Memorial and the Washington Mall: Philosophical Thoughts on Political Iconography," in *Critical Issues in Public Art: Content, Context, and Controversy*, Harriet F. Seine and Sally Webster, eds., 71–100 (Washington, DC: Smithsonian Institute Press, 1992), 74.

11. Parliament Square is a center of tourist and civil exchange. It sits on a tourist path from the Houses of Parliament and Westminster Abby and at the top of Pall Mall, which leads to Buckingham Palace. The National Gallery, the Admiralty, and St. Martin-in-the Fields church are also on the square.

12. Alice Thomson of the *Daily Telegraph* was quoted in Cederwell.

13. Lapper, 236.

14. Lapper, 234.

15. Miles.

16. At the south end of the square is an equestrian statue of Charles I in a conventional pose suggesting royalty and conquest, which is based on a famous Roman statue of Marcus Aurelius and was also the favored position of Louis XV and Napoleon to emphasize their military strength and leadership (for example in David's triumphant, Neoclassical portrait *Napoleon Crossing the Alps* (1801), which served as Imperial propaganda). On either side of Nelson's Column are the bronze statues of Sir Henry Havelock and Sir Charles James Napier, and fronting the north wall of Trafalgar Square are busts of Generals Beatty, Jellicoe, and Cunningham, all famous military leaders. All of the "heroes" are significantly honored for their participation in the colonization of India, Egypt, and the Caribbean, and were known as brutal leaders of mutinous soldiers, who were often of the nationality of the countries they fought to dominate.

17. This opinion was expressed, for example, in the following newspaper quote: "Roy Hattersley, in the *Daily Mail*, agreed that while the sculpture was 'a celebration of both courage and motherhood', it was nevertheless 'the wrong statue in the wrong place.' The Trafalgar Square plinth is crying out for 'individual examples of national achievement and British greatness,' he said. Hattersley drew up his own shortlist of likely greats, including Shakespeare, Milton, Elgar, Newton and Wren. 'Most of us will share the view that Lapper is someone to admire . . . but the simple truth is that Trafalgar Square is meant for something else.'" Quoted from Cederwell.

18. Jeanette Hart, Letter to the editor, *The Guardian*, September 21, 2005.

19. Paul Usherwood, "The Battle of Trafalgar Square," *Art Monthly* 2, no. 4 (2004), 43.

20. Rodney Mace, *Trafalgar Square: Emblem of Empire* (Southampton, UK: Camelot Press, 1976).

21. For more on Gil, see Ann Millett-Gallant, "Little Displays: The Photography of Ricardo Gil," *Review of Disability Studies: An International Journal* 2, v.4 (2009).

SELECTED BIBLIOGRAPHY

Cederwell, William. "What they said about … the fourth plinth," *The Guardian*, March 18, 2004. Fourth Plinth Project website: www.fourthplinth.co.uk/

Gisbourne, Mark. "The Self and Others" in *Contemporary (U.K.)* no. 2 (February, 2002): 52–7.

Hall, Kim Q. "Pregnancy, Disability and Gendered Embodiment: Rethinking Alison Lapper Pregnant," lecture delivered at the Society for Disability Studies Conference, Bethesda, MD, June 17, 2006.

Hutchinson, Ray, ed. *Constructions of Urban Space*. Stamford, CT: Jai Press, 2000.

Januszczak, Waldemar. "Matter of life and death—Art—Profile—Marc Quinn," *The Sunday Times*, December 10, 2000.

Jones, Jonathan. "Bold, graphic, subversive—but bad art," *The Guardian*, March 16, 2004.

Kemp, M. and M. Wallace. *Spectacular Bodies: The Art and Science of the Human Body from Leonardo to Now*. London, Hayward Gallery; Los Angeles: University of California Press, 2000.

Kennedy, Maev. "Pregnant and proud: Statue of artist wins place in Trafalgar Square," *The Guardian*, March 16, 2004.

Lacy, Suzanne, ed. *Mapping the Terrain: New Genre Public Art*. Seattle: Bay Press, 1995.

Lapper, Alison. *My Life in My Hands*. London: Simon & Schuster, 2005.

Mace, Rodney. *Trafalgar Square: Emblem of Empire*. Southampton, UK: Camelot Press, 1976.

Miles, Malcolm. *Art, Space, and the City: Public Art and Urban Futures*. London: Routledge, 1997.

Mitchell, David T. and Snyder, Sharon L. *Narrative Prosthesis: Disability and the Dependencies of Discourse*. Ann Arbor: University of Michigan Press, 2000.

Preece, Robert. "Just a Load of Shock? An Interview with Marc Quinn," *Sculpture* 19, no. 8 (2000): 14–19.

Seine, H. F. and Webster, S., eds. *Critical Issues in Public Art: Content, Context, and Controversy*. Washington, DC: Smithsonian Institute Press, 1992.

Selwood, Sara. *The Benefits of Public Art: The Polemics of Public Places*. Poole, UK: Policy Studies Institute Publications, 1995.

Usherwood, Paul. "The Battle of Trafalgar Square," *Art Monthly* 2, no. 4 (2004): 43.

Warner, Marina. *Monuments and Maidens: The Allegory of the Female Form*. New York: Atheneum, 1985.

CHAPTER 31

Blindness and Visual Culture:
An Eyewitness Account

Georgina Kleege

SUMMARY

Blind figures have often served as props for theories of consciousness or for highlighting the importance of metaphorical sight. By confronting appearances of the "Hypothetical Blind Man" in philosophy and visual studies, Georgina Kleege makes the case that when blindness is made into a conceptual device, it overlooks the reality of blind experience.

For example, blind musician Ray Charles was asked whether he was relieved to have not "seen" the terrorist attacks on September 11, 2001. Kleege points out that for most people the images of the attacks, rather than the events themselves, provoke emotional responses, but this doesn't justify the belief that blind people would be immune to the significance of the historical events. In this way, the Hypothetical Blind Man (the version of blind experience imagined by sighted people) would be detached or indifferent to the nation's collective grief. The use of hypothetical blindness has long been used to inaccurately describe inattention, ignorance, or prejudice—none of which define the lived experience of blindness.

Several works by blind authors, including Helen Keller, attempt to loosen the grip that the Hypothetical Blind Man holds on sighted people's imaginations. And as a debate between a blind philosopher and his sighted colleague shows, there is a possibility of representing blindness as something besides the absence of sight. Kleege thus calls for an interrogation of the binary opposition between blindness and sight, instead conceptualizing a spectrum of variation in visual acuity.

In April 2004, I was invited to speak at a conference on visual culture at the University of California, Berkeley. Speakers were asked to respond to an essay by W. J. T. Mitchell titled, "Showing Seeing: A Critique of Visual Culture," which offers a series of definitions of the emergent field of visual studies, distinguishing it from the more established disciplines of art history, aesthetics, and media studies. As an admitted outsider to the field of visual studies, I chose to comment on the following statement:

"Visual culture entails a meditation on blindness, the invisible, the unseen, the unseeable, and the overlooked" (Mitchell, 2002: 170). In my last book, *Sight Unseen*, I attempted to show blindness through my own experience, and a survey of representations of blindness in literature and film. At the same time, I wanted to show seeing, to sketch my understanding of vision, drawn from a lifetime of living among the sighted in this visual culture we share. I started from the premise that the average blind person knows more about what it means to be sighted than the average sighted person knows about what it means to be blind. The blind grow up, attend school, and lead adult lives among sighted people. The language we speak, the literature we read, the architecture we inhabit, were all designed by and for the sighted.

If visual studies entails a meditation on blindness, it is my hope that it will avoid some of the missteps of similar meditations of the past. Specifically, I hope that visual studies can abandon one of the stock characters of the western philosophical tradition—"the Hypothetical Blind Man" (Gitter, 2001: 58). The Hypothetical Blind Man—or the Hypothetical as I will call him for the sake of brevity—has long played a useful, though thankless, role as a prop for theories of consciousness. He is the patient subject of endless thought experiments where the experience of the world through four senses can be compared to the experience of the world through five. He is asked to describe his understanding of specific visual phenomena—perspective, reflection, refraction, color, form recognition—as well as visual aids and enhancements— mirrors, lenses, telescopes, microscopes. He is understood to lead a hermit-like existence, so far at the margins of his society, that he has never heard this visual terminology before the philosophers bring it up. Part of the emotional baggage he hauls around with him comes from other cultural representations of blindness, such as Oedipus and the many Biblical figures whose sight is withdrawn by the wrathful God of the Old Testament or restored by the redeemer of the New. His primary function is to highlight the importance of sight and to elicit a frisson of awe and pity which promotes gratitude among the sighted theorists for the vision they possess.

I will not attempt to survey every appearance of the Hypothetical throughout the history of philosophy. It is enough to cite a few of his more memorable performances, and then to suggest what happens when he is brought face to face with actual blind people through their own first-hand, eye-witness accounts. Professor Mitchell alludes to the passages in Descartes' *La Dioptrique* where he compares vision to the Hypothetical's use of sticks to grope his way through space. Descartes' references to the Hypothetical are confusing and are often conflated by his readers. In one instance, he compares the way the Hypothetical's stick detects the density and resistance of objects in his path, to the way light acts on objects the eye looks at. In a later passage, Descartes performs a thought experiment, giving the Hypothetical a second stick which he could use to judge the distance between two objects by calculating the angle formed when he touches each object with one of the sticks. Descartes does not explain how the Hypothetical is supposed to make this calculation or how he can avoid running into things while doing so. I doubt that Descartes actually believed that any blind person ever used two sticks in this way. In fact, the image that illustrates his discussion shows the Hypothetical's dog sound asleep on the ground, indicating that the Hypothetical is going nowhere. Even so, Descartes' description of the way a blind person uses one stick reflects a basic misunderstanding. He imagines that the blind use the stick to construct a mental image, or its equivalent, of their surroundings, mapping the location of specifically identified objects. In fact, then as now, a stick or cane is a poor tool for this kind of mental imaging. The stick serves merely to announce the presence of an obstacle, not to determine if it is a rock or a tree root, though there are sound cues—a tap versus a thud—that might help make this distinction. In many situations, the cane is more of an auditory than a tactile tool. It seems that in Descartes' desire to describe vision as an extension of or hypersensitive form of touch, he recreates the blind man in his own image, where the eye must correspond to the hand extended by one or perhaps two sticks.

The most detailed depiction of the Hypothetical came about in 1693, when William Molyneux wrote his famous letter to John Locke. He proposed a thought experiment where a blind man who had learned to recognize geometric forms such as a cube and a sphere by touch, would have his sight restored through an operation. Would he be able to distinguish the two forms merely by looking at them? The Molyneux question continues to be debated today, even though the history of medicine is full of case studies of actual blind people who have had their sight restored by actual operations. Apparently, Molyneux was married to a blind woman, which has always led me to wonder why he did not pose his hypothetical question about her. Perhaps he knew that others would object that marriage to a philosopher might contaminate the experimental data. There was a risk that the philosopher might prime her answers or otherwise rig the results. Certainly in commentary on actual cases of restored sight, debaters of the Molyneux question are quick to disqualify those who were allowed to cast their eyes upon, for instance the faces of loved ones, before directing their gaze at the sphere and the cube.

Denis Diderot's 1749 "Letter on the Blind for the Use of Those Who See" is generally credited with urging a more enlightened, and humane attitude toward the blind. His blind man of Puiseaux and Nicholas Saunderson, the English mathematician, were both real rather than hypothetical blind men. As he introduces the man from Puiseaux, Diderot is at pains to supply details of his family history and early life to persuade his reader that this is a real person. Significantly the man from Puiseaux is first encountered helping his young son with his studies,

demonstrating both that he is a loving family man, and capable of intellectual activity. But the questions Diderot poses generally fall under the purview of the Hypothetical. Certainly, many of his remarks help support Descartes' theory relating vision to touch:

> One of our company thought to ask our blind man if he would like to have eyes. "If it were not for curiosity," he replied, "I would just as soon have long arms: it seems to me my hands would tell me more of what goes on in the moon than your eyes or your telescopes."
>
> (Diderot, 1999: 153)

Diderot praises the blind man's ability to make philosophical surmises about vision, but does not have a high opinion of blind people's capacity for empathy:

> As of all the external signs which raise our pity and ideas of pain the blind are affected only by cries, I have in general no high thought of their humanity. What difference is there to a blind man between a man making water and one bleeding in silence?
>
> (Diderot, 1999: 156)

The phrasing of the question here suggests an afterthought. I imagine Diderot, at his table, conjuring up two men, one pissing, one bleeding. While his visual imagination is practiced in making these sorts of mental images he is less adept at tuning his mind's ear. He recognizes that for the blood to be spilt at a rate sufficient to create the same sound as the flowing urine, the bleeding man would normally cry out in pain. So he imagines, in effect, a bleeding mute. But he fails to take into account the relative viscosity, not to mention the different odors, of the two fluids. But Diderot cannot think of everything.

Now I imagine a blind man wandering onto the scene. My blind man is not quite the one Diderot imagines. For one thing he is a bit preoccupied; the philosophers have dropped by again. They talk at him and over his head, bandying about names that are now familiar to him: Locke, Molyneux, Descartes. They question him about his ability to conceptualize various things: windows, mirrors, telescopes—and he responds with the quaint and winsome answers he knows they have come for. Anything to get rid of them. Distracted as he is, the sound of the bleeding mute's plashing blood registers on his consciousness. Lacking Diderot's imagination, however, the thought does not occur to him that this sound emanates from a bleeding mute. His reason opts instead for the explanation that the sound comes from some man relieving his bladder—a far more commonplace phenomenon, especially in the mean streets where the blind man resides. It is not that the blind man has no fellow feeling for the mute. Come to think of it, the mute would make a good companion. He could act as a guide and keep an eye out for marauding philosophers, while the blind man could do all the talking. But the blind man does not have enough information to recognize the mute's dilemma. The only hope for the bleeding mute is to find some way to attract the blind man's attention, perhaps by throwing something. But surely, such a massive loss of blood must have affected his aim. While the blind man, living as he does at the margins of his society, is accustomed to being spurned by local homeowners and merchants who find his presence unsightly, and so might flee the bleeding mute's missiles without suspecting that his aid is being solicited.

The blind man quickens his pace as best he can. The mute succumbs at last to his mortal wound. And the philosopher shifts to another topic.

I am wrong to make fun of Diderot, since his treatment of blindness was at once far more complex and far more compassionate than that of other philosophers. And it is not as if his low opinion of the blind's ability to empathize with others' pain has ceased to contribute to attitudes about blindness. Consider this anecdote from recent history. Some weeks after September 11, 2001, the blind musician Ray Charles was interviewed about his rendition of "America the Beautiful," which received a good deal of air time during the period of heightened patriotism that followed that event. The interviewer, Jim Gray, commented that Charles should consider himself lucky that his blindness prevented him from viewing the images of the World Trade Center's collapse, and the Pentagon in flames: "Was this maybe one time in your life where not having the ability to see was a relief?" Like Diderot, the interviewer assumed that true horror can only be evinced through the eyes. Many eyewitness accounts of the event however, were strikingly nonvisual. Many people who were in the vicinity of Ground Zero during and soon after the disaster found it hard to put what they saw into words, in part because visibility in the area was obscured by smoke and ash, and in part because what they were seeing did not correspond to any visual experience for which they had language. People described instead the sound of falling bodies hitting the ground, the smell of the burning jet fuel, and the particular texture of the ankle deep dust that filled the streets. But for the majority of television viewers, eye-witnesses from a distance, those events are recalled as images, indelible, powerful and eloquent. To many, like the reporter interviewing Ray Charles, it is the images rather than the mere fact of the events that produce the emotional response. The assumption seems to be that because the blind are immune to images they must also be immune to the significance of the events, and therefore must be somehow detached from or indifferent to the nation's collective horror and grief.

It is fortunate for anyone interested in dismantling the image of blindness fostered by the Hypothetical Blind Man, that we have today a great many first-hand accounts of blindness. In recent decades, memoirs, essays, and other texts by actual blind people attempt to loosen the grip the Hypothetical still seems to hold on the sighted imagination. Thanks to work by disability historians, we are also beginning to have older accounts of blindness drawn from archives of institutions and schools for the blind around the world. One such account is a text written in 1825, by a 22-year-old blind French woman named Thérèse-Adèle Husson. Born in Nancy into a petit bourgeois household, Husson became blind at nine months following a bout of smallpox. Her case attracted the attention of the local gentry who sponsored a convent education for her, and encouraged her to cultivate her interests in literature and music. At the age of 20 she left home for Paris where she hoped to pursue a literary career. Her first text, "Reflections on the Moral and Physical Condition of the Blind" seems to have been written as a part of her petition for aid from the Hôpital des Quinze-Vingts, an institution that provided shelter and financial support to the indigent blind of Paris. For the most part, her text follows the example of comportment and educational manuals of the time, offering advice to parents and caretakers on the correct way to raise a blind child, and to young blind people themselves on their role in society. It is by turns formulaically obsequious and radically assertive, since she writes from the premise—revolutionary for the time— that her first-hand experience of blindness gives her a level of expertise that equals or surpasses that of the institution's sighted administrators. While it is unlikely that Husson's convent education would have exposed her to the work of Descartes or Diderot, she considers some of the same questions previously posed to the Hypothetical. It is possible that the provincial

aristocrats, who took up her education, may have engaged in amateurish philosophizing in her presence. For instance, like Diderot's blind man of Puiseaux, she prefers her sense of touch to the sight she lacks. She recounts how, at the time of her first communion, her mother promised her a dress made of chiffon, then, either as a joke or in an attempt to economize, purchased cheaper percale instead. When the young Husson easily detected the difference through touch, her mother persisted in her deception, and even brought in neighbor women to corroborate. Whether playing along with the joke, or as a genuine rebuke of her mother's attempt to deceive her, Husson retorted:

> I prefer my touch to your eyes, because it allows me to appreciate things for what they really are, whereas it seems to me that your sight fools you now and then, for this is percale and not chiffon.
>
> (Husson, 2001: 25)

In a later discussion of her ability to recognize household objects through touch, her impatience seems out of proportion, unless we imagine that she frequently found herself the object of philosophical speculation by literal-minded practitioners:

> We know full well that a chest of drawers is square, but more long than tall. Again I hear my readers ask what is a square object! I am accommodating enough to satisfy all their questions. Therefore, I would say to them that it is easy enough to know the difference between objects by touching them, for not all of them have the same shape. For example, a dinner plate, a dish, a glass can't begin to be compared with a chest of drawers, for the first two are round, while the other is hollow; but people will probably point out that it is only after having heard the names of the articles that I designate that it became possible for me to acquire the certainty that they were hollow, round, square. I will admit that they are right, but tell me, you with the eyes of

Argus, if you had never heard objects described, would you be in any better position to speak of them than I?

(Husson, 2001: 41)

Her emphasis on square versus round objects as well as her tone and her taunt, "You with the eyes of Argus," suggests an irritation that may come from hearing the Molyneux question one too many times. She is also arguing against the notion that such words as "square" and "round" designate solely visual phenomena, to which the blind have no access and therefore no right to use these words.

Almost a century later, Helen Keller gives vent to a similar irritation at literal-minded readers. In her 1908 book, *The World I Live In*, she gives a detailed phenomenological account of her daily experience of deaf-blindness. Early on, she footnotes her use of the verb "see" in the phrase, "I was taken to see a woman":

> The excellent proof-reader has put a query to my use of the word "see." If I had said "visit," he would have asked no questions, yet what does "visit" mean but "see" (*visitare*)? Later I will try to defend myself for using as much of the English language as I have succeeded in learning.
>
> (Keller, 2003: 19)

Keller makes good use of her Radcliffe education to show that the more one knows about language the harder it is to find vocabulary that does not have some root in sighted or hearing experience. But, she argues, to deny her the use of seeing-hearing vocabulary would be to deny her the ability to communicate at all.

In their 1995 book, *On Blindness*, two philosophers, one sighted and one blind, conduct an epistolary debate that might seem to put to rest all the old hypothetical questions. Unfortunately, Martin Milligan, the blind philosopher, died before the discussion was fully underway. If he had lived, we can assume not only that he and his sighted colleague, Bryan Magee, would have gotten further with their debate, but also that they would have edited some testy quibbles about which terms to use and which translation of Aristotle is more accurate. Milligan, who worked primarily in moral and political philosophy, and was an activist in blind causes in the United Kingdom, forthrightly resists the impulse to allow the discussion to stray far from the practical and social conditions that affect the lives of real blind people. For instance, he cites an incident from his early life, before he found an academic post, when he was turned down for a job as a telephone typist on a newspaper because the employer assumed that he would not be able to negotiate the stairs in the building. He identifies this as one of thousands of examples of the exaggerated value sighted people place on vision. Any thinking person has to recognize that sight is not required to climb or descend stairs. He asserts that the value of sight would be that it would allow him to move around unfamiliar places with greater ease. He concedes that vision might afford him some aesthetic pleasure while viewing a landscape or painting, but insists that he can know what he wants to know about the visible world from verbal descriptions, and that this knowledge is adequate for his needs, and only minimally different from the knowledge of sighted people. He accuses Magee of voicing "visionist"—or what I might call "sightist"—attitudes that the differences between the sighted and the blind must be almost incomprehensibly vast, and that vision is a fundamental aspect of human existence. Milligan says that these statements seem

> to express the passion, the zeal of a missionary preaching to the heathen in outer darkness. Only, of course, your "gospel" isn't "good" news to us heathens, for the message seems to be that ours is a "darkness" from

which we can never come in—not the darkness of course that sighted people can know, but the darkness of never being able to know *that* darkness, or of bridging the vast gulf that separates us from those who do.

(Magee and Milligan, 1995: 46)

This prompts Magee to cite his own early work on race and homosexuality, as proof of his credentials as a liberal humanist. He also speculates, somewhat sulkily, about whether the first 18 months of Milligan's life when his vision was presumed to be normal, might disqualify him as a spokesman for the blind, since he might retain some vestige of a visual memory from that period. Later, Magee consults with a neurologist who assures him that the loss of sight at such an early age would make Milligan's brain indistinguishable from that of a person born blind. And so the discussion continues.

Along the way, Magee makes some claims about sight that seem to me to be far from universal. For instance, he states that:

By the sighted, seeing is felt as a *need*. And it is the feeding of this almost ungovernable craving that constitutes the ongoing pleasure of sight. It is as if we were desperately hungry all the time, in such a way that only if we were eating all the time could we be content—so we eat all the time.

(Magee and Milligan, 1995: 104)

Magee asserts that when sighted people are obliged to keep their eyes closed even for a short time, it induces a kind of panic. To illustrate his point, he notes that a common method of mistreating prisoners is to keep them blindfolded, and this mistreatment can lead them to feel anxious and disoriented. I suspect that his example is influenced by traditional metaphors that equate blindness with a tomb-like imprisonment. Surely a blind prisoner, accustomed to the privation of sight, might still

have similar feelings of anxiety and disorientation, due to the threat, whether stated or implied, of pending bodily harm.

To his credit, Magee does allow that some blind experiences are shared by the sighted. Milligan describes how many blind people negotiate new environments, and can feel the presence of large objects even without touching them as "atmosphere-thickening occupants of space." Magee reports that when he

was a small child I had a vivid non-visual awareness of the nearness of material objects. I would walk confidently along a pitch black corridor in a strange house and stop dead a few inches short of a closed door, and then put out my hand to grope for the knob. If I woke up in the dark in a strange bedroom and wanted to get to a light-switch on the opposite side of the room I could usually circumnavigate the furniture in between, because I could "feel" where the larger objects in the room were. I might knock small things over, but would almost invariably "feel" the big ones. I say "feel" because the sensation, which I can clearly recall, was as of a feeling-in-the-air with my whole bodily self. Your phrase "atmosphere-thickening occupants of space" describes the apprehension exactly. I suddenly "felt" a certain thickness in the air at a certain point relative to myself in the blackness surrounding me. ... This illustrates your point that the blind develop potentialities that the sighted have also been endowed with but do not develop because they have less need of them.

(Magee and Milligan, 1995: 97–8)

Here, and in a few other places in the correspondence, Magee and Milligan seem to be moving in a new direction. It is not merely that they discover a shared perceptual experience, but one that is not easy to categorize as belonging to one of the five traditional senses. Here, a "feeling" is not the experience of texture or form through physical contact, but an apprehension, of an atmospheric change, experienced kinesthetically, and by the body as a whole. This seems to point toward a need for a theory of multiple senses where each of the traditional five could be subdivided into a number of discrete sensory activities, which function sometimes in concert with and sometimes in counterpoint to others. Helen Keller identified at least three different aspects of touch that she found meaningful: texture, temperature, and vibration. In fact, she understands sound as vibrations that the hearing feel in their ears while the deaf can feel them through other parts of their bodies. Thus she could feel thunder by pressing the palm of her hand against a windowpane, or someone's footsteps by pressing the soles of her feet against floorboards.

What these blind authors have in common is an urgent desire to represent their experiences of blindness as something besides the absence of sight. Unlike the Hypothetical, they do not feel themselves to be deficient or partial—sighted people minus sight—but whole human beings who have learned to attend to their nonvisual senses in different ways. I have deliberately chosen to limit my discussion here to works by people who became blind very early in life. One of the most striking features of the Hypothetical Blind Man is that he is always assumed to be both totally and congenitally blind. Real blindness, today as in the past, rarely fits this profile. Only about 10–20 percent of people designated as legally blind, in countries where there is such a designation, are without any visual perception at all. It is hard to come by statistics on people who are born totally blind, in part because it only becomes an issue when the child, or her parents, seek services for the blind, which tends to occur only when the child reaches school age. We can assume that more infants were born blind in the past, since some of the most prevalent causes of infantile blindness have been eliminated by medical innovations in the nineteenth and twentieth centuries. Nevertheless, in the past, as now, the leading causes of blindness occur later in life, and often leave some residual vision. Some may retain the ability to distinguish light from darkness, while others may continue to perceive light, color, form, and movement to some degree. Some people may retain the acuity to read print or facial expressions, while lacking the peripheral vision that facilitates free movement through space. And regardless of the degree or quality of residual vision, blind people differ widely in the ways they attend to, use, or value these perceptions.

Although the situation of the Hypothetical is rare, his defenders are quick to discount anyone with any residual sight or with even the remotest possibility of a visual memory. In traditional discussions of blindness, only total, congenital blindness will do. In a review of my book *Sight Unseen*, Arthur Danto asserted that I had too much sight to claim to be blind (Danto, 1999: 35. He quoted a totally blind graduate student he once knew who said that he could not conceptualize a window, and that he was surprised when he learned that when a person's face is said to glow, it does not in fact emit light like an incandescent light bulb. Danto does not tell us what became of this student or even give his name, using him only as a modern-day version of the Hypothetical. Then he goes on to relate the history of the Molyneux question.

If only the totally blind can speak of blindness with authority, should we make the same restriction on those who talk about vision? Is there such a thing as total vision? We know that a visual acuity of 20/20 is merely average vision. There are individuals whose acuity measures better than 20/20, 20/15 or even 20/10. Such individuals can read every line of the familiar Snellan eye chart, or, as in the case of Ted Williams, can read the print on a baseball whizzing toward their bat at a speed close to 90 miles per hour. How many scholars of visual culture, I wonder but won't ask, can claim such a level of visual acuity?

What visual studies can bring to these discussions is an interrogation of the binary opposition between blindness and sight. It is clearly more useful to think in terms of a spectrum of variation in visual acuity, as well as a spectrum of variation in terms of visual awareness or skill. The visual studies scholar, highly skilled in understanding images, who loses some or even all her sight, will not lose the ability to analyze images and to communicate her observations. In his essay, "Showing Seeing," W. J. T. Mitchell describes a classroom exercise where students display or perform some feature of visual culture as if to an audience that has no experience of visual culture. The exercise assumes that some students will be better at the task, while others might improve their performance with practice, and in all cases their aptitude would have little, if anything, to do with their visual acuity. The skill, as I understand it, is in the telling as much as it is in the seeing—the ability to translate images in all their complexity and resonance into words.

And as we move beyond the simple blindness versus sight binary, I hope we can also abandon the clichés that use the word "blindness" as a synonym for inattention, ignorance, or prejudice. If the goal is for others to see what we mean it helps to say what we mean. Using the word in this way seems a vestigial homage to the Hypothetical, meant to stir the same uncanny frisson of awe and pity. It contributes on some level to the perception of blindness as a tragedy too dire to contemplate, which contributes in turn to lowered expectations among those who educate and employ the blind. It also contributes to the perception among the newly blind themselves that the only response to their new condition is to retire from view.

I will leave you with a futuristic image of blindness. In Deborah Kendrick's story, "20/20 with a Twist," Mary Seymour, chief administrator of the department of visual equality, looks back on her life from the year 2020. In this blind Utopia, the major handicaps of blindness have been eliminated; private automobiles were phased out a decade earlier and technologies to convert print to Braille or voice had become ubiquitous and transparent. Of course, Mary reflects, it was not always like this. Back in the dark ages of the 1980s and 1990s, Braille proficiency had ceased to be a requirement for teachers of blind children, Braille production facilities and radio reading services were shut down, and blind children were no longer being educated at all. Mary and other blind people who had grown up in an earlier, slightly more enlightened period, banded together to lead a nonviolent, visionary rebellion to bring down the oppressive regime. They tampered with the power supply—since darkness is no impediment to blind activity—scrambled computer transmissions, and disrupted television broadcasts. All across the country, television screens went blank while the audio continued, interrupted periodically by the revolutionary message: "You, too, can function without pictures."

The rebel leaders were captured, however, and forced to undergo implantation of optic sensors, which, the captors reasoned, would transform them into sighted people who would see the error of their ways and abandon the cause. But the rebels persisted. The power supply was shut down completely. The government fell, and the captured leaders were liberated in triumph.

Significantly, the optic sensors did not transform the revolutionary leaders into sighted people. Rather, each acquired only a facet of visual experience. One gained the ability to perceive color. Another developed a sort of telepathic vision, allowing him to form images of places at great distances.

Mary's sensor gave her a kind of literal hindsight, making her able to create a detailed mental picture of a room, only after she had left it. These bits and pieces of vision serve as a badge of the former rebels' heroic past, and allow them to perform entertaining parlor tricks, but are otherwise easy to disregard.

This is a far cry from the Hypothetical. In Deborah Kendrick's image of the future, blindness is a simple physical characteristic rather than an ominous mark of otherness. If the Hypothetical Blind Man once helped thinkers form ideas about human consciousness surely his day is done. He does too much damage hanging around. It is time to let him go. Rest in peace.

REFERENCES

Charles, Ray. Interview. *The Today Show*. NBC Television, October 4, 2001.

Danto, Arthur. (1999) "Blindness and Sight." *The New Republic* 220.16: 34–36.

Diderot, Denis. (1999) *Thoughts on the Interpretation of Nature and Other Philosophical Works*. David Adams (ed.). Manchester: Clinaman Press.

Gitter, Elisabeth. (2001) *The Imprisoned Guest: Samuel Howe and Laura Bridgman, the Original Deaf-Blind Girl*. New York: Farrar, Straus and Giroux.

Husson, Thérèse-Adèle. (2001) *Reflections: The Life and Writing of a Young Blind Woman in Post-Revolutionary France*. Catherine J. Kudlick and Zina Weygand (eds). New York: New York University Press.

Keller, Helen. (2003) *The World I Live In*. Roger Shattuck (ed.). New York: New York Review Books.

Kendrick, Deborah. (1987) "20/20 with a Twist," in Marsha Saxton and Florence Howe (eds) *With Wings: An Anthology of Literature by and about Women with Disabilities*. New York: Feminist Press at the City University of New York.

Magee, Bryan and Milligan, Martin. (1995) *On Blindness*. Oxford: Oxford University Press.

Mitchell, W. J. T. (2002) "Showing Seeing: A Critique of Visual Culture." *Journal of Visual Culture* 1.2: 165–181.

CHAPTER 32

Disability, Life Narrative, and Representation

G. Thomas Couser

SUMMARY

Before the advent of Disability Studies, disabled identity often escaped theoretical scrutiny, even when it was over-represented in the cultural mainstream. Historically, the representation of disability has functioned at the expense of disabled people, but contemporary memoirists and autobiographers are increasingly taking control of their own life narratives. In this essay, G. Thomas Couser suggests that the recent proliferation of books by disabled writers is significant because it is a cultural manifestation of the disability rights movement. Disability autobiography should be seen as a response to the traditional misrepresentation of disability.

Before World War II, there was very little autobiographical writing by disabled authors, but the return of injured soldiers and the polio epidemic spurred production of life-narratives in the postwar period. Since then, HIV/AIDS, breast cancer, and autism have all been written about at an increasing rate, and a wide variety of conditions from ALS to Down syndrome became relatively common subjects at the end of the twentieth century.

Scholars must work to define the political and ethical meaning of these texts. Couser points out that bodily variations often become a reason for storytelling in everyday interactions. Disabled people are regularly called upon to account for their differences, and in many cases these accounts are expected to conform to preconceived notions of the public. Culture inscribes narratives on the bodies of disabled people, and so disabled autobiographers often begin from a position of marginalization and pre-inscription. But autobiography allows writers the chance for self-representation from within their experience to "counter their historical subjection by occupying the subject position." Thus disabled autobiographers speak both *for* and *about* disability.

Disability is an inescapable element of human existence and experience. Although it is as fundamental an aspect of human diversity as race, ethnicity, gender, and sexuality, it is rarely acknowledged as such. This is odd, because in practice disability often trumps other minority statuses. That is, for people who differ from the hegemonic identity in more than one way, certain impairments—such as blindness or deafness—may function as their primary defining characteristic, their "master status." In this sense, disability may be *more* fundamental than racial, ethnic, and gender distinctions. Yet until the recent advent of Disability Studies, it escaped the critical scrutiny, theoretical analysis, and recognition accorded other forms of human variation.

At the same time, disability has had a remarkably high profile in both high and popular culture, both of which are pervaded with images of disability. Unlike other marginalized groups, then, disabled people have been *hyper*-represented in mainstream culture; they have not been disregarded so much as they have been subjected to objectifying notice in the form of mediated staring. To use an economic metaphor that is a literal truth, disability has been an extremely valuable cultural commodity for thousands of years. The cultural representation of disability has functioned at the expense of disabled people, however, in part because they have rarely controlled their own images. In the last several decades, however, this situation has begun to change, most notably in life writing, especially autobiography: in late twentieth century life writing, disabled people have initiated and controlled their own narratives in unprecedented ways and to an extraordinary degree.

Indeed, one of the most significant developments—if not *the* most significant development—in life writing in North America over the last three decades has been the proliferation of book-length accounts (from both first- and third-person points of view) of living with illness and disability. Whereas in the 1970s it was difficult to find *any* representation of most disabling conditions in life writing, today one can find *multiple* representations of many conditions. Equally significant, and more remarkable, one can find *autobiographical* accounts of conditions that would seem to preclude first-person testimony altogether—for example, autism, locked-in syndrome, and early Alzheimer's disease.

A comprehensive history of disability life writing has yet to be written, but it is safe to say that there was not much in the way of published autobiographical literature before World War II. War both produces and valorizes certain forms of disability; not surprisingly, then, disabled veterans produced a substantial number of narratives after the war. Polio generated even more narratives; indeed, polio may be the first disability to have engendered its own substantial autobiographical literature

(Wilson). In the 1980s and 1990s, HIV/AIDS and breast cancer provoked significant numbers of narratives; many of these challenge cultural scripts of the conditions (such as that AIDS is an automatic death sentence or that breast cancer negates a woman's sexuality [Couser]). A dramatic example of the generation of autobiographical literature devoted to a particular condition is the advent of autobiographies by people with autism (sometimes referred to as "autiebiographies"). Before 1985 these were virtually nonexistent; since 1985, nearly 100 have been produced. (This number does not include the many narratives written by parents of autistic children.) Thus, one major post-World War II cultural phenomenon was the generation of large numbers of narratives about a small number of conditions.

A complementary phenomenon has been the production of small numbers of narratives about a large number of conditions, some quite rare and some only recently recognized. Among these conditions are ALS (also known as Lou Gehrig's disease), Alzheimer's, aphasia, Asperger's syndrome, asthma, cerebral palsy, chronic fatigue syndrome, cystic fibrosis, diabetes, disfigurement, Down syndrome, epilepsy, locked-in syndrome, multiple sclerosis, obesity, obsessive-compulsive disorder, stuttering, stroke, and Tourette syndrome. As the twentieth century drew to a close, then, many disabilities came out of the closet into the living room of life writing.

Like life writing by other marginalized groups—women, African Americans, and gays and lesbians—life writing by disabled people is a cultural manifestation of a human rights movement; significantly, the rise in personal narratives of disability has roughly coincided with the disability rights movement, whose major legal manifestation in the U.S. is the Americans with Disabilities Act, which was passed in 1990 (but which, some would argue, has never been fully implemented). The first flowering of disability autobiography is also part of a disability renaissance involving other arts and media. Disability autobiography should be seen, then, not as spontaneous "self-expression" but as a response—indeed a retort—to the traditional misrepresentation of disability in Western culture generally.

This rich body of narrative can be approached in a number of ways. One way of getting at the relation between somatic variation and life narrative is through an everyday phenomenon: the way deviations from bodily norms often provoke a demand for explanatory narrative in everyday life. Whereas the unmarked case—the "normal" body—can pass without narration, the marked case—the scar, the limp, the missing limb, or the obvious prosthesis—calls for a story. Entering new situations, or reentering familiar ones, people with anomalous bodies are often called upon to account for them, sometimes quite explicitly: they may be asked, "What happened to *you*?" Or, worse, they may be addressed as if their stories are already known. Evidence of this is necessarily anecdotal. Let one compelling example suffice: Harriet McBryde Johnson, a Charleston lawyer and disability rights advocate who has a congenital muscle-wasting disease, reports remarks made by strangers she encounters on the street as she drives her power chair to the office:

> "I admire you for being out: most people
>   would give up."
> "God bless you! I'll pray for you."
> "You don't let the pain hold you back, do
>   you?"
> "If I had to live like you, I think I'd kill
>   myself."
>
> (2)

One of the social burdens of disability, then, is that it exposes affected individuals to inspection, interrogation, interpretation, and violation of privacy.

In effect, people with extraordinary bodies are held responsible for them, in two senses. First, they are required to account for them, often to complete strangers; second, the expectation is that their accounts will serve to relieve their auditors' discomfort. The elicited narrative is expected to conform to, and thus confirm, a cultural script. For example, people diagnosed with lung cancer or HIV/AIDS are expected to admit to behaviors that have induced the condition in question—to acknowledge having brought it upon themselves. Thus, one fundamental connection between life narrative and somatic anomaly is that to have certain conditions is to have one's life written *for* one. For people with many disabilities, culture inscribes narratives *on* their bodies, willy nilly.

Disability autobiographers typically begin from a position of marginalization, belatedness, and pre-inscription. Yet one can see why autobiography is a particularly important form of life writing about disability: written from inside the experience in question, it involves *self*-representation by definition and thus offers the best-case scenario for revaluation of that condition. Long the objects of others' classification and examination, disabled people have only recently assumed the initiative in representing themselves; in disability autobiography particularly, disabled people counter their historical subjection by occupying the subject position. In approaching this literature, then, one should attend to the politics and ethics of representation, for the "representation" of disability in such narratives is a political as well as a mimetic act—a matter of speaking *for* as well as speaking *about*.

With particularly severe or debilitating conditions, particularly those affecting the mind or the ability to communicate, the very existence of first-person narratives makes its own point: that people with condition "X" are capable of self-representation.

The autobiographical act models the agency and self-determination that the disability rights movement has fought for, even or especially when the text is collaboratively produced. One notable example is *Count Us In: Growing Up with Down Syndrome*, a collaborative narrative by two young men with the syndrome in question. Not only is the title cast in the imperative mood— "count us in"—the subtitle puns on "up" and "down," a bit of verbal play that challenges conventional ideas about mental retardation, such as that those with it never really mature. Autobiography, then, can be an especially powerful medium in which disabled people can demonstrate that they *have* lives, in defiance of others' commonsense perceptions of them. Indeed, disability autobiography is often in effect a postcolonial, indeed an anti-colonial, phenomenon, a form of autoethnography, as Mary Louise Pratt has defined it: "instances in which colonized subjects undertake to represent themselves in ways that engage with [read: contest] the colonizer's own terms" (7).

People with disabilities have become increasingly visible in public spaces and open about their disabilities. But their physical presence in public life represents only a rather limited kind of access. Properly conceived and carried out (admittedly, a large qualifier), life narrative can provide the public with controlled access to lives that might otherwise remain opaque or exotic to them. Further, much disability life writing can be approached as "qualify-of-life" writing because it addresses questions discussed under that rubric in philosophy, ethics, and especially biomedical ethics. It should be required reading, then, for citizens in a world with enormous technological capability to sustain life and repair bodies in the case of acute illness and injury but with very little commitment to accommodate and support chronic disability. Because disability life narratives can counter the too often moralizing, objectifying, pathologizing, and marginalizing representations of disability in contemporary culture, they offer an important, if not unique, entrée for inquiry into one of the fundamental aspects of human diversity.

WORKS CITED

Couser, G. Thomas. *Recovering Bodies: Illness, Disability, and Life Writing*. Madison: University of Wisconsin Press, 1997.

Johnson, Harriet McBryde. *Too Late to Die Young: Nearly True Tales from a Life*. New York: Henry Holt, 2005.

Kingsley, Jason, and Mitchell Levitz. *Count Us In: Growing Up with Down Syndrome*. New York: Harcourt, 1994.

Pratt, Mary Louise. *Imperial Eyes: Travel Writing and Transculturation*. New York: Routledge, 1992.

Wilson, Daniel J. "Covenants of Work and Grace: Themes of Recovery and Redemption in Polio Narratives." *Literature and Medicine* 13.1 (Spring 1994): 22–41.

CHAPTER 33

Why Disability Identity Matters: From Dramaturgy to Casting in John Belluso's *Pyretown*

Carrie Sandahl

SUMMARY

Should disabled characters be played exclusively by disabled actors? How does a play give meaning to disability beyond a form of impairment? Carrie Sandahl addresses the use of disability in dramaturgy at both the level of the play (the words and actions of the play) and the production (who is employed and cast in the making of the play). In this chapter, she focuses on disabled playwright John Belluso and describes a "watershed" moment in the entertainment industry after disabled rights groups have forced producers, directors, and casting agents to pay more attention to disabled people working the field. Sandahl suggests that disability identity matters for dramatists because even though identity might be socially constructed, it is still the primary organizing principle for the distribution of resources and opportunities.

Belluso's play *Pyretown* focuses on the lived experience of impairment and disability in stark contrast to the routine use of impairment to launch an "overcoming narrative." By rejecting the narrative about overcoming disability, the play can instead show how rugged individualism distracts people from shared struggles for social justice. Sandahl demonstrates how the play introduces "objective knowledge" about class, gender, and disability that can unite communities. New disability plays allow characters and the audience to create imaginative identifications across social differences, and they can lay the groundwork for collective social action.

The decisions to cast disabled actors or employ disabled workers is also important. Sandahl argues that the politics of production in new disability theatre, especially surrounding issues of casting, adds as much to "objective knowledge" of disability as the text itself. The challenge for any actor is to ally with the character he or she plays, and in an ideal world any actor could play any character. But with so few roles available to disabled actors, their demand for these roles becomes important economically, aesthetically, and politically. Disabled actors can portray the intimate depths and complex embodiment of disability, and the disability community can show solidarity by demanding disabled actors be cast. Sandahl concludes this essay by describing how a nondisabled actor in *Pyretown* challenged her to question assumptions about new disability theatre as it is embodied, not only as it lives on the page.

In November 2005, I found myself in a situation that I had fantasized about but never believed would actually happen. I was at the Public Theater in New York City facilitating an open discussion between a panel of disabled theatre artists and an audience of nearly 150 entertainment industry professionals. This audience included directors, designers, writers, producers, funders, actors, and casting agents in not only theatre but film and television as well. The conversation centered on increasing the participation of disabled people in the performing arts, and, in the process, reframing the structures and ways of thinking that excluded us in the first place. In other words, I had a rarified opportunity to argue precisely why disability identity matters to an audience that had the power to put our arguments directly into action by changing the exclusionary practices of the entertainment industry's business-as-usual.

This meeting was spearheaded by the Disability Theatre Initiative, an advocacy group formed by two New York women: Sharon Jensen of the Non-Traditional Casting Project and Simi Linton, a disability studies scholar and founder of the consulting business Disability/Arts.[1] I had participated in such events before, speaking about disability and performance mostly to groups of academics, students, and fellow artists. Jensen and Linton alerted me that the event at the Public, though, was going to be different, that it was going to be well attended by professional luminaries—but I was not about to believe it until I saw it for myself. After all, attendance at the event was completely voluntary, and past events often included the "usual suspects." Normally, such events included people we already knew in the disability arts community. But there we were. And there they were. And the conversation that took place was extraordinary. Participants openly shared their concerns, fears, desires, best practices, and worst failures in including disabled people at all levels of the profession. And, unlike at many consciousness-raising events I have attended, the non-disabled participants were enthusiastic about what disabled people had to offer. They were not primarily worried about compliance with civil rights laws. That evening, a group of participants committed to continuing the conversation. In April 2006, the Disability Theatre Initiative, Disability/Arts, the Non-Traditional Casting Project, the Screen Actors Guild, and the Dramatists Guild held another well-attended event for industry professionals on issues of disability at HBO headquarters in New York City.[2]

I am getting old enough to recognize a watershed moment when it is happening. I have been thinking about why the change in conversation is happening now. Why is the industry beginning to pay more positive attention to disabled artists? For years, disabled artists have formed advocacy groups within the Screen Actors Guild, Actor's Equity, and the American Federation of Television and Radio Artists. These groups have fought ableist discrimination in the entertainment industry. Additionally, disabled activists and academics have long produced trenchant critiques of media representation of disability and offered solutions for change.[3] Not only are we gaining more attention—the tenor of conversation around disability issues is changing as well. Past events too often put disabled people and their allies on the offensive and non-disabled people on the defensive. However, more recent conversations have been two-way exchanges of information. Non-disabled entertainment industry professionals are expressing genuine interest in the talent, stories, and perspectives of disabled people.

As I think about what has brought us to these changes, I recognize that this moment is a logical link in a long chain of political, academic, artistic, and social accomplishments by disabled people. While I cannot explicate all the links in this chain in this article, I am going to focus on one of the most important: the accomplishments of a disabled writer named John Belluso. Belluso's successful career as a playwright and television writer generated great interest in new disability theatre. New disability theatre aims to explore the lived experience of disability, rather than the usual dramaturgical use of disability as a metaphor for non-disabled people's sense of outsiderness. Belluso was on the panel at the Public's November event, and it seemed as if everyone on the panel and in the audience knew him personally. Although he was not the official host of the evening's event, it was clear to me that it was his great talent, magnetic personality, and advocacy efforts that were in large part responsible for the turnout.

Just a few months after this event, Belluso died unexpectedly of a heart attack. The shockwaves are still being felt throughout both the theatre and disability communities. I was grief-stricken when I heard the news. During the November event, I had spent a lot of time with Belluso. I had given him the good news that I had been granted tenure, and his response was, "Yay for us!" He truly saw any one of our accomplishments as a win for the entire disability community. Belluso was one year younger than I, making both of us members of the first generation of disabled children mainstreamed by law into public schools, the first generation to benefit from laws that required our inclusion into universities, into theatre spaces, and into theatre schools. He recognized that his success, that our success, was enabled by the activism of those who came before us. In an artist statement, he explains:

> I think of myself as a writer who is born of the contemporary disability civil rights movement of the mid-to-late 1970s. I've always felt that it was the creators of that movement who paved the way for the life I live now. Without the civil rights laws they struggled so hard to force into passage, without the history they changed, I doubt I would have been afforded the opportunity to create a life for myself in the theatre arts.
>
> (Lewis, *Beyond* 163)

After our presentation at the Public, Belluso and I, along with mutual friend Ann Stocking (a professionally trained, Los Angeles-based disabled actor who is also of the same generation), stayed up until 4 a.m. in Belluso's hotel room talking about changes that were happening for disabled people. Much of the conversation centered on why disability identity matters. In particular, we debated why it is important that disabled people write from their own experiences and why disabled people must be cast in the roles of disabled characters. This article is my way of remembering why Belluso's identity mattered (and still does), by discussing his work in that context and by documenting our debates surrounding his work.

I will discuss the significance of disability identity at work on two primary levels: the level of the play and the level of production. At the level of the play, I will explore the dramaturgical use of disability in Belluso's 2004 play *Pyretown*. Then, at the level of production, I will explore how casting decisions affected my reception of the play at the Victory Gardens Theater in Chicago, Illinois, in 2004.

THE LEVEL OF THE PLAY

In this discussion, when I refer to disability identity at work at the level of the play, I mean how disability functions dramaturgically in new disability plays. How is disability used to create meaning in the text beyond the fact of impairment? To address this question, recent work by postpositivist realists (or simply realists, as they have become known for short) becomes useful. Realists are scholars arguing for the continued relevance of identity politics as a basis of critical analysis, political organizing, and efforts to enact social justice. Realists have been developing theoretical models that attempt to reconcile the debate between two groups of scholars: one group believes that the social construction of identity casts aspersions on claims to knowledge based on personal experience, while the other believes that identity is essential, fixed, and therefore unassailable

(Moya and Hames-García 3). Instead, realists such as Paula Moya argue that identities are both constructed and real. Moya explains that identity, even if it is socially constructed, remains the primary organizing structure by which rights and access to material goods are conferred.

Those who experience the deleterious, real effects of this distribution system have what realists call "epistemic privilege," which is a "special advantage with respect to possessing or acquiring knowledge about how fundamental aspects of our society (such as race, class, gender, and sexuality) operate to sustain matrices of power" (Moya 38). Realists clarify that their definition of epistemic privilege is not to be confused with unmediated, raw perception or uncomplicated essences, but is what they call "interpreted experience" or experience that is understood through social relations. Such knowledge is constantly reinterpreted and revised through interactions with others, creating a richer and more—in the words of realists—"objective" picture of oppressive social systems. This picture, then, becomes a useful basis for strategizing within and among identity groups for social change. Belluso's play *Pyretown* illustrates this process through the relationship of the play's three characters as they compare, contrast, and ultimately revise their knowledge gained from individual epistemic privilege. Each character's knowledge base is circumscribed by different but overlapping experiences of social class, gender, prejudice, oppression, and the failing health care system.

Belluso's focus on the lived experience of impairment and disability stands in stark contrast to representation's use of the onset of impairment to launch an "overcoming narrative." An overcoming narrative focuses on a disabled character's psychological process of mitigating or overcoming physical injury and impairment.[4] This process becomes a stand-in

for the favorite American fable of pulling yourself up by the bootstraps—even when paralyzed. A good example of this myth is Lanford Wilson's play *Fifth of July* (1975), in which Kenneth Talley, Jr., a wounded war veteran, accepts and overcomes his physical impairment. His journey becomes a metaphor for the United States' process of making sense of and healing from the aftermath of the Vietnam War.

Dramaturgically, new disability playwrights do not reject the metaphorical use of disability altogether, but they tend to create fresh metaphors that are more closely aligned with the lived reality of disability experiences. Belluso himself rejects the typical overcoming narrative and instead represents the experience of impairment and disability as a generative source of knowledge that reveals unjust social systems of power at work. In the case of *Pyretown*, Belluso is particularly interested in how disability can reveal the ways in which the myth of rugged American individualism keeps us from recognizing shared struggles for social justice. Belluso said in an interview that

> disability itself is an experience where no man can be an island, just because of the way that society is built, both literally and metaphorically. We're really at a key place in this country where we're starting to have to question our connection to people—in other nations and in our own country. What do we owe them? What connects us to people who need care and are not receiving it?
>
> (Lewis, "Radical" 38)

While everyone exists in relationships of care and dependency, they are more overt when one is disabled, especially in relation to the American health care system. Belluso's play explores relationships of care through the story of a May–December romance between Harry, a 22-year-old wheelchair user, and Louise (Lou for short), a 39-year-old, non-disabled, impoverished, single mother. Their relationship is forged as they battle an uncaring and ridiculously bureaucratic health maintenance organization (HMO). Interestingly, the HMO is not personified by a merciless white male bureaucrat in a business suit, but by a third character, Rebecca. Rebecca is a well-meaning physician who, at the beginning of the play, is seven months pregnant. Throughout the course of the play, each character spends time as both victim and oppressor as changing circumstances dictate advancement at another character's expense. Even though the characters are pitted against one other's interests for survival, they find ways to come together in support of one another in temporary, albeit ambiguously effective, coalition building.

The play's structure is a series of 21 relatively short, chronologically organized scenes. The scenes alternate between two stories, which sometimes intersect. Each story is written and performed in a different theatrical style. One set of scenes plays out Harry and Lou's romance; stylistically, these scenes are realistic, respecting the fourth wall. Framing and interrupting these scenes are Rebecca's monologues, which break the fourth wall. Rebecca speaks directly to the audience; her language is poetic, and she comments directly on the play's action in a Brechtian manner. Because the two theatrical styles intersect throughout the play, the audience is not allowed to identify smoothly with any of the characters. Rebecca's Brechtian interruptions provide moments of reflection for audience members to consider both the conflicts between the characters' interpretive frameworks and between their own and the characters'.

My analysis of the play here follows the play's story arc: Harry and Lou's hesitant courtship, brief romance, and their ultimate break-up. In the parallel story arc, Rebecca moves from being an idealistic young doctor who believes that she can bring compassion to the HMO system, to power junkie who derives sadistic pleasure from denying patients care, to mother of a newborn who has left her profession and regained her humanity. Along the way, the characters forge connections across identity differences, connections that reveal and revise what the characters think they know about the most effective means of navigating their social worlds. Ironically, what they learn from one another ultimately leads to choices for survival that drive the characters apart, but in the process they create a clearer picture of oppressive social matrices for the audience.

The play's prologue establishes its main theme: interconnectedness. The lights rise on a clearly pregnant Rebecca wearing a doctor's coat. She speaks directly to the audience, musing:

> There are slivers of something inside our bodies. Fragile strings inside us, slivers, thin, like the most delicate of veins. But they are not veins, they are made of a different Substance.
>
> They are contained within each body, but they also break outward; breaking out of the skin, connecting themselves, to other bodies. Tight, taut, radiant threads of Interconnection, threads constructed of Power and Desire.
>
> (Belluso 41)

Embarrassed by her poetic revelry, Rebecca excuses herself and explains to the audience that she's a doctor who is in love with Romantic poetry. She then finds herself inside a memory (or perhaps a dream) during which she describes a moment between Harry and Lou that illustrates these threads of connection. In contrast to her poetic explication of these threads, the moment between Harry and Lou is mundane, taking place in a grocery store before the two have even officially met. Rebecca describes Lou's simple act of taking a box of cereal off a high shelf for Harry, while the action is performed the actors:

> A swift and simple gesture. She twists her body, stretches her arm upward, he senses her forward movement, he pulls back, sort of like an improvised dance step between a woman on legs and a man on wheels. No words spoken between them, barely even a look exchanged, the smallest of smiles maybe, then each move on with their shopping.
>
> (Belluso 41)

This prologue is deceptively simple, seeming to be an act of kindness provided with neither fanfare nor pity, but with a tender matter-of-factness that leaves Harry's masculine dignity intact. But this quotidian scenario takes on complex significance as the play progresses, by illustrating how Rebecca's, Harry's, and Lou's circumstances are intertwined—socially and politically. Their differences and relationships are forged through networks of care that are as practical as they are romantic. As Belluso said in an interview, "Being disabled is a constant set of negotiations, just as falling in love is a constant set of negotiations" (Lewis, "Radical" 40).

Following this prologue, the play proper opens with Lou imploring an unseen receptionist in a hospital emergency room to have her toddler daughter, Bea, seen by a doctor. After responding that, yes, she has filled out the appropriate forms, that yes, she has been waiting for hours, and that yes, she is certain her daughter has an ear infection, Lou says in exasperation,

> I made this diagnosis because she points at her ear and says, "Owee, Owee, Mommy, Owee," to me that means ear infection. ... I'm really not a cranky person, I swear I'm not, but I have two

kids with me who have not had naps, I have another kid who I need to pick up from day care in...seventeen minutes, and I have a Yankee pot roast which I need to cook. ... I'm tired of waiting. I want to see a doctor, NOW!

> (Belluso 42)

Just when she is about to break down, she hears Harry's voice from behind: "I think I'm next" (42). She scowls at him, but he responds by volunteering to let her and Bea ahead of him in line. Then he proceeds to coach her about how to work the system to get seen more quickly. And here they connect.

The scenes that develop their courtship continue the pattern established in the prologue and initial scene: recognizing shared needs across his disability oppression and her class oppression and assisting one another with kindness and biting humor that deflects pity. Both use epistemic privilege to help one another. Their sameness allows them to empathize with one another, and their differences provide them with resources that the other needs. Rebecca's monologues are woven throughout the play, telling the story of Pyretown's hospital closure and her need to take a job in an HMO call center as a "utilization review physician." Her job is to determine which patients' cases warrant medical attention, to determine when to give referrals for tests and specialists, and to keep patient care at "capitation," or the spending limit per patient. She is compelled to take this job because her extended family lives in Pyretown, her husband has a factory job there, and as the due date of her baby nears, her options have become more limited.

The audience learns at the outset that both Harry and Lou are living in poverty: Harry lives on Social Security disability income and Lou on welfare. They both rely on the same Medicaid-sponsored HMO for their health care. Harry, though, has no dependents and only needs to take care of himself, while Lou must gather resources to support herself and her children. We also learn that both Harry and Lou have suffered trauma.

He became paraplegic as the result of a diving accident during his teen years. However, Belluso departs from the traditional overcoming narrative that this revelation would normally launch. The immediate trauma of disablement is not the cause of Harry's recent troubles. Instead, it is his ongoing relationship with the health care system. He claims that he "got over" his impairment, but has been unable to move on with his life or connect with other people since his mother passed away. His mother had been his caregiver and helped him through his rehabilitation, then she herself became ill with cancer, and he became her caregiver. He blames her death on barriers to care erected by the HMO, which is now erecting similar barriers to Harry's ongoing medical needs due to his paraplegia.

Lou has also suffered trauma as an abused wife. She has recently separated from her husband and is trying to raise three young children. She relates to Harry's experience of being an overwhelmed caregiver, as the needs of her children outstrip her abilities to meet them, especially as Bea has been suffering recurrent illnesses. The HMO, as personified by Rebecca, has been downplaying the seriousness of Bea's illnesses, resulting in denial of services. These shared experiences of poverty and fighting for the needs of a loved one bring Harry and Lou even closer.

At first Lou deflects Harry's sexual advances because of their seemingly insurmountable age difference; however, over the course of the play Lou responds to Harry's advances as they become closer friends through taking care of each other in both small and large ways. For instance, Lou drives Harry to places and helps him with his shopping, a seemingly insignificant task but one that consumes Harry's time because of a terrible public transportation system and bad weather. Harry, a highly educated perpetual student, helps Lou get into a community college program to earn a nursing degree and becomes her tutor. Harry not only tutors her in her nursing coursework, but tutors her on the ins and outs of challenging the HMO bureaucracy. This advice becomes increasingly valuable as Bea's illness becomes more and more urgent: an ear infection leads to chronic coughing and spitting up blood. As an experienced mother, Lou knows Bea's situation is serious and feels helpless as her daughter's health deteriorates; Rebecca tells Lou on the phone that Bea's symptoms are merely the result of usual childhood illnesses.

This phone conversation marks the first real interaction between the characters in the play's two storylines. Even though earlier in the play Rebecca romanticized her observations of Lou and Harry's evolving romance, when she finally connects with Lou on the phone, she is cruel to her. Rebecca downplays Lou's concerns for Bea and eventually hangs up on her, leaving Lou sobbing. Rebecca is driven to such cruelty after she is severely reprimanded for approving too many referrals and then given financial rewards for keeping patients at capitation. She is in the untenable situation of wanting to help her patients physically and emotionally but needing to earn income for her family. As she encounters growing pressures from the HMO, desperate patients, and her husband's insecurity due to her breadwinner status, Rebecca exerts power where she has it: by hurting the people she claims to help.

The evolving romance between Harry and Lou is also untenable, and not as smooth as my description of their mutual understanding and teamwork against the evils of the HMO may seem to portray. Throughout their hesitant courtship, differences in the lived experience of their social positions emerge that eventually push the two apart. Although Harry has the skills necessary to pull himself out of poverty, he chooses not to. Instead he sells and smokes pot, takes classes, reads the same books over and over, and designs websites for leftist political organizations. Harry refuses to participate in corporations that profit from what he considers to be exploitation of the masses—corporations like the one that he believes killed his mother and that exploit the disabled for profit. He exacts his revenge by being a sponge on the capitalist system, continuing to accept government aid for the disabled without ever graduating. Lou sees clearly that Harry's immature choices do nothing to affect the battles he's waging. Harry's choices are a form of privilege that he fails to acknowledge. Lou must prioritize getting food on the table and health care for her children over romance, pot smoking, political grandstanding, and intellectual debate. Harry is also an avowed atheist, while Lou is a practicing Catholic. Harry's dismissal of Lou's Catholic values drives another wedge between them.

Lou wants to be self-sufficient and tries to follow Harry's advice about obtaining an education. However, over the course of the play, the demands of Bea's frightening illness derail her efforts. At first, Harry's attentions take her away from the hardships of her life, but soon she resents anything that keeps her from focusing on her daughter's needs. The play's turning point is a short scene in which Lou is up in the middle of the night with a very sick Bea. Lou's failed attempts to soothe her daughter devolve into screams. Lou loses control and throws a glass of water that shatters near her sobbing daughter's head. The scene immediately following portrays Lou on the phone making an appeal to Rebecca, who has refused to schedule tests for Bea. In a misguided attempt to help Lou, Harry gets on the other line and continually interrupts their conversation, angrily demanding services, spouting Marxist rhetoric, and threatening legal action. Rebecca hangs up on Lou, who then erupts in rage at Harry. She throws Harry out into the rain.

Near the end of the play, Lou rejects what Harry has been teaching her about working the system and getting an education. Lou makes a personal trip to Rebecca's office, which is against the institution's policy, and begs for help. This is the first time in the play that Rebecca and Lou interact face to face. The two women make an emotional connection with each other, and Rebecca regains her humanity when she sees Lou's desperation as a mother. Their epistemic experiences of motherhood allow them to connect. Lou gets the referral she needs. In the final scene, Lou breaks up with Harry, telling him that she has quit school and has got back together with her husband, as her husband has promised her that he has cleaned up his act, has taken anger management courses, and has a new well-paying job. Bea indeed has a serious medical condition, perhaps cystic fibrosis or mastoiditis, and Lou needs to marshal all her resources for the survival of herself and her children. The end of the play finds Lou back together with an abusive husband, Harry alone, and Rebecca fired from her job for giving too many referrals.

In the play's epilogue, Rebecca is giving her newborn baby boy a bath, admiring his beauty and returning to the poetic language she used at the beginning of the play, this time with a difference. She explains:

There are slivers of something inside of our bodies. Fragile strings, slivers thin as the most delicate veins. They are the Defining Property of us; Mutualism, Interconnection. That's what I believe these slivers can be, if they are fed by *Mercy*.

(Belluso 59)

With this ambiguous ending, Belluso reveals the complexity of each character's situation. Lou and Harry's romance enriches and revises what each character thinks they know through their individual epistemic privilege. Lou is changed by her relationship with Harry—she more effectively works the system by getting her daughter what she needs, but in a way that Harry finds repugnant. Likewise, Harry is changed by his relationship with Lou—he begins to see that Lou's survival tactics are keeping her child alive, whereas his own abrasive strategies failed to get his mother what she needed. He realizes that he does need to connect with other people and spend less time alone. Rebecca has regained her humanity, but loses her job. Her baby boy represents the future, but a financially uncertain one. Each character has shown each other mercy, even if mercy is temporary and has its limits.

Belluso says of the play's ending, "Yeah, it's not the kind of happy ending my mother would have liked. But I do think that the characters have affected each other's lives through moments of exchange and connection that are hopeful, in a sense" (Lewis, "Radical" 38). Just as the play's characters reveal and revise their interpretive frameworks in negotiating their relationships with one another, audience members are invited to go through the same process as they experience the play. Realist theorist Brent Henze explains:

Outsiders wishing to support the liberatory work of the oppressed must form responsible and imaginative alliances—alliances grounded in appropriate reconceptions of their experiences in relation to others.

That is, we should not work toward *imaginary* identifications of ourselves with others, in which we make claims about our "sameness" without regard for the real differences in our experiences and lives; rather, we should work toward *imaginative* identifications of ourselves with others, in which we interrogate our own experience, seeking points where common ground or empathy might be actively constructed between us while remaining conscious of the real differences between our experiences and lives.

(248)

New disability theatre provides audiences with the opportunity to make imaginative identifications across difference with the plays' characters, rather than imaginary identifications with the same old idealistic narrative of overcoming. The traditional overcoming narrative relies on simplistic metaphors about the similarity between coping with disability and coping with other life hardships. Harry's lived experience of disability, his past relationship as a caregiver to his mother, and his recent relationship as a caregiver to Lou provide him particular knowledge of the oppressiveness of the health care system. Lou's lived experience of disability through her relationships of care to Harry and Bea has given her knowledge that leads to a hard and far-from-ideal choice necessary to provide resources for her family's endurance. Harry's and Lou's different experiences of disability and their failure to overcome them in the traditional sense illuminate interlocking systems of oppression that complicate overcoming in real life. Both Belluso's characters and the audience have the opportunity to come to greater clarity, or, as the post-positivist realists would argue, "objective knowledge" about the social matrices of class, gender, and ability that restrict the choices available to oppressed people for survival. This knowledge lays the groundwork for collective social change. And that's where hope lies.

THE LEVEL OF PRODUCTION

My argument so far has been that Belluso's work creates opportunities for both characters and audiences to create imaginative identifications with one another across forms of social difference. These identifications reveal how interlocking forms of oppression operate to restrict liberation. I have also argued that Belluso uses instances of the lived experience of disability to launch and sustain his narratives. Disability remains a metaphor for the characters' obstacles, but Belluso complicates his metaphor by intersecting it with other layers of social identity (class, gender, religion, age, etc.), thus refusing to make disability carry the burden of signifying the primary "problem" that needs rectifying within the narrative.

The terms I have been using in this article to describe the interactions between the characters in the play and between the audience and the characters—terms such as "alliance," "identification," and "intersecting interpretive frameworks"—imply a sort of emotional and intellectual exchange between members of different groups. Unfortunately, historical power imbalances mean that resources have not been equally distributed across groups, so the real costs and benefits of this exchange are not equivalent among participants. The ways in which this inequality manifests itself become apparent at the level of production, particularly around issues of casting.

Because Belluso himself was closely tied to the disability rights movement and his message is so closely tied to disability identity, the identity of the actor cast as Harry matters a great deal. While Belluso expressed a clear preference for casting a disabled actor in the role, Harry has been performed by non-disabled actors, a choice that adds extra-textual layers of meaning to the production. The politics of production in new disability theatre, especially surrounding issues of casting, adds as much to the emerging "objective knowledge" of disability oppression in the United States as does the text itself. It is worth spending some time surveying some of these issues regarding casting before exploring how the casting of Harry created meaning in the Chicago production of *Pyretown*.

It would be easy to argue that the actor's job is to form imaginative alliances with the characters he or she plays. Through the rehearsal process, actors excavate and then make use of personal life experiences that are similar to their characters' to bring a sense of authenticity to their roles. When an actor's repertoire of life experience is different from the character's, he or she researches the character's differences and works to inhabit them with his or her own body, mind, and affect. Most actors relish the opportunity to take on characters that radically differ from themselves. In so doing, they practice their art at the highest level. And audiences love to see actors transform. Think of our most cherished film actors, like Meryl Streep, Robert DeNiro, and Anthony Hopkins, whose chameleon-like acting wins praise from critics and audiences alike. No matter the theatrical style, it is the actor's level of commitment to inhabiting the similarities as well as the differences between him or herself and the character that is paramount to seducing the audience to engage with the character, and to believe in the character's desires, obstacles, and circumstances. In an ideal world, any actor should be able to inhabit any character. Any actor should have the opportunity to use his or her artistry to form an imaginative alliance with the character for the benefit of the audience. Unfortunately, too often the art world reduces this opportunity through the use of type-casting, or matching the actor's identity as closely as possible to that of the character. Typecasting is congruent with what Henze would call an imaginary (rather than imaginative) identification "in which we make claims about our 'sameness' without regard for the real differences in our experiences and lives" (Henze 248).

Ideally any actor should be able to play any character. However, our world is far from ideal, especially for disabled actors. While type-casting is the dominant form of casting today, exceptions, or casting against type, are made for actors from more socially dominant locations. Convention dictates which identities are considered acceptable to take on other identities in performance. And these conventions change over time. In the Elizabethan era, for example, male actors had license to play female characters. In the late nineteenth and early twentieth centuries, convention allowed white actors to blacken their faces to play African American characters. Currently, a trend has emerged that allows, even encourages, slender actors to play large-sized characters. Svelte actors like Gwyneth Paltrow (*Shallow Hal*, 2001) and Renée Zellweger (*Bridget Jones's Diary*, 2001) have either donned "fat suits" or bulked up for a role. Martin Lawrence (*Big Momma's House*, 2000) and John Travolta (*Hairspray*, 2007) have crossed body size and gender lines by wearing fat suits in drag. And currently, in the case of disability, non-disabled actors have been famously cast as disabled characters: Macaulay Culkin as wheelchair-using teen Roland in *Saved* (2004), Patrick Stewart as wheelchair-using Professor Charles Xavier in the recent *X-Men* films (2000, 2003, 2006), and Sean Penn as developmentally disabled Sam Dawson in *I am Sam* (2001). In the disability arts and activist communities, casting non-disabled actors as disabled characters is called pejoratively

"cripping up," referencing the outdated practice of white actors "blacking up" to play African American characters.[5] In "cripping up," and in each of the other examples I have listed, an actor is cast to play a character from a less dominant social position. Rarely is an actor of color, a woman, or a disabled person cast against type to play a character from a more dominant social position. Actors from marginalized groups must battle on two fronts, then: to be cast in roles that resemble their own identities and to be cast in roles that do not.

Disabled actors' demands to play disabled characters are based on economics, aesthetics, and politics. In terms of economics, disabled actors rarely make a living in their profession because so few roles are available to them; they are neither type-cast nor cast against type. Even professionally trained disabled actors have difficulty getting cast at all. They are routinely passed over for traditionally non-disabled roles because it is assumed that their impairments will confuse the audience if the impairment is not explained by the text. After all, audiences are trained by convention to read disability as a metaphor, or meaning-maker, in the play. If the disability cannot be explained by the script, then the actor's impairment will be a supposed distraction, or will create meanings unintended by the playwright or the director. Even when a character is written as disabled, non-disabled actors are still routinely chosen over disabled ones. The most commonly reason cited for this choice is that there are simply not enough professionally trained disabled actors in the casting pool. In terms of aesthetics, disabled actors argue that non-disabled actors, no matter how good their technical skill at imitating the physicality of a disabled character (and most often verisimilitude is not achieved) or how good their research into the lives of disabled people, they lack the lived experience of disability necessary to bring these characters fully to life. Non-disabled people, even fine actors, understand the disability experience primarily through stereotypes available in mainstream media. These actors often focus on getting the outward shell of the characterization right (how a disabled person might move, speak, carry the body, etc.) but have little access to the lived experience of disability. Experiences such as being stared at, using personal assistants for activities of daily living, living with pain, dealing with access issues, and navigating social services and the medical establishment are unavailable to most non-disabled actors. Even if a disabled actor has not personally experienced all of these situations, it is likely that he or she has better access to them because of related disability experiences or ties to the disability community in general.

In the epilogue to her anthology *Beyond Victims and Villains: Contemporary Plays by Disabled Playwrights*, disabled theatre artist and scholar Victoria Lewis discusses the casting difficulties disabled actors face. She writes that Belluso

> struggled to convince producers and directors to cast disabled actors . . . arguing that disability is a social identity with a long history, not a biological medical condition to be mimicked. Belluso points to the many hours of rehearsal time spent trying to familiarize nondisabled actors with the "given circumstances" of life lived with a disability.
>
> (389)

The concept of disability as a social identity and not just a physical condition explains casting choices in which a disabled actor is cast in a role in which his or her impairment significantly differs from the character's. This form of casting is, paradoxically, both within and against type. In Belluso's play *Body of Bourne*, developed and produced by the Mark Taper Forum Theatre (2001), disabled actor Clark Middleton was cast as protagonist Randolf Bourne. Middleton's impairment somewhat physically resembled that of the character. One could say, then, that Middleton was typecast in this role. His understudy Christopher Thornton, though, was cast against type. Thornton is a wheelchair user and went onstage as Bourne in Middleton's place on a number of occasions. Although Thornton's impairment significantly differed from Middleton's and the character's, his own disability experience provided him with epistemic privilege useful to inhabiting the character of Bourne.[6] Disabled playwright Mike Ervin explains that in addition to the valuable life experience disabled actors bring to playing disabled characters, casting disabled actors is important for their professional advancement. He told Victoria Lewis:

> There is no substitute for casting actors with disabilities. That doesn't mean you'll always be able to find one. You may be forced to punt and go with a walkie-talkie. But if you do, something will always be missing. I thought it was important to hire one of our own for symbolic and solidarity reasons. If we don't give them a break, who the hell else ever will? Also, their conspicuous absence would make the statement that there just aren't any of us who are good enough to cut it.
>
> (*Beyond* 388)

Casting actors with disabilities, especially in new disability theatre, is an important choice economically for the livelihood of disabled actors, aesthetically in terms of portraying the intimate depths and complex life experiences of the disabled character, and politically as a form of solidarity. As a theatre artist and disability activist, I deeply believed that casting disabled actors in new disability theatre was the only way to produce the work. My beliefs, though, were challenged in November 2004, when I had the opportunity to see *Pyretown* at the Victory Gardens Theater in Chicago.

As a fan and friend of Belluso's, I know that I would see something vital to the disability art and culture movement. I looked forward not only to seeing the play, but to seeing some high quality acting by a disabled actor. The afternoon before the performance, I met with playwright Mike Ervin, who is also the Access Project Coordinator at Victory Gardens. The Access Project is a remarkable program that provides an enviably high level of disability access and accommodations for both audiences and performers, supports the development of disabled playwrights' work, and holds disability culture events. Given the theatre's commitment to disability culture and Ervin's involvement, I was surprised to learn that their production of *Pyretown* starred non-disabled actor Aaron Roman Weiner in the role of Harry. Despite the production team's best efforts, they were "forced to punt and go with a walkie-talkie" as they were unable to find an actor with a disability appropriate to the role at the time. I was extremely disappointed but curious about how Weiner would do in this role, and how he would be able to portray Harry's complexities.

The performance took place in a small black box theatre set up with thrust seating, so audience members were in very close proximity to the actors. This event was one of the most interesting audience experiences I have had. My viewing of the play oscillated between scrutinizing Weiner's physicality (focusing on Weiner-the-actor in the intimate, black-box setting) and being fully engaged with the world of the play (focusing on Harry-the-character). Weiner is a fine young actor, and his portrayal of Harry was spot-on: sexy, nuanced, and engaging. Most of the time, his embodiment of paraplegia rang true; he moved as a wheelchair-using person

with paraplegia would. What gave him away as a non-disabled person to me were his legs and torso. Although he adopted the posture and mannerisms of a paraplegic, his legs and torso seemed clearly not impaired: symmetrically muscular and "normal-looking." I cannot be sure whether my viewing of the play would have been different had I not known the actor's identity, but knowing it did add layer upon layer of meanings for me during the production and resonated in my thoughts and discussions long afterwards.

What triggered my most visceral response was how director Tim Farrell chose to block the scene changes and curtain call. Because the play consists of 21 short scenes that shift from location to location almost cinematically, the set must be reconfigured often and quickly. During these changes, the actors moved the scenery in semidarkness, remaining in character. Weiner stayed in the chair and worked with the assistance of other actors to move the sparse set pieces on and off and around the set. The choreography of these scene changes was fascinating—how the actors worked together to move the set while accommodating Harry's disability.

I describe my response to this choreography as "visceral" because I found it both thematically interesting and politically infuriating. On the one hand, the scene changes reinforced the themes of the play, extending the characters' caregiving with a quiet matter-of-factness. This choice created echoes of the play's prologue, in which Lou reaches the box of cereal for Harry—which Rebecca describes for the audience as a "an improvised dance step between a woman on legs and a man on wheels." The themes of accommodation, caring for one another, and cooperating at the level of the play were reinforced at the level of production. On the other hand, I found myself getting angry, my face flushing in the darkened auditorium. How dare

Weiner "crip up" during the scene changes? During the intermission, I heard audience members behind me debating whether Weiner was really disabled. In the lobby, I heard another audience member commenting on how wonderful it was that they had been able to find a disabled actor for the role. These comments added fuel to my anger. How many other audience members were "fooled" into thinking that an actual disabled actor had found work and had performed stunningly? If they knew Weiner was non-disabled, would they think there were no disabled actors who could, in Ervin's words, "cut it"? I both loved the play and was very disturbed by the comments circulating around me.

After the intermission, my reception continued to oscillate through the second half of the show, but the curtain call enraged me. As is customary, the actors returned to the stage for their applause— as themselves, having dropped their characters. Weiner, though, took his curtain call as a disabled actor. He clearly had dropped the affect of Harry, but retained Harry's physicality. I was perplexed by this choice and felt betrayed as a member of the disability activist community. This seemed to me an instance of "cripping up" unnecessarily.

After leaving the theatre, I went out for dinner and drinks with a group of friends from the disability community (some of whom had impairments and others who did not).[7] We spent the evening debating the casting of Harry (some of us had been convinced that Weiner was actually disabled and others had not been). In the course of this conversation, my anger softened and transformed into a serious questioning of my previously held values. We raised many questions. Is it more important that this significant piece of new disability theatre be performed, and performed well, than to not perform it at all if a qualified disabled actor could not be

found? Should solidarity for disabled actors outweigh solidarity for the work itself? Would Weiner's effective portrayal of Harry have been lessened if he had dropped his disability identity during the scene changes and curtain call? Would audience members have then turned their attention from the play's themes and instead focused on Weiner's technical skill at mimicking paraplegia? Why did we not demand that the role of Rebecca be played by a pregnant actor? How does disability identity matter? Why does it matter? When does it matter? We all proposed different answers to these questions, but one answer seemed pretty consistent in the group: it was preferable for Weiner not to break the illusion that he was disabled for the sake of the play. I would continue this conversation with others long after that evening's performance, and each time I have this conversation my perspective is enriched, and my previously held, righteous position that solidarity with disabled actors, especially in new disability theatre, should take precedence above all else is challenged.

Fast forward to that conversation with Belluso in New York almost a year after I saw *Pyretown* in Chicago. Belluso admitted to Ann and me that he was disappointed that Harry had not been played by a disabled actor. But then he said something to us, the same thing he said to Marge Betley, dramaturge of Geva Theatre's premiere of *Pyretown* in Rochester:

> When an able-bodied actor plays a wheelchair role, inevitably there is a moment when the play is over and the actors *stand* to take a bow. That's a moment of loss, a reductive moment for me; it lets the audience off the hook.
>
> (62)[8]

I got it. Had Weiner stood to take his bow, the audience would no longer have been asked to make an imaginative identification with both the disabled character and the disabled actor. The non-disabled audience members might then have made an imaginary identification with the likewise non-disabled actor. I did not like this revelation, but I understood it.

The questions raised by Victory Garden's version of *Pyretown* at both the level of the play and the level of production challenged me, and pushed me (and I am sure many others) from the comfort of what I thought I knew in many ways. These challenges arise from new disability theatre itself: theatre as it is embodied, not only as it lives on the page. As Belluso reminded us, disability is a constant set of negotiations. Like the characters in *Pyretown* who must make sacrifices in this imperfect world, the production made sacrifices that ultimately clarified for us, added to our knowledge of, the always complex process of living life with a disability.

NOTES

Earlier versions or portions of this article were presented at Florida State University's Film and Literature conference in February 2006, Stanford University's "Future of Minority Studies" seminar in May 2006, the Society for Disability Studies conference in Bethesda MD in June 2006, and the Association for Theatre Higher Education's conference in Chicago in 2006. The author would like to thank audiences at these events for their insightful comments, which guided the development of this material.

1. This panel was called, "Broadening Diversity: Theatre and Disability," and was held at the Public Theater in New York in November 2005. The panel included John Belluso, Susan Nussbaum, Lynn Manning, and Troy Kastur. We spoke the next day at Columbia University's disability studies seminar at an event entitled "Casting Tradition to the Wind: Disability and Theatre in the 21st Century." For information about Simi Linton's consulting work, see www.similinton.com. The Non-Traditional Casting Project is now known as Alliance for Inclusion in the Arts; see www.ntcp.org.
2. This event was called "Written on the Body: A Conversation about Disability" and held at HBO Headquarters in New York, April 2006. For a transcript of the conversations at this event, see www.ntcp.org.
3. Much has been written about disability stereotypes and their function in dramatic narrative; for two seminal works on this topic see Longmore and Norden.
4. For more information about the use of disability as a narrative device, see Mitchell and Snyder.
5. I became aware of the term "cripping up" from the disability arts community describing non-disabled actors playing disabled roles. I believe that this term was coined by Kaite O'Reilly, a disabled UK playwright (see Komporály).
6. For an interview with Clark Middleton and Christopher Thornton about playing Randolf Bourne, see Weinart. Also, it is important to note the contribution of Victoria Lewis, founder and past director of the Other Voices Project at the Mark Taper Forum Theatre. The Other Voices Project supported the development of disabled theatre artists and advocated for disability-themed work, access, and accommodations at the Taper and nationally. *Body of Bourne* was developed and supported by the Project. Lewis and Belluso co-directed Other Voices from 1999 to 2000. Belluso continued to direct Other Voices until 2005.
7. I want to thank the friends who entered into this conversation with me after the show, especially Jim Ferris, David Linton, and Gretchen Case.
8. See Betley for a provocative discussion of how the Geva Theatre's commitment to casting a disabled actor in the role of Harry influenced the production both politically and aesthetically, and of how the production has had a lasting impact on the theatre company. Interestingly, Betley also found meaning in the play's set changes as disabled actor Christopher Thornton, who played Harry, navigated the space in his wheelchair.

REFERENCES

Belluso, John. *Body of Bourne*. Dir. Lisa Peterson. Perf. Clark Middleton and Christopher Thornton. Mark Taper Forum, Los Angeles. May 27–July 15, 2001.

——. *Pyretown*. Dir. Tim Ferrell. Perf. Aaron Roman Weiner. Victory Gardens Theater, Chicago. November 2004.

——. *Pyretown*. *American Theatre* April 2004: 39–59.

Betley, Marge. "How Geva Got Harry on Stage." *American Theatre* April 2004: 60–2.

Henze, Brent. "Who Says Who Says?: The Epistemological Grounds for Agency in Liberatory Political Projects." Eds. Paula M. L. Moya and Michael Hames-García. *Reclaiming Identity: Realist Theory and the Predicament of Postmodernism.* Berkeley: University of California Press, 2000. 229–50.

Komporály, Jozefina. "'Cripping Up Is the Twenty-first Century's Answer to Blacking Up': Conversation with Kaite O'Reilly on Theatre, Feminism, and Disability, 6 June 2005, British Library, London." *Gender Forum: Illuminating Gender* 12 (2005). 29 August 2007 <www.genderforum.uni-koeln.de/illuminating/interview_oreilly.html>.

Lewis, Victoria. *Beyond Victims and Villains: Contemporary Plays by Disabled Playwrights.* New York: Theatre Communications Group, 2006.

——. "Radical Optimism: An Interview with the Playwright." *American Theatre* April 2004: 40.

Longmore, Paul. "Screening Stereotypes: Images of Disabled People in Television and Motion Pictures." *Social Policy* 16.1 (1985): 31–7.

Mitchell, David, and Sharon Snyder. *Narrative Prosthesis: Disability and the Dependencies of Discourse.* Ann Arbor: University of Michigan Press, 2001.

Moya, Paula M. L. *Learning From Experience: Minority Identities, Multicultural Struggles.* Berkeley: University of California Press, 2002.

Moya, Paula M. L., and Michael Hames-García. *Reclaiming Identity: Realist Theory and the Predicament of Postmodernism.* Berkeley: University of California Press, 2000.

Norden, Martin. *The Cinema of Isolation: A History of Physical Disability in the Movies.* New Brunswick, NJ: Rutgers University Press, 1994.

Weinart, Laura. "Clark Middleton and Christopher Thornton." *Back Stage West* 31 May 2001. 3 September 2007 <www.allbusiness.com/services/amusement-recreation-services/4373483-1.html>.

CHAPTER 34

The Autistic Victim: *Of Mice and Men*

Sonya Freeman Loftis

SUMMARY

Autistic people are particularly likely to be killed by parents or caregivers. In this chapter, Sonya Freeman Loftis identifies the "fluid boundary" between fiction and reality when it comes to killing autistic characters and the way autistic people are treated in the real world. These characters might have varying degrees of similarity to real autistic people, but their popularity can influence the assumptions and discourses that surround autistic people. When fictional narratives treat autistic people as objects to "cure or kill," it reinforces beliefs about the justifications for the filicide of autistic people.

Loftis examines the well-known character of Lennie Small from John Steinbeck's novel *Of Mice and Men* in part because Texas courts use this character as a way to decide whether a person should be exempt from the death penalty. The book is also widely taught in high schools and even in classes on medical ethics; it is woven into the public conversation about disability and euthanasia. Yet the book has rarely been analyzed from a disability studies perspective that would present Lennie's subjectivity.

The novel's plot centers on Lennie and his companion, George, as they aid each other as migrant farm workers—Lennie's physical strength makes him a superior worker while George helps him take care of himself and find work. After Lennie accidentally kills a woman, George shoots his friend rather than giving him over to the other farmhands. Loftis argues that Lennie's death is "authorized" by cultural discourses that depict autistic people as violent and lacking subjectivity. George's actions are often interpreted as justified—or as merciful—only because of a belief that the autistic body is an empty frame that must be suffering. Furthermore, the novel relies on this view of autism to depict Lennie's death as a mercy killing; the plot simply wouldn't make sense if Lennie were neurotypical. In order to acknowledge Lennie's subjectivity, the ethical debate around *Of Mice and Men* must move away from George's choice for euthanasia and toward Lennie's death as a victim of cultural discourses.

We must be concerned not merely about who murdered them, but about the system, the way of life, the philosophy which produced the murderers.

> (Martin Luther King Jr., "Eulogy for the Martyred Children")

Autistic people are particularly likely to be the victims of filicide.[1] The collection *Loud Hands: Autistic People, Speaking,* edited by Julia Bascom and published by the Autistic Self Advocacy Network in 2012, is dedicated to 36 people, all of them disabled (most of them autistic), all of them killed by caregivers or family members (most of them parents). Neurodiversity.com, dedicated to autism-related issues and managed by Kathleen Seidel, maintains a list of names under the heading "Murder of Autistic Persons."[2] The list is long. Such cases often garner great attention from the media—but the focus is rarely on the autistic victim.[3] As Stuart Murray notes, "In the majority of these cases the focus of the media coverage is not on the child who has died, but rather on the parent."[4] Media coverage of these "mercy killings" often solicits sympathy for the killer.[5] To give only one example, after Daniela Dawes killed her 10-year-old son, Jason, ABC reported that

> Jason Dawes was diagnosed as autistic when he was 18 months old. At the age of 10 he had the mental age of a 3-year-old. He couldn't speak and he needed constant help to eat, bathe, and go to the toilet. Most of that responsibility fell to his mother, Daniela Dawes. … It all got too much for her on August the fourth last year. That day she suffocated her son and then tried to kill herself.[6]

When the victim of the crime is disabled, the killer may even be more likely to receive a reduced sentence. (Dawes's sentence was reduced: she pleaded guilty to murder in 2004 but was "ultimately sentenced to a five-year good-behavior bond.")[7] Media coverage that is sympathetic to autistic filicide, presenting parents as overwhelmed by their children's care or depicting murder as an act of mercy (highlighting the pain the disabled child was believed to be suffering), works together with reduced sentences to suggest a lack of cultural value placed on autistic personhood. In this chapter, I want to explore the fluid boundary between fiction and reality in literature about autistic characters in order to contemplate the various ways in which reality influences fiction (and fiction influences reality) in cultural discourses about characters (and people) with autistic characteristics. I am not arguing that any real-life tragedy was inspired

by any fictional event, only that assumptions that devalue autistic identity and stereotypes that create fear and discrimination may be in dialogue between media interpretations of actual events and depictions of characters in fictional works. Fictional depictions found in literary texts and the public interpretation of actual events become mutually sustaining social artifacts that forge a cultural connection between autism and death. The interconnection of the "cure or kill" trope of disability studies and real-life events tragically reinforces cultural attitudes that regard neurotypical subjectivity as the only subjectivity.[8]

OF MICE AND MEN AND AUTISTIC FILICIDE

Some might argue that actual deaths have little to do with fictional depictions of people on the spectrum: the Texas legal system's appropriation and interpretation of Steinbeck's novella *Of Mice and Men* is a reminder of the powerful impact that fictional representations of disability can have on the actual perceptions of cognitively disabled subjectivity. In 2002 the U.S. Supreme Court ruled that individuals with intellectual disability (those with IQs measured to be below the average range) could not receive the death penalty.[9] The state of Texas, however, has continued to execute individuals who qualify as intellectually disabled under guidelines established by the American Association on Intellectual and Developmental Disabilities.[10] Instead of using clinical tests developed by psychologists to diagnose intellectual disability, Texas courts use characteristics known as "the Briseño factors."[11] This group of criteria was developed by the Texas Court of Criminal Appeals and is based on Steinbeck's character Lennie Small.[12] As the court explains, "Most Texas citizens might agree that Steinbeck's

Lennie should, by virtue of his lack of reasoning ability and adaptive skills, be exempt" from the death penalty.[13] The literary character has become adapted into law, as the court rules that individuals judged to be less impaired than the fictional Lennie may be executed, while those judged to be more impaired than the literary character may not.[14] Steinbeck's son has objected strenuously to this use of his father's novella: "I had no idea that the great state of Texas would use a fictional character that my father created…as a benchmark to identify whether defendants with intellectual disability should live or die."[15] The Texas law using a literary character to define intellectual disability is a startling reminder of the influence that fictional depictions can have on public opinions. Indeed, *Of Mice and Men* is so deeply woven into our cultural narratives of disability and euthanasia that it has sometimes been taught in classes on medical ethics, forming part of the education of another professional group called upon to make life and death decisions.[16] Steinbeck's fictional account of a cognitively disabled man influencing death penalty laws in Texas shows that literary depictions of disabled subjectivity can have a strong influence on public policy.

Although *Of Mice and Men* is a staple of the U.S. high school curriculum and the book has received abundant attention from literary critics, the novella has seldom received analysis from a disability studies perspective: this dearth of disability approaches to the novella may be connected to Lennie's perceived lack of subjectivity as a cognitively disabled character. As Sally Chivers argues, "Though overtly 'about' disability, Steinbeck's novella *Of Mice and Men* has largely escaped notice in the emerging field of disability studies, likely because of its simple moral lesson that leaves little room for complex analysis."[17] In fact, Steinbeck's presentation of Lennie as a character lacking in human subjectivity may motivate this avoidance on the part of disability studies scholars. One dangerous cultural perception that ignores autistic subjectivity is the tendency to see autistic characters (and people) only as they relate to neurotypicals. Many disability studies critics have noted that disabled characters in literary works and films are often minor characters: while they may prove central to the plot, these figures generally appear on the margins of the story. This is a particularly pervasive and significant facet of characterization for figures with intellectual disabilities, reflecting real-life perceptions that deny the subjectivity of those with cognitive differences. While Lennie is a major character, he is completely subordinated to George in the course of the novella's plot: the reader is subtly guided to empathize with George and to see Lennie only through his relationship with his neurotypical friend. As Patrick McDonagh explains, "In literature characters with intellectual disability are rarely considered on their own terms so much as in their relationships to other people. The same holds true beyond the text."[18] Disability studies scholar Licia Carlson, who specializes in intellectual disability, is often disturbed when people ask her if she has a disabled family member: "As I have delved deeper into the margins of philosophy, this relatively benign question has come to represent far more troubling beliefs that I have encountered. First, the intellectually disabled are not persons. They are owed respect and justice only by virtue of their relationship to nondisabled family members who are persons."[19] In other words, a disability studies reading of Lennie as autistic requires a critical approach to a character deemed (in literary and cultural discourses) as a virtual nonentity, and a lack of critical attention to his perceived absence or vacancy in the narrative may be part of larger cultural trends that categorically deny cognitively disabled subjectivity.

No literary critic has ever suggested that Lennie may be on the autism spectrum; it is clear, however, that autistic traits are key to Lennie's character. Reading Lennie as autistic gives his death an uncomfortably contemporary political dimension in relation to recent media depictions of autistic filicide and raises moral questions regarding public perceptions of autistic subjectivity.[20] It is clear that Lennie adheres to many of the stereotypes commonly perpetuated about people with intellectual disability. However, Lennie is also depicted as a recognizably autistic character. At least one theatrical production has made the decision to represent Lennie as overtly autistic, clarifying the exact nature of his intellectual disability for the audience.[21] Certainly, Lennie's special interest in animals is one of the defining attributes of his character. He talks endlessly about his desire to own rabbits: "I wish't we'd get the rabbits pretty soon, George."[22] He also engages in stimming: when overstimulated or stressed, Lennie "flapped his big hands" or "rocked himself back and forth" (67, 83). He relies strongly on ritual and routine (especially the ritual of George repeatedly narrating the story of their imagined farm).[23] His social naïveté, trusting nature, and intellectual disability present serious challenges to his self-care skills (it is likely that he could not find and maintain work without George's help). Furthermore, Lennie's sensory difference leads to the novella's climactic conflict, as his desire for sensory stimulation (stroking soft animals or materials) ultimately results in an accidental death.[24] While studies have shown that it is virtually unheard of for autistic sensory issues to contribute to violent behavior, Steinbeck's popular novella offers sensory integration

dysfunction as the primary cause in a murder.[25] Although this turn of events is extremely improbable, it may give modern readers (who are generally more aware of autistic traits than a 1930s audience would have been) a feeling of unease, causing them to perceive people on the spectrum as potentially dangerous. Ultimately, Lennie's death is "authorized" by cultural discourses that depict autistic people as violent and threatening because of a perceived lack of human subjectivity.

Multiple stereotypes regarding autism and intellectual disability help to reduce the reader's perception of Lennie's subjectivity and thus to validate the supposed heroism of George's mercy killing.[26] For example, Steinbeck depicts Lennie as both childlike and unusually large and strong.[27] During the early 1900s, "popular discussions of intellectual disability constructed it in two ways: the body could be seen as physically incompetent, a reflection of the mind's vacancy, or it could become dangerously healthy, an exemplar of the body without a mind to control it."[28] Although autism conveys no particular physical attributes, public perceptions of those on the spectrum as unusually large and strong are still prevalent today.[29] Benjy Compson of *The Sound and the Fury* (see the discussion in chapter 4 [original volume]) is another autistic character who is depicted as being an unusually large man (he is much taller than his caregiver, Luster, and Faulkner compares him to a lumbering bear). Indeed, Faulkner's description of Benjy is remarkably similar to Steinbeck's description of Lennie. Steinbeck describes Lennie as "a huge man, shapeless of face, with large, pale eyes, with wide, sloping shoulders; he walked heavily, dragging his feet a little, the way a bear drags his paws. His arms did not swing at his sides, but hung loosely."[30] As Martin Halliwell argues, "Lennie's 'shapeless' features and 'heavy' walk mark him out as an idiot figure, with his large size, his proximity to animals (bear) and objects (pendulum) reinforcing his lack of freewill and rationality."[31] A plethora of stereotypes combine in Steinbeck's description: the autistic Lennie is unusually large, animal-like, mechanical, clumsy, and symbolically deprived of "freewill and rationality." Indeed, Lennie's strong connection with (and frequent comparison to) animals is an example of an overarching literary trend: "The relationship between intellectual disability and animality has a long history."[32] As many critics have noted, Steinbeck constantly compares Lennie to animals throughout the novella.[33] This literary depiction participates in a larger philosophical trend:

> Animal rights theorists have paid special attention to those with cognitive disabilities. Some have averred that we need to parse our moral universe so that "normal" human and nonhuman beings who possess the capacity for reason constitute one category, while nonhuman animals and intellectually subpar humans together constitute another. If these philosophers are right, then people who are lacking the capacity ... for rational deliberation cannot be our equals—they are non-persons. ... The controversy indicates the extent to which the moral status of individuals with cognitive disabilities remains unsettled.[34]

Writing in 2009, Carlson noted that even with an ever-increasing awareness of disability rights, "when I looked for contemporary discussions about this group [people with intellectual disabilities], most of the references I found were in discussions of animal rights, asking pointedly whether the severely mentally retarded can be distinguished from non-human animals in any meaningful sense."[35] These stereotypes (dangerous uncontrollable size and animal metaphors) work together in forming the

literary (and cultural) texts that reduce Lennie's perceived subjectivity and humanity, thus "authorizing" Lennie's autistic filicide.

In the novella, Steinbeck builds on common stereotypes of mental disability to transform an actual murder that he witnessed into a fictional tale: these alterations to the real-life events work to reduce Lennie's subjectivity and agency. In reality, Steinbeck's Lennie was based on a man whom Steinbeck had known in his own days working as a migrant worker:

> The characters are composites to some extent. Lennie was a real person. He's in an insane asylum in California right now. I worked alongside him for many weeks. He didn't kill a girl. He killed a ranch foreman. Got sore because the boss had fired his pal and stuck a pitchfork right through his stomach. I hate to tell you how many times. I saw him do it. We couldn't stop him until it was too late.[36]

The actual event on which Steinbeck's work was based was wildly different from the situation presented in the novella. In reality, the murder had a different motive (in Steinbeck's opinion, the man committed murder because "the boss had fired his pal"), the victim of the crime is altered (the foreman is killed, not his wife), the manner of death is more overtly violent (a deliberate stabbing as opposed to an accident), and the disability status of the killer is highly ambiguous (Steinbeck perceived the man as having some kind of intellectual disability, although his depiction of Lennie highlights traits strongly associated in the public mind with autism). By altering the perceived level of violence and the motive for the murder, Steinbeck clearly depicts the crime in the novella as accidental rather than deliberate, thus creating an ambiguous moral dilemma that has tortured generations of high school students. More importantly,

Steinbeck's alterations of his real-life source material highlight Lennie's disability and difference. The change of perceived motive for the crime—a move from social motivation to sensory motivation—emphasizes Lennie's fundamental Otherness: neurotypical readers are not likely to share Lennie's intense sensory responses. Significantly, Steinbeck presents Lennie's sensory issues as a force that controls his character. A murder driven by sensory needs greatly reduces Lennie's agency: he seems to be controlled by his impairment. In short, Steinbeck alters his real-life source material in ways that highlight Lennie's autistic nature and that may reduce the character's subjectivity.

However, the most telling alteration from the real-life case is that of the gender of the victim: the circumstances surrounding the death of Curley's wife invoke stereotypical fears of disabled sexuality, depicting sexuality as an uncontrollable force that overrides Lennie's agency. The fear of disabled sexuality has a long cultural lineage, and the eugenics movement of the early twentieth century created an environment that only served to reinforce "societal fears that cognitively disabled men are always potentially violent sexual predators."[37] During this time period, "sexual criminality was seen as synonymous with cognitive impairment."[38] Indeed, many literary critics have noted the implied potential for sexual violence underlying the accidental death in Steinbeck's novella. Although Lennie's encounter with Curley's wife is clearly not a rape, "the implication of sexual danger exists at the level of word transfer: petting animals versus petting women changes the whole nature of the event."[39] Leo Gurko agrees: "Lennie is ... presented as a violent sexual predator."[40] In fact, one of the official "articles of belief" (published in 1912) justifying the eugenics movement stated that "feeble-minded persons, especially females,

have abnormally strong sex drives which they are unable to control."[41] Unfortunately, these stereotypes regarding disabled sexuality have persisted into modern discourses in various ways. There are still false rumors on the Internet that men with Asperger's are more likely to commit rape than their neurotypical counterparts, although there is no evidence to support such claims (these rumors may be based on a misplaced fear that difficulty decoding social cues might result in an inability to recognize a woman's lack of consent). Sensory issues that involve hypersensitivity to touch may also be misinterpreted or falsely sexualized. As Halliwell argues, "Lennie's love of fur and soft material is certainly an indication of his polymorphous sexuality."[42] Interpreting Lennie as autistic, I would argue that his intense desire for this kind of sensory input is a result of sensory integration needs that have little or no relationship to sexuality.[43] In general, cultural depictions of people on the spectrum display the two stereotypical extremes accorded by our society to disabled sexuality in general (people with disabilities are imagined as either asexual or as hypersexual/sexually deviant).[44] While the stereotype of the asexual savant has been more popular in the past two decades (think of television characters such as Spencer Reid and Dr. Sheldon Cooper of *The Big Bang Theory*), people with cognitive impairments were more likely to be imagined as hypersexual in the 1920s and 1930s. Clearly, these attitudes contributed to the widespread sterilization and institutionalization of people with mental disabilities during this era.[45]

In fact, the implied potential for sexual violence in Lennie's depiction is reinforced by the proposed punishment for his crime: Curley and the other ranch workers threaten to lynch the cognitively disabled man, thus intertwining cultural narratives of eugenics and ableism with historical discourses surrounding rape and racism. According to Michelle Jarman, in "the early twentieth century . . . discourses surrounding white-on-black lynching and the eugenic castration of cognitively disabled men," while forming "distinct historical practices, . . . are actually profoundly interconnected."[46] Jarman goes on to explore the "link . . . between eugenic narratives of abnormal sexuality and the rape stories used to mobilize racist mob violence," explaining that "the 'black rapist' and the sexually aggressive 'moron' represented tangible threats to the sanctity of white domesticity. White men . . . cast themselves as chivalrous heroes who rescued 'their' women and families by eliminating these menaces."[47] Like the imaginary threat to women supposedly posed by victims of lynching, the popular construction of cognitively disabled men as hypersexualized set up a particular minority group as a perceived threat to a normative ideal of white heterosexual marriage.[48] It is significant that Lennie (as a representative of disabled sexuality) kills a married woman rather than a single one, as he symbolically comes between Curley and his wife. In Steinbeck's novella, however, it is George who is depicted as heroic, as his killing of his friend serves to protect normative sexuality from the uncontrollable and hypersexualized disabled body, symbolically "protecting" his society from the possibility that Lennie will pass on a genetic legacy of mental disability. Overall, the fictional female victim draws attention to larger cultural fears of disabled sexuality and ultimately suggests that Lennie, driven by sexual need, is out of control and lacking in agency.

Yet George's act of euthanasia is culturally authorized by more than just hints of potential sexual violence: animal metaphors are again brought into play to justify his actions and to present Lennie as lacking in human subjectivity. Edward E. Waldron has noted that "Steinbeck uses Candy's early behavior toward his dog as both a foreshadowing and an example against which to measure George's behavior toward Lennie."[49] As Stephanie Jensen-Moulton explains, "In the novel, Steinbeck does not afford Lennie fully human stature. He is cruelly executed in exactly the same manner as Candy's old dog."[50] Approval of these actions is directly provided by Slim, "the prince of the ranch" whose "word is law." Slim approves of both the killing of Candy's dog and George's execution of Lennie: "This confirmation of the necessity of his action might not comfort George, but it does affirm for the reader the lightness of George's action in the value scheme of the novel."[51] Waldron and Jensen-Moulton have both noted that Steinbeck's use of animal imagery is an underlying argument for Lennie's death. According to Waldron, "A point often made by proponents of active euthanasia for hopelessly dying patients is that we accept such actions on behalf of animals in our society."[52] In sum, Lennie's comparison to animals validates his death by denying that people with cognitive disabilities have human subjectivity.

Ultimately, Lennie's death might serve as a theoretical example of the ways in which the cultural denial of autistic subjectivity informs violence: the death of a cognitively disabled person may be read through the lens of euthanasia regardless of circumstance. The belief that there is no subjectivity within the intellectually disabled body, that the autistic body is an empty frame that must inevitably be suffering, seems to underpin common responses to Steinbeck's novella. George's killing of Lennie is most often understood as a form of euthanasia.[53] Waldron's interpretation is typical of this common approach: "George knows that Lennie will die as the result of his killing Curley's wife, either by being blasted by Curley and the other hands or by being locked up in an institution. Lennie is, in effect, 'terminally ill,' that is, he faces imminent death. George chooses to provide a more tolerable form of dying for his friend."[54] As a matter of fact, Lennie isn't terminally ill. He is about to be lynched. What if Lennie were not disabled but were instead part of another cultural minority group? If Lennie were African American, would his white friend George be portrayed as a hero for shooting him in order to prevent a lynching?[55] If we imagine Lennie as part of a different cultural group, the pivotal role of society and discrimination in George's "merciful" decision is suddenly all too apparent. As Jarman explains, our society views racial issues as "volatile, divisive, and political," while disability issues are generally viewed as "medical and individual."[56] The political and public aspect of Lennie's death (threatened lynching) is obfuscated in critical discussions of Steinbeck's work because readers and critics usually focus on the isolated and private aspect of Lennie's death (what is culturally read as euthanasia). Such an approach denies disability as a social and political issue, insisting that impairment be read as a private tragedy.[57]

Furthermore, stereotypes about autism work in subtle ways to culturally authorize George's criminal act. Lennie is depicted as being unable to understand the full magnitude of what he has done and as having so little control that he may not be able to prevent doing it again in the future. In effect, the novella is *only* able to present mercy killing as a viable moral option because Lennie is disabled—the plot of the novella simply would not make sense in our cultural imagination if Lennie were neurotypical. George kills his autistic friend because Lennie faces social discrimination that the novella presents as natural, justified, and unchangeable. In fact, the novella was first titled *Something That Happened:* "Steinbeck was not interested in exploring the reasons why events transpired in a particular way, but tried to focus on a particular occurrence and its consequences."[58] Of course, Lennie's

death, while depicted as though divorced from both past and future, an unpreventable tragedy in which no other course is possible, is not just "something that happened" but a choice that George (and Steinbeck) make as a result of a certain set of cultural ideologics. Because the autistic victim is presented as being without true subjectivity, readers may falsely perceive George's choice as the only option when in fact other options exist. Shouldn't George try to stop the mob? Or try to turn his friend in to authorities who will prevent the mob violence? Or even try to help his friend escape because George knows that the court system will not render true justice? On a larger scale, the novella does not address the role of good care, education, and therapy for Lennie. Lennie's material conditions and socioeconomic status come into play here: George cannot afford to find appropriate care and therapy.[59] Shouldn't those circumstances be changed? Placing Lennie in an institution is also disregarded as a viable option because psychiatric institutions are perceived to be places of suffering. Shouldn't such institutions be changed? If a jury is perceived as being unable to render true justice for Lennie, shouldn't the prejudices of the jury be changed? George finds that shooting his autistic friend is easier than answering any of these questions.

If Lennie is an autistic character, then his death at George's hands gains contemporary relevance in comparison to recent media depictions of autistic filicide: media representations of these tragedies broach the division between literary fiction and reality, as these cultural texts (televised reports, newspaper articles, and online blogs) deny autistic subjectivity and assume the lens of euthanasia. George is Lennie's only "family," and Steinbeck presents him as both guardian and father figure for his infantilized friend:

> George's voice became deeper. He repeated his words rhythmically as though he had

said them many times before. "Guys like us, that work on ranches, are the loneliest guys in the world. They got no family. They don't belong no place. ..."

Lennie broke in. "*But not us! An' why? Because ... because I got you to look after me, and you got me to look after you, and that's why.*"

(14–15, second ellipses in the original)

Violence against people with autism is often perpetrated by family members.[60] Rosemarie Garland-Thomson has written about "the cultural logic of euthanasia":

The logic of "cure or kill," accompanied by today's faith in technology, is that if the disabled body cannot be normalized, it must be eliminated. If it does not respond to being improved, if it refuses to register the success of the rescuer's moral or technological efforts, the disabled body becomes intolerable, a witness to the human inability to perfect the world.[61]

Many readers see George, in his role as both father and killer, as Lennie's "rescuer."[62] The critical history of Steinbeck's work seems to affirm the supposition that Lennie is without subjectivity, that he does not exist without his neurotypical friend. In the end, the ethical debate that has engaged generations of critics (and generations of high school students) is not really about Lennie's death so much as it is about George's decision.

NOTES

1. See studies such as Mark T. Palermo, "Preventing Filicide in Families with Autistic Children," *Offender Therapy and Comparative Criminology* 47, no. 1 (2003): 47–57: "Autism ... has been associated with an increased risk of social victimization, and a recent rise in number of acts of filicide of developmentally disabled children has included several cases of autism" (ibid., 47); and Rohini Coorg and Anne Tournay, "Filicide-Suicide

Involving Children with Disabilities," *Journal of Child Neurology* 28, no. 6 (2013): 745–751. Although official record keeping is difficult, Coorg and Tournay found that 54 percent of disabled filicide victims were autistic: "Children with autism may be at risk for filicide-suicide, but accurate record keeping is needed to determine the incidence and risk factors" (ibid., 745). Many disability rights activists have noted the prevalence of autistic filicides. For example, see Cevick, "Invisible Autistic Filicide Victims."

2. Throughout this introduction, I'm indebted to Stuart Murray's excellent discussion of autistic filicide in *Representing Autism*, 167–171.

3. Ibid., 168. Cevick comments that "murder apologists continue to respond in posted comments about the difficulties in parenting autistic children rather than reacting to the horrific nature of this pattern of filicide-suicide. ... Children and disabled adult victims are treated as collateral damage for exhausted parents" ("Invisible Autistic Filicide Victims").

4. Murray, *Representing Autism*, 168.

5. Ibid., 168–169. This is part of what Michelle Jarman describes as "media inattention to disability oppression" ("Dismembering the Lynch Mob: Intersecting Narratives of Disability, Race, and Sexual Menace," in *Sex and Disability*, ed. Robert McRuer and Anna Mollow [Durham, NC: Duke University Press, 2012], 89–107, quote at 91).

6. ABC news story quoted in Murray, *Representing Autism*, 169.

7. Ibid.

8. On the "cure or kill" trope in literary works, see Rosemarie Garland-Thomson, "Seeing the Disabled: Visual Rhetorics of Disability in Popular Photography," in *New Disability History*, ed. Paul K. Longmore and Lauri Umansky (New York: New York University Press, 2001), 355.

9. Ed Pilkington, "Texas Set to Execute Death Row Inmate Diagnosed as 'Mentally Retarded,'" *Guardian*, 5 August 2012, www.theguardian.com/world/2012/aug/05/texas-death-row-mentally-retarded, accessed 24 July 2014.

10. Ibid.

11. Ibid.

12. Ibid.

13. Quoted in ibid.

14. See Pilkington's discussion in ibid.

15. Rania Khalek, "Steinbecks: Leave Lennie Alone," *Salon*, 8 August 2012, www.salon.com/2012/08/08/steinbecks_leave_lennie_alone/, accessed 24 July 2014.

16. See Edward E. Waldron, "Using Literature to Teach Ethical Principles in Medicine: *Of Mice*

and Men and the Concept of Duty," *Literature and Medicine* 7 (1988): 170–176.

17. Sally Chivers, "Disability Studies and the Vancouver Opera's *Of Mice and Men*," *Disability Studies Quarterly* 23, no. 1 (2003), http://dsq-sds.org/article/view/402/551; Mitchell and Snyder include both *Of Mice and Men* and *Flowers for Algernon* on their list of novels about disability that have shaped U.S. education (*Narrative Prosthesis*, 167).

18. Patrick McDonagh, "Literature and the Notion of Intellectual Disability," *Disability Studies Quarterly* 17, no. 4 (1997): 272.

19. Licia Carlson, *The Faces of Intellectual Disability* (Bloomington: Indiana University Press, 2010), 3.

20. See Stephanie Jensen-Moulton, "Intellectual Disability in Carlisle Floyd's *Of Mice and Men*," *American Music* 30, no. 2 (2012): 129–156. Jensen-Moulton comes closest by comparing Lennie to Kanner's early description: "Steinbeck's understanding of intellectual disability was grounded not only in his own experience working alongside the man on whom he later based Lennie's character, but would also have found its basis in contemporary thought. Psychiatrist Leo Kanner had already established himself as a prominent teacher and scholar by the early 1930s, specializing in the intellectual disability he would later call autism. As Kanner writes—albeit with dated terminology—'mental defectives were viewed as a menace to civilization, incorrigible at home, burdens to the school, sexually promiscuous, breeders of feebleminded offspring, victims and spreaders of poverty, degeneracy, crime and disease.' Clearly, Steinbeck's Lennie—whose seemingly innocent desire to touch soft things results in such a tragic outcome—falls somewhere within the categories outlined above by Kanner, thereby reinforcing negative stereotypes about cognitive differences" (ibid., 146–147).

21. Elaine Liner, "Theatre Arlington Stages a Solid and Serious *Of Mice and Men*," *Dallas Observer*, 31 October 2013, www.dallasobserver.com/2013-10-31/culture/theatre-arlington-stages-a-solid-and-serious-of-mice-and-men/full/, accessed 25 July 2014.

22. John Steinbeck, *Of Mice and Men* (New York: Penguin Books, 1994), Kindle edition, page 11. Hereafter cited parenthetically in the text.

23. See Martin Halliwell, *Images of Idiocy: The Idiot Figure in Modern Fiction and Film* (Aldershot: Ashgate, 2004). As Halliwell explains, "Retelling the story of the farm is a ritual to comfort Lennie when he feels vulnerable or tired" (ibid., 147).

24. As Jensen-Moulton notes, "Lennie's need for sensory stimulation would, in the end, be the downfall of their dream" ("Intellectual Disability," 131).

25. Marianne Mordre et al., "Is Long-Term Prognosis for Pervasive Developmental Disorder Not Otherwise Specified Different from Prognosis for Autistic Disorder? Findings from a 30-Year Follow-Up Study," *Journal of Autism and Developmental Disorders* 42, no. 6 (2011): 920–928.

26. See Susan Baglieri and Arthur Shapiru, *Disability Studies and the Inclusive Classroom* (New York: Routledge, 2012), 226. Lennie is a classic example of at least two established tropes for disabled characters: "the victim of violence" and "the Holy innocent or the eternal child" (ibid.).

27. See Chivers, "Disability Studies," for further discussion of Lennie's size.

28. Janice Brockley quoted in ibid.

29. I have a friend who teaches in a classroom in which all of the children are autistic. When people find out where she works, they often ask with concern, "Are your students big?" This odd question seems to be inspired by a fear for my friend's physical safety (she is a very petite woman). Although there is no scientific basis for the belief that autistic people will be larger than neurotypical people, my friend and I have often wondered if this perception may be based on cultural fears that all autistic people are uncontrollable and need to be physically restrained.

30. Steinbeck, *Of Mice and Men*, 4.

31. Halliwell, *Images of Idiocy*, 144. In this chapter, some of my sources refer to medical terminology used to describe mental disabilities in previous eras (such as "feebleminded," "moron," "idiot," and "retarded"). These terms are outdated and offensive and are not my terms.

32. Carlson quoted in Jensen-Moulton, "Intellectual Disability," 140. See also Anupama Iyer, "Portrayal of Intellectual Disability in Fiction," in *Mindreadings: Literature and Psychiatry*, ed. Femi Oyebode (London: RCPsych Publications, 2009), Kindle edition. Iyer notes that "resemblance to and kinship with animals is often called forth to emphasize the difference of people with intellectual disabilities and signal that they are not quite human" (locator 2665).

33. As Jensen-Moulton notes, Steinbeck "perpetuates the stereotype of the intellectually disabled as animalistic or subhuman in behavior as well as level of communication and predictability" ("Intellectual Disability," 140).

34. Licia Carlson and Eva Feder Kittay quoted in ibid., 145. As Jensen-Moulton argues, "Steinbeck's novel unsubtly reflects the link between intellectual disability and animal rights through the litany of small animals left dead in Lennie's wake and his motivic use of animals in the novel. While Steinbeck himself was no animal rights activist, the animals in the novel represent both the fragility of life

and the connection between these innocent creatures' deaths and Lennie's euthanasia" (ibid., 146).

35. Carlson, *The Faces of Intellectual Disability*, 2.

36. "Men, Mice, and Mr. Steinbeck: *New York Times/*
1937," in *Conversations with John Steinbeck*, ed.
Thomas Fensch (Jackson: University Press of
Mississippi, 1988), 8–10.

37. Jensen-Moulton, "Intellectual Disability," 131.
Jarman also explores "the presumed sexual threat
of cognitively disabled men" during Steinbeck's
lifetime ("Dismembering the Lynch Mob," 91).

38. Jarman, "Dismembering the Lynch Mob," 100.

39. Jensen-Moulton, "Intellectual Disability," 149.

40. Leo Gurko, "The War between Good and Evil,"
Readings on "Of Mice and Men" (San Diego, CA:
Greenhaven, 1998), 62.

41. Baglieri and Shapiru, *Disability Studies*, 227.

42. Halliwell, *Images of Idiocy*, 148.

43. Anecdotal evidence on "Wrong Planet" seems to
suggest that autistics who are hypersensitive to
touch may be less likely to engage in sexual
activity, although I'm not aware of any studies on
this subject.

44. Disabled people are often portrayed as "sexual predators" or "sexual innocents" (Heather Garrison,
"Adolescents' Perceptions of the Sociocultural
Construct of Disability When Responding to Literature: *Of Mice and* Men," 44, *ETD Collection for Ford-
ham University*, http://fordham.bepress.com/
dissertations/AAI3302114, accessed 7 August 2014).

45. See Jarman's discussion in "Dismembering the
Lynch Mob." For an approach to eugenics specific
to *Of Mice and Men*, see Baglieri and Shapiru:
"The character, Lennie, exemplifies a view of intellectually disabled persons as social menaces
contributing to the genetic decline and social dis-
organization that proliferated during the era of
eugenics" (*Disability Studies*, 227).

46. Jarman, "Dismembering the Lynch Mob," 89–90.

47. Ibid., 93.

48. Ibid.

49. Waldron, "Using Literature," 172. Chivers
("Disability Studies") and Halliwell (*Images of
Idiocy*) also make the same point.

50. Jensen-Moulton, "Intellectual Disability," 152.

51. Waldron, "Using Literature," 176.

52. Ibid.

53. Many critics have viewed *Of Mice and Men* as a
novella about euthanasia (e.g., see Waldron,
"Using Literature"; Chivers "Disability Studies";
and Jensen-Moulton, "Intellectual Disability").

54. Waldron, "Using Literature," 175.

55. I am not arguing that racism and ableism are
parallel cultural phenomena (these two forms
of discrimination are distinct entities that function in different ways; see Jarman's discussion
in "Dismembering the Lynch Mob," 103). It is
important to note both the ways that discourses
of race and disability overlap and inform each
other and the key ways in which they differ. I'm
merely using this imaginary exercise in an
attempt to highlight the ways in which the disability rights movement has lagged far behind
the civil rights movement.

56. Jarman, "Dismembering the Lynch Mob," 90.

57. See Jarman's discussion of private versus public in
lynching and castration (ibid., 104).

58. Halliwell, *Images of Idiocy*, 138.

59. Many autistic self-advocates have critiqued media
rhetoric that seems to "blame" autistic filicide on a
lack of appropriate support for caregivers. Such
rhetoric seems to imply that autistic filicide could
be prevented if only caregivers received more
social and financial support. Arguing that a caregiver
who becomes a killer simply needed more resources
evokes sympathy for the killer and draws attention
away from the autistic victim. By saying that better
care, education, and therapy might improve the
fictional Lennie's prospects, I am not espousing that
kind of rhetoric. Do autistics and their families need
better services and support? Of course they do. Is a
lack of services and support an extenuating circumstance that justifies homicide? Of course it isn't. In
this chapter, I am arguing that cultural attitudes that
devalue and deny autistic subjectivity and personhood contribute to autistic filicide, not that a lack of
services encourages filicide.

60. See Jarman's discussion of disability, family, and
violence ("Dismembering the Lynch Mob," 104).

61. Garland-Thomson, "Seeing the Disabled," 355.
See Jensen-Moulton's discussion in "Intellectual
Disability."

62. See Jensen-Moulton, "Intellectual Disability," for
further discussion.

PART VII

Fiction, Memoir, and Poetry

CHAPTER 35

Stones in My Pockets, Stones in My Heart

Eli Clare

SUMMARY

Eli Clare is the author of a book of essays titled *Exile and Pride: Disability, Queerness, and Liberation* and a collection of poetry, *The Marrow's Telling: Words in Motion*. His work focuses on disability, queer, and trans identities, and social justice.

In "Stones in My Pocket, Stones in My Heart," Clare writes about the ways that disability, class, sexuality, and race are inevitably "piling into a single human body." The memoir begins in Clare's teen years and raises questions about the connections between his gender status and sexual abuse at the hands of his father. For Clare, understanding his sexuality is always tied to the power relationship with his father.

Clare gives context to his experience by explaining that part of the transgender/transsexual movement is the deconstruction of a gender binary that automatically links femininity to female-bodied people and masculinity to male-bodied people. Those who maintain the binary, Clare suggests, inherently maintain the hierarchy of power that structures situations of abuse. Thus he understands his father's abusive actions in a larger context of socially constructed gender binaries.

Even as Clare recalls a period of increasing comfort with butch identity, he must also investigate the ways that a lower-class childhood and disabled body affect social situations. While claiming gender ambiguity, Clare asks if disabled people can also refuse the binaries of disabled and non-disabled in an effort to reclaim their bodies. Clare describes a scene of his tremoring hands "trembling with CP, with desire, with the last remnants of fear, trembling because this is how my body moves."

Gender reaches into disability; disability wraps around class; class strains against abuse; abuse snarls into sexuality; sexuality folds on top of race...everything finally piling into a single human body. To write about any aspect of identity, any aspect of the body, means writing about this entire maze. This I know, and yet the question remains: where to start? Maybe with my white skin, stubbly red hair, left ear pierced, shoulders set slightly off center, left riding higher than right, hands tremoring, traced with veins, legs well-muscled. Or with me in the mirror, dressing to go out, knotting my tie, slipping into my blazer, curve of hip and breast vanishing beneath my clothes. Or possibly with the memory of how my body felt swimming in the river, chinook fingerlings nibbling at my toes. There are a million ways to start, but how do I reach beneath the skin?

* * *

Age 13, hair curling down around my ears, glasses threatening to slide off my nose, I work with my father every weekend building a big wooden barn of a house. I wear overalls, my favorite flannel shirt, sleeves rolled up over a long-john top, and well-worn work boots. Over the years, my mother and I have fought about my hair. I want to cut the curls off; she thinks they're pretty. All morning I have sawed 2 × 12 girders to length, helped my father pound them into place. I come home from the building site to pick up a crowbar and eat lunch. A hammer hangs from my hammer loop; a utility knife rides in my bib pocket. I ask my mother, "Am I feminine?" My memory stops here. I do not remember what possessed me to ask that question, what I wanted to know, what my mother answered.

* * *

Feminine. Female. Girl. I watched my younger sister spend hours in the bathroom with a curling iron, my mother with her nail file and eyebrow tweezers. I watched and listened to the girls in my school talk about boys, go behind the equipment shed to kiss them, later whisper in algebra class about fucking them. I watched from the other side of a stone wall, a wall that was part self-preservation, part bones and blood of aloneness, part the impossible assumptions I could not shape my body around.

Dresses. Make-up. High heels. Perfume. I tried wearing the skirts my mother sewed for me. She urged me into Girl Scouts, slumber parties, the 4-H knitting and sewing clubs. I failed, not wanting any part of these activities. I loved my work boots and overalls long after all the other girls had discovered pantyhose and mini-skirts. But failing left a hole in my heart; I wanted to belong somewhere.

Am I feminine? Maybe I meant: "What am I, a girl, a boy, something else entirely?" Maybe I meant: "Can I be a girl *like this*?" Or maybe I was simply trying to say: "Mama, I don't understand." What did I want her to

say? At 13, I didn't have a clue what it meant to be feminine or, for that matter, masculine. Those words were empty signifiers, important only because I knew I was supposed to have an attachment to femininity. At 13, my most sustaining relations were not in the human world. I collected stones—red, green, gray, rust, white speckled with black, black streaked with silver—and kept them in my pockets, their hard surfaces warming slowly to my body heat. Spent long days at the river learning what I could from the salmon, frogs, and salamanders. Roamed the beaches at high tide and low, starfish, mussels, barnacles clinging to the rocks. Wandered in the hills thick with moss, fern, liverwort, bramble, tree. Only here did I have a sense of body. Those stones warm in my pockets, I knew them to be the steadiest, only inviolate parts of myself. I wanted to be a hermit, to live alone with my stones and trees, neither a boy nor a girl. And now 20 years later, how do I reach beneath the skin to write, not about the stones, but the body that warmed them, the heat itself?

* * *

I could start with the ways my body has been stolen from me. Start slowly, reluctantly, with my parents. My father who raised me, his eldest daughter, as an almost son. My father who started raping me so young I can't remember when he first forced his penis into me. My mother who tells me she didn't know about his violence. I believe her because I know how her spirit vacated the premises, leaving only her body as a marker. My mother who closed her eyes and turned her back, who said to my father, "She's yours to raise as you see fit." My mother who was shaped entirely by absence and my father who taught me the hills and woods: they were the first thieves.

But tell me, if I start here by placing the issues of violence and neglect on the table alongside my queerness, what will happen next? Will my words be used against me, twisted to bolster the belief that sexual abuse causes homosexuality, contorted to provide evidence that transgressive gender identity is linked directly to neglect? Most feminist and queer activists reject these linkages and for good reason. Conservatives often use them to discredit lesbian, gay, bi, and trans identities and to argue for our conversion rather than our liberation. But this strategy of denial, rejecting any possibility of connection between abuse and gender identity, abuse and sexuality, slams a door on the messy reality of how our bodies are stolen.

* * *

I question my mother about that day when I asked, "Am I feminine?" I hope she will remember my question and her answer and offer me some clues about what I wanted to know. She has no memory of that day, but reminds me of something else. One year during the long rainy season we called winter, the Lions Club held a carnival in the old, falling-down junior high gymnasium. I wasted money on "the man-eating fish," only to see Tiny Lawrence eating tuna from a can, laughed at the boys throwing wet sponges at the volunteer firemen, then stood watching a woman draw quick cartoon-like portraits, each signed "Betsy Hammond" with a flourish. She was new to town, and I, curious, eventually paid my dollar to sit down in front of her easel. I recognized myself in the resulting drawing, liked the hard lines that defined my face, the angle of my jaw, the toughness in my mouth.

Weeks later in the grocery store, my mother introduced herself to Betsy. They started talking about husbands and children, and soon my mother mentioned me, her eldest daughter, and the portrait I had brought home from the carnival. Betsy didn't know what my mother was talking about. Finally after much confusion, she asked, "Didn't I draw your son?" I remember the complete joy I felt when my mother came home with this story. I looked again and again at the portrait, thinking, "Right here, right now, I am a boy." It made me smile secretly for weeks, reach down into my pockets to squeeze a stone tight in each fist. I felt as if I were looking in a mirror and finally seeing myself, rather than some distorted fun-house image.

* * *

How do I write not about the stones, but the heat itself? I could start by asking some hard, risky questions. Really, I'd rather hang out with my ten-year-old self and share in her moment of glee as she looked in the mirror. But truly, those questions feel inevitable, and my boyhood pleasure turns cold when I dip into the messy reality of how my body was stolen. So, whatever the risk, let me ask.

How did my father's violence, his brutal taking of me over and over again, help shape and damage my body, my sexuality, my gender identity? How did his gendered abuse—and in this culture vaginal rape is certainly gendered—reinforce my sense of not being a girl? How did his non-abusive treatment of me as an almost son interact with the ways in which his fists and penis and knives told me in no uncertain terms that I was a girl? How did watching him sexually abuse other children—both boys and girls—complicate what I knew of being girl, being boy? How did my mother's willful ignorance of the hurt he inflicted on me influence what I absorbed about femininity and masculinity?

* * *

Little did I know back then as I carried that carnival caricature home with me that the experience of being called sir, assumed to be a young man, would become a regular occurrence. This gender ambiguity, being seen as a woman at one turn and a teenage boy at the next, marks to a large extent my queerness. When people stumble over their pronouns, stammer, blush, or apologize in embarrassment, I often think of Riki Anne Wilchins' description of her friend Holly Boswell:

> Holly is a delicate Southern belle of long acquaintance. .... S/he has tender features, long, wavy blonde hair, a soft Carolina accent, a delicate feminine bosom, and no interest in surgery. Holly lives as an open transgendered mother of two in Ashville, North Carolina. Her comforting advice to confused citizens struggling with whether to use Sir or Madam is, "Don't give it a second thought. You don't have a pronoun yet for me."[1]

Sometimes when I'm read as a woman, I actively miss hearing "sir," "ma'am" sounding foreign, distant, unfamiliar, even wrong to me. Usually I feel safer, somewhat buffered from men's violence against women, walking the streets after dark, knowing my night-time outline and stride are frequently read as male. But mostly, I feel matter-of-fact: "Oh yeah, this is happening again."

Many dykes feel angered, irritated, dismayed, shamed by the experience of being read as male, feel the need to assert their womanhood. And in the same vein, I hear all the time about gay men who pump up their masculinity. To defend and strengthen one's authentic gender identity is important. But all too often I hear defensiveness in the argument that butch dykes don't mimic men but carve out new ways of being women; in the gay male personals that dismiss femmes and drag queens out of hand. Is this our one and only response to a heterosexist world that refuses to recognize feminine males and masculine females, that challenges our very queerness?

In the past decade, the burgeoning transgender/transsexual movement has questioned and started to wage a struggle against the binary gender system that automatically links female-bodied people to femininity to womanhood and male-bodied people to masculinity to manhood. Even the binary of female-bodied and male-bodied appears more and more to be a social construction as intersexed people—people who for any number of reasons are born with or develop ambiguous genitals, reproductive organs, and/or secondary sex characteristics—begin to speak publicly of their lives and the medical intrusion they've faced. How natural are the rigid, mutually exclusive definitions of male and female if they have to be defended by genital surgery performed on intersexed people? The trans movement suggests a world full of gender and sex variation, a world much more complex than one divided into female-bodied women and male-bodied men. Many trans activists argue for an end, not to the genders of woman and man, but to the socially constructed binary.

Within this context, to answer the homophobes becomes easy, those folks who want to dehumanize, erase, make invisible the lives of butch dykes and nellie fags. We shrug. We laugh. We tell them: your definitions of woman and man suck. We tell them: your binary stinks. We say: here we are in all our glory—male, female, intersexed, trans, butch, nellie, studly, femme, king, androgynous, queen, some of us carving out new ways of being women, others of us new ways of being men, and still others new ways of being something else entirely. *You don't have pronouns yet for us.*

* * *

How do I write not about the stones, but the heat itself? I could start with the brutal, intimate details of my father's thievery, of his hands clamping around my neck, tearing into me, claiming my body as his own. The brutal, intimate details, but listen: I get afraid that the homophobes are right, that maybe in truth I live as a transgendered butch because he raped me, my mother neglected me. I lose the bigger picture, forget that woven through and around the private and intimate is always the public and political.

We live in a time of epidemic child abuse, in a world where sexual and physical violence against children isn't only a personal tragedy and a symptom of power run amok, but also a form of social control. When a father rapes his daughter, a mother beats her son, a white schoolteacher sexually fondles a Black student, a middle-class man uses a working-class boy to make child pornography, a nondisabled caregiver leaves a disabled kid to sit in her/his urine for hours, these adults teach children bodily lessons about power and hierarchy, about being boys, being girls, being children, being Black, being working-class, being disabled.

What better way to maintain a power structure—white supremacy, male supremacy, capitalism, a binary and rigid gender system—than to drill the lessons of who is dominant and who is subordinate into the bodies of children. No, not every individual perpetrator thinks, "This kid has stepped too far outside. I need to beat/rape her back into line." But certainly the power imbalances out of which child abuse arises are larger than any individual perpetrator's conscious intentions. Social control happens exactly at the junctures where the existing power structure is—consciously or not—maintained and strengthened.

And here is the answer to my fear. Child abuse is not the cause of but rather a response to—among other things—transgressive gender identity and/or sexuality. The theory I'm trying to shape is not as simple as "My father abused me because I was a queer child who—by the time I had any awareness of gender—was not at all sure of my girlness," although some genderqueer kids do get raped specifically because of their queerness. Rather I want to say, "My father raped me for many reasons, and inside his acts of violence I learned about what it meant to be female, to be a child, to live in my particular body, and those lessons served the larger power structure and hierarchy well."

* * *

At the same time, our bodies are not merely blank slates upon which the powers-that-be write their lessons. We cannot ignore the body itself: the sensory, mostly non-verbal experience of our hearts and lungs, muscles and tendons, telling us and the world who we are. My childhood sense of being neither girl nor boy arose in part from the external lessons of abuse and neglect, from the confusing messages about masculinity and femininity that I could not comprehend; I would be a fool to claim otherwise. But just as certainly, there was a knowing that resided in my bones, in the stretch of my legs and arch of my back, in the stones lying against my skin, a knowing that whispered, "not girl, not boy."

Butch, nellie, studly, femme, king, androgynous, queen: how have we negotiated the lies and thievery, the ways gender is influenced by divisions of labor, by images of masculinity and femininity, by racism, sexism, classism, ableism, by the notions of "real" men and "real" women? And how, at the same time, have we listened to our own bodies? For me the answer is not simple.

I think about my disabled body. For too long, I hated my trembling hands, my precarious balance, my spastic muscles so repeatedly overtaken by tension and tremor, tried to hide them at all costs. More than once I wished to amputate my right arm so it wouldn't shake. Self-mutilation is shame of the baldest kind. All the lies contained in the words *retard, monkey, defect*; in the gawking, the pats on my head, and the tears cried on my shoulder; in the moments where I became someone's supercrip or tragedy: all those lies became my second skin.

I think about my disabled body, how as a teenager I escaped the endless pressure to have a boyfriend, to shave my legs, to wear make-up. The same lies that cast me as genderless, asexual, and undesirable also framed a space in which I was left alone to be my quiet, bookish, tomboy self, neither girl nor boy. Even then, I was grateful. But listen, if I had wanted to date boys, wear lipstick and mascara, play with feminine clothes—the silk skirt and pumps, the low-cut blouse, the outrageous prom dress—I would have had to struggle much longer and harder than my nondisabled counterparts. The sheer physical acts of shaving my legs and putting on make-up would have been hard enough. Harder still would have been the relentless arguing with my parents, resisting their image of me as asexual or vulnerable to assault, persuading them that I could in truth take care of myself at the movies with Brent Miller or Dave Wilson.[2] But in truth I didn't want to date Brent or wear the low-cut blouse. I shuddered at the thought. How would I have reacted to the gendered pressures my younger, nondisabled sister faced? For her the path of least resistance pointed in the direction of femininity; for me it led toward not-girl-not-boy. But to cast my abiding sense of gendered self simply as a reaction to ableism is to ignore my body and what it had to tell me. When I look around me in disability community, I see an amazing range of gender expression, running the gamut from feminine to androgynous to masculine, mixed and swirled in many patterns. Clearly we respond in a myriad of ways to the ableist construction of gender.

How do we negotiate the lies and listen to our bodies? I think about my disabled body, my queer butch body read as a teenage boy. The markers of masculinity—my shaved head and broad stance, direct gaze and muscled arms—are unmistakable. And so are the markers of disability—my heavy-heeled gait; my halting, uneven speech; the tremors in my hands, arms, and shoulders. They all twine together to shape me in the ableist world as either genderless or a teenage boy. The first is all too familiar to disabled people. The second arises from the gender binary, where if I am not recognized as a woman, then I am presumed to be a man or more likely, given my lack of height and facial hair, a teenage boy. These external perceptions match in large part my internal sense of gender, my bodily comfort with gender ambiguity. But if the external and internal didn't match, what then?

Once I sat in a writing workshop with straight, feminine, disabled women, and we talked for an entire afternoon about gender identity, precisely because of the damage inflicted when the external ableist perceptions don't match the internal sense of self. All too often, the thieves plant their lies, and our bodies absorb them as the only truth. Is it any surprise that sometimes my heart fills with small gray stones, which never warm to my body heat?

* * *

The work of thieves: certainly external perception, stereotypes, lies, false images, and oppression hold a tremendous amount of power. They define and create who we are, how we think of our bodies, our gendered selves. How do I write not about the stones, but the body that warms them, the heat itself? That question haunts me because I lived by splitting body from mind, body from consciousness, body from physical sensation, body from emotion as the bullies threw rocks and called *retard,* as my father and his buddies tied me down, pulled out their knives. My body became an empty house, one to which I seldom returned. I lived in exile; the stones rattling in my heart, resting in my pockets, were my one and only true body.

But just as the stolen body exists, so does the reclaimed body. I think of disabled people challenging the conception of a "perfect" body/mind. Ed Roberts sits out front of his house talking about crip liberation. Ellen Stohl shapes herself into a sex symbol for the disability community. I think of queer people pushing upon the dominant culture's containment of gender, pleasure, and sex. Drag queens and kings work the stage. Dykes take to the streets. Gay men defend public sex. Trans people of all varieties say, "This is how we can be men, women, how we can inhabit all the spaces in between." Radical faeries swirl in their pagan finery. Bisexual people resist a neat compartmentalizing of sexuality. I think of people of color, poor people, working-class people all thumbing their noses at the notion of assimilation. Over and over again, we take the lies and crumble them into dust.

But how do I write about *my* body reclaimed, full of pride and pleasure? It is easy to say that abuse and ableism and homophobia stole my body away, broke my desire, removed me from my pleasure in the stones warm against my skin, the damp sponginess of moss growing on a rotten log, the taste of spring water dripping out of rock. Harder to express how that break becomes healed, a bone once fractured, now whole, but different from the bone never broken. And harder still to follow the path between the two. How do I mark this place where my body is no longer an empty house, desire whistling lonely through the cracks, but not yet a house fully lived in? For me the path from stolen body to reclaimed body started with my coming out as a dyke.

* * *

I was 18 and had just moved to the city. I didn't want to be a girl, nor was I a boy. I hid my body, tried as much as possible to ignore it. During my first week of college, I started meeting dykes. In three weeks I began asking, "Am I a lesbian?" Once before, I had faced this question and known the answer. The summer I was 12, two women, friends of my parents, came visiting from Arkansas. I adored Suzanne and Susan, showed them my favorite spots, the best blackberry brambles, where the muskrat built her den. I wanted them to stay with me in my river valley. They came out to my parents, and later I overheard my father say that Suzanne was gay, his face growing tight and silent. Somehow I knew what that word meant, even though I barely understood *homosexual* and had only heard *lesbian* as a taunt. It made me smile. The image of Suzanne and Susan holding hands as we walked Battle Rock Beach stuck with me for weeks. I knew somewhere deep inside me, rising up to press against my sternum, that I was like them. This I knew, but by the time I turned 13, it had vanished.

Now at the age of 18, I picked the question up again. I had never kissed a boy, never had a boyfriend or girlfriend. I knew nothing about sexual desire. For me sex was bound together with abuse. I had learned the details from my father just as I had learned how to mix a wheelbarrow of concrete, frame a stud wall. Sex meant rape—that simple, that complicated. The only thing I knew about desire was the raw, split-openness that rampaged through me after he was done, how those feelings could overtake my body again late at night in my own bed, mounting up uncontainably. I was not in love with a woman; I didn't even have a crush. And yet the question "Am I a lesbian?" hung with me.

I went to dyke events, read dyke books, listened to dyke music, hung out at my first dyke bar, went to my first dyke dance. I adored watching those women talk, laugh, hold hands, dance, kiss. Those soft butch women who would never have claimed their butchness then, during the lesbian-feminist androgyny of the '70s and early '80s. Those women with buzzed hair and well-defined biceps, jeans faded and soft. Those women who looked me in the eye. Watching them was like polishing my favorite stone to its brightest glint. I knew I could be *this* kind of woman and so slowly over the course of that year came to know myself as a dyke. I waited another four years to kiss a woman.

My coming out wasn't as much about discovering sexual desire and knowledge as it was about dealing with gender identity. Simply put, the disabled, mixed-class tomboy who asked her mother, "Am I feminine?" didn't discover a sexuality among dykes, but rather a definition of woman large enough to be comfortable for many years. And if that definition hadn't been large enough, what then? Would I have sought out hormones and/or surgery? If I had been born a hundred years ago when a specifically lesbian definition didn't exist, would I have been a "passing woman"? If I live long enough to see the world break free of the gender binary, will I find home not as a butch dyke, a woman by default, but as some third, fourth, fifth gender? Some gender that seems more possible since trans people have started to organize, build community, speak out about our lives. Some gender that I have already started reaching toward.

* * *

In queer community, I found a place to belong and abandoned my desire to be a hermit. Among crips, I learned how to embrace my strong, spastic body. Through feminist work around sexual violence—political activism, theoretical analysis, emotional recovery—I came to terms with the sexual abuse and physical torture done to me. And somewhere along the line, I pulled desire to the surface, gave it room to breathe. Let me write not about the stones, but the heat itself.

I think of the first woman I dated. She and I spent many nights eating pizza, watching movies, and talking halfway until dawn. I fell in love but never even kissed her, too afraid to even say, "This is what I want," much less to lean over and put my lips to hers. It made sense only years later when my memories of rape came flooding back. I think of the butch woman, once my lover, now a good friend. One night as we lay in bed, she told me, "I like when your hands tremble over my body. It feels good, like extra touching." Her words pushed against the lies. But all too often, sex was a bodiless, mechanical act for me as I repeatedly fled my body. We decided we'd be happier as friends. I think of the woman who called me her dream butchy *shiksa* and made me smile. I took so long to realize what had flared between us she almost gave up waiting. With her, desire traced my body, vivid and unmistakable, returning me to the taste of spring water, the texture of tree bark as I climbed toward sky. With her, I understood finally what it meant to want my hand on a lover's skin, the weight of a lover's body against mine. A bone long fractured, now mending.

I turn my pockets and heart inside out, set the stones—quartz, obsidian, shale, agate, scoria, granite—along the scoured top of the wall I once lived behind, the wall I still use for refuge. They shine in the sun, some translucent to the light, others dense, solid, opaque. I lean my body into the big unbreakable expanse, tracing which stones need to melt, which will crack wide, geode to crystal, and which are content just as they are.

* * *

But before I make it too simple, let me tell another story about coming to queer community, queer identity. Five or six years after I came out, I lived in Oakland, California, still learning the habits and manners of urban dykes. I remember a weekend when 20 of us, mostly dykes, helped move a friend from north Oakland to west Berkeley. The apartment filled with laughter as we carried endless boxes to the moving van, flexed our muscles over the couch, teased the lovers who sneaked a kiss in the empty closet. That mix of friends, lovers, and ex-lovers, butch dykes, femme dykes, androgynous dykes: we elbowed and jostled and gossiped. Leslie and I hauled a table to the van. On our way back, she off-handedly said how she was glad to be wearing her steel-toed boots, but that her feet were beginning to hurt. I wanted to get to know Leslie better. She was butch and knew it. I liked watching her from across the room, feeling something less than attraction but more than curiosity. I hadn't yet named myself butch but knew I had much in common with Leslie's butchness. So when she mentioned her steel-toed boots, I asked where she worked, assuming she'd have a story about forklifts or hi-los, a warehouse, bailer, mill, factory, or mine. I thought about the summer I was 15 working in the woods. I was the only girl who started the summer with work boots already broken in. The other girls envied me for weeks as they nursed their blistered feet. Leslie said, "I just bought them as a fashion statement." I felt as if I'd been exposed as a hick yet again, caught assuming she was someone I might have grown up with. *A fashion statement.* What did I have in common with Leslie? I felt the stones in my heart grind deep.

Today, more than decade after watching Leslie from across the room, I have settled into a certain butch identity. Often I don't feel drawn to the urban markers of being butch—the leather jacket, the steel-toed boots, the black-on-black look, the arc of chain from wallet to belt loop—but I do understand how certain clothes make me feel inside my body. I learned to dress by watching the loggers and fishermen I grew up around, learned to love t-shirts and torn jeans, dusty work boots and faded flannel shirts from them. The girls with whom I went to school also wore their share of flannel and denim, but when it came time to learn how to dress like "women," they turned to *Vogue* and *Glamour*. To emulate the dress of their working-class mothers was somehow shameful. They wanted their lessons to come from the middle- and upper-class beauty mags. The boys on the other hand never thought to dress like anyone except the working-class men around them. For me, *Vogue* and *Glamour* held none of the appeal that Walt Maya did, dressed in his checked shirt, cowboy boots, and wide-brimmed hat. I joined the boys in their emulation.

I knew early on the feel of boots and denim, knew I would never learn to walk in a skirt. I loved how my body felt as I swung an ax, how my mind felt as I worked through the last and hardest algebra problem in Mr. Johnson's advanced math class, the most elusive metaphor in Mr. Beckman's poetry class. I knew I never wanted a child or a husband. I knew these things but could never have put words to them, knew them in spite of all that stole me away from my body.

How did I "know" I never wanted a husband, would never learn to walk in a skirt? What does it mean when I write that I "felt" like neither a girl nor a boy? The words *know* and *feel* are slippery in their vagueness. I pull out an old photo of myself from the night of my high school graduation. I stand outside on our front deck; behind me are the deep greens of western Oregon in May. I wear a white dress, flowers embroidered on the front panel, the plainest, simplest dress my mother would let me buy. I look painfully uncomfortable, as if I have no idea what to do with my body, hands clasped awkwardly behind me, shoulders caved inward, immobilized, almost fearful beneath my smile. I am in clumsy, unconsenting drag. This is one of the last times I wore a dress. This is my body's definition of *know* and *feel*.

And yet those things I knew and felt were also deeply shaped and colored by the rural, white, working-class culture of Port Orford. They were cradled not so much by an unconscious baby butch sensibility, but in a working-class town where at weddings and funerals everyone looked as if they had been stuffed into their dress clothes. They were nurtured in the small town hardware store and lumber yard, where, even though George always asked if I could handle the 50-pound bags of cement, I was Bob's eccentric, "handicapped" kid and was never told to stop. They were underlined by my parents' desperate upward scramble toward the middle class and their corresponding passion for formal education. They were molded by the common knowledge that most of the girls in town would catch their lives on too many kids, most of the boys on alcohol and guns, and only a few of us would leave the county for good.

* * *

The stolen body, the reclaimed body, the body that knows itself and the world, the stone and the heat which warms it: my body has never been singular. Disability snarls into gender. Class wraps around race. Sexuality strains against abuse. *This is how to reach beneath the skin.*

Friday nights I go to the local queer bar, nurse a single Corona, hang out with my dyke friends. Mostly I go to watch one of the wait staff, a woman with long brown hair, sharp nose, and ready smile. She flirts with everyone, moving table to table, making eye contact, hunkering down to have a quiet word or laugh amidst the noise. She flirts with me too, catching me in her wide smile, appreciative gaze. I am under no illusion: this is simply how she works her job. But after a lifetime of numbness I adore her attention, adore tipping back my chair, spreading my legs wide, and watching her from across the room.

I want to take the stone between my tremoring hands—trembling with CP, with desire, with the last remnants of fear, trembling because this is how my body moves—and warm it gentle, but not, as I have always done before, ride roughshod over it. I want to enter as a not-girl-not-boy transgendered butch—gendered differently than when I first came out, thinking simply, "*This* is how I'll be a woman," never imagining there might be a day when the word *woman* was too small; differently from the tomboy who wanted to be a hermit; but still connected to both. Enter with my pockets and heart half-full of stone. Enter knowing that the muscled grip of desire is a wild, half-grown horse, ready to bolt but too curious to stay away.

* * *

In the end, I will sit on the wide, flat top of my wall, legs dangling over those big, uncrackable stones, weathered smooth and clean. Sit with butch women, femme dykes, nellie men, studly fags, radical faeries, drag queens and kings, transsexual people who want nothing more than to be women and men, intersexed people, hermaphrodites with attitudes, transgendered, pangendered, bigendered, polygendered, ungendered, androgynous people of many varieties and trade stories long into the night. Laugh and cry and tell stories. Sad stories about bodies stolen, bodies no longer here. Enraging stories about false images, devastating lies, untold violence.

Bold, brash stories about reclaiming our bodies and changing the world.

NOTES

1. Wilchins, Riki Anne, *Read My Lips* (Ithaca, NY: Firebrand Books, 1997), p. 118.
2. I now recognize the disturbing irony of this, given the ways in which my father was sexually using me.

CHAPTER 36

Unspeakable Conversations

Harriet McBryde Johnson

SUMMARY

When philosopher Peter Singer invites Harriet McBryde Johnson to discuss selective infanticide, she accepts the invitation to Princeton despite the fact that his ideas place her among the people who would be permissible to kill. She hopes to erect some kind of bridge between their discourses and to make clear to anyone listening that the presence or absence of disability doesn't predict quality of life.

The relationship between the pair began years before during a contentious debate in which McBryde Johnson found herself "sucked into a civil discussion about whether I ought to exist." Through a series of correspondence Singer and McBryde Johnson were able to arrive at the heart of the matter: the world's preeminent philosopher believed disability makes a person "worse off." Their disagreement over this point spurred the invitation to speak at Princeton.

McBryde Johnson and Singer balance etiquette with their ideological commitments during the Princeton forum. Neither side is able to persuade the other to alter their positions. But after the trip, McBryde Johnson admits that she believes Singer "actually is human" despite his flawed assumption that disabled people have a lower quality of life. To argue with this assumption, she writes that she only needs to invoke the "undeniable reality of disabled lives well lived."

McBryde Johnson wrote a memoir, *Too Late to Die Young: Nearly True Tales from a Life,* and a novel titled *Accidents of Nature.* In addition to her writing, McBryde Johnson was an activist and attorney. "Unspeakable Conversations" was published in *The New York Times Magazine* in 2003.

He insists he doesn't want to kill me. He simply thinks it would have been better, all things considered, to have given my parents the option of killing the baby I once was, and to let other parents kill similar babies as they come along and thereby avoid the suffering that comes with lives like mine and satisfy the reasonable preferences of parents for a different kind of child. It has nothing to do with me. I should not feel threatened.

Whenever I try to wrap my head around his tight string of syllogisms, my brain gets so fried it's . . . almost fun. Mercy! It's like "Alice in Wonderland."

It is a chilly Monday in late March, just less than a year ago. I am at Princeton University. My host is Prof. Peter Singer, often called—and not just by his book publicist—the most influential philosopher of our time. He is the man who wants me dead. No, that's not at all fair. He wants to legalize the killing of certain babies who might come to be like me if allowed to live. He also says he believes that it should be lawful under some circumstances to kill, at any age, individuals with cognitive impairments so severe that he doesn't consider them "persons." What does it take to be a person? Awareness of your own existence in time. The capacity to harbor preferences as to the future, including the preference for continuing to live.

At this stage of my life, he says, I am a person. However, as an infant, I wasn't. I, like all humans, was born without self-awareness. And eventually, assuming my brain finally gets so fried that I fall into that wonderland where self and other and present and past and future blur into one boundless, formless all or nothing, then I'll lose my personhood and therefore my right to life. Then, he says, my family and doctors might put me out of my misery, or out of my bliss or oblivion, and no one count it murder.

I have agreed to two speaking engagements. In the morning, I talk to 150 undergraduates on selective infanticide. In the evening, it is a convivial discussion, over dinner, of assisted suicide. I am the token cripple with an opposing view.

I had several reasons for accepting Singer's invitation, some grounded in my involvement in the disability rights movement, others entirely personal. For the movement, it seemed an unusual opportunity to experiment with modes of discourse that might work with very tough audiences and bridge the divide between our perceptions and theirs. I didn't expect to straighten out Singer's head, but maybe I could reach a student or two. Among the personal reasons: I was sure it would make a great story, first for telling and then for writing down.

By now I've told it to family and friends and colleagues, over lunches and dinners, on long car trips, in scads of e-mail messages and a couple of formal speeches. But it seems to be a story that just won't settle down. After all these tellings, it still lacks a coherent structure; I'm miles away from a rational argument. I keep getting interrupted by questions—like these:

Q: Was he totally grossed out by your physical appearance?

A: He gave no sign of it. None whatsoever.

Q: How did he handle having to interact with someone like you?

A: He behaved in every way appropriately, treated me as a respected professional acquaintance and was a gracious and accommodating host.

Q: Was it emotionally difficult for you to take part in a public discussion of whether your life should have happened?

A: It was very difficult. And horribly easy.

Q: Did he get that job at Princeton because they like his ideas on killing disabled babies?

A: It apparently didn't hurt, but he's most famous for animal rights. He's the author of "Animal Liberation."

Q: How can he put so much value on animal life and so little value on human life?

That last question is the only one I avoid. I used to say I don't know; it doesn't make sense. But now I've read some of Singer's writing, and I admit it does make sense—within the conceptual world of Peter Singer. But I don't want to go there. Or at least not for long.

So I will start from those other questions and see where the story goes this time.

That first question, about my physical appearance, needs some explaining.

It's not that I'm ugly. It's more that most people don't know how to look at me. The sight of me is routinely discombobulating. The power wheelchair is enough to inspire gawking, but that's the least of it. Much more impressive is the impact on my body of more than four decades of a muscle-wasting disease. At this stage of my life, I'm Karen Carpenter thin, flesh mostly vanished, a jumble of bones in a floppy bag of skin. When, in childhood, my muscles got too weak to hold up my spine, I tried a brace for a while, but fortunately a skittish anesthesiologist said no to fusion, plates and pins—all the apparatus that might have kept me straight. At 15, I threw away the back brace and let my spine reshape itself into a deep twisty S-curve. Now my right side is two deep canyons. To keep myself upright, I lean forward, rest my rib cage on my lap, plant my elbows beside my knees. Since my backbone found its own natural shape, I've been entirely comfortable in my skin.

I am in the first generation to survive to such decrepitude. Because antibiotics were available, we didn't die from the childhood pneumonias that often come with weakened respiratory systems. I guess it is natural enough that most people don't know what to make of us.

Two or three times in my life—I recall particularly one largely crip, largely lesbian cookout halfway across the continent—I have been looked at as a rare kind of beauty. There is also the bizarre fact that where I live, Charleston, S.C., some people call me Good Luck Lady: they consider it propitious to cross my path when a hurricane is coming and to kiss my head just before voting day. But most often the reactions are decidedly negative. Strangers on the street are moved to comment:

> I admire you for being out; most people would give up.
> God bless you! I'll pray for you.
> You don't let the pain hold you back, do you?
> If I had to live like you, I think I'd kill myself.

I used to try to explain that in fact I enjoy my life, that it's a great sensual pleasure to zoom by power chair on these delicious muggy streets, that I have no more reason to kill myself than most people. But it gets tedious. God didn't put me on this street to provide disability awareness training to the likes of them. In fact, no god put anyone anywhere for any reason, if you want to know.

But they don't want to know. They think they know everything there is to know, just by looking at me. That's how stereotypes work. They don't know that they're confused, that they're really expressing the discombobulation that comes in my wake.

So. What stands out when I recall first meeting Peter Singer in the spring of 2001 is his apparent immunity to my looks, his apparent lack of discombobulation, his immediate ability to deal with me as a person with a particular point of view.

Then, 2001. Singer has been invited to the College of Charleston, not two blocks from my house. He is to lecture on "Rethinking Life and Death." I have been dispatched by Not Dead Yet, the national organization leading the disability-rights opposition to legalized assisted suicide and disability-based killing. I am to put out a leaflet and do something during the Q. and A.

On arriving almost an hour early to reconnoiter, I find the scene almost entirely peaceful; even the boisterous display of South Carolina spring is muted by gray wisps of Spanish moss and mottled oak bark.

I roll around the corner of the building and am confronted with the unnerving sight of two people I know sitting on a park bench eating veggie pitas with Singer. Sharon is a veteran activist for human rights. Herb is South Carolina's most famous atheist. Good people, I've always thought—now sharing veggie pitas and conversation with a proponent of genocide. I try to beat a retreat, but Herb and Sharon have seen me. Sharon tosses her trash and comes over. After we exchange the usual courtesies, she asks, "Would you like to meet Professor Singer?"

She doesn't have a clue. She probably likes his book on animal rights. "I'll just talk to him in the Q. and A."

But Herb, with Singer at his side, is fast approaching. They are looking at me, and Herb is talking, no doubt saying nice things about me. He'll be saying that I'm a disability rights lawyer and that I gave a talk against assisted suicide at his secular humanist group a while back. He didn't agree with everything I said, he'll say, but I was brilliant. Singer appears interested, engaged. I sit where I'm parked. Herb makes an introduction. Singer extends his hand.

I hesitate. I shouldn't shake hands with the Evil One. But he is Herb's guest, and I simply can't snub Herb's guest at the college where Herb teaches. Hereabouts, the rule is that if you're not prepared to shoot on sight, you have to be prepared to shake hands. I give Singer the three fingers on my right hand that still work. "Good afternoon, Mr. Singer. I'm here for Not Dead Yet." I want to think he flinches just a little. Not Dead Yet did everything possible to disrupt his first week at Princeton. I sent a check to the fund for the 14 arrestees, who included comrades in power chairs. But if Singer flinches, he instantly recovers. He answers my questions about the lecture format. When he says he looks forward to an interesting exchange, he seems entirely sincere.

It is an interesting exchange. In the lecture hall that afternoon, Singer lays it all out. The "illogic" of allowing abortion but not infanticide, of allowing withdrawal of life support but not active killing. Applying the basic assumptions of preference util-itarianism, he spins out his bone-chilling argument for letting parents kill disabled babies and replace them with nondisabled babies who have a greater chance at happiness. It is all about allowing as many individuals as possible to fulfill as many of their preferences as possible.

As soon as he's done, I get the micro-phone and say I'd like to discuss selective infanticide. As a lawyer, I disagree with his jurisprudential assumptions. Logical inconsistency is not a sufficient reason to change the law. As an atheist, I object to his using religious terms ("the doctrine of the sanctity of human life") to characterize his critics. Singer takes a note pad out of his pocket and jots down my points, apparently eager to take them on, and I proceed to the heart of my argument: that the presence or absence of a disability doesn't predict quality of life. I question his replacement-baby theory, with its assump-tion of "other things equal," arguing that people are not fungible. I draw out a comparison of myself and my nondisabled brother Mac (the next-born after me), each of us with a combination of gifts and flaws so peculiar that we can't be measured on the same scale.

He responds to each point with clear and lucid counterarguments. He proceeds with the assumption that I am one of the people who might rightly have been killed at birth. He sticks to his guns, conceding just enough to show himself open-minded and flexible. We go back and forth for 10 long minutes. Even as I am horrified by what he says, and by the fact that I have been sucked into a civil discussion of whether I ought to exist, I can't help being dazzled by his verbal facility. He is so respectful, so free of condescension, so focused on the argument, that by the time the show is over, I'm not exactly angry with him. Yes, I am shaking, furious, enraged— but it's for the big room, 200 of my fellow Charlestonians who have listened with polite interest, when in decency they should have run him out of town on a rail.

My encounter with Peter Singer merits a mention in my annual canned letter that December. I decide to send Singer a copy. In response, he sends me the nicest possible e-mail message. Dear Harriet (if he may)...Just back from Australia, where he's from. Agrees with my comments on the world situation. Supports my work against institutionalization. And then some pointed questions to clarify my views on selective infanticide.

I reply. Fine, call me Harriet, and I'll reciprocate in the interest of equality, though I'm accustomed to more formality. Skipping agreeable preambles, I answer his questions on disability-based infanticide and pose some of my own. Answers and more questions come back. Back and forth over several weeks it proceeds, an engaging discussion of baby killing, disability prejudice and related points of law and philosophy. Dear Harriet. Dear Peter.

Singer seems curious to learn how someone who is as good an atheist as he is could disagree with his entirely reasonable views. At the same time, I am trying to plumb his theories. What has him so convinced it would be best to allow parents to kill babies with severe disabilities, and not other kinds of babies, if no infant is a "person" with a right to life? I learn it is partly that both biological and adoptive parents prefer healthy babies. But I have trouble with basing life-and-death decisions on market considerations when the market is structured by prejudice. I offer a hypothetical comparison: "What about mixed-race babies, especially when the combination is entirely nonwhite, who I believe are just about as unadoptable as babies with disabilities?" Wouldn't a law allowing the killing of these undervalued babies validate race prejudice? Singer agrees there is a problem. "It would be horrible," he says, "to see mixed-race babies being killed because they can't be adopted, whereas white ones could be." What's the difference? Preferences based on race are unreasonable. Preferences based on ability are not. Why? To Singer, it's pretty simple: disability makes a person "worse off."

Are we "worse off"? I don't think so. Not in any meaningful sense. There are too many variables. For those of us with congenital conditions, disability shapes all we are. Those disabled later in life adapt. We take constraints that no one would choose and build rich and satisfying lives within them. We enjoy pleasures other people enjoy, and pleasures peculiarly our own. We have something the world needs.

Pressing me to admit a negative correlation between disability and happiness, Singer presents a situation: imagine a disabled child on the beach, watching the other children play.

It's right out of the telethon. I expected something more sophisticated from a professional thinker. I respond: "As a little girl playing on the beach, I was already aware that some people felt sorry for me, that I wasn't frolicking with the same level of frenzy as other children. This annoyed me, and still does." I take the time to write a detailed description of how I, in fact, had fun playing on the beach, without the need of standing, walking or running. But, really, I've had enough. I suggest to Singer that we have exhausted our topic, and I'll be back in touch when I get around to writing about him.

He responds by inviting me to Princeton. I fire off an immediate maybe.

Of course I'm flattered. Mama will be impressed.

But there are things to consider. Not Dead Yet says—and I completely agree—that we should not legitimate Singer's views by giving them a forum. We should not make disabled lives subject to debate. Moreover, any spokesman chosen by the opposition is by definition a token. But even if I'm a token, I won't have to act like one. And anyway, I'm kind of stuck. If I decline, Singer can make some hay: "I offered them a platform, but they refuse rational discussion." It's an old trick, and I've laid myself wide open.

My invitation is to have an exchange of views with Singer during his undergraduate course. He also proposes a second "exchange," open to the whole university, later in the day. This sounds a lot like debating my life—and on my opponent's turf, with my opponent moderating, to boot. I offer a counterproposal, to which Singer proves amenable. I will open the class with some comments on infanticide and related issues and then let Singer grill me as hard as he likes before we open it up for the students. Later in the day, I might take part in a discussion of some other disability issue in a neutral forum. Singer suggests a faculty–student discussion group sponsored by his department but with cross-departmental membership. The topic I select is "Assisted Suicide, Disability Discrimination and the Illusion of Choice: A Disability Rights Perspective." I inform a few movement colleagues of this turn of events, and advice starts rolling in. I decide to go with the advisers who counsel me to do the gig, lie low and get out of Dodge.

I ask Singer to refer me to the person who arranges travel at Princeton. I imagine some capable and unflappable woman like my sister, Beth, whose varied job description at a North Carolina university includes handling visiting artists. Singer refers me to his own assistant, who certainly seems capable and unflappable enough. However, almost immediately Singer jumps back in via e-mail. It seems the nearest hotel has only one wheelchair-accessible suite, available with two rooms for $600 per night. What to do? I know I shouldn't be so accommodating, but I say I can make do with an inaccessible room if it has certain features. Other logistical issues come up. We go back and forth. Questions and answers. Do I really need a lift-equipped vehicle at the airport? Can't my assistant assist me into a conventional car? How wide is my wheelchair?

By the time we're done, Singer knows that I am 28 inches wide. I have trouble controlling my wheelchair if my hand gets cold. I am accustomed to driving on rough, irregular surfaces, but I get nervous turning on steep slopes. Even one step is too many. I can swallow purées, soft bread and grapes. I use a bedpan, not a toilet. None of this is a secret; none of it cause for angst. But I do wonder whether Singer is jotting down my specs in his little note pad as evidence of how "bad off" people like me really are.

I realize I must put one more issue on the table: etiquette. I was criticized within the movement when I confessed to shaking Singer's hand in Charleston, and some are appalled that I have agreed to break bread with him in Princeton. I think they have a very good point, but, again, I'm stuck. I'm engaged for a day of discussion, not a picket line. It is not in my power to marginalize Singer at Princeton; nothing would be accomplished by displays of personal disrespect. However, chumminess is clearly inappropriate. I tell Singer that in the lecture hall it can't be Harriet and Peter; it must be Ms. Johnson and Mr. Singer.

He seems genuinely nettled. Shouldn't it be Ms. Johnson and Professor Singer, if I want to be formal? To counter, I invoke the ceremonial low-country usage, Attorney Johnson and Professor Singer, but point out that Mr./Ms. is the custom in American political debates and might seem more normal in New Jersey. All right, he says. Ms./Mr. it will be.

I describe this awkward social situation to the lawyer in my office who has served as my default lunch partner for the past 14 years. He gives forth a full-body shudder.

"That poor, sorry son of a bitch! He has no idea what he's in for."

Being a disability rights lawyer lecturing at Princeton does confer some cachet at the Newark airport. I need all the cachet I can get. Delta Airlines has torn up my power chair. It is a fairly frequent occurrence for any air traveler on wheels.

When they inform me of the damage in Atlanta, I throw a monumental fit and tell them to have a repair person meet me in Newark with new batteries to replace the ones inexplicably destroyed. Then I am told no new batteries can be had until the morning. It's Sunday night. On arrival in Newark, I'm told of a plan to put me up there for the night and get me repaired and driven to Princeton by 10 a.m.

"That won't work. I'm lecturing at 10. I need to get there tonight, go to sleep and be in my right mind tomorrow."

"What? You're lecturing? They told us it was a conference. We need to get you fixed tonight!"

Carla, the gate agent, relieves me of the need to throw any further fits by undertaking on my behalf the fit of all fits.

Carmen, the personal assistant with whom I'm traveling, pushes me in my disabled chair around the airport in search of a place to use the bedpan. However, instead of diaper-changing tables, which are functional though far from private, we find a flip-down plastic shelf that doesn't look like it would hold my 70 pounds of body weight. It's no big deal; I've restricted my fluids. But Carmen is a little freaked. It is her first adventure in power-chair air travel. I thought I prepared her for the trip, but I guess I neglected to warn her about the probability of wheelchair destruction. I keep forgetting that even people who know me well don't know much about my world.

We reach the hotel at 10:15 p.m., four hours late.

I wake up tired. I slept better than I would have slept in Newark with an unrepaired chair, but any hotel bed is a near guarantee of morning crankiness. I tell Carmen to leave the TV off. I don't want to hear the temperature.

I do the morning stretch. Medical people call it passive movement, but it's not really passive. Carmen's hands move my limbs, following my precise instructions, her strength giving effect to my will. Carmen knows the routine, so it is in near silence

that we begin easing slowly into the day. I let myself be propped up to eat oatmeal and drink tea. Then there's the bedpan and then bathing and dressing, still in bed. As the caffeine kicks in, silence gives way to conversation about practical things. Carmen lifts me into my chair and straps a rolled towel under my ribs for comfort and stability. She tugs at my clothes to remove wrinkles that could cause pressure sores. She switches on my motors and gives me the means of moving without anyone's help. They don't call it a power chair for nothing.

I drive to the mirror. I do my hair in one long braid. Even this primal hairdo requires, at this stage of my life, joint effort. I undo yesterday's braid, fix the part and comb the hair in front. Carmen combs where I can't reach. I divide the mass into three long hanks and start the braid just behind my left ear. Section by section, I hand it over to her, and her unimpaired young fingers pull tight, crisscross, until the braid is fully formed.

A big polyester scarf completes my costume. Carmen lays it over my back. I tie it the way I want it, but Carmen starts fussing with it, trying to tuck it down in the back. I tell her that it's fine, and she stops.

On top of the scarf, she wraps the two big shawls that I hope will substitute for an overcoat. I don't own any real winter clothes. I just stay out of the cold, such cold as we get in Charleston.

We review her instructions for the day. Keep me in view and earshot. Be instantly available but not intrusive. Be polite, but don't answer any questions about me. I am glad that she has agreed to come. She's strong, smart, adaptable and very loyal. But now she is digging under the shawls, fussing with that scarf again.

"Carmen. What are you doing?"

"I thought I could hide this furry thing you sit on."

"Leave it. Singer knows lots of people eat meat. Now he'll know some crips sit on sheepskin."

The walk is cold but mercifully short. The hotel is just across the street from Princeton's wrought-iron gate and a few short blocks from the building where Singer's assistant shows us to the elevator. The elevator doubles as the janitor's closet—the cart with the big trash can and all the accouterments is rolled aside so I can get in. Evidently there aren't a lot of wheelchair people using this building.

We ride the broom closet down to the basement and are led down a long passageway to a big lecture hall. As the students drift in, I engage in light badinage with the sound technician. He is squeamish about touching me, but I insist that the cordless lavaliere is my mike of choice. I invite him to clip it to the big polyester scarf.

The students enter from the rear door, way up at ground level, and walk down stairs to their seats. I feel like an animal in the zoo. I hadn't reckoned on the architecture, those tiers of steps that separate me from a human wall of apparent physical and mental perfection, that keep me confined down here in my pit.

It is 5 before 10. Singer is loping down the stairs. I feel like signaling to Carmen to open the door, summon the broom closet and get me out of here. But Singer greets me pleasantly and hands me Princeton's check for $500, the fee he offered with apologies for its inadequacy.

So. On with the show.

My talk to the students is pretty Southern. I've decided to pound them with heart, hammer them with narrative and say "y'all" and "folks." I play with the emotional tone, giving them little peaks and valleys, modulating three times in one 45-second patch. I talk about justice. Even beauty and love. I figure they haven't been getting much of that from Singer.

Of course, I give them some argument too. I mean to honor my contractual obligations. I lead with the hypothetical about mixed-race, nonwhite babies and build the ending around the question of who should have the burden of proof as to the quality of disabled lives. And woven throughout the talk is the presentation of myself as a representative of a minority group that has been rendered invisible by prejudice and oppression, a participant in a discussion that would not occur in a just world.

I let it go a little longer than I should. Their faces show they're going where I'm leading, and I don't look forward to letting them go. But the clock on the wall reminds me of promises I mean to keep, and I stop talking and submit myself to examination and inquiry.

Singer's response is surprisingly soft. Maybe after hearing that this discussion is insulting and painful to me, he doesn't want to exacerbate my discomfort. His reframing of the issues is almost pro forma, abstract, entirely impersonal. Likewise, the students' inquiries are abstract and fairly predictable: anencephaly, permanent unconsciousness, eugenic abortion. I respond to some of them with stories, but mostly I give answers I could have e-mailed in.

I call on a young man near the top of the room.

"Do you eat meat?"

"Yes, I do."

"Then how do you justify—"

"I haven't made any study of animal rights, so anything I could say on the subject wouldn't be worth everyone's time."

The next student wants to work the comparison of disability and race, and Singer joins the discussion until he elicits a comment from me that he can characterize as racist. He scores a point, but that's all right. I've never claimed to be free of prejudice, just struggling with it.

Singer proposes taking me on a walk around campus, unless I think it would be too cold. What the hell? "It's probably warmed up some. Let's go out and see how I do."

He doesn't know how to get out of the building without using the stairs, so this time it is my assistant leading the way. Carmen has learned of another elevator, which arrives empty. When we get out of the building, she falls behind a couple of paces, like a respectful chaperone.

In the classroom there was a question about keeping alive the unconscious. In response, I told a story about a family I knew as a child, which took loving care of a nonresponsive teenage girl, acting out their unconditional commitment to each other, making all the other children, and me as their visitor, feel safe. This doesn't satisfy Singer. "Let's assume we can prove, absolutely, that the individual is totally unconscious and that we can know, absolutely, that the individual will never regain consciousness."

I see no need to state an objection, with no stenographer present to record it; I'll play the game and let him continue.

"Assuming all that," he says, "don't you think continuing to take care of that individual would be a bit—weird?"

"No. Done right, it could be profoundly beautiful."

"But what about the caregiver, a woman typically, who is forced to provide all this service to a family member, unable to work, unable to have a life of her own?"

"That's not the way it should be. Not the way it has to be. As a society, we should pay workers to provide that care, in the home. In some places, it's been done that way for years. That woman shouldn't be forced to do it, any more than my family should be forced to do my care."

Singer takes me around the architectural smorgasbord that is Princeton University by a route that includes not one step, unramped curb or turn on a slope. Within the strange limits of this strange assignment, it seems Singer is doing all he can to make me comfortable.

He asks what I thought of the students' questions.

"They were fine, about what I expected. I was a little surprised by the question about meat eating."

"I apologize for that. That was out of left field. But—I think what he wanted to know is how you can have such high respect for human life and so little respect for animal life."

"People have lately been asking me the converse, how you can have so much respect for animal life and so little respect for human life."

"And what do you answer?"

"I say I don't know. It doesn't make a lot of sense to me."

"Well, in my view—"

"Look. I have lived in blissful ignorance all these years, and I'm not prepared to give that up today."

"Fair enough," he says and proceeds to recount bits of Princeton history. He stops. "This will be of particular interest to you, I think. This is where your colleagues with Not Dead Yet set up their blockade." I'm grateful for the reminder. My brothers and sisters were here before me and behaved far more appropriately than I am doing.

A van delivers Carmen and me early for the evening forum. Singer says he hopes I had a pleasant afternoon.

Yes, indeed. I report a pleasant lunch and a very pleasant nap, and I tell him about the Christopher Reeve Suite in the hotel, which has been remodeled to accommodate Reeve, who has family in the area.

"Do you suppose that's the $600 accessible suite they told me about?"

"Without doubt. And if I'd known it was the Christopher Reeve Suite, I would have held out for it."

"Of course you would have!" Singer laughs. "And we'd have had no choice, would we?"

We talk about the disability rights critique of Reeve and various other topics. Singer is easy to talk to, good company.

Too bad he sees lives like mine as avoidable mistakes.

I'm looking forward to the soft vegetarian meal that has been arranged; I'm hungry. Assisted suicide, as difficult as it is, doesn't cause the kind of agony I felt discussing disability-based infanticide. In this one, I understand, and to some degree can sympathize with, the opposing point of view—misguided though it is.

My opening sticks to the five-minute time limit. I introduce the issue as framed by academic articles. Not Dead Yet recommended for my use. Andrew Batavia argues for assisted suicide based on autonomy, a principle generally held high in the disability rights movement. In general, he says, the movement fights for our right to control our own lives; when we need assistance to effect our choices, assistance should be available to us as a matter of right. If the choice is to end our lives, he says, we should have assistance then as well. But Carol Gill says that it is differential treatment—disability discrimination—to try to prevent most suicides while facilitating the suicides of ill and disabled people. The social-science literature suggests that the public in general, and physicians in particular, tend to underestimate the quality of life of disabled people, compared with our own assessments of our lives. The case for assisted suicide rests on stereotypes that our lives are inherently so bad that it is entirely rational if we want to die.

I side with Gill. What worries me most about the proposals for legalized assisted suicide is their veneer of beneficence—the medical determination that, for a given individual, suicide is reasonable or right. It is not about autonomy but about nondisabled people telling us what's good for us.

In the discussion that follows, I argue that choice is illusory in a context of pervasive inequality. Choices are structured by oppression. We shouldn't offer assistance with suicide until we all have the assistance we need to get out of bed in the morning and live a good life. Common causes of suicidality—dependence, institutional confinement, being a burden—are entirely curable. Singer, seated on my right, participates in the discussion but doesn't dominate it. During the meal, I occasionally ask him to put things within my reach, and he competently complies.

I feel as if I'm getting to a few of them, when a student asks me a question. The words are all familiar, but they're strung together in a way so meaningless that I can't even retain them—it's like a long sentence in Tagalog. I can only admit my limitations. "That question's too abstract for me to deal with. Can you rephrase it?"

He indicates that it is as clear as he can make it, so I move on.

A little while later, my right elbow slips out from under me. This is awkward. Normally I get whoever is on my right to do this sort of thing. Why not now? I gesture to Singer. He leans over, and I whisper, "Grasp this wrist and pull forward one inch, without lifting." He follows my instructions to the letter. He sees that now I can again reach my food with my fork. And he may now understand what I was saying a minute ago, that most of the assistance disabled people need does not demand medical training.

A philosophy professor says, "It appears that your objections to assisted suicide are essentially tactical."

"Excuse me?"

"By that I mean they are grounded in current conditions of political, social and economic inequality. What if we assume that such conditions do not exist?"

"Why would we want to do that?"

"I want to get to the real basis for the position you take."

I feel as if I'm losing caste. It is suddenly very clear that I'm not a philosopher. I'm like one of those old practitioners who used to visit my law school, full of bluster about life in the real world. Such a bore! A once-sharp mind gone muddy! And I'm only 44—not all that old.

The forum is ended, and I've been able to eat very little of my puréed food. I ask Carmen to find the caterer and get me a container. Singer jumps up to take care of it. He returns with a box and obligingly packs my food to go.

When I get home, people are clamoring for the story. The lawyers want the blow-by-blow of my forensic triumph over the formidable foe; when I tell them it wasn't like that, they insist that it was. Within the disability rights community, there is less confidence. It is generally assumed that I handled the substantive discussion well, but people worry that my civility may have given Singer a new kind of legitimacy. I hear from Laura, a beloved movement sister. She is appalled that I let Singer provide even minor physical assistance at the dinner. "Where was your assistant?" she wants to know. How could I put myself in a relationship with Singer that made him appear so human, even kind?

I struggle to explain. I didn't feel disempowered; quite the contrary, it seemed a good thing to make him do some useful work. And then, the hard part: I've come to believe that Singer actually is human, even kind in his way. There ensues a discussion of good and evil and personal assistance and power and philosophy and tactics for which I'm profoundly grateful.

I e-mail Laura again. This time I inform her that I've changed my will. She will inherit a book that Singer gave me, a collection of his writings with a weirdly appropriate inscription: "To Harriet Johnson, So that you will have a better answer to questions about animals. And thanks for coming to Princeton. Peter Singer. March 25, 2002." She responds that she is changing her will, too. I'll get the autographed photo of Jerry Lewis she received

as an M.D.A. poster child. We joke that each of us has given the other a "reason to live."

I have had a nice e-mail message from Singer, hoping Carmen and I and the chair got home without injury, relaying positive feedback from my audiences—and taking me to task for a statement that isn't supported by a relevant legal authority, which he looked up. I report that we got home exhausted but unharmed and concede that he has caught me in a generalization that should have been qualified. It's clear that the conversation will continue.

I am soon sucked into the daily demands of law practice, family, community and politics. In the closing days of the state legislative session, I help get a bill passed that I hope will move us one small step toward a world in which killing won't be such an appealing solution to the "problem" of disability. It is good to focus on this kind of work. But the conversations with and about Singer continue. Unable to muster the appropriate moral judgments, I ask myself a tough question: am I in fact a silly little lady whose head is easily turned by a man who gives her a kind of attention she enjoys? I hope not, but I confess that I've never been able to sustain righteous anger for more than about 30 minutes at a time. My view of life tends more toward tragedy.

The tragic view comes closest to describing how I now look at Peter Singer. He is a man of unusual gifts, reaching for the heights. He writes that he is trying to create a system of ethics derived from fact and reason, that largely throws off the perspectives of religion, place, family, tribe, community and maybe even species—to "take the point of view of the universe." His is a grand, heroic undertaking.

But like the protagonist in a classical drama, Singer has his flaw. It is his unexamined assumption that disabled people are inherently "worse off," that we "suffer," that we have lesser "prospects of a happy life." Because of this all-too-common prejudice, and his rare courage in taking it to its logical conclusion, catastrophe looms. Here in the midpoint of the play, I can't look at him without fellow-feeling.

I am regularly confronted by people who tell me that Singer doesn't deserve my human sympathy. I should make him an object of implacable wrath, to be cut off, silenced, destroyed absolutely. And I find myself lacking a logical argument to the contrary.

I am talking to my sister Beth on the phone. "You kind of like the monster, don't you?" she says.

I find myself unable to evade, certainly unwilling to lie. "Yeah, in a way. And he's not exactly a monster."

"You know, Harriet, there were some very pleasant Nazis. They say the SS guards went home and played on the floor with their children every night."

She can tell that I'm chastened; she changes the topic, lets me off the hook. Her harshness has come as a surprise. She isn't inclined to moralizing; in our family, I'm the one who sets people straight.

When I put the phone down, my argumentative nature feels frustrated. In my mind, I replay the conversation, but this time defend my position.

"He's not exactly a monster. He just has some strange ways of looking at things."

"He's advocating genocide."

"That's the thing. In his mind, he isn't. He's only giving parents a choice. He thinks the humans he is talking about aren't people, aren't 'persons.'"

"But that's the way it always works, isn't it? They're always animals or vermin or chattel goods. Objects, not persons. He's repackaging some old ideas. Making them acceptable."

"I think his ideas are new, in a way. It's not old-fashioned hate. It's a twisted, misinformed, warped kind of beneficence. His motive is to do good."

"What do you care about motives?" she asks. "Doesn't this beneficent killing make disabled brothers and sisters just as dead?"

"But he isn't killing anyone. It's just talk."

"Just talk? It's talk with an agenda, talk aimed at forming policy. Talk that's getting a receptive audience. You of all people know the power of that kind of talk."

"Well, sure, but—"

"If talk didn't matter, would you make it your life's work?"

"But," I say, "his talk won't matter in the end. He won't succeed in reinventing morality. He stirs the pot, brings things out into the open. But ultimately we'll make a world that's fit to live in, a society that has room for all its flawed creatures. History will remember Singer as a curious example of the bizarre things that can happen when paradigms collide."

"What if you're wrong? What if he convinces people that there's no morally significant difference between a fetus and a newborn, and just as disabled fetuses are routinely aborted now, so disabled babies are routinely killed? Might some future generation take it further than Singer wants to go? Might some say there's no morally significant line between a newborn and a 3-year-old?"

"Sure. Singer concedes that a bright line cannot be drawn. But he doesn't propose killing anyone who prefers to live."

"That overarching respect for the individual's preference for life—might some say it's a fiction, a fetish, a quasi-religious belief?"

"Yes," I say. "That's pretty close to what I think. As an atheist, I think all preferences are moot once you kill someone. The injury is entirely to the surviving community."

"So what if that view wins out, but you can't break disability prejudice? What if you wind up in a world where the disabled person's 'irrational' preference to live must yield to society's 'rational' interest in reducing the incidence of disability? Doesn't horror kick in somewhere? Maybe as you watch the door close behind whoever has wheeled you into the gas chamber?"

"That's not going to happen."

"Do you have empirical evidence?" she asks. "A logical argument?"

"Of course not. And I know it's happened before, in what was considered the most progressive medical community in the world. But it won't happen. I have to believe that."

Belief. Is that what it comes down to? Am I a person of faith after all? Or am I clinging to foolish hope that the tragic protagonist, this one time, will shift course before it's too late?

I don't think so. It's less about belief, less about hope, than about a practical need for definitions I can live with.

If I define Singer's kind of disability prejudice as an ultimate evil, and him as a monster, then I must so define all who believe disabled lives are inherently worse off or that a life without a certain kind of consciousness lacks value. That definition would make monsters of many of the people with whom I move on the sidewalks, do business, break bread, swap stories and share the grunt work of local politics. It would reach some of my family and most of my nondisabled friends, people who show me personal kindness and who sometimes manage to love me through their ignorance. I can't live with a definition of ultimate evil that encompasses all of them. I can't refuse the monster-majority basic respect and human sympathy. It's not in my heart to deny every single one of them, categorically, my affection and my love.

The peculiar drama of my life has placed me in a world that by and large thinks it would be better if people like me did not exist. My fight has been for accommodation, the world to me and me to the world.

As a disability pariah, I must struggle for a place, for kinship, for community, for connection. Because I am still seeking acceptance of my humanity, Singer's call to get past species seems a luxury way beyond my reach. My goal isn't to shed the perspective that comes from my particular experience, but to give voice to it. I want to be engaged in the tribal fury that rages when opposing perspectives are let loose.

As a shield from the terrible purity of Singer's vision, I'll look to the corruption that comes from interconnectedness. To justify my hopes that Singer's theoretical world—and its entirely logical extensions—won't become real, I'll invoke the muck and mess and undeniable reality of disabled lives well lived. That's the best I can do.

CHAPTER 37

"I Am Not One of The" and "Cripple Lullaby"

Cheryl Marie Wade

SUMMARY

Cheryl Marie Wade was a poet, performer, and activist considered a pioneer in the disability arts movement. In 1985 she founded Wry Crips, a theater group that presented poetry, skits, and dramatic readings from disabled women. An unapologetic feminist and playwright, Wade developed two groundbreaking solo shows, A Woman with Juice and Sassy Girl: Memoirs of a Poster Child Gone Awry.

In her poem "I Am Not One of The," Wade confronts various identities that are socially constructed around a disabled body. The speaker of the poem rejects these assumptions in favor of embracing her body and "withered legs hidden with a blanket." After invoking feminist icons, the poem's speaker insists "I'm the Gimp/I'm the Cripple/I'm the Crazy Lady/I'm The Woman With Juice." Wade said this poem was dedicated "to all my disabled sisters, to the activists in the streets and on the stages, to the millions of Sharon Kowalskis without a Karen Thompson, to all my sisters and brothers in the pits, closets, and institutions of enlightened societies everywhere." It originally appeared in *Sinister Wisdom*.

In "Cripple Lullaby," Wade extends her investigation of disabled identity. In this poem, the speaker reclaims, rather than denies, the common images of disability, often placing those images into contexts in which they aren't assumed to belong: "I'm homeless in the driveway of your manicured street/I'm Evening Magazine's SuperCrip of the Week." Although the speaker embraces images that disturb ableist misconceptions, the poem also repeats the insistence that disability is not, as some might imagine it, "a reason to die."

I AM NOT ONE OF THE

I am not one of the physically challenged—

I'm a sock in the eye with a gnarled fist
I'm a French kiss with cleft tongue
I'm orthopedic shoes sewn on a last of your
    fears

I am not one of the differently abled—

I'm an epitaph for a million imperfect
    babies left untreated

I'm an ikon carved from bones in a mass
    grave in Tiergarten, Germany—
I'm withered legs hidden with a blanket
I am not one of the able disabled—

I'm a black panther with green eyes and
    scars like a picket fence
I'm pink lace panties teasing a stub of milk
    white thigh
I'm the Evil Eye

I'm the first cell divided
I'm mud that talks

I'm Eve   I'm Kali
I'm The Mountain That Never Moves
I've been forever   I'll be here forever
I'm the Gimp
I'm the Cripple
I'm the Crazy Lady

I'm The Woman With Juice

CRIPPLE LULLABY

I'm trickster coyote in a gnarly-bone suit
I'm a fate worse than death in shit-kickin'
  boots

I'm the nightmare booga you flirt with in
  dreams
'Cause I emphatically demonstrate: It ain't
  what it seems

I'm a whisper, I'm a heartbeat, I'm "that
  accident," and goodbye
One thing I am not is a reason to die.

I'm homeless in the driveway of your
  manicured street
I'm Evening Magazine's SuperCrip of the
  Week

I'm the girl in the doorway with no
  illusions to spare
I'm a kid dosed on chemo, so who said life
  is fair

I'm a whisper, I'm a heartbeat, I'm "let's
  call it suicide," and a sigh
One thing I am not is a reason to die

I'm the poster child with doom-dipped
  eyes
I'm the ancient remnant set adrift
  on ice

I'm that Valley girl, you know, dying of
  thin
I'm all that is left of the Cheshire Cat's
  grin

I'm the Wheelchair Athlete, I'm every dead
  Baby Doe
I'm Earth's last volcano, and I am ready to
  blow

I'm a whisper, I'm a heartbeat, I'm a
  genocide survivor, and Why?
One thing I am not is a reason to die.

I am not a reason to die.

CHAPTER 38

Selections from *Planet of the Blind*

Steve Kuusisto

SUMMARY

This excerpt from Stephen Kuusisto's memoir *Planet of the Blind* begins with his enrollment at a university where a first-floor dorm room was "the extent of the campus's support services for disabled students in 1973." As he immerses himself in the world of literature, he must also find ways to negotiate a setting where he carries a white cane in order to help sighted people understand him.

Kuusisto falls in love with poetry and with one of his classmates, and his coming-of-age experiences are structured by his way of seeing. His sense of touch helps him to understand his world, but he also desires a sense of belonging. The opportunity to handle birds in the school's ornithology collection leads to a love of bird-watching with others. After one afternoon of describing birds with his friend Jim, Kuusisto writes, "I think Jim imagines I've seen some birds, and maybe I have."

Planet of the Blind details Kuusisto's childhood in a community and school unprepared for his blindness. The memoir confronts the stigma of disability while detailing Kuusisto's journey into adulthood and a successful writing career. Kuusisto is a poet, memoirist, and public speaker whose work focuses on disability, diversity, education, and public policy. After publishing *Planet of the Blind* in 1998, he published two collections of poetry and another memoir titled *Eavesdropping: A Memoir of Blindness and Listening.*

I believe that in every blind person's imagination there are landscapes. The world is gray and marine blue, then a clump of brown shingled houses stands revealed by rays of sun, appearing now as bison—shaggy and still. These are the places learned by rote, their multiple effects of color made stranger by fast-moving clouds. The unknown is worse, an epic terrain that, in the mind's eye, could prevent a blind person from leaving home.

Since I know the miniature world of Geneva, New York, I decide to attend college there. On campus, though, there are sudden skateboards. I wish for a magic necklace to ward them away. The quadrangle is a world of predatory watching, and so I begin affecting a scowl. I look serious, as if my corpuscles have turned into hot pearls. I'm the angriest-looking boy on earth.

The dean's office knows about my eyes. I have a first-floor room in the dorm in case of fire. The theory is that with a vision impairment, I might not make it down the fire escape. This is the extent of the campus's support service for disabled students in 1973. The unreadable print in books, the dark dormitory room, the inaccessible library books—all these are things left to my dissemblings.

In the classroom I gravitate toward literature. The prevailing pedagogy is still centered on the New Criticism, a method of reading and analysis born in the years after World War II. This is a lucky break for me: the stress here is on the close reading of texts.

One simply has to read a poem to death.

The professor chain-smokes and takes the class line by line through turgid Victorian prosody. We crawl in the nicotine haze through the comma splices of Thomas Hardy.

I listen, hunched in my chair as the machinery of poets is dissected. We are eighteenth-century clock makers: nothing is too small for our rational little universe.

In the dim library I move through the stacks, pressing my nose to the spines. In my pocket I carry a letter from the eye doctor addressed "To Whom It May Concern"—it avows that too much reading is dangerous for me. "The scanning motions inherent in reading make retinal tearing more likely. Therefore Mr. Kuusisto should read in moderation."

Like all true talismans, this letter is frightening. It's designed to protect me from professors who may demand too much from me. But in my pocket it feels like a letter bomb.

Reading is hazardous!

And to me the words of poetry are onions, garlic, fennel, basil; the book itself an earthenware vessel.

Reading alone with a magnifying glass, nothing on earth makes more sense to me than Wallace Stevens's poem "The Pleasures of Merely Circulating": "The angel flew round in the garden/the garden flew round with the clouds,/and the clouds flew around, and the clouds flew around,/and the clouds flew around with the clouds."

My spastic eye takes in every word like a red star seen on a winter night. Every syllable is acquired with pain. But poetry furnishes me with a lyric anger, and

suddenly poems are wholly necessary. Robert Bly's book *The Light Around the Body*, for example, expresses an almost mystical combination of wonder and rage about "the Great Society." He depicts a world gone so awry that the very pine stumps start speaking of Goethe and Jesus, the insects dance, there are murdered kings in the light bulbs outside movie theaters. All of it is glorious, and like my boyhood discovery of Caruso in the attic, Bly's voice, among others—Breton, Nerval, Lorca—follows me in the dark.

* * *

I move in a solitude fueled by secrecy. O Lord, let me never be seen with the white cane. Let me roll through the heavy oceans like the beluga whale, filled with dark seeds, always coursing forward. Let no one find me out! This is my lacerating tune. Leaning over my private page, I shake with effort.

Weakness and *lack of affect* are the synonyms for the word *blind*. In Roget's Thesaurus one finds also: *ignorant, oblivious, obtuse, unaware, blocked, concealed, obstructed, hidden, illiterate, backward, crude, uneducated,* and worst of all, *unversed.*

At twilight I walk in the botanical gardens, the night smells richly of lilac. I've read that Immanuel Kant could not bear to visit his friends in sickness; after they died, he would repress all memories of them. There are limits to cognition and reason. What would he think in the mad purple twilight where I live. Would he visit himself?

I hear radios and TV sets from the open windows on campus.

Under the violet streetlights my glasses, thick as dishes, fill with aberrations at the edges of their thick curves.

College is brutally difficult for me. One poem must take the place of the bulky novel I cannot read, or at least not read in a week. I often go home from the library with the few words I've been able to see and absorb still vivid in my imagination. Alone, I take the words apart and rearrange them like Marcel Duchamp playing chess with his own private rules. Still, I need extra time for every assignment. But exploring what words can do when placed side by side, I'm starting to build the instrument that will turn my blindness into a manner of seeing.

Still, walking around, feigning sight, I step in the rain-washed gutter, brush the street sign, and make a hundred slapstick gestures. In a flash I'm Stan Laurel, the angel of nutty innocence. This can happen without warning. It might be the telephone that does it. A friend calls, saying she'll meet me downstairs in half an hour. She drives a red Chrysler.

I walk down to the street and approach the car. I reach for the door on the passenger's side and give it a tug, but it's locked. I rap on the window, but my friend doesn't seem to hear. I rap again, tug on the door, rap and tug. Then I walk around to her side of the car. Is she in some Wagnerian trance, Brünn-hilde at the wheel? When I lean down to her window, I see at last the face of a genuinely terrified Chinese woman. I motion to her to roll down her window. She won't. I try to explain my mistake in sign language—pointing to my eyes, telling her loudly that I've mistaken her car for that of a friend. I begin backing away from her into the street like an ungainly kid on roller skates.

My embarrassments are legion. I know the white cane has become a necessity for the maintenance of my psychological health. I enter bathrooms marked "Ladies," and entering restaurants, I trip down short flights of steps. I appear misty eyed and drunk and walk about in circles looking for exits and entrances.

Without the cane, who will understand me? But it will be another eighteen years before I receive proper Orientation and Mobility training. Before I will accept it.

* * *

In one of my last trips without a cane I visit the great Prado museum in Madrid, where I find I cannot see the famous paintings of Velázquez and Goya because they are hanging behind ropes that prohibit the vandals from drawing too close. Since I can't draw near, I see oceans of mud in vast gilded frames instead of the ceremonial world of court or the sprawl of lusty peasants.

I've waited years to get to the Prado, and now I'm wandering through its broad hall-ways thwarted by guards and ropes. Of course I should be carrying a white cane. But of course I'm carrying nothing except my sense of not-quite-belonging, which I'm fighting like a man swatting hornets.

At a souvenir counter I buy a museum guide—I'll read about the paintings I can't see—but the print is microscopic. Instead of a book, I find I'm holding a little cup full of sand.

The light in the Prado is alternately prismatic, then dark as a jail. I stand in the sunbeams under the oval skylights and watch the world break up into rainbows, then turn a corner into a great vaulted darkness, where an important painting hangs behind a veil, black as an abandoned lighthouse.

But I've traveled so far to see the paintings, and I hate to be circumscribed by tricks of the light, so I fall in with a group of American tourists. They are dutifully following a Spanish woman tour-guide who is describing paintings in the gallery at which I've arrived. But she spots me as an impostor, a freeloading listener, and as I strain to see the fetlock of a painted horse, she points me out to the group.

"This man is not in our tour," she says. "Sir, you will have to leave."

And I walk from the museum, a flapping windmill of a man, and find myself doing a muddy umbrella-dance in the icy wet park. Two students approach and ask if I'll buy a comic book to help disabled schoolchildren. I give them some money and think that some kid will get a break.

* * *

Dusk is the hour when I'm most likely to misjudge the speed and flow of traffic. It's rush hour—people hurrying home in the autumn rush hour, some on foot, some in cars. In such moments I often feel prematurely aged: I want some help in crossing the street. I want to reach for someone's arm.

Ironically, though, as things visual are in doubt, they grow in unconventional beauty. Dear Jackson Pollock, I've entered your *Autumn Rhythm*. The irregular or sometimes certain flight of color and shape is a wild skein, a tassel of sudden blue here, a wash of red. The very air has turned to hand-blown glass with its imperfect bubbles of amethyst or hazel blue. I stand on the ordinary street corner as if I've awakened at the bottom of a stemware vase. The glassblower's molten rose has landed in my eyes.

I shift my glasses—a slow moon rises on my path, things appear and disappear, and the days are like Zen-autumn.

* * *

A benevolent Shakespeare professor finds me a reader. Enter Ramona, a classics major who comes in the afternoons three days a week.

We sit in a sunbeam in a steep room somewhere toward the rear of the library. It's a storage space, old encyclopedias line the shelves. The librarian thinks no one will hear Ramona reading to me in this spot. He's given us two wooden chairs. We stack our books on them and sit on the floor. Soon we have a blanket, which we

assiduously roll up and store each night in a closet.

Ramona is a tremendous reader, the shadowy forms of things, ideas, gestalt, whatever, they move as she talks. Together we cross the ancient hot plateaus where words are as mighty as numbers. She reads Gilgamesh, the poems of the Cid. And flat on my back in that tall room, I never fall asleep. What stranger miracles are there? Sometimes she stops, and I learn not to interrupt her silence: she's performing a calculation. It's a lesson for me in absorption. My own nervousness tends to exclude such moments.

Oddly enough, eros, syllables, and alchemy are facts, particularly in the lives of young people. Beside Ramona, listening, my habitual shyness around women begins to fall away. Outside the library, I find myself conversing with my female classmates with ease. For the first time, I discover how conversations between men and women can be like warm soap dissolving in a bath.

In the old student pub—a dark cellar, I meet a strange new girl named Bettina. We talk and drink German beer. Bettina is a polymath, angry, rebelling against her father, who is an executive at a television network.

"The bastard, he'd have been comfortable during the Crusades!" she says, and stubs her cigarette out in an ashtray on the bar.

With this altogether irreverent young woman, I experience puppy love. She's an Irish country girl with long, thrilling, unkempt red hair. Red leaning back toward gold.

Bettina cooks spaghetti over a gas ring in a basement. (She never has an apartment of her own, instead she occupies other people's places without self-consciousness. She knows everyone.) I accept a glass of wine, I'm wrapped in earth tones and sparks. My hands stink of Gauloises cigarettes, my fingers spasm from the nicotine.

She squeezes the juice of a lemon into the salad. Puts Tabasco in the pasta sauce. She throws raw carrot chunks in there too.

"Why are you putting carrots in the tomato sauce? That's disgusting!"

"Oh, shut up, if you'd eaten more carrots, your eyes would be better."

"I ate lots of carrots! My eyes went bad from masturbation!"

"Well, maybe you don't need to do that anymore."

I can't speak, because she's kissing me. It's a potent kiss, her tongue is wet and vital in my mouth.

She draws me to the floor, pulls down my pants, guides me inside her. I can't believe how quickly she does it, my brain is still stuck on the word *carrot*.

She's on top, loosening buttons down the front of her black dress. As her breasts touch my outstretched hands, I come with every ounce of my viscera. I come the way all virgin-boys should—with surrender and reverence. I'm trying to say something.

"It's okay," she whispers. "I'm wearing a diaphragm."

I start to rise on my elbows.

"I'm sorry, I—"

"Shhhhh!"

Her face closes in, her red hair falls over my eyes, tickles, smells faintly of shampoo. She guides my fingers gently to her clitoris. She's an open meadow! A birch tree at midsummer, the sunlight seeming to be above and inside her.

Like all virgins, I'm a narcissist: surely no one has ever experienced this abundant wet circle of girl before? Not like this!

I'm on a rug in a spot of lamplight. The sauce simmers behind us. There's a clatter of water pipes, there are apartments above. Dishes rattle somewhere. Bettina is astride me, and leaning, she kisses me forcefully, filling my mouth with her sip of cabernet.

For the first time the vast silence that follows sex expands in my chest.

"I love you!" I say it "I love you!"

I begin to cry. I who cannot see a woman's face, who can't look someone in the eye, I, I, who, what, never thought this could happen. I'm crying in earnest, copious sparkles.

"Shhhhh!"

She arches her back, I slip from her, a little fish, laughing and weeping.

Bettina refastens her dress, retrieves a tortoiseshell hair clasp, arranges it, sings very softly some lines from Yeats: "'Ah penny, brown penny, I am looped in the loops of her hair.'"

* * *

Nights. November. Books. Smoke. Pierre Reverdy. Emily Dickinson. The windows open, a sweet smell of fallen leaves. I stroke Bettina's neck as she reads from Rexroth's Chinese poems: "'The same clear glory extends for ten thousand miles. The twilit trees are full of crows.'"

I'm unimaginably blessed. The crystallography of sharpened syntax, image, her voice behind it, wash of water on stones.

"'My soul wandered, happy, sad, unending.'" (Neruda)

"'The branches are dying of love.'" (Lorca)

"'Show me, dear Christ, thy spouse, so bright and clear.'" (Donne)

"'Here is the shadow of truth, for only the shadow is true.'" (Warren)

* * *

In the library Bettina finds a box of discarded records. These are Caedmon recordings of Yeats, an actor reading Baudelaire, poems by Carl Sandburg, John Crowe Ransom. The recordings are in miserable condition. And there at the bottom of the pile is a recorded bird-watching disk. A British narrator talks the listener through encounters with dozens of different birds. The birds sing on command, precise, silver, optimistic.

"Listen to the plover!" says the voice.

"He's stirring on a spring morning!"

The plover obeys, lets loose its porous notes.

"Now the nightingale. Bird of poetry!"

The nightingale sounds brighter and better rested than the plover. Clearly it is a happy bird.

"The blackbird."

"The oriole."

In some places the needle sticks. The oriole hiccups over and over.

Here come the wild swans.

I'm completely jazzed: all my life I've been a stranger in this neighborhood. I've never seen a bird. Now, hearing them has made a place in my imagination. The birds! The damned birds! I've been missing out on something huge. But where are they?

Someone tells me about the ornithology collection in the biology building. I go there alone on a Saturday, when I know that the building will be deserted. The birds are arranged in display cases on both sides of the first-floor corridor. I press my nose to the glass specimen case and try not to breathe, for breathing fogs the glass. I see cocoon shapes, brown as cordovan shoes. These are the taxidermied and long-fallen members of the parliament, as strange to me as Roman coins and nails.

The labs are empty, the lights off. There is a hum of large refrigerators, a percolating sound. I tap the glass case with my forefinger, and it swings open as if by magic! Perhaps some student assistant has forgotten to lock the case!

Imagine never having seen a bird. And now your hands are free to explore the vagaries of the bird-tomb. How weightless they are, light as dinner rolls! But the feathers are stiff, almost lacquered, like the tiny ribs of a corset I once held in an antique shop.

This can't be what a live bird's plumage would feel like. These birds are stiff, Victorian, spent.

But what a miracle of pipe stems and ligatures, the legs and wings joined with such supple delicacy.

I lift a large thing from its perch, hold it to my face, just barely making out its predatory look. A hawk? It's large as a basketball, light as a throwaway newspaper.

Here I am, twentysomething, standing in a deserted corridor, fondling birds. I feel like a frotteurist: a person who has orgasms from casual touch with strangers. I'm some kind of pervert, alone with these dead birds, running my hands over their heads, tracing their beaks with my fingernails. What if a security guard were to appear and ask me what I'm doing?

"I'm blind, sir, and this is my first experience with birds!"

"My name is Kid Geronimo, and I live in the elevator!"

"Have you ever touched a plover, sir?"

"My name is Wigglesworth, I'm searching for insects."

This is a lifelong habit, imaginary conversations with authority figures, usually when I'm touching something, when I'm on the verge of an understanding.

All the birds smell like vintage hats. As I run my hands over their prickly backs, I put names to them, since I have no idea what they are.

"Leather-breasted barnacle chomper."

"Blue-throated Javanese son of Zero."

Outside I sit under a tree and listen to the living catbirds, a thrush, the chickadee. What I wish for is to see a live bird. So one afternoon shortly thereafter, I convince my friend and teacher Jim Crenner to go bird-watching with me. Jim is a poet, a student of anything that possesses color. He is a mosaic man with a Peterson's guide and at least two pairs of binoculars.

We walk into a meadow, talking of poets, Leopardi, Rumi, Eliot.

Jim knows I can't see well but figures he can point me to colors, fix me on a glittering stone from Ravenna, a goldfinch on a fencepost.

"Hold still, right there is a fat finch big as a Spanish gold piece!" he says, whispering through his mustache, as if he were reading aloud in one of his classes.

"There's a red-winged blackbird."

"A vireo."

"A scarlet tanager."

How toothsome they all sound! How thrilling it must be to spy them on their April branches, blond chaff from the skies, afterthoughts of a blue atmosphere.

When I look through binoculars, I see a coral blue/green bubble, perhaps my own eye, but nothing like a bird. I can't quite bring myself to tell this to Jim, who is in a rapture of color and evolutionary wonder.

"To think these things evolved from primal mud without a god!" he says, alert to the sheer improbability of our planet. But by now I realize I am looking at the blue dish of self. My field glasses are trained on my own optic nerves.

I have a major bird thirst, something untranslatable, I can't share it, can't cry aloud at my frustration. Instead I pretend.

"Can you see him? He's right on that post, fat and horny," says Jim, and I look into my own dish of thickened green and say, "Look at him jump!" At the moment I say it, I mean it. I can see that bird hopping up and down, that goldfinch jumping like a penny on a railroad track.

I agree with everything Jim sees, adding my own intensifier and adjectives. I don't want to tell him I can't see the damned things, fearing it will make him self-conscious, for then our outing will become an exercise in description. He'll have to tell me what they look like. And I will have to appreciate them all the more. By pretending to see, I'm sparing us an ordeal. Sure I'm faking it with the binoculars, gloating over imaginary bluejays, but I'm alone with my own imagination, listening casually to an enthusiastic friend, my blindness locked away for the time.

I think Jim imagines I've seen some birds, and maybe I have.

CHAPTER 39

"The Magic Wand"

Lynn Manning

SUMMARY

In "The Magic Wand," Lynn Manning focuses on a moment of disclosing his disability—"I whip out my folded cane"—that brings his identity as a black man into relief with his identity as a blind man. The poem juxtaposes the stereotyping of a black man as a "wizard of roundball" or a "sociopathic gangbanger" with the stereotypes that might apply to a blind man: a savant composer, an "all-seeing soul," or a "motherless child." The poem's speaker identifies the black man as the "white man's burden" but a disabled man as "every man's burden."

Cataloging the "profound metamorphosis" from black man to blind man brings the viewer no closer to the speaker's experience of these identities. Both sets of assumptions about these identities originate outside of the speaker's conception of himself; he says that "My final form is never of my choosing." Even if the speaker might "wield the wand" to transform into another version of himself, Manning's poem implicates "You"—the reader and the viewer of a blind black man—as the "magician" who dictates his final appearance.

Manning is an award winning poet, playwright, actor, and former World Champion of Blind Judo. He was blinded by a gunshot wound at the age of 23. Manning has written several critically acclaimed plays, including *Weights*, which garnered three NAACP Theater awards. In 1996, he co-founded the Watts Village Theater Company, and he has also served as the president of the Firehouse Theater Company, dedicated to the inclusion of people with disabilities in all aspects of the theatre arts.

THE MAGIC WAND

Quick-change artist extraordinaire,
I whip out my folded cane
and change from black man to blind
   man
with a flick of my wrist.

It is a profound metamorphosis—
From God gifted wizard of roundball
dominating backboards across America,
To God-gifted idiot savant composer
pounding out chart-busters on a cockeyed
   whim;
From sociopathic gangbanger with death
   for eyes
to all-seeing soul with saintly spirit;
From rape deranged misogynist
to poor motherless child;
From welfare-rich pimp
to disability-rich gimp;
And from 'white man's burden'
to every man's burden.

It is always a profound metamorphosis.
Whether from cursed by man to cursed
    by God;
or from scriptures condemned to God
    ordained,

My final form is never of my choosing;
I only wield the wand;
You are the magicians.

CHAPTER 40

Biohack Manifesto

Jillian Weise

SUMMARY

"A poem is like a walk," Jillian Weise writes in her 2015 poem "Biohack Manifesto." By repeating that "A poem is like going on a walk/A walk is like a poem," the experience of the poem is juxtaposed with the experience of embodiment. But the metaphor of walking and poetry assumes a certain functionality that fails in reality; the stanza finishes with Weise telling us that "I was walking the other day and a poem tripped me."

The solution to such a poetic problem might be to biohack it, in Weise's terms: "can somebody hack me/can somebody change my settings." In her manifesto, she wants to make space for disabled bodies despite the way society might try to exclude them. "My people are just trying to get born," she writes of the disabled people who are potentially targets of selective abortion, "like please don't test us/we are going to fail." She concludes the poem with a contemplation of her role as poet, suggesting that the disabled artist is expected to always be sorry.

Weise is the author of *The Book of Goodbyes*, which received the 2013 James Laughlin Award from the Academy of American Poets. Her debut poetry collection, *The Amputee's Guide to Sex*, was published by Soft Skull Press in 2007. Weise is also the author of the novel *The Colony*.

BIOHACK MANIFESTO

It is terrible to be trapped
   at DEF CON
with not even Ray Kurzweil's
daughter to gaze upon
I know some of you wish
I would go wherever
my people go, the factory,
physical therapy,
   a telethon

No! says my mentor
Not this. This is too angry
This is too much about
Not that. Not that

I like to hack, sometimes,
the Hebrew Bible

I don't think my mentor hacks
the Bible b/c it has too much
lame deaf blind circumcised in it

Not that. Not that in poetry
Didn't we already have
Judd Woe? He was so good to us
so good and sad and sorry

The great thing about Judd Woe
is that now we don't have to
keep looking for a disabled poet
We got him

Everybody together now: We got him
Thank YHWH he's a man

I am so relieved, aren't you?
I am so cock blocked, aren't you?

Here I am at the cobbler

Please, please can you make
all my high heels into wedges

Here I am at Wal-Mart

Please, please, can you make
your children stop following me

Here I am at Advanced Prosthetics

Please, please, can you
change my settings

THIS IS NOT POETRY, they said

Be happy with what we give you
We got you

Insurance: You are allowed ten socks/year

Insurance: You are not allowed to walk in
    oceans
Insurance: If you had fought for us, if you
had lost your leg for us, for freedom, then
we would cover the leg that walks in
    oceans

AND WHY IS IT ALWAYS A POEM IS A WALK?

A poem is like a walk
A poem is like going on a walk
A walk is like a poem
I was walking the other day and a poem
    tripped me

Don't leave
Don't I have any other ideas
Be a man, mortality, zip it

Call in the aubades
I wish I would read an aubade
Is it morning yet? This manifesto
is so so long. Too angry
Who you bangin' on my door?

JUDY GRAHN

Thank YHWH. It was getting hot
    in here
Ray Kurzweil's daughter is in Hawaii

I was about to give up

Yes
Yes
I know

I am trying to walk the treadmill
My leg beeps at 3 mph
This is the conference for hackers
Can somebody hack me
Can somebody change my settings

Yes
Yes
I know

JENNY HOLZER

So glad you could make it
Come in, JUDY is here
What do y'all do with all the men in our
    heads

Yes
Yes
It is terrible

My people are just trying to get born
like please don't test us
we are going to fail
and the test comes back
and says YOUR BABY IS FUCKED

JUDY, JENNY, I have been your student
   faithfully

I have kissed some ass, tho, hoping
if they like me enough—what
if they like me enough—why

JUDY, do you need a coaster?
Thy cup runneth over

The glass slipper, amenities
The manifesto must go on

BIOHACK IT

CUT ALL OF IT my mentor says
This is not poetry

My mentor says: A poem is a walk
Get well soon, I pray for you

Must go   Poem about coed
virility   aging   dahlias

Recurrent word to describe beauty
hacked from the Hebrew Bible: Ruddy

Don't leave   In the morning
I will vacuum this up Scansion, feet

I am sorry if you offended me
Role of disabled artist:
Always be sorry

Contributors

H-Dirksen L. Bauman is Professor of Deaf Studies at Gallaudet University where he serves as Coordinator of the MA program in Deaf Studies. He is the editor of *Open Your Eyes: Deaf Studies Talking* (2008) and co-editor of *Signing the Body Poetic: Essays in American Sign Language Literature* (2006). Dr. Bauman is also an executive editor of the *Deaf Studies Digital Journal*.

Douglas C. Baynton, Associate Professor of History at the University of Iowa, is the author of *Forbidden Signs: American Culture and the Campaign Against Sign Language* (1996), and co-author with Jack Gannon and Jean Bergey of *Through Deaf Eyes: A Photographic History of an American Community* (2007).

Chris Bell is a PhD student in English at the Nottingham Trent University where his research examines cultural responses to the AIDS crisis. His essays and articles have appeared in *Positively Aware, On the Move: Mobility and Identity, Culture and the Condom*, and *The Faces of AIDS: Living in the Heartland*.

Liat Ben-Moshe is an Assistant Professor of Disability Studies at the University of Toledo. Her work examines the connections between prison abolition and deinstitutionalization in the U.S. She is the co-editor (with Allison Carey and Chris Chapman) of *Disability Incarcerated: Imprisonment and Disability in the United States and Canada* (2014). In addition, she has written on such topics as disability, anti-capitalism and anarchism; queerness, gender, race and disability; politics of abolition; inclusive pedagogy; and representations of disability.

Michael Bérubé is the Paterno Family Professor in Literature at Pennsylvania State University and the author of *Life As We Know It: A Father, A Family, and an Exceptional Child* (1996).

David Bolt PhD is an Associate Professor in the Department of Disability and Education at Liverpool Hope University, where he is also director of the Centre for Culture and Disability Studies. He is editor in chief of the *Journal of Literary and Cultural Disability Studies*, joint editor of the Literary Disability Studies book series, and author of numerous interdisciplinary works about disability, literary representation, culture, language, and education.

Eli Clare, writer and activist, lives in the Green Mountains of Vermont and is the author of a book of essays *Exile and*

Pride: Disability, Queerness, and Liberation and a collection of poetry *The Marrow's Telling: Words in Motion.*

Lerita M. Coleman-Brown is Ayse I. Carden Distinguished Professor of Psychology and Director of the Science Center for Women at Agnes Scott College in Decatur, Georgia. Professor Brown's early work centered on nonverbal behavior (particularly communicated toward stigmatized individuals), and stigma, identity and self-concept. Her most recent articles include, "Advising a Diverse Student Body: Lessons I've Learned from Trading Places" published in *Liberal Education* and "An Ordinary Mystic: Contemplation, Inner Authority, and Spiritual Direction in the Life and Work of Howard Thurman," published in *Presence: An International Journal of Spiritual Direction.*

G. Thomas Couser retired in 2011 from Hofstra University, where he was a professor of English and founding director of the Disability Studies Program. He is the author of *American Autobiography: The Prophetic Mode* (1979), *Altered Egos: Authority in American Autobiography* (1989), *Recovering Bodies: Illness, Disability, and Life Writing* (1997), *Vulnerable Subjects: Ethics and Life Writing* (2004), *Signifying Bodies: Disability in Contemporary Life Writing* (2009), and *Memoir: An Introduction* (2012). He has completed a memoir of his father and is writing a book about contemporary American patriography (memoirs of fathers).

Lennard J. Davis, the editor of this volume, is Distinguished Professor of Liberal Arts and Sciences at the University of Illinois at Chicago in the Departments of Disability and Human Development, English, and Medical Education. He is the author of *Enforcing Normalcy: Disability, Deafness and the Body; Bending Over Backwards: Disability, Dismodernism, and*

Other Difficult Positions; Obsession: A History, for which he received a Guggenheim Fellowship, and *The End of Normal: Identity in a Biocultural Era.*

Jay Dolmage is Associate Professor and Associate Chair of English at the University of Waterloo. He is the founding editor of the *Canadian Journal of Disability Studies* and is the author of *Disability Rhetoric* (2014) which won a PROSE Award from the Professional and Scholarly Publishing Division of the Association of American Publishers in 2015. His essays on rhetoric, writing, and disability studies have appeared in edited collections and journals, including *Cultural Critique, Disability Studies Quarterly, Journal of Literary & Cultural Disability Studies, Pedagogy,* and *Rhetoric Review.* He grew up in the disability rights movement in Canada and remains committed to promoting greater access within higher education and across society.

Nirmala Erevelles is Professor of Social and Cultural Studies in Education at the University of Alabama. Her book, *Disability and Difference in Global Contexts: Enabling a Transformative Body Politic,* was published in 2011. She has published articles in journals such as *Educational Theory, Teachers College Record,* the *American Educational Research Journal, Disability & Society,* among others in the areas of sociology of education, disability studies, transnational feminist theory, and curriculum studies.

Rosemarie Garland-Thomson is Professor of Women's Studies and English at Emory University. Her fields of study are feminist theory, American literature, and disability studies. Her work develops the field of disability studies in the humanities and women's and gender studies. Her most recent book is *Staring: How We Look.*

Erving Goffman was Professor of Sociology at the University of California at Berkeley and University of Pennsylvania. He was the author of numerous books on social interaction including *The Presentation of Self in Everyday Life* (1956) and *Stigma* (1963).

Alison Kafer is Professor of Feminist Studies at Southwestern University, where she also teaches in the Race and Ethnicity Studies and Environmental Studies programs. She is the author of *Feminist, Queer, Crip*.

Eva Feder Kittay PhD is Distinguished Professor of Philosophy at Stony Brook University/SUNY. Her interests focus on cognitive disability and feminist care ethics. She is the recipient of a NEH and a Guggenheim Fellowship for *Disabled Minds and Things That Matter*, a work in progress. Publications include *Love's Labor: Essays on Women, Equality, and Dependency, Cognitive Disability and the Challenge to Moral Philosophy, Blackwell Guide to Feminist Philosophy, The Subject of Care: Theoretical Perspectives on Dependency and Women,* and *Women and Moral Theory.*

Georgina Kleege teaches creative writing and disability studies at the University of California, Berkeley. Her recent books include: *Sight Unseen* (1999) and *Blind Rage: Letters to Helen Keller* (2006). Kleege's current work is concerned with blindness and visual art: how blindness is represented in art, how blindness affects the lives of visual artists, how museums can make visual art accessible to people who are blind and visually impaired. She has lectured and served as consultant to art institutions around the world including the Metropolitan Museum of Art in New York and the Tate Modern in London.

Stephen Kuusisto teaches in the Center on Human Policy, Law, and Disability Studies at Syracuse University. He is the author of the memoirs *Planet of the Blind* and *Eavesdropping* as well as two collections of poems, *"Only Bread, Only Light"* and *"Letters to Borges."*

Bradley Lewis MD, PhD is an Associate Professor at New York University's Gallatin School of Individualized Study. He has interdisciplinary training in humanities and psychiatry and writes at the interface of psychiatry, cultural studies, and disability studies. His recent books are *Narrative Psychiatry: How Stories Shape Clinical Practice* and *Depression: Integrating Science, Culture, and Humanities.*

Sonya Freeman Loftis is an Assistant Professor of English at Morehouse College, where she specializes in Shakespeare and disability studies. She is the author of two monographs: *Shakespeare's Surrogates* (2013) and *Imagining Autism* (2015). She currently serves on the editorial review board for *Disability Studies Quarterly*, and her work on drama and disability has appeared in journals such as *Shakespeare Bulletin, SHAW: The Annual of Bernard Shaw Studies, South Atlantic Review,* and *The Brecht Yearbook.* In 2015, Dr. Loftis received honorable mention for the Society for Disability Studies Irving K. Zola Award for "best emerging scholar in the field of disability studies."

Paul K. Longmore (1946–2010) was Professor of History at San Francisco State University and winner of the Henry B. Betts Award from the American Association of People with Disabilities. An activist and a scholar, he published two key books in disability studies, *The New Disability History: American Perspectives* (ed. with Lauri Umansky, 2001) and *Why I Burned My Book and Other Essays on Disability* (2003). A team of disability historians who benefited from the field he founded is completing his book on Telethons.

Harriet McBryde Johnson (July 8, 1957–June 4, 2008) was a lawyer, writer, and disability activist. Her writing on disability appeared in numerous publications including *New Mobility, South Carolina Lawyer, Review of Public Personnel Administration*, and the *New York Times*. She is the author of the memoir *Too Late to Die Young: Nearly True Tales from a Life* (2005) and the novel *Accidents of Nature* (2006).

Robert McRuer is Professor of English and Chair of the Department of English at The George Washington University. He is author of *Crip Theory: Cultural Signs of Queerness and Disability* (2006) and *The Queer Renaissance: Contemporary American Literature and the Reinvention of Lesbian and Gay Identities* (1997). With Anna Mollow, he co-edited *Sex and Disability* (2012). His articles have appeared in *PMLA, Radical History Review, GLQ: A Journal of Lesbian and Gay Studies*, and numerous other locations.

Lynn Manning (April 30, 1955–August 3, 2015) was an American playwright, poet, and actor known for his autobiographical work that explores the complexities of life as a blind African-American man.

Helen Meekosha is an Honorary Associate Professor in the School of Social Sciences at the University of New South Wales, Sydney, Australia. Her research in Critical Disability Studies has broken new ground in setting disability in a context of neoliberalism and globalization. Her most recent research has been on the experience of disability from the perspective of those who live in rural and remote communities in Australia. Her work and publications on disability and the global South has led to invitations to give keynote addresses at conferences in Asia, the U.S. and Europe. She has been active in the disability movement since 1981, is a lifetime member of

Women With Disabilities Australia and is currently vice president of the Society of Disability Studies (U.S.). Her recent book (with Karen Soldatic) is *The Global Politics of Impairment and Disability Processes and Embodiments*.

Ann Millett-Gallant is an art historian and a lecturing fellow for the University of North Carolina at Greensboro. Her research focuses on representations of the disabled body in art and visual culture, and her book, *The Disabled Body in Contemporary Art* (2010) is the first to cross the disciplines of art history and disability studies. She has also published essays and reviews of art and film in disability studies journals and art magazines.

Andrea Minear is Assistant Professor of Elementary Education in the Department of Elementary Education at the University of West Alabama. Her areas of expertise are early childhood literacy, social justice and equity in education, and narrative research.

David Mitchell and **Sharon Snyder** are the authors of *Narrative Prosthesis: Disability and the Dependencies of Discourse* (2000) and *Cultural Locations of Disability* (2006). They are also the creators of three award-winning films about disability arts, history, and culture. Together they helped found the Committee on Disability Issues in the Profession at the Modern Languages Association as well as researched, wrote, and curated a Chicago Disability History Exhibit for Bodies of Work: Disability Arts and Culture Festival. Currently, they are completing work on a new book titled, *The Geo-Politics of Disability*, and also producing a new film on the social and surgical issues involved with esophageal atresia.

Joseph J. Murray is Associate Professor of ASL and Deaf Studies at Gallaudet

University. He is co-editor of *Deaf Gain: Raising the Stakes for Human Diversity* (2014) and *In Our Hands: Essays in Deaf History, 1770–1970* (2016). He has published in deaf history, deaf studies, and language planning and language rights.

Catherine Prendergast is Professor of English at the University of Illinois at Urbana-Champaign. An editorial board member of the *Journal of Literary and Cultural Disability Studies*, she is co-editor with Elizabeth Donaldson of a special issue of that journal on "Representing Emotion and Disability" (2011).

Margaret Price is an Associate Professor of Writing at Spelman College and co-editor of reviews for *Disability Studies Quarterly*. Her book *Mad at School: Rhetorics of Mental Disability and Academic Life* appeared in 2011. She is at work on a second book about the naming and un-naming of mental disability among faculty.

Ato Quayson did his BA at the University of Ghana and his PhD at the University of Cambridge. He is currently Professor of English and inaugural Director of the Centre for Diaspora and Transnational Studies at the University of Toronto. His publications include *Calibrations: Reading for the Social* (2003), *Aesthetic Nervousness: Disability and the Crisis of Representation* (2007) and he was also editor of the 2-volume *Cambridge History of Postcolonial Literature* (2012).

Harilyn Rousso is a disability activist, feminist, psychotherapist, writer, and painter who has worked on issues of women and girls with disabilities for more than 30 years. She is the founder of the Networking Project for Disabled Women and Girls of the YWCA/NYC, executive producer of the documentary *Positive Images: Portraits of Women with Disabilities*, and author of numerous publications on gender and disability including *Disabled, Female and Proud: Stories of Ten Women with Disabilities, Double Jeopardy: Addressing Gender Equity in Special Education*, and *Don't Call Me Inspirational: A Disabled Feminist Talks Back*.

Ellen Samuels is Assistant Professor of Gender & Women's Studies and English at the University of Wisconsin at Madison. Her critical writing on disability has appeared in numerous journals and anthologies, and was awarded the Catherine Stimpson Prize for Outstanding Feminist Scholarship in 2011.

Carrie Sandahl is Associate Professor at the University of Illinois at Chicago in the Department of Disability and Human Development. She directs Chicago's Bodies of Work, an organization that supports the development of disability arts and culture. Her research and creative activity focus on disability identity in live performance and film. Sandahl's publications include a co-edited anthology, *Bodies in Commotion: Disability and Performance*, which garnered the Association for Theatre in Higher Education award for Outstanding Book in Theatre Practice and Pedagogy (2006). She is collaborating on a documentary, *Code of the Freaks*, a critique of disability representations in cinema.

Marsha Saxton is the executive director of the Project on Women and Disability at the Massachusetts Office of Disability. She is a trainer, consultant, and organizer in peer counseling for disabled people. She is the editor of *With Wings: An Anthology of Literature By and About Women With Disabilities*.

Tom Shakespeare is a sociologist and bioethicist. After researching and teaching at the Universities of Cambridge, Sunderland, Leeds and Newcastle, he moved to the World Health Organization in 2008. His books include *Disability Rights and Wrongs, The Sexual Politics of Disability* and *Genetic Politics: From Eugenics to Genome.*

Russell Shuttleworth PhD, MSW is a senior lecturer in the School of Health and Social Development at Deakin University. His education and training is in medical anthropology and social work. He has conducted critical, disability-related qualitative and ethnographic research on subjects such as sexuality, masculinity, communication, technology and leadership. His most recent research is on facilitated sex and disability in Victoria, Australia. He is the editor (with Teela Sanders) of the book, *Sex and Disability: Politics, Identity and Access.*

Tobin Siebers is V. L. Parrington Collegiate Professor of English and Art and Design at the University of Michigan. He is the author of 13 books, including *The Body Aesthetic: From Fine Art to Body Modification* (2000), *Disability Theory* (2008), and *Disability Aesthetics* (2010). Siebers is a past fellow of the Michigan Society of Fellows, the Mellon Foundation, the Columbia Society of Fellows, and the Guggenheim Foundation. In 2011 he was named the recipient of the Senior Scholar Award of the Society for Disability Studies.

Tanya Titchkosky is Professor at the University of Toronto in the Department of Social Justice Education of the Ontario Institute for Studies in Education. Her books include *The Question of Access: Disability, Space, Meaning* and *Reading and Writing Disability Differently: The Textured Life of Embodiment and Disability, Self and Society*. Tanya works to draw out the meaning made of narrated perceptions of embodied differences by relying on phenomenological and hermeneutic-oriented sociological approaches of inquiry within Race, Queer and Disability Studies.

Cheryl Marie Wade is a poet, playwright, videomaker, and performer. She is the editor of Gnarlybone News, a free online "cut and paste" disability culture newsletter. Her performance video "Body Talk" received an Award of Achievement from Superfest XXI. She is the recipient of the 1994 National Endowment for the Arts Solo Theater Artist's Fellowship and the CeCe Robinson Award for disability writing and performing.

Jillian Weise is the author of *The Amputee's Guide to Sex*, the novel *The Colony*, and *The Book of Goodbyes*, which won the 2013 James Laughlin Award from the Academy of American Poets. Her essays on being a cyborg have appeared in the *New York Times* and *Narrative Inquiry in Bioethics.*

Susan Wendell is the author of *The Rejected Body: Feminist Philosophical Reflections on Disability* (1996). She is Professor Emerita at Simon Fraser University. She has lived with ME disease (CFIDS) since 1985.

Credit Lines

[1] Lennard J. Davis, "Constructing Normalcy." Reprinted by permission.

[2] Douglas C. Baynton, "Disability and the Justification of Inequality in American History" in *The New Disability History: American Perspectives*, edited by Paul K. Longmore and Lauri Umansky. Copyright © 2001. Reprinted with the permission of New York University Press.

[3] Paul K. Longmore, "'Heaven's Special Child': The Making of Poster Children." Reprinted with permission.

[4] Dolmage, Jay. "Disabled Upon Arrival: The Rhetorical Construction of Disability and Race at Ellis Island." *Cultural Critique* 77 (2011): 24–69.

[5] Martha Saxton, "Disability Rights and Selective Abortion." Reprinted by permission.

[6] Michael Bérubé, "Disability, Democracy, and the New Genetics" from *Genetics, Disability, and Deafness*, edited by John Vickrey Van Cleve. Copyright © 2004 Gallaudet University. Reprinted with permission.

[7] Bradley Lewis, "A Mad Fight: Psychiatry and Disability Activism." Reprinted by permission.

[8] Liat Ben-Moshe, "The Institution Yet to Come: Analyzing Incarceration Through a Disability Lens" published in part as "Disabling Incarceration: Connecting Disability to Divergent Confinements in the USA" in *Critical Sociology* 37.7 (2012). Copyright © 2012 by Sage Publications, Inc. Reprinted with permission.

[9] From *Stigma: Notes on the Management of Spoiled Identity* by Erving Goffman. Copyright © 1963 by Simon & Schuster, Inc.

[10] Lerita M. Coleman-Brown, "Stigma: An Enigma Demystified" from *The Dilemma of Difference: A Multidisciplinary View of Stigma* by Stephen C. Ainlay, Gaylene Becker, and Lerita M. Coleman. Reprinted by permission of Plenum.

[11] Susan Wendell, "Unhealthy Disabled: Treating Chronic Illnesses as Disabilities" from *Hypatia* 16.4 (Autumn 2001). Copyright © 2010 by Hypatia, Inc. Reprinted with the permission of John Wiley & Sons, Inc.

[12] Meekosha, Helen and Russell Shuttleworth. "What's So 'Critical' about Critical Disability Studies?" from *Australian Journal of Human Rights* 15.1 (2009): 47–75.

[13] Tom Shakespeare, "The Social Model of Disability." Reprinted by permission.

[14] David T. Mitchell and Sharon L. Snyder, excerpt from *Narrative Prosthesis: Disability and the Dependencies of Discourse*. Copyright © 2001 by The University of Michigan. Reprinted with permission.

[15] Ato Quayson, excerpt from *Aesthetic Nervousness: Disability and the Crisis of Representation*. Copyright © 2007 by Columbia University Press. Reprinted with the permission of the publisher.

[16] Catherine Prendergast, "The Unexpected Schizophrenic: A Post-Postmodern Introduction." Reprinted by permission.

[17] H-Dirksen L. Baumann and Joseph J. Murray, "Deaf Studies in the 21st Century: 'Deaf-Gain' and the Future of Human Diversity" in *The Oxford Handbook of Deaf Studies, Language, and Education, Volume 2*. Copyright © 2010 by Oxford University Press. Reprinted with permission.

[18] "Aesthetic Blindness: Symbolism, Realism and Reality" by David Bolt from *Mosaic* 46.3 (2013): 93–108. This article originally appeared in *Mosaic*, a journal for the interdisciplinary study of literature.

[19] Titchkosky, Tanya. "Life with Dead Metaphors: Impairment Rhetoric in Social Justice Praxis." *Journal of Literary and Cultural Disability Studies* 9.1 (2015).

[20] Kafer, Alison. "At the Same Time, Out of Time: The Case of Ashley X" in *Feminist Queer Crip*. Indiana University Press (2013).

[21] Kittay, Eva. "Centering Justice on Dependency and Recovering Freedom." *Hypatia* 30.1 (2015): 285–291.

[22] Tobin Siebers, "Disability and the Theory of Complex Embodiment—For Identity Politics in a New Register" from *Disability Theory*. Copyright © 2008. Reprinted with the permission of The University of Michigan Press.

[23] Margaret Price, "Naming and Definition" from "Introduction" from *Mad at School: Rhetorics of Mental Disability and Academic Life*. Copyright © 2011 University of Michigan. Reprinted with permission. This contains excerpts from Johnnie Lacy, "Director, Community Resources For Independent Living: An African-American Woman's Perspective on The Independent Living Movement in The Bay Area, 1960s–1980s" (interview conducted by David Landes, 1998) and "Minority vs. Disability Identity," both from *Disability Rights and Independent Living Movement Oral History Series* (UC Berkeley, 2000). Also excerpts from Donald Galloway, from "Blind Services and Advocacy and the Independent Living Movement in Berkeley" interviews conducted by Sharon Bonney and Fred Pelka (2000–2002) in *Disability Rights and Independent Living Movement Oral History Series* (UC Berkeley, 2004). All courtesy The Bancroft Library, University of California, Berkeley.

[24] Ellen Samuels, "My Body, My Closet: Invisible Disability and the Limits of Coming-Out Discourse" from *GLQ: A Journal of Lesbian and Gay Studies* 9, 1–2 (2003): 233–255. Copyright © 2003 by Duke University Press. Reprinted by permission of the publisher, www.dukepress.edu

[25] Rosemarie Garland-Thomson, "Integrating Disability, Transforming Feminist Theory" from *National Women's Studies Association Journal* 14.3 (Fall 2002). Copyright © 2002. Reprinted with permission.

Index